BRITAIN
Tourist & Motoring Atlas
2008

Edition 2008 by Manufacture Française des Pneumatiques Michelin
Société en commandite par actions au capital de 304 000 000 EUR
Place des Carmes-Déchaux - 63 Clermont-Ferrand (France)
R.C.S. Clermont-Fd B 855 200 507

© Michelin et Cie, Propriétaires-Editeurs 2007

First edition 2007
First impression 2007

Cartography by Philip's
Copyright © 2007 Philip's

Ordnance Survey®

Data for the speed cameras provided by PocketGPSWorld.com Ltd.

Information for Tourist Attractions shown on the mapping supplied by VisitBritain.

Information for National Parks, National Trails and Country Parks in Wales supplied by the Countryside Council for Wales.

Information for National Parks, National Trails and Country Parks in England supplied by the Countryside Agency. Data for Regional Parks, Long Distance Footpaths and Country Parks in Scotland provided by Scottish Natural Heritage.

Gaelic name forms used in the Western Isles provided by Comhairle nan Eilean.

Data for the National Nature Reserves in England provided by English Nature. Data for the National Nature Reserves in Wales provided by Countryside Council for Wales. Darparwyd data'n ymwneud â Gwarchodfeydd Natur Cenedlaethol Cymru gan Gyngor Cefn Gwlad Cymru.

Information on the location of National Nature Reserves in Scotland was provided by Scottish Natural Heritage.

In spite of the care taken in the production of this book, it is possible that a defective copy may have escaped our attention. If this is so, please return it to your bookseller, who will exchange it for you, or contact:

Michelin
Maps & Guides – Hannay House – 39 Clarendon Road
Watford Herts WD 17 1JA

www.ViaMichelin.com

Printed in Italy by Rotolito

Contents

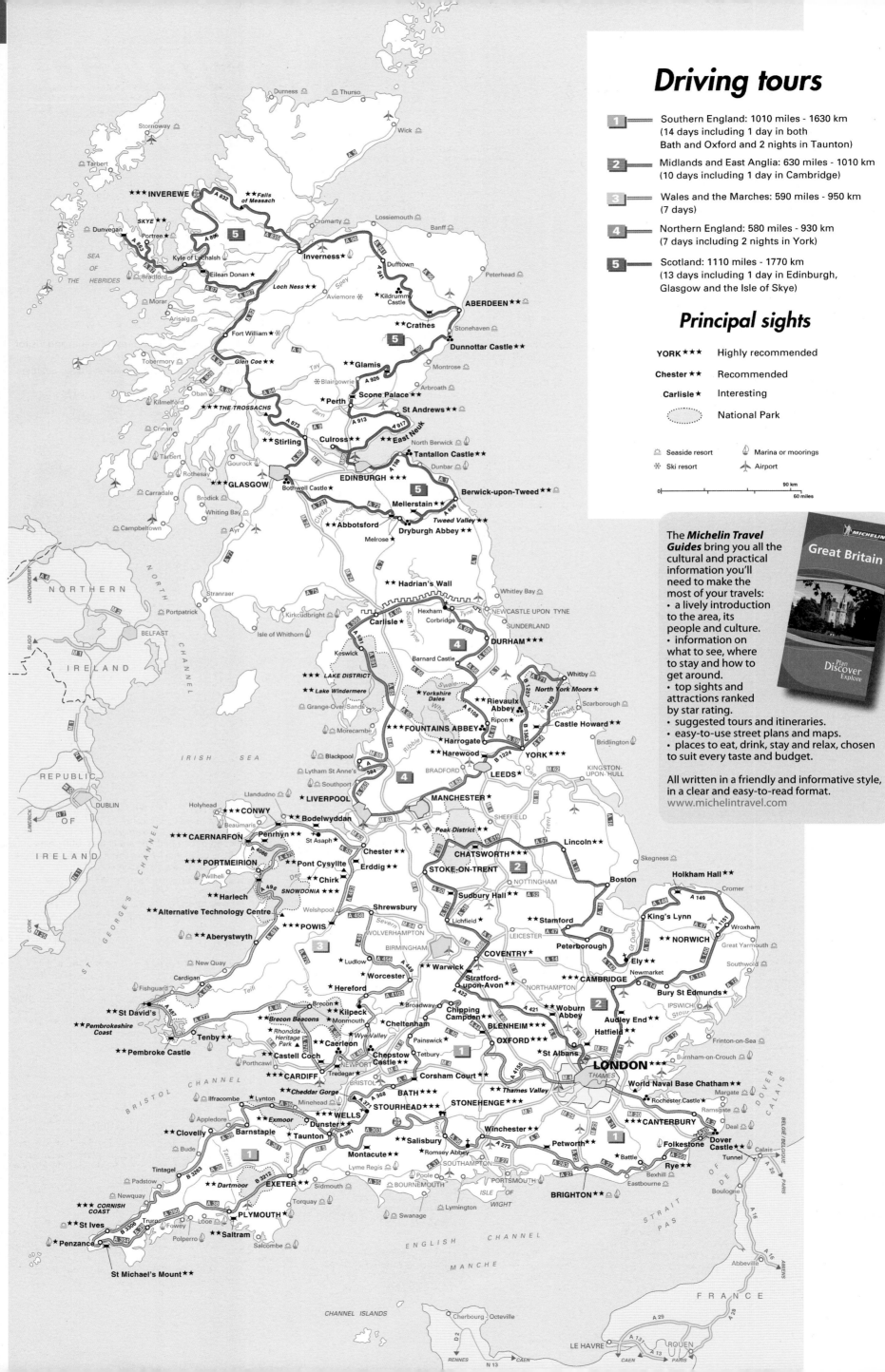

Driving tours

1 ━━━ Southern England: 1010 miles - 1630 km
(14 days including 1 day in both
Bath and Oxford and 2 nights in Taunton)

2 ━━━ Midlands and East Anglia: 630 miles - 1010 km
(10 days including 1 day in Cambridge)

3 ━━━ Wales and the Marches: 590 miles - 950 km
(7 days)

4 ━━━ Northern England: 580 miles - 930 km
(7 days including 2 nights in York)

5 ━━━ Scotland: 1110 miles - 1770 km
(13 days including 1 day in Edinburgh,
Glasgow and the Isle of Skye)

Principal sights

YORK ★★★   Highly recommended

Chester ★★   Recommended

Carlisle ★   Interesting

⬭   National Park

⌂ Seaside resort   ⚓ Marina or moorings

❄ Ski resort   ✈ Airport

0 ┤─────────────┤ 90 km
0 ┤─────────────┤ 60 miles

The **Michelin Travel Guides** bring you all the cultural and practical information you'll need to make the most of your travels:
• a lively introduction to the area, its people and culture.
• information on what to see, where to stay and how to get around.
• top sights and attractions ranked by star rating.
• suggested tours and itineraries.
• easy-to-use street plans and maps.
• places to eat, drink, stay and relax, chosen to suit every taste and budget.

All written in a friendly and informative style, in a clear and easy-to-read format.
www.michelintravel.com

MICHELIN
Great Britain
Plan Discover Explore

DRIVING TOURS IN GREAT BRITAIN

Selection of main sights
Symbols in the text

🛈 Tourist information - ♿ Wheelchair access
⊛ Tips to help improve your experience
🕐 Hours of operation - 🕐 Periods of closure
Kids Sights of interest to children
🚶 Walking tours
💶 Entry fees

1 SOUTHERN ENGLAND
1010 miles - 1630 km (14 days)

Landscapes and nature

The Southeast
"London's Countryside" is highly urbanised but its varied relief and an abundance of trees, woods and parkland make an attractive habitat for its generally prosperous population. The inland rim of the basin containing Greater London is formed by gracefully sculpted chalk hills. The **Chiltern Hills** (northwest) are famous for their beechwoods. The **North Downs** (south) define a great east-west arc. Between them and the **South Downs** lies the **Weald** (deriving from *wald*, the German word for forest), a tract (100 mi/160km) of dense oakwoods, sandy hills and clay vales. To the east is the great **estuary of the Thames**, flanked by creeks and inlets and by orchards and market gardens.
The coastal fringe, facing continental Europe with which it has many links, has changed in outline over the centuries; erosion by the sea has been balanced by the gain of such tracts of rich pastureland as Romney Marsh.

Central Southern England
The high and airy chalklands centred on Salisbury Plain were the heart of prehistoric England. Innumerable lesser earthworks and other traces form the setting for the greater monuments like **Stonehenge**.
Later populations have settled in the gentle river valleys and in the ports and resorts of the coast. The great arms of the sea, which are sheltered from the Channel by the pretty **Isle of Wight**, are an amateur sailor's paradise. West of the beautiful woods and heaths of the **New Forest** is the geologically complex and scenically fascinating **Dorset coast**.

The West Country
A granite backbone runs through **Devon** and **Cornwall,** showing itself in rugged high moorlands topped by wind-blasted "tors." The Exmoor National Park in North Devon is formed of red sandstone, which in the Devon lowlands yields rich agricultural soils. The county's particularly luxuriant version of the English patchwork field pattern gives way in the harsher environment of Cornwall to smaller fields often of ancient origin, bounded by earthen hedge-banks or stone walls.

R. Besse/MICHELIN

Cornwall: Lizard coastline

The long coastline of the peninsula is unsurpassed; most varieties of coastal scenery are represented; spectacular rocky bastions under fierce attack from Atlantic rollers contrast with sheltered bays and beautifully wooded inlets running far inland.

LONDON

London is the commercial, political and artistic capital of the United Kingdom, and one of the great financial centres of the world. Although the one city plays several roles, it has twin centres – the City of London, known as The City, for trade and commerce, and the City of Westminster, known as the West End, for royal palaces and parliament, theatres and entertainment, art and fashion.

▶ **Orient Yourself**: Most sightseeing and tourist activites are confined to Westminster, the West End and Kensington. The underground is the most effective way of getting around town, though buses will allow you to see more. Taxis are expensive. Always catch a (licensed) black taxi cab unless your hotel recommends another taxi company. Short distances are best covered on foot. There are various bus sightseeing tours, of which The Big Bus Company is among the best: www.bigbustours.com

⊛ **Don't Miss**: The BA London Eye, British Museum, National Gallery, Covent Garden, Westminster Abbey, Tower of London, Kew Gardens, Hampton Court Palace, Greenwich by river boat.

🕐 **Organizing Your Time**: Allow at least 4 days.

Kids **Especially for Kids**: Natural History Museum; hands-on fun in the Science Museum; buskers and toyshops in Covent Garden; London Zoo; London Dungeon (teens only).

🚶 **Walking Tours**: There are many walking tour operators, the best is the Original London Walks: www.london.walks.com

Canterbury

The ecclesiastical capital of England, rich in medieval atmosphere, is dominated by its renowned cathedral. Long open to influences from the Continent, the city lies on Watling Street, the great Roman thoroughfare linking London (some 56 miles/90 km west) with the port of Dover. It also forms the terminus of the Pilgrims' Way, a trackway of prehistoric origin used by some of the worshippers at the shrine of St Thomas, England's best-known martyr.

🛈 12/13 Sun Street, The Buttermarket ☎ 01227 378 100 ; canterburyinformation@canterbury.gov.uk; www.canterbury.co.uk.

⊛ **Don't Miss**: The Cathedral, especially the tomb of the Black Prince

🕐 **Organizing Your Time**: allow half to a full day

Kids **Especially for Kids**: The Canterbury Tales; Howlett's Wild Animal Park

A.F. Kersting/MICHELIN

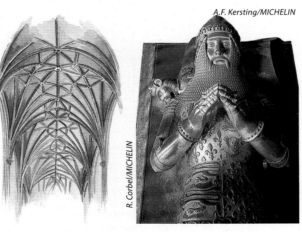

R. Corbel/MICHELIN

Left: Nave vault with liernes (linking ribs not joined to central boss or springer) Canterbury cathedral c 1390 - 1405 - Right: Black Prince's effigy

Stonehenge

Stonehenge, Britain's most celebrated prehistoric monument, is 4 000 years old; radiocarbon dating indicates that its construction was begun in c2950 BC and completed in three phases by c 1550 BC. In context with other comparable feats of civil engineering, it is several centuries later than the Great Pyramid in Egypt, contemporary with Minoan culture in Crete, a millennium earlier than the first Great Wall of China, 2 000 years earlier than the Aztec constructions (and carved stone calendars) of Mexico and 3 500 years older than the figures on Easter Island. For centuries it has sent writers, painters and every sort of visitor into flights of fancy, for its purpose remains an enigma. Although many of the stones have fallen or disappeared it is still possible, from the centre of the circle, to see the sun rise over the Heel Stone (at the entrance) on midsummer's day; there are suggestions that it was constructed as an astronomical observatory or a sanctuary for a sun-worshipping cult, or even a combination of the two. The main axis has always been aligned with the midsummer sunrise and Stonehenge must have been a ceremonial centre celebrating the sun and marking the seasons. Certainly it was not "built by the Druids", the priesthood of the Celtic peoples who reached Britain in 250 BC, long after the completion of the final phase of the building.

Visit
🕐 Open daily, 9.30am (9am Jun-Aug) to 6pm (7pm Jun-Aug; 5pm mid-Oct to late-Oct; 4pm late-Oct to mid-Mar). 🕐 Closed 1 Jan and 24-26 Dec. £4.40 Audio tour (9 languages). Parking. Refreshments. ☎ 01980 624 715;

www.stonehengemasterplan.org
www.english-heritage.org.uk

New Forest

William I made the area near his castle in Winchester a royal forest for hunting; severe penalties were imposed on poachers or anyone who harmed the deer or trees. The Crown ceded jurisdiction of the forest (144sq mi/373km2) to the Forestry Commission in 1924 and in 2005 it was given the status of National Park. Ponies, donkeys, deer, cattle and occasionally pigs still roam freely in the unspoilt woodland, heath and marshland and not infrequently by the roadside. Motorists should drive slowly and always with extreme care.

🛈 High Street. Lyndhurst; ☎ 023 8028 3444; www.newforestmuseum.org.uk www.newforestnpa.gov.uk

▶ Orient Yourself: The New Forest Museum and Visitor Centre is the best place to start.

⊛ **Don't Miss:** One of the Ornamental Drives; Beaulieu Motor Museum; Buckler's Hard.

🕐 **Organizing Your Time:** Allow two days.

Kids **Especially for Kids:** Beaulieu National Motor Museum; Wildlife Conservation Park.

🚶 **Walking Tours:** Ask at the visitor centre.

A. Williams/MICHELIN

The venerable Knightwood Oak (New Forest)

In the Forest
Bolderwood Ornamental Drive – This is a lovely drive through several enclosures created in the 19C and now containing many fine, mature trees, especially oak and beech. The **Bolderwood Walks**, at the beginning of the drive, enable visitors to see some of the forest deer at close quarters from observation platforms. Further along, some of the oak and beech pollards are at least 300 years old. At the end of the drive just before the A 35 is the venerable Knightwood Oak reputedly 375 years old.

Lyndhurst – Capital of the New Forest, this bustling and attractive town was where the forest verderers held court in the 17C Queen's House. The bold red-brick Victorian church is notable for its Burne-Jones windows and an 1864 fresco by Lord Leighton. In the churchyard is the grave of Alice Hargreaves, née Liddell, who inspired Lewis Carroll to write Alice in Wonderland.

The New Forest Museum and Visitor Centre, (High Street. 🕐 Open daily 10am-5pm, 🕐 Closed Christmas Eve from 12 noon, 25-26 Dec. 💶 £3. ☎ 023 8028 3444) offers an excellent introduction to the area with displays on every aspect of life in the New Forest: a film; computer interactives; the 25' long New Forest embroidery; and children's activities.
www.newforestmuseum.org.uk

Stourhead

The garden at Stourhead is one of the supreme examples of English landscape style. This idyllic scenery was created by the banker Henry Hoare II (1705-85), whose father had built a Classical house here in 1721, designed by the architect Colen Campbell, pioneer of English Palladianism. Henry Hoare was influenced in his garden design by the landscapes he saw on his travels and even more by the paintings of Claude Lorraine and Nicholas Poussin, in which nature is presented in luminous shades and focal points are provided by statuary or Classical buildings.

Visit
♿Garden: 🕐 Open daily, 9am-7pm/dusk. House: Open late-Mar to early-Nov, Sat-Wed and Good Friday, noon-5.30pm/dusk. Garden and house £8.70; garden or house £4.90; garden only, Nov-Feb £3.80. Restaurant. Refreshments. Parking. ☎ 01747 841 152;
www.nationaltrust.org.uk

Dartmoor National Park

Largest and wildest stretch of open country in southern Britain. Two plateaux, rising to over 2 000ft/610m and covered with blanket bog and heather moorland, are divided by the River Dart. Ponies – descendants of those turned out in the Middle Ages – still graze much of the lower-lying heather moorland and there are hundreds of ancient sites – chambered tombs, hillforts, stone circles, medieval crosses and waymarks.

Cornish Coast

Remoteness and wildness are the charms of the Cornwall peninsula with its long rugged coastline. The Cornwall Coast Path – part of the larger South West Way – winds a sinuous course (268mi/430km) above the sheer cliffs and indented coves and is the ideal way to discover the scenic splendours of the peninsula. The footpath is clearly waymarked and there is a wide choice of inland paths as short cuts.

R. Besse/MICHELIN

Penwith coastline, near St Ives

Exmoor National Park

Rising to 1 500ft/460m, from Chapman Barrows to Dunkery Beacon, the heartland is still the windswept haunt of falcon and hawk; cliffs, broken by deep valleys with waterfalls, make protected breeding sites for seabirds. With the Quantocks, Exmoor is the last secure habitat in the south of England for the red deer and a small breeding herd has been established to maintain the declining numbers of Exmoor ponies.

Wells

The calm of the cathedral within its precinct contrasts majestically with the bustle of the Market Square in England's smallest cathedral city. Together with the other Mendip towns (Frome, Glastonbury, Shepton Mallet and Street), Wells prospered as a centre of the wool trade in the Middle Ages. The social history of Wells and the Mendip area are outlined in the Wells Museum in the Chancellor's House on the Cathedral Green.

- 🛈 Town Hall, Market Place ☎ 01749 672 552; www. wells.gov.uk.
- Don't Miss: The Cathedral, particularly its West Front; Cheddar Gorge and Caves.
- 🕐 Organizing Your Time: Allow half a day in Wells.
- Especially for Kids: Wookey Hole.
- 👣 Also See: Bath, Bristol, Glastonbury, Laycock.
- 🚶 Walking Tours: During the summer season there are guided walks of Wells departing from the tourist information centre.

Bath

In the 18C Bath was transformed in a fashionable spa town, where people came to seek a cure for ill health or to enjoy the social life. People still flock to Bath, not for a physical cure but to capture a taste of 18C society; to admire the graceful Georgian terraces and villas, built in the local honey-coloured stone, rising up the seven hills beside the river Avon, or to follow in the footsteps of Jane Austen and some of the characters in her novels.

A. Taverner/MICHELIN

Georgian terrace architecture in Bath

- 🅿 Parking: A Park and Ride system is in operation (follow the signs).
- Don't Miss: The Baths, Royal Crescent and by way of contrast (out of town) the American Museum.
- 🕐 Organizing Your Time: Allow at least two full days.
- Especially for Kids: The Baths, if they are studying the Romans at school. The American Museum.
- 👣 Also See: Bristol, Cheltenham, The Cotswolds, Devizes, Glastonbury, Gloucester, Lacock, Longleat, Stonehenge, Stourhead, Wells.
- 🚶 Walking Tours:

  Jane Austen Walking Tour – 🕐 *daily at 11am from the Tourist Information Centre, tours last 1 ½ hours.* ⚲£4.50. www.janeausten.co.uk/centre/walking_tours.

  Ghost Walks of Bath – 🕐 *Apr-Oct, Mon-Sat 8pm; Nov-Mar, Fri at 8pm, tours last about two hours.* ⚲£6. ☎ 01225 463 618; www.ghostwalksofbath.co.uk;

  Mayor's Guides walking tours – 🕐 *daily 10.30am and Sun-Fri 2pm., also May-Sep Tue, Fri, Sat 7pm, depart from outside the Roman Baths entrance, tours last 2 hours.*

The Cotswolds

Rising gently from the Upper Thames valley in the southeast to a dramatic escarpment overlooking the Severn Vale in the west, the Cotswolds offer the essence of rural England in concentrated form. Airy open uplands, sheltered in places by stately belts of beech trees, alternate with deep valleys enfolding exquisite villages and small towns.

- ▶ Orient Yourself: There are various bus tours of the area, departing from the surrounding towns of Oxford, Stratford, Cheltenham and Bath, including City Sightseeing (*mid May-late Sept* ☎ 01708 866000; www.citysightseeing.co.uk.
- Don't Miss: Bibury,Cirencester Chastleton House, Snowshill Manor, Chipping Campden, Hidcote Manor Garden.
- 🕐 Organizing Your Time: Allow 3 days to see the area at a leisurely pace.
- Especially for Kids: Cotswold Wildlife Park and various attractions at Bourton-on-the-Water.

R. Corbel/MICHELIN

Typical stone cottage, Gloucestershire

Blenheim Palace

Built 1705-22 by Sir John Vanbrugh, this greatest building of the English Baroque, residence of the Dukes of Marlborough, is matched in splendour by the sublime landscape of its vast park, transformed between 1764-74 by Lancelot "Capability" Brown, whose masterpiece it is. At the park gates is the elegant town of **Woodstock**, built of mellow Cotswold stone, where old coaching inns and antique shops cluster round the Classical town hall.

Visit

🕐 Park: Open daily (except 25 Dec and one Sat in Nov), 9am-4.45pm. Palace: Open mid Feb-mid Dec, daily (🕐 closed Mon-Tue during Nov-Dec), 10.30am-4.45pm (4.45pm last admission). ⚲ Palace and park (including garden attractions) £13, Park and gardens only £8. 🚶 Guided tour (1hr,4 languages) every 10min; Guide book (£4; 6 languages). Parking. Restaurant, cafeteria. ☎ 01993 811 325 (24hr recorded information); www.blenheimpalace.com

R. Corbel/MICHELIN

Bleinhem Palace and its gardens

Oxford

The city of Oxford, on the Thames, 58 mi/93km northwest of London, incorporates England's oldest University and smallest cathedral.

- ▶ Orient Yourself: Oxford is compact and can be covered on foot.
- Don't Miss: Punting on the river; Christ Church; Bodleian Library; Ashmolean Museum; University Museum of Natural History/Pitt Rivers Museum.
- 🕐 Organizing Your Time: Allow at least three days. Many of the colleges are open only in the afternoon; visiting times are usually displayed at the porter's lodge. All college opening times can be seen on www. www.ox.ac.uk/visitors.
- Especially for Kids: Family Walking Tour - Children must be accompanied by an adult with a maximum of 4 children per adult. *School hols, daily 2.30pm.* ⚲ *Adults £5 and children 6-16 years £3;* The Oxford Story.
- 🚶 Walking Tours: City and Colleges Tour – 🕐 *Daily 11am, 2pm, additional tours on Saturday at 10.30am and 1pm.* ⚲*£6.50.* City and College Tour including Christ Church – 🕐 *Fri-Sat 2pm.* ⚲ *£7.50.* Ghost Tour 🕐 *June-Oct, Fri-Sat 7.45pm.* ⚲ *£5.* Inspector Morse Tour – 🕐 *Sat 1:30pm; advisable to book in advance at TIC or* ☎ *01865 726871;* ⚲ *£7.*

2 MIDLANDS & EAST ANGLIA

630 miles - 1010 km (10 days)

Landscapes and nature

The centre of England is firmly defined to the west by the mountains of Wales and to the north by the southern end of the **Pennines**. To the south and east a less marked boundary is formed by a succession of broad vales watered by slowly moving rivers overlooked by the escarpments of hill ranges. The most prominent hill range is the belt of oolitic limestone, which extends from Dorset to the River Humber, and is at its widest in the **Cotswolds**. It is the fine Cotswold stone which gives the built landscape such a distinctive character.

Elsewhere there is a less coherent pattern of modest blocks of hill country, in mixed farming except for heath and woodland tracts such as Cannock Chase (Staffordshire), Charnwood Forest (Leicestershire) and the **Royal Forest of Dean** (Gloucestershire).

England's most extensive area of low relief is a region of great individuality; densely populated in medieval times, it is unequalled in its wealth of ancient villages and small towns. Its dry climate and generally good soils mean that much of its gently undulating farmland is in arable cultivation; fields are large and many trees and hedges have been removed. East of Norwich, the regional capital, are the **Norfolk Broads,** extensive shallow stretches of water formed by peat extraction, rich in wildlife and thronged with pleasure craft.

Building styles express past links with the Netherlands; it was Dutch engineers who carried out much of the work which transformed the marshes and fens around the Wash into the country's richest tract of arable land.

The regular pattern of ancient county towns set at the centre of their shires (Gloucester, Northampton, Lincoln) is overlaid by the later one of the Industrial Revolution. Heavy industry began at Ironbridge and was fuelled by the diverse mineral resources of the region. It caused Birmingham to swell to metropolitan size and engendered the chaotic urban sprawls of the Black Country and the Potteries. The derelict land caused by recent industrial decline is being transformed into parkland.

Cambridge

England's second oldest university city (after Oxford), Cambridge lies 58 mi/41km due north of London on the western edge of the East Anglian fenlands situated on the River.

- ▶ Orient Yourself: All the main colleges and the Fitzwilliam Museum are tightly clustered in the centre of town. There is a hop-on hop-off bus tour (*see Address Book for details*).
- 🅿 Parking: Park and ride system in operation. City centre closed to motor vehicles during the week from 10am to 4pm.
- Don't Miss: St John's College; punting on the river Cam; King's College chapel, particularly when the Choir is in voice.
- 🕐 Organizing Your Time: Allow two full days.
- Especially for Kids: Imperial War Museum, Duxford.
- 🚶 Walking Tours: Guided walking tours and ghost tours are organised daily by the tourist information centre ☎ 01223 457 574; tours@cambridge.gov.uk.

  Christian Heritage Walking Tours depart Sun at 2.30pm and Wed at 11am; £3. ☎ 01223 311 602; www.christianheritageuk.org.uk

Chatsworth

The original Chatsworth was begun in 1551 by Sir William Cavendish and Bess of Hardwick, that indomitable Elizabethan who was married four times and multiplied her wealth with each marriage. She first exercised her passion for building at Chatsworth, where she created a Renaissance palace, but, on deciding that her third husband, the Earl of Shrewsbury, was a "knave, fool and beast" and that he had had an affair with his prisoner, Mary Queen of Scots, Bess returned to her Hardwick property fifteen miles away and built another. Chatsworth was transformed between 1686 and 1707 by the first Duke of Devonshire into a Baroque palace, which was greatly extended between 1820 and 1827 by the 6th Duke. In 1854 Charles de Saint-Amant described it as "le second Versailles".

A.F. Kersting/MICHELIN

State Drawing Room, Chatsworth

Visit

♿ House only ◷ Open Mar to mid-Dec, daily, 11am-5.30pm (6pm/dusk garden). House and garden ↔ House and garden £9.50; garden £5.75. ↔ Guided tour by appointment only, £17 per head (minimum 8 people). Brochure (6 languages). Parking. Refreshments. ☎ 01246 582 204; www.chatsworth.org

Peak District National Park

The deep dales and stone-walled fields of the White Peak are surrounded to east, west and north by the dramatic moors and peat bogs of the Dark Peak. In addition to walking, people come to fish and to cycle. Rock climbing on the gritstone edges has been joined by gliding, hang-gliding and wind-surfing as leisure activities.

Stratford-upon-Avon

Stratford is Arden country; its timber frames were hewn from the surrounding Forest of Arden and its favourite son's mother was called Mary Arden. William Shakespeare (1564-1616) forsook his home town and his wife, Anne Hathaway, for London, where success came to him as a jobbing playwright, who was able to distil sex and violence, farce and philosophy into the most potent lines in the language. He returned to Stratford in 1611, rich and famous enough to acquire a coat of arms, and lived at New Place until his death. Stratford is now one of England's most popular tourist destinations and as a result can be very congested, especially during the summer months.

A. Williams/MICHELIN

Mary Arden's House, home of Shakespeare's mother, near Stratford

▸ **Orient Yourself:** The centre is small enough to comfortably cover most attractions on foot. A hop-on, hop-off City Sightseeing Bus covers the rest. ☎ 01789 299 866; www.citysightseeing.co.uk.

🚫 **Don't Miss:** Hall's Croft; a night at the Royal Shakespeare Theatre; Mary Arden's House and the Shakespeare Countryside Museum.

◷ **Organizing Your Time:** Allow two days plus time for excursions.

↔ **Walking Tours:** Town Walk Mon- Wed 11am, Thur- Sun 2pm. (Times vary Christmas and New Year). ↔ £5. Meet at the Swan Fountain, Waterside (opposite Sheep Street), near The Royal Shakespeare Theatre. Booking not necessary. ☎ 01789 292 478, 07855 760 377. Ghost Walk Thur and Friday 7:30pm. Booking necessary. ☎ 01789 292 478, 07855 760 377.

3️⃣ WALES & THE MARCHES

590 miles - 950 km (7 days)

Landscapes and nature

The principality is approached from the east via the English **Marches**, attractive farming country interspersed with hill ranges anticipating the mountains beyond. In the south, marking the border near Chepstow, is the luxuriantly wooded gorge of the Wye. To the west lies Cardiff, the capital, flanked by the other former coal ports of the coast which were supplied by the immense coalfield of South Wales, a high plateau deeply cut by valleys filled with mining settlements. North of the mining country is the great bastion of the red sandstone escarpment of the **Brecon Beacons.**

Further west the scene is rural, rolling country ending in the cliffs and rocks of the **Pembrokeshire Coast National Park.** The gentle swelling forms of the sheep-grazed uplands of Mid-Wales contrast with the drama of the mountains of **Snowdonia**, true highlands of great grandeur. To the west extends the remote **Lleyn Peninsula.** The narrow coastal plain of North Wales abounds in seaside resorts. Offshore across the Menai Strait is the Isle of Anglesey.

Cardiff

Cardiff, capital city (and also the most southerly part) of Wales, arose around the Roman fort guarding the crossing of the Taff, on the road between Caerleon and Carmarthen. It was the world's principal coal port at the start of the 20C and much of its appearance today can be directly attributed to this era. Rugby football, the national sport of Wales, has its headquarters in the Millennium Stadium (formerly Cardiff Arms Park).

▸ **Orient Yourself:** The sights are spread over quite a large area so the City Sightseeing/Guide Friday (hop on-hop off) bus tour is a good way to get around. Operates Mar to late-Oct, daily. £7. ☎ 029 2038 4291, 01789 284 466; www.guidefriday.com.

🚫 **Don't Miss:** National Museum of Wales; Cardiff Castle exotic interiors; a major sporting or musical event at the Millennium Stadium if possible.

🚫 **Please Consider:** Be aware that large events at the Millennium Stadium will mean congestion on the roads and may mean city centre accommodation is in short supply.

◷ **Organizing Your Time:** Allow at least a full day.

Kids **Especially for Kids:** Techniquest for hands-on fun.

Brecon Beacons

High red sandstone mountains divide the ancient rocks of mid-Wales from the coalfields and industrialisation farther south. Along the southern edge of the Park a limestone belt provides a dramatic change in scenery and there are hundreds of sink-holes and cave systems, the most spectacular being the Dan-yr-Ogof Caves at the head of the Tawe valley.

Pembrokeshire Coast

Second smallest of the Parks, for much of its length it is less than three miles wide. Steep cliffs display spectacularly folded and twisted rock formations; sheltered bays invite bathing and scuba-diving. Offshore islands such as Skomer and Skokholm support huge colonies of seabirds.

Snowdonia

Snowdonia was designated a National Park in 1951; it covers 840 sq mi/2 180km2 of wild beauty amongst the scenic mountains of North Wales and is the second largest of such parks in England and Wales. Yr Wyddfa Fawr, The Great Tumulus, or Snowdon (3 560ft/1 085m), as it is called in English, dominates the northern sector, Cader Idris (2 930ft/830m) the south. There are 96 peaks of over 1 970ft/600m in the park.

ℹ Snowdonia National park Headquarters: ☎ 01766 770 274. Gwynedd Council: ☎ 01286 672 255.

🚫 **Don't Miss:** Snowdon Mountain railway and the vew from the summit; Llechwed Slate Caverns; Machynlleth Centre for Alternative Technology.

◷ **Organizing Your Time:** Allow at least three days

Kids **Especially for Kids:** Either of the mountain railways; Celtica.

🧗 **Mountaineering:** National Mountain Centre ◷ Open mid-Jul to early-Sep, daily, 9.30am-5.30pm; courses (2hr)

at 9.30am, noon and 3pm in abseiling, climbing, canoeing (participants must be able to swim; change of clothes advisable) and skiing (long trousers, long sleeves and gloves); ↔ £10 per course. Booking available. Equipment provided. ☎ 01690 720 214; Fax 01690 720 394; www.pyb.co.uk.

↔ **Skiing:** Rhiw Goch Ski and Mountain Bike Centre.

🚲 **Mountain Biking:** Rhiw Goch Ski and Mountain Bike Centre. Also Coed-y-Brenin Forest Park and Gwydir Forest.

↔ **Walking:** Ask about park ranger-guided walks at any tourist office; Coed-y-Brenin Forest Park and Gwydir Forest are good locations.

Portmeirion

Built on a wooded peninsula, with wonderful views over the shining waters and sweeping sandbanks of Traeth Bach, and with the mountains of Snowdonia as a backdrop, this dream village was the creation of the ever-fertile imagination of the long-lived architect and pioneer preservationist, Sir Clough Williams-Ellis (1893-1978). It has often been used as the setting for films and television programmes, the most famous of which was The Prisoner (1966-67), a TV series which gained cult status, starring Patrick McGoohan.

ℹ High Street, Harlech ☎ 01766 780 658 (seasonal); Fax 01766 780 658; www.gwynedd.gov.uk.

ℹ High Street, Porthmadog ☎ 01766 512 981; porthmadog.tic@gwynedd.gov.uk

Caernarfon

The strategic site of Caernarfon, at the southwestern end of the Menai Strait and offering views stretching north to Anglesey and south over the hills and mountains of Snowdonia, has been appreciated from earliest times. It was the most westerly position of the Romans in Wales, who built their fort of Segontium nearby; the Normans chose the castle's present site for their wooden stronghold, which was probably replaced by a stone castle even before Edward I began his mighty structure, bristling with towers and turrets and designed as a seat of power. Caernarfon's name itself derives from the Welsh for "Fort on the Shore."

R. Corbel/MICHELIN

The town today, still watched over by the castle and partly encircled within its walls, is a centre for visitors to Snowdonia and for yachtsmen eager to make use of the town's proximity to the waters of the strait and Caernarfon Bay.

ℹ Oriel Pendeitsh, Castle Street LL55 1ES ☎ 01286 672 232; Fax 01286 678 209; www.visitcaernarfon.com

🚫 **Don't Miss:** Caernarfon Castle, viewed from the water if possible

◷ **Organizing Your Time:** Allow 2 hours to se the castle and town

Kids **Especially for Kids:** Beaches at Port Donorwic (east) and at Dinas Dinlle (south west)

Conwy

Viewed from the east bank, the River Conwy and bestriding bridges, the walled town and **Conwy Castle**, massive and bristling with towers, make a breathtaking sight against the mountain background. Llywelyn the Great chose this ideal site, controlling the estuary, for his future burial place and to this end endowed a Cistercian abbey. Later, with the building of Edward I's mighty fortress and garrison town, the monks were moved upstream to Maenan. All of Edward I's castles in Wales – with the exception of Harlech – were built in association with a "bastide", a town laid out on a rectangular grid. The town developed with the castle but remained contained by its circuit of walls.

ℹ Conwy Castle Visitor Centre LL32 8LD ☎ 01492 592 248; Fax : 01492 573 545; conwytic@virgin.net

▸ **Orient Yourself:** City Sightseeing buses operate a service between here and Llandudno - mid May-late Sept ☎01708 866 000; www.citysightseeing.co.uk.

🚫 **Don't Miss:** Conwy Castle; a trip on the Princess Christine northeast.

◷ **Organizing Your Time:** Allow 2 hours to see town and castle.

Kids **Especially for Kids:** beaches at the Conwy Marina and Penmaenmawr (west); Conwy Butterfly Jungle.

Powis

The town of Welshpool (Y Trallwng) lies at the northern end of the ridge on which is built **Powis Castle**. The barony of the la Pole was granted to Gruffyd ap Gwenwynwyn in 1277 on condition that his son renounce all Welsh princely titles. The massive twin towers of the gateway date from the decades prior to 1300. In 1587 the castle was bought by Sir Edward Herbert who quickly adapted it to Elizabethan standards of comfort. The Long Gallery, with its mid-17C *trompe-l'œil* panelling, is dated 1592-93 while the Dining Room and Oak Drawing Room were remodelled in the early 20C. The castle houses the collections of the first **Lord Clive** (1725-74) victor of Plassey and founder of British India, and many fine paintings.

The **gardens**, their Italianate terraces enhancing the castle's craggy site, were created towards the end of the 17C. They were not later subjected to the fashionable attentions of Capability Brown and are one of the rare remaining masterpieces of the period.

Castle and museum: Open Jul-Aug, Tue-Sun; late-Mar to Jun and Sep to early Nov, Wed-Sun and Bank Hol Mon, 1-5pm. Garden: Open as castle, 11am-6pm. £7.50; garden only, £5. No dogs. Parking. Licensed restaurant. 01938 551 920; 01938 551 944 (infoline); www.nationaltrust.org.uk

R. Corbel/MICHELIN

Cruck Cottage, Herefordshire (Late medieval timber construction)

4 NORTHERN ENGLAND

580 miles - 930 km (7 days)

Landscapes and nature

At a certain latitude not easy to define the personality of the English landscape changes decisively. A less kindly climate, high moorlands and rugged mountains predominate; building stones lend themselves to bold rather than refined treatment; the impact of industry is widespread. These factors combine to give a distinct and strong identity to "The North".

The long mountain chain of the **Pennines** is the region's central feature, though it is flanked by extensive lowlands; to the west lie the **Cheshire** and **Lancashire** plains, the former as lush and tidy as any southern county, the latter much built over but growing horticultural crops on its reclaimed "mosses".

To the east, beyond the densely populated **Yorkshire** coalfield, is equally fertile country, prolonged northwards by the **Vale of York** and bounded along the coast by chalk wolds divided by the great estuary of the **Humber**.

The **Pennine Chain**, with its three National Parks, is far from homogeneous in character. In the far North, the wild and lonely **Cheviots** of the Northumberland National Park are the well-rounded remains of ancient volcanoes. In the **Yorkshire Dales** the characteristic features of limestone country are well developed tablelands rising to high, flat-topped eminences like **Pen-y-Ghent** (2273ft/693m), gorges, cliffs, caves and underground streams. Here and in that part of the **Peak District** where pale carboniferous limestone occurs the rock has been used to build a harmonious landscape of stone, sterner than but similar to the Cotswold Country. Between the Peak District, the mountain playground for much of industrial Lancashire, and the Yorkshire Dales lie many upland miles of even more severe country, underlain by the sombre millstone grit. The abundant rainfall pours off the mountains in fast-flowing streams, which drove the mills and factories in the densely built-up valleys or fed the unspoilt rivers of Dales and Peak. East of the Pennines, the **North York Moors** National Park forms a vast heather-covered tableland which reaches the sea in an undeveloped coastline of great beauty.

To the west is the **Lake District**, where the highest peaks in England (**Scafell Pike** 3 206ft/978m) dominate an inexhaustible variety of mountain scenery ranging from the wildest of storm-blasted crags to the exquisite park and scenery reflected in **Lake Windermere**.

In **Northumbria**, the northernmost province in England, where the fells draw ever closer to the coast, the windy farmlands contrast with deep wooded denes and the trio of riverside conurbations flanking the **Tyne, Wear** and **Tees**.

Lake District

"I do not know of any tract of country in which, in so narrow a compass, may be found an equal variety in the influences of light and shadow upon the sublime and beautiful". The words of the poet William Wordsworth express something of the attraction that draws vast numbers of visitors to the Lake District. Most of the area is incorporated in the Lake District National Park (880sq mi/2 280km2) of which one quarter is conserved by the National Trust. The Lake District can be appreciated in many ways – exploring the narrow and often congested lanes by car, taking a trip in a launch, sailing or windsurfing on the lakes and best of all by walking or climbing in the fells.

A. Williams/MICHELIN

Lake Windermere

Hawkshead *LA22 0NT* *015394 36525*

Beckside Car Park (Ullswater), Glenridding, Penrith, CA11 0PD 017684 82414;

Bowness on Windermere LA23 3HJ 01539 442 895; www.lake-district.gov.uk.

Orient Yourself: Visit the Brockhole National Park Visitor Centre to get an overall view of the district; Ambleside and Windermere make good touring bases; half-day and full-day guided tours in mini-coaches are available from several companies including Lakes Supertours, *1 High Street, Windermere* *01539 442 751, 01539 488 133;* www.lakes-supertours.com and Mountain Goat tours, *Victoria Street, Windermere,* *01539 445 161;* www.lakes-pages.co.uk

Don't Miss: A boat trip; a walk (for as long as you can manage!);

Please Consider: Motorists should note that some mountain roads are narrow with sharp bends and severe gradients, sometimes over 1:3/30%.
Walkers and fell climbers are advised to choose routes suited to their experience; to tell someone of their intended route and time of return; to take the necessary maps and equipment; to wear appropriate footwear and clothing; not to set out in failing daylight or deteriorating weather conditions: Hill Top (Beatrix Potter's cottage) is hugely popular, and you may well have to wait to get in *(timed ticket system)*. **Organizing Your Time**: Allow at least three days if you want to get a flavour of the area.

Kids **Especially for Kids**: Hill Top (Beatrix Potter's cottage) for little ones.

Walking Tours: There are many guided walks and rambles, ask at your nearest TIC. Advance registration essential. Park in Grange and take the train to Arnside. Those who grow tired during the walk (8mi/13km; at least 3hr) can be picked up by a tractor and trailer. Sturdy shoes are advised as the foreshore at the start is rocky; Wellington boots or jeans are not advised as you will get wet during the river crossing (approx 2ft deep); at any time of year wear several layers rather than one thick covering; in summer suntan lotion and hats are necessary but it may also be windy; bring water and a towel for cleaning the mud off your feet at the end. *01539 534 026;* www.morecambebay.org.uk

Bicycle Trails: Cycles are available for hire from many places, including Windermere railway station.

Sailing: Lake Windermere has many sailing and watersports options. A popular venue is Coniston Boating Centre, Coniston Water *015394 41366.*

Hadrian's Wall

In AD 122, during a tour of the western provinces of the Empire, the Roman Emperor Hadrian visited Britain. He ordered the building of a defensive wall across the northernmost boundary of the Empire from Wallsend on the Tyne, to Bowness on the Solway Firth (73mi/117km). Although Hadrian's Wall has come to represent the frontier between England and Scotland it is well south of the modern border between the countries. Parts of this wall can still be seen today and museums, camps and settlements give a picture of military and civilian life on Rome's "Northwest Frontier".

Wentworth Car Park, Hexham, Northumberland, NE46 1QE 01434 652220; www.hadrians-wall.org

Visit

Housesteads Roman Fort Open daily, 10am-6pm (4pm Oct -Mar). Closed Jan 1 and 24-26 Dec. £3.60. Informations panels (4 languages). Parking. Refreshments. 01434 344 363; www.english-heritage.org.uk. The fort (5 acres/2ha) is perched high on the ridge and is the most complete example on the Wall. Still clearly visible are the foundations of the large courtyard house of the commandant, the granaries, barracks, headquarters building, the four main gateways, the hospital and 24-seater latrine block as well as part of the civilian settlement, clustering round the south gate.
The Wall is visible to east and west as it undulates over the whinsill ridge.

Durham

The quiet streets of the little medieval city with its castle are the perfect foil for the great sandstone mass of the Norman cathedral rising above the deep wooded gorge of the River Wear in a sublime fusion of architecture and landscape, in what is a truly remarkable setting.

2 Millennium Place, Durham, DH1 1WA *0191 384 3720;* www. durhamcity.gov.uk

Orient Yourself: You can see this compact little city quite easily on foot; for an alternative view, boat trips are available and rowing boats are for hire.

Don't Miss: The Cathedral's Chapel of the Nine Altars; the riverside views from or near Prebend's Bridge.

Organizing Your Time: Allow half a day.

Yorkshire Dales

Nearly half of the Dales is farmland. Over four centuries the monasteries' sheep walks developed into the start of a road system across the fells, the best known today being the green lane between Kilnsey and Malham Cove and Tarn. The unique limestone pavement "grykes" provide sheltered habitats for lime- and shade-loving plants. The "Dales" themselves, (Ribble-, Swale-, Wensley- and Wharfe-) have welcoming villages in rich valley pastures, while the limestone peaks of Ingleborough and Pen-y-Ghent present a more rugged face.

Fountain's Abbey

Set in the wooded valley of the little River Skell 3 miles/5km west of Ripon, in the glorious North Yorkshire countryside, these Cistercian ruins are wonderfully evocative of monastic life in the Middle Ages.

In 1132 a small band of Benedictines, in revolt against slack discipline at their abbey in York, were granted land in this "place remote from all the world." Accepted by St Bernard into his austere order, the monks set about transforming the northern wilderness into the flourishing and productive countryside characteristic of Cistercian endeavour. Within a century, Fountains was the centre of an enormous enterprise, managing fish-farms and ironworkings, as well as forests and vast tracts of agricultural land, the profits from which paid for an ambitious building programme.

The great complex fell into decay following the Dissolution but in 1768 it was bought by the Aislabie family, who had long desired it as the ultimate in picturesque ruins to complete their lavish landscaping of the adjacent Studley Royal estate.

Visitor Centre – The Centre provides information on the history of the abbey, the Cistercian rule and the construction of the gardens of Studley Royal.

From the Visitor Centre take the minibus or take the steep and direct path (5min) or the longer less steep path with view points (10min); at the gate fork right to Fountains Hall or left to the abbey ruins and the gardens. Open Mar-Oct, daily, 10am-5pm (3pm, 12-13 Jul, and Oct); Nov-Jan, Sat-Thu, 10am-4pm/dusk); Feb-Mar, daily, 10am-4pm. Deerpark open daily during daylight hours. Last admission 1 hr before closing. Closed 1 Jan and 24-25 Dec. £5.50. Guided tour of abbey, water garden and mill. Deer park £2. Licensed restaurant. 01765 608 888 (infoline); www.fountainsabbey.org.uk.

North York Moors

A relatively quiet Park. The moors are clearly defined, rising sharply from Tees in the north to Pickering and the Vale of York in the south. The eastern boundary is the sea. The Park contains Staithes, home of Captain Cook, and Whitby, famous for jet – a fossilised black amber – so popular with the Victorians, also Rievaulx and Rosedale Abbeys.

York

Formerly an economic centre based on the wool trade, York is marked by many elegant Georgian buildings that reflect the wealth of those moving from the north into what has become an important centre of social and cultural life.

Orient Yourself: Most of the city's attractions are within the old walls and is best explored on foot. There are lots of guided walks (*see www.york-tourism.co.uk*) but for a general introduction try Yorkwalk (*daily Feb-Nov 10.30am, 2.15pm; Sat-Sun only 10.30am, 2.15pm Dec-Jan* *01904 622 303; www.yorkwalk.co.uk*). Just turn up at their

Museum Street office. City Sightseeing operate hop-on, hop-off open top bus tours (⊙ *daily Easter-September, Sat-Sun Oct* ☎ *01904 655 585; www. yorktourbuses.co.uk*) buy your ticket on the bus.

- ⊕ **Don't Miss:** The stained glass in York Minster; National Railway Museum; The Shambles; Castle Howard, particularly its park.
- ⊙ **Organizing Your Time:** Allow 2-3 days for the city centre alone.
- **Kids Especially for Kids:** National Railway Museum; Jorvik Viking Centre.
- **Bicycle Trails:** York is a cycle-friendly city; for cycle routes and information go to www.york.gov.uk/cycling/index. html.

5 SCOTLAND

1110 miles - 1770 km (13 days)

Landscapes and nature

While many elements of the English landscape – enclosed fields, parklands – are repeated in Scotland, often in a neater, simplified form, the country's scenic personality is quite distinct; mountains and moorlands predominate; the climate is noticeably more rigorous (albeit with many compensations, mild winters in the west, sparkling air in the east); human activity is highly concentrated in the lowlands and parts of the coast, leaving much of the surface of the land free from urban intrusions and exhilaratingly open to the influences of Nature. This rich and varied landscape can be broken down into three main regions.

The **Southern Uplands,** sparsely inhabited borderlands, consist of gently rounded moors penetrated in the west by deep, narrow dales, in the east by the broader, cultivated valleys of the **Tweed** and its tributaries.

The **Central Lowlands,** dramatically pierced by the great firths of **Tay, Clyde** and **Forth,** are densely populated and the focus of the urban and industrial life of Scotland. The area is rich in minerals and has a prosperous agriculture. The region, which is low-lying only in contrast to the mountains to the north and south, is enlivened by numerous hill ranges, the Pentland Hills and Campsie Fells forming a background to Edinburgh and Glasgow, the high **Ochils** seeming to bar the way northwards.

A. Williams/MICHELIN

The famous Forth Bridge (1883-1890)

The **Highlands and Islands,** the third main region of Scotland, includes the highest peak in Britain, **Ben Nevis** (4 406ft/1 344m) and the **Cairngorm Mountains,** dominated by **Ben Macdui** (4 296ft/1 309m). Much of the area lies above 2 000ft/610m and rises above 4 000ft/1 220m. A complex geological history has left landforms as varied as the smoothly rounded **Grampians,** the towering **Cuillins** of the Isle of Skye and the spectacular mountain and cliff scenery of **Wester Ross.** Water is everywhere; tumbling peat-brown burns feed fine rivers; there are salt- and fresh-water lochs and in the west, the sea defines an extraordinarily indented coastline.

Cotton grass and heather clothe the mountains; tree cover becomes ever sparser northwards, though there are magnificent remains of the ancient Caledonian pine forest at Glenmore.

The thinly spread human presence favours wildlife; the coast is thronged with seabirds, including puffins; there are grey and common seals; inland the red deer is abundant, and in the wilder places live the wild cat, the eagle, and the recently re-established osprey.

Beyond the mainland lie nearly 800 islands, many uninhabited, each with its own character, like wind-swept **Islay,** almost in sight of Ireland; **Skye,** with its unsurpassed mountain and coastal scenery; **Orkney,** rich in prehistoric remains, and far-off **Shetland,** stern and treeless.

Edinburgh

Edinburgh, capital of Scotland, lies on the Firth of Forth, a deep inlet gouged into the east coast. The city is spectacularly located on a series of volcanic hills, each giving a different and often spectacular vantage point. Perhaps the best known is Arthur's Seat (823ft/251m), overlooking Holyrood Park. Edinburgh boasts a past rich in history; the Old Town, huddled for years on the ridge running down from the Castle Rock, contrasts with the New Town, with its elegant Georgian streets and squares.

- ▶ **Orient Yourself:** Edinburgh is compact. You can visit all the Old Town and much of the New Town on foot (there are several guided walking tours; bus tours of the city depart from Waverley Bridge next to the station www.citysightseeing.co.uk
- ℗ **Parking:** Difficult and expensive; don't drive in central Edinburgh.
- ⊕ **Don't Miss:** The Royal Mile; an underground tour; the Scottish Parliament Building; the views from the Nelson Monument and Arthur's Seat; Charlotte Square; the Festival Fringe; Royal Museum and Museum of Scotland; Royal Yacht Britannia; Forth Bridges view from South Queensferry.
- ⊙ **Organizing Your Time:** Allow at least three days.
- **Kids Especially for Kids:** a (not too scary) ghost tour; Edinburgh Zoo, Our Dynamic Earth; Deep Sea World (at North Queensferry).
- **Walking Tours:** The Edinburgh Literary Pub Tour ☎ 0131 226 6665; www.edinburghliterarypubtour.co.uk Mercat Tours; City of the Dead Tours (not recommended for children or the faint hearted).

Glasgow

Glasgow, Scotland's most populous city, is an important industrial centre and port, lying 44 miles/70km west of Edinburgh, just a few miles inland of the east coast. It is currently enjoying a renaissance as a cultural centre.

R. Corbel/MICHELIN

The Glasgow School of Art (1897-1909), built by Charles Rennie Mackintosh, combines strict utility of purpose with innovative, near-abstract forms and decorative Art Nouveau elements.

- ▶ **Orient Yourself:** Since Glasgow's main sights are well scattered about, it is advisable to use public transport. The underground stations are indicated on the town plan below. City tours in open-topped buses leave from George Square. Contact Scotguide Tours Services for further information. ☎ 0141 204 0444; www.scotguide.com.
- ⊕ **Don't Miss:** The Burrell Collection, Glasgow Cathedral; Hunterian Art Gallery Mackintosh wing; Museum of Transport, an excursion to New Lanark.
- ⊙ **Organizing Your Time:** Allow at least three days in the city itself.
- **Kids Especially for Kids:** Glasgow Science Centre.

The Trossachs

Occupying Scotland's midriff area, the Trossachs is one of the country's most famous scenic areas, with rugged mountains and wooded slopes reflected in the waters of many lochs. From Callander and Loch Venachar in the east, to Loch Katrine and even to the shores of Loch Lomond in the west, this whole area of great scenic beauty is easily accessible.

- 🄳 *Ancester Square,Callander* ☎ *08707 200 628; www.lochlomond-trossachs.org www.trossachs.org.uk*
- 🄳 *National Park Headquarters, The Old Station, Balloch Road, Balloch G83 8BF* ☎ *01389 722600; www.lochlomond-trossachs.org*
- ▶ **Orient Yourself:** Callander is a good base. Outdoor explorers should make the National Park Headquarters their first stop.
- ⊕ **Don't Miss:** Loch Katrineand the panorama closeby; Loch Lomond; Ben Lomond.
- ⊙ **Organizing Your Time:** Allow 2-3 days.
- 🄰 **Also See:** Perth, Stirling.
- **Walking:** Callander is a centre for hill walking with several "Munros" (peaks over 3,000 feet/914m) close by, go to *www. trossachs.org.uk* for more details; Queen Elizabeth Forest Park.
- **Bicycle Trails:** Cycle hire from Loch Katrine Visitor Centre and Queen Elizabeth Forest Park. For more details, go to the activities page on: www.trossachs.org.uk
- **Fishing:** Lake of Menteith, Queen Elizabeth Forest Park.

Wester Ross and Inverewe Garden

The Atlantic seaboard of Wester Ross is wild and dramatic, with magnificent mountains and placid lochs. The main touring centres are Kyle of Lochalsh, Gairloch and Ullapool, and from these the visitor may drive, walk, climb, fish or sail, to enjoy to the full this glorious area.

- 🄳 *Auchtercairn, Gairloch* ☎ *01445 712 130.*
- 🄳 *Car Park, Kyle of Lochalsh DD8 4EF* ☎ *01599 534 276;*
- 🄳 *Argyle Street, Ullapool* ☎ *01854 612135; www.ullapool.com.*
- ⊕ **Don't Miss:** Inverewe Garden; Loch Maree; Eilean Donan Castle.
- ⊕ **Be Careful:** Do not underestimate distances. Single track and winding lochside roads need time. Remember to keep the gas tank well topped-up.
- ⊙ **Organizing Your Time:** Allow 2-3 days.
- ▶ **Also See:** Inverness, Oban, Isle of Skye, Western Isles.

Visit

Inverewe Garden – ⅀⅁ ⊙ *(NTS) Open daily, late-Mar-Oct, 9am-9pm; Nov to late-Mar, 9.30am-5pm.* ⊞ *£7 Guide book (3 languages). Visitor Centre: Open late-Mar to Oct, daily, 10am-5pm. Parking. Licensed restaurant.* ☎ *01445 781 200; Fax 01445 781 497;* www.nts.org.uk.

These outstanding gardens, in a magnificent coastal setting, show many sorts of plants to their best advantage. The gardens (64 acres/26ha) are made possible so far north, on the same latitude as Leningrad, by the influence of the Gulf Stream. The property, a barren peninsula with an acid peat soil exposed to the Atlantic gales, was bought for Osgood Mackenzie in 1862. A rabbit-proof fence was erected, Scots and Corsican pines were planted as wind-breaks and soil was imported. A lifetime of planning and planting, continued after his death by his daughter, has created this memorial to him. Colour is found at most seasons, with azaleas and rhododendrons in May, the rock garden in June, herbaceous borders in mid-summer and heathers and maples in the autumn.

R. Corbel/MICHELIN

House at Culross, 16C

Other sightseeing and themed tours

Natural settings

The 12 National Parks in England and Wales and four forest parks in Scotland are areas of scenic attraction for recreation. In addition to marked trails there are picnic sites, visitor centres and facilities for various activities (boating, sailing, canoeing, pony trekking, rambling).

Council for National Parks
6/7 Barnard Mews, London SW11 1QU ☎ 020 7924 4077; www.cnp.org.uk.
The parks provide some of the best walking and rambling country.

Forestry Commission
Headquarters, 231 Corstorphine Road, Edinburgh, Lothian EH12 7AT. ☎ 0131 334 0303; www.forestry.gov.uk
Conservation is the main aim of the **national reserves** (wildfowl sanctuaries, sand dunes, moorland).

Royal Society for the Protection of Birds
The Lodge, Sandy, Bedfordshire SG19 2DL.
☎ 01767 680 551;
www.rspb.org.uk

Wildfowl and Wetlands Trust, National Centre
Slimbridge, Gloucestershire GL2 7BT, ☎ 0870 334 4000; www.wwt.org.uk

Scottish Wildlife Trust
Cramond House, Kirk Cramond, Cramond Glebe Road, Edinburgh EH4 6NS. ☎ 0131 312 7765;
www.swt.org.uk

Scottish Natural Heritage
12 Hope Terrace, Edinburgh EH9 2AS. ☎ 0131 447 4784;
www.snh.org.uk

Restricted motorway junctions

M1	Northbound	Southbound
2	No exit	No access
4	No exit	No access
6a	No exit	No access
	Access from M25 only	Exit to M25 only
7	No exit	No access
	Access from M10 only	Exit to M10 only
17	No access	No exit
	Exit to M45 only	Access from M45 only
19	No exit to A14	No access from A14
21a	No access	No exit
23a	Exit to A42 only	
24a	No access	No access
35a	No access	No exit
43	No exit to M621 northbound	
48	No exit to A1 southbound	

M2	Eastbound	Westbound
1	Access from A2 eastbound only	Exit to A2 westbound only

M3	Eastbound	Westbound
8	No exit	No access
10	No access	No exit
13	No access to M27 eastbound	
14	No exit	No access

M4	Eastbound	Westbound
1	Exit to A4 eastbound only	Access from A4 westbound only
2	Access to A4 eastbound only	Access to A4 westbound only
21	No exit	No access
23	No access	No exit
25	No exit	No access
25a	No exit	No access
29	No exit	No access

M4	Eastbound	Westbound
38		No access
39	No exit or access	No exit
41	No access	No exit
41a	No exit	No access
42	Exit to A483 only	Access from A483 only
42	Access from A483 only	Exit to A483 only

M5	Northbound	Southbound
10	No exit	No access
11a	No access from A417 eastbound	No exit to A417 westbound

M6	Northbound	Southbound
3a	No access	No exit
	Exit to M42 northbound only	Access from M6 eastbound only
4a	No exit	No access
	Access from M42 southbound only	Exit to M42 only
5	No access	No exit
10a	No access	No exit
	Exit to M54 only	Access from M54 only
11a	No exit / access	No access / exit
	No access to M6 Toll	
20	No exit to M56 eastbound	No access from M56 westbound
24	No exit	No access
25	No access	No exit
30	No exit	No access
	Access from M61 northbound only	Exit to M61 southbound
31a	No access	No exit

M6 Toll	Northbound	Southbound
T1		
T2	No exit / access	No access
T5	No exit	No access
T7	No access	No exit
T8	No access	No exit

M8	Eastbound	Westbound
8	No exit to M73 northbound	No access from M73 southbound
9	No access	No exit
13	No exit southbound	No access
14	No access	No exit
16	No exit	No access
17	No exit	No access
18		No exit
19	No exit to A814 eastbound	No access from A814 westbound
20	No exit	No access
21	No access	No exit
22	No exit	No access
	Access from M77 only	Exit to M77 only
23	No exit	No access
25	Exit to A739 northbound only	Exit to A739 northbound only
	Access from A739 southbound only	Access from A739 southbound only
25a	No exit	No access
28	No exit	No access
28a	No exit	No access

M9	Eastbound	Westbound
1a	No exit	No access
2	No access	No exit
3	No exit	No access
6	No access	No exit
8	No exit	No access

M11	Northbound	Southbound
4	No exit	No access
5	No access	No exit
9	No access	No exit
13	No access	No exit
14	No exit to A428 westbound	No exit
		Access from A14 westbound only

Continued on page XIII

Restricted motorway junctions

Continuation from page XI

M20	Eastbound	Westbound
2	No access	No exit
3	No exit	No access
	Access from M26 eastbound only	Exit to M26 westbound only
11a	No access	No exit

M23	Northbound	Southbound
7	No exit to A23 southbound	No access from A23 northbound
10a	No exit	No access

M25	Clockwise	Anticlockwise
5	No exit to M26 eastbound	No access from M26 westbound
19	No access	No exit
21	No exit to M1 southbound	No exit to M1 southbound
	Access from M1 southbound only	Access from M1 southbound only
31	No exit	No access

M27	Eastbound	Westbound
10	No exit	No access
12	No access	No exit

M40	Eastbound	Westbound
3	No exit	No access
7	No exit	No access
8	No exit	No access
13	No exit	No access
14	No access	No exit
16	No access	No exit

M42	Northbound	Southbound
1	No exit	No access
7	No access	No exit
	Exit to M6 northbound only	Access from M6 northbound only
7a	No access	No exit
	Exit to M6 only	Access from M6 northbound only
8	No exit	Exit to M6 northbound
	Access from M6 southbound only	Access from M6 southbound only

M45	Eastbound	Westbound
M1 junc 17	Access to M1 southbound only	No access from M1 southbound
With A45 (Dunchurch)	No access	No exit

M48	Eastbound	Westbound
M4 junc 21	No exit to M4 westbound	No access from M4 eastbound
M4 junc 23	No access from M4 westbound	No exit to M4 eastbound

M49	Southbound	
18a	No exit to M5 northbound	

M53	Northbound	Southbound
11	Exit to M56 eastbound only	Exit to M56 eastbound only
	Access from M56 westbound only	Access from M56 westbound only

M56	Eastbound	Westbound
2	No exit	No access
3	No access	No exit
4	No exit	No access
7		No access
8	No exit or access	No exit
9	No access from M6 northbound	No access to M6 southbound
15	No exit to M53	No access from M53 northbound

M57	Northbound	Southbound
3	No exit	No access
5	No exit	No access

M58	Eastbound	Westbound
1	No exit	No access

M60	Clockwise	Anticlockwise
2	No exit to A34 northbound	No exit to A34 northbound
3	No access to M56	No exit to M56
4	No exit to A5103 southbound	No exit to A5103 northbound
5	No exit to A580	No access from A580
14	No exit	No access
16	No access	No exit
20		No access
22	No access	
25	No exit or access	
26		No exit or access
27	No exit	No access

M61	Northbound	Southbound
2	No access from A580 eastbound	No exit to A580 westbound
3	No access from A580 eastbound	No exit to A580 westbound
	No access from A666 southbound	
M6 junc 30	No exit to M6 southbound	No access from M6 northbound

M62	Eastbound	Westbound
23	No access	No exit

M65	Eastbound	Westbound
9	No access	No exit
11	No exit	No access

M66	Northbound	Southbound
1	No access	No exit

M67	Eastbound	Westbound
1a	No access	No exit
2	No exit	No access

M69	Northbound	Southbound
2	No exit	No access

M73	Northbound	Southbound
2	No access from M8	No exit to M8
	or A89 eastbound	or A89 westbound
	No exit to A89	No access from A89
3	Exit to A80 northbound only	Access from A80 southbound only

M74	Northbound	Southbound
2	No access	No exit
3	No exit	No access
7	No exit	No access
9	No exit or access	No access
10		No exit
11	No exit	No access
12	No access	No exit

M77	Northbound	Southbound
4	No exit	No access
6	No exit	No access
7	No exit or access	
8	No access	No access
M8 junc 22	Exit to M8 eastbound only	Access from M8 westbound only

M80	Northbound	Southbound
3	No access	No exit
5	No access from M876	No exit to M876

M90	Northbound	Southbound
2a	No access	No exit
7	No exit	No access
8	No access	No exit
10	No access from A912	No exit to A912

M180	Northbound	Southbound
1	No access	

M621	Eastbound	Westbound
2a	No exit	No access
4	No exit or access	
5	No exit	No access
6	No access	No exit

M876	Northbound	Southbound
2	No access	No exit

A1(M)	Northbound	Southbound
2	No access	No exit
3		No access
5	No exit	No access
40	No access	No exit
44	No exit, access from M1 only	Exit to M1 only
57	No access	No exit
65	No access	No exit

A3(M)	Northbound	Southbound
1		No access
4	No access	No exit

A38(M)	Northbound	Southbound
With Victoria Road (Park Circus) Birmingham	No exit	No access

A48(M)	Northbound	Southbound
M4 Junc 29	Exit to M4 eastbound only	Access from M4 westbound only
29a	Access from A48 eastbound only	Exit to A48 westbound only

A57(M)	Eastbound	Westbound
With A5103	No access	No exit
With A34	No access	No exit

A58(M)	Southbound	
With Park Lane and Westgate, Leeds	No access	

A64(M)	Eastbound	Westbound
With A58 Clay Pit Lane, Leeds	No access	No exit
With Regent Street, Leeds	No access	No access

A74(M)	Northbound	Southbound
18	No access	No exit
22	No access	No exit

A167(M)	Northbound	Southbound
With Camden St, Newcastle	No exit	No exit or access

A194(M)	Northbound	Southbound
A1(M) junc 65 Gateshead Western Bypass	Access from A1(M) northbound only	Exit to A1(M) southbound only

Distance table

How to use this table

Distances are shown in miles and, in *italics*, kilometres.
For example, the distance between Aberdeen and Bournemouth is 564 miles or *908* kilometres.

London

Aberdeen
517
832

Aberystwyth
211 445
340 716

Ayr
394 183 317
634 295 510

Berwick-upon-Tweed
352 182 311 134
567 293 501 216

Birmingham
117 420 114 289 274
188 676 183 465 441

Blackpool
226 308 153 180 181 123
364 496 246 290 291 198

Bournemouth
107 564 207 436 412 147 270
172 908 333 702 663 237 435

Braemar
482 59 405 143 148 385 281 524
776 95 652 230 238 620 452 843

Brighton
52 573 253 446 409 163 286 92 534
84 922 407 718 658 262 460 148 859

Bristol
122 493 125 370 362 81 204 82 477 147
196 793 201 595 583 130 328 132 768 237

Cambridge
54 471 214 357 306 100 208 154 438 116 169
87 758 344 575 493 161 335 248 705 187 272

Cardiff
157 505 105 382 368 103 209 117 483 182 45 190
253 813 169 615 592 166 336 188 778 293 72 306

Carlisle
301 221 224 93 87 196 87 343 196 370 277 264 289
484 356 360 150 140 315 140 552 316 596 446 425 465

Doncaster
171 344 176 235 184 94 94 235 310 175 209 142
275 554 283 378 296 151 151 378 499 380 282 187 336 229

Dover
71 588 297 478 424 194 312 174 553 82 202 125 238 389 242
114 947 478 769 683 312 502 280 890 132 325 201 383 626 390

Dundee
448 67 376 117 113 349 239 495 52 441 406 441 152 275 523
721 108 605 188 182 562 385 797 84 832 692 654 710 245 443 842

Edinburgh
390 125 320 73 57 292 183 439 91 456 373 345 385 96 219 462 56
628 201 515 117 92 470 295 707 146 734 600 555 620 154 352 744 90

Exeter
181 569 201 446 428 157 282 82 550 184 76 249 112 297 247 331 460 399
291 916 323 718 689 253 454 132 885 296 122 401 195 568 404 399 834 724

Fishguard
260 504 56 373 371 170 209 222 493 291 154 270 112 297 247 331 460 399 230
418 811 90 600 597 274 336 357 794 468 248 435 180 478 398 533 740 642 370

Fort William
510 149 430 133 190 392 296 539 125 575 486 479 485 206 383 622 132 158 450
821 240 692 214 306 631 476 867 201 926 782 771 781 332 575 959 204 232 901 782

Glasgow
397 145 320 33 101 292 183 439 110 468 373 372 385 96 249 488 83 44 449 376 101
639 233 515 53 163 470 295 707 177 753 600 599 620 154 401 786 134 71 723 605 163

Gloucester
109 468 102 330 318 56 174 99 443 159 23 123 56 247 150 191 410 349 111 153 454 346
175 753 164 531 512 90 280 159 713 256 56 198 90 398 241 307 660 562 179 246 731 557

Great Yarmouth
128 517 294 402 345 180 252 240 477 180 275 82 284 320 167 185 484 386 335 366 527 419 225
206 832 473 647 555 290 406 386 768 290 443 132 457 515 269 298 779 621 539 589 848 674 362

Harwich
76 535 281 425 372 167 275 187 504 128 217 67 246 336 194 125 469 413 333 337 543 432 196 82
122 861 452 684 599 269 443 301 811 206 349 108 396 541 312 201 755 665 449 542 874 695 316 132

Holyhead
269 439 111 305 311 148 141 288 426 334 206 270 216 231 181 360 394 333 282 167 438 330 191 334 349
433 707 179 491 501 238 227 463 686 538 332 435 348 372 291 580 634 536 454 269 705 531 307 538 562

Inverness
550 105 486 199 215 458 348 597 75 617 539 505 549 262 383 622 132 158 542 66 166 504 553 569 474
885 169 782 320 346 737 560 961 121 993 867 813 884 422 617 1001 212 254 995 872 106 267 811 890 916 763

John o' Groats
663 232 601 328 342 574 478 724 202 741 668 630 680 391 507 746 259 285 744 671 195 295 628 677 693 603 129
1067 373 967 528 550 924 769 1165 325 1193 1075 1014 1094 629 816 1201 417 459 1197 1080 314 475 1011 1090 1116 970 208

Kingston upon Hull
184 364 283 251 185 134 127 264 327 245 233 139 244 158 47 256 295 234 309 280 369 254 169 207 196 231 394 518
296 586 359 404 298 216 204 425 526 394 375 224 393 254 76 412 475 451 594 409 272 333 316 372 316 372 634 834

Kyle of Lochalsh
586 189 499 212 263 471 372 618 159 651 552 555 564 275 432 671 186 216 628 567 79 179 528 602 611 514 84 189 445
943 304 803 341 423 758 599 995 256 1048 888 893 908 443 695 1080 299 348 1011 913 127 288 850 969 983 827 135 304 716

Land's End
297 692 313 570 552 281 405 205 665 308 200 374 245 477 374 381 642 574 123 353 686 573 235 446 390 405 741 868 421 763
478 1114 503 888 452 652 330 1070 496 342 602 394 768 602 613 1033 924 197 568 1104 922 378 718 628 652 1193 1397 678 1228

Leeds
189 327 169 212 156 113 72 255 293 260 194 145 232 119 29 260 258 202 270 237 329 215 174 196 223 176 360 487 55 394 405
304 526 272 341 251 182 116 410 472 419 312 233 373 192 47 418 415 325 435 381 530 346 280 315 359 283 579 784 89 634 652

Leicester
97 414 153 299 252 39 140 158 389 166 120 68 154 206 74 185 349 296 196 209 422 314 85 140 147 190 461 588 102 500 320 95
156 666 246 481 406 63 225 254 626 267 193 109 248 332 119 298 562 476 315 336 679 505 137 225 237 306 742 947 164 805 515 153

Lincoln
131 383 199 274 224 90 128 209 357 197 183 85 208 191 39 202 314 258 247 272 399 291 159 128 155 216 427 554 44 476 371 68 51
211 616 320 441 360 145 206 336 575 317 295 137 335 307 63 325 505 415 398 438 642 468 256 206 249 348 687 892 71 766 597 109 82

Liverpool
202 341 104 213 219 93 49 234 318 272 161 194 169 120 86 299 286 216 237 160 329 216 140 240 265 102 382 511 130 407 361 75 130 129
325 549 167 343 352 150 79 377 512 438 259 312 272 193 138 481 460 348 381 257 530 348 225 386 427 164 615 822 209 655 581 121 209 208

Manchester
185 340 119 212 156 80 48 227 318 250 161 165 183 119 61 276 281 219 255 126 212 228 134 197 329 215 126 212 228 34 41 373 600 35 56
298 547 208 341 315 129 77 365 512 414 259 266 295 192 98 444 459 346 380 317 530 346 203 341 367 200 600 805 153 654 581 64 148 135 56

Newcastle upon Tyne
286 235 257 149 64 207 129 347 201 352 299 241 325 57 114 358 166 110 364 329 253 148 266 281 308 272 268 395 132 318 498 92 187 159 168 132
460 378 414 240 103 333 208 558 323 567 481 388 523 92 183 576 267 177 586 529 407 238 428 452 496 438 431 636 212 512 802 148 301 256 270 212

Norwich
114 496 276 382 328 166 232 214 457 175 252 62 262 289 147 174 452 360 343 504 385 204 20 311 529 654 198 52 61 185 264
183 798 444 615 528 267 373 344 735 282 406 100 422 465 237 280 729 589 496 552 811 620 328 32 117 501 852 1053 240 937 678 283 192 169 354 298 425

Nottingham
122 393 164 274 221 50 111 183 353 193 145 83 172 194 43 205 328 262 221 220 401 293 110 153 150 185 430 557 90 479 345 70 25 35 98 73 157 130
196 633 264 441 356 80 179 295 568 311 233 134 277 312 69 330 528 422 356 354 646 472 177 246 241 298 692 896 145 771 555 113 40 56 158 118 253 209

Oban
499 178 412 94 180 384 285 530 141 565 465 468 477 198 346 585 117 123 568 477 84 148 515 524 427 307 419 387 308 307 233 492 390
803 286 663 151 290 618 459 853 227 910 748 753 768 303 557 942 188 198 884 774 79 148 710 829 843 687 188 393 557 206 1070 494 674 623 496 494 375 792 628

Oxford
57 483 154 353 324 64 187 90 465 108 74 83 108 260 145 141 433 372 156 205 472 356 52 200 145 238 532 656 192 550 274 168 73 137 172 144 260 145 109 462
92 777 248 568 521 103 301 145 749 174 119 134 174 418 233 227 697 599 251 330 760 573 84 322 233 383 856 1056 309 885 441 270 117 221 277 232 418 233 175 744

Plymouth
218 615 237 492 474 203 328 128 587 226 293 167 299 300 552 496 167 124 454 392 195 84 343 426 410 338 262 359 263 585 220 330 298 221 290 158 403 290 148 379 199
351 990 382 792 763 327 528 206 945 361 196 472 269 642 477 483 888 798 74 425 958 797 253 365 588 497 528 1069 1271 571 1085 143 509 389 472 455 455 660 552 430 945 320

Portsmouth
70 560 222 430 401 141 264 52 547 48 97 144 142 348 234 130 514 453 135 251 555 448 119 221 166 311 613 737 269 633 259 257 162 201 254 236 337 207 191 545 77 176
113 901 357 692 645 227 425 84 881 77 156 232 229 560 377 209 827 729 217 404 893 721 192 356 267 501 987 1186 433 1019 417 414 261 323 409 380 542 333 307 877 124 283

Sheffield
159 360 159 245 190 76 86 216 320 193 138 54 160 187 168 187 393 520 67 159 361 189 64 137 339 135 455 370
256 579 256 394 306 122 138 348 515 364 165 193 312 245 29 394 468 378 381 346 560 399 203 218 187 301 632 837 105 687 581 53 100 74 116 61 201 235 60 546 217 455 370

Shrewsbury
160 399 77 269 265 45 98 185 371 226 103 159 111 176 179 330 274 179 145 382 272 77 225 240 113 438 567 169 451 303 109 84 133 58 69 201 205 93 364 106 225 207 82
258 642 124 433 426 72 158 298 597 364 166 256 179 283 404 531 441 288 233 615 438 124 362 386 182 705 912 272 726 488 175 135 214 93 111 323 330 150 586 171 362 333 132

Southampton
77 537 213 417 388 128 251 31 532 61 76 148 121 324 209 143 500 438 105 221 543 432 106 176 530 64 151 21 199 185
124 880 323 671 624 206 404 50 856 98 122 238 195 521 336 230 805 705 169 375 871 697 169 354 264 472 963 1164 412 995 367 373 220 328 385 356 521 332 283 853 103 243 34 320 298

Stranraer
402 228 325 51 170 297 188 444 194 475 378 379 390 101 257 496 167 124 454 392 195 84 343 426 410 338 262 359 263 585 220 330 298 221 290 158 403 290 148 379 500 461 263 277 445
647 367 523 82 274 478 303 715 312 765 608 610 628 163 414 798 269 200 731 631 314 135 552 686 660 544 422 610 417 423 942 354 531 480 356 354 649 467 238 610 805 742 446 716

Swansea
194 507 31 372 359 151 216 167 505 222 81 309 232 274 167 329 267 184 572 696 84 637 319 137 108 798 658 143 329 267 184 296 921 1120 425 956
312 816 117 610 616 192 348 269 813 357 137 365 301 441 761 663 259 108 798 658 143 329 267 184 296 921 1120 425 956 459 399 285 375 314 301 559 485 192 506 141 206 217 118 161 417

York
207 319 195 214 148 130 96 269 285 275 222 165 244 121 34 282 250 194 287 261 330 217 189 201 228 204 352 479 37 407 411 24 108 75 99 64 84 181 77 309 181 333 278 52 133 258 222 272
333 513 314 344 238 209 154 433 459 443 357 266 393 195 55 454 402 312 462 420 531 349 304 323 367 328 566 771 60 655 661 39 174 121 159 103 135 291 124 497 291 536 448 84 214 415 357 438

Map of Great Britain with towns: John o' Groats, Kyle of Lochalsh, Inverness, Aberdeen, Braemar, Fort William, Dundee, Oban, Edinburgh, Glasgow, Berwick-upon-Tweed, Ayr, Stranraer, Newcastle upon Tyne, Carlisle, York, Kingston upon Hull, Leeds, Blackpool, Manchester, Doncaster, Liverpool, Holyhead, Sheffield, Lincoln, Nottingham, Shrewsbury, Leicester, Norwich, Great Yarmouth, Aberystwyth, Birmingham, Cambridge, Harwich, Fishguard, Gloucester, Oxford, London, Swansea, Cardiff, Bristol, Southampton, Brighton, Portsmouth, Dover, Exeter, Bournemouth, Plymouth, Land's End.

Road map symbols

M6	Motorway, toll motorway
4 5	Motorway junction – full, restricted access
S S	Motorway service area – full, restricted access
	Motorway under construction
A453	Primary route – dual, single carriageway
S	Service area
	Roundabout
	Multi-level junction
4 5	Numbered junction – full, restricted access
	Primary route under construction
	Narrow primary route
Derby	Primary destination
A34	A road – dual, single carriageway
	A road under construction
	Narrow A road
B2135	B road – dual, single carriageway
	B road under construction
	Narrow B road
	Minor road
	Minor road with restricted access
2	Distance in miles
	Scenic route
	Speed camera – single, multiple
TOLL	Toll
	Steep gradient – arrow points downhill
	Tunnel
	National trail – England and Wales
	Long distance footpath – Scotland
	Railway with station
	Railway with level crossing
	Tunnel
	Preserved railway with station
	National boundary
	County / unitary authority boundary
	Car ferry, catamaran
	Passenger ferry, catamaran
	Hovercraft, freight ferry
CALAIS 1:15	Ferry destination, journey time – hrs : mins
Ferry	Car ferry – river crossing
	Principal airport
	Other airport
	National park
	Woodland
	Beach
	Linear antiquity
	Roman road

	✕ 1066	Hillfort, battlefield – with date
	▲ 795	Viewpoint, spot height – in metres
	▲	Nature reserve, youth hostel
		Golf course, sporting venue
		Camp site, caravan site, camping and caravan site
	P&R	Shopping village, park and ride
29		Adjoining page number – road maps

Road map scale 1: 200 000 or 3·15 miles to 1 inch

```
0   1   2   3   4   5   6 miles
0 1 2 3 4 5 6 7 8 9 10 km
```

Tourist information

✝	Abbey, cathedral or priory
	Ancient monument
	Aquarium
	Art gallery
	Bird collection or aviary
	Castle
	Church
	Country park England and Wales Scotland
	Farm park
	Garden
	Historic ship
	House
	House and garden
	Motor racing circuit
	Museum
	Picnic area
	Preserved railway
	Race course
	Roman antiquity
	Safari park
	Theme park
	Tourist information centre open all year open seasonally
	Zoo
✦	Other place of interest

Speed Cameras

Fixed camera locations are shown using the ▢ symbol.

In congested areas the ▣ symbol is used to show that there are two or more cameras on the road indicated.

Due to the restrictions of scale the camera locations are only approximate and cannot indicate the operating direction of the camera. Mobile camera sites, and cameras located on roads not included on the mapping are not shown. Where two or more cameras are shown on the same road, drivers are warned that this may indicate that a SPEC system is in operation. These cameras use the time taken to drive between the two camera positions to calculate the speed of the vehicle.

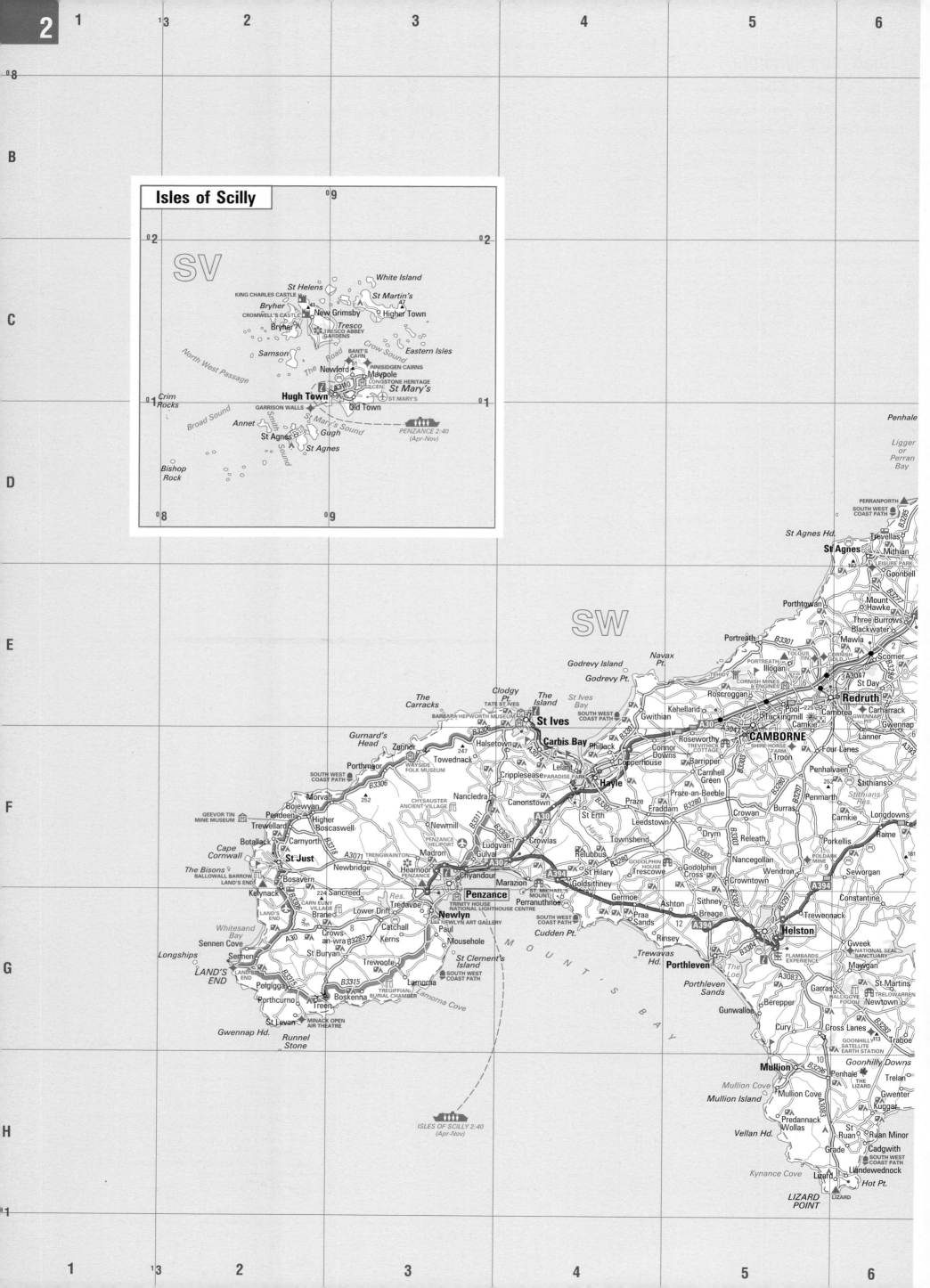

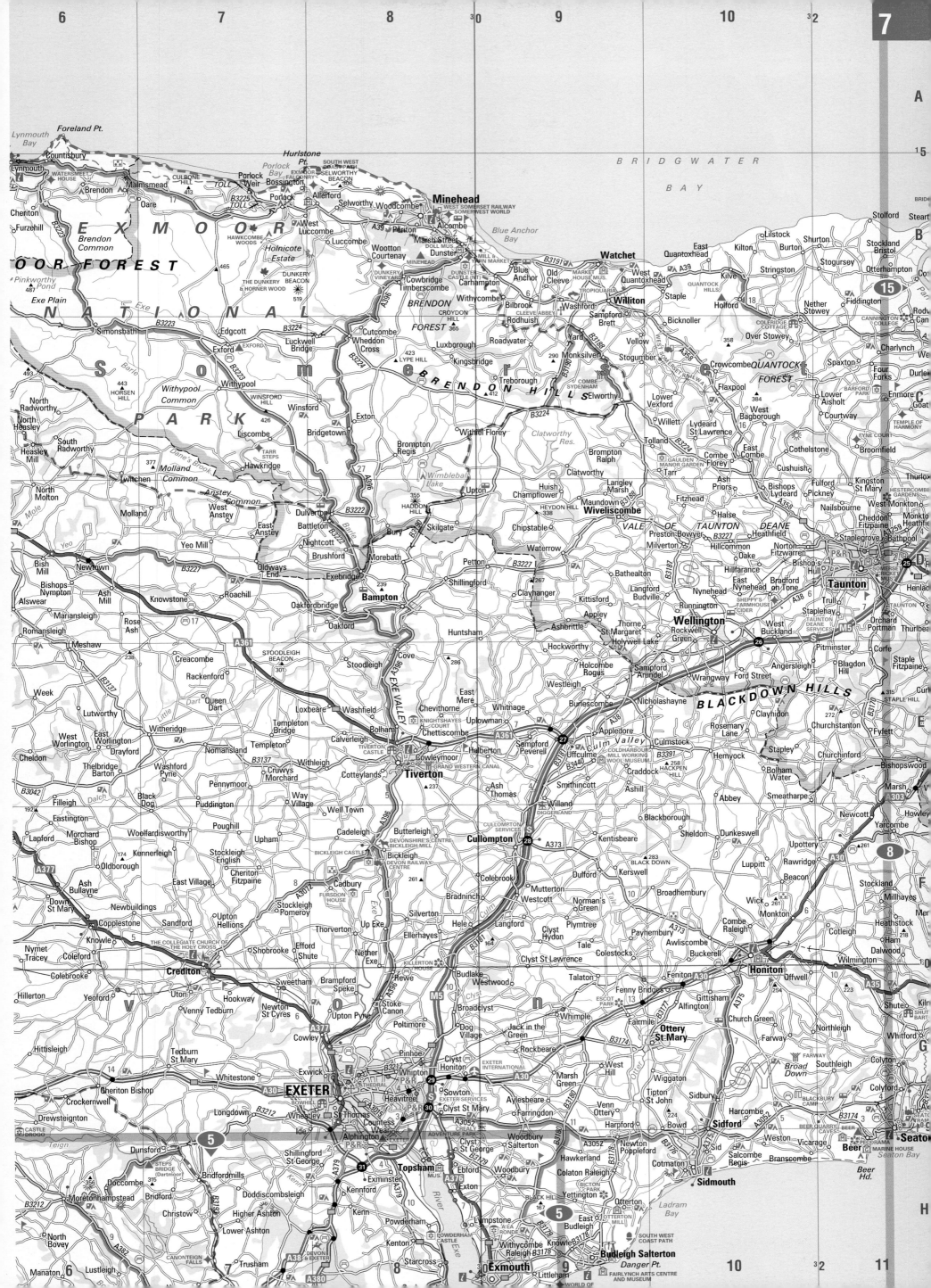

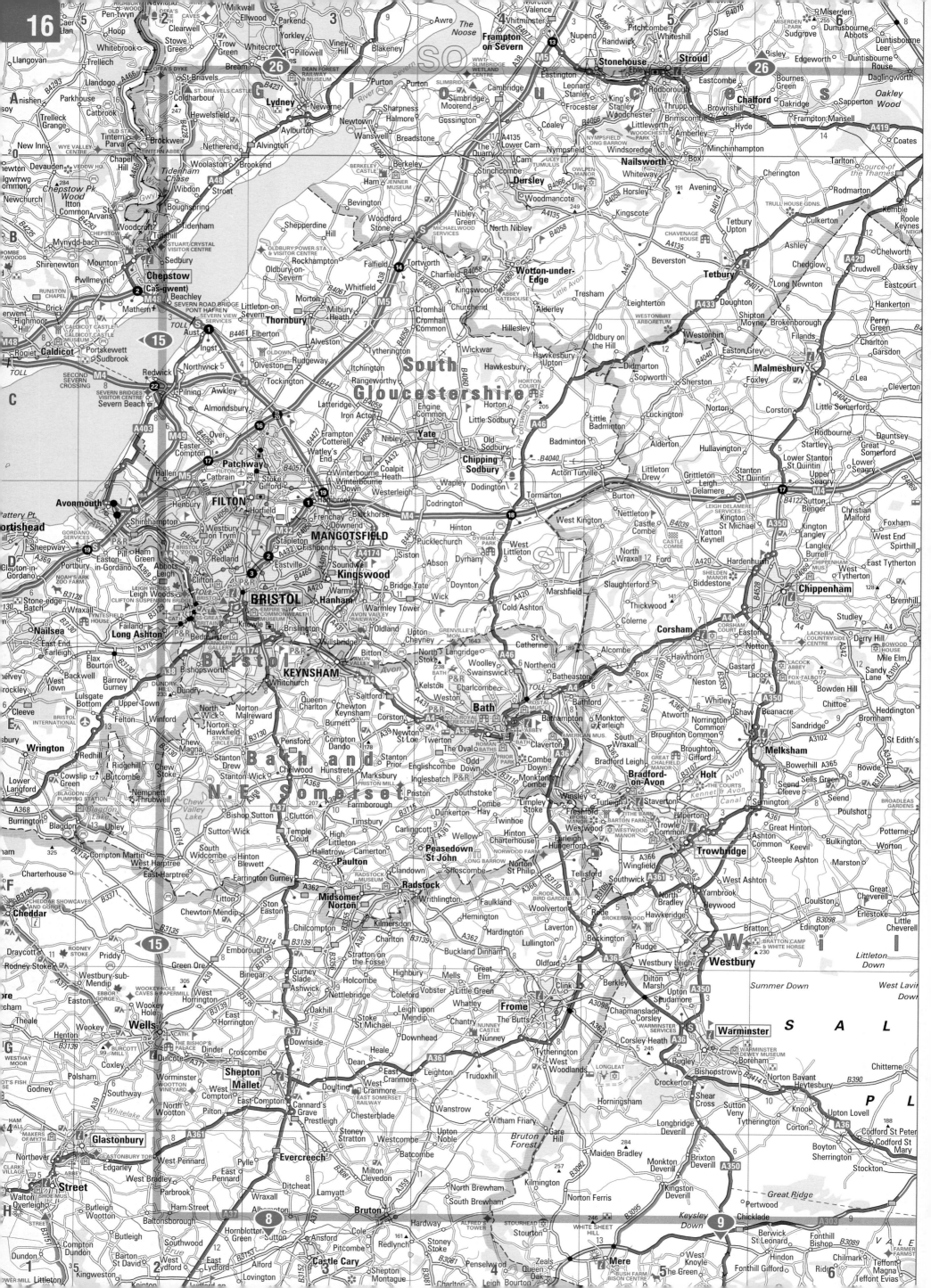

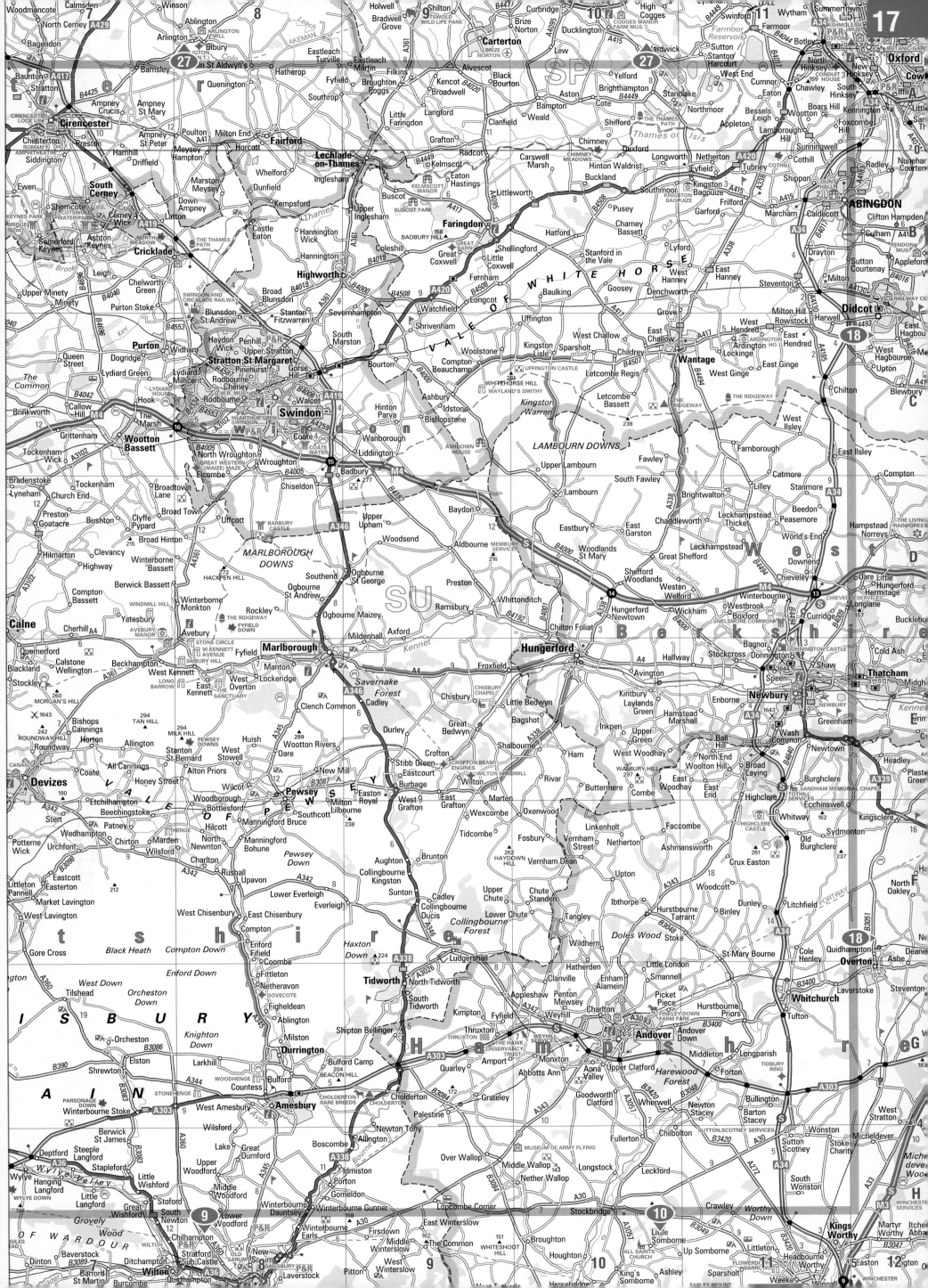

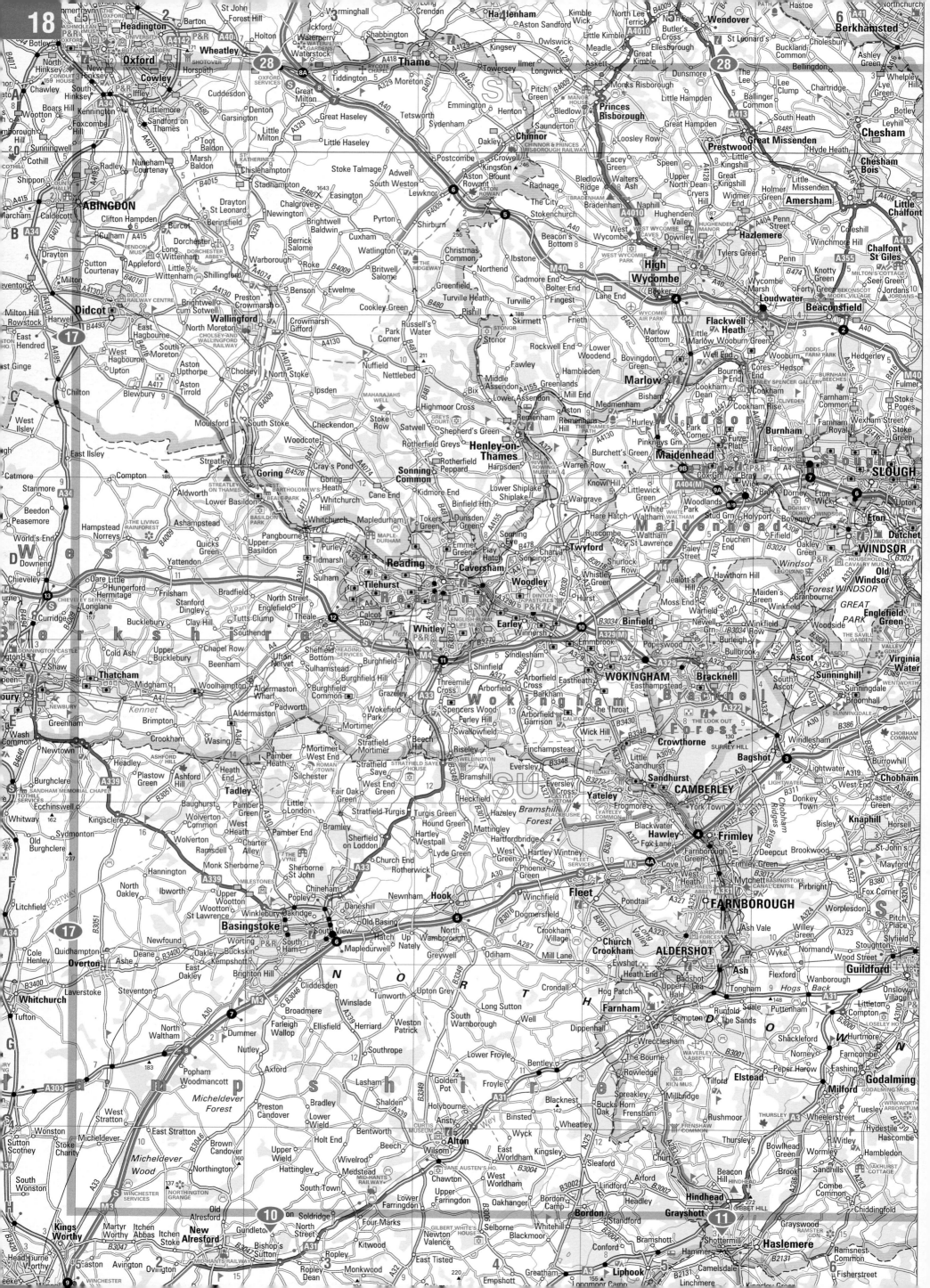

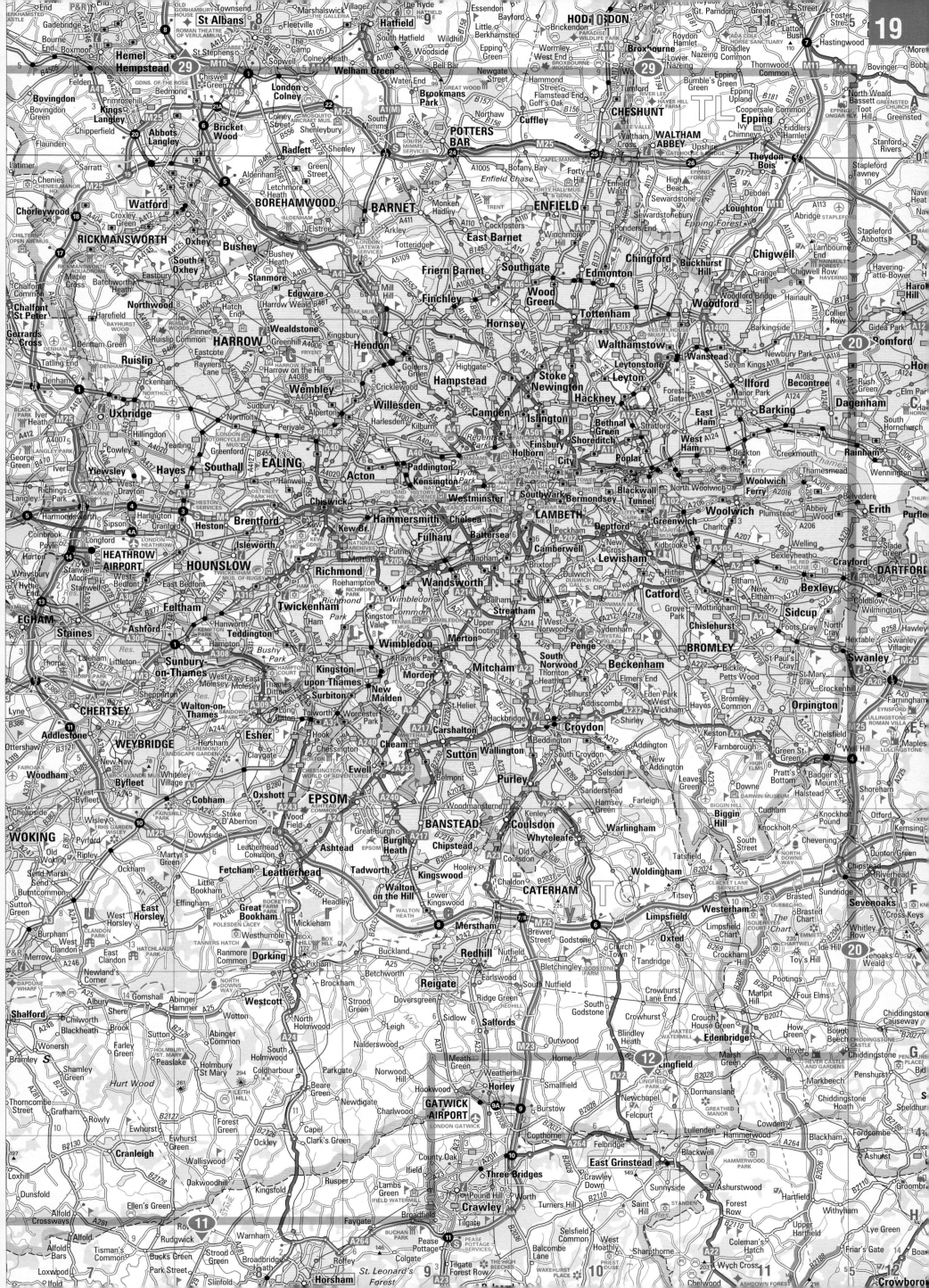

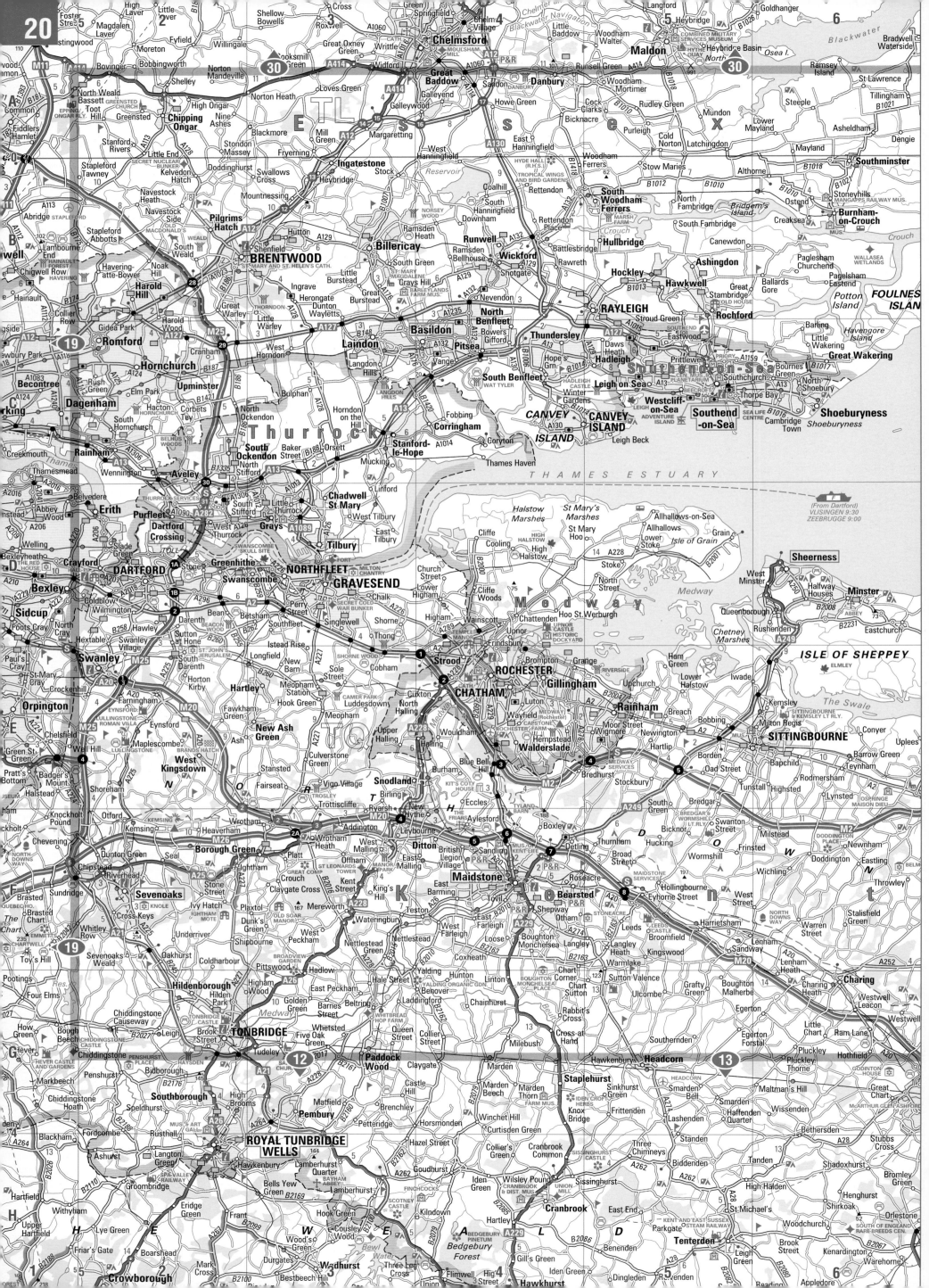

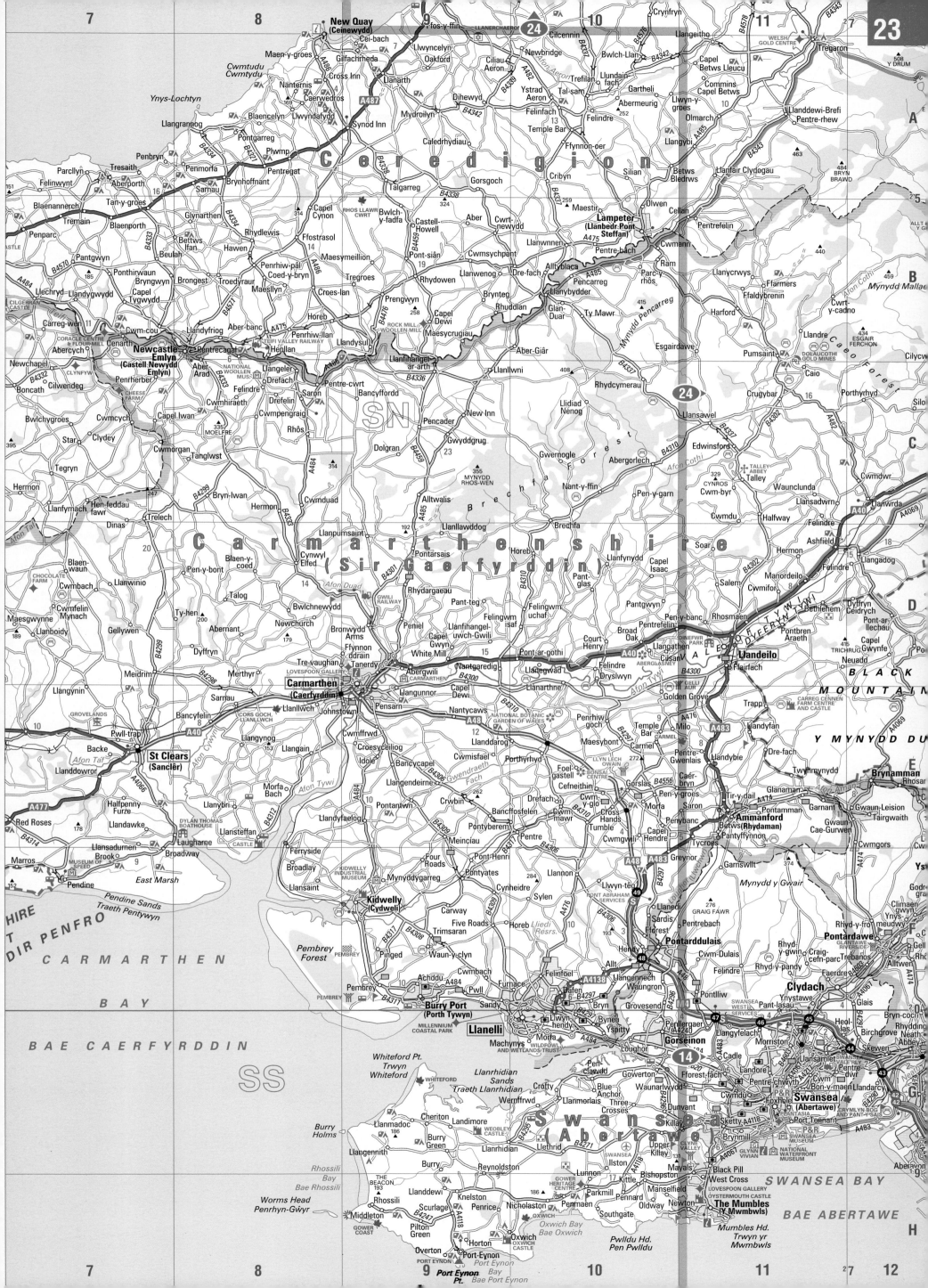

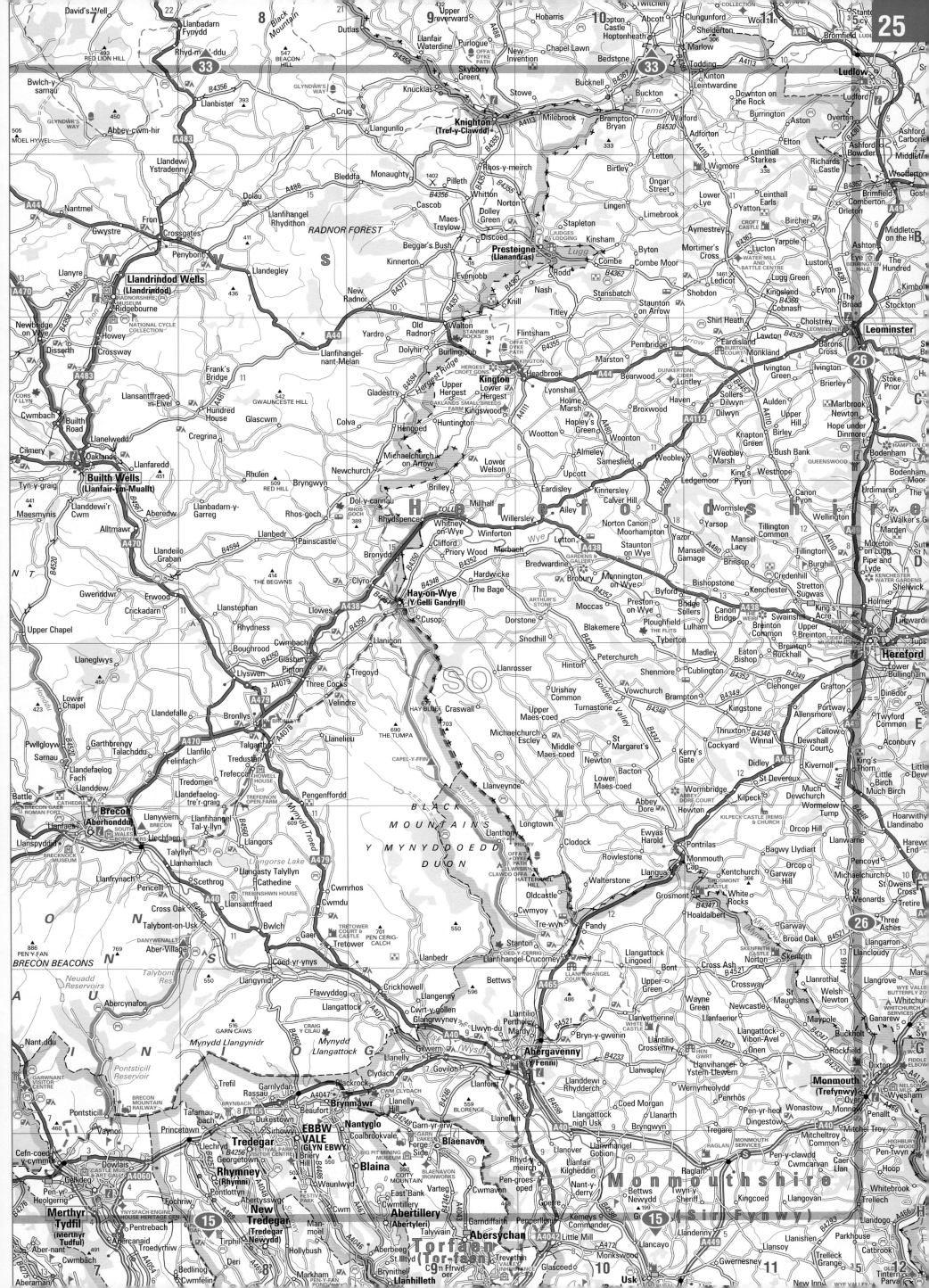

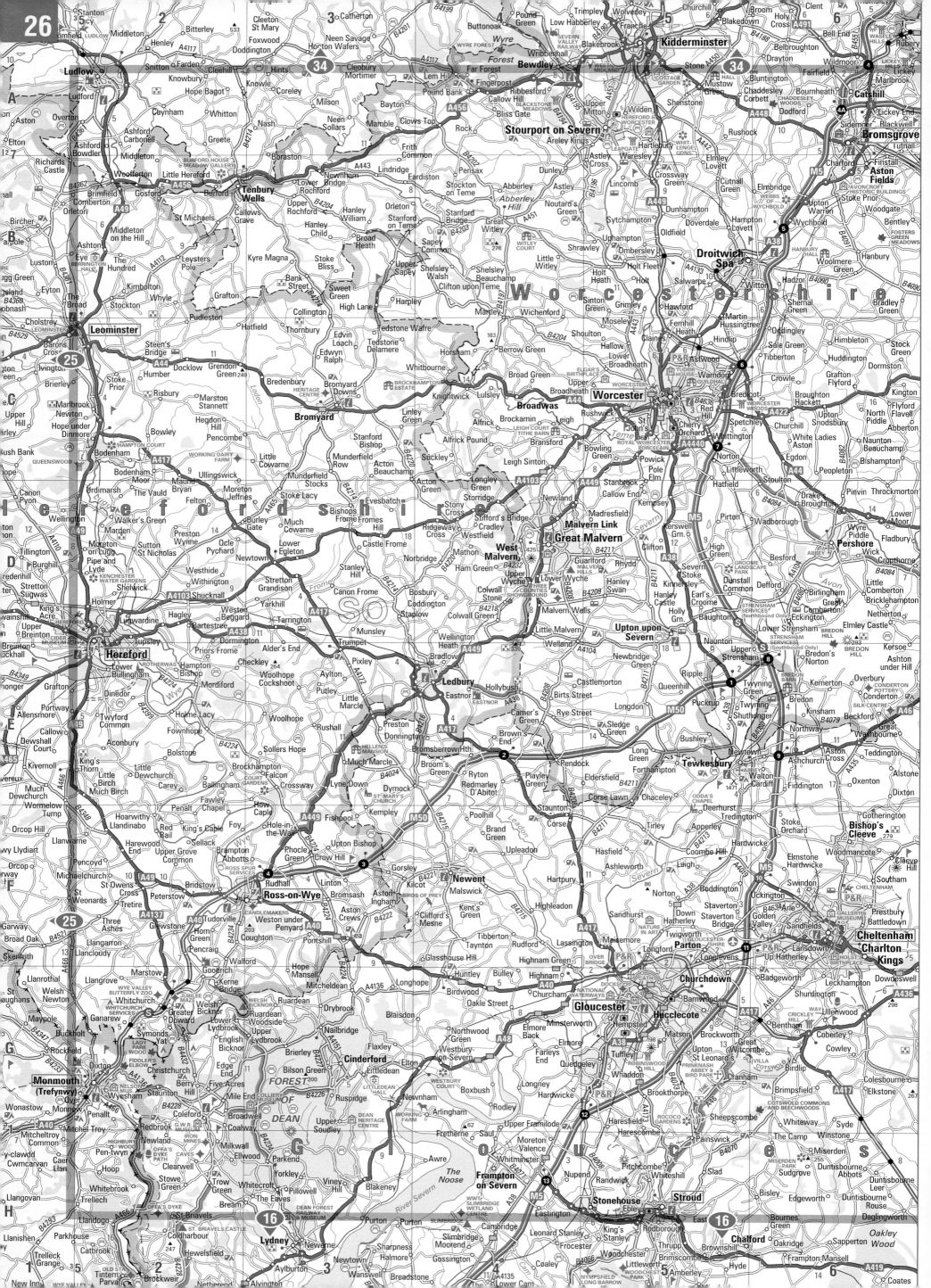

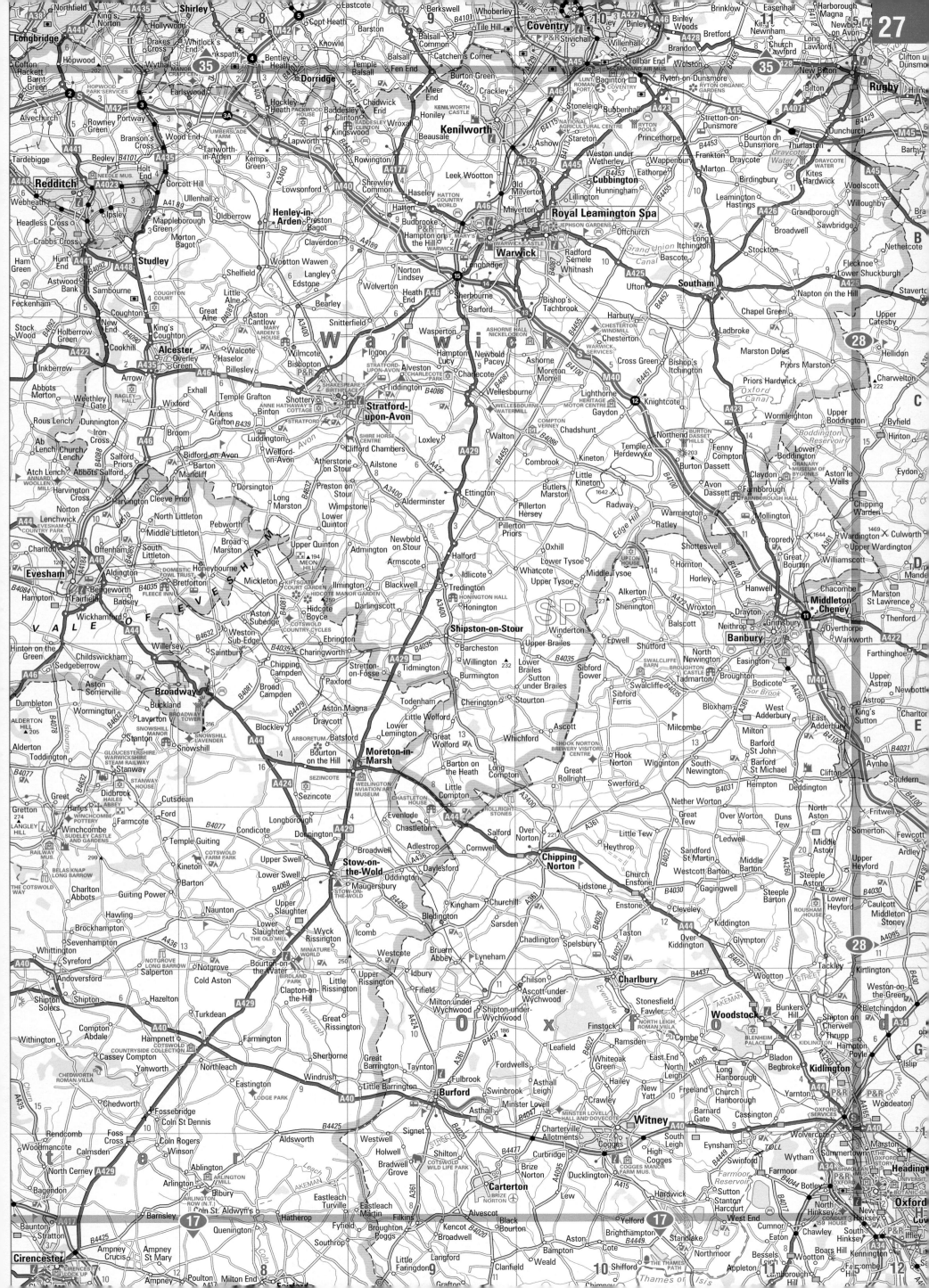

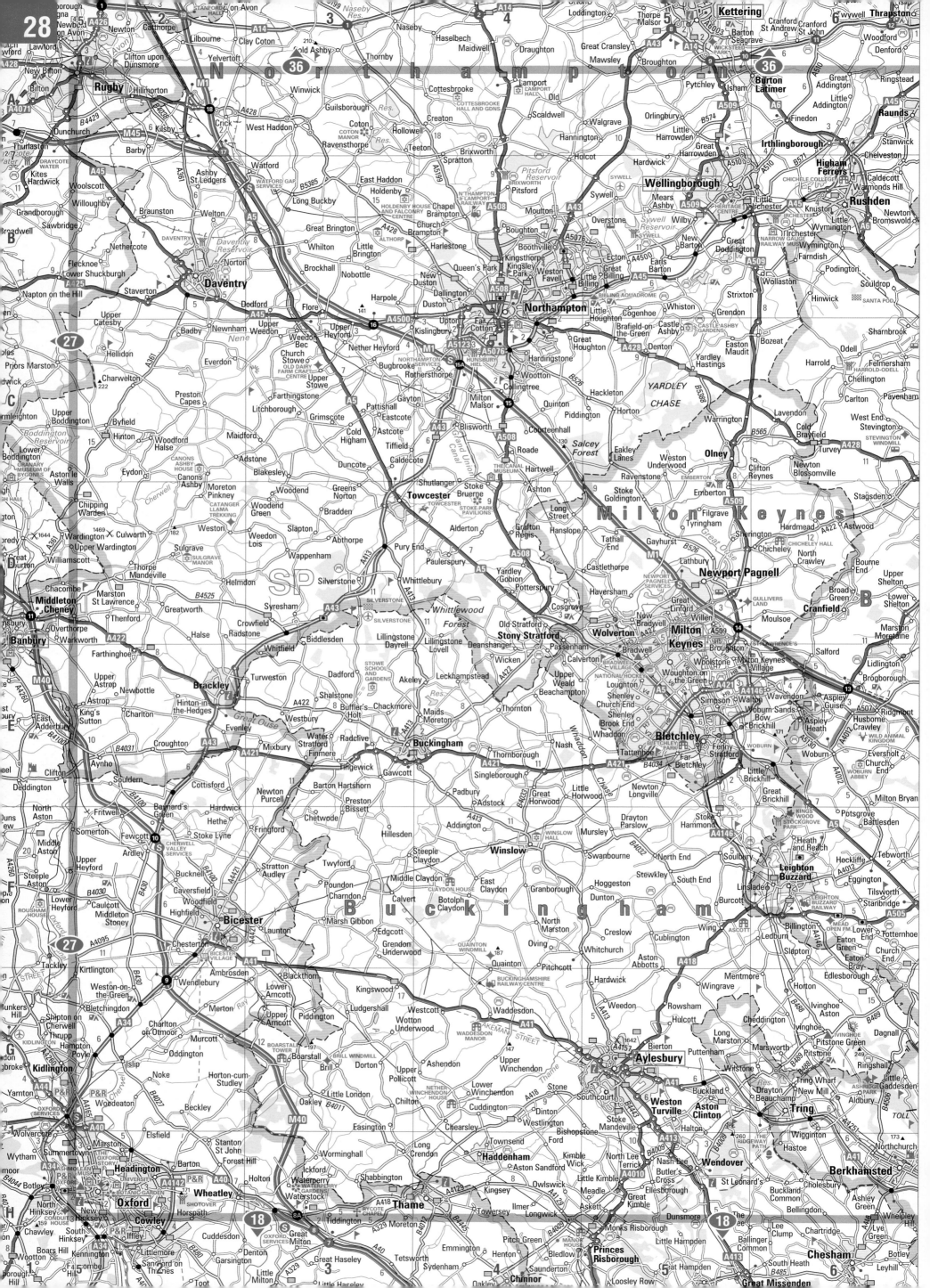

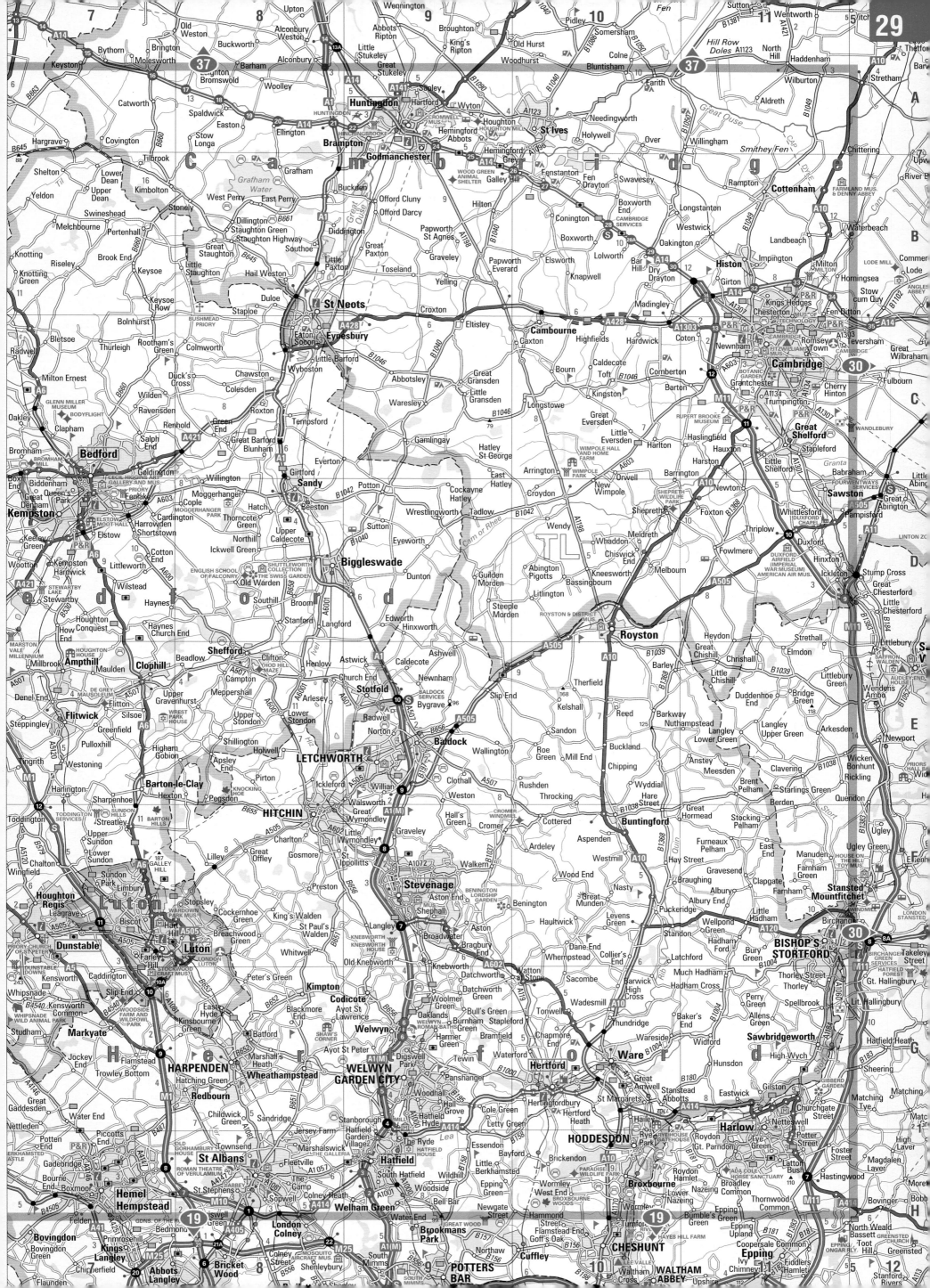

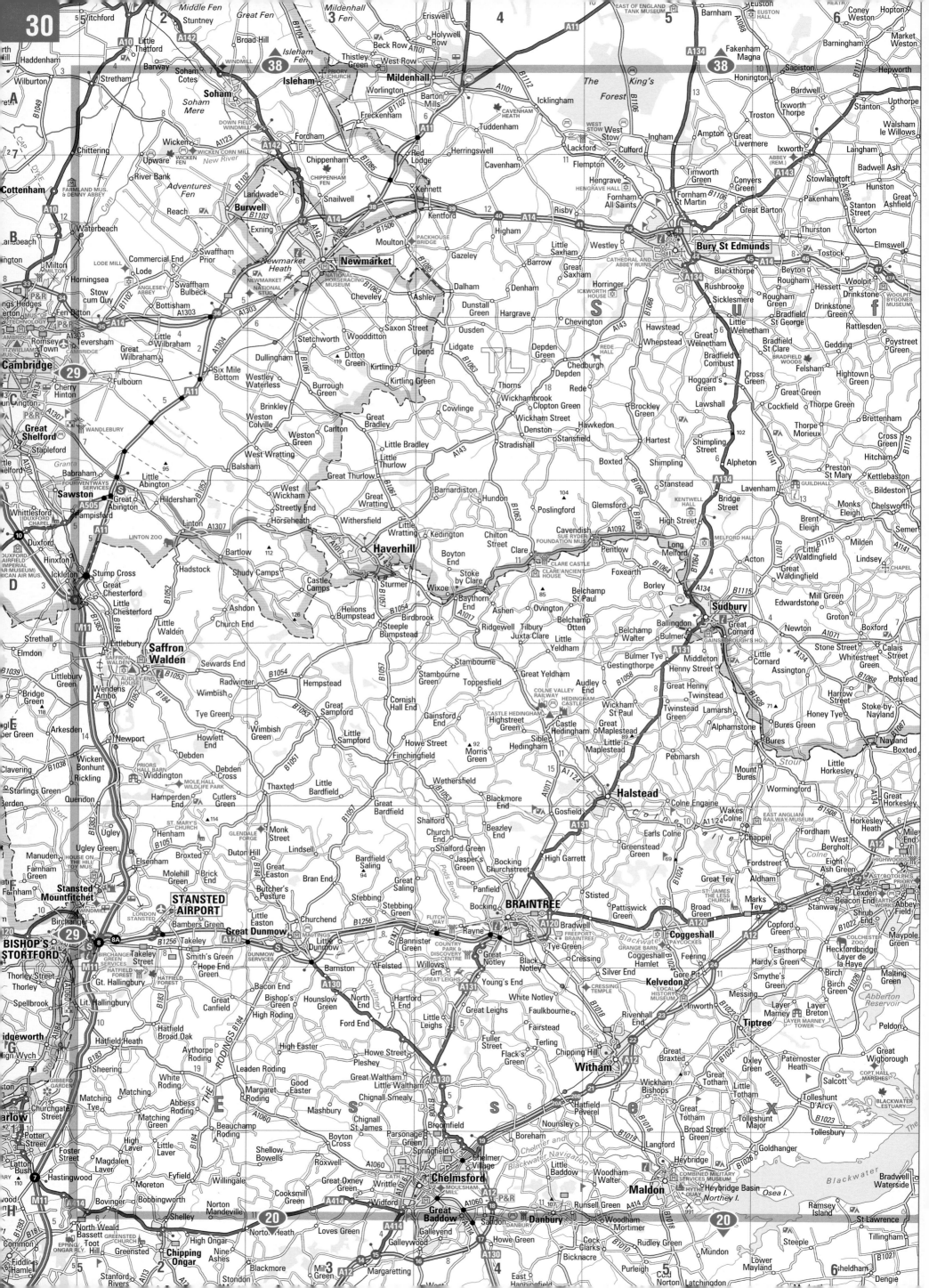

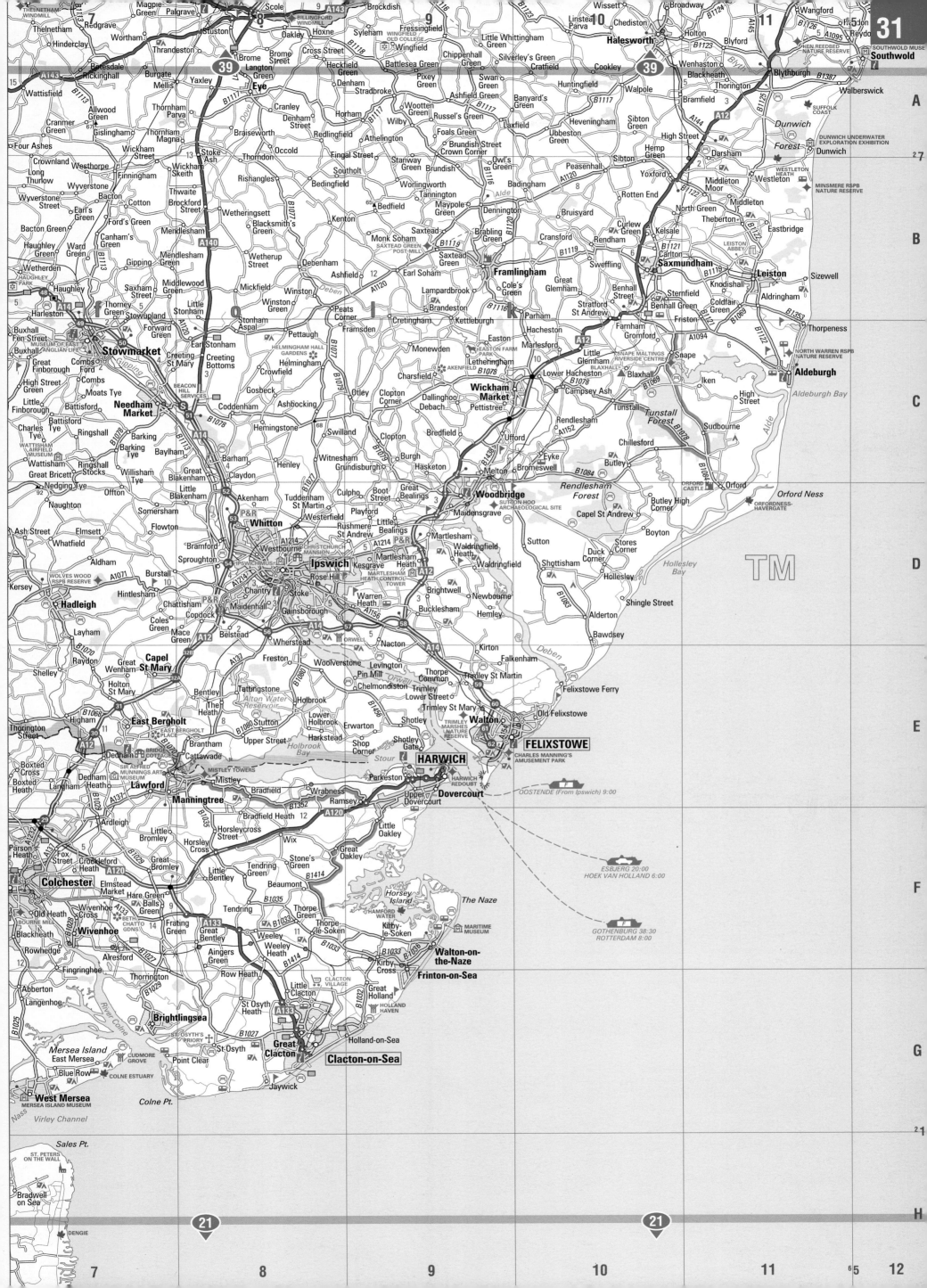

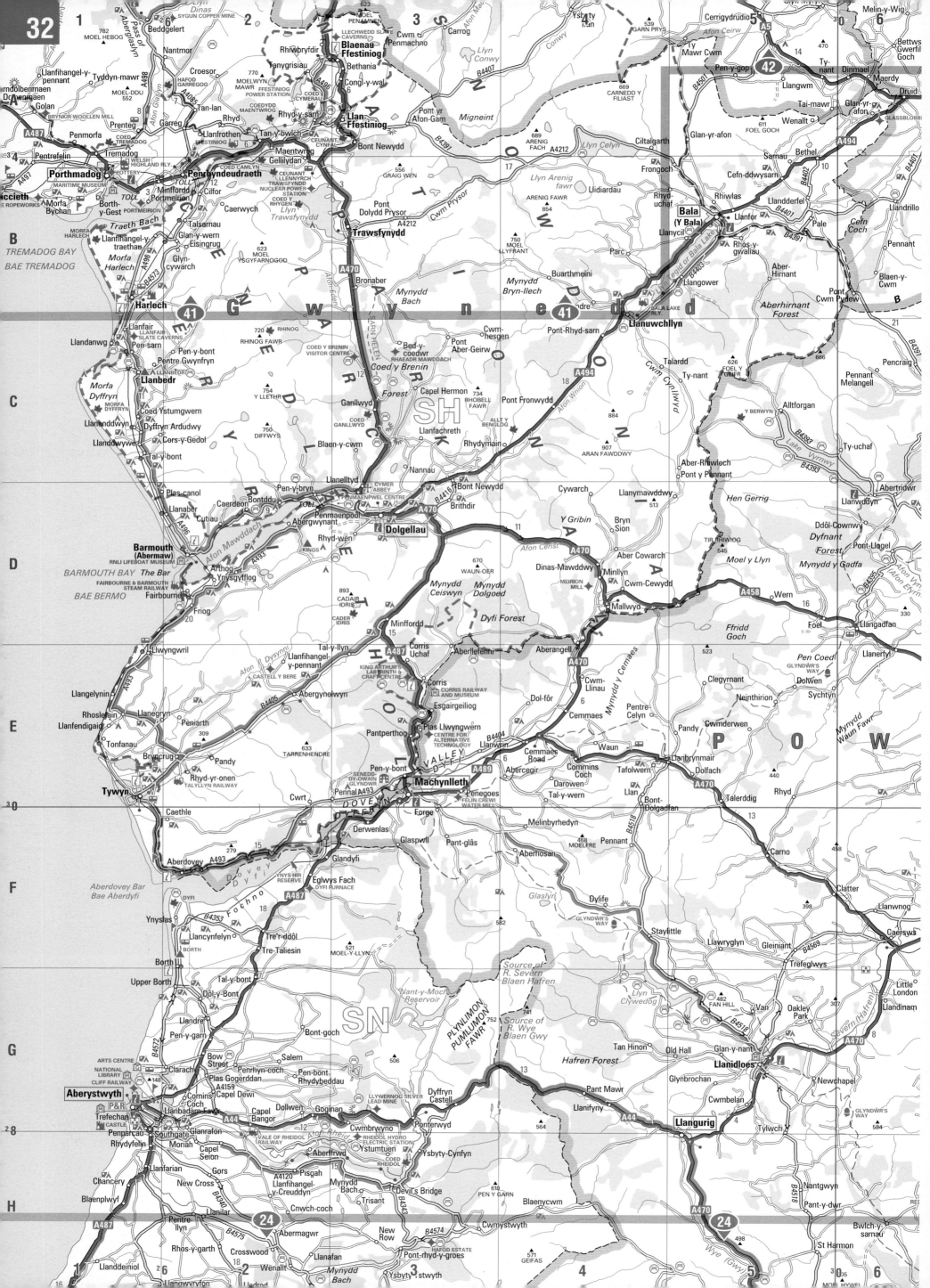

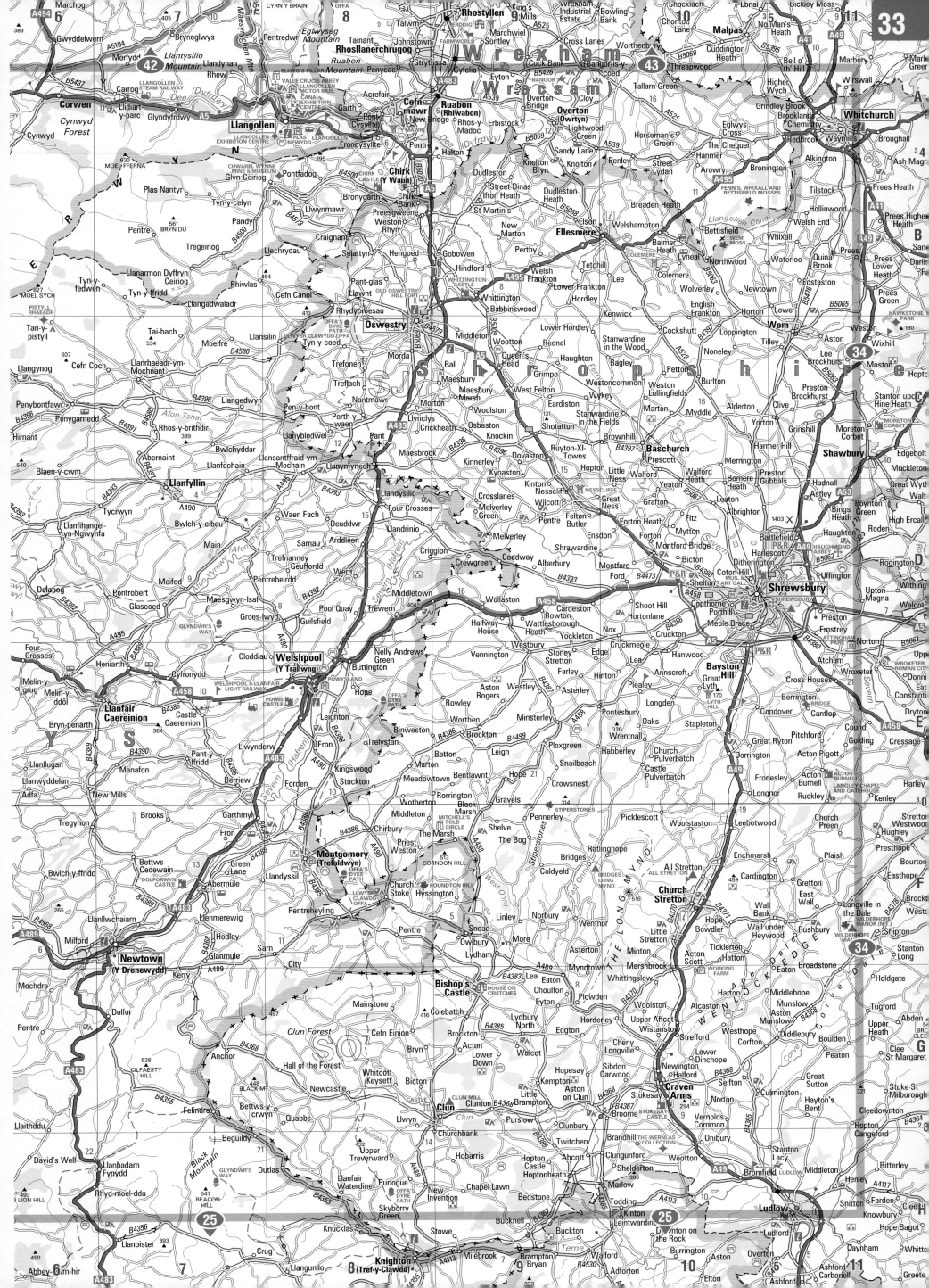

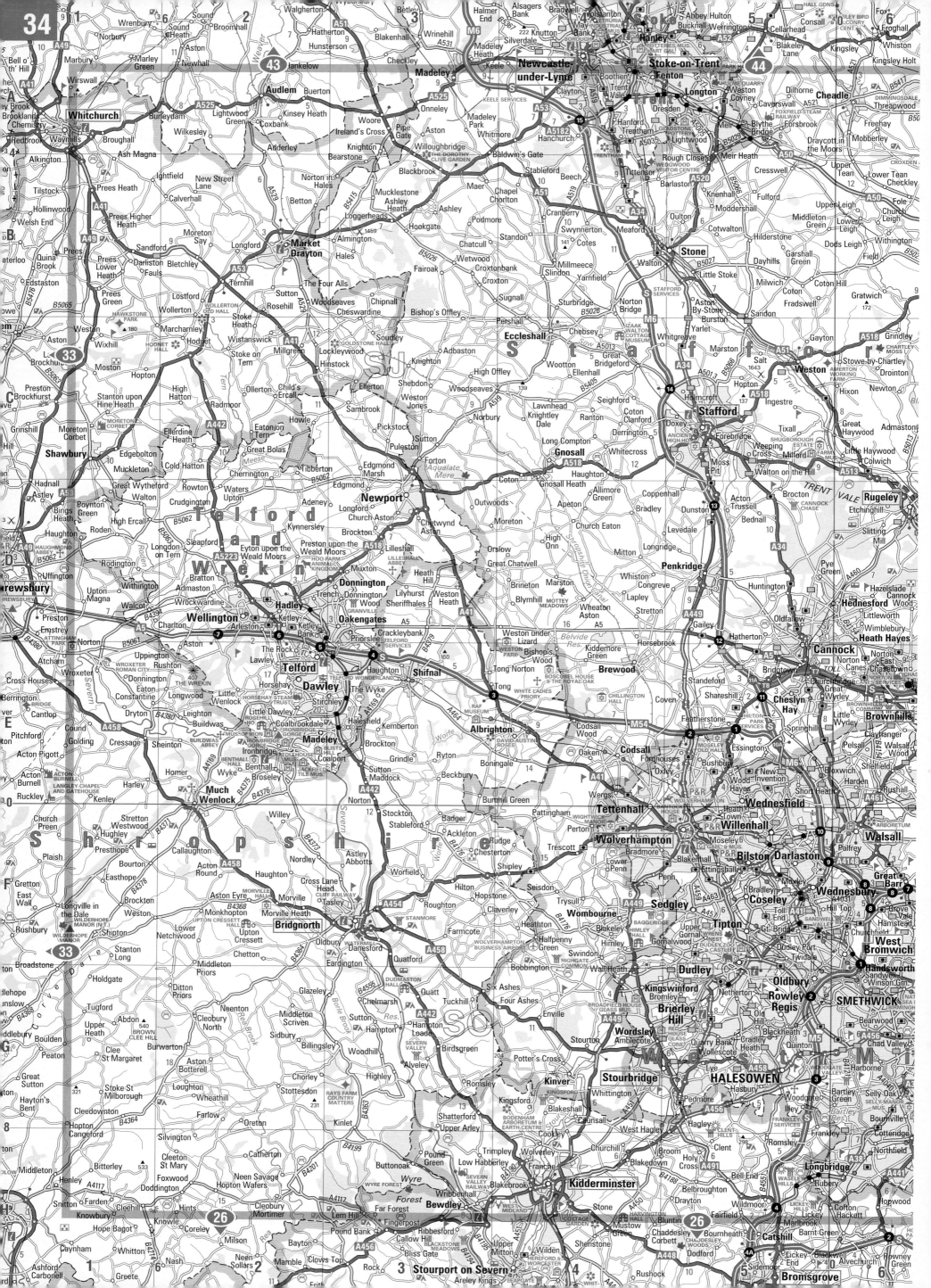

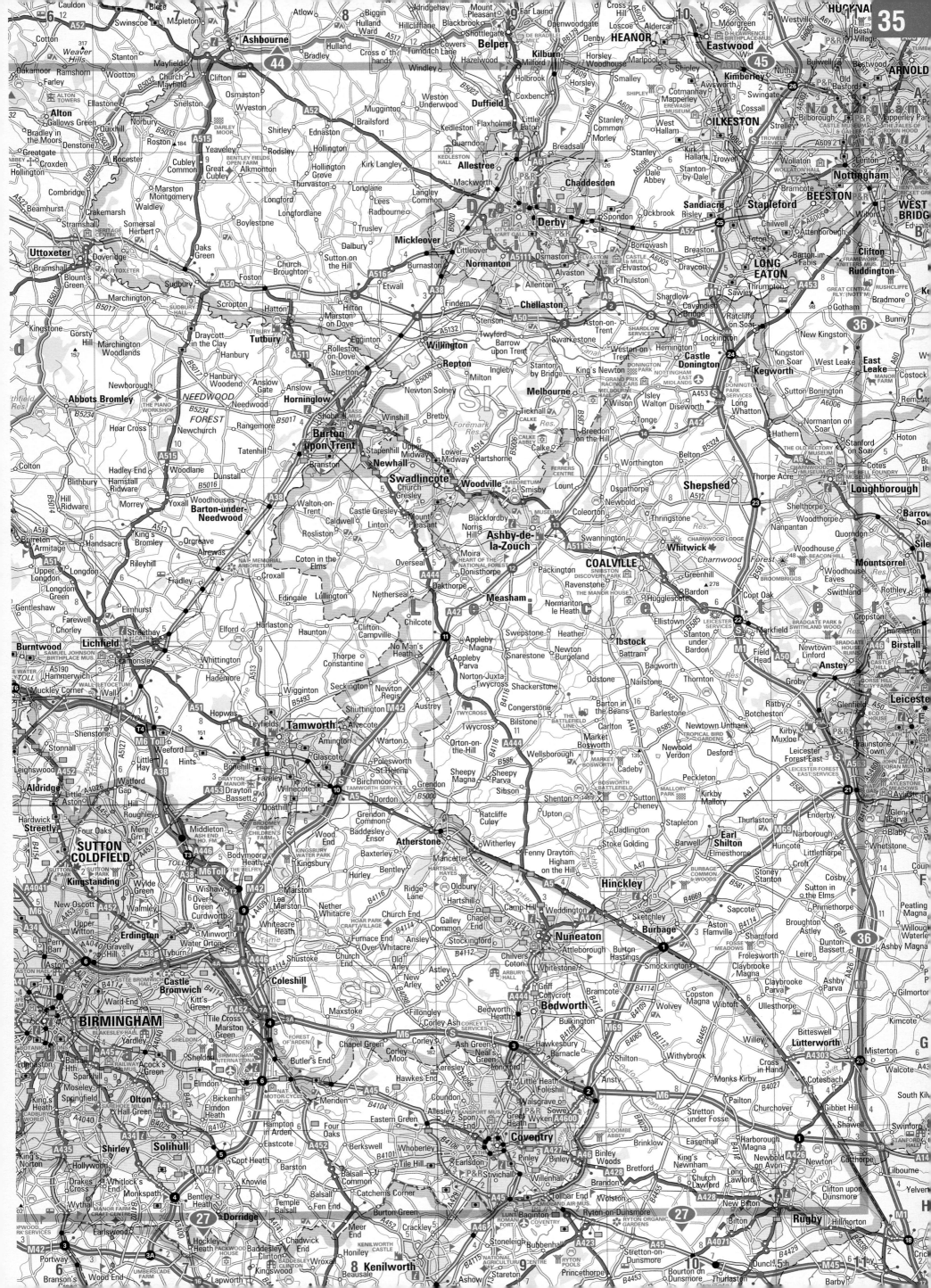

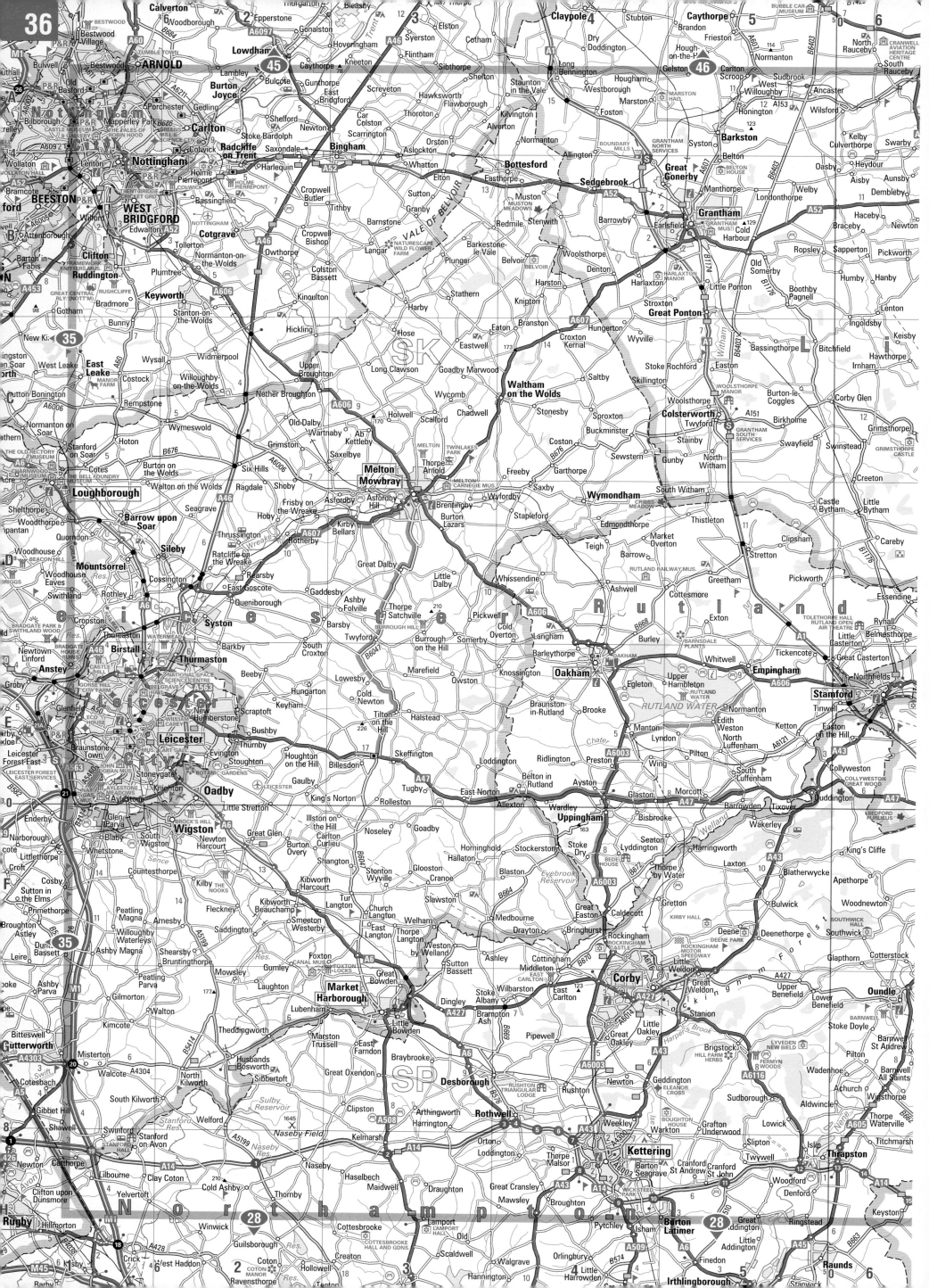

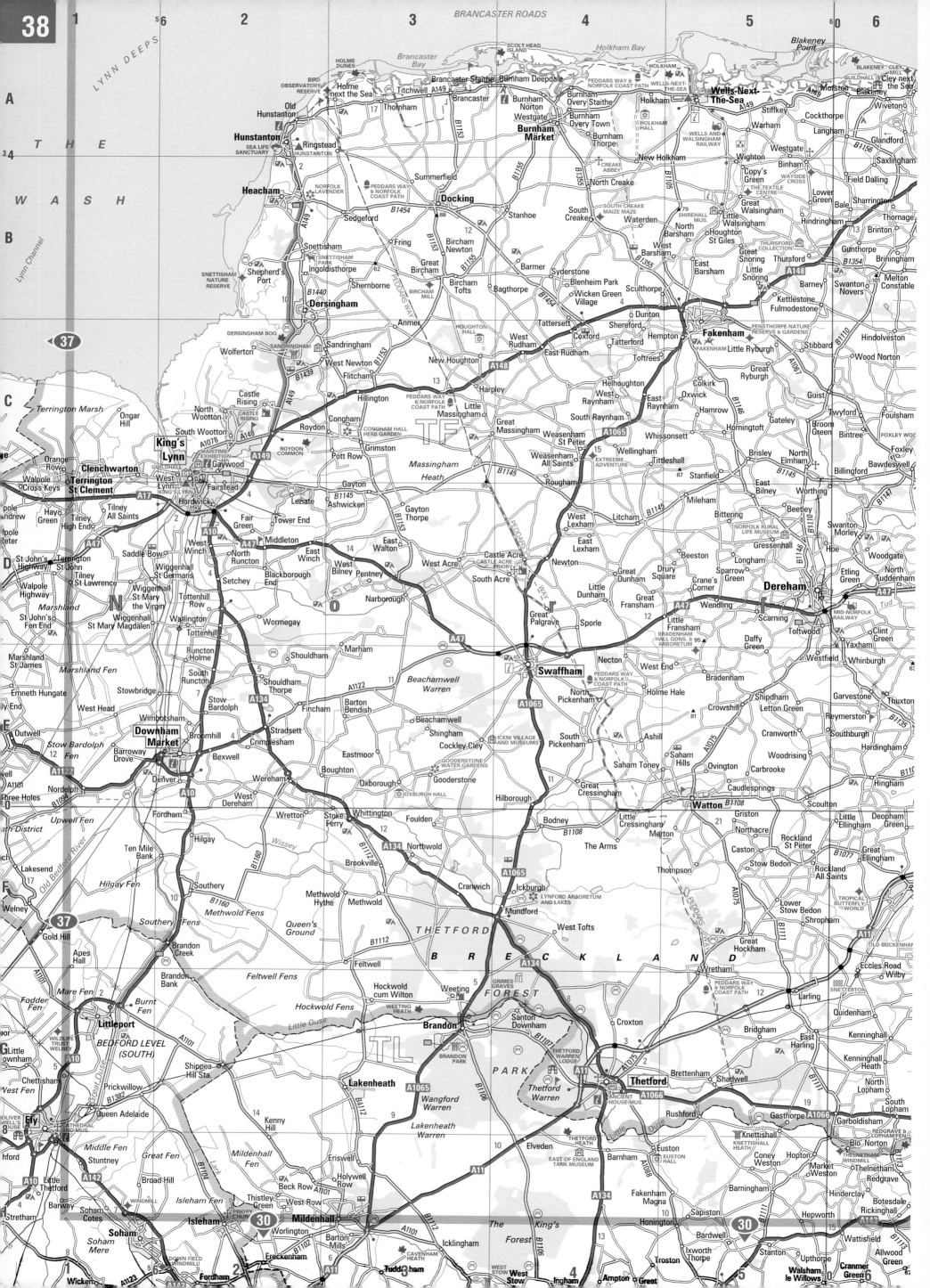

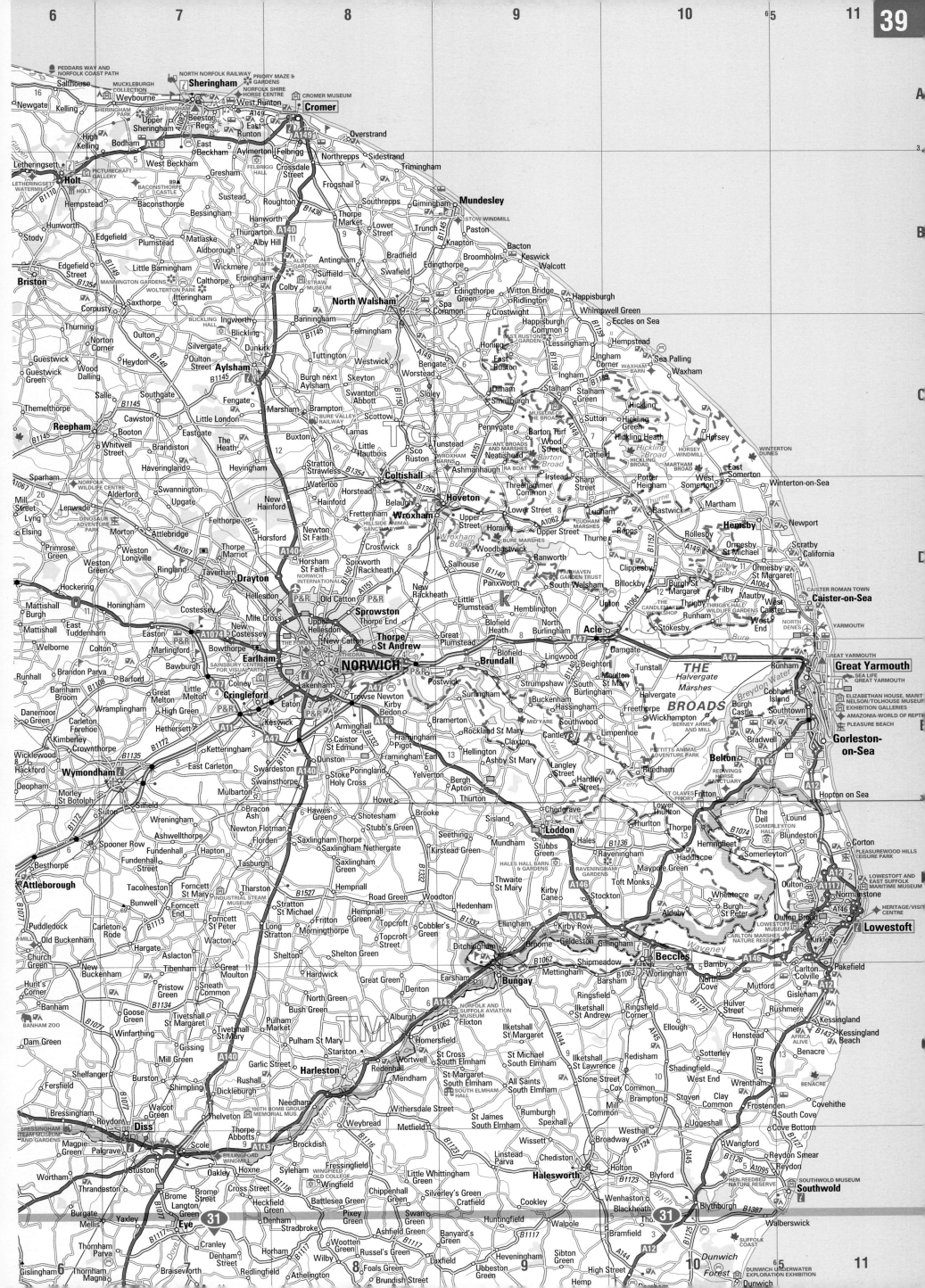

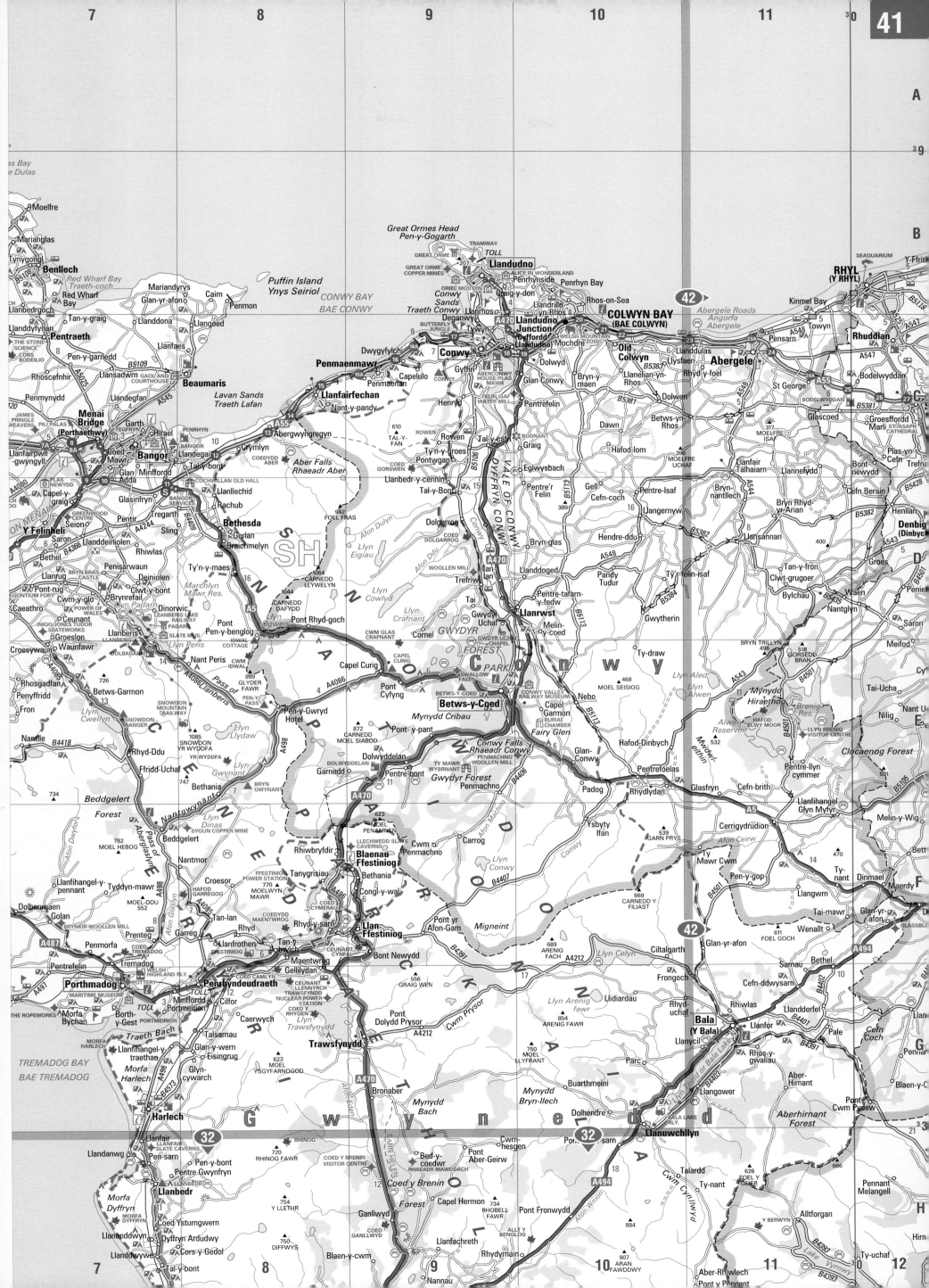

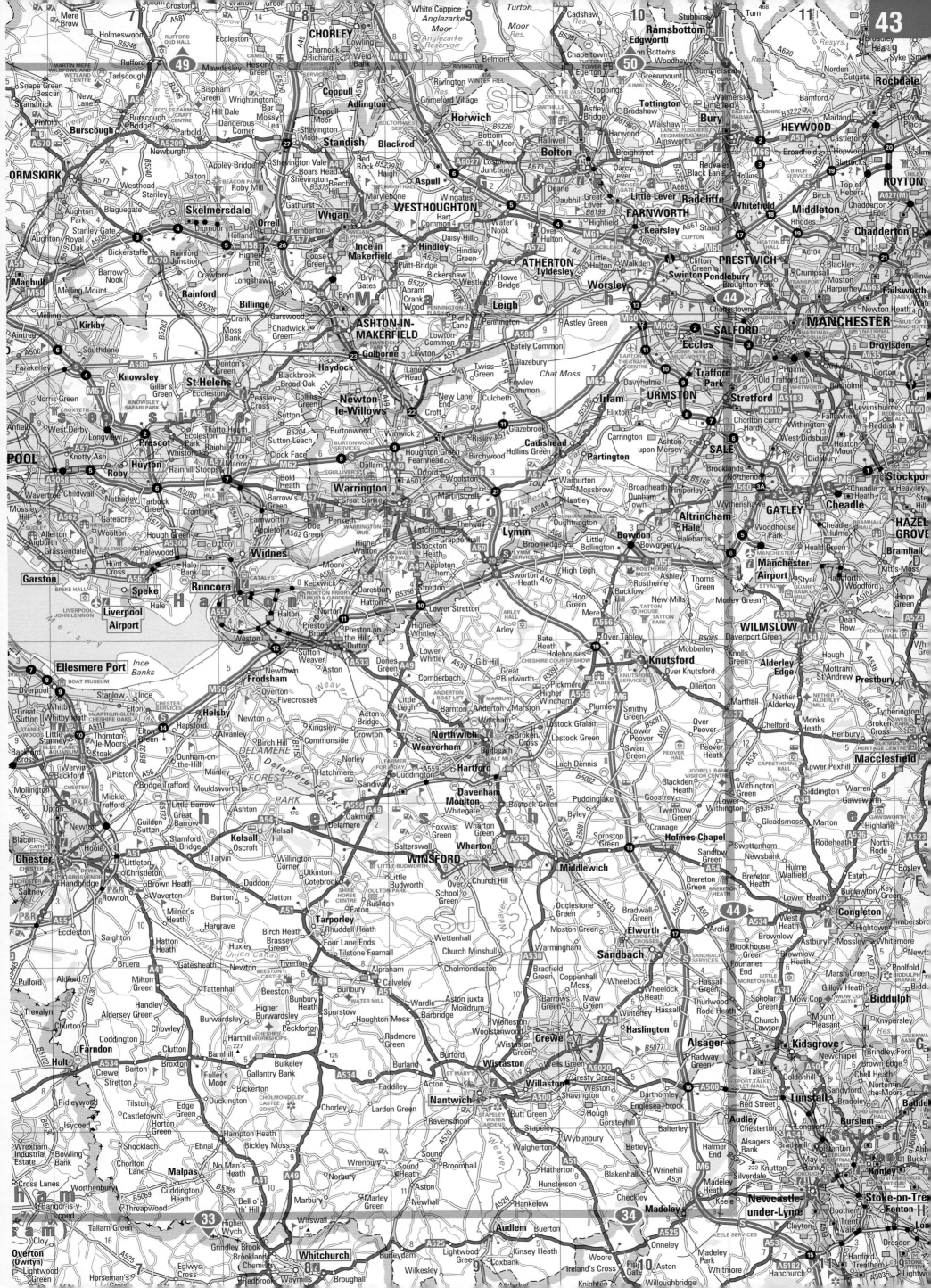

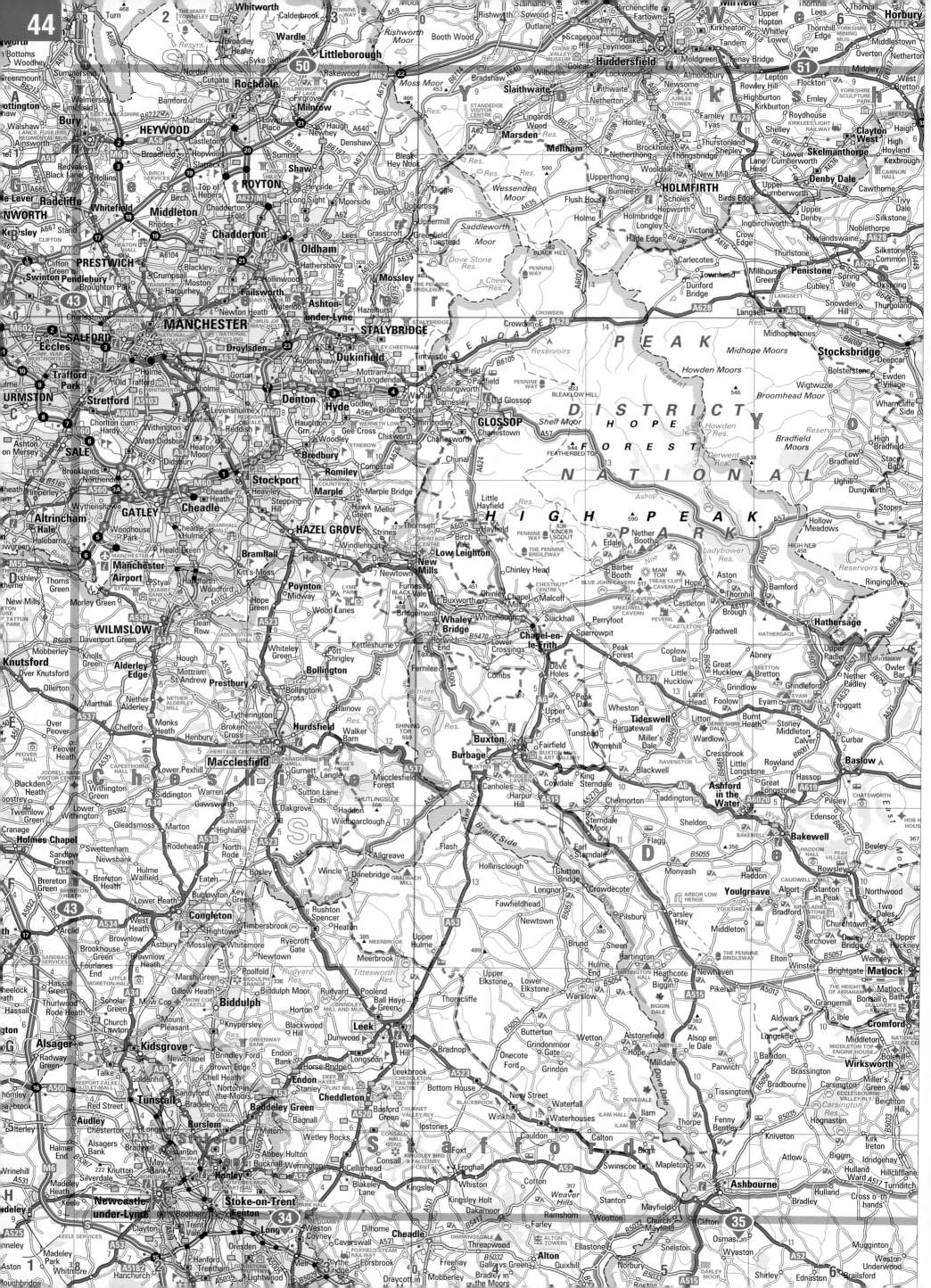

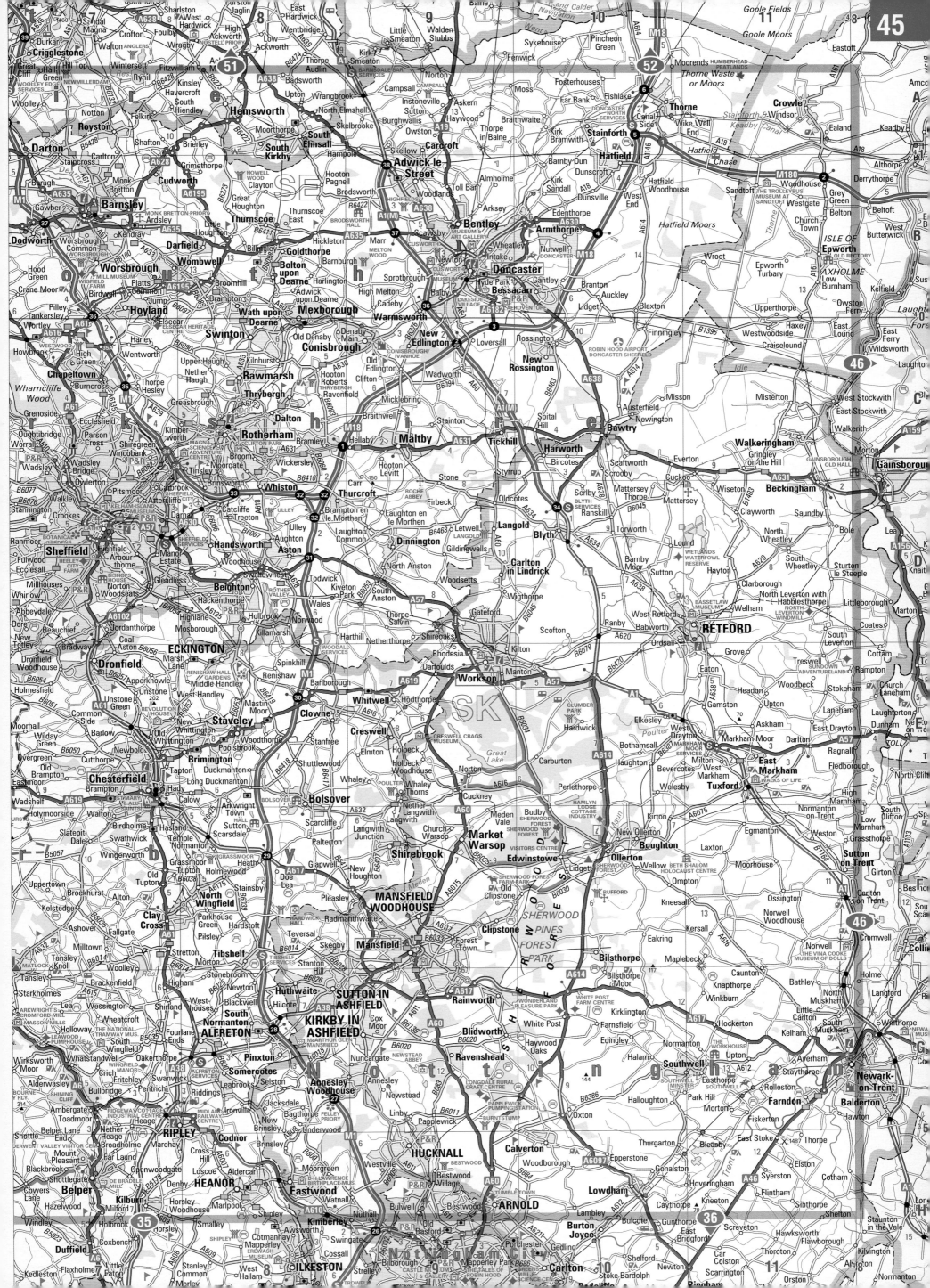

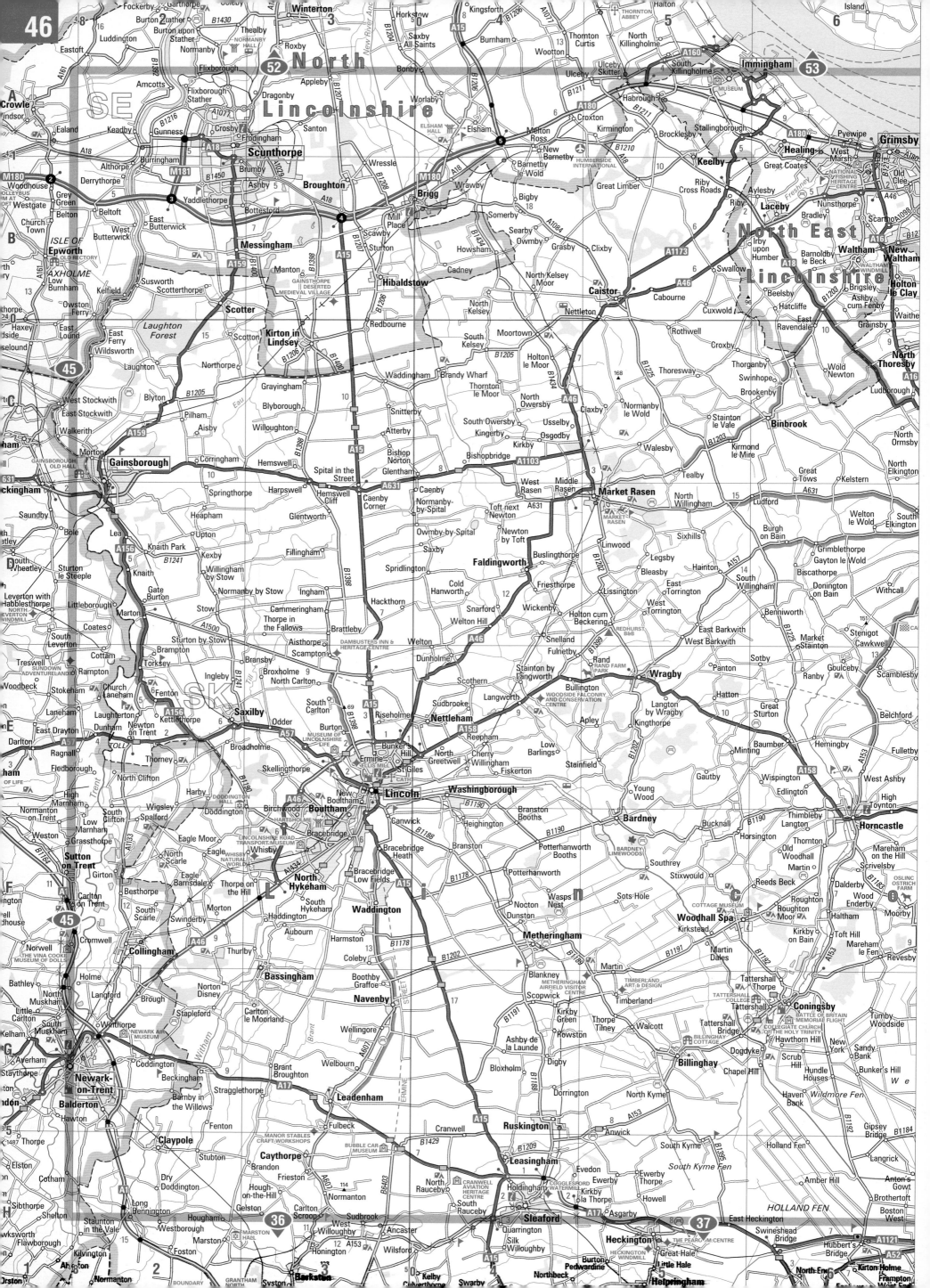

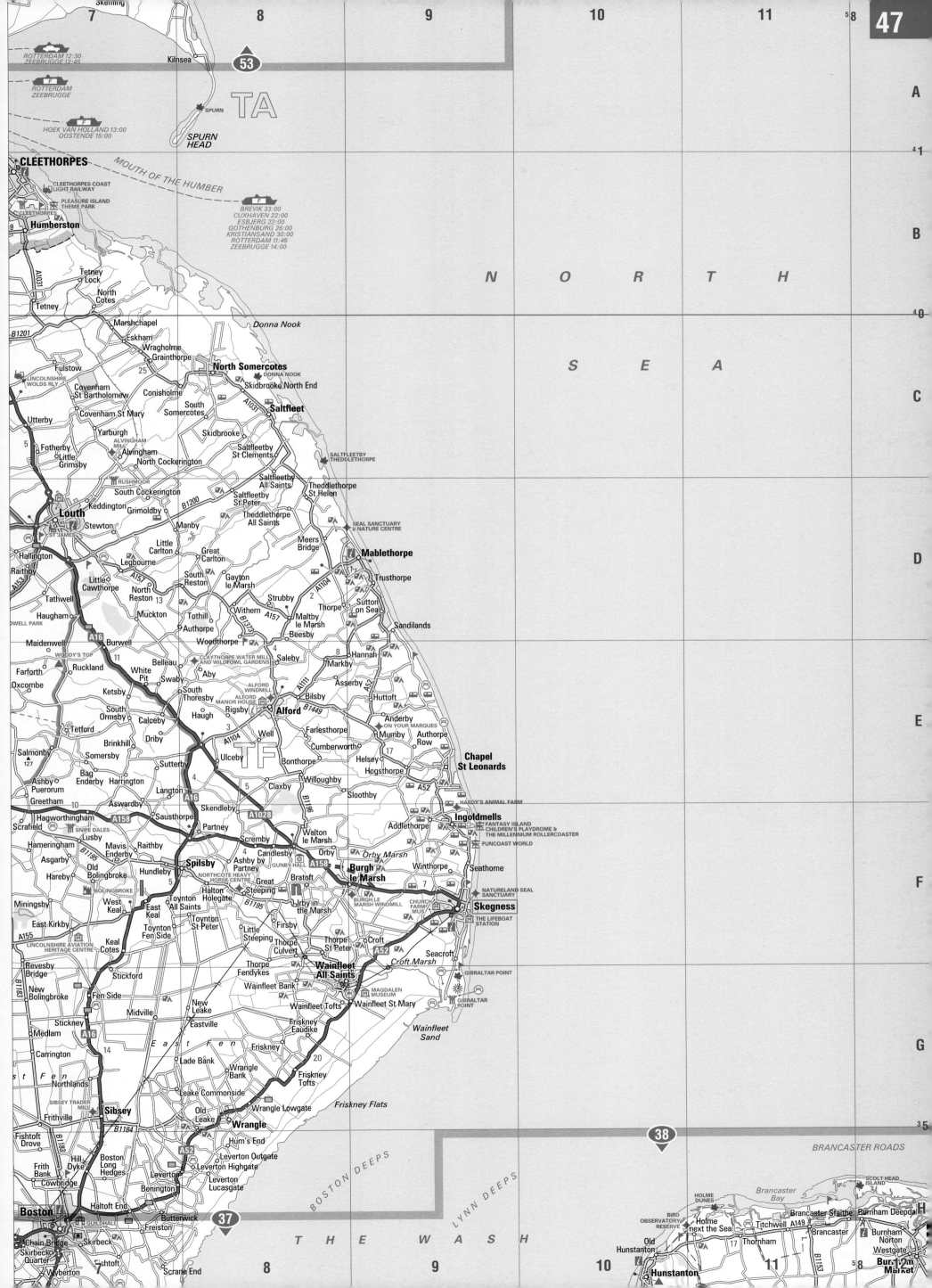

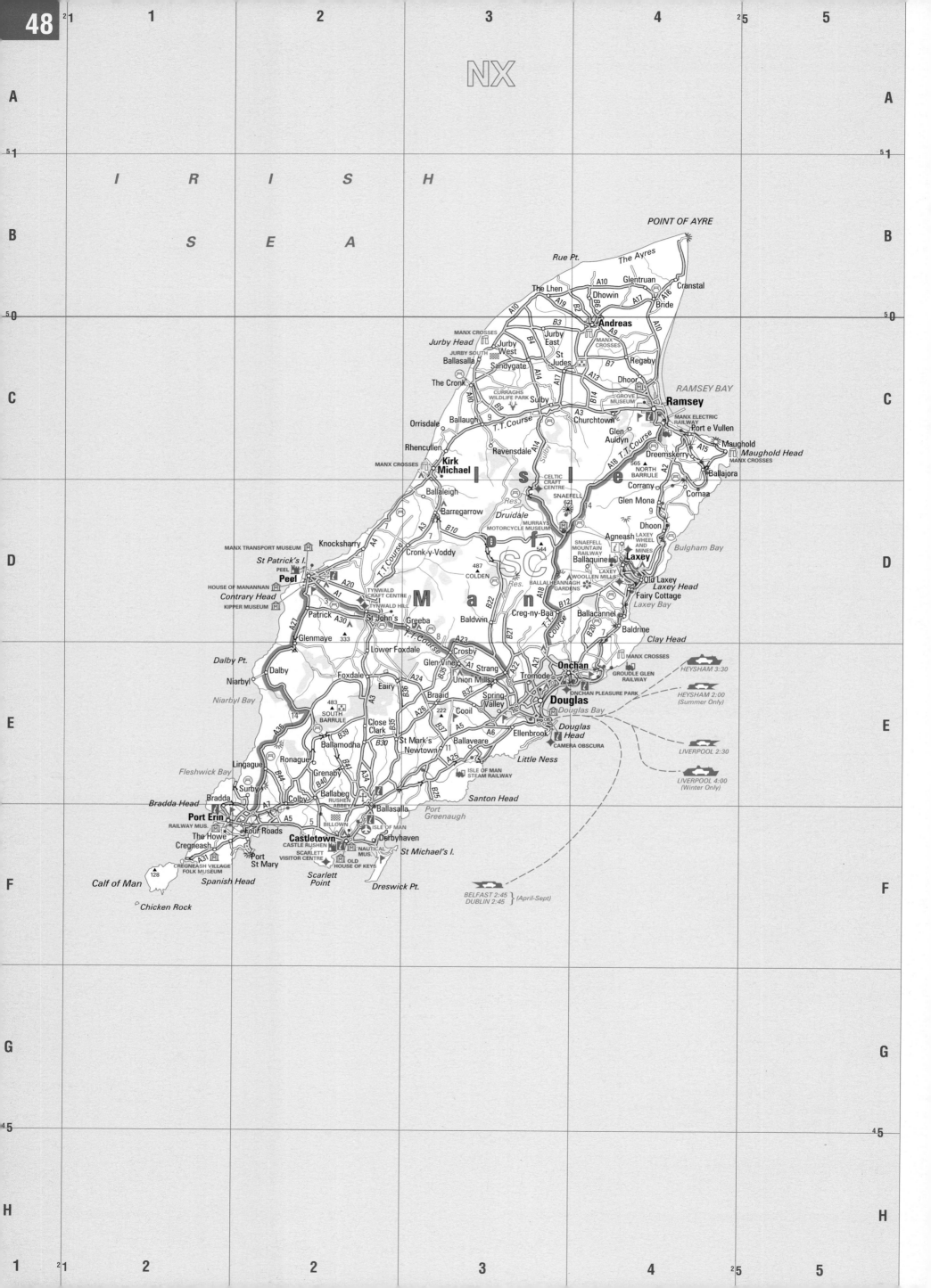

NX

IRISH

SEA

POINT OF AYRE

The Ayres

Rue Pt.

The Lhen
Glentruan
Cranstal

A10
Dhowin
Bride

A19
B2
B6
A17
A16

B3
Andreas
A9

MANX CROSSES
Jurby East
MANX CROSSES

Jurby Head
Jurby West
St Judes
B7
Regaby

JURBY SOUTH
B4
A17
Ballasalla
Sandygate
A13
Dhoor

The Cronk
A14
RAMSEY BAY

A10
CURRAGHS WILDLIFE PARK
GROVE MUSEUM
Ramsey

Orrisdale
Ballaugh
Sulby
A3
Churchtown
MANX ELECTRIC RAILWAY

9
T.T.Course
Glen Auldyn
Port e Vullen

Rhencullen
Ravensdale
Dreemskerry
A15
Maughold

A14
Sulby
565 NORTH BARRULE
A2
Maughold Head

MANX CROSSES
CELTIC CRAFT CENTRE
A18 T.T.Course
Ballajora

Kirk Michael
ISLE
e
Corrany
MANX CROSSES

Ballaleigh
SNAEFELL 621
Glen Mona
Cornaa

Barregarrow
Druidale
MURRAYS MOTORCYCLE MUSEUM
9
Dhoon

B10
of
Agneash
LAXEY WHEEL AND MINES
Bulgham Bay

MANX TRANSPORT MUSEUM
Knocksharry
Cronk-y-Voddy
SNAEFELL MOUNTAIN RAILWAY
Ballaquine
Laxey

St Patrick's I.
487 COLDEN
544
S C
BALLALHEANNAGH GARDENS
LAXEY WOOLLEN MILLS

Peel
PEEL
Res.
Old Laxey

HOUSE OF MANANNAN
A20
M
a
n
Laxey Head

Contrary Head
TYNWALD CRAFT CENTRE
B22
Ballacannel
Fairy Cottage

KIPPER MUSEUM
A1
Baldwin
Creg-ny-Baa
A18 T.T.Course
Laxey Bay

Patrick A30
TYNWALD HILL
St John's
Greeba
B21
Baldrine

Glenmaye
333
8
A23
Crosby
Clay Head

A27
T.T.Course
Glen Vine
A1
Strang
HEYSHAM 3:30

Dalby Pt.
Lower Foxdale
A22
Onchan
GROUDLE GLEN RAILWAY
HEYSHAM 2:00 (Summer Only)

Niarbyl
Dalby
Foxdale
A24
Braaid
B32
Union Mills
Tromode
ONCHAN PLEASURE PARK

Niarbyl Bay
483 SOUTH BARRULE
A3
Eairy
B35
Spring Valley
Douglas
LIVERPOOL 2:30

14
B39
Close Clark
222
Cooil
Douglas Bay

Ballamodha
B30
St Mark's
A5
Ballaveare
Ellenbrook
Douglas Head
LIVERPOOL 4:00 (Winter Only)

Lingague
Ronague
Newtown
11
A25
CAMERA OBSCURA

Fleshwick Bay
Surby
Grenaby
A34
Little Ness

Bradda Head
Colby
Ballabeg
B25
ISLE OF MAN STEAM RAILWAY

Bradda
A1
Ballasalla
Santon Head

Port Erin
RUSHEN ABBEY
Port Greenaugh

RAILWAY MUS.
Four Roads
5
BILLOWN
ISLE OF MAN

The Howe
A5
Castletown
Derbyhaven

Cregneash
A31
CASTLE RUSHEN
NAUTICAL MUS.

CREGNEASH VILLAGE FOLK MUSEUM
Port St Mary
SCARLETT VISITOR CENTRE
OLD HOUSE OF KEYS
St Michael's I.

128
Spanish Head
Scarlett Point
Dreswick Pt.

Calf of Man
BELFAST 2:45
DUBLIN 2:45 (April-Sept)

Chicken Rock

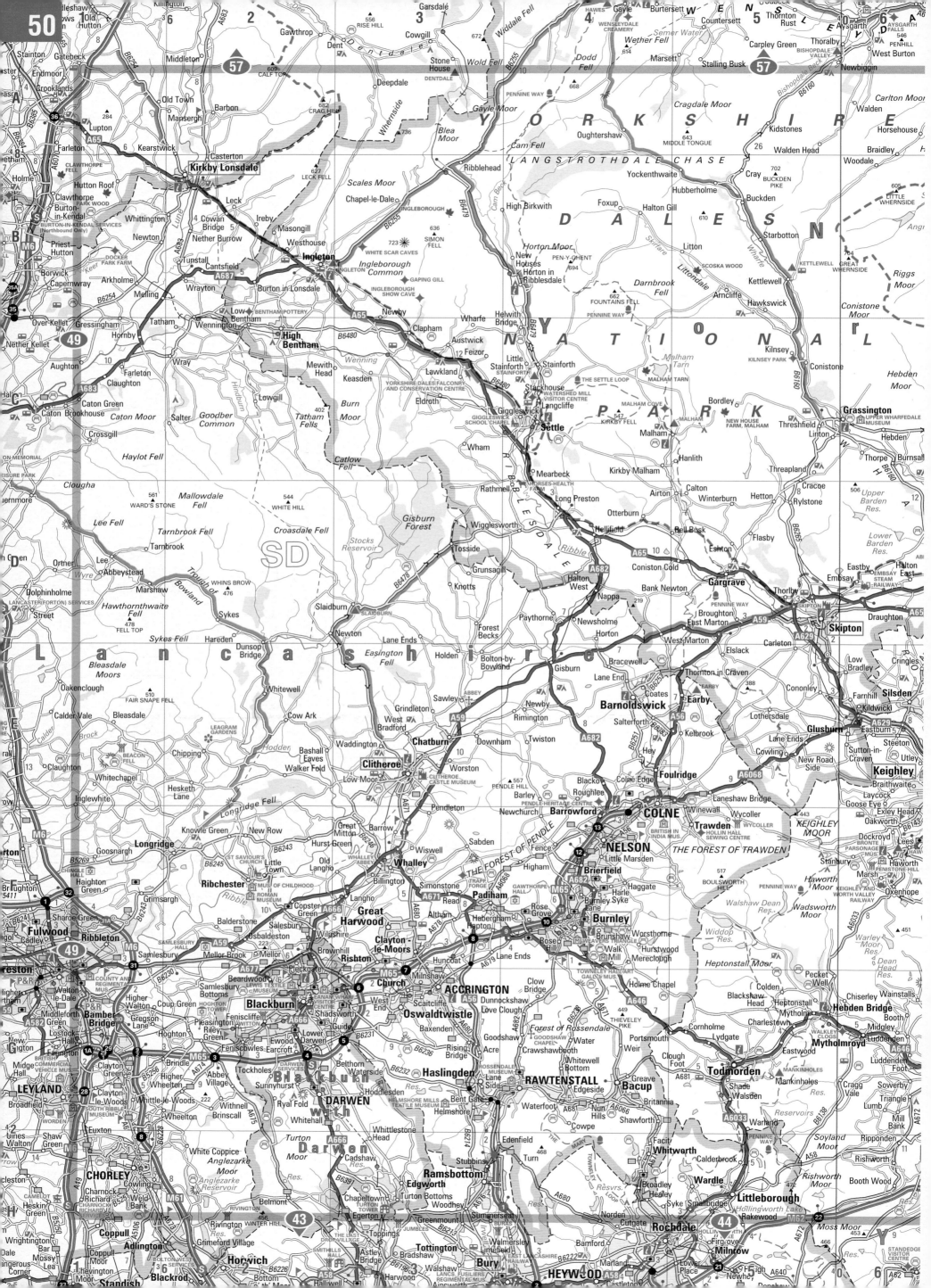

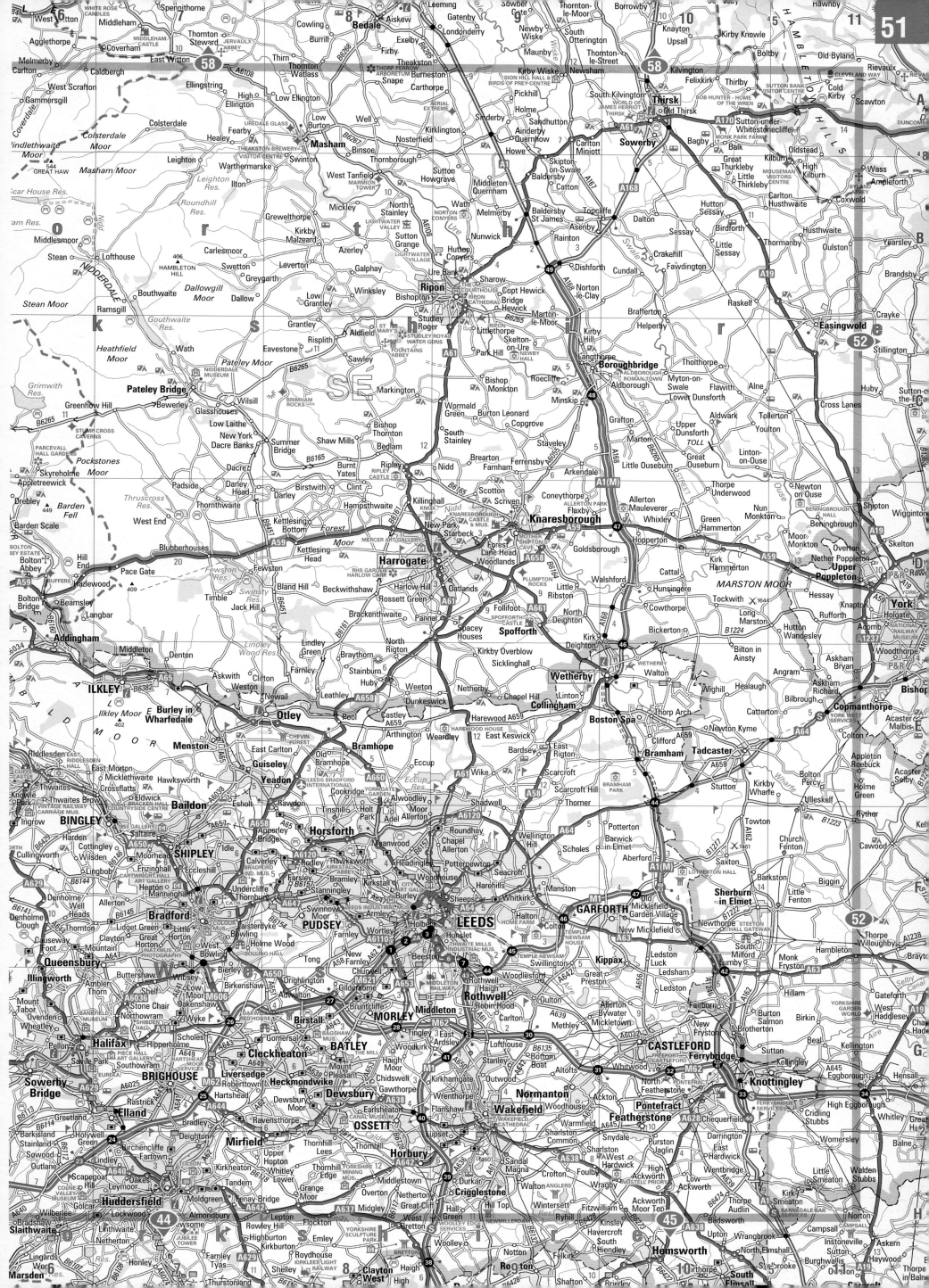

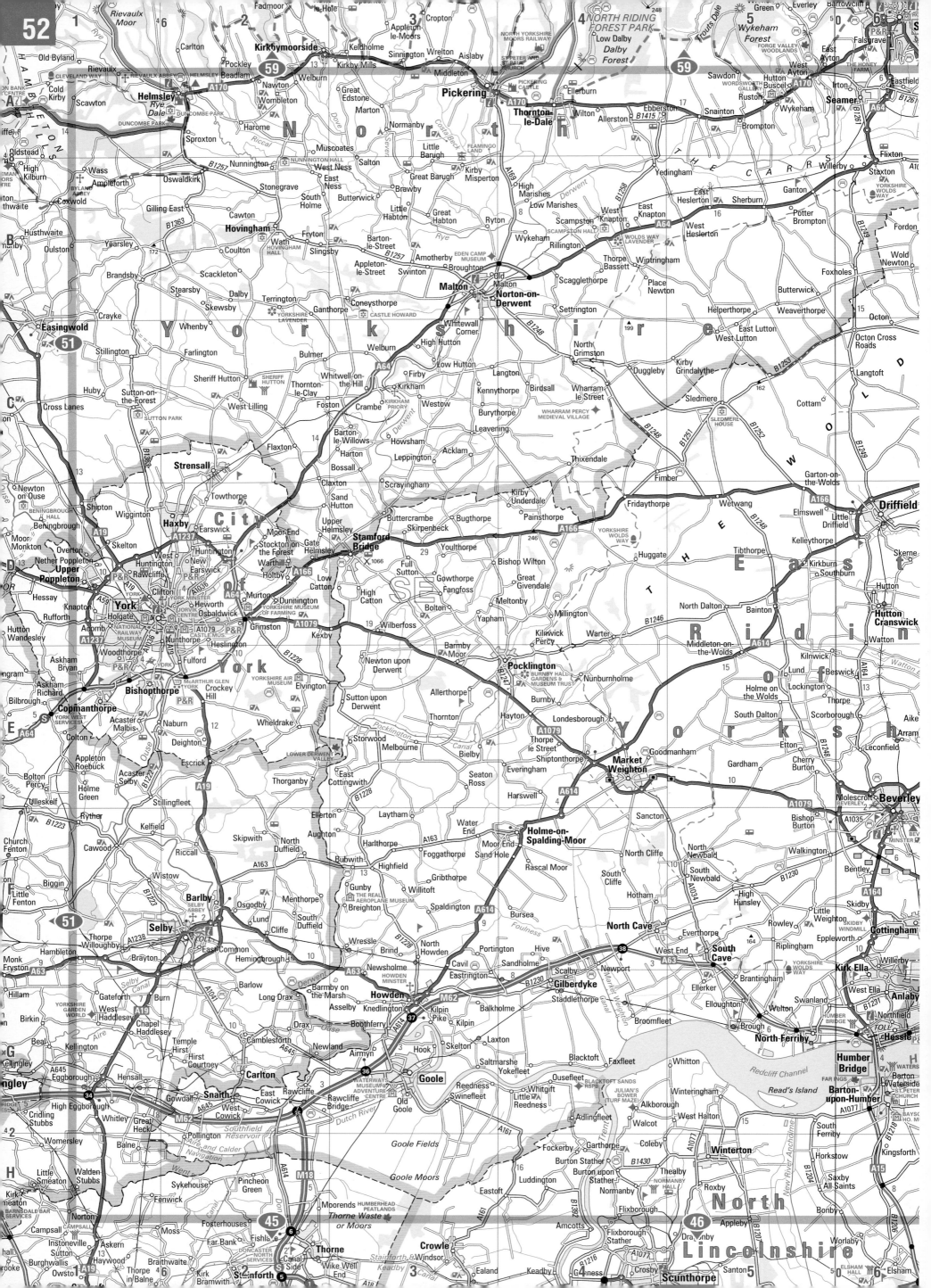

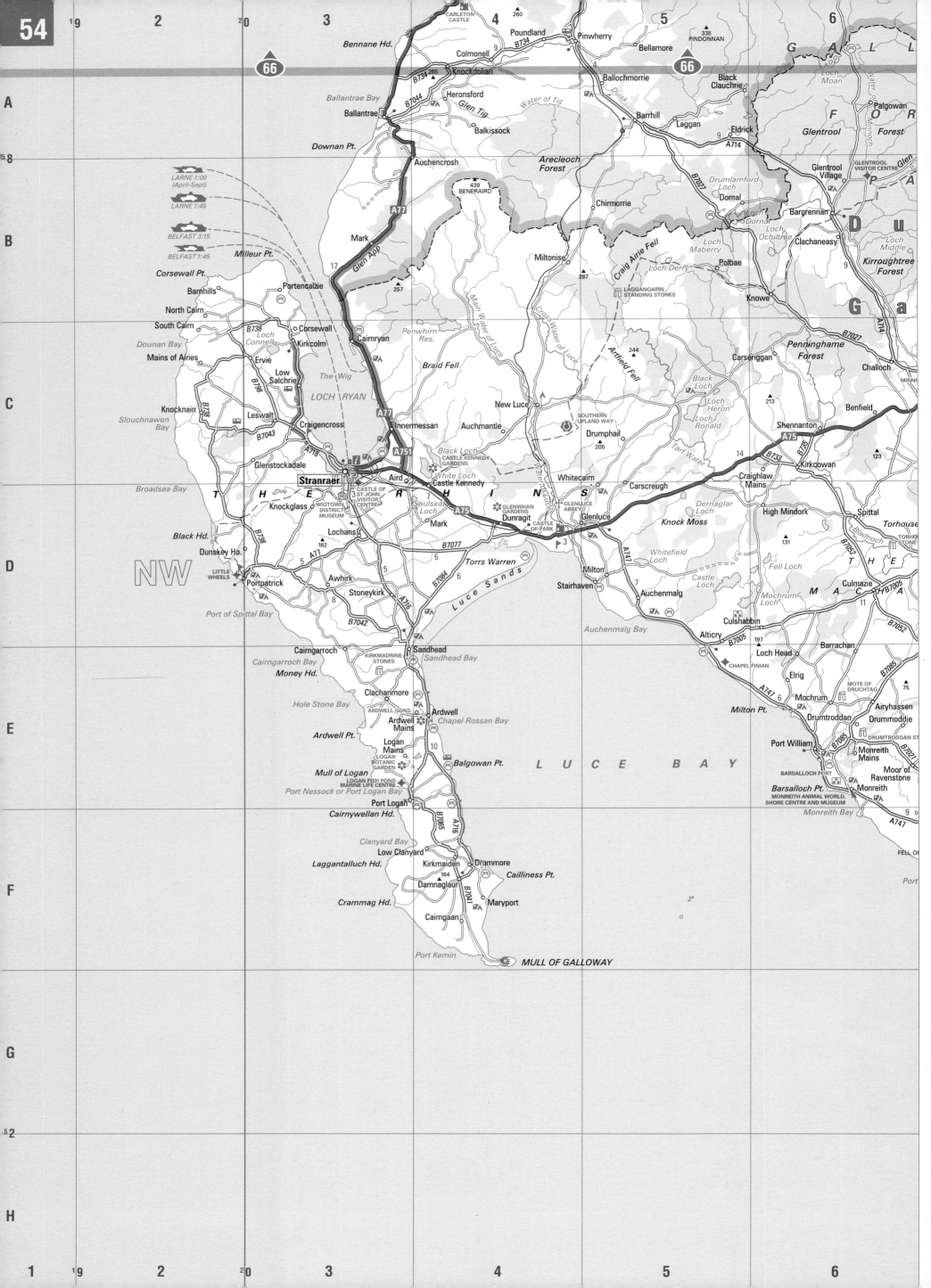

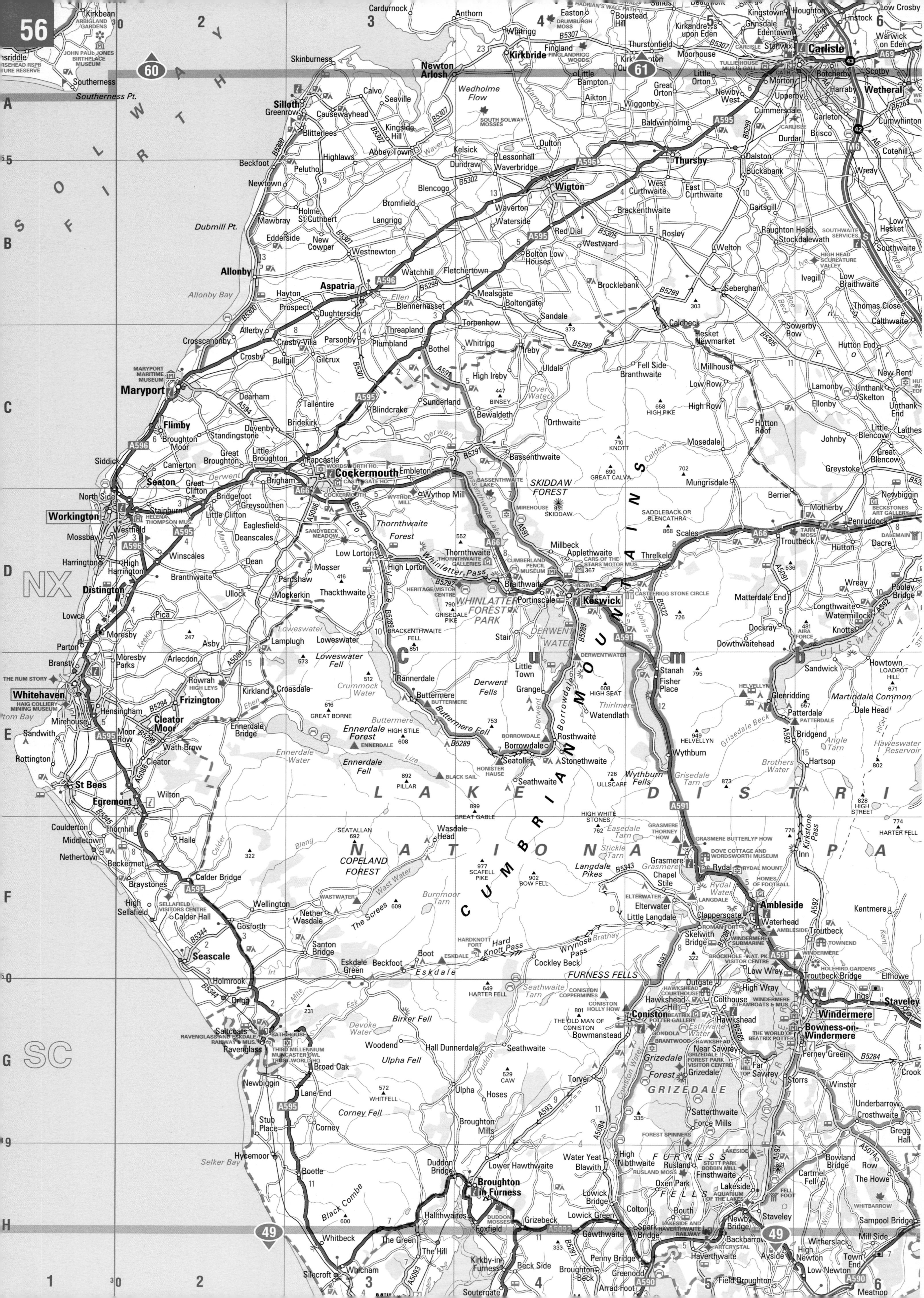
SOLWAY FIRTH
Kirkbean
Arbigland Gardens
John Paul Jones Birthplace Museum
Southerness
Southerness Pt.
Cardurnock
Anthorn
Easton
Boustead Hill
Burgh by Sands
Beaumont
Kingstown
Houghton
Linstock
Low Crosby
Glasson
Drumburgh Moss
Whitrigg
Kirkbride
Fingland
Finglandrigg Woods
Kirkandrews upon Eden
Grinsdale
Edentown
Stanwix
Carlisle
Warwick on Eden
Thurstonfield
Kirkbampton
Moorhouse
Tullie House Museum & Gall.
Botcherby
Scotby
Skinburness
Newton Arlosh
Little Bampton
Great Orton
Little Orton
Morton
Harraby
Wetheral
Silloth
Greenrow
Calvo
Seaville
Wedholme Flow
Aikton
Newby West
Upperby
Causewayhead
Kingside Hill
South Solway Mosses
Wiggonby
Cummersdale
Carleton
Blitterlees
Abbey Town
Baldwinholme
Durdar
Brisco
Cumwhinton
Cotehill
Beckfoot
Highlaws
Kelsick
Lessonhall
Oulton
Thursby
Dalston
Pelutho
Dundraw
Waverbridge
Wigton
Buckabank
Wreay
Newtown
Blencogo
West Curthwaite
East Curthwaite
Bromfield
Waverton
Gaitsgill
Mawbray
Holme St Cuthbert
Langrigg
Waterside
Brackenthwaite
Low Hesket
Dubmill Pt.
Edderside
New Cowper
Red Dial
Westward
Rosley
Raughton Head
Stockdalewath
Southwaite Services
Southwaite
Westnewton
Bolton Low Houses
Welton
High Head Sculpture Valley
Allonby
Aspatria
Watchhill
Fletchertown
Brocklebank
Ivegill
Low Braithwaite
Sebergham
Allonby Bay
Hayton
Ellen
Blennerhasset
Mealsgate
Boltongate
Thomas Close
Calthwaite
Prospect
Oughterside
Sandale
Caldbeck
Hesket Newmarket
Sowerby Row
Crosscanonby
Allerby
Torpenhow
Threapland
Crosby Villa
Parsonby
Plumbland
Bothel
Whitrigg
Ireby
Hutton End
Crosby
Bullgill
Gilcrux
Uldale
Fell Side
Branthwaite
Millhouse
New Rent
Maryport
Maryport Maritime Museum
Dearham
High Ireby
Binsey
Over Water
Low Row
Lamonby
Unthank
Skelton
Tallentire
Sunderland
Blindcrake
High Pike
High Row
Ellonby
Flimby
Bridekirk
Bewaldeth
Orthwaite
Hutton Roof
Broughton Moor
Dovenby
Standingstone
Little Broughton
Knott
Mosedale
Johnby
Little Blencow
Great Blencow
Laithes
Siddick
Camerton
Great Broughton
Papcastle
Derwent
Bassenthwaite
Caldew
Seaton
Great Clifton
Brigham
Cockermouth
Wordsworth Ho.
Castlegate Ho.
Embleton
Bassenthwaite Lake
Great Calva
Skiddaw Forest
Mungrisdale
Greystoke
North Side
Stainburn
Bridgefoot
Greysouthen
Wythop Mill
Berrier
Newbiggin
Workington
Helena Thompson Mus.
Little Clifton
Mirehouse
Skiddaw
Saddleback or Blencathra
Motherby
Beckstones Art Gallery
Penruddock
Mossbay
Westfield
Eaglesfield
Sandybeck Meadow
Thornthwaite Forest
Scales
Tarn Moss
Troutbeck
Dacre
Deanscales
Lorton
Thornthwaite
Thornthwaite Galleries
Millbeck
Applethwaite
Threlkeld
Hutton
Dalemain
Harrington
High Harrington
Winscales
Dean
Low Lorton
High Lorton
Whinlatter Pass
Cumberland Pencil Museum
Cars of the Stars Motor Mus.
Wreay
Pooley Bridge
Distington
Branthwaite
Mosser
Pardshaw
Thackthwaite
Heritage/Visitor Centre
Whinlatter Forest Park
Braithwaite
Portinscale
Keswick
Castlerigg Stone Circle
Matterdale End
Longthwaite
Watermillock
Ullock
Mockerkin
Grisedale Pike
Brackenthwaite Fell
Stair
Derwent Water
Aira Force
Knotts
Ullswater
Lowca
Pica
Moresby
Loweswater
Lamplugh
Dockray
Dowthwaitehead
Parton
Asby
Arlecdon
Loweswater Fell
Derwentwater
Howtown
Loadpot Hill
Bransty
Moresby Parks
Rowrah
High Leys
Crummock Water
Rannerdale
Little Town
Stanah
Fisher Place
Sandwick
The Rum Story
Whitehaven
Haig Colliery Mining Museum
Frizington
Kirkland
Croasdale
Derwent Fells
Grange
High Seat
Helvellyn
Glenridding
Martindale Common
Hensingham
Cleator Moor
Ehen
Buttermere
Great Borne
Watendlath
Thirlmere
Patterdale
Dale Head
Mirehouse
Sandwith
Moor Row
Ennerdale Bridge
Ennerdale Forest
High Stile
Buttermere Fell
Borrowdale
Rosthwaite
Bridgend
Angle Tarn
Haweswater Reservoir
Wath Brow
Cleator
Ennerdale Water
Ennerdale Fell
Liza
Black Sail
Seatoller
Honister Hause
Stonethwaite
Wythburn
Grisedale Tarn
Brothers Water
Hartsop
Rottington
St Bees
Egremont
Wilton
Pillar
Seathwaite
Ullscarf
Wythburn Fells
LAKE DISTRICT NATIONAL PARK
CUMBRIAN MOUNTAINS
Great Gable
High Street
Coulderton
Thornhill
High White Stones
Grasmere Thorney How
Harter Fell
Middletown
Seatallan
Wasdale Head
Easedale Tarn
Grasmere Butterlyp How
Kirkstone Pass
Haile
Nethertown
Beckermet
Copeland Forest
Bleng
Stickle Tarn
Dove Cottage and Wordsworth Museum
Inn
Scafell Pike
Bow Fell
Langdale Pikes
Grasmere
Rydal
Rydal Mount
Calder Bridge
Chapel Stile
Homes of Football
Braystones
Wastwater
Wast Water
Burnmoor Tarn
Rydal Water
Kentmere
High Sellafield
Sellafield Visitors Centre
Calder Hall
Wellington
Nether Wasdale
The Screes
Elterwater
Langdale
Ambleside
Waterhead
Troutbeck
Little Langdale
Clappersgate
Roman Fort
Gosforth
Hardknott Fort
Hard Knott Pass
Wrynose Pass
Brathay
Skelwith Bridge
Windermere Submarine
Townend
Seascale
Santon Bridge
Eskdale Green
Beckfoot
Boot
Eskdale
Cockley Beck
Brockhole Nat. Pk. Visitor Centre
Holehird Gardens
Holmrook
Irt
Furness Fells
Low Wray
Troutbeck Bridge
Elfhowe
Harter Fell
Seathwaite Tarn
Coniston Coppermines
Outgate
High Wray
Drigg
Mite
Coniston Fell
Hawkshead Courthouse
Hawkshead Hill
Colthouse
Windermere Steamboats & Mus.
Ings
Staveley
Saltcoats
Ravenglass and Eskdale Railway & Mus.
Bath House
Ravenglass
Devoke Water
Birker Fell
The Old Man of Coniston
Coniston
Ruskin Museum
Beatrix Potter Gallery
Hawkshead
Windermere
Bowness-on-Windermere
The World of Beatrix Potter
Bowmanstead
Gondola
Brantwood
Esthwaite Water
Third Millennium Muncaster Owl Trust World HQ
Woodend
Hall Dunnerdale
Grizedale Forest Park Visitor Centre
Near Sawrey
Far Sawrey
Hill Top
Ferney Green
Crook
Broad Oak
Ulpha Fell
Grizedale Forest
Grizedale
Newbiggin
Caw
Torver
Storrs
Winster
Whitfell
Lane End
Ulpha
Hoses
Coniston Water
Underbarrow
Crosthwaite
Corney Fell
Stub Place
Corney
Broughton Mills
Satterthwaite
Force Mills
Gregg Hall
Forest Spinners
Selker Bay
Hycemoor
Duddon Bridge
Lower Hawthwaite
Water Yeat
Blawith
High Nibthwaite
Furness Fells
Rusland
Rusland Moss
Stott Park Bobbin Mill
Lakeside
Finsthwaite
Bowland Bridge
Row
Bootle
Broughton in Furness
Oxen Park
Lakeside Aquarium of the Lakes
Cartmel Fell
The Howe
Fell Foot
Black Combe
Lowick Bridge
Lowick Green
Colton
Bouth
Whitbarrow
Hallthwaites
Duddon Mosses
Foxfield
Grizebeck
Newby Bridge
Lakeside and Haverthwaite Railway
Staveley
Sampool Bridge
Gawthwaite
Spark Bridge
Backbarrow
Artcrystal
Mill Side
Witherslack
Whitbeck
The Green
The Hill
Haverthwaite
Ayside
High Newton
Town End
Low Newton
Kirkby-in-Furness
Beck Side
Penny Bridge
Broughton Beck
Greenodd
Silecroft
Whicham
Field Broughton
Meathop
Souterage
Arrad Foot
NX
SC
A
B
C
D
E
F
G
H
1
2
3
4
5
6
60
61
49
A7
A69
A6
M6
A595
A596
A66
A591
A592
A593
A5092
A5086
A594
A5091
A5084
A5074
A5093
A590
B5300
B5302
B5307
B5301
B5299
B5305
B5291
B5292
B5289
B5294
B5295
B5345
B5344
B5343
B5322
B5285
B5286
B5284
B5281
B6263
B6264
B5288
B5263
B5320
B6413

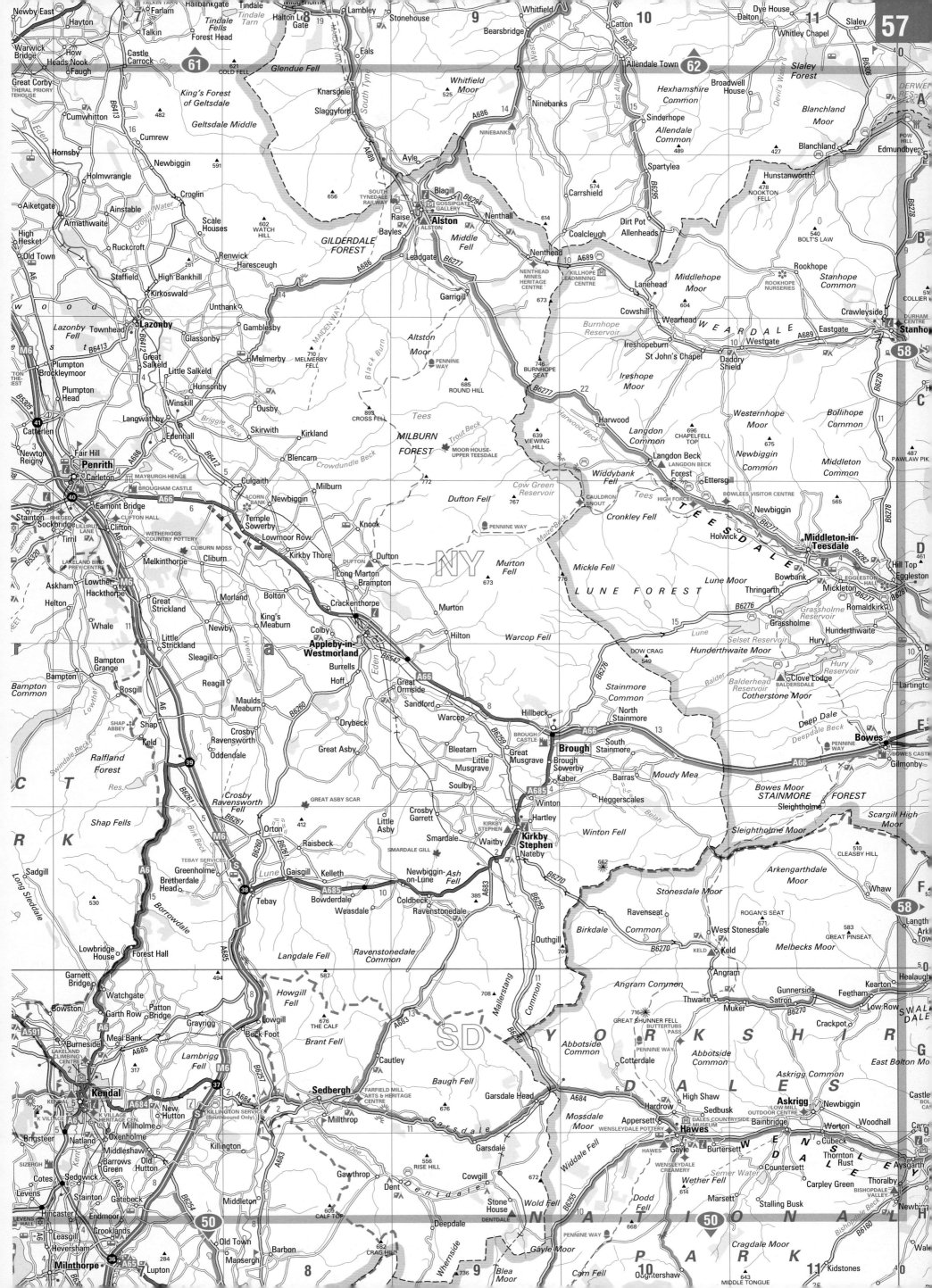

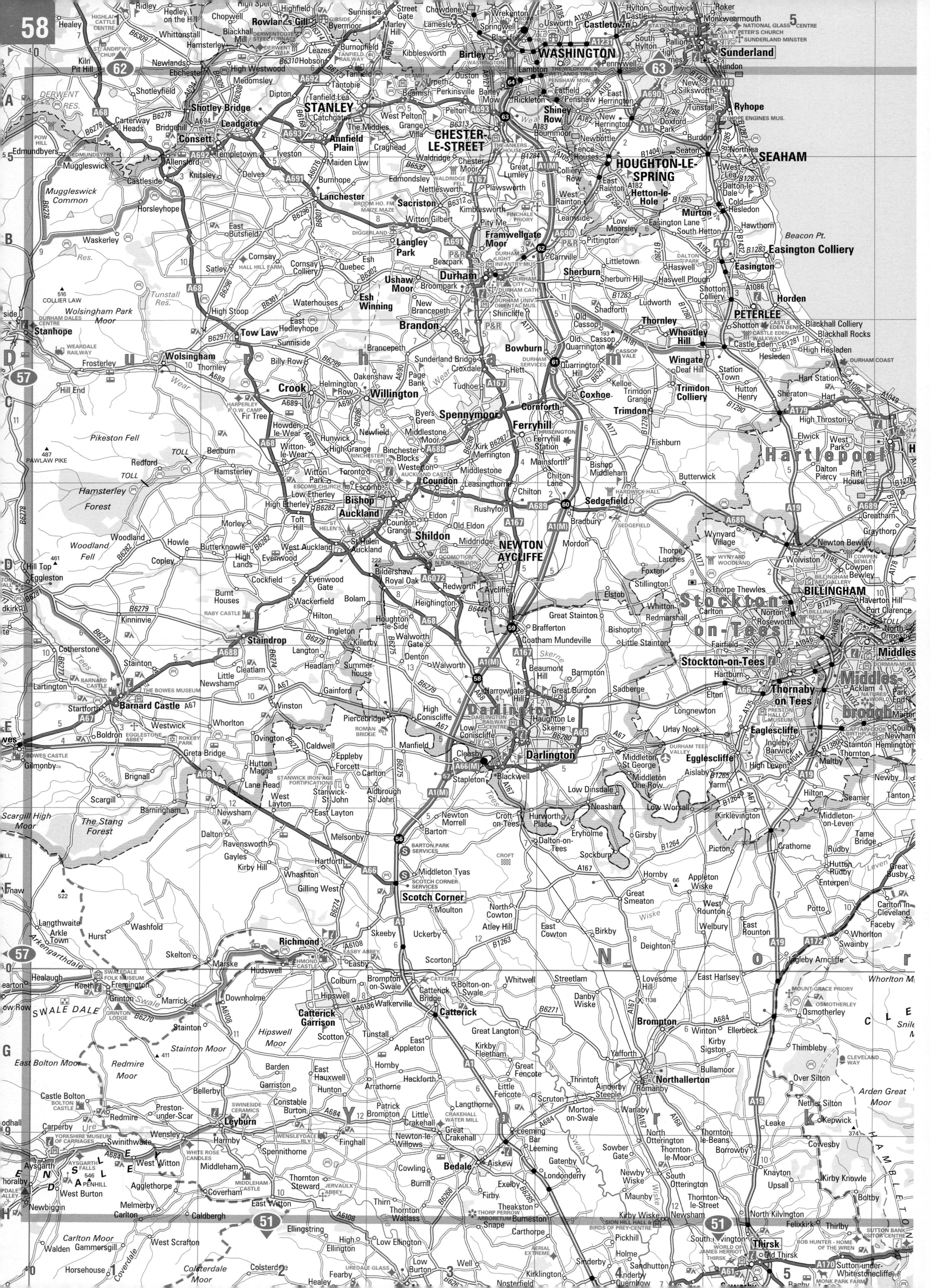

SEAHAM

WASHINGTON

Sunderland

STANLEY

CHESTER-LE-STREET

HOUGHTON-LE-SPRING

Consett

Leadgate

Durham

Easington Colliery

Easington

PETERLEE

Horden

Crook

Willington

Spennymoor

Ferryhill

Trimdon

Wingate

Bishop Auckland

Shildon

NEWTON AYCLIFFE

Sedgefield

Stockton-on-Tees

BILLINGHAM

Hartlepool

Barnard Castle

Darlington

Thornaby-on-Tees

MIDDLES-brough

Eaglescliffe

Egglescliffe

Scotch Corner

Richmond

Catterick Garrison

Catterick

Brompton

Northallerton

Bedale

Leyburn

Thirsk

NZ

SE

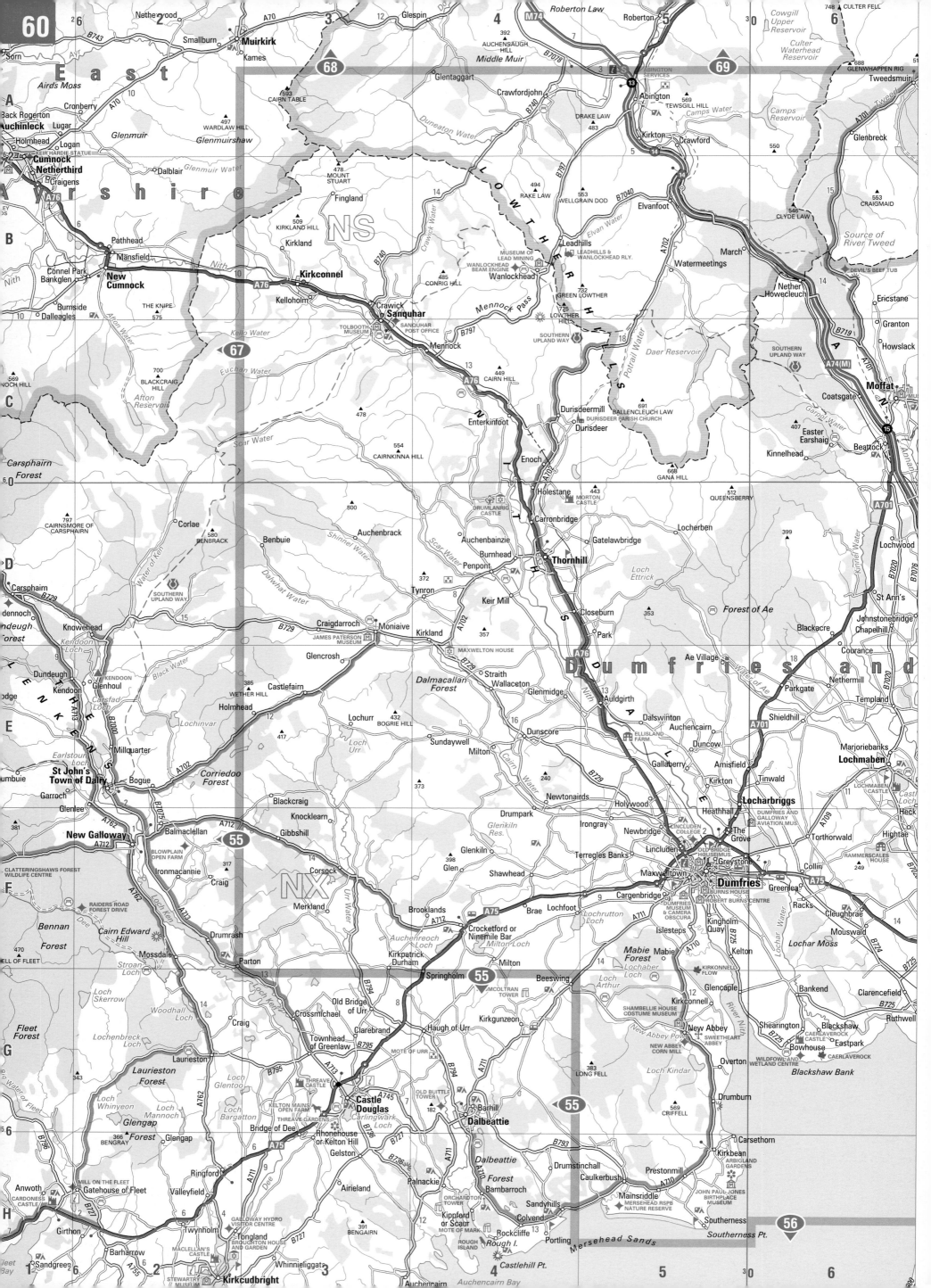

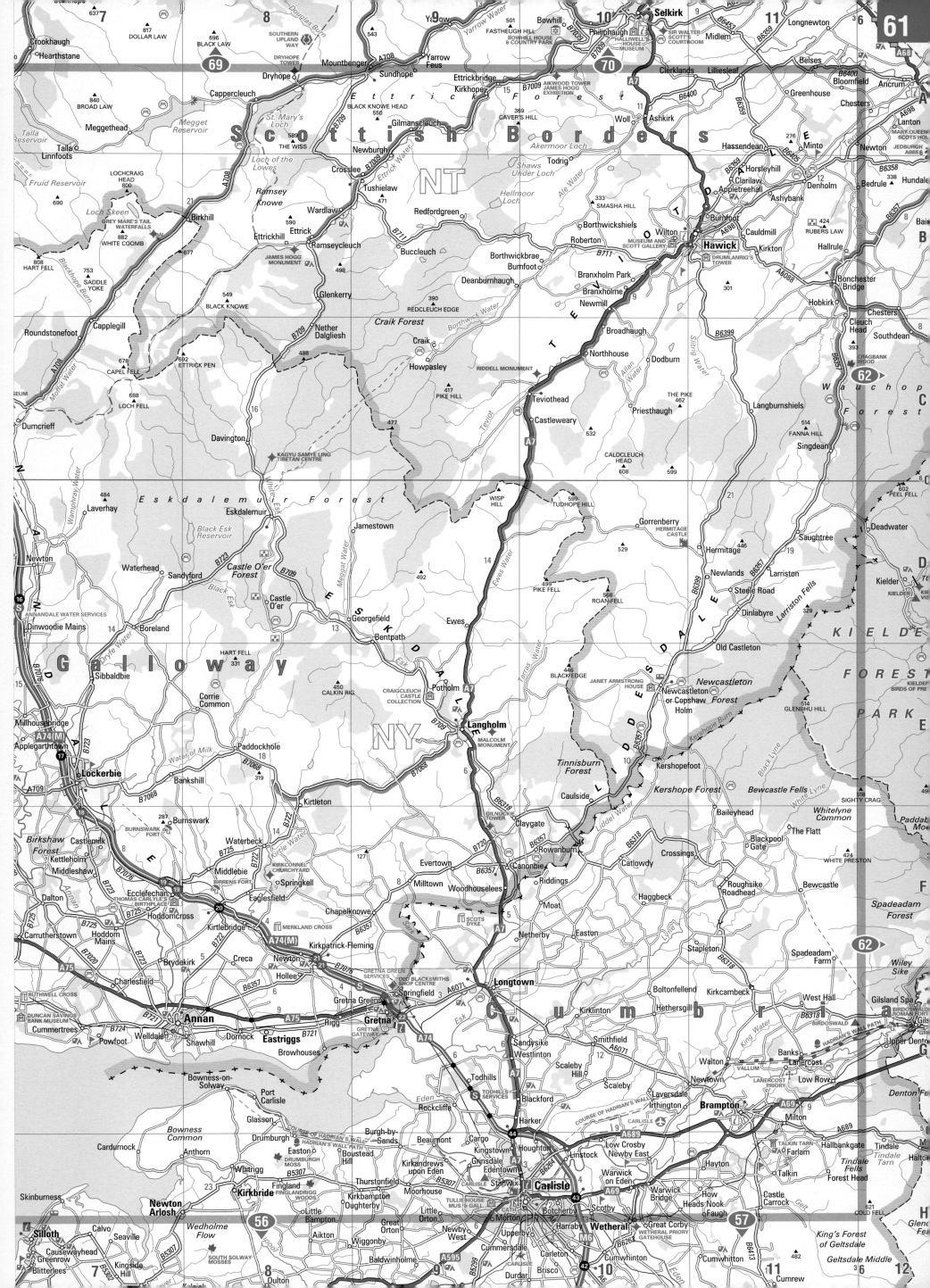

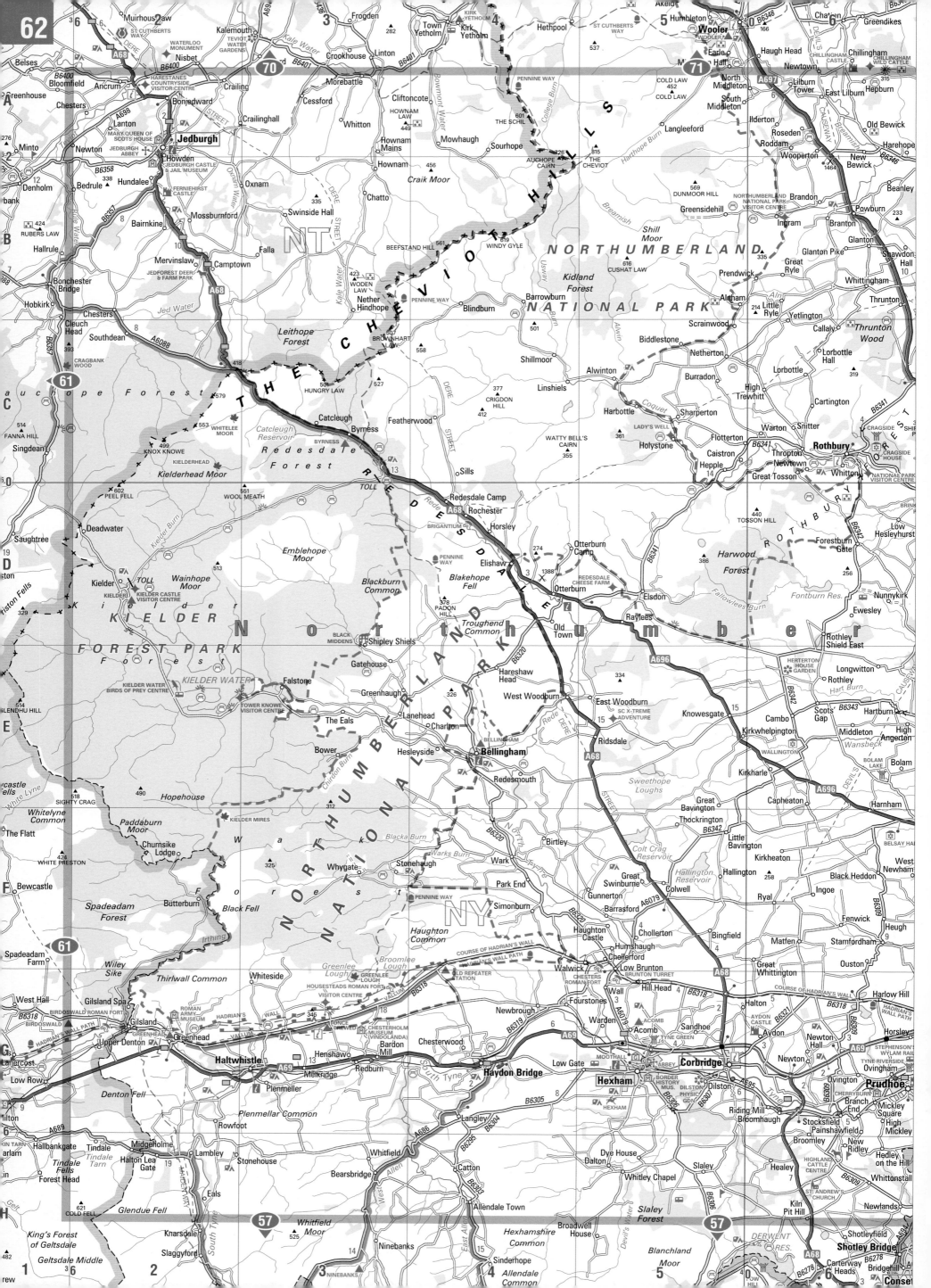

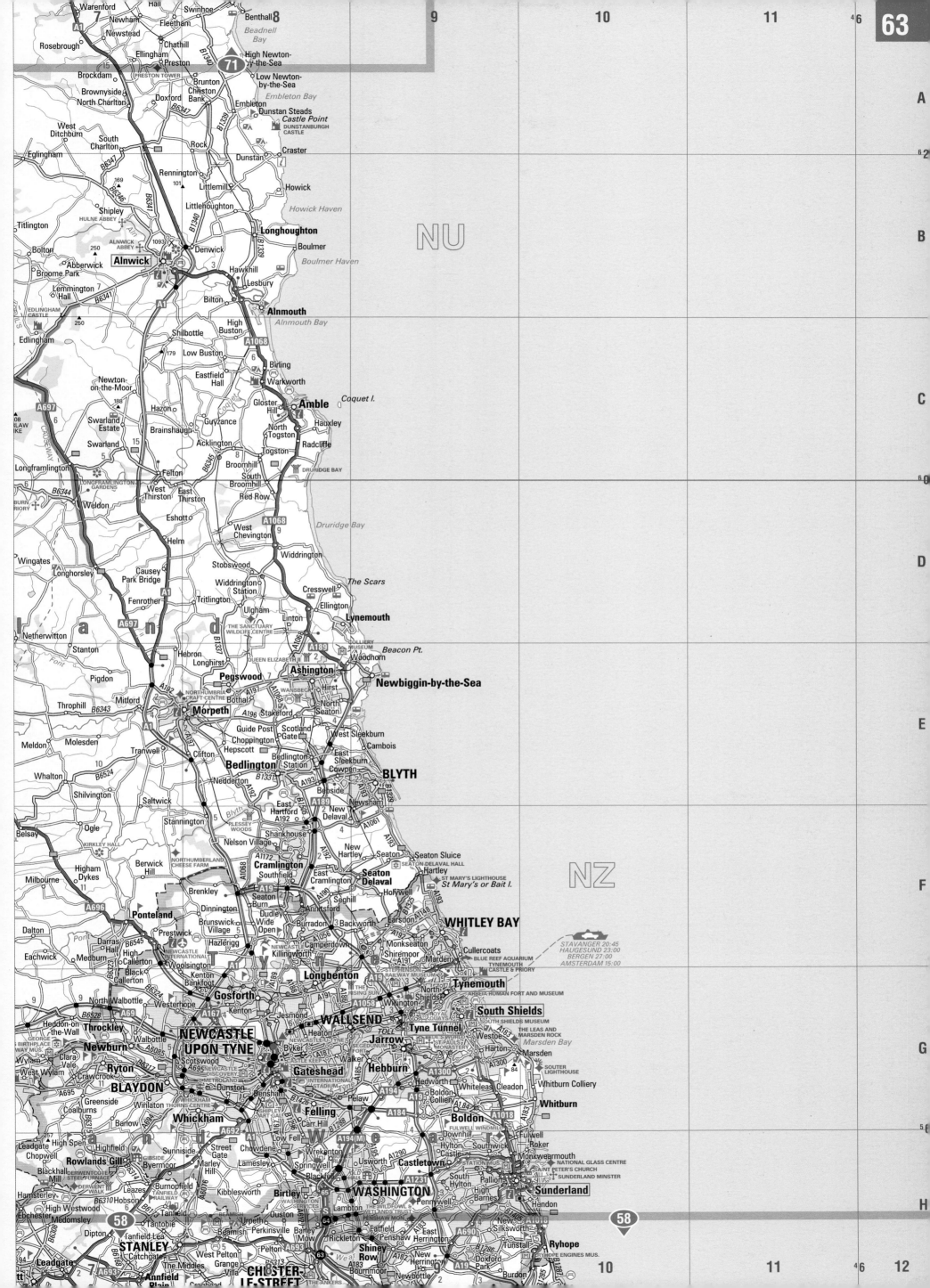

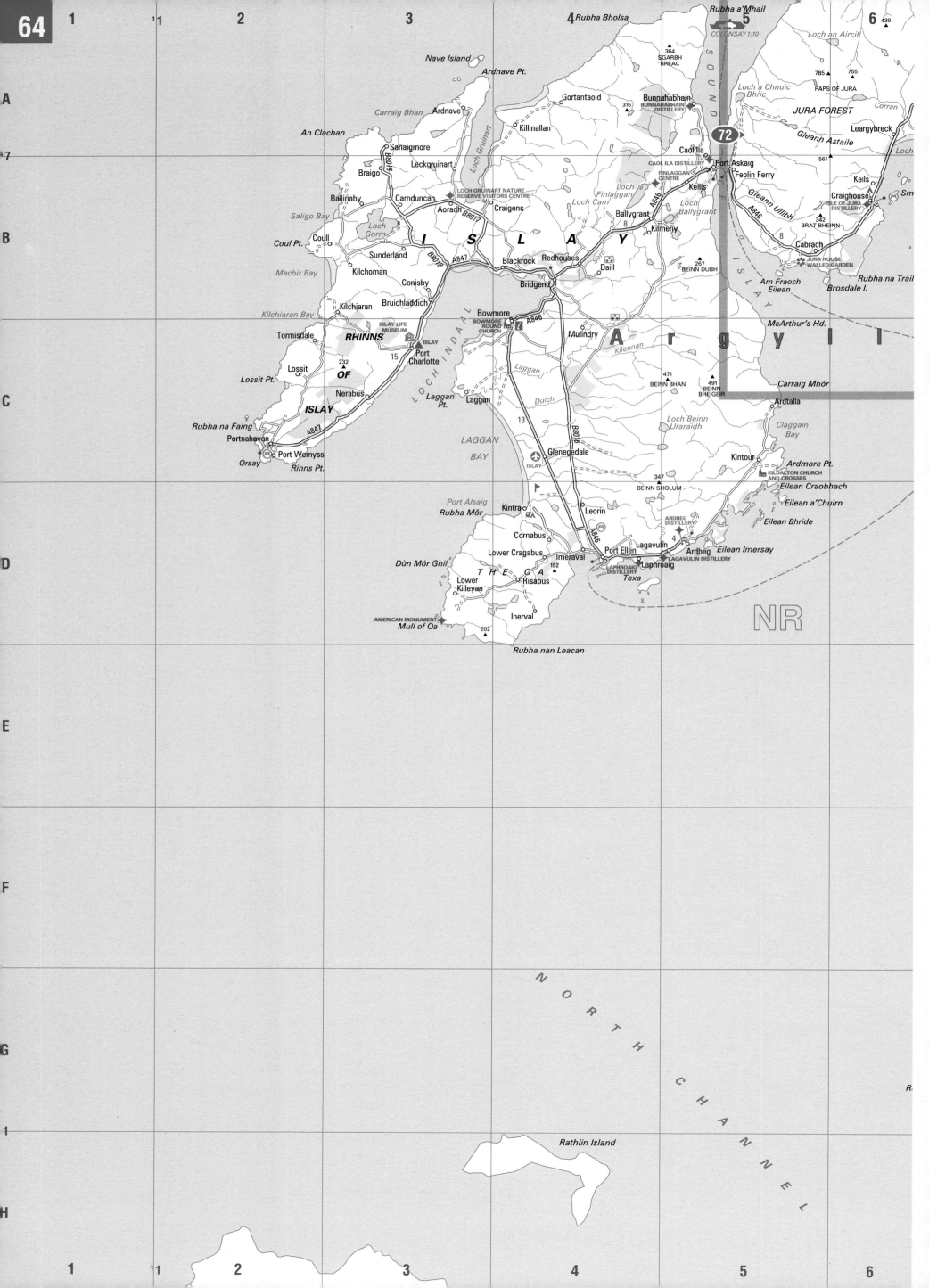

MOTHERWELL HAMILTON WISHAW Newmains Morningside Larkhall Carluke
Bothwell Stevenston Cleland Bonkle Braidwood Lanark New Lanark World Heritage Village
East Kilbride Strathaven Stonehouse Blackwood Kirkmuirhill Lesmahagow Coalburn Douglas

Newton Mearns Eaglesham Drumclog Darvel Newmilns Galston Greenholm Muirkirk Kames Glenbuck
Neilston Uplawmoor Stewarton Fenwick Kilmaurs Kilmarnock Crookedholm Hurlford Moscow

Dreghorn Riccarton Crosshouse Tarbolton Mauchline Catrine Sorn Smallburn Cronberry Lugar
Monkton Mossblown Annbank Drongan Auchinleck Cumnock Netherthird Logan Cairn Table 593

Dalrymple Patna Waterside Dalmellington New Cumnock Pathhead Mansfield Kirkconnel Kelloholm Kirkconnel Sanquhar Crawick Wanlockhead

Carsphairn Forest Carsphairn Dalmellington Enoch Hill Blackcraig Hill 700 Afton Reservoir
DUMFRIES and GALLOWAY Moniaive Penpont Drumlanrig Castle Thornhill

CARRICK FOREST GALLOWAY FOREST PARK Loch Doon Loch Bradan Merrick 843 Loch Enoch
St John's Town of Dalry Corsock Corriedoo Forest Dalmacallan Forest

EAST AYRSHIRE SOUTH LANARKSHIRE SOUTH AYRSHIRE RENFREWSHIRE

A77 A76 A71 A70 A713 A723 M74 M77 A702 A721 A72 A719

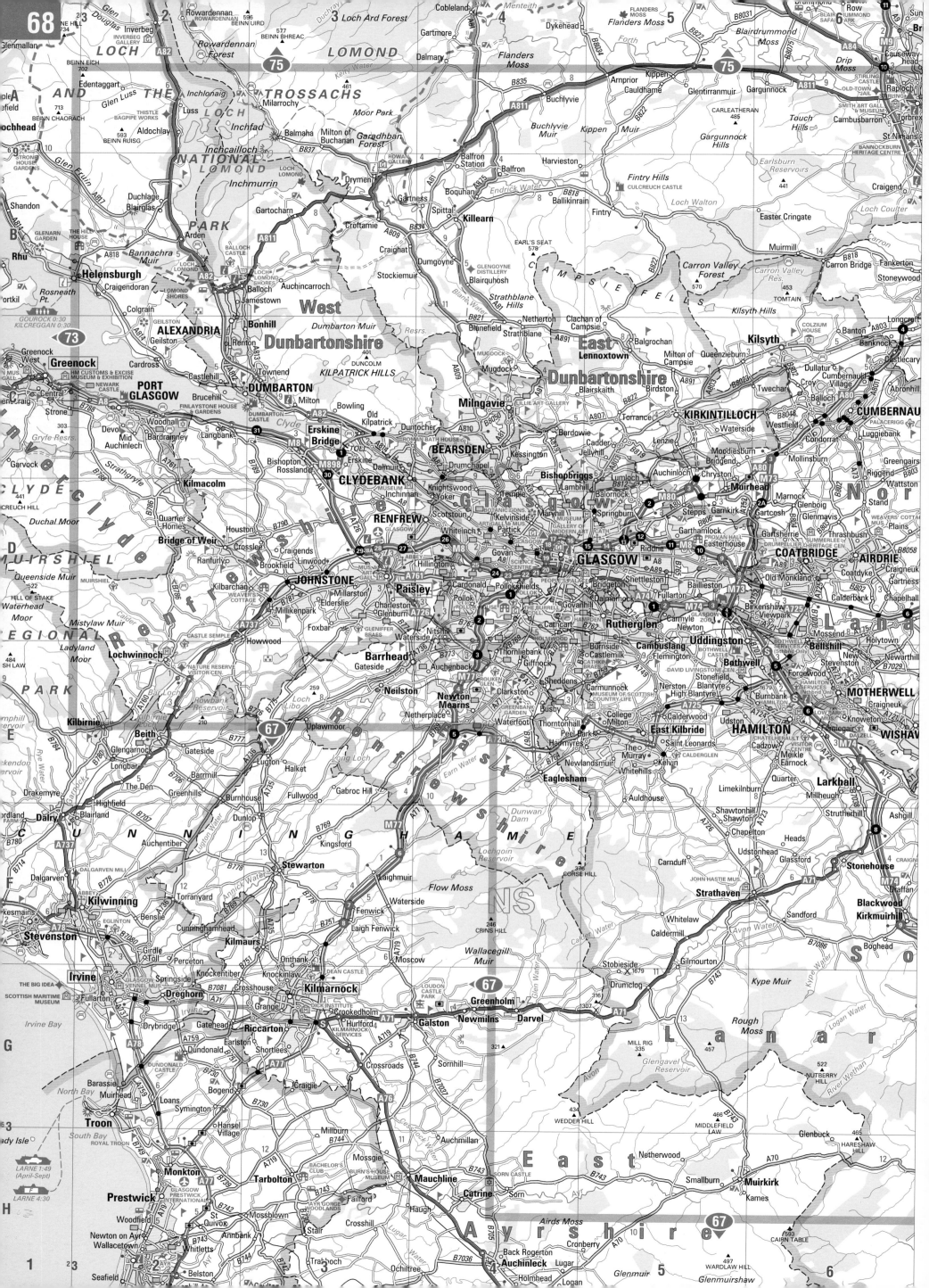

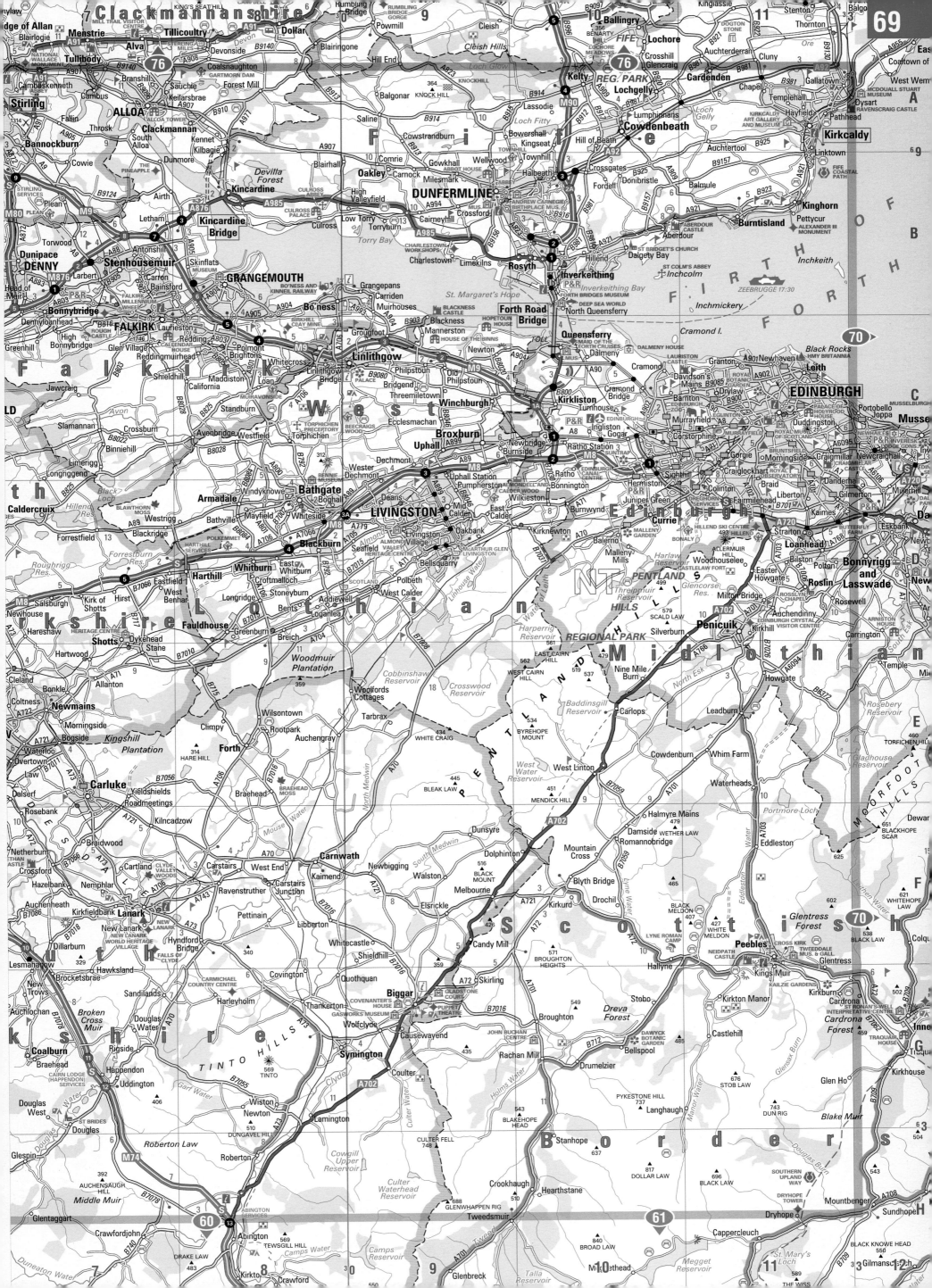

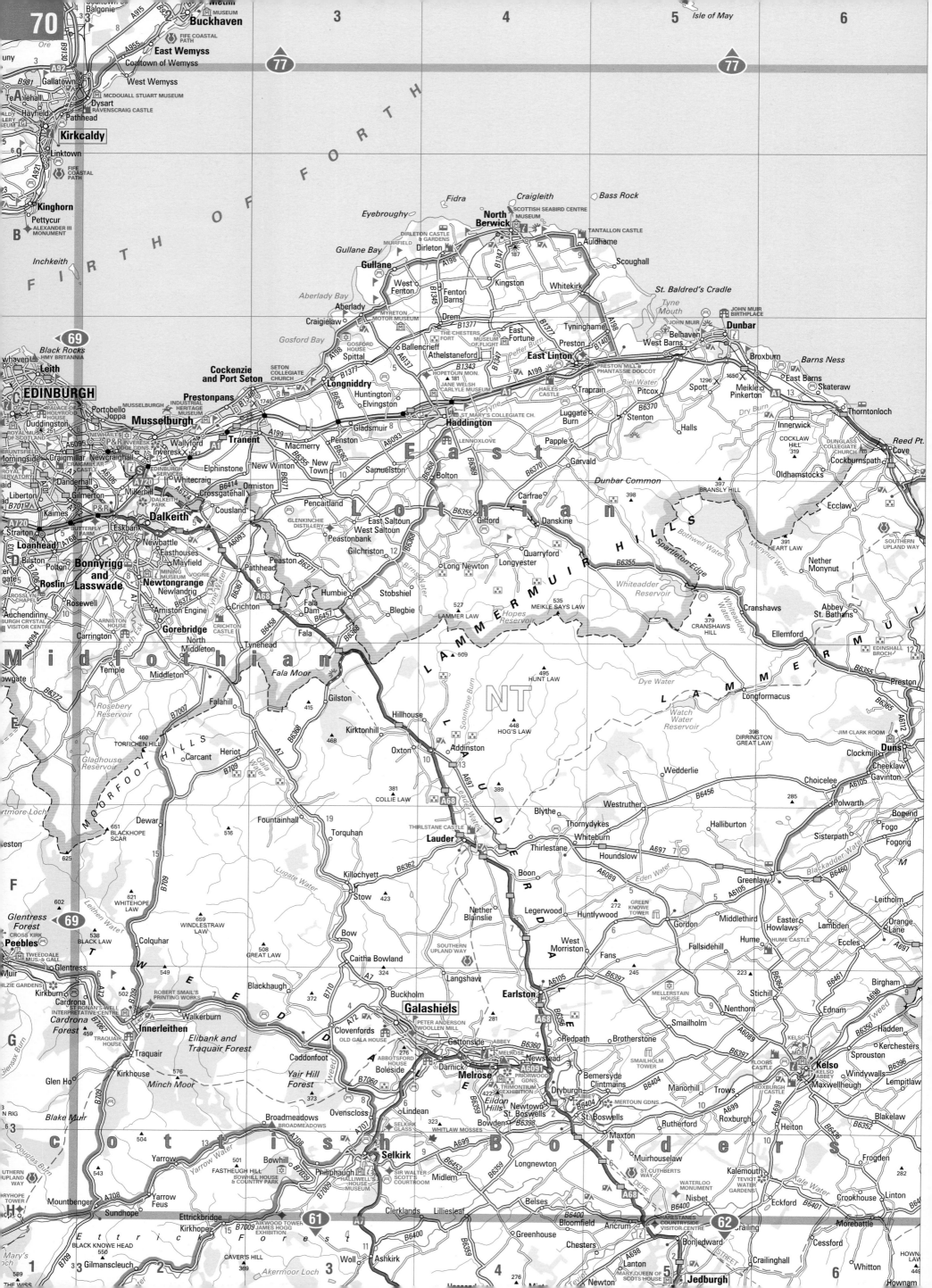

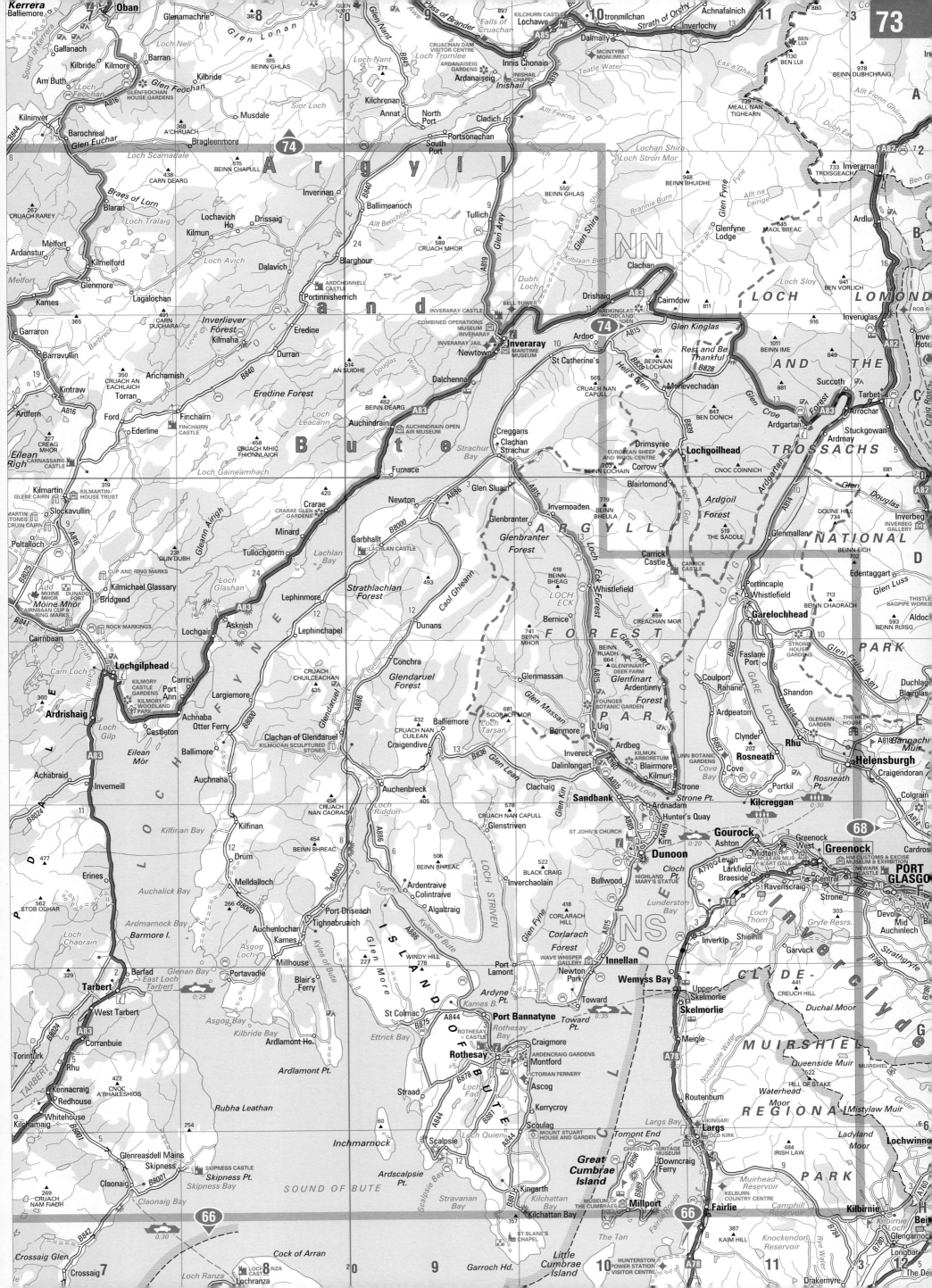

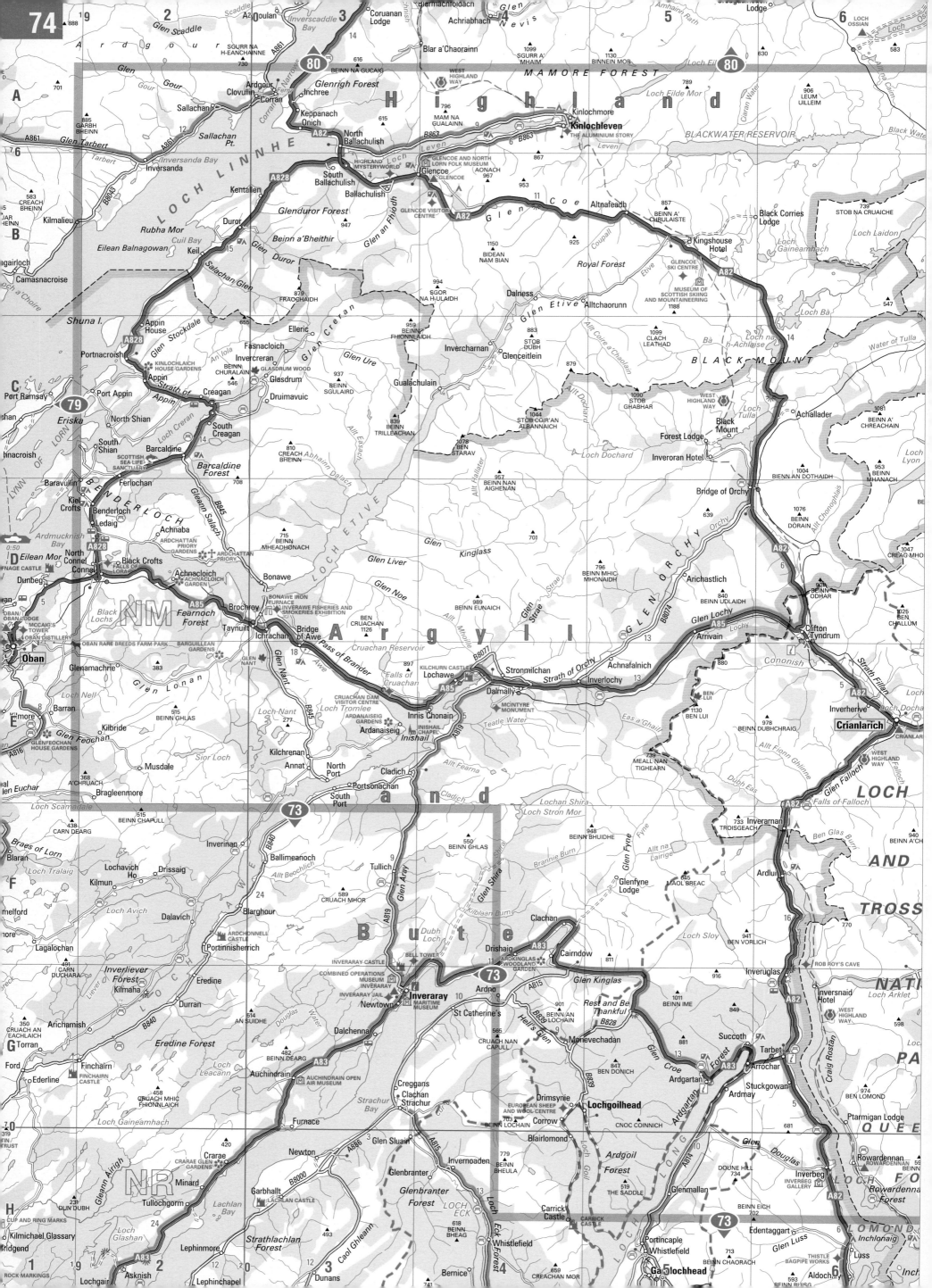

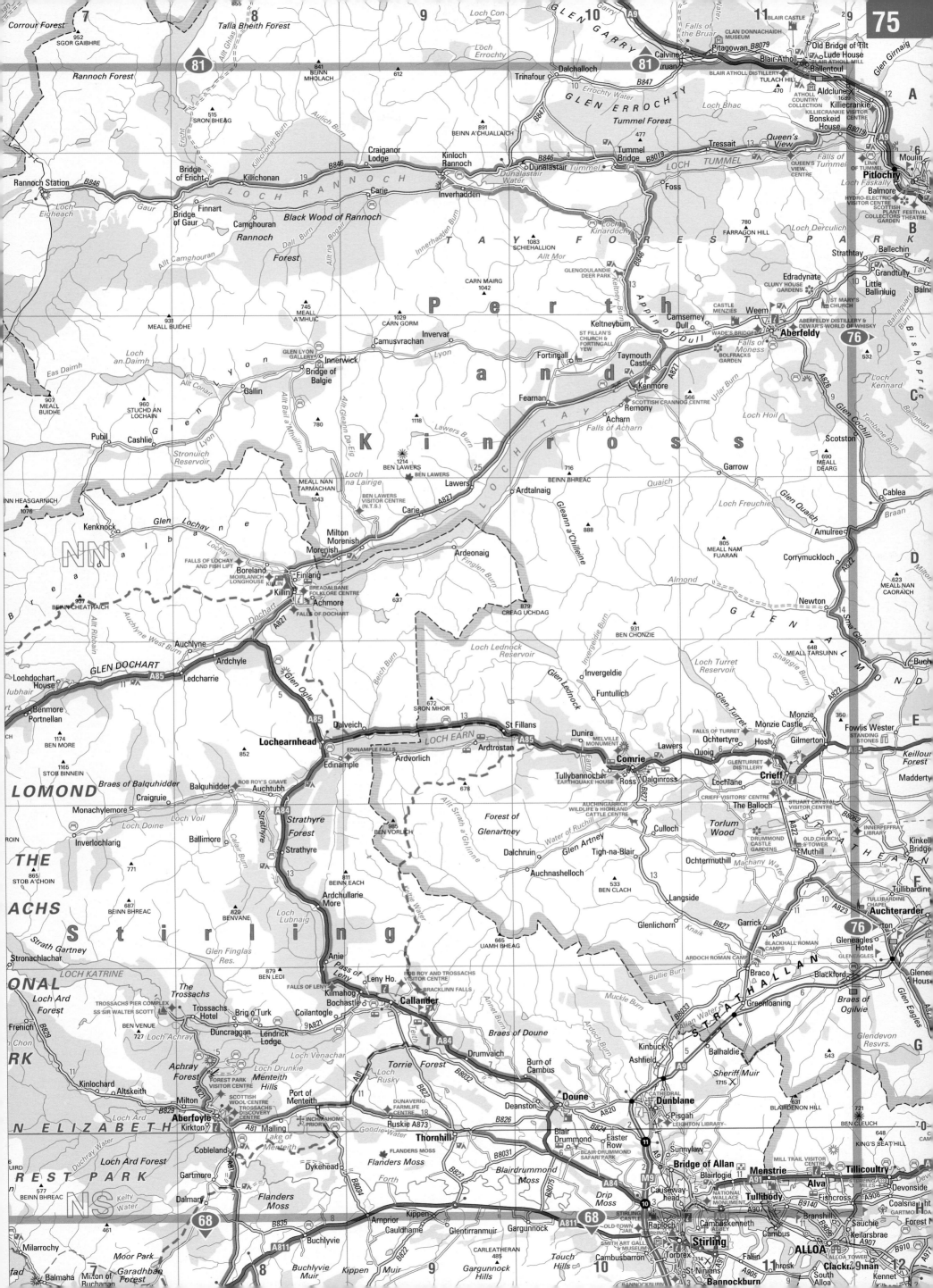

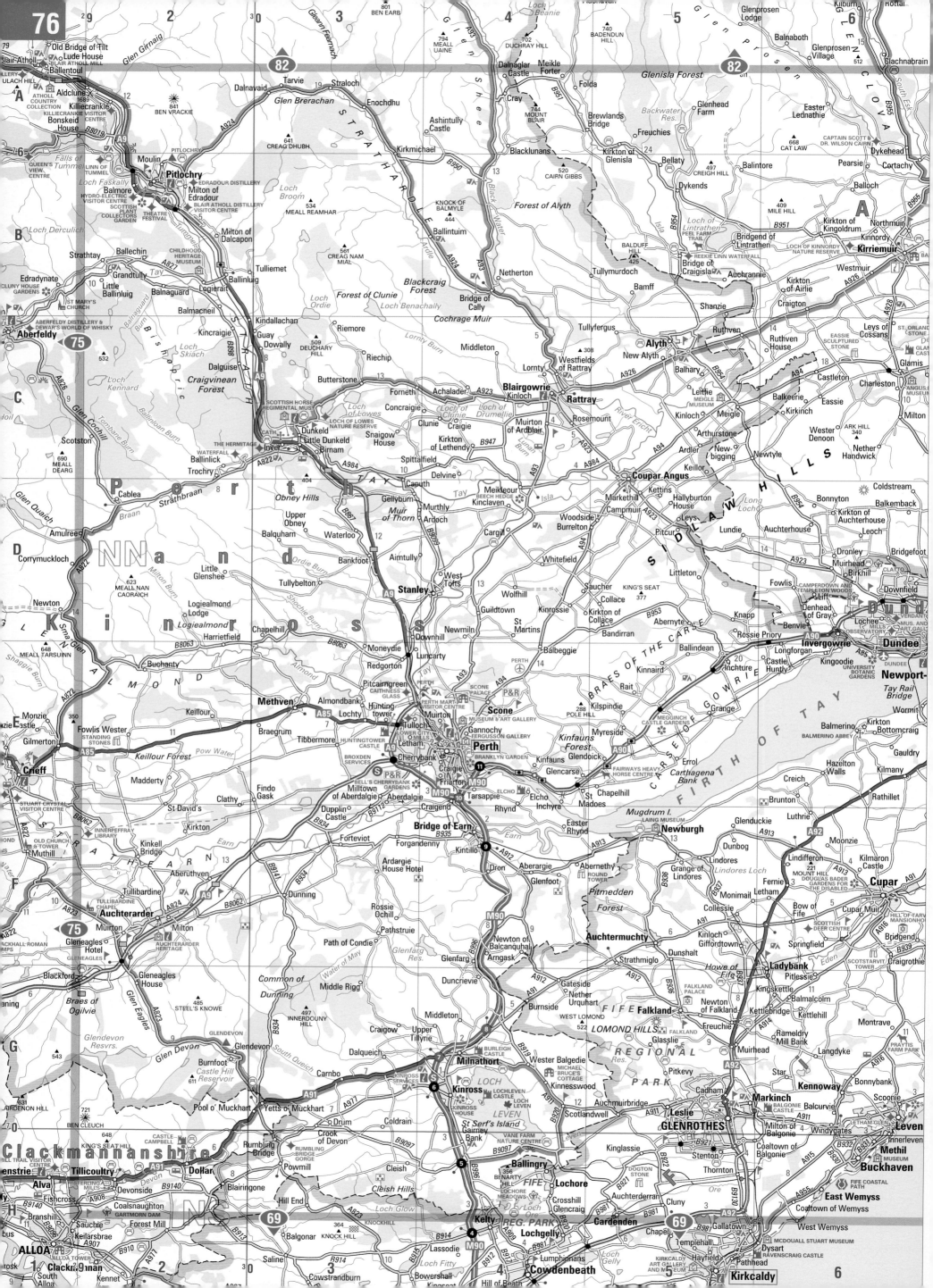

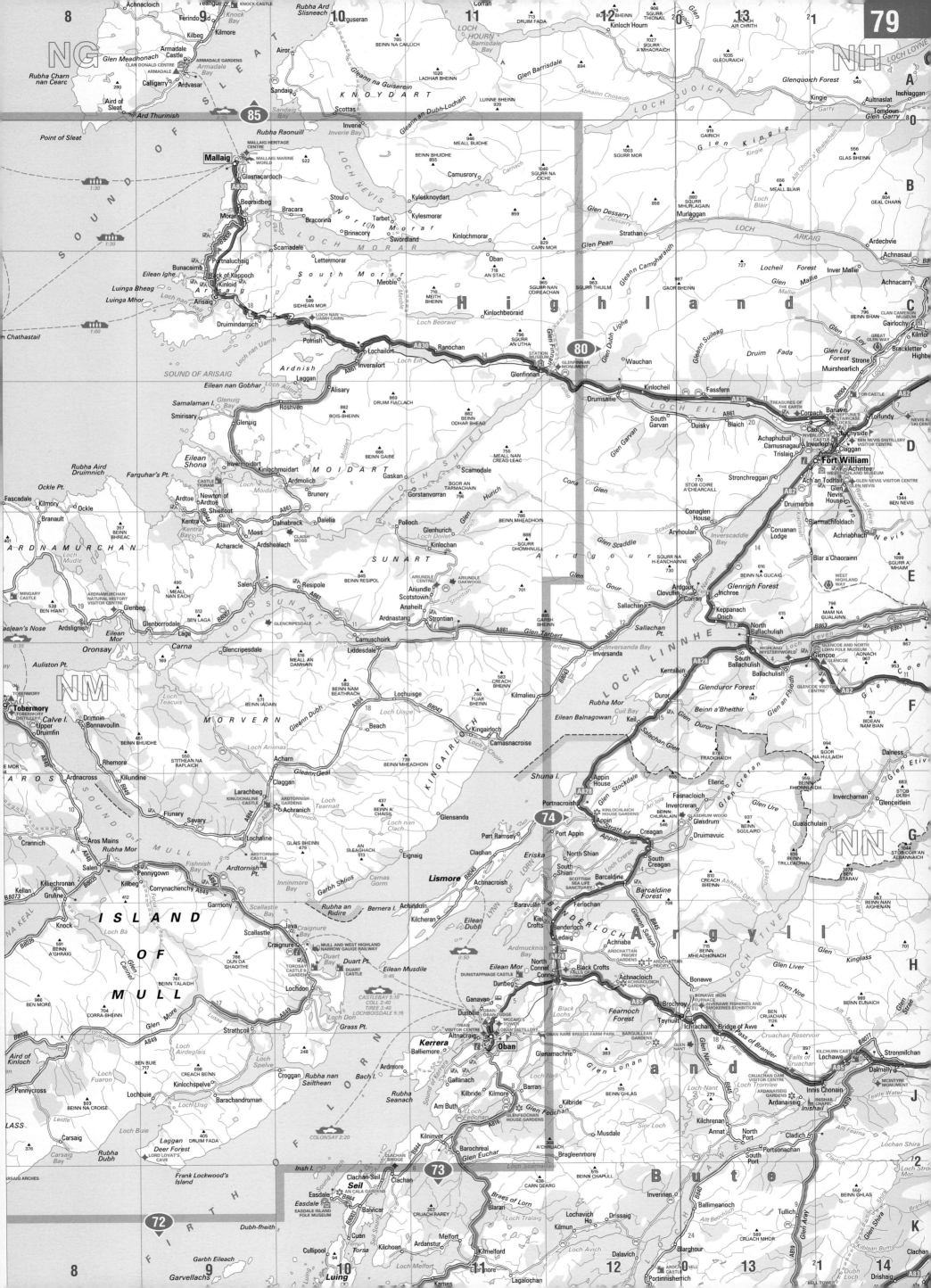

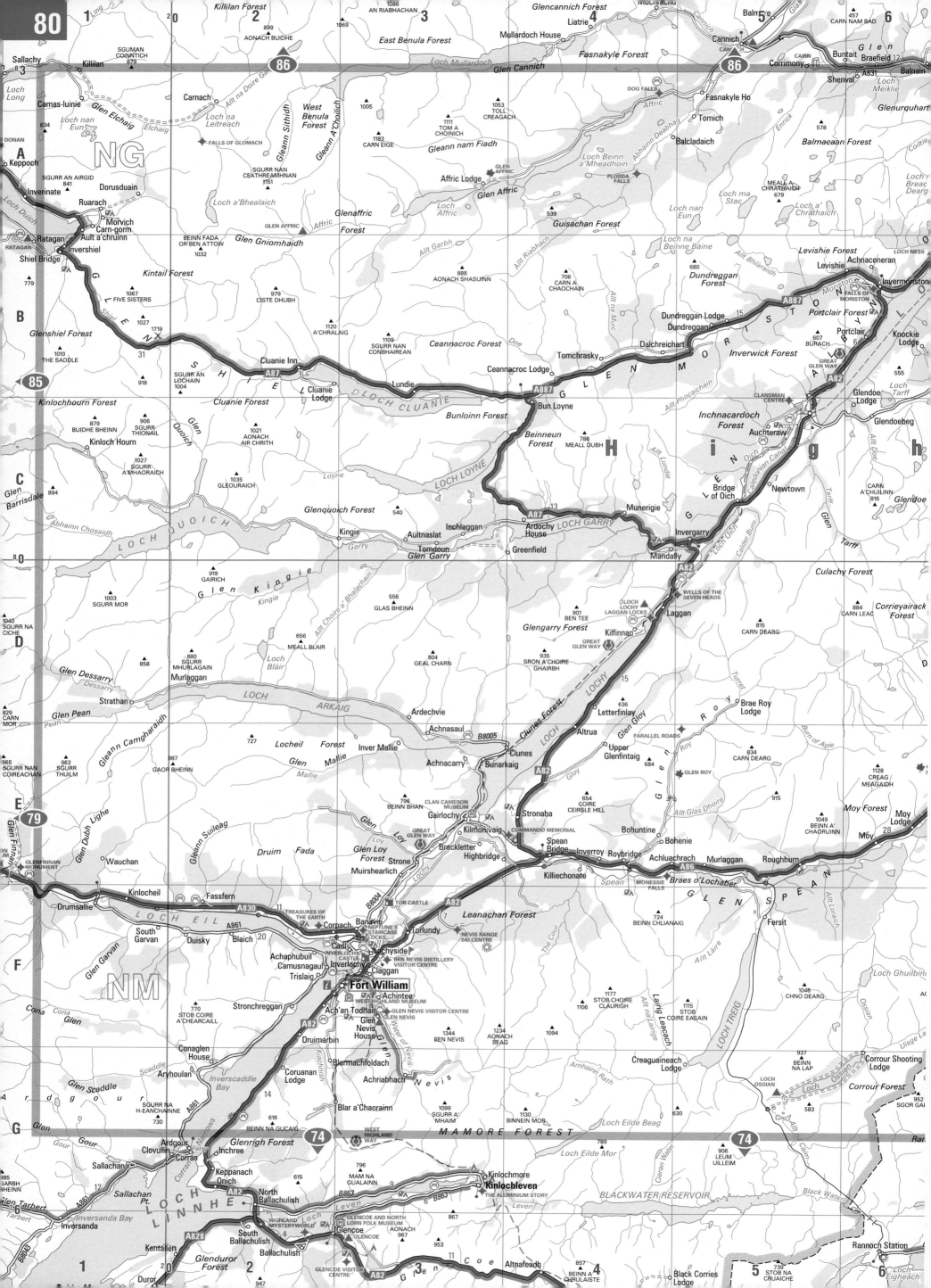

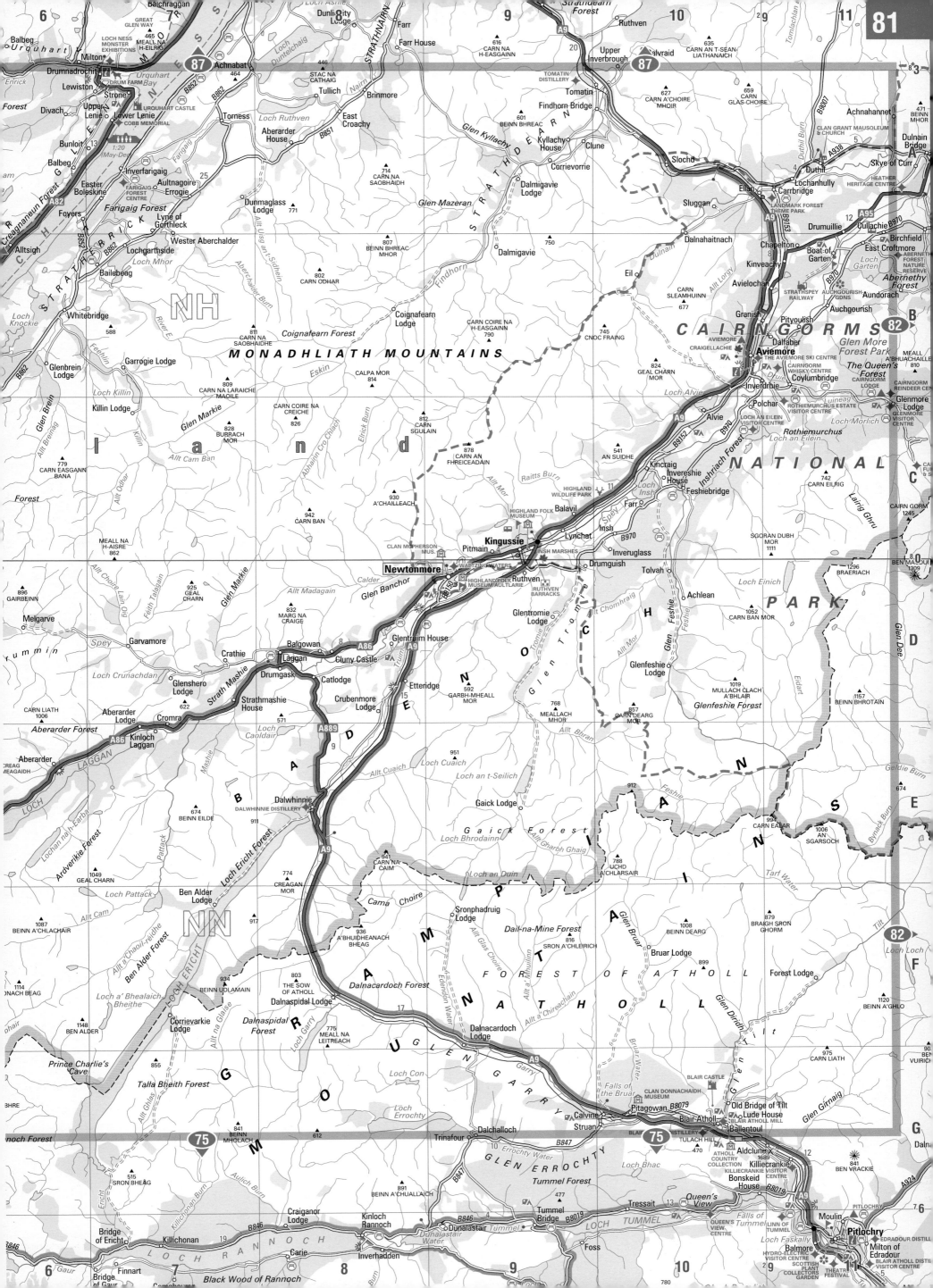

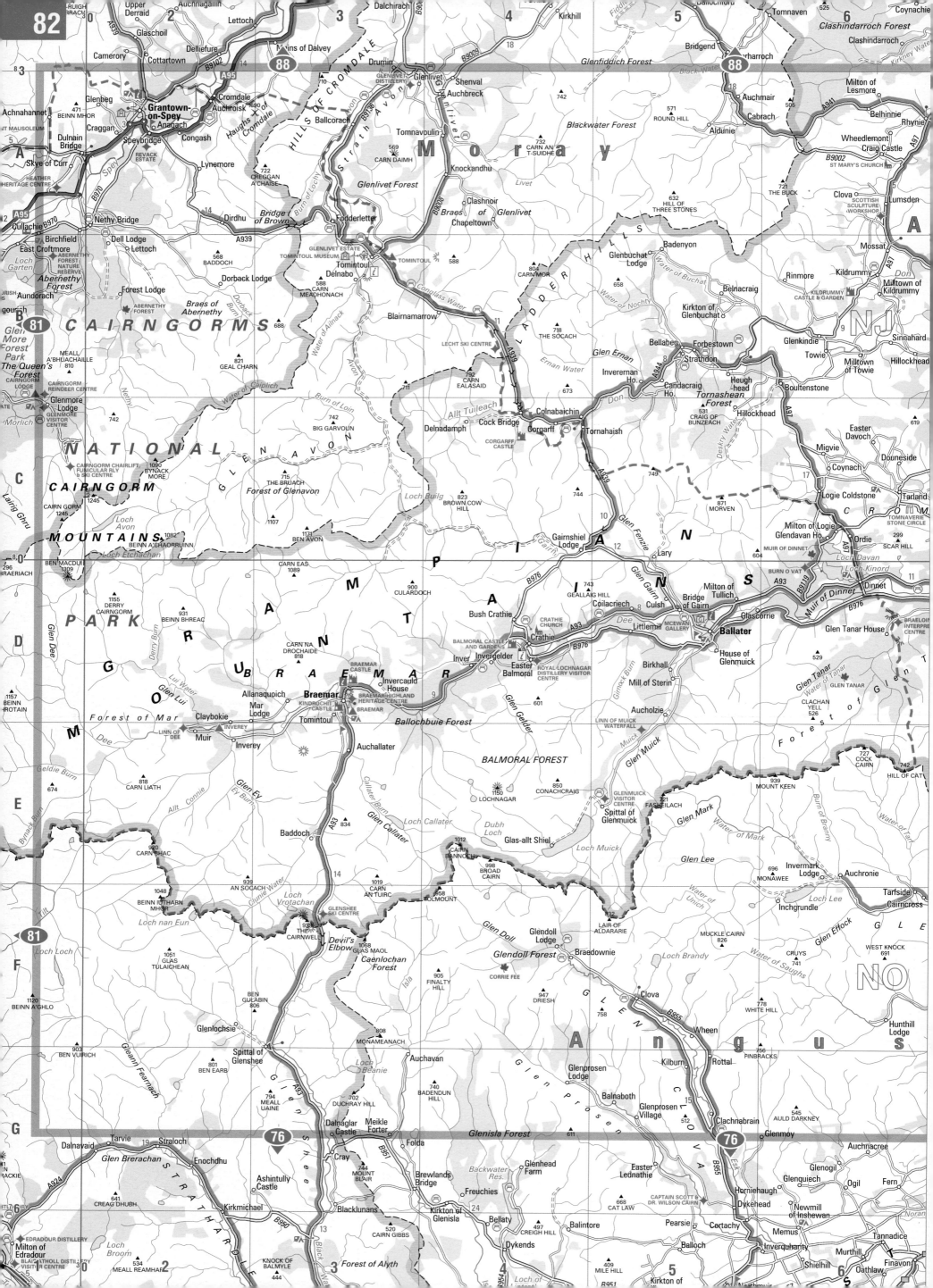

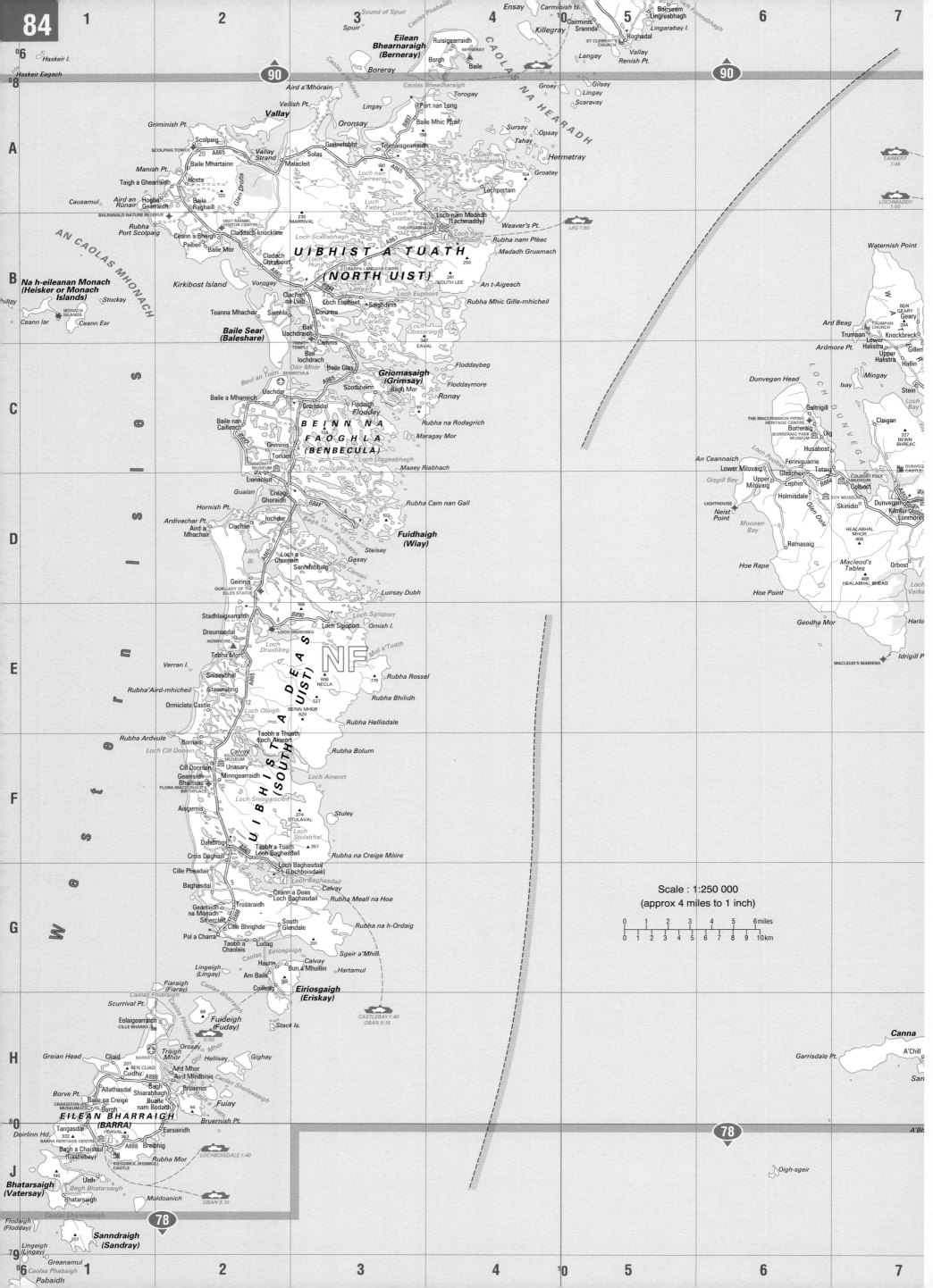

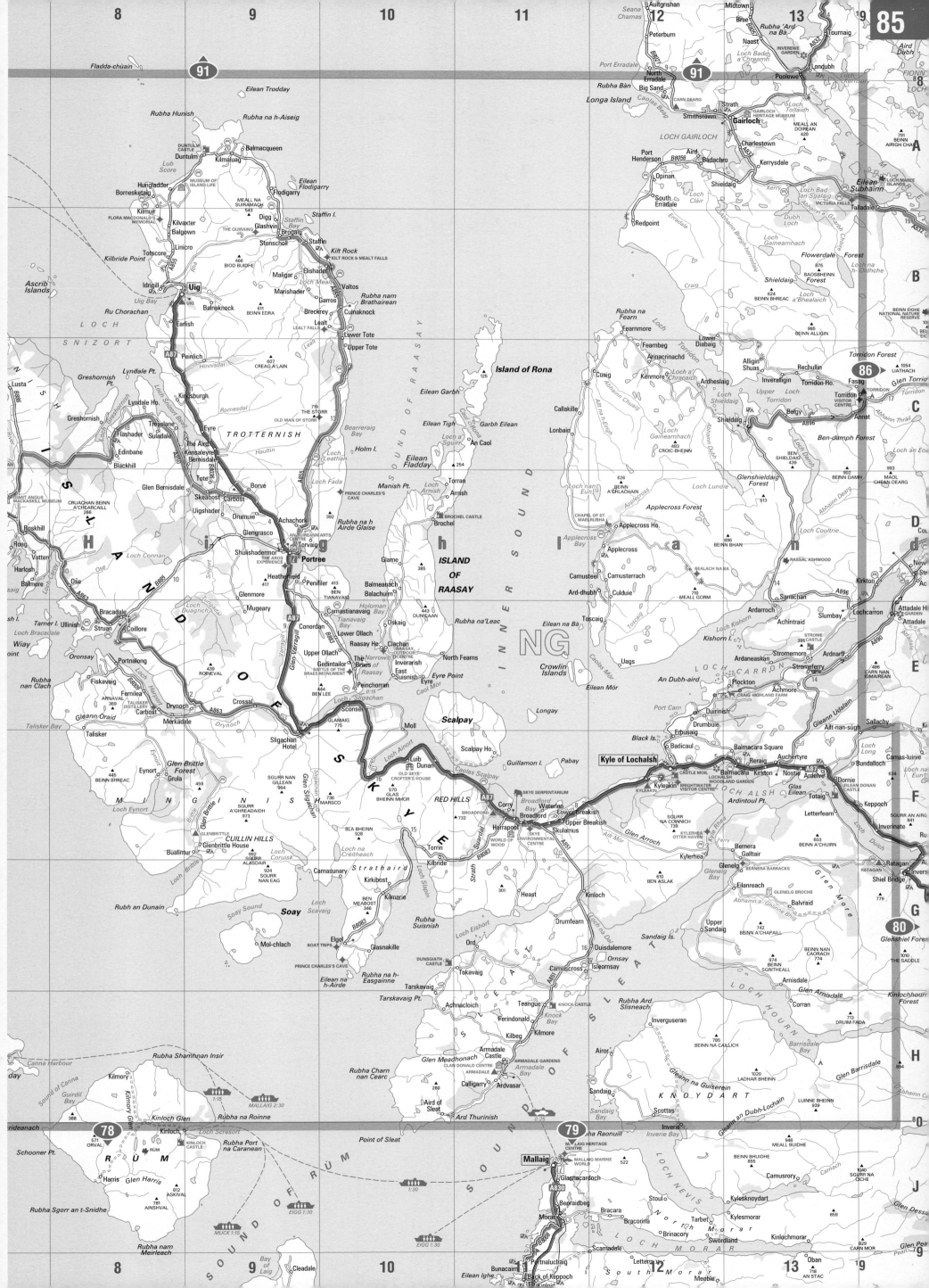

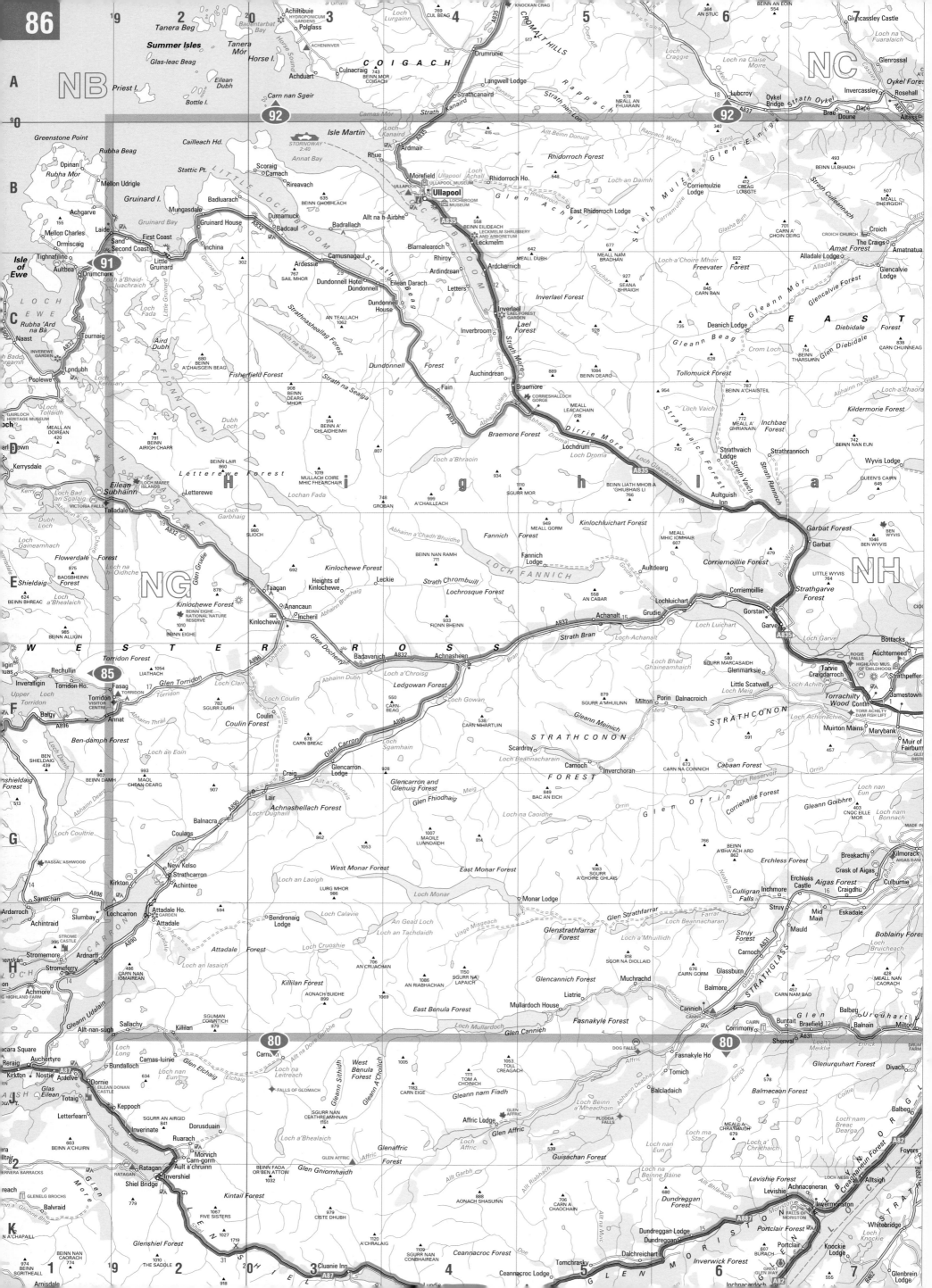

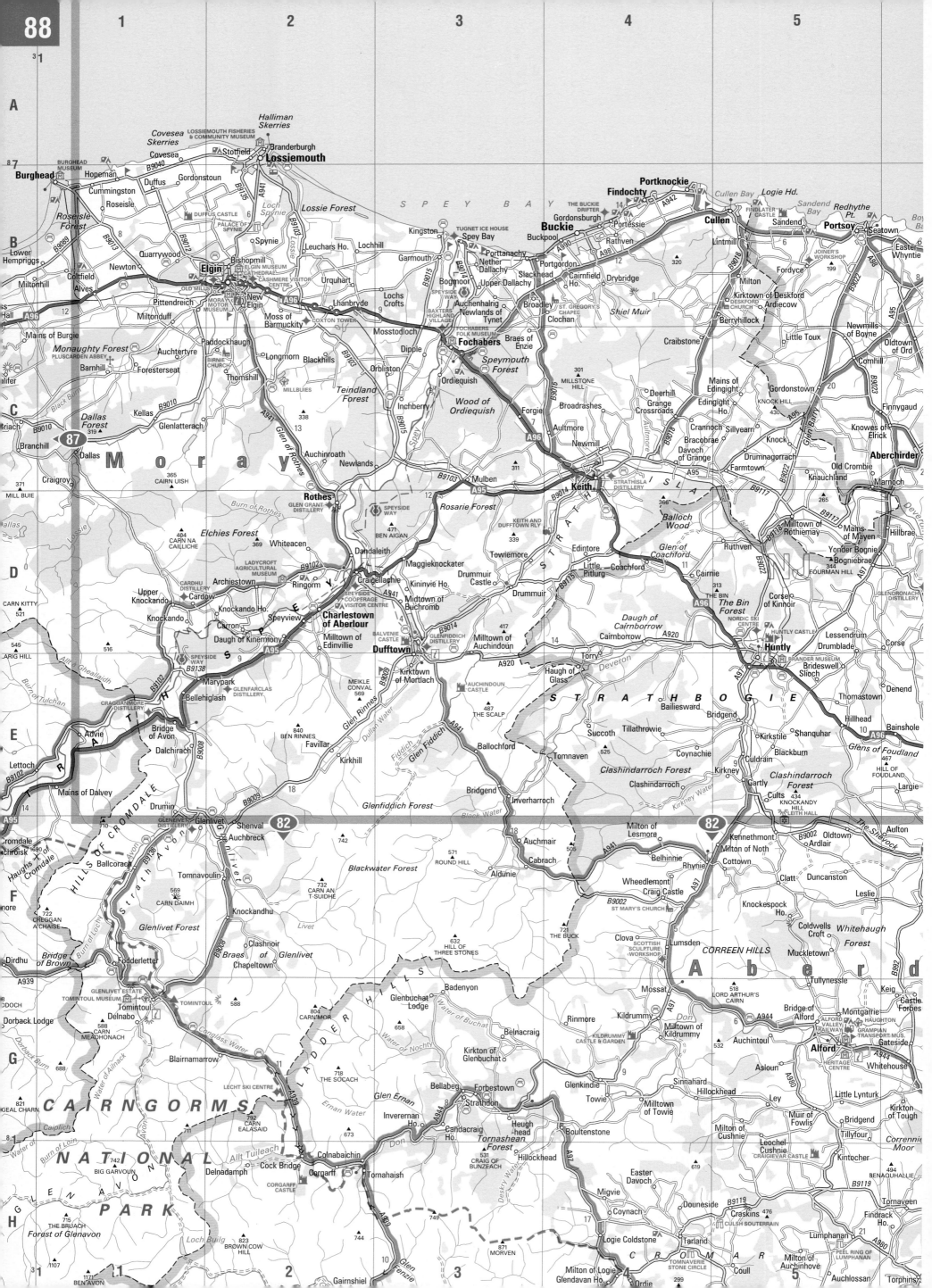

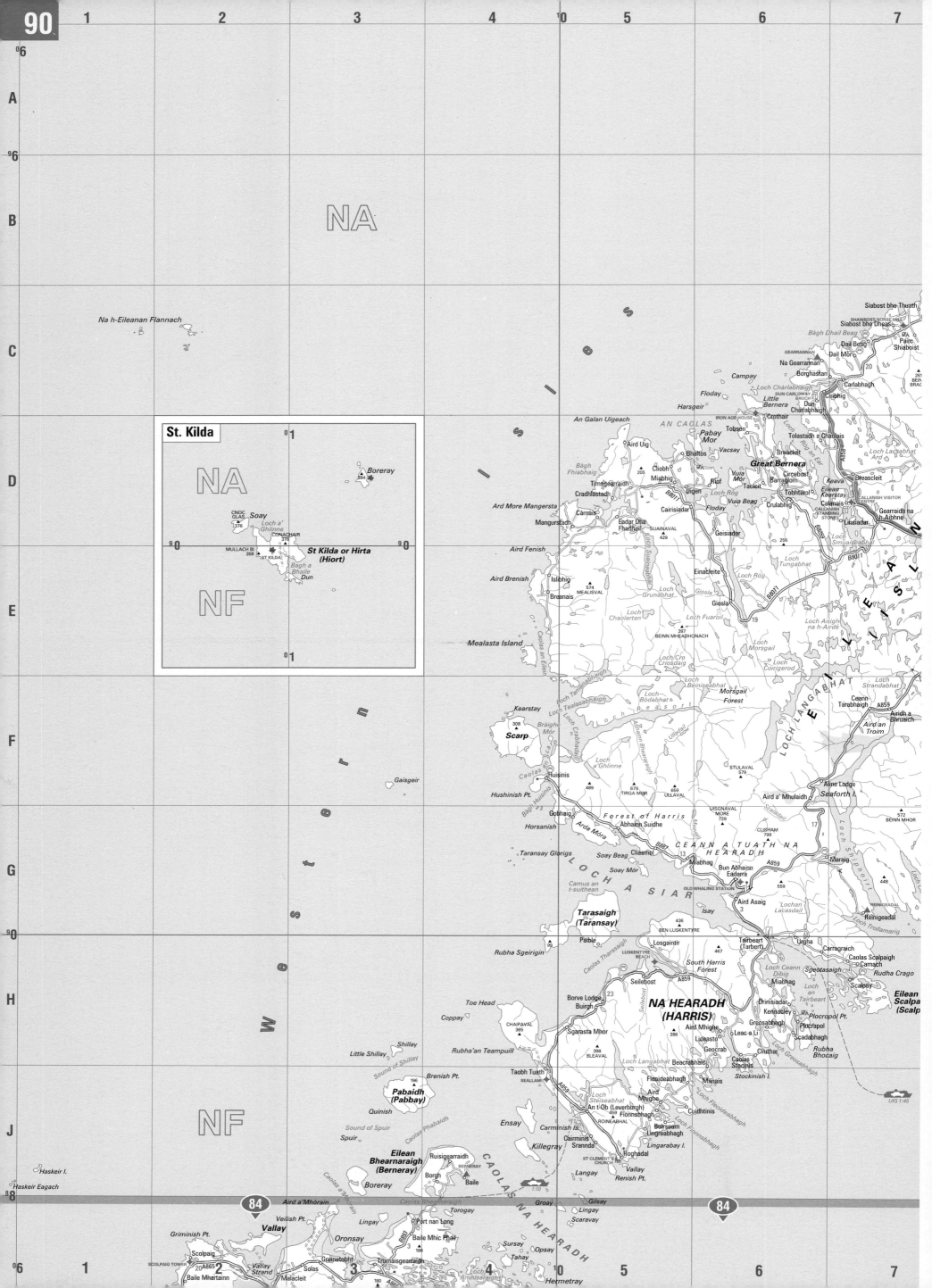

RUBHA ROBHANAIS
(BUTT OF LEWIS)

CHURCH OF ST MOLVAG
Cunndal
Eòropaidh   Coig Peighinnean
                   B8014
                   HARBOUR VIEW GALLERY
Cross Sands   Lional
Suainebost   Port Nis
Aird Dhail   Cros   Tabost
Dail bho Dheas   Sgiogarstaigh
         Dail bho Thuath

Gabhsann bho Thuath
Gabhsann bho Dheas   A857
Mealabost Bhuirgh   Cuiashader
Bail Àrd Bhuirgh
Coig Peighinnean Bhuirgh   15
Siadar   Cellar Head
Rubha Leathann   Siadar Iàrach
Aird Barvas   Siadar Uarach
TRUSHAL   Baile an Truiseil
STONE

BLACK HOUSE
MUSEUM   Barabhas Iarach
Labost   Barabhas Uarach
Bragar Arnol Barabhas
        Brù   248
Labost A858   MUIRNEAG   Baili Ur Tholastaidh
                              Tolastadh bho Thuath
                              Tolsta Head
                  Loch
                  Sgeireach
                  Mòr   Gleann Tholàstaidh
                           Port Bun
                  Griais   a'Ghlinne
                  Grìais
                  Bac   Creag Fhraoch
                  Col
Loch Scarabhat Mhòr Col Uarach Vatisker Pt.
         292   Coll Sands
BEINN MHOLACH   Breibhig
Loch   Aird Thunga BROAD BAY
nan Stearnag A857   Tunga   OR
              B895   Sròn Ruadh   LOCH A TUATH
An Gleann Ur   Port Nan Giùran Rubha an t-Siumpain
Newmarket   Cnoc
Loch Urabhal Lacasdal   Amhlaigh Port Mholair
              STORNOWAY   A866   Aird
Grioda Stornoway   Sulaisiadar Seisiadar
        Sanndabhaig Mealabost Garrabost EYE
Loch a'   A866   Aiglnis   PENINSULA
Ghainmhich   Tolm   Pabail Uarach
Acha Mòr 14   An Cnoc Pabail Iarach
                      Suardail Bàgh Phabail
          Arnish Moor Holm I.
                       A'Chearc
Loch
Orasaigh
Griomsidar Ben Casgro
Lurbost   ULLAPOOL
Loch Tobhta   2:40
Bridein
Ranais   Raerinish Pt.
Soval Lodge
Crosbost
        Barkin Is. Tabhaidh Mhor
        Eilean Chaluim
        Chille   Eilean Orasaidh
Lacasaidh Ceos
Baile   Eireasort Cromor
Ailein   Gearraidh Bhaird Eilean Thoraidh
Slidinis   Cabharstadh
Tabost   Cearsiadar
Ceann Shiphoirt Marbhig
Loch   Calbost
nan
Eilean
Taobh a' Ghlinne Grabhair
           Loch Odhairn
P A R K   Kebock Head
O R
P A I R C
           Orasaigh
           Eisgean Leumrabhagh
Loch Shell or Loch Sealg
           Srianach
470   Eilean Iubhard
CRIONAIG

Mol Truisg

Gob Rubh'Uisenis
Loch
Bhrollum Rubha Bhrollum
Rubha
a'Bhaird
        CAOLAS NAN EILEAN
        Garbh
        Eilean   Eilean Mhuire
Na h-Eileanan Mòra   Eilean an Tighe
(Shiant Islands)

Scale : 1:250 000
(approx 4 miles to 1 inch)

0 1 2 3 4 5 6 miles
0 1 2 3 4 5 6 7 8 9 10km

NB

NG

Fladda-chùain

85
Eilean Troddam

Rubha Hunish   Rubha na h-Aiseig

DUNTULM
CASTLE   20
Duntulm Macqueen
Kilmaluag

Greenstone Point
Rubha Beag
Eilean Mullagra
Glas-leac Mòr
Glas-leac
Beag
92
Priest I.   Bottle

Rubha Mor
Mellon Udrigle
Opinan
Sròn a' Gheodha   Eilean   Achgarve Gruinard I.
Dhuibh   Furadh Mór   Mur
Rubha Reidh Camas 155   Gruinard Bay
             Mòr   Laide
                   Mellon Charles Sand First Coast
             Loch an Ormiscaig Second Coast
Cove   Draing Isle of Tighnafiline 86
             296   Ewe   Aultbea Drumchork Little
             AN CUAIDH   Loch 'Bhaid- Gruinard
Melvaig   Inverasdale luachraich
Aultgrishan Loch-Sguod Midtown L O C H
Brae   Rubha 'Ard E W E
Seana   na Bà   Loch
Chamas   Naast   Fada
Peterburn   INVEREWE Tournaig
            GARDEN
            Loch Bad Rubha
Port Erradale a'Chrearnh Dubh
North   Londubh Aird
Erradale   CÀRN Poolewe   Dubh
Rubha Bàn   DEARG Big Sand FIONN
Longa Island 85   LOCH
            GAIRLOCH
            HERITAGE
Smithstown MUSEUM 791
            Gairloch MEALL AN BEINN
                      DOIREAN AIRIGH CHARR
                      420
Port   Aird Charlestown
Henderson Badachro
           B8056
LOCH GAIRLOCH

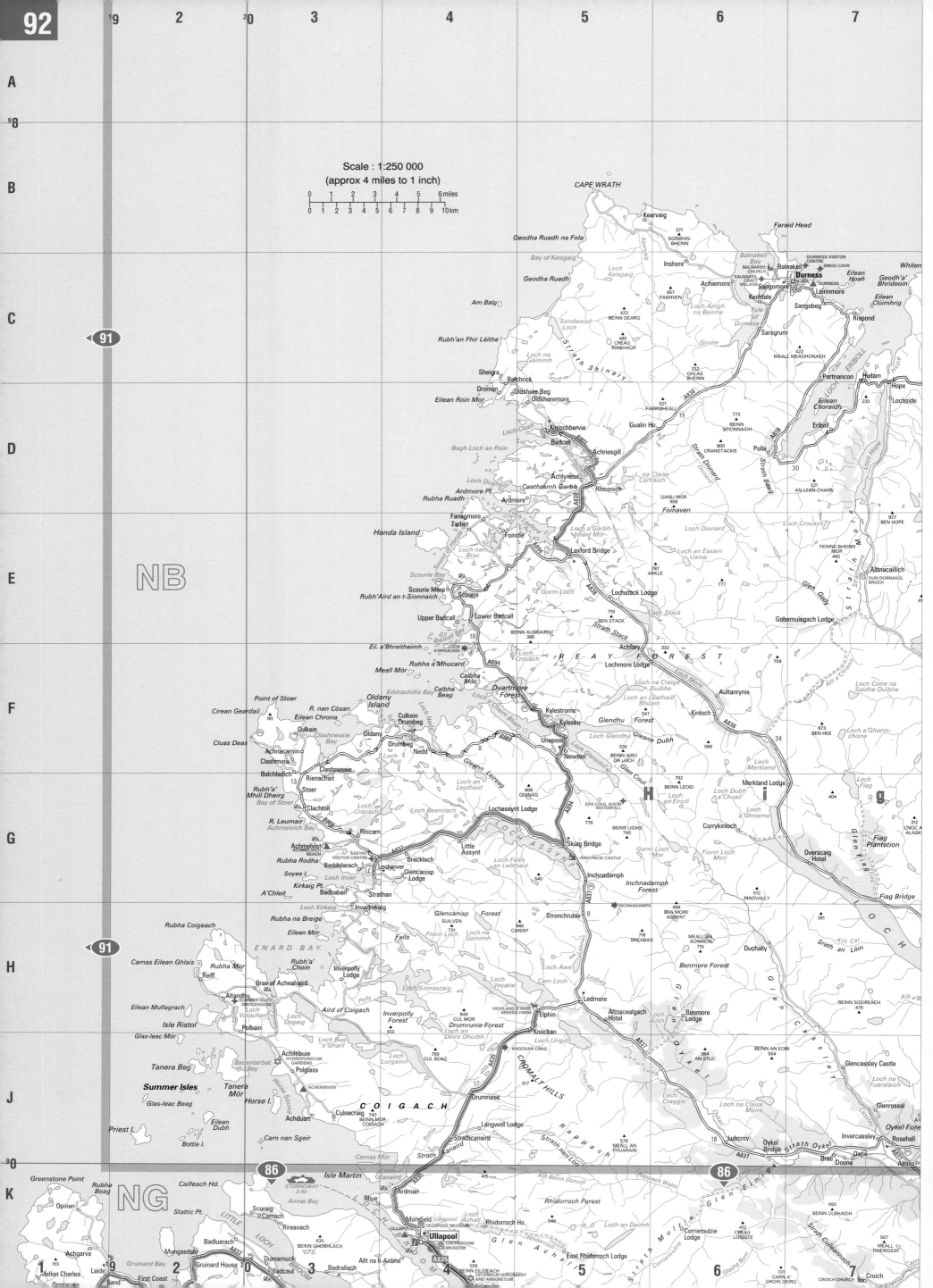

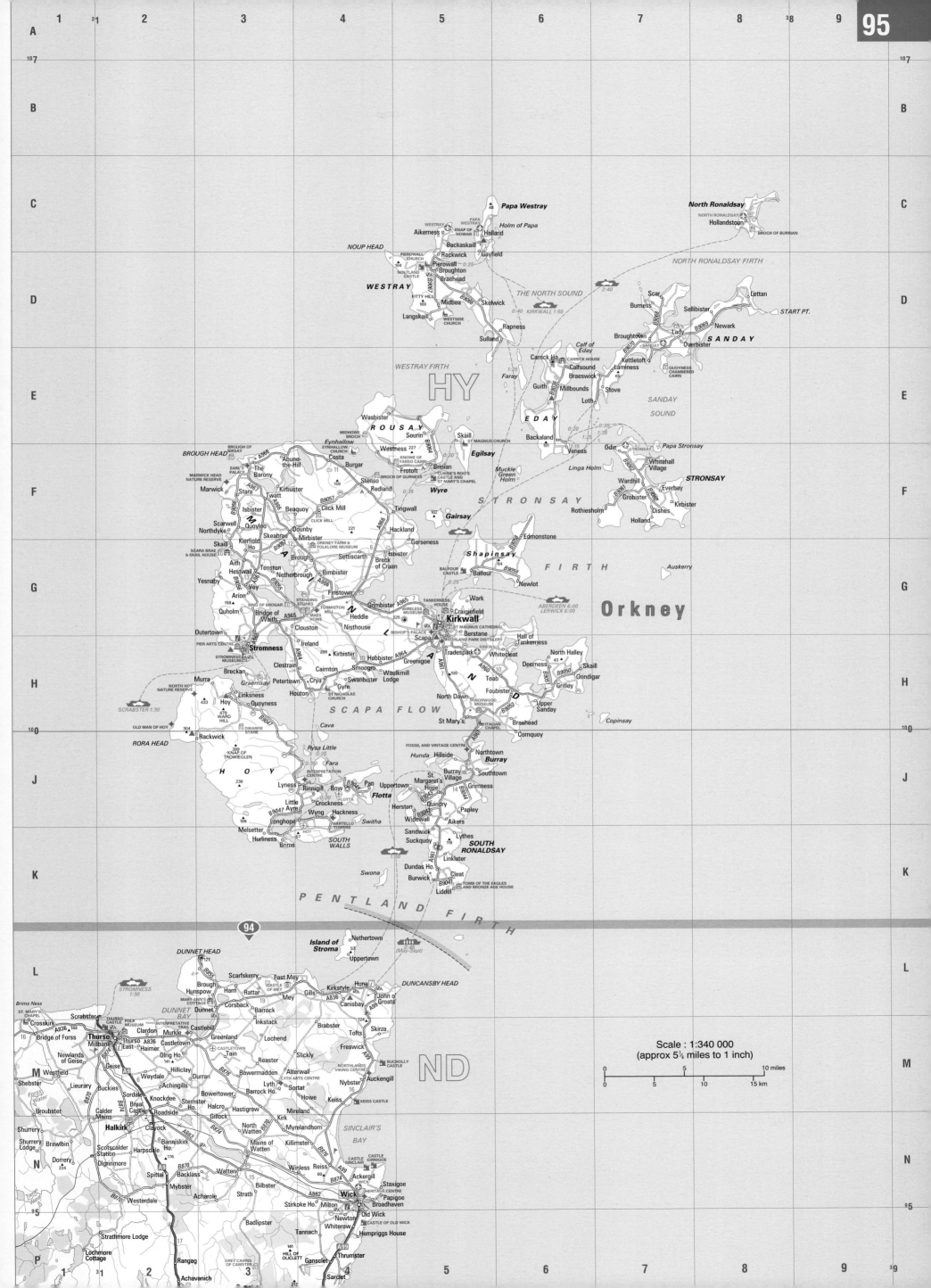

Scale : 1:340 000
(approx 5¼ miles to 1 inch)

0   5   10 miles
0   5   10   15 km

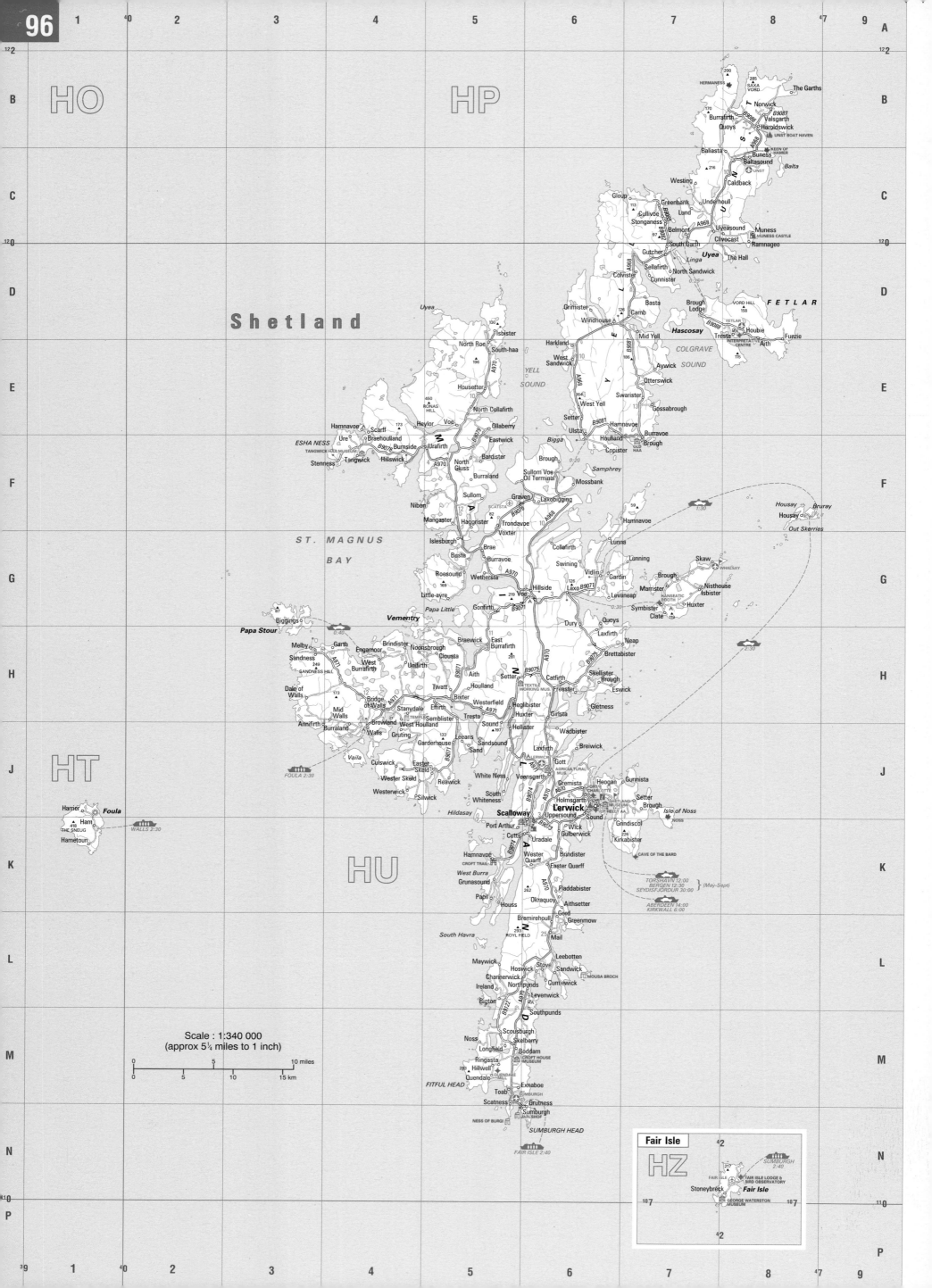

Key to Town Plan Symbols

Motorway		Railway	
Primary Route Dual/Single		Tramway with Station	
A Road Dual/Single		Railway/ Bus Station	
B Road Dual/Single		Shopping Precinct/ Retail Park	
Minor Through Road/ One Way Street		Park	
Pedestrian Roads		Congestion Charging Zone	
Shopping Streets			

✝	Abbey/Cathedral	🚉	Railway Station
	Ancient Monument		Roman Antiquity
🐟	Aquarium		Safari Park
G	Art Gallery		Shopmobility
	Bird Collection/Aviary	🎭	Theatre
	Building of Public Interest	i	Tourist Information Centre (open all year)
	Castle	i	Tourist Information Centre (open seasonally)
	Church of interest		Zoo
	Cinema	◆	Other Place of Interest
✿	Garden		Underground/ Metro Station
⛵	Historic Ship	H	Hospital
	House	P	Parking
	House & Garden		Police
M	Museum	PO	Post Office
	Preserved Railway	▲	Youth Hostel

Aberdeen

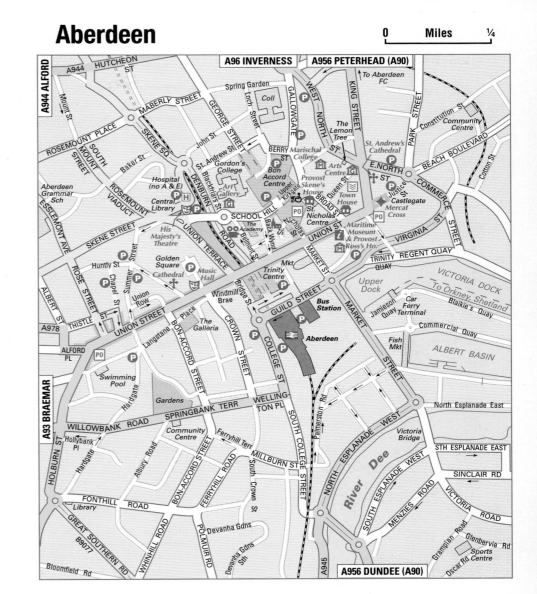

Bath

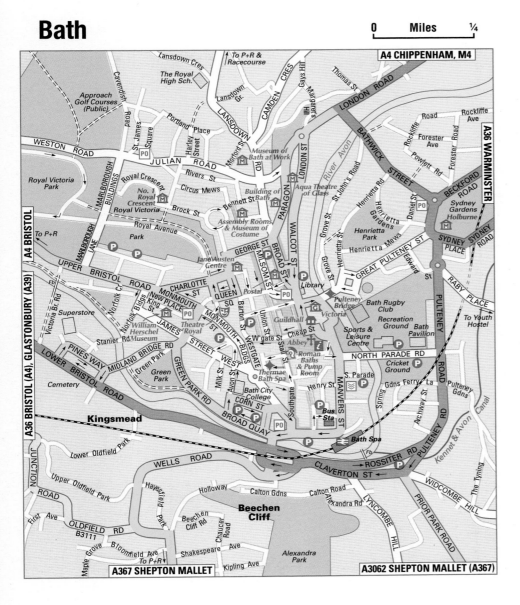

Blackpool

Birmingham

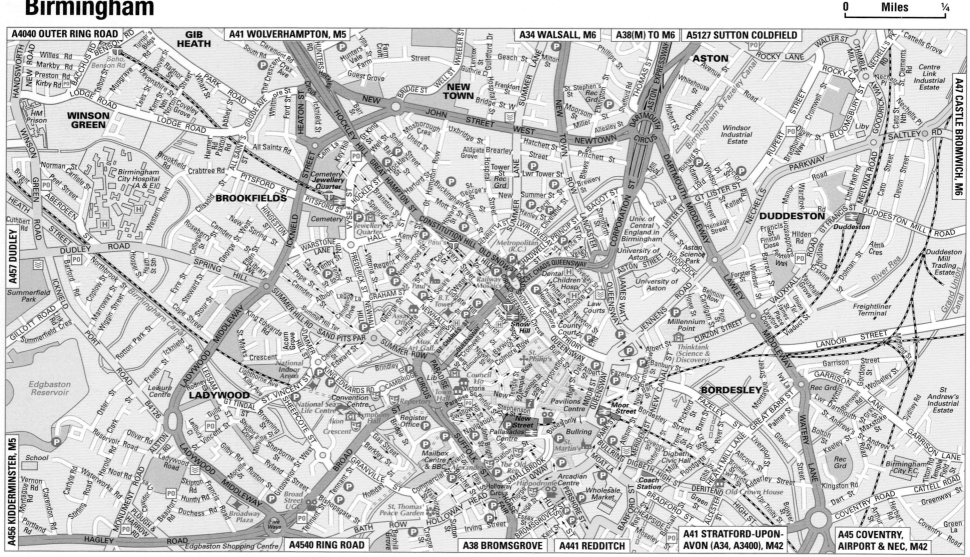

Bournemouth

Bradford

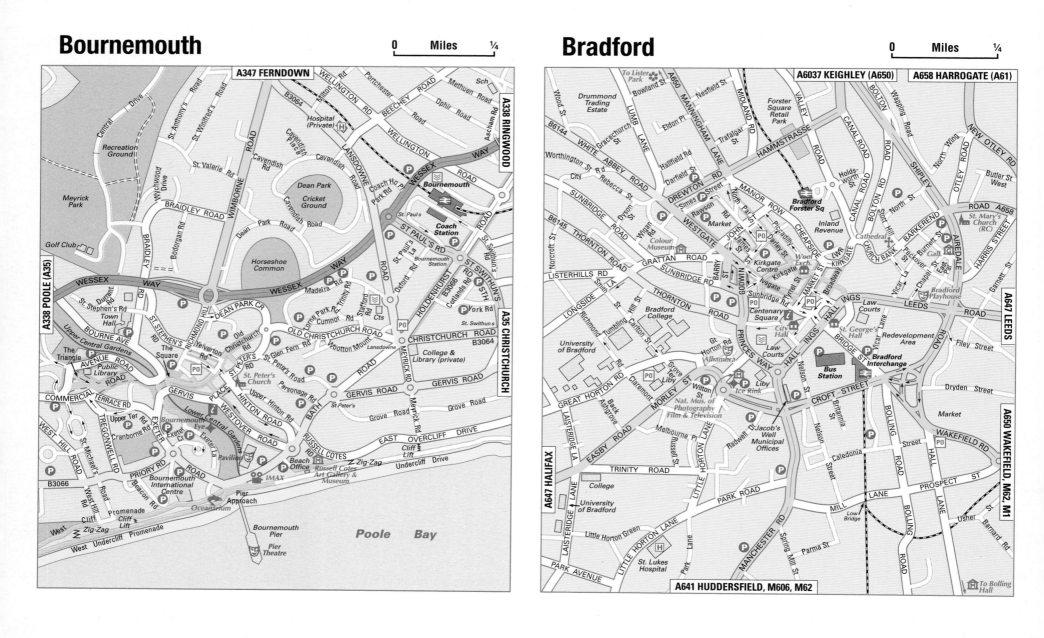

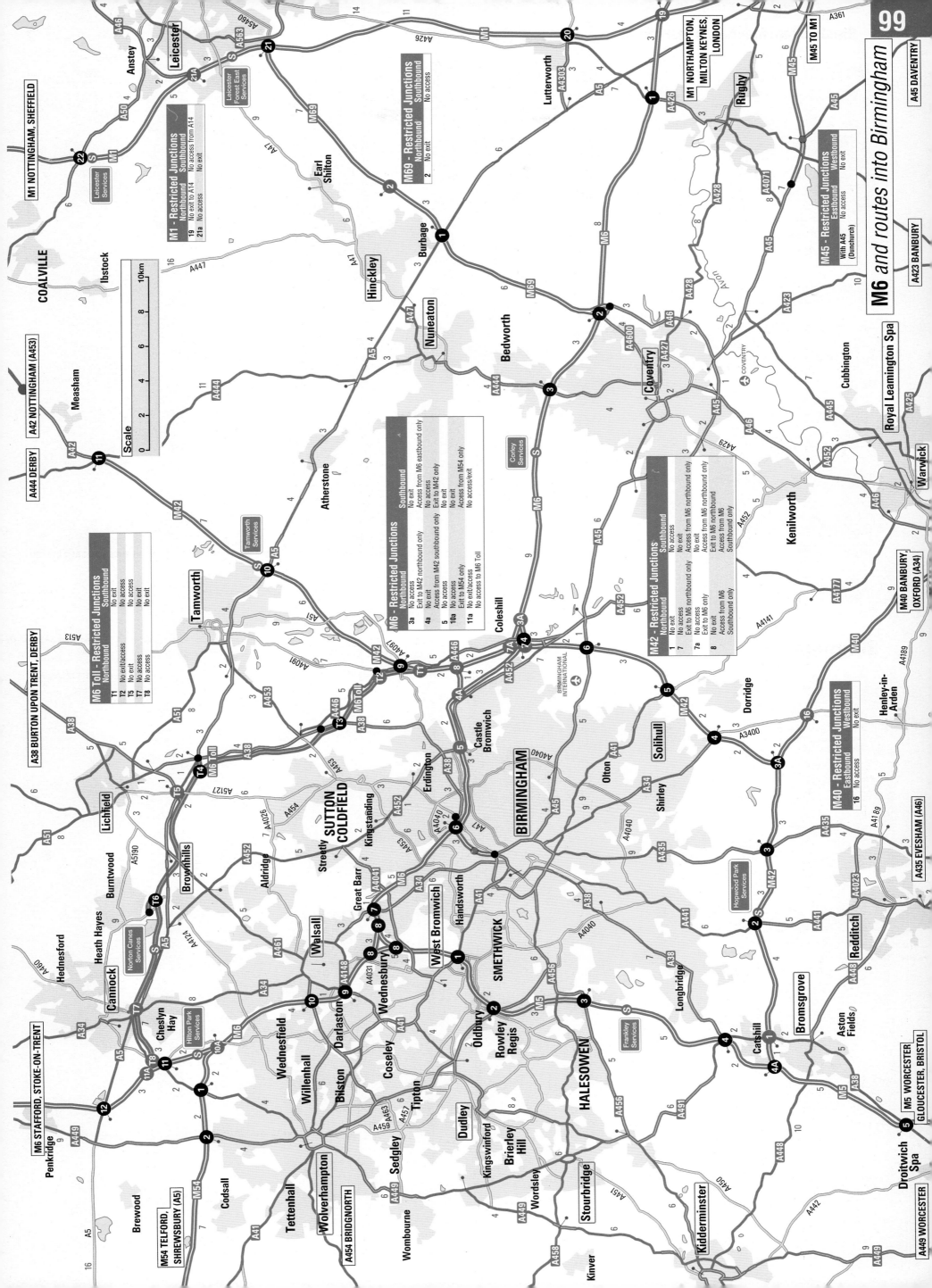

M6 and routes into Birmingham

M1 - Restricted Junctions
	Northbound	Southbound
19	No exit to A14	No access from A14
21a	No access	No exit

M69 - Restricted Junctions
	Northbound	Southbound
2	No exit	No access

M45 - Restricted Junctions
	Eastbound	Westbound
With A45 (Dunchurch)	No access	No access

M6 - Restricted Junctions
	Northbound	Southbound
3a	No exit	No exit
4a	Exit to M42 northbound only	Access from M6 eastbound only
5	Access from M42 southbound only	No access
10a	No access	Exit to M42 only
11a	Exit to M54 only	No exit
	No access to M6 Toll	Access from M54 only/exit
		No access/exit

M42 - Restricted Junctions
	Northbound	Southbound
1	No exit	No access
7	No access	No exit
7a	Exit to M6 northbound only	Access from M6 northbound only
8	Exit to M6 only	Exit to M6 northbound only
	Access from M6 Southbound only	Access from M6 Southbound only

M6 Toll - Restricted Junctions
	Northbound	Southbound
T1		No exit
T2	No exit/access	No exit
T5	No exit	No access
T7	No access	
T8	No access	

M40 - Restricted Junctions
	Eastbound	Westbound
16	No access	No exit

M54 TELFORD, SHREWSBURY (A5)

M6 STAFFORD, STOKE-ON-TRENT

M5 WORCESTER, GLOUCESTER, BRISTOL

M1 NORTHAMPTON, MILTON KEYNES, LONDON

Scale
0 2 4 6 8 10km

Bristol

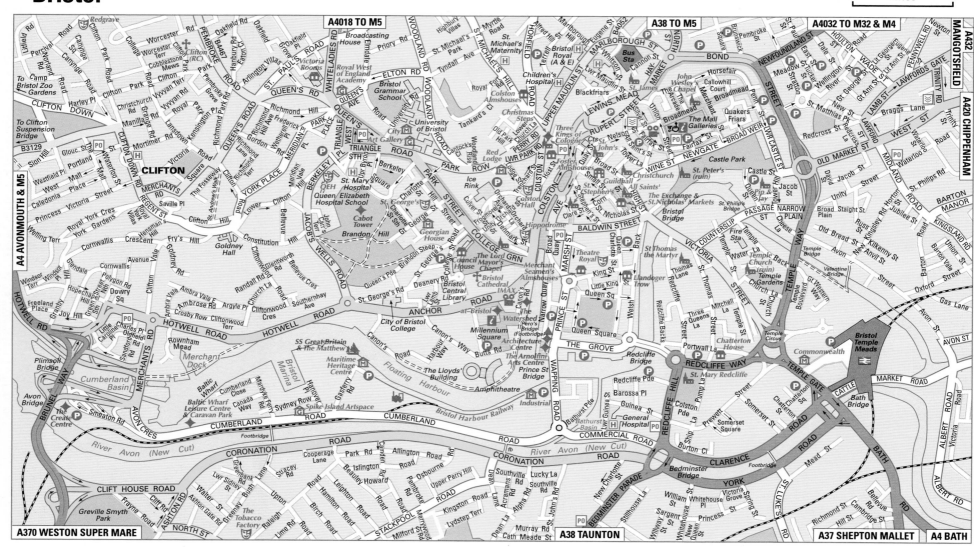

Brighton

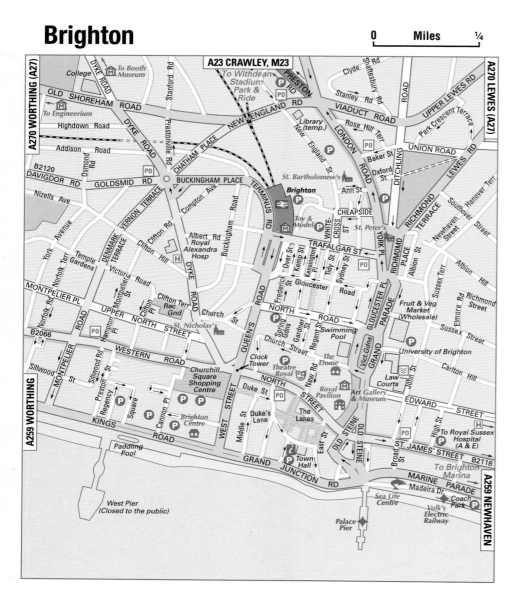

Cambridge

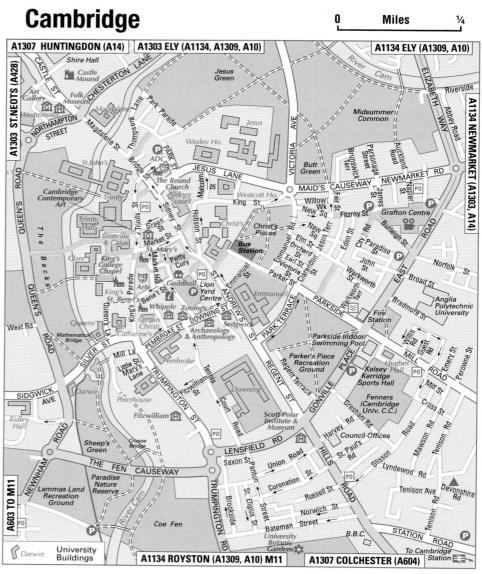

Cardiff / Caerdydd

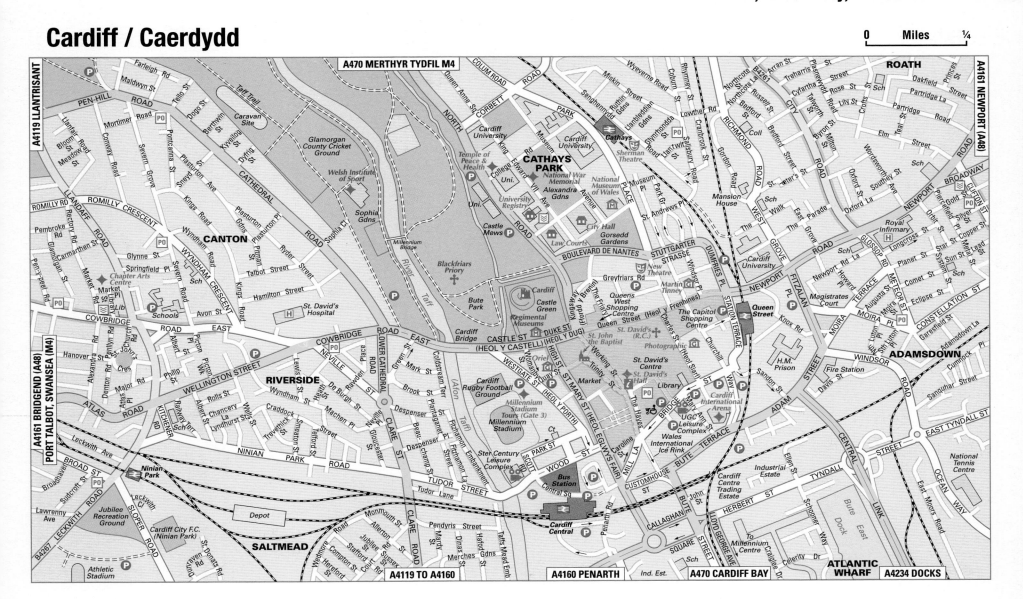

Canterbury

Cheltenham

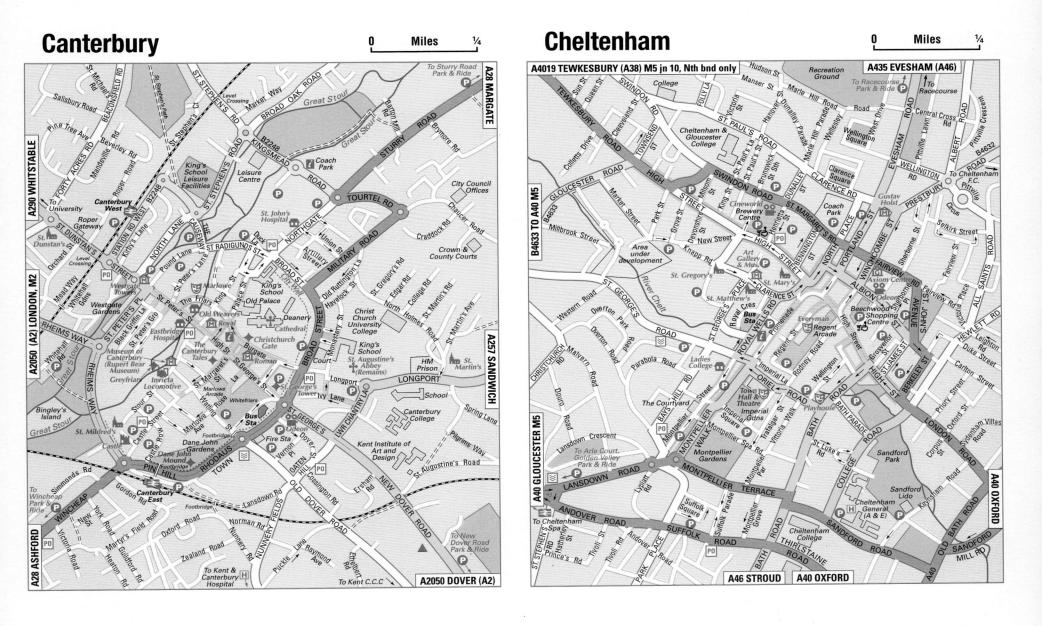

Chester

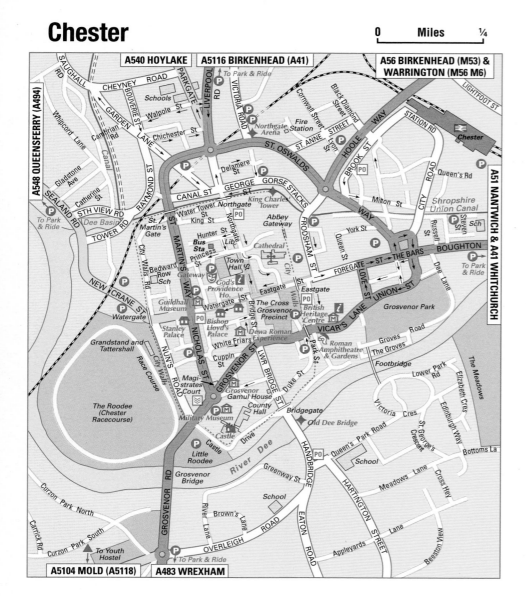

Coventry

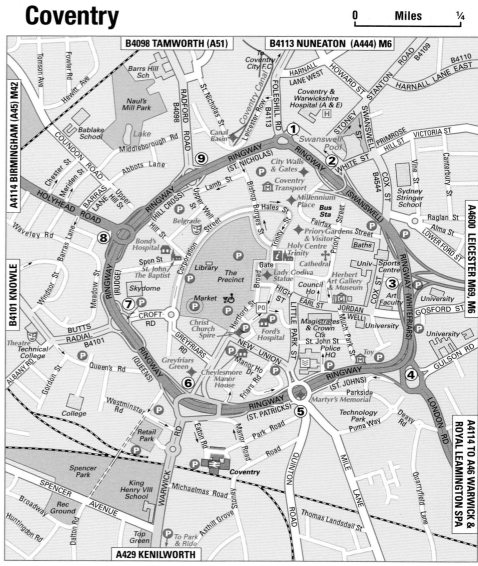

Derby

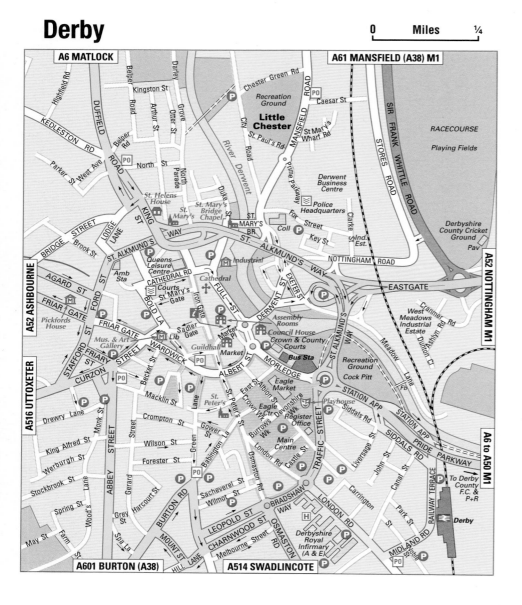

Port of Dover

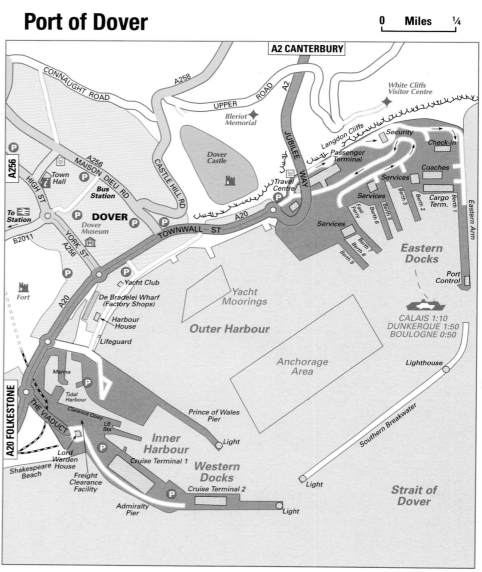

Durham

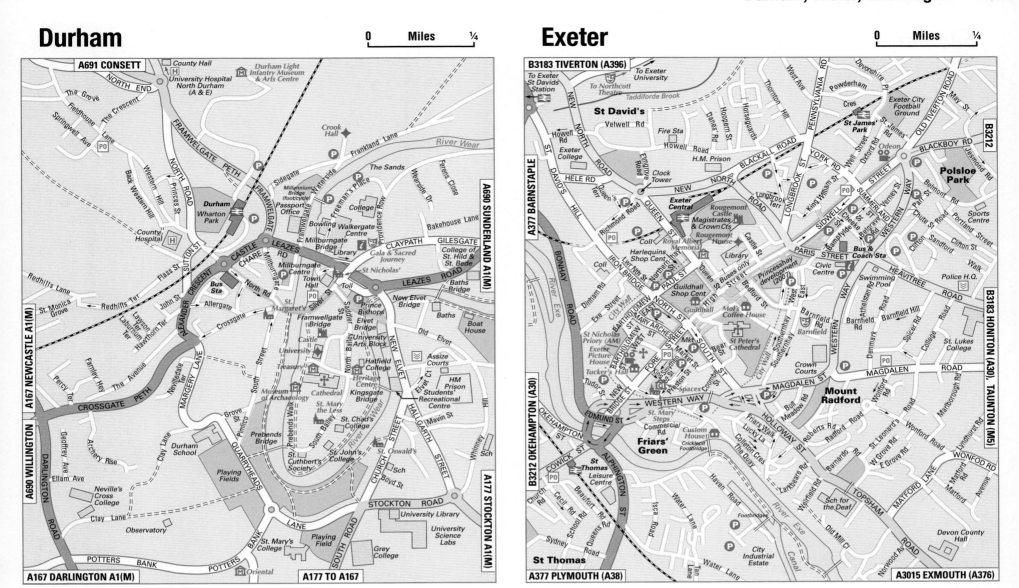

Exeter

Edinburgh

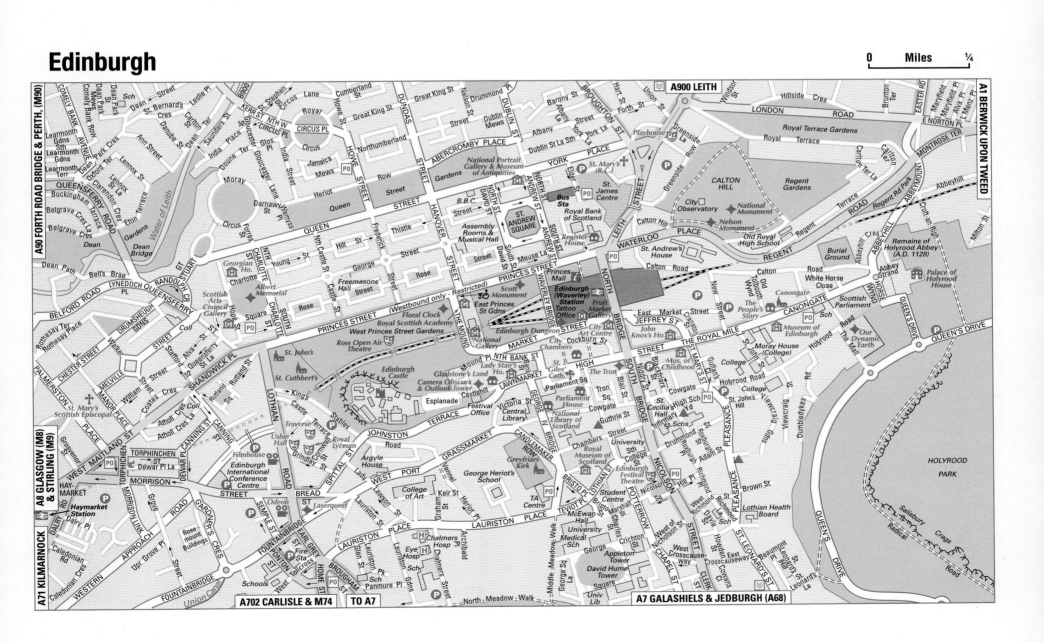

Glasgow

0 Miles ¼

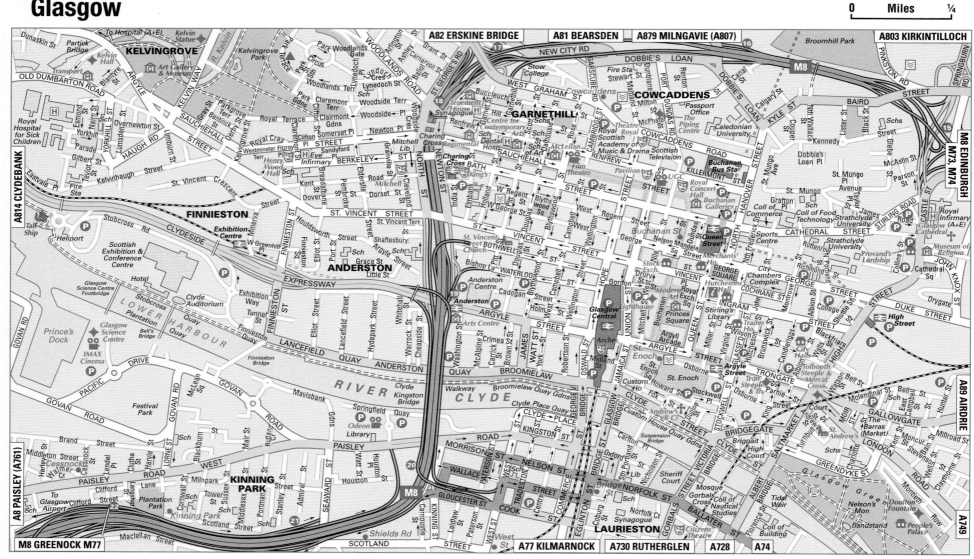

Gloucester

0 Miles ¼

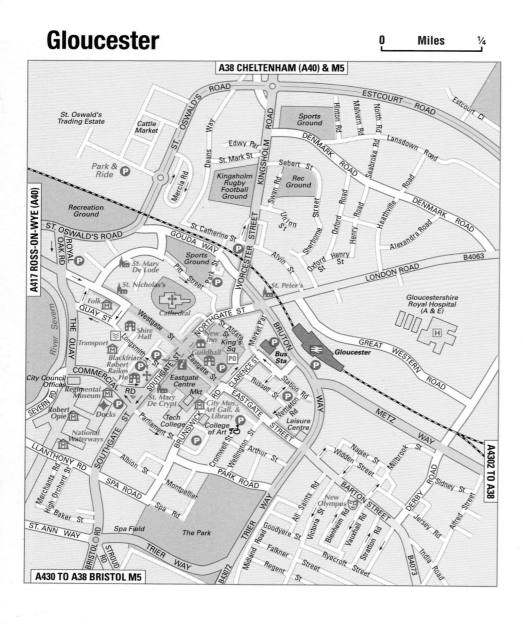

Hanley (Stoke-on-Trent)

0 Miles ¼

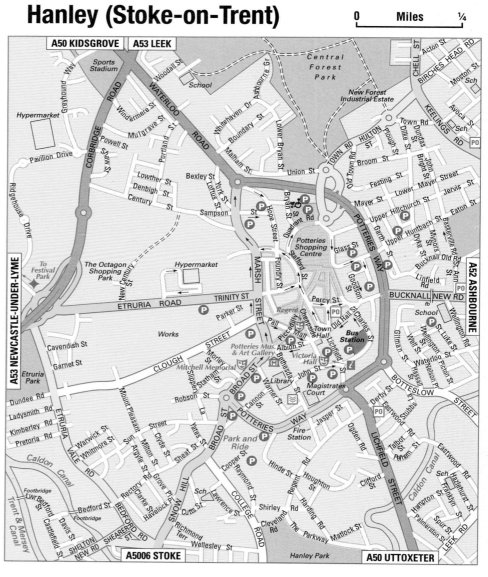

Hull

Ipswich

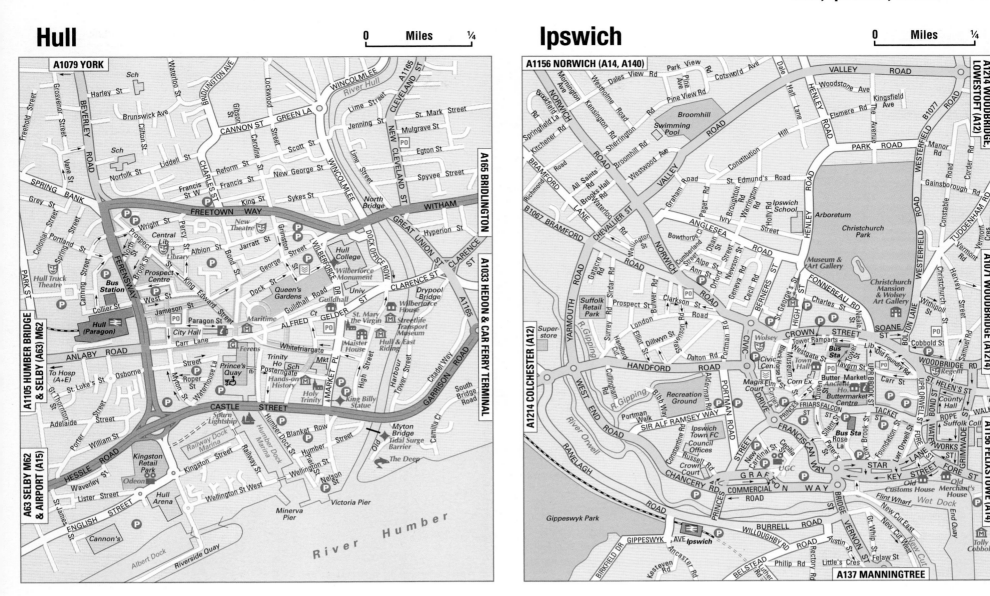

Leeds

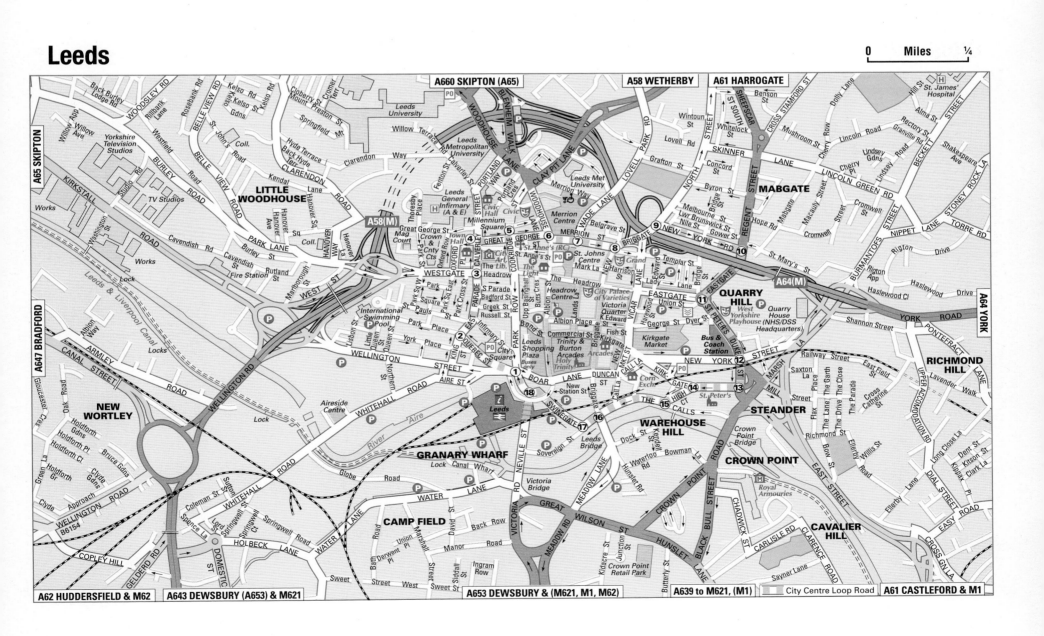

Leicester

Lincoln

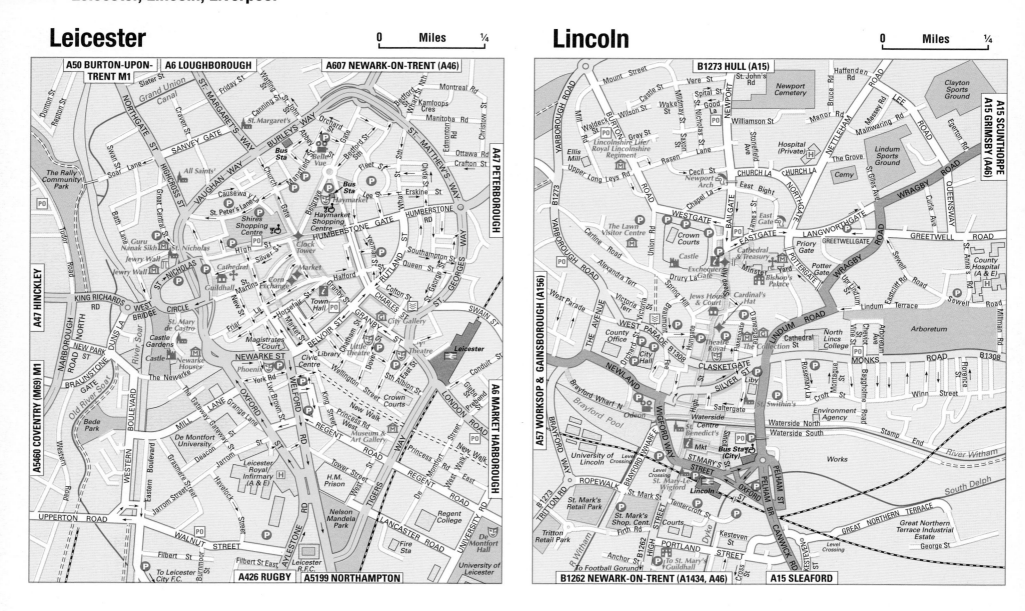

Liverpool

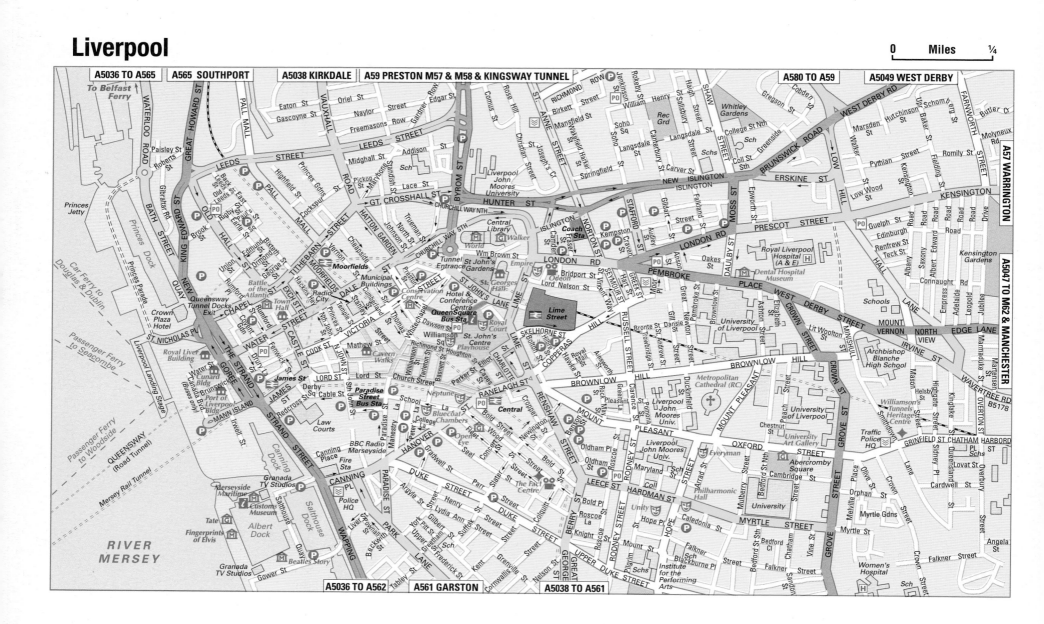

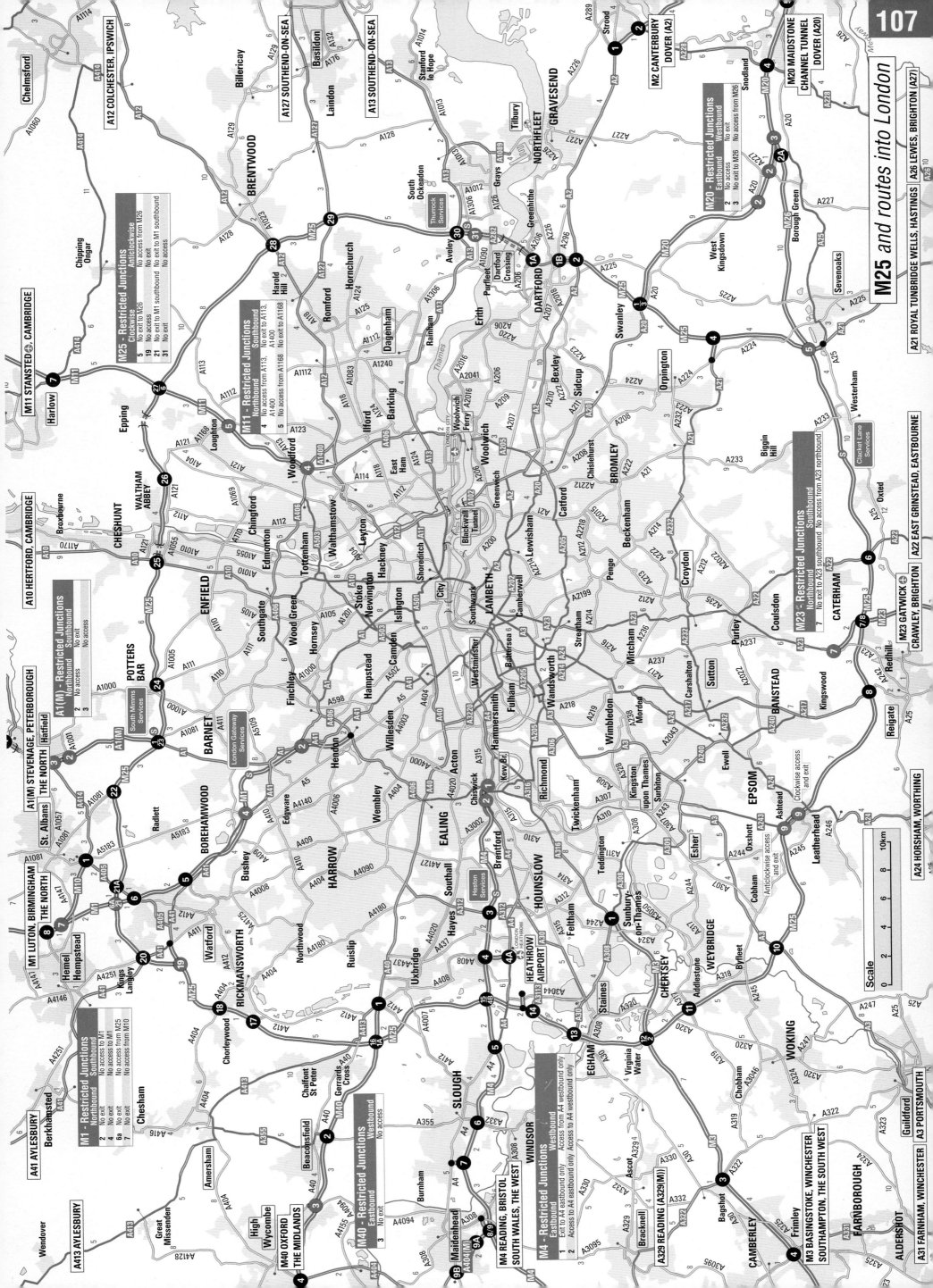

M25 and routes into London

London Docklands

Congestion Charging Zone

Uncharged Roads

0   Miles   1

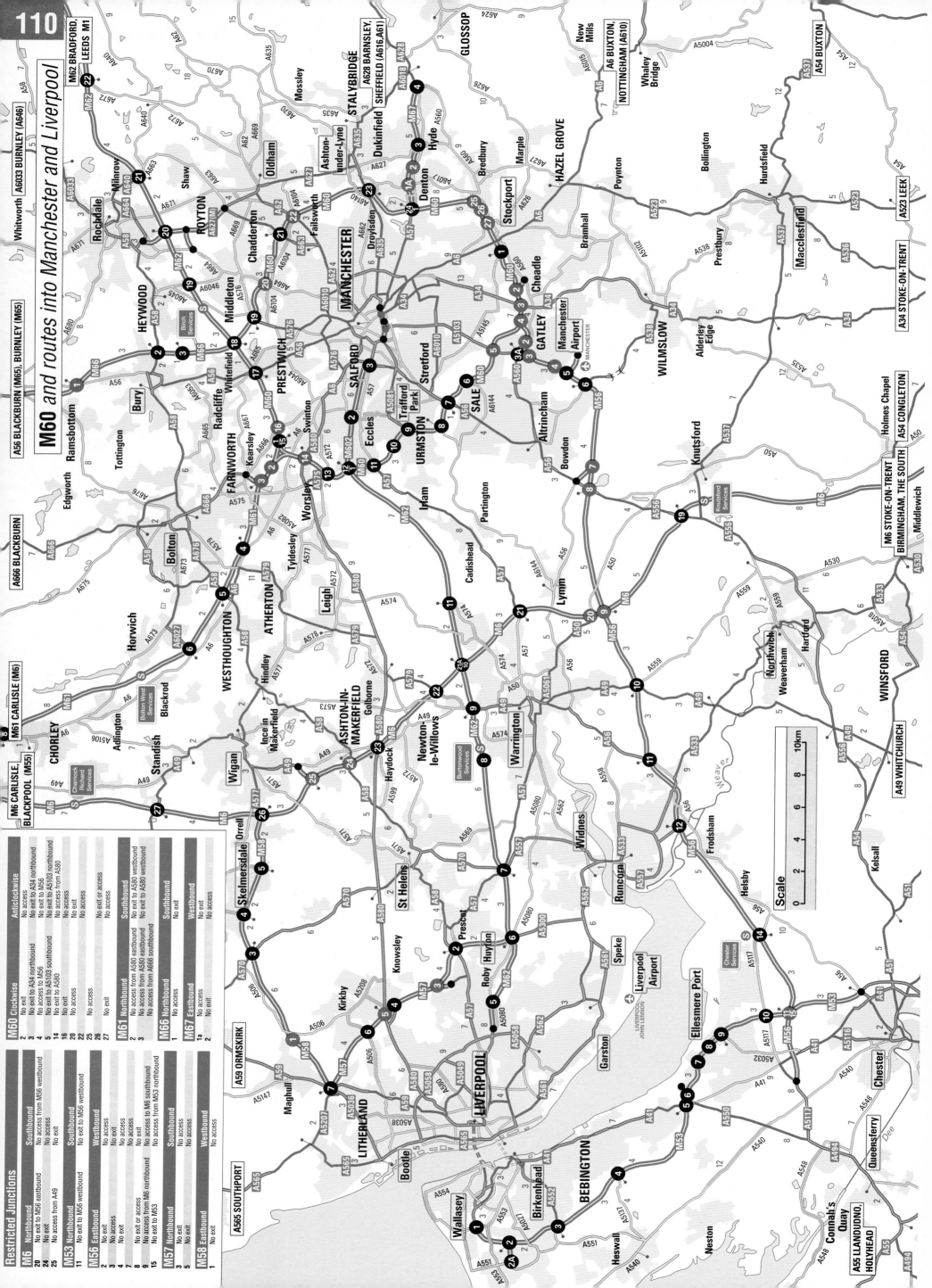

M60 and routes into Manchester and Liverpool

Manchester

Middlesbrough

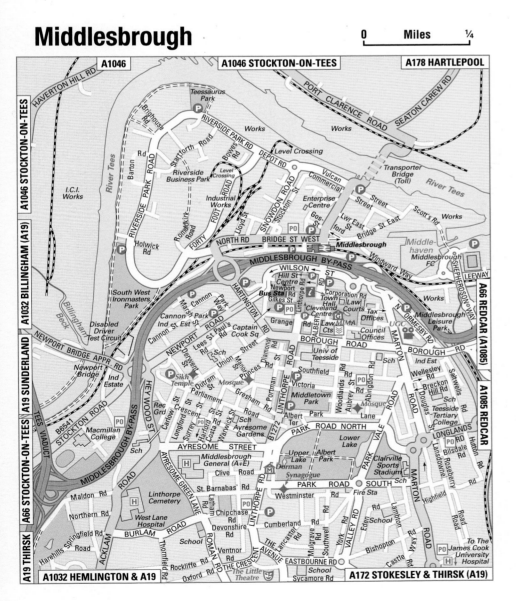

Milton Keynes

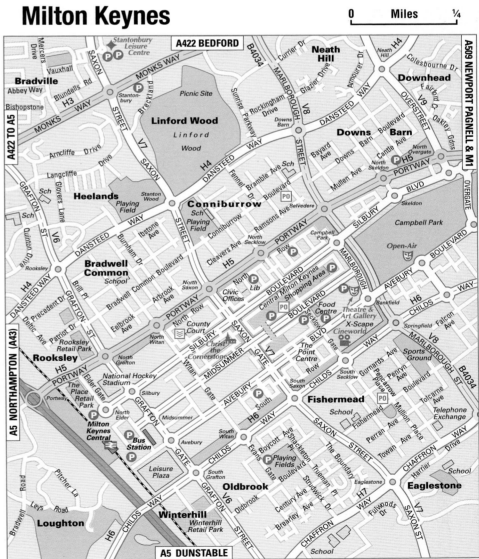

Newcastle upon Tyne

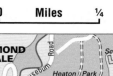

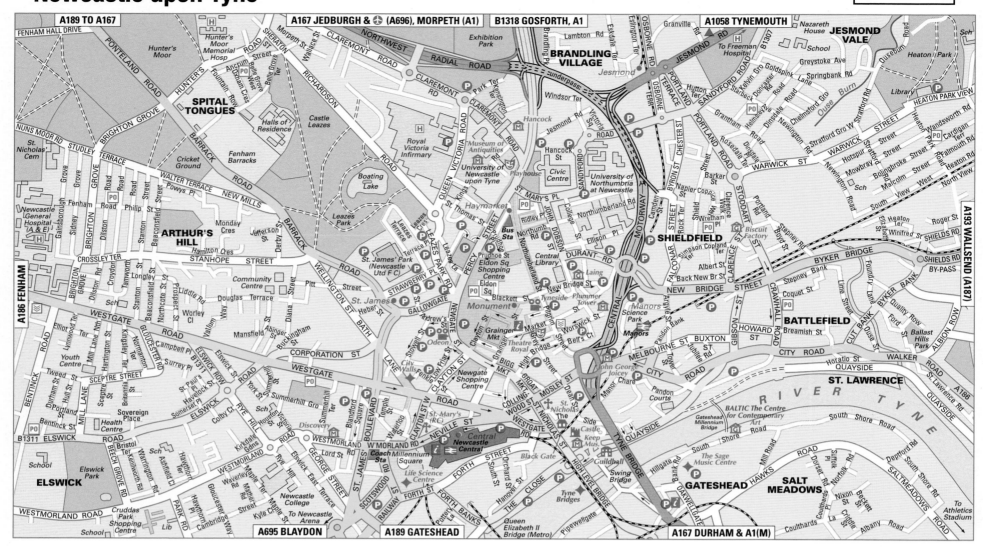

Northampton

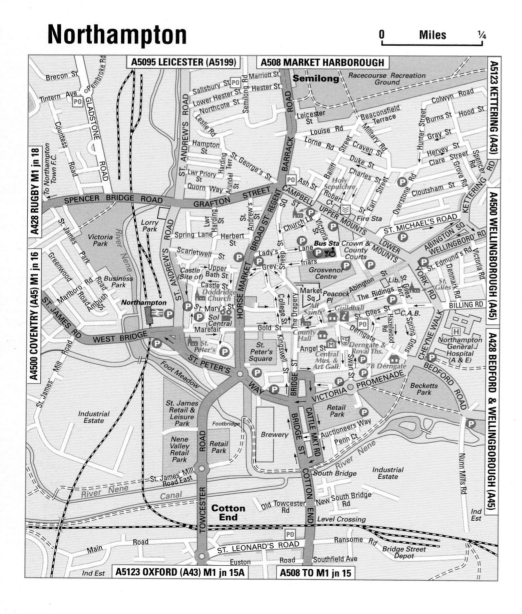

Norwich

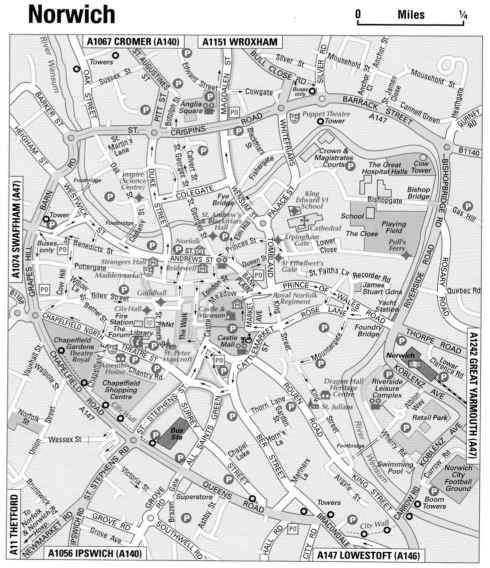

Nottingham

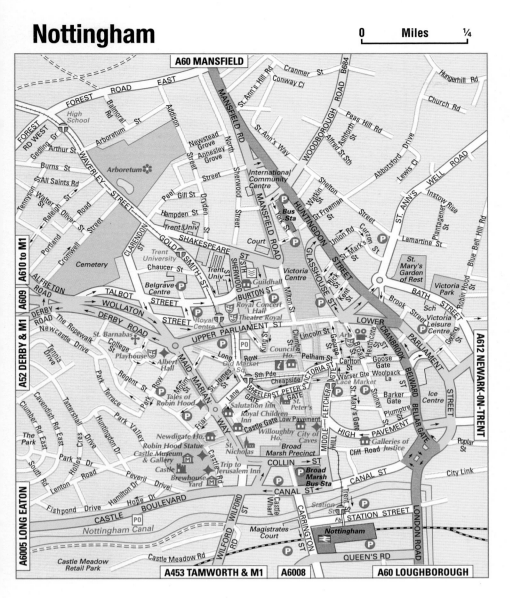

Oxford

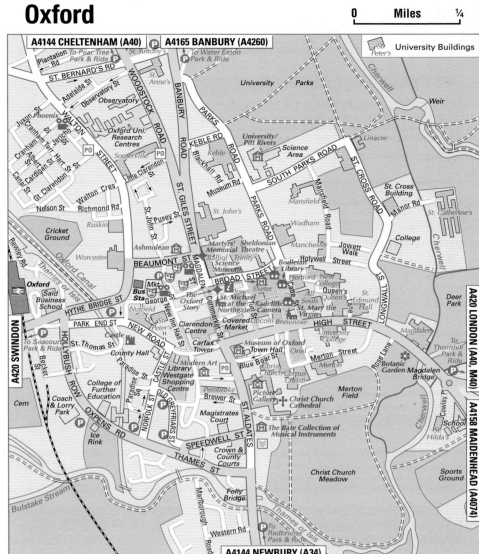

Plymouth

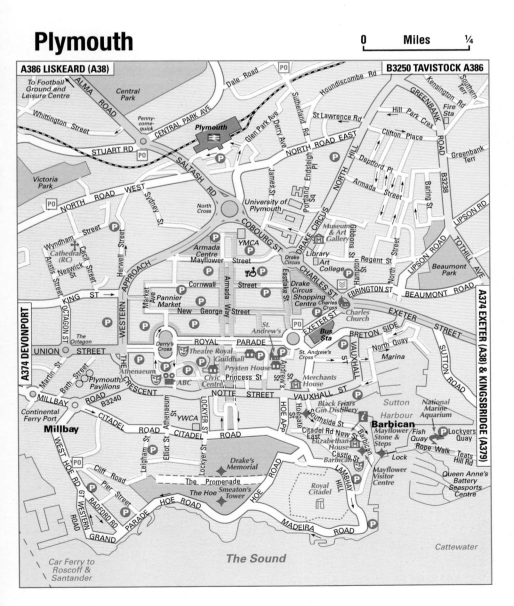

Portsmouth

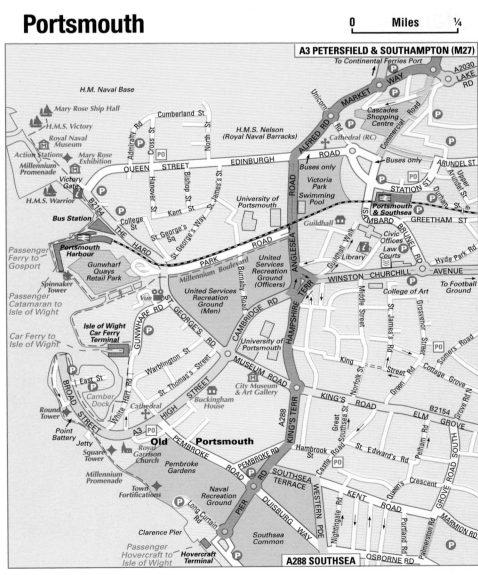

Reading

0   Miles   ¼

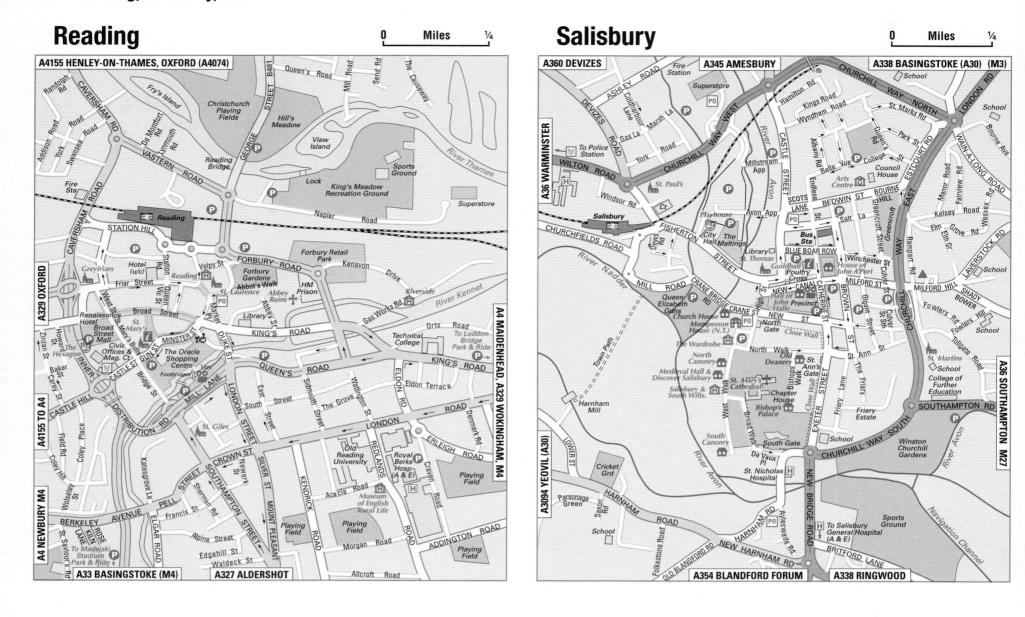

Salisbury

0   Miles   ¼

Sheffield

0   Miles   ¼

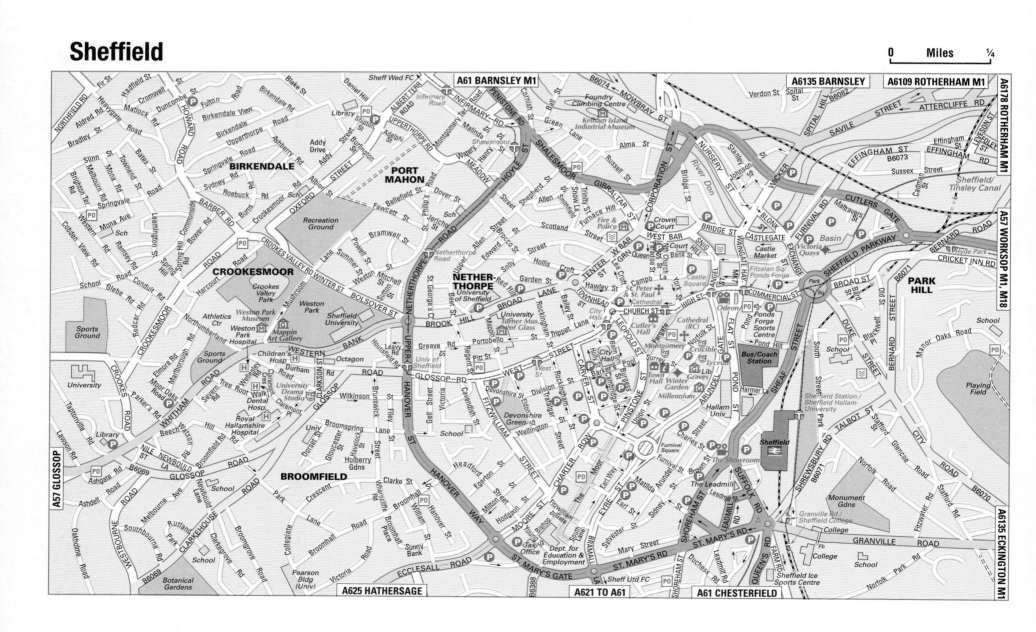

Southampton

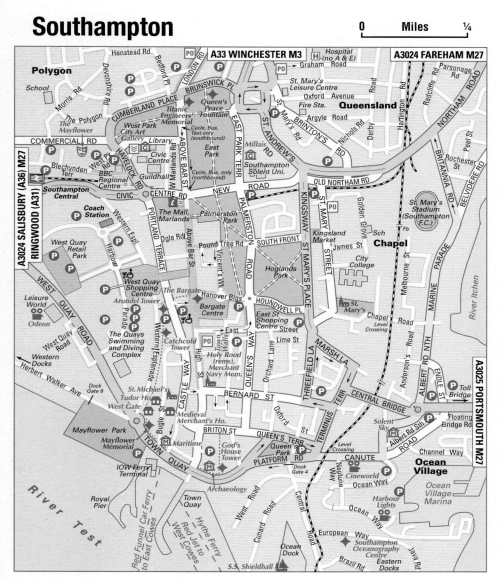

Stratford-upon-Avon

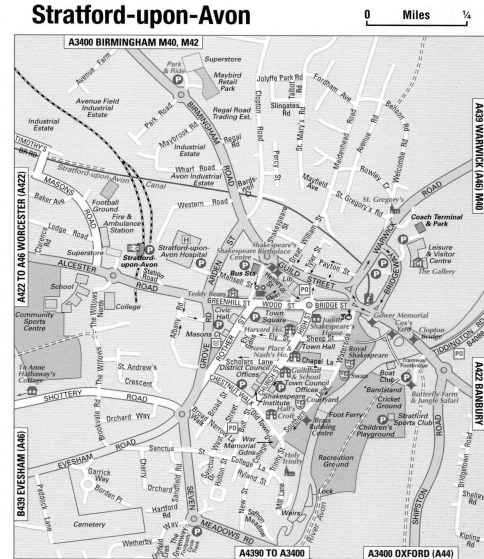

Sunderland

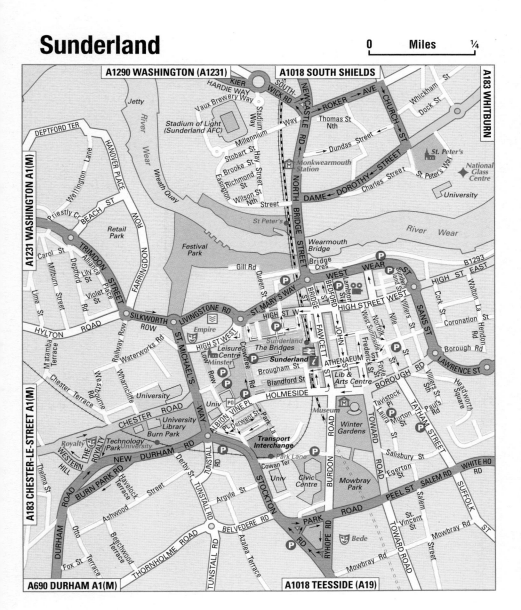

Swansea / Abertawe

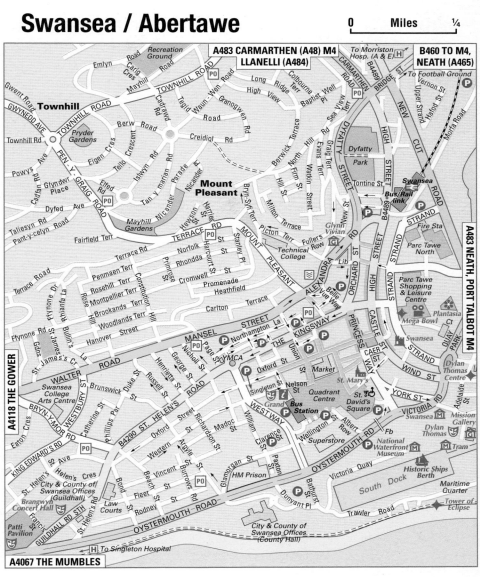

Swindon

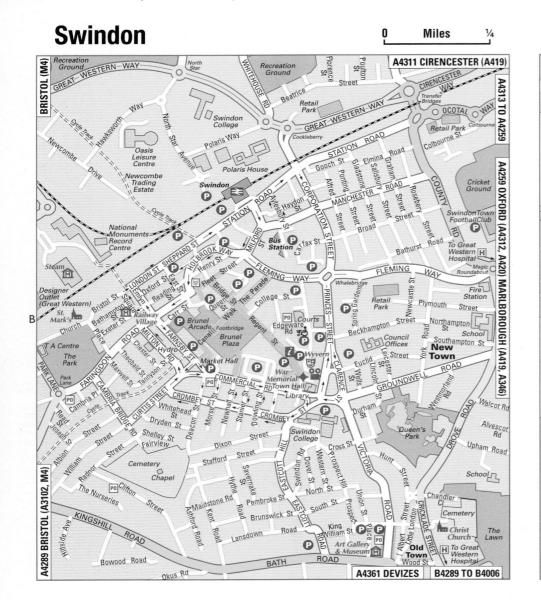

Winchester

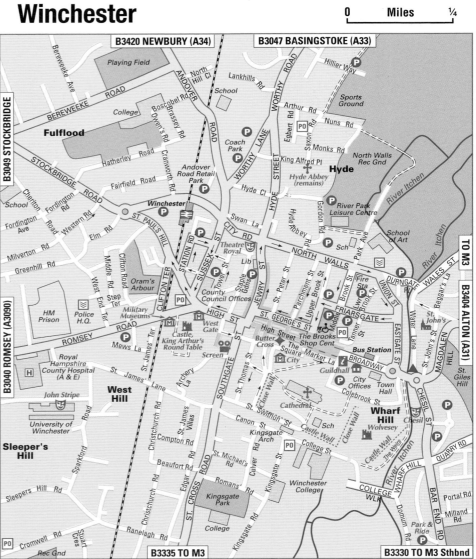

Worcester

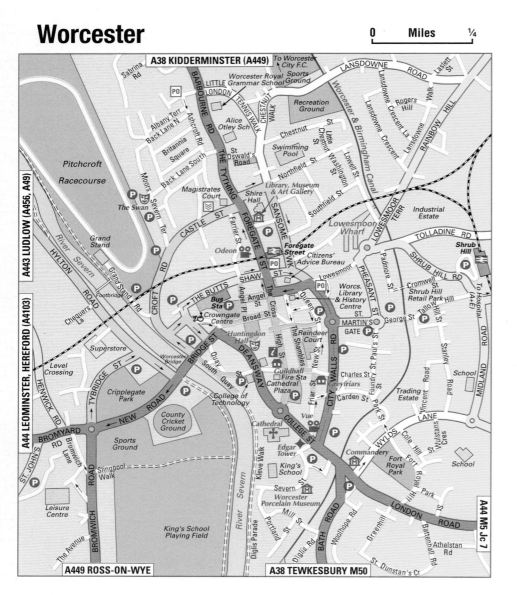

York

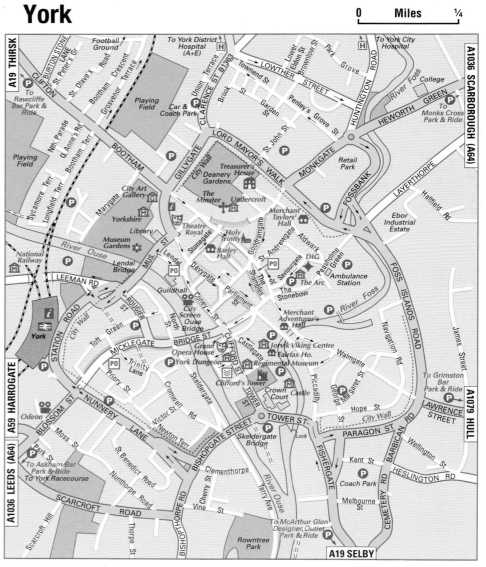

How to use the index

Example

Whimple Devon 7 G9
- grid square
- page number
- county or unitary authority

Index to road maps of Britain

Abbreviations used in the index

Aberdeen Aberdeen City	Derbys Derbyshire	I o W Isle of Wight	Nottingham City of Nottingham	Stoke Stoke-on-Trent
Aberds Aberdeenshire	Devon Devon	Invclyd Inverclyde	Notts Nottinghamshire	Suff Suffolk
Ald Alderney	Dorset Dorset	Jersey Jersey	Orkney Orkney	Sur Surrey
Anglesey Isle of Anglesey	Dumfries Dumfries and Galloway	Kent Kent	Oxon Oxfordshire	Swansea Swansea
Angus Angus	Dundee Dundee City	Lancs Lancashire	P'boro Peterborough	Swindon Swindon
Argyll Argyll and Bute	Durham Durham	Leicester City of Leicester	Pembs Pembrokeshire	T & W Tyne and Wear
Bath Bath and North East Somerset	E Ayrs East Ayrshire	Leics Leicestershire	Perth Perth and Kinross	Telford Telford and Wrekin
Beds Bedfordshire	E Dunb East Dunbartonshire	Lincs Lincolnshire	Plym Plymouth	Thurrock Thurrock
Bl Gwent Blaenau Gwent	E Loth East Lothian	London Greater London	Poole Poole	Torbay Torbay
Blkburn Blackburn with Darwen	E Renf East Renfrewshire	Luton Luton	Powys Powys	Torf Torfaen
Blkpool Blackpool	E Sus East Sussex	M Keynes Milton Keynes	Ptsmth Portsmouth	V Glam The Vale of Glamorgan
Bmouth Bournemouth	E Yorks East Riding of Yorkshire	M Tydf Merthyr Tydfil	Reading Reading	W Berks West Berkshire
Borders Scottish Borders	Edin City of Edinburgh	M'bro Middlesbrough	Redcar Redcar and Cleveland	W Dunb West Dunbartonshire
Brack Bracknell	Essex Essex	Medway Medway	Renfs Renfrewshire	W Isles Western Isles
Bridgend Bridgend	Falk Falkirk	Mers Merseyside	Rhondda Rhondda Cynon Taff	W Loth West Lothian
Brighton City of Brighton and Hove	Fife Fife	Midloth Midlothian	Rutland Rutland	W Mid West Midlands
Bristol City and County of Bristol	Flint Flintshire	Mon Monmouthshire	S Ayrs South Ayrshire	W Sus West Sussex
Bucks Buckinghamshire	Glasgow City of Glasgow	Moray Moray	S Glos South Gloucestershire	W Yorks West Yorkshire
Caerph Caerphilly	Glos Gloucestershire	N Ayrs North Ayrshire	S Lnrk South Lanarkshire	Warks Warwickshire
Cambs Cambridgeshire	Gtr Man Greater Manchester	N Lincs North Lincolnshire	S Yorks South Yorkshire	Warr Warrington
Cardiff Cardiff	Guern Guernsey	N Lnrk North Lanarkshire	Scilly Scilly	Wilts Wiltshire
Carms Carmarthenshire	Gwyn Gwynedd	N Som North Somerset	Shetland Shetland	Windsor Windsor and Maidenhead
Ceredig Ceredigion	Halton Halton	N Yorks North Yorkshire	Shrops Shropshire	Wokingham Wokingham
Ches Cheshire	Hants Hampshire	NE Lincs North East Lincolnshire	Slough Slough	Worcs Worcestershire
Clack Clackmannanshire	Hereford Herefordshire	Neath Neath Port Talbot	Som Somerset	Wrex Wrexham
Conwy Conwy	Herts Hertfordshire	Newport City and County of Newport	Soton Southampton	York City of York
Corn Cornwall	Highld Highland	Norf Norfolk	Staffs Staffordshire	
Cumb Cumbria	Hrtlpl Hartlepool	Northants Northamptonshire	Sthend Southend-on-Sea	
Darl Darlington	Hull Hull	Northumb Northumberland	Stirl Stirling	
Denb Denbighshire	I o M Isle of Man		Stockton Stockton-on-Tees	
Derby City of Derby				

Ashford Hill Hants 18 E2
Ashford in the Water Derbys 44 F5
Ashgill S Lnrk 68 F6
Ashill Devon 7 E9
Ashill Norf 38 E4
Ashill Som 8 C2
Ashingdon Essex 20 B5
Ashington Northumb 63 E8
Ashington Som 8 B4
Ashington W Sus 11 C10
Ashintully Castle Perth 76 A4
Ashkirk Borders 61 A10
Ashlett Hants 10 D3
Ashleworth Glos 26 F5
Ashley Cambs 30 B3
Ashley Ches 43 D10
Ashley Devon 6 E5
Ashley Dorset 9 D10
Ashley Glos 16 B6
Ashley Hants 10 E1
Ashley Hants 10 A2
Ashley Northants 36 F3
Ashley Staffs 34 B3
Ashley Green Bucks 28 H6
Ashley Heath Dorset 9 D10
Ashley Heath Staffs 34 B3
Ashmanhaugh Norf 39 C9
Ashmansworth Hants 17 F11
Ashmansworthy Devon 6 E2
Ashmore Dorset 9 C8
Ashorne Warks 27 C10
Ashover Derbys 45 F7
Ashow Warks 27 A10
Ashprington Devon 5 F9
Ashreigney Devon 6 E5
Ashtead Sur 19 F8
Ashton Ches 43 F8
Ashton Corn 2 G5
Ashton Hants 10 C4
Ashton Hereford 26 B2
Ashton Invclyd 73 F11
Ashton Northants 28 D4
Ashton Northants 37 G6
Ashton Common Wilts 16 F5
Ashton-In-Makerfield Gtr Man 43 C8
Ashton Keynes Wilts 17 B7
Ashton under Hill Worcs 26 E6
Ashton-under-Lyne Gtr Man 44 C3
Ashton upon Mersey Gtr Man 43 C10
Ashurst Hants 10 C2
Ashurst Kent 12 C4
Ashurst W Sus 11 C10
Ashurstwood W Sus 12 C3
Ashwater Devon 6 G2
Ashwell Herts 29 E9
Ashwell Rutland 36 D4
Ashwell Som 8 C2
Ashwellthorpe Norf 39 F7
Ashwick Som 16 G3
Ashwicken Norf 38 D3
Ashybank Borders 61 B11
Askam in Furness Cumb 49 B2
Askern S Yorks 45 A9
Askerswell Dorset 8 E4
Askett Bucks 28 H5
Askham Cumb 57 D7
Askham Notts 45 E11
Askham Bryan York 52 E1
Askham Richard York 51 E11
Asknish Argyll 73 D8
Askrigg N Yorks 57 G11
Askwith N Yorks 51 E7
Aslackby Lincs 37 B6
Aslacton Norf 39 F7
Aslockton Notts 36 B3
Asloun Aberds 83 B7
Aspatria Cumb 56 B3
Aspenden Herts 29 F10
Asperton Lincs 37 B8
Aspley Guise Beds 28 E6
Aspley Heath Beds 28 E6
Aspull Gtr Man 43 B9
Asselby E Yorks 52 G3
Asserby Lincs 47 E8
Assington Suff 30 E6
Assynt Ho. Highld 87 E8
Astbury Ches 44 F2
Astcote Northants 28 C3
Asterley Shrops 33 E9
Asterton Shrops 33 F9
Asthall Oxon 27 G9
Asthall Leigh Oxon 27 G10
Astley Shrops 33 D11
Astley Warks 35 G9
Astley Worcs 26 B4
Astley Abbotts Shrops 34 F3
Astley Bridge Gtr Man 43 A10
Astley Cross Worcs 26 B5
Astley Green Gtr Man 43 C10
Aston Ches 43 H9
Aston Ches 43 E8
Aston Derbys 44 D6
Aston Hereford 25 A11
Aston Herts 29 F9
Aston Oxon 17 A10
Aston Shrops 33 C11
Aston Staffs 34 A3
Aston S Yorks 45 D8
Aston Telford 34 E2
Aston W Mid 35 G6
Aston Wokingham 18 C4
Aston Abbotts Bucks 28 F5
Aston Botterell Shrops 34 G2
Aston-By-Stone Staffs 34 B5
Aston Cantlow Warks 27 C8
Aston Clinton Bucks 28 G5
Aston Crews Hereford 26 F3
Aston Cross Glos 26 E6
Aston End Herts 29 F9
Aston Eyre Shrops 34 F2
Aston Fields Worcs 26 B6
Aston Flamville Leics 35 F10
Aston Ingham Hereford 26 F3
Aston juxta Mondrum Ches 43 G9
Aston le Walls Northants 27 C11
Aston Magna Glos 27 E8
Aston Munslow Shrops 33 G11
Aston on Clun Shrops 33 G9
Aston-on-Trent Derbys 35 C10
Aston Rogers Shrops 33 E9
Aston Rowant Oxon 18 B4
Aston Sandford Bucks 28 H4
Aston Somerville Worcs 27 E7
Aston Subedge Glos 27 D8
Aston Tirrold Oxon 18 C2
Aston Upthorpe Oxon 18 C2
Astrop Northants 28 E2
Astwick Beds 29 E9
Astwood M Keynes 28 D6
Astwood Worcs 26 C5
Astwood Bank Worcs 27 B7
Aswarby Lincs 37 B6
Aswardby Lincs 47 E7
Atch Lench Worcs 27 C7
Atcham Shrops 33 E11
Athelhampton Dorset 9 E6
Athelington Suff 31 A9
Athelney Som 8 B2
Athelstaneford E Loth 70 C4
Atherington Devon 6 D4
Atherstone Warks 35 F9
Atherstone on Stour Warks 27 C9
Atherton Gtr Man 43 B9
Atley Hill N Yorks 58 F3
Atlow Derbys 44 H6
Attadale Highld 86 H2
Attadale Ho. Highld 86 H2
Attenborough Notts 35 B11
Atterby Lincs 46 C3
Attercliffe S Yorks 45 D7
Attleborough Norf 38 F6
Attleborough Warks 35 F9
Attlebridge Norf 39 D7
Atwick E Yorks 53 D7
Atworth Wilts 16 E5
Aubourn Lincs 46 F3
Auchagallon N Ayrs 66 C1
Auchallater Aberds 82 E3
Aucharnie Aberds 89 D6
Auchattie Aberds 83 D8
Auchavan Angus 82 G3
Auchbreck Moray 82 A4
Auchenback E Renf 68 E4
Auchenbainzie Dumfries 60 D4
Auchenblae Aberds 83 F9
Auchenbrack Dumfries 60 D3
Auchenbreck Argyll 73 E9
Auchencairn Dumfries 55 D10
Auchencairn Dumfries 60 E5
Auchencairn N Ayrs 66 D3
Auchencrosh S Ayrs 54 B4
Auchencrow Borders 71 D7
Auchendinny Midloth 69 D11
Auchengray S Lnrk 69 E8
Auchenhalrig Moray 88 B3
Auchenheath S Lnrk 69 F7
Auchenlochan Argyll 73 F8
Auchenmalg Dumfries 54 D5
Auchensoul S Ayrs 66 G5
Auchentiber N Ayrs 67 B6
Auchertyre Highld 85 F13
Auchgourish Highld 81 B11
Auchincarroch W Dunb 68 B3
Auchindrain Argyll 73 C9
Auchindrean Highld 86 C4
Auchininna Aberds 89 D6
Auchinleck E Ayrs 67 D8
Auchinloch N Lnrk 68 C5
Auchinroath Moray 88 C2
Auchintoul Aberds 83 B7
Auchiries Aberds 89 E10
Auchlee Aberds 83 D10
Auchleven Aberds 83 A8
Auchlochan S Lnrk 69 G7
Auchlossan Aberds 83 C7
Auchlunies Aberds 83 D10
Auchlyne Stirl 75 E8
Auchmacoy Aberds 89 E9
Auchmair Moray 82 A5
Auchmantle Dumfries 54 C4
Auchmillan E Ayrs 67 D8
Auchmithie Angus 77 C9
Auchmuirbridge Fife 76 G5
Auchmull Angus 83 F7
Auchnacree Angus 77 A7
Auchnagallin Highld 87 H13
Auchnagatt Aberds 89 D9
Auchnaha Argyll 73 E8
Auchnashelloch Perth 75 F10
Aucholzie Aberds 82 D5
Auchrannie Angus 76 B5
Auchroisk Highld 82 A2
Auchronie Angus 82 E6
Auchterarder Perth 76 F2
Auchteraw Highld 80 C5
Auchterderran Fife 76 H5
Auchterhouse Angus 76 D6
Auchtermuchty Fife 76 F5
Auchterneed Highld 86 F7
Auchtertool Fife 69 A11
Auchtertyre Moray 88 C1
Auchtubh Stirl 75 E8
Auckengill Highld 94 D5
Auckley S Yorks 45 B10
Audenshaw Gtr Man 44 C3
Audlem Ches 34 A2
Audley Staffs 43 G10
Audley End Essex 30 E5
Auds Aberds 89 B6
Aughton E Yorks 52 F3
Aughton Lancs 43 B6
Aughton Lancs 50 C1
Aughton S Yorks 45 D8
Aughton Wilts 17 F9
Aughton Park Lancs 43 B7
Auldearn Highld 87 F12
Aulden Hereford 25 C11
Auldgirth Dumfries 60 E5
Auldhame E Loth 70 B4
Auldhouse S Lnrk 68 E5
Ault a'chruinn Highld 85 F14
Aultanrynie Highld 92 F6
Aultbea Highld 91 J13
Aultdearg Highld 86 E5
Aultgrishan Highld 91 J12
Aultguish Inn Highld 86 D6
Aultibea Highld 93 G13
Aultiphurst Highld 93 C11
Aultmore Moray 88 C4
Aultnagoire Highld 81 A7
Aultnamain Inn Highld 87 C9
Aultnaslat Highld 80 C3
Aulton Aberds 83 A8
Aundorach Highld 82 B1
Aunsby Lincs 36 B6
Auquhorthies Aberds 89 F8
Aust S Glos 16 C2
Austendike Lincs 37 C8
Austerfield S Yorks 45 C10
Austrey Warks 35 E8
Austwick N Yorks 50 C3
Authorpe Lincs 47 D8
Authorpe Row Lincs 47 E9
Avebury Wilts 17 E8
Aveley Thurrock 20 C2
Avening Glos 16 B5
Averham Notts 45 G11
Aveton Gifford Devon 5 G7
Avielochan Highld 81 B11
Aviemore Highld 81 B10
Avington Hants 10 A4
Avington W Berks 17 E10
Avoch Highld 87 F10
Avon Hants 9 E10
Avon Dassett Warks 27 D11
Avonbridge Falk 69 C8
Avonmouth Bristol 15 D11
Avonwick Devon 5 F8
Awbridge Hants 10 B2
Awhirk Dumfries 54 D3
Awkley S Glos 16 C2
Awliscombe Devon 7 F10
Awre Glos 26 H4
Awsworth Notts 35 A10
Axbridge Som 15 F10
Axford Hants 18 G3
Axford Wilts 17 D9
Axminster Devon 8 E1
Axmouth Devon 8 E1
Axton Flint 42 D4
Aycliff Kent 21 G10
Aycliffe Durham 58 D3
Aydon Northumb 62 G6
Aylburton Glos 16 A3
Ayle Northumb 57 B9
Aylesbeare Devon 7 G9
Aylesbury Bucks 28 G5
Aylesby NE Lincs 46 B6
Aylesford Kent 20 F4
Aylesham Kent 21 F9
Aylestone Leicester 36 E1
Aylmerton Norf 39 B7
Aylsham Norf 39 C7
Aylton Hereford 26 E3
Aymestrey Hereford 25 B11
Aynho Northants 28 E2
Ayot St Lawrence Herts 29 G8
Ayot St Peter Herts 29 G9
Ayr S Ayrs 66 D6
Aysgarth N Yorks 58 H1
Ayside Cumb 49 A3
Ayston Rutland 36 E4
Aythorpe Roding Essex 30 G2
Ayton Borders 71 D8
Aywick Shetland 96 E7
Azerley N Yorks 51 B8

B

Babbacombe Torbay 5 E10
Babbinswood Shrops 33 B9
Babcary Som 8 B4
Babel Carms 24 E5
Babell Flint 42 E4
Babraham Cambs 30 C2
Babworth Notts 45 D10
Bac W Isles 91 C9
Bachau Anglesey 40 B6
Back of Keppoch Highld 79 C9
Back Rogerton E Ayrs 67 D8
Backaland Orkney 95 E6
Backaskaill Orkney 95 C5
Backbarrow Cumb 49 A3
Backe Carms 23 E7
Backfolds Aberds 89 C10
Backford Ches 43 E7
Backford Cross Ches 43 E6
Backhill Aberds 89 E7
Backhill Aberds 89 E10
Backhill of Clackriach Aberds 89 D9
Backhill of Fortree Aberds 89 D9
Backhill of Trustach Aberds 83 D8
Backies Highld 93 J11
Backlass Highld 94 E4
Backwell N Som 15 E10
Backworth T & W 63 F9
Bacon End Essex 30 G3
Baconsthorpe Norf 39 B7
Bacton Hereford 25 E10
Bacton Norf 39 B9
Bacton Suff 31 B7
Bacton Green Suff 31 B7
Bacup Lancs 50 G4
Badachro Highld 85 A12
Badanloch Lodge Highld 93 F10
Badavanich Highld 86 F4
Badbury Swindon 17 C8
Badby Northants 28 C2
Badcall Highld 92 D5
Badcaul Highld 86 B3
Baddeley Green Stoke 44 G3
Baddesley Clinton Warks 27 A9
Baddesley Ensor Warks 35 F8
Baddidarach Highld 92 G3
Baddoch Aberds 82 E3
Baddock Highld 87 F10
Badenscoth Aberds 89 E7
Badenyon Aberds 82 B5
Badger Shrops 34 F3
Badger's Mount Kent 19 E11
Badgeworth Glos 26 G6
Badgworth Som 15 F9
Badicaul Highld 85 F12
Badingham Suff 31 B10
Badlesmere Kent 21 F7
Badlipster Highld 94 F4
Badluarach Highld 86 B2
Badminton S Glos 16 C5
Badnaban Highld 92 G3
Badninish Highld 87 B10
Badrallach Highld 86 B3
Badsey Worcs 27 D7
Badshot Lea Sur 18 G5
Badsworth W Yorks 45 A8
Badwell Ash Suff 30 B6
Bae Colwyn = Colwyn Bay Conwy 41 C10
Bag Enderby Lincs 47 E7
Bagby N Yorks 51 A10
Bagendon Glos 27 H7
Bagh a Chaisteil = Castlebay W Isles 84 J1
Bagh Mor W Isles 84 C3
Bagh Shiarabhagh W Isles 84 H2
Baghasdal W Isles 84 G2
Bagillt Flint 42 E5
Baginton Warks 27 A10
Baglan Neath 14 B3
Bagley Shrops 33 C10
Bagnall Staffs 44 G3
Bagnor W Berks 17 E11
Bagshot Sur 18 E6
Bagshot Wilts 17 E10
Bagthorpe Norf 38 B3
Bagthorpe Notts 45 G8
Bagworth Leics 35 E10
Bagwy Llydiart Hereford 25 F11
Bail Àrd Bhuirgh W Isles 91 B9
Bail Uachdraich W Isles 84 B3
Baildon W Yorks 51 F7
Baile W Isles 90 J4
Baile a Mhanaich W Isles 84 C2
Baile Ailein W Isles 91 E7
Baile an Truiseil W Isles 91 B8
Baile Boidheach Argyll 72 F6
Baile Glas W Isles 84 C3
Baile Mhartainn W Isles 84 A2
Baile Mhic Phail W Isles 84 A3
Baile Mor Argyll 78 J5
Baile Mor W Isles 84 B2
Baile na Creige W Isles 84 H1
Baile nan Cailleach W Isles 84 C2
Baile Raghaill W Isles 84 A2
Bailebeag Highld 81 B7
Baileyhead Cumb 61 F11
Bailiesward Aberds 88 E4
Baillieston Glasgow 68 D5
Bail'lochrach W Isles 84 C3
Bail'Ur Tholastaidh W Isles 91 C10
Bainbridge N Yorks 57 G11
Bainsford Falk 69 B7
Bainshole Aberds 88 E6
Bainton E Yorks 52 D5
Bainton P'boro 37 E6
Bairnkine Borders 62 B2
Baker Street Thurrock 20 C3
Baker's End Herts 29 G10
Bakewell Derbys 44 F6
Bala = Y Bala Gwyn 32 B5
Balachuirn Highld 85 D10
Balavil Highld 81 C9
Balbeg Highld 81 A6
Balbeg Highld 86 H7
Balbeggie Perth 76 E4
Balbithan Aberds 83 B9
Balbithan Ho. Aberds 83 B10
Balblair Highld 87 E10
Balblair Highld 87 B8
Balby S Yorks 45 B9
Balchladich Highld 92 F3
Balchraggan Highld 87 H8
Balchraggan Highld 87 G8
Balchrick Highld 92 D4
Balchrystie Fife 77 G7
Balcladaich Highld 80 A4
Balcombe W Sus 12 C2
Balcombe Lane W Sus 12 C2
Balcomie Fife 77 F9
Balcurvie Fife 76 G6
Baldersby N Yorks 51 B9
Baldersby St James N Yorks 51 B9
Balderstone Lancs 50 F2
Balderton Ches 42 F6
Balderton Notts 46 G2
Baldhu Corn 3 E6
Baldinnie Fife 77 F7
Baldock Herts 29 E9
Baldovie Dundee 77 D7
Baldrine I o M 48 D4
Baldslow E Sus 13 E6
Baldwin I o M 48 D3
Baldwinholme Cumb 56 A5
Baldwin's Gate Staffs 34 A3
Bale Norf 38 B6
Balearn Aberds 89 C10
Balemartine Argyll 78 G2
Balephuil Argyll 78 G2
Balerno Edin 69 D10
Balevullin Argyll 78 G2
Balfield Angus 83 G7
Balfour Orkney 95 G5
Balfron Stirl 68 B4
Balfron Station Stirl 68 B4
Balgaveny Aberds 89 D6
Balgavies Angus 77 B8
Balgonar Fife 69 A9
Balgove Aberds 89 E8
Balgowan Highld 81 D8
Balgown Highld 85 B8
Balgrochan E Dunb 68 C5
Balgy Highld 85 C13
Balhaldie Stirl 75 G11
Balhalgardy Aberds 83 A9
Balham London 19 D9
Balhary Perth 76 C5
Baliasta Shetland 96 C8
Baligill Highld 93 C11
Balintore Angus 76 B5
Balintore Highld 87 D11
Balintraid Highld 87 D10
Balk N Yorks 51 A10
Balkeerie Angus 76 C6
Balkemback Angus 76 D6
Balkholme E Yorks 52 G3
Balkissock S Ayrs 54 A4
Ball Shrops 33 C9
Ball Haye Green Staffs 44 G3
Ball Hill Hants 17 E11
Ballabeg I o M 48 E2
Ballacannel I o M 48 D4
Ballachulish Highld 74 B3
Ballajora I o M 48 C4
Ballaleigh I o M 48 D3
Ballamodha I o M 48 E2
Ballantrae S Ayrs 54 A3
Ballaquine I o M 48 D4
Ballards Gore Essex 20 B6
Ballasalla I o M 48 C3
Ballasalla I o M 48 E2
Ballater Aberds 82 D5
Ballaugh I o M 48 C3
Ballaveare I o M 48 E3
Ballcorach Moray 82 A3
Ballechin Perth 76 B2
Balleigh Highld 87 C10
Ballencrieff E Loth 70 C3
Ballentoul Perth 81 G10
Ballidon Derbys 44 G6
Balliemore Argyll 73 E9
Balliemore Argyll 79 J11
Ballikinrain Stirl 68 B4
Ballimeanoch Argyll 73 B9
Ballimore Argyll 73 E8
Ballimore Stirl 75 F8
Ballinaby Argyll 64 B3
Ballindean Perth 76 E5
Ballingdon Suff 30 D5
Ballinger Common Bucks 18 A6
Ballingham Hereford 26 E2
Ballingry Fife 76 H4
Ballinlick Perth 76 C2
Ballinluig Perth 76 B2
Ballintuim Perth 76 B4
Balloch Angus 76 B6
Balloch Highld 87 G10
Balloch N Lnrk 68 C6
Balloch W Dunb 68 B2
Ballochan Aberds 83 D7
Ballochford Moray 88 E3
Ballochmorrie S Ayrs 54 A5
Balls Cross W Sus 11 B8
Balls Green Essex 31 F7
Ballygown Argyll 78 G7
Ballygrant Argyll 64 B4
Ballyhaugh Argyll 78 F4
Balmacara Highld 85 F13
Balmacara Square Highld 85 F13
Balmaclellan Dumfries 55 B9
Balmacneil Perth 76 B2
Balmacqueen Highld 85 A9
Balmae Dumfries 55 E9
Balmaha Stirl 68 A3
Balmalcolm Fife 76 G6
Balmeanach Highld 85 D10
Balmedie Aberds 83 B11
Balmer Heath Shrops 33 B10
Balmerino Fife 76 E6
Balmerlawn Hants 10 D2
Balmichael N Ayrs 66 C2
Balmirmer Angus 77 D8
Balmore Highld 85 D7
Balmore Highld 86 H6
Balmore Highld 87 G11
Balmore Perth 76 B2
Balmule Fife 69 B11
Balmullo Fife 77 E7
Balmungie Highld 87 F10
Balnaboth Angus 82 G5
Balnabruaich Highld 87 E10
Balnabruich Highld 94 H3
Balnacoil Highld 93 H11
Balnacra Highld 86 G2
Balnafoich Highld 87 H9
Balnagall Highld 87 C11
Balnaguard Perth 76 B2
Balnahard Argyll 72 D3
Balnahard Argyll 78 H7
Balnain Highld 86 H7
Balnakeil Highld 92 C6
Balnaknock Highld 85 B9
Balnapaling Highld 87 E10
Balne N Yorks 52 H1
Balochroy Argyll 65 C8
Balone Fife 77 F7
Balornock Glasgow 68 D5
Balquharn Perth 76 D3
Balquhidder Stirl 75 E8
Balsall W Mid 35 H8
Balsall Common W Mid 35 H8
Balsall Heath W Mid 35 G6
Balscott Oxon 27 D10
Balsham Cambs 30 C2
Baltasound Shetland 96 C8
Balterley Staffs 43 G10
Baltersan Dumfries 55 C7
Balthangie Aberds 89 C8
Baltonsborough Som 8 A4
Balvaird Highld 87 F8
Balvicar Argyll 72 B6
Balvraid Highld 85 G13
Balvraid Highld 87 H11
Bamber Bridge Lancs 50 G1
Bambers Green Essex 30 F2
Bamburgh Northumb 71 G10
Bamff Perth 76 B5
Bamford Derbys 44 D6
Bamford Gtr Man 44 A2
Bampton Cumb 57 E7
Bampton Devon 7 D8
Bampton Oxon 17 A10
Bampton Grange Cumb 57 E7
Banavie Highld 80 F3
Banbury Oxon 27 D11
Bancffosfelen Carms 23 E9
Banchory Aberds 83 D8
Banchory-Devenick Aberds 83 C11
Bancycapel Carms 23 E9
Bancyfelin Carms 23 E8
Bancyffordd Carms 23 C9
Bandirran Perth 76 D5
Banff Aberds 89 B6
Bangor Gwyn 41 C7
Bangor-is-y-coed Wrex 43 H6
Banham Norf 39 G6
Bank Hants 10 D1
Bank Newton N Yorks 50 D5
Bank Street Worcs 26 B3
Bankend Dumfries 60 G6
Bankfoot Perth 76 D3
Bankglen E Ayrs 67 E9
Bankhead Aberdeen 83 B10
Bankhead Aberds 83 C8
Banknock Falk 68 C6
Banks Cumb 61 G11
Banks Lancs 49 G3
Bankshill Dumfries 61 E7
Banningham Norf 39 C8
Banniskirk Ho. Highld 94 E3
Bannister Green Essex 30 F3
Bannockburn Stirl 69 A7
Banstead Sur 19 F9
Bantham Devon 5 G7
Banton N Lnrk 68 C6
Banwell N Som 15 F9
Banyard's Green Suff 31 A9
Bapchild Kent 20 E6
Bar Hill Cambs 29 B10
Barabhas W Isles 91 C8
Barabhas Iarach W Isles 91 C8
Barabhas Uarach W Isles 91 B8
Barachandroman Argyll 79 J9
Barassie S Ayrs 66 C6
Baravullin Argyll 79 H11
Barbaraville Highld 87 D10
Barber Booth Derbys 44 D5
Barbieston S Ayrs 67 E7
Barbon Cumb 50 A2
Barbridge Ches 43 G9
Barbrook Devon 6 B6
Barby Northants 28 A2
Barcaldine Argyll 74 C2
Barcheston Warks 27 E9
Barcombe E Sus 12 E3
Barcombe Cross E Sus 12 E3
Barden N Yorks 58 G2
Barden Scale N Yorks 51 D6
Bardennoch Dumfries 67 G8
Bardfield Saling Essex 30 F3
Bardister Shetland 96 F5
Bardney Lincs 46 F5
Bardon Leics 35 D10
Bardon Mill Northumb 62 G3
Bardowie E Dunb 68 C4
Bardrainney Invclyd 68 C2
Bardsea Cumb 49 B3
Bardsey W Yorks 51 E9
Bardwell Suff 30 A6
Bare Lancs 49 C4
Barfad Argyll 73 G7
Barford Norf 39 E7
Barford Warks 27 B9
Barford St John Oxon 27 E11
Barford St Martin Wilts 9 A9
Barford St Michael Oxon 27 E11
Barfrestone Kent 21 F9
Bargod = Bargoed Caerph 15 B7
Bargoed = Bargod Caerph 15 B7
Bargrennan Dumfries 54 B6
Barham Cambs 37 H7
Barham Kent 21 F9
Barham Suff 31 C8
Barharrow Dumfries 55 D9
Barhill Dumfries 55 C11
Barholm Lincs 37 D6
Barkby Leics 36 E2
Barkestone-le-Vale Leics 36 B3
Barkham Wokingham 18 E4
Barking London 19 C11
Barking Suff 31 C7
Barking Tye Suff 31 C7
Barkingside London 19 C11
Barkisland W Yorks 51 H6
Barkston Lincs 36 A5
Barkston N Yorks 51 F10
Barkway Herts 29 E10
Barlaston Staffs 34 B4
Barlavington W Sus 11 C8
Barlborough Derbys 45 E8
Barlby N Yorks 52 F2
Barlestone Leics 35 E10
Barley Herts 29 E10
Barley Lancs 50 E4
Barley Mow T & W 58 A3
Barleythorpe Rutland 36 E4
Barling Essex 20 C6
Barlow Derbys 45 E7
Barlow N Yorks 52 G2
Barlow T & W 63 G7
Barmby Moor E Yorks 52 E3
Barmby on the Marsh E Yorks 52 G2
Barmer Norf 38 B4
Barmoor Castle Northumb 71 G8
Barmoor Lane End Northumb 71 G9
Barmouth = Abermaw Gwyn 32 D2
Barmpton Darl 58 E4
Barmston E Yorks 53 D7
Barnack P'boro 37 E6
Barnacle Warks 35 G9
Barnard Castle Durham 58 E1
Barnard Gate Oxon 27 G11
Barnardiston Suff 30 D4
Barnbarroch Dumfries 55 D11
Barnburgh S Yorks 45 B8
Barnby Suff 39 G10
Barnby Dun S Yorks 45 B10
Barnby in the Willows Notts 46 G2
Barnby Moor Notts 45 D10
Barnes Street Kent 20 G3
Barnet London 19 B9
Barnetby le Wold N Lincs 46 B4
Barney Norf 38 B5
Barnham Suff 38 H4
Barnham W Sus 11 D8
Barnham Broom Norf 39 E6
Barnhead Angus 77 B9
Barnhill Ches 43 G7
Barnhill Dundee 77 D7
Barnhill Moray 88 C1
Barnhills Dumfries 54 B2
Barningham Durham 58 E1
Barningham Suff 38 H5
Barnoldby le Beck NE Lincs 46 B6
Barnoldswick Lancs 50 E4
Barns Green W Sus 11 B10
Barnsley Glos 27 H7
Barnsley S Yorks 45 B7
Barnstaple Devon 6 C4
Barnston Essex 30 G3
Barnston Mers 42 D5
Barnstone Notts 36 B3
Barnt Green Worcs 27 A7
Barnton Ches 43 E9
Barnton Edin 69 C10
Barnwell All Saints Northants 36 G6
Barnwell St Andrew Northants 36 G6
Barnwood Glos 26 G5
Barochreal Argyll 79 J11
Barons Cross Hereford 25 C11
Barr S Ayrs 66 G5
Barra Airport W Isles 84 H1
Barra Castle Aberds 83 A9
Barrachan Dumfries 54 E6
Barrack Aberds 89 D8
Barraglom W Isles 90 D6
Barrahormid Argyll 72 E6
Barran Argyll 79 J11
Barrapol Argyll 78 G2
Barras Aberds 83 E10
Barras Cumb 57 E10
Barrasford Northumb 62 F5
Barravullin Argyll 73 C7
Barregarrow I o M 48 D3
Barrhead E Renf 68 E3
Barrhill S Ayrs 54 A5
Barrington Cambs 29 D10
Barrington Som 8 C2
Barripper Corn 2 F5
Barrmill N Ayrs 67 A6
Barrock Highld 94 C4
Barrock Ho. Highld 94 D4
Barrow Lancs 50 F3
Barrow Rutland 36 D4
Barrow Suff 30 B4
Barrow Green Kent 20 E6
Barrow Gurney N Som 15 E11
Barrow Haven N Lincs 53 G6
Barrow-in-Furness Cumb 49 C2
Barrow Island Cumb 49 C1
Barrow Nook Lancs 43 B7
Barrow Street Wilts 9 A7
Barrow upon Humber N Lincs 53 G6
Barrow upon Soar Leics 36 D1
Barrow upon Trent Derbys 35 C9
Barroway Drove Norf 38 E1
Barrowburn Northumb 62 B4
Barrowby Lincs 36 B4
Barrowcliff N Yorks 59 H11
Barrowden Rutland 36 E5
Barrowford Lancs 50 F4
Barrows Green Ches 43 G9
Barrows Green Cumb 57 H7
Barrow's Green Mers 43 D8
Barry Angus 77 D8
Barry = Y Barri V Glam 15 E7
Barry Island V Glam 15 E7
Barsby Leics 36 D2
Barsham Suff 39 G9
Barston W Mid 35 H8
Bartestree Hereford 26 D2
Barthol Chapel Aberds 89 E8
Barthomley Ches 43 G10
Bartley Hants 10 C2
Bartley Green W Mid 34 G6
Bartlow Cambs 30 D2
Barton Cambs 29 C11
Barton Ches 43 G7
Barton Glos 27 F8
Barton Lancs 42 B6
Barton Lancs 49 F5
Barton N Yorks 58 F3
Barton Oxon 28 H2
Barton Torbay 5 E10
Barton Warks 27 C8
Barton Bendish Norf 38 E3
Barton Hartshorn Bucks 28 E3
Barton in Fabis Notts 35 B11
Barton in the Beans Leics 35 E9
Barton-le-Clay Beds 29 E7
Barton-le-Street N Yorks 52 B3
Barton-le-Willows N Yorks 52 C3
Barton Mills Suff 30 A4
Barton on Sea Hants 9 E11
Barton on the Heath Warks 27 E9
Barton St David Som 8 A4
Barton Seagrave Northants 36 H4
Barton Stacey Hants 17 G11
Barton Turf Norf 39 C9
Barton-under-Needwood Staffs 35 D7
Barton-upon-Humber N Lincs 52 G6
Barton Waterside N Lincs 52 G6
Barugh S Yorks 45 B7
Barway Cambs 37 H11
Barwell Leics 35 F10
Barwick Herts 29 G10
Barwick Som 8 C4
Barwick in Elmet W Yorks 51 F9
Baschurch Shrops 33 C10
Bascote Warks 27 B11
Basford Green Staffs 44 G3
Bashall Eaves Lancs 50 E2
Bashley Hants 9 E11
Basildon Essex 20 C4
Basingstoke Hants 18 F3
Baslow Derbys 44 E6
Bason Bridge Som 15 G9
Bassaleg Newport 15 C8
Bassenthwaite Cumb 56 C4
Bassett Soton 10 C3
Bassingbourn Cambs 29 D10
Bassingfield Notts 36 B2
Bassingham Lincs 46 F3
Bassingthorpe Lincs 36 C5
Basta Shetland 96 D7
Baston Lincs 37 D7
Bastwick Norf 39 D10
Baswick Steer E Yorks 53 E6
Batchworth Heath Herts 19 B7
Batcombe Dorset 8 D5
Batcombe Som 16 H3
Bate Heath Ches 43 E9
Batford Herts 29 G8
Bath Bath 16 E4
Bathampton Bath 16 E4
Bathealton Som 7 D9
Batheaston Bath 16 E4
Bathford Bath 16 E4
Bathgate W Loth 69 D8
Bathley Notts 45 G11
Bathpool Corn 4 D3
Bathpool Som 8 B1
Bathville W Loth 69 D8
Batley W Yorks 51 G8
Batsford Glos 27 E8
Battersby N Yorks 59 F6
Battersea London 19 D9
Battisborough Cross Devon 5 G6
Battisford Suff 31 C7
Battisford Tye Suff 31 C7
Battle E Sus 12 E6
Battle Powys 25 E7
Battledown Glos 26 F6
Battlefield Shrops 33 D11
Battlesbridge Essex 20 B4
Battlesden Beds 28 F6
Battlesea Green Suff 39 H8
Battleton Som 7 D8
Battram Leics 35 E10
Battramsley Hants 10 E2
Baughton Worcs 26 D5
Baughurst Hants 18 F2
Baulking Oxon 17 B10
Baumber Lincs 46 E6
Baunton Glos 17 A7
Baverstock Wilts 9 A9
Bawburgh Norf 39 E7
Bawdeswell Norf 38 C6
Bawdrip Som 15 H9
Bawdsey Suff 31 D10
Bawtry S Yorks 45 C10
Baxenden Lancs 50 G3
Baxterley Warks 35 F8
Baybridge Hants 10 B4
Baycliff Cumb 49 B2
Baydon Wilts 17 D9
Bayford Herts 29 H10
Bayford Som 8 B6
Bayles Cumb 57 B9
Baylham Suff 31 C8
Baynard's Green Oxon 28 F2
Bayston Hill Shrops 33 E10
Baythorn End Essex 30 D4
Bayton Worcs 26 A3
Beach Highld 79 F10
Beachampton Bucks 28 E4
Beachamwell Norf 38 E3
Beachans Moray 87 G13
Beacharr Argyll 65 D7
Beachborough Kent 21 H8
Beachley Glos 16 B2
Beacon Devon 7 F10
Beacon End Essex 30 F6
Beacon Hill Sur 18 H5
Beacon's Bottom Bucks 18 B4
Beaconsfield Bucks 18 C6
Beacrabhaic W Isles 90 H6
Beadlam N Yorks 52 A2
Beadlow Beds 29 E8
Beadnell Northumb 71 H11
Beaford Devon 6 E4
Beal Northumb 71 F9
Beal N Yorks 51 G11
Beamhurst Staffs 35 B6
Beaminster Dorset 8 D3
Beamish Durham 58 A3
Beamsley N Yorks 51 D6
Bean Kent 20 D2
Beanacre Wilts 16 E6
Beanley Northumb 62 B6
Beaquoy Orkney 95 F4
Bear Cross Bmouth 9 E9
Beardwood Blkburn 50 G2
Beare Green Sur 19 G8
Bearley Warks 27 B8
Bearnus Argyll 78 G6
Bearpark Durham 58 B3
Bearsbridge Northumb 62 H3
Bearsden E Dunb 68 C4
Bearsted Kent 20 F4
Bearstone Shrops 34 B3
Bearwood Hereford 25 C10
Bearwood Poole 9 E9
Bearwood W Mid 34 G6
Beattock Dumfries 60 C6
Beauchamp Roding Essex 30 G2
Beauchief S Yorks 45 D7
Beaufort Bl Gwent 25 G8
Beaufort Castle Highld 87 G8
Beaulieu Hants 10 D2
Beauly Highld 87 G8
Beaumaris Anglesey 41 C8
Beaumont Cumb 61 H9
Beaumont Essex 31 F8
Beaumont Hill Darl 58 E3
Beausale Warks 27 A9
Beauworth Hants 10 B4
Beaworthy Devon 6 G3
Beazley End Essex 30 F4
Bebington Mers 42 D6
Bebside Northumb 63 E8
Beccles Suff 39 G10
Becconsall Lancs 49 G4
Beck Foot Cumb 57 G8
Beck Hole N Yorks 59 F9
Beck Row Suff 38 H2
Beck Side Cumb 49 A2
Beckbury Shrops 34 E3
Beckenham London 19 E10
Beckermet Cumb 56 F2
Beckfoot Cumb 56 H3
Beckfoot Cumb 56 B2
Beckford Worcs 26 E6
Beckhampton Wilts 17 E7
Beckingham Lincs 46 G2
Beckingham Notts 45 D11
Beckington Som 16 F5
Beckley E Sus 13 D7
Beckley Hants 9 E11
Beckley Oxon 28 G2
Beckton London 19 C11
Beckwithshaw N Yorks 51 D8
Becontree London 19 C11
Bed-y-coedwr Gwyn 32 C3
Bedale N Yorks 58 H3
Bedburn Durham 58 C2
Bedchester Dorset 9 C7
Beddau Rhondda 14 C6
Beddgelert Gwyn 41 F7
Beddingham E Sus 12 F3
Beddington London 19 E10
Bedfield Suff 31 B9
Bedford Beds 29 C7
Bedham W Sus 11 B9
Bedhampton Hants 10 D6
Bedingfield Suff 31 B8
Bedlam N Yorks 51 C8
Bedlington Northumb 63 E8
Bedlington Station Northumb 63 E8
Bedlinog M Tydf 14 A6
Bedminster Bristol 16 D2
Bedmond Herts 19 A7
Bednall Staffs 34 D5
Bedrule Borders 62 B2
Bedstone Shrops 33 H9
Bedwas Caerph 15 C7
Bedworth Warks 35 G9
Bedworth Heath Warks 35 G9
Beeby Leics 36 E2
Beech Hants 18 H3
Beech Staffs 34 B4
Beech Hill Gtr Man 43 B8
Beech Hill W Berks 18 E3
Beechingstoke Wilts 17 F7
Beedon W Berks 17 D11
Beeford E Yorks 53 D7
Beeley Derbys 44 F6
Beelsby NE Lincs 46 B6
Beenham W Berks 18 E2
Beeny Corn 4 B2
Beer Devon 7 H11
Beer Hackett Dorset 8 C4
Beercrocombe Som 8 B2
Beesands Devon 5 G9
Beesby Lincs 47 D8
Beeson Devon 5 G9
Beeston Beds 29 D8
Beeston Ches 43 G8
Beeston Norf 38 D5
Beeston Notts 35 B11
Beeston W Yorks 51 F8
Beeston Regis Norf 39 A7
Beeswing Dumfries 55 C11
Beetham Cumb 49 B4
Beetley Norf 38 D5
Begbroke Oxon 27 G11
Begelly Pembs 22 F6
Beggar's Bush Powys 25 B9
Beguildy Powys 33 H7
Beighton Norf 39 E9
Beighton S Yorks 45 D8
Beighton Hill Derbys 44 G6
Beith N Ayrs 66 A6
Bekesbourne Kent 21 F8
Belaugh Norf 39 D8
Belbroughton Worcs 34 H5
Belchamp Otten Essex 30 D5
Belchamp St Paul Essex 30 D4
Belchamp Walter Essex 30 D5
Belchford Lincs 46 E6
Belford Northumb 71 G10
Belhaven E Loth 70 C5
Belhelvie Aberds 83 B11
Belhinnie Aberds 82 A6
Bell Bar Herts 29 H9
Bell Busk N Yorks 50 D5
Bell End Worcs 34 H5
Bell o'th'Hill Ches 43 H8
Bellabeg Aberds 82 B5
Bellamore S Ayrs 66 H5
Bellanoch Argyll 72 D6
Bellaty Angus 76 B5
Belleau Lincs 47 E8
Bellehiglash Moray 88 E1
Bellerby N Yorks 58 G2
Bellever Devon 5 D7
Belliehill Angus 77 A8
Bellingdon Bucks 28 H6
Bellingham Northumb 62 E4
Belloch Argyll 65 E7
Bellochantuy Argyll 65 E7
Bells Yew Green E Sus 12 C5
Bellsbank E Ayrs 67 F7
Bellshill N Lnrk 68 D6
Bellshill Northumb 71 G10
Bellspool Borders 69 G10
Bellsquarry W Loth 69 D9
Belmaduthy Highld 87 F9
Belmesthorpe Rutland 36 D6
Belmont Blkburn 50 H2
Belmont London 19 E9
Belmont S Ayrs 66 D6
Belmont Shetland 96 C7
Belnacraig Aberds 82 B5
Belowda Corn 3 C8
Belper Derbys 45 H7
Belper Lane End Derbys 45 H7
Belsay Northumb 63 F7
Belses Borders 70 H4
Belsford Devon 5 F8
Belstead Suff 31 D8
Belston S Ayrs 67 D6
Belstone Devon 6 G5
Belthorn Lancs 50 G3
Beltinge Kent 21 E8
Beltoft N Lincs 46 B2
Belton Leics 35 C10
Belton Lincs 36 B5
Belton Norf 39 E10
Belton N Lincs 45 B11
Belton in Rutland Rutland 36 E4
Beltring Kent 20 G3
Belts of Collonach Aberds 83 D8
Belvedere London 19 D11
Belvoir Leics 36 B4
Bembridge I o W 10 F5
Bemersyde Borders 70 G4
Bemerton Wilts 9 A10
Bempton E Yorks 53 B7
Ben Alder Lodge Highld 81 F7
Ben Armine Lodge Highld 93 H10
Ben Casgro W Isles 91 E9
Benacre Suff 39 G11
Benbecula Airport W Isles 84 C2
Benbuie Dumfries 60 D3
Benderloch Argyll 74 D2
Bendronaig Lodge Highld 86 H3
Benenden Kent 13 C7
Benfield Dumfries 54 C6
Bengate Norf 39 C9
Bengeworth Worcs 27 D7
Benhall Green Suff 31 B10
Benhall Street Suff 31 B10
Benholm Aberds 83 G10
Beningbrough N Yorks 51 D11
Benington Herts 29 F9
Benington Lincs 47 H7
Benllech Anglesey 41 B7
Benmore Argyll 73 E10
Benmore Stirl 75 E7
Benmore Lodge Highld 92 H6
Bennacott Corn 6 G1
Bennan N Ayrs 66 D2
Benniworth Lincs 46 D6
Benover Kent 20 G4
Bensham T & W 63 G8
Benslie N Ayrs 66 B6
Benson Oxon 18 B3
Bent Aberds 83 F8
Bent Gate Lancs 50 G3
Benthall Northumb 71 H11
Benthall Shrops 34 E2
Bentham Glos 26 G6
Benthoul Aberdeen 83 C10
Bentlawnt Shrops 33 E9
Bentley E Yorks 52 F6
Bentley Hants 18 G4
Bentley Suff 31 E8
Bentley S Yorks 45 B9
Bentley Warks 35 F8
Bentley Worcs 26 B6
Bentley Heath W Mid 35 H7
Benton Devon 6 C5
Bentpath Dumfries 61 D9
Bents W Loth 69 D8
Bentworth Hants 18 G3
Benvie Dundee 76 D6
Benwick Cambs 37 F9
Beoley Worcs 27 B7
Beoraidbeg Highld 79 B9
Bepton W Sus 11 C7
Berden Essex 29 F11
Bere Alston Devon 4 E5
Bere Ferrers Devon 4 E5
Bere Regis Dorset 9 E7
Berepper Corn 2 G5
Bergh Apton Norf 39 E9
Berinsfield Oxon 18 B2
Berkeley Glos 16 B3
Berkhamsted Herts 28 H6
Berkley Som 16 G5
Berkswell W Mid 35 H8
Bermondsey London 19 D10
Bernera Highld 85 F13
Bernice Argyll 73 D10
Bernisdale Highld 85 C9
Berrick Salome Oxon 18 B3
Berriedale Highld 94 H3
Berrier Cumb 56 D5
Berriew Powys 33 E7
Berrington Northumb 71 F9
Berrington Shrops 33 E11
Berrow Som 15 F9
Berrow Green Worcs 26 C4
Berry Down Cross Devon 6 B4
Berry Hill Glos 26 G2
Berry Hill Pembs 22 B5
Berry Pomeroy Devon 5 E9
Berryhillock Moray 88 B5
Berrynarbor Devon 6 B4
Bersham Wrex 42 H6
Berstane Orkney 95 G5
Berwick E Sus 12 F4
Berwick Bassett Wilts 17 D7
Berwick Hill Northumb 63 F7
Berwick St James Wilts 17 H7
Berwick St John Wilts 9 B8
Berwick St Leonard Wilts 9 A8
Berwick-upon-Tweed Northumb 71 E8
Bescar Lancs 43 A6
Besford Worcs 26 D6
Bessacarr S Yorks 45 B10
Bessels Leigh Oxon 17 A11
Bessingby E Yorks 53 C7
Bessingham Norf 39 B7
Bestbeech Hill E Sus 12 C5
Besthorpe Norf 39 F6
Besthorpe Notts 46 F2
Bestwood Nottingham 36 A1
Bestwood Village Notts 45 H9
Beswick E Yorks 52 E6
Betchworth Sur 19 G9
Bethania Ceredig 24 B2
Bethania Gwyn 41 E8
Bethania Gwyn 41 F8
Bethel Anglesey 40 C5
Bethel Gwyn 41 D7
Bethel Gwyn 32 B5
Bethersden Kent 13 B8
Bethesda Gwyn 41 D8
Bethesda Pembs 22 E5
Bethlehem Carms 24 F3
Bethnal Green London 19 C10
Betley Staffs 43 H10
Betsham Kent 20 D3
Betteshanger Kent 21 F10
Bettiscombe Dorset 8 E2
Bettisfield Wrex 33 B10
Betton Shrops 33 E9
Betton Shrops 34 B2
Bettws Bridgend 14 C5
Bettws Mon 25 G9
Bettws Newport 15 B8
Bettws Cedewain Powys 33 F7
Bettws Gwerfil Goch Denb 42 H3
Bettws Ifan Ceredig 23 B8
Bettws Newydd Mon 25 H10
Bettws-y-crwyn Shrops 33 G8
Bettyhill Highld 93 C10
Betws Carms 24 G3
Betws Bledrws Ceredig 23 A10
Betws-Garmon Gwyn 41 E7
Betws-y-Coed Conwy 41 E9
Betws-yn-Rhos Conwy 42 E2
Beulah Ceredig 23 B7
Beulah Powys 24 C6
Bevendean Brighton 12 F2
Bevercotes Notts 45 E10
Beverley E Yorks 52 F6
Beverston Glos 16 B5
Bevington Glos 16 B3
Bewaldeth Cumb 56 C4
Bewcastle Cumb 61 F11
Bewdley Worcs 34 H3
Bewerley N Yorks 51 C7
Bewholme E Yorks 53 D7
Bexhill E Sus 12 F6
Bexley London 19 D11
Bexleyheath London 19 D11
Bexwell Norf 38 E2
Beyton Suff 30 B6
Bhaltos W Isles 90 D5

Bhatarsaigh W Isles 84 J1
Bibury Glos 27 H8
Bicester Oxon 28 F2
Bickenhall Som 8 C1
Bickenhill W Mid 35 G7
Bicker Lincs 37 B8
Bickershaw Gtr Man 43 B9
Bickerstaffe Lancs 43 B7
Bickerton Ches 43 G8
Bickerton N Yorks 51 D10
Bickington Devon 5 D8
Bickington Devon 6 C4
Bickleigh Devon 7 F8
Bickleigh Devon 4 E6
Bickleton Devon 6 C4
Bickley London 19 E11
Bickley Moss Ches 43 H8
Bicknacre Essex 20 A4
Bicknoller Som 7 C10
Bicknor Kent 20 F5
Bickton Hants 9 C10
Bicton Shrops 33 D10
Bicton Shrops 33 G8
Bidborough Kent 12 B4
Biddenden Kent 13 C7
Biddenham Beds 29 D7
Biddestone Wilts 16 D5
Biddisham Som 15 F9
Biddlesden Bucks 28 D3
Biddlestone Northumb 62 C5
Biddulph Staffs 44 G2
Biddulph Moor Staffs 44 G3
Bideford Devon 6 D3
Bidford-on-Avon Warks 27 C8
Bidston Mers 42 C5
Bielby E Yorks 52 E3
Bieldside Aberdeen 83 C10
Bierley I o W 10 G4
Bierley W Yorks 51 F7
Bierton Bucks 28 G5
Big Sand Highld 85 A12
Bigbury Devon 5 G7
Bigbury on Sea Devon 5 G7
Bigby Lincs 46 B4
Biggar Cumb 49 C1
Biggar S Lnrk 69 G9
Biggin Derbys 44 G5
Biggin Derbys 44 H6
Biggin N Yorks 51 F11
Biggin Hill London 19 F11
Biggings Shetland 96 G3
Biggleswade Beds 29 D8
Bighouse Highld 93 C11
Bighton Hants 10 A5
Bignor W Sus 11 C8
Bigton Shetland 96 L5
Bilberry Corn 3 C9
Bilborough Nottingham 35 A11
Bilbrook Som 7 B9
Bilbrough N Yorks 51 E11
Bilbster Highld 94 E4
Bildershaw Durham 58 D3
Bildeston Suff 30 D6
Billericay Essex 20 B3
Billesdon Leics 36 E3
Billesley Warks 27 C8
Billingborough Lincs 37 B7
Billinge Mers 43 B8
Billingford Norf 38 C6
Billingham Stockton 58 D5
Billinghay Lincs 46 G5
Billingley S Yorks 45 B8
Billingshurst W Sus 11 B9
Billingsley Shrops 34 G3
Billington Beds 28 F6
Billington Lancs 50 F3
Billockby Norf 39 D10
Billy Row Durham 58 C2
Bilsborrow Lancs 49 F5
Bilsby Lincs 47 E8
Bilsham W Sus 11 D8
Bilsington Kent 13 C9
Bilson Green Glos 26 G3
Bilsthorpe Notts 45 F10
Bilsthorpe Moor Notts 45 G10
Bilston Midloth 69 D11
Bilston W Mid 34 F5
Bilstone Leics 35 E9
Bilting Kent 21 G7
Bilton E Yorks 53 F7
Bilton Northumb 63 B8
Bilton Warks 27 A11
Bilton in Ainsty N Yorks 51 E10
Bimbister Orkney 95 G4
Binbrook Lincs 46 C6
Binchester Blocks Durham 58 C3
Bincombe Dorset 8 F5
Bindal Highld 87 C12
Binegar Som 16 G3
Binfield Brack 18 D5
Binfield Heath Oxon 18 D4
Bingfield Northumb 62 F5
Bingham Notts 36 B3
Bingley W Yorks 51 F7
Bings Heath Shrops 33 D11
Binham Norf 38 B5
Binley Hants 17 F11
Binley W Mid 35 H9
Binley Woods Warks 35 H9
Binniehill Falk 69 C7
Binsoe N Yorks 51 B8
Binstead I o W 10 E4
Binsted Hants 18 G4
Binton Warks 27 C8
Bintree Norf 38 C6
Binweston Shrops 33 E9
Birch Essex 30 G6
Birch Gtr Man 44 B2
Birch Green Essex 30 G6
Birch Heath Ches 43 F8
Birch Hill Ches 43 E8
Birch Vale Derbys 44 D4
Bircham Newton Norf 38 B3
Bircham Tofts Norf 38 B3
Birchanger Essex 30 F2
Birchencliffe W Yorks 51 H7
Bircher Hereford 25 B11
Birchfield Highld 82 A1
Birchgrove Cardiff 15 D7
Birchgrove Swansea 14 B3
Birchington Kent 21 E9
Birchmoor Warks 35 E8
Birchover Derbys 44 F6
Birchwood Lincs 46 F3
Birchwood Warr 43 C9
Bircotes Notts 45 C10
Birdbrook Essex 30 D4
Birdforth N Yorks 51 B10
Birdham W Sus 11 E7
Birdholme Derbys 45 F7
Birdingbury Warks 27 B11
Birdlip Glos 26 G6
Birds Edge W Yorks 44 B6
Birdsall N Yorks 52 C4
Birdsgreen Shrops 34 G3
Birdsmoor Gate Dorset 8 D2
Birdston E Dunb 68 C5
Birdwell S Yorks 45 B7
Birdwood Glos 26 G4
Birgham Borders 70 G6
Birkby N Yorks 58 F4
Birkdale Mers 49 H3
Birkenhead Mers 42 D6
Birkenhills Aberds 89 D7
Birkenshaw N Lnrk 68 D5
Birkenshaw W Yorks 51 G8
Birkhall Aberds 82 D5
Birkhill Angus 76 D6
Birkhill Dumfries 61 B8
Birkholme Lincs 36 C5
Birkin N Yorks 51 G11
Birley Hereford 25 C11
Birling Kent 20 E3
Birling Northumb 63 C8
Birling Gap E Sus 12 G4
Birlingham Worcs 26 D6
Birmingham W Mid 35 G6
Birmingham International Airport W Mid 35 G7
Birnam Perth 76 C3
Birse Aberds 83 D7
Birsemore Aberds 83 D7
Birstall Leics 36 E1
Birstall W Yorks 51 G8
Birstwith N Yorks 51 D8
Birthorpe Lincs 37 B7
Birtley Hereford 25 B10
Birtley Northumb 62 F4
Birtley T & W 63 H8
Birts Street Worcs 26 E4
Bisbrooke Rutland 36 F4
Biscathorpe Lincs 46 D6
Biscot Luton 29 F7
Bish Mill Devon 7 D6
Bisham Windsor 18 C5
Bishampton Worcs 26 C6
Bishop Auckland Durham 58 D3
Bishop Burton E Yorks 52 F5
Bishop Middleham Durham 58 C4
Bishop Monkton N Yorks 51 C9
Bishop Norton Lincs 46 C3
Bishop Sutton Bath 16 F2
Bishop Thornton N Yorks 51 C8
Bishop Wilton E Yorks 52 D3
Bishopbridge Lincs 46 C4
Bishopbriggs E Dunb 68 D5
Bishopmill Moray 88 B2
Bishops Cannings Wilts 17 E7
Bishop's Castle Shrops 33 G9
Bishop's Caundle Dorset 8 C5
Bishop's Cleeve Glos 26 F6
Bishops Frome Hereford 26 D3
Bishop's Green Essex 30 G3
Bishop's Hull Som 7 D11
Bishop's Itchington Warks 27 C10
Bishops Lydeard Som 7 D10
Bishops Nympton Devon 7 D6
Bishop's Offley Staffs 34 C3
Bishop's Stortford Herts 29 F11
Bishop's Sutton Hants 10 A5
Bishop's Tachbrook Warks 27 B10
Bishops Tawton Devon 6 C4
Bishop's Waltham Hants 10 C4
Bishop's Wood Staffs 34 E4
Bishopsbourne Kent 21 F8
Bishopsteignton Devon 5 D10
Bishopstoke Hants 10 C3
Bishopston Swansea 23 H10
Bishopstone Bucks 28 G5
Bishopstone E Sus 12 F3
Bishopstone Hereford 25 D11
Bishopstone Swindon 17 C9
Bishopstone Wilts 9 B9
Bishopstrow Wilts 16 G5
Bishopswood Som 8 C1
Bishopsworth Bristol 16 E2
Bishopthorpe York 52 E1
Bishopton Darl 58 D4
Bishopton Dumfries 55 E7
Bishopton N Yorks 51 B9
Bishopton Renfs 68 C3
Bishopton Warks 27 C8
Bishton Newport 15 C9
Bisley Glos 26 H6
Bisley Sur 18 F6
Bispham Blkpool 49 E3
Bispham Green Lancs 43 A7
Bissoe Corn 3 E6
Bisterne Close Hants 9 D11
Bitchfield Lincs 36 C5
Bittadon Devon 6 B4
Bittaford Devon 5 F7
Bittering Norf 38 D5
Bitterley Shrops 34 H1
Bitterne Soton 10 C3
Bitteswell Leics 35 G11
Bitton S Glos 16 E3
Bix Oxon 18 C4
Bixter Shetland 96 H5
Blaby Leics 36 F1
Black Bourton Oxon 17 A9
Black Callerton T & W 63 G7
Black Clauchrie S Ayrs 54 A5
Black Corries Lodge Highld 74 B5
Black Crofts Argyll 74 D2
Black Dog Devon 7 F7
Black Heddon Northumb 62 F6
Black Lane Gtr Man 43 B10
Black Marsh Shrops 33 F9
Black Mount Argyll 74 C5
Black Notley Essex 30 F4
Black Pill Swansea 14 B2
Black Tar Pembs 22 F4
Black Torrington Devon 6 F3
Blackacre Dumfries 60 D6
Blackadder West Borders 71 E7
Blackawton Devon 5 F9
Blackborough Devon 7 F9
Blackborough End Norf 38 D2
Blackboys E Sus 12 D4
Blackbrook Derbys 45 H7
Blackbrook Mers 43 C8
Blackbrook Staffs 34 B3
Blackburn Aberds 88 E5
Blackburn Aberds 83 B10
Blackburn Blkburn 50 G2
Blackburn W Loth 69 D8
Blackcraig Dumfries 60 E3
Blackden Heath Ches 43 E10
Blackdog Aberds 83 B11
Blackfell T & W 63 H8
Blackfield Hants 10 D3
Blackford Cumb 61 G9
Blackford Perth 75 G11
Blackford Som 15 G10
Blackford Som 8 B5
Blackfordby Leics 35 D9
Blackgang I o W 10 G3
Blackhall Colliery Durham 58 C5
Blackhall Mill T & W 63 H7
Blackhall Rocks Durham 58 C5
Blackham E Sus 12 C3
Blackhaugh Borders 70 G3
Blackheath Essex 31 F7
Blackheath Suff 31 A11
Blackheath Sur 19 G7
Blackheath W Mid 34 G5
Blackhill Aberds 89 D10
Blackhill Aberds 89 C10
Blackhill Highld 85 C8
Blackhills Highld 87 F12
Blackhills Moray 88 C2
Blackhorse S Glos 16 D3
Blackland Wilts 17 E7
Blackley Gtr Man 44 B2
Blacklunans Perth 76 A4
Blackmill Bridgend 14 C5
Blackmoor Hants 11 A6
Blackmoor Gate Devon 6 B5
Blackmore Essex 20 A3
Blackmore End Essex 30 E4
Blackmore End Herts 29 G8
Blackness Falk 69 C9
Blacknest Hants 18 G4
Blacko Lancs 50 E4
Blackpool Blkpool 49 F3
Blackpool Devon 5 G9
Blackpool Pembs 22 E5
Blackpool Airport Lancs 49 F3
Blackpool Gate Cumb 61 F11
Blackridge W Loth 69 D7
Blackrock Argyll 64 B4
Blackrock Mon 25 G9
Blackrod Gtr Man 43 A9
Blackshaw Dumfries 60 G6
Blackshaw Head W Yorks 50 G5
Blacksmith's Green Suff 31 B8
Blackstone W Sus 11 C11
Blackthorn Oxon 28 G3
Blackthorpe Suff 30 B6
Blacktoft E Yorks 52 G4
Blacktop Aberdeen 83 C10
Blacktown Newport 15 C8
Blackwall Tunnel London 19 D10
Blackwater Corn 2 E6
Blackwater Hants 18 F5
Blackwater I o W 10 F4
Blackwaterfoot N Ayrs 66 D1
Blackwell Darl 58 E3
Blackwell Derbys 44 E5
Blackwell Derbys 45 G8
Blackwell Warks 27 D9
Blackwell Worcs 26 A6
Blackwell W Sus 12 C2
Blackwood S Lnrk 68 F6
Blackwood = Coed Duon Caerph 15 B7
Blackwood Hill Staffs 44 G3
Blacon Ches 43 F6
Bladnoch Dumfries 55 D7
Bladon Oxon 27 G11
Blaen-gwynfi Neath 14 B4
Blaen-waun Carms 23 D7
Blaen-y-coed Carms 23 D8
Blaen-y-Cwm Denb 32 B6
Blaen-y-cwm Gwyn 32 C3
Blaen-y-cwm Powys 33 C6
Blaenannerch Ceredig 23 B7
Blaenau Ffestiniog Gwyn 41 F9
Blaenavon Torf 25 H9
Blaencelyn Ceredig 23 A8
Blaendyryn Powys 24 E6
Blaenffos Pembs 22 C6
Blaengarw Bridgend 14 B5
Blaengwrach Neath 24 H5
Blaenpennal Ceredig 24 B3
Blaenplwyf Ceredig 32 H1
Blaenporth Ceredig 23 B7
Blaenrhondda Rhondda 14 A5
Blaenycwm Ceredig 32 H4
Blagdon N Som 15 F11
Blagdon Torbay 5 E9
Blagdon Hill Som 7 E11
Blagill Cumb 57 B9
Blaguegate Lancs 43 B7
Blaich Highld 80 F2
Blain Highld 79 E9
Blaina Bl Gwent 25 H9
Blair Atholl Perth 81 G10
Blair Drummond Stirl 75 H10
Blairbeg N Ayrs 66 C3
Blairdaff Aberds 83 B8
Blairglas Argyll 68 B2
Blairgowrie Perth 76 C4
Blairhall Fife 69 B9
Blairingone Perth 76 H2
Blairland N Ayrs 66 B6
Blairlogie Stirl 75 H11
Blairlomond Argyll 74 H4
Blairmore Argyll 73 E10
Blairnamarrow Moray 82 B4
Blairquhosh Stirl 68 B4
Blair's Ferry Argyll 73 G8
Blairskaith E Dunb 68 C4
Blaisdon Glos 26 G4
Blakebrook Worcs 34 H4
Blakedown Worcs 34 H4
Blakelaw Borders 70 G6
Blakeley Staffs 34 F4
Blakeley Lane Staffs 44 H3
Blakemere Hereford 25 D10
Blakeney Glos 26 H3
Blakeney Norf 38 A6
Blakenhall Ches 43 H10
Blakenhall W Mid 34 F5
Blakeshall Worcs 34 G4
Blakesley Northants 28 C3
Blanchland Northumb 57 A11
Bland Hill N Yorks 51 D8
Blandford Forum Dorset 9 D7
Blandford St Mary Dorset 9 D7
Blanefield Stirl 68 C4
Blankney Lincs 46 F4
Blantyre S Lnrk 68 E5
Blar a'Chaorainn Highld 80 G3
Blaran Argyll 73 B7
Blarghour Argyll 73 B8
Blarmachfoldach Highld 80 G2
Blarnalearoch Highld 86 B4
Blashford Hants 9 D10
Blaston Leics 36 F4
Blatherwycke Northants 36 F5
Blawith Cumb 56 H4
Blaxhall Suff 31 C10
Blaxton S Yorks 45 B10
Blaydon T & W 63 G7
Bleadon N Som 15 F9
Bleak Hey Nook Gtr Man 44 B4
Blean Kent 21 E8
Bleasby Lincs 46 D5
Bleasby Notts 45 H11
Bleasdale Lancs 50 E1
Bleatarn Cumb 57 E9
Blebocraigs Fife 77 F7
Bleddfa Powys 25 B9
Bledington Glos 27 F9
Bledlow Bucks 18 A4
Bledlow Ridge Bucks 18 B4
Blegbie E Loth 70 D3
Blencarn Cumb 57 C8
Blencogo Cumb 56 B3
Blendworth Hants 10 C6
Blenheim Park Norf 38 B4
Blennerhasset Cumb 56 B3
Blervie Castle Moray 87 F13
Bletchingdon Oxon 28 G2
Bletchingley Sur 19 F10
Bletchley M Keynes 28 E5
Bletchley Shrops 34 B2
Bletherston Pembs 22 D5
Bletsoe Beds 29 C7
Blewbury Oxon 18 C2
Blickling Norf 39 C7
Blidworth Notts 45 G9
Blindburn Northumb 62 B4
Blindcrake Cumb 56 C3
Blindley Heath Sur 19 G10
Blisland Corn 4 D2
Bliss Gate Worcs 26 A4
Blissford Hants 9 C10
Blisworth Northants 28 C4
Blithbury Staffs 35 C6
Blitterlees Cumb 56 A3
Blockley Glos 27 E8
Blofield Norf 39 E9
Blofield Heath Norf 39 D9
Blo'Norton Norf 38 H6
Bloomfield Borders 61 A11
Blore Staffs 44 H5
Blount's Green Staffs 35 B6
Blowick Mers 49 H3
Bloxham Oxon 27 E11
Bloxholm Lincs 46 G4
Bloxwich W Mid 34 E5
Bloxworth Dorset 9 E7
Blubberhouses N Yorks 51 D7
Blue Anchor Som 7 B9
Blue Anchor Swansea 23 G10
Blue Row Essex 31 G7
Blundeston Suff 39 F11
Blunham Beds 29 C8
Blunsdon St Andrew Swindon 17 C8
Bluntington Worcs 26 A5
Bluntisham Cambs 29 A10
Blunts Corn 4 E4
Blyborough Lincs 46 C3
Blyford Suff 39 H10
Blymhill Staffs 34 D4
Blyth Notts 45 D10
Blyth Northumb 63 E9
Blyth Bridge Borders 69 F10
Blythburgh Suff 39 H10
Blythe Borders 70 F4
Blythe Bridge Staffs 34 A5
Blyton Lincs 46 C2
Boarhills Fife 77 F8
Boarhunt Hants 10 D5
Boars Head Gtr Man 43 B8
Boars Hill Oxon 17 A11
Boarshead E Sus 12 C4
Boarstall Bucks 28 G3
Boasley Cross Devon 6 G3
Boat of Garten Highld 81 B11
Boath Highld 87 D8
Bobbing Kent 20 E5
Bobbington Staffs 34 F4
Bobbingworth Essex 30 H2
Bocaddon Corn 4 F2
Bochastle Stirl 75 G9
Bocking Essex 30 F4
Bocking Churchstreet Essex 30 F4
Boddam Aberds 89 D11
Boddam Shetland 96 M5
Boddington Glos 26 F5
Bodedern Anglesey 40 B5
Bodelwyddan Denb 42 E3
Bodenham Hereford 26 C2
Bodenham Wilts 9 B10
Bodenham Moor Hereford 26 C2
Bodermid Gwyn 40 H3
Bodewryd Anglesey 40 A5
Bodfari Denb 42 E3
Bodffordd Anglesey 40 C6
Bodham Norf 39 A7
Bodiam E Sus 13 D6
Bodicote Oxon 27 E11
Bodieve Corn 3 B8
Bodinnick Corn 4 F2
Bodle Street Green E Sus 12 E5
Bodmin Corn 4 E1
Bodney Norf 38 F4
Bodorgan Anglesey 40 D5
Bodsham Kent 21 G8
Boduan Gwyn 40 G5
Bodymoor Heath Warks 35 F7
Bogallan Highld 87 F9
Bogbrae Aberds 89 E10
Bogend Borders 70 F6
Bogend S Ayrs 67 C6
Boghall W Loth 69 D8
Boghead S Lnrk 68 F6
Bogmoor Moray 88 B3
Bogniebrae Aberds 88 D5
Bognor Regis W Sus 11 E8
Bograxie Aberds 83 B9
Bogside N Lnrk 69 E7
Bogton Aberds 89 C6
Bogue Dumfries 55 A9
Bohenie Highld 80 E4
Bohortha Corn 3 F7
Bohuntine Highld 80 E4
Boirseam W Isles 90 J5
Bojewyan Corn 2 F2
Bolam Durham 58 D2
Bolam Northumb 62 E6
Bolberry Devon 5 H7
Bold Heath Mers 43 D8
Boldon T & W 63 G9
Boldon Colliery T & W 63 G9
Boldre Hants 10 E2
Boldron Durham 58 E1
Bole Notts 45 D11
Bolehill Derbys 44 G6
Boleside Borders 70 G3
Bolham Devon 7 E8
Bolham Water Devon 7 E10
Bolingey Corn 3 D6
Bollington Ches 44 E3
Bollington Cross Ches 44 E3
Bolney W Sus 12 D1
Bolnhurst Beds 29 C7
Bolshan Angus 77 B9
Bolsover Derbys 45 E8
Bolsterstone S Yorks 44 C6
Bolstone Hereford 26 E2
Boltby N Yorks 58 H5
Bolter End Bucks 18 B4
Bolton Cumb 57 D8
Bolton E Loth 70 C4
Bolton E Yorks 52 D3
Bolton Gtr Man 43 B10
Bolton Northumb 63 B7
Bolton Abbey N Yorks 51 D6
Bolton Bridge N Yorks 51 D6
Bolton-by-Bowland Lancs 50 E3
Bolton le Sands Lancs 49 C4
Bolton Low Houses Cumb 56 B4
Bolton-on-Swale N Yorks 58 G3
Bolton Percy N Yorks 51 E11
Bolton Town End Lancs 49 C4
Bolton upon Dearne S Yorks 45 B8
Boltonfellend Cumb 61 G10
Boltongate Cumb 56 B4
Bolventor Corn 4 D2
Bomere Heath Shrops 33 D10
Bon-y-maen Swansea 14 B2
Bonar Bridge Highld 87 B9
Bonawe Argyll 74 D3
Bonby N Lincs 52 H6
Boncath Pembs 23 C7
Bonchester Bridge Borders 61 B11
Bonchurch I o W 10 G4
Bondleigh Devon 6 F5
Bonehill Devon 5 D8
Bonehill Staffs 35 E7
Bo'ness Falk 69 B8
Bonhill W Dunb 68 C2
Boningale Shrops 34 E4
Bonjedward Borders 62 A2
Bonkle N Lnrk 69 E7
Bonnavoulin Highld 79 F8
Bonnington Edin 69 D10
Bonnington Kent 13 C9
Bonnybank Fife 76 G6
Bonnybridge Falk 69 B7
Bonnykelly Aberds 89 C8
Bonnyrigg and Lasswade Midloth 70 D2
Bonnyton Aberds 89 E6
Bonnyton Angus 76 D6
Bonnyton Angus 77 B9
Bonsall Derbys 44 G6
Bonskeid House Perth 75 A11
Bont Mon 25 G10
Bont-Dolgadfan Powys 32 E4
Bont-goch Ceredig 32 G2
Bont-newydd Conwy 42 E3
Bont Newydd Gwyn 41 F9
Bont Newydd Gwyn 32 C3
Bontddu Gwyn 32 D2
Bonthorpe Lincs 47 E8
Bontnewydd Ceredig 24 B3
Bontnewydd Gwyn 40 E6
Bontuchel Denb 42 G3
Bonvilston V Glam 14 D6
Booker Bucks 18 B5
Boon Borders 70 F4
Boosbeck Redcar 59 E7
Boot Cumb 56 F3
Boot Street Suff 31 D9
Booth W Yorks 50 G6
Booth Wood W Yorks 50 H6
Boothby Graffoe Lincs 46 G3
Boothby Pagnell Lincs 36 B5
Boothen Stoke 34 A4
Boothferry E Yorks 52 G3
Boothville Northants 28 B4
Bootle Cumb 56 H3
Bootle Mers 42 C6
Booton Norf 39 C7
Boquhan Stirl 68 B4
Boraston Shrops 26 A3
Borden Kent 20 E5
Borden W Sus 11 B7
Bordley N Yorks 50 C5
Bordon Hants 18 H5
Bordon Camp Hants 18 H4
Boreham Essex 30 H4
Boreham Wilts 16 G5
Boreham Street E Sus 12 E5
Borehamwood Herts 19 B8
Boreland Dumfries 61 D7
Boreland Stirl 75 D8
Borgh W Isles 84 H1
Borgh W Isles 90 J4
Borghastan W Isles 90 C7
Borgie Highld 93 D9
Borgue Dumfries 55 E9
Borgue Highld 94 H3
Borley Essex 30 D5
Bornais W Isles 84 F2
Bornesketaig Highld 85 A8
Borness Dumfries 55 E9
Borough Green Kent 20 F3
Boroughbridge N Yorks 51 C9
Borras Head Wrex 42 G6
Borreraig Highld 84 C6
Borrobol Lodge Highld 93 G11
Borrowash Derbys 35 B10
Borrowby N Yorks 58 H5
Borrowdale Cumb 56 E4
Borrowfield Aberds 83 D10
Borth Ceredig 32 F2
Borth-y-Gest Gwyn 41 G7
Borthwickbrae Borders 61 B10
Borthwickshiels Borders 61 B10
Borve Highld 85 D9
Borve Lodge W Isles 90 H5
Borwick Lancs 49 B5
Bosavern Corn 2 F2
Bosbury Hereford 26 D3
Boscastle Corn 4 B2
Boscombe Bmouth 9 E10
Boscombe Wilts 17 H9
Boscoppa Corn 3 D9
Bosham W Sus 11 D7
Bosherston Pembs 22 G4
Boskenna Corn 2 G3
Bosley Ches 44 F3
Bossall N Yorks 52 C3
Bossiney Corn 4 C1
Bossingham Kent 21 G8
Bossington Som 7 B7
Bostock Green Ches 43 F9
Boston Lincs 37 A9
Boston Long Hedges Lincs 47 H7
Boston Spa W Yorks 51 E10
Boston West Lincs 46 H6
Boswinger Corn 3 E8
Botallack Corn 2 F2
Botany Bay London 19 B9
Botcherby Cumb 61 H10
Botcheston Leics 35 E10
Botesdale Suff 38 H6
Bothal Northumb 63 E8
Bothamsall Notts 45 E10
Bothel Cumb 56 C3
Bothenhampton Dorset 8 E3
Bothwell S Lnrk 68 E6
Botley Bucks 18 A6
Botley Hants 10 C4
Botley Oxon 27 H11
Botolph Claydon Bucks 28 F4
Botolphs W Sus 11 D10
Bottacks Highld 86 E7
Bottesford Leics 36 B4
Bottesford N Lincs 46 B2
Bottisham Cambs 30 B2
Bottlesford Wilts 17 F8
Bottom Boat W Yorks 51 G9
Bottom House Staffs 44 G4
Bottom of Hutton Lancs 49 G4
Bottom o'th'Moor Gtr Man 43 A9
Bottomcraig Fife 76 E6
Botusfleming Corn 4 E5
Botwnnog Gwyn 40 G4
Bough Beech Kent 19 G11
Boughrood Powys 25 E8
Boughspring Glos 16 B2
Boughton Norf 38 E2
Boughton Notts 45 F10
Boughton Northants 28 B4
Boughton Aluph Kent 21 G7
Boughton Lees Kent 21 G7
Boughton Malherbe Kent 20 G5
Boughton Monchelsea Kent 20 F4
Boughton Street Kent 21 F7
Boulby Redcar 59 E8
Boulden Shrops 33 G11
Boulmer Northumb 63 B8
Boulston Pembs 22 E4
Boultenstone Aberds 82 B6
Boultham Lincs 46 F3
Bourn Cambs 29 C10
Bourne Lincs 37 C6
Bourne End Beds 28 D6
Bourne End Bucks 18 C5
Bourne End Herts 29 H7
Bournemouth Bmouth 9 E9
Bournemouth International Airport Dorset 9 E10
Bournes Green Glos 16 A6
Bournes Green Sthend 20 C6
Bournheath Worcs 26 A6
Bournmoor Durham 58 A4
Bournville W Mid 34 G6
Bourton Dorset 9 A6
Bourton N Som 15 E9
Bourton Oxon 17 C9
Bourton Shrops 34 F1
Bourton on Dunsmore Warks 27 A11
Bourton on the Hill Glos 27 E8
Bourton-on-the-Water Glos 27 F8
Bousd Argyll 78 E5
Boustead Hill Cumb 61 H8
Bouth Cumb 56 H5
Bouthwaite N Yorks 51 B7
Boveney Bucks 18 D6
Boverton V Glam 14 E5
Bovey Tracey Devon 5 D9
Bovingdon Herts 19 A7
Bovingdon Green Bucks 18 C5
Bovingdon Green Herts 19 A7
Bovinger Essex 30 H2
Bovington Camp Dorset 9 F7
Bow Borders 70 F3
Bow Devon 6 F6
Bow Orkney 95 J4
Bow Brickhill M Keynes 28 E6
Bow of Fife Fife 76 F6
Bow Street Ceredig 32 G2
Bowbank Durham 57 D11
Bowburn Durham 58 C4
Bowcombe I o W 10 F3
Bowd Devon 7 G10
Bowden Borders 70 G4
Bowden Devon 5 G9
Bowden Hill Wilts 16 E6
Bowderdale Cumb 57 F8
Bowdon Gtr Man 43 D10
Bower Northumb 62 E3
Bower Hinton Som 8 C3
Bowerchalke Wilts 9 B9
Bowerhill Wilts 16 E6
Bowermadden Highld 94 D4
Bowers Gifford Essex 20 C4
Bowershall Fife 69 A9
Bowertower Highld 94 D4
Bowes Durham 57 E11
Bowgreave Lancs 49 E4
Bowgreen Gtr Man 43 D10
Bowhill Borders 70 H3
Bowhouse Dumfries 60 G6
Bowland Bridge Cumb 56 H6
Bowley Hereford 26 C2
Bowlhead Green Sur 18 H6
Bowling W Dunb 68 C3
Bowling W Yorks 51 F7
Bowling Bank Wrex 43 H6
Bowling Green Worcs 26 C5
Bowmanstead Cumb 56 G5
Bowmore Argyll 64 C4
Bowness-on-Solway Cumb 61 G8
Bowness-on-Windermere Cumb 56 G6
Bowsden Northumb 71 F8
Bowside Lodge Highld 93 C11
Bowston Cumb 57 G6
Bowthorpe Norf 39 E7
Box Glos 16 A5
Box Wilts 16 E5
Box End Beds 29 D7
Boxbush Glos 26 G4
Boxford Suff 30 D6
Boxford W Berks 17 D11
Boxgrove W Sus 11 D8
Boxley Kent 20 F4
Boxmoor Herts 29 H7
Boxted Essex 30 E6
Boxted Suff 30 C5
Boxted Cross Essex 31 E7
Boxted Heath Essex 31 E7
Boxworth Cambs 29 B10
Boxworth End Cambs 29 B10
Boyden Gate Kent 21 E9
Boylestone Derbys 35 B7
Boyndie Aberds 89 B6
Boynton E Yorks 53 C7
Boysack Angus 77 C9
Boyton Corn 6 G2
Boyton Suff 31 D10
Boyton Wilts 16 H6
Boyton Cross Essex 30 H3
Boyton End Suff 30 D4
Bozeat Northants 28 C6
Braaid I o M 48 E3
Braal Castle Highld 94 D3
Brabling Green Suff 31 B9
Brabourne Kent 13 B9
Brabourne Lees Kent 13 B9
Brabster Highld 94 D5
Bracadale Highld 85 E8
Bracara Highld 79 B10
Braceborough Lincs 37 D6
Bracebridge Lincs 46 F3
Bracebridge Heath Lincs 46 F3
Bracebridge Low Fields Lincs 46 F3
Braceby Lincs 36 B6
Bracewell Lancs 50 E4
Brackenfield Derbys 45 G7
Brackenthwaite Cumb 56 B4
Brackenthwaite N Yorks 51 D8
Bracklesham W Sus 11 E7
Brackletter Highld 80 E3
Brackley Argyll 65 D8
Brackley Northants 28 E2
Brackloch Highld 92 G4
Bracknell Brack 18 E5
Braco Perth 75 G11
Bracobrae Moray 88 C5
Bracon Ash Norf 39 F7
Bracorina Highld 79 B10
Bradbourne Derbys 44 G6
Bradbury Durham 58 D4
Bradda I o M 48 F1
Bradden Northants 28 D3
Braddock Corn 4 E2
Bradeley Stoke 44 G2
Bradenham Bucks 18 B5
Bradenham Norf 38 E5
Bradenstoke Wilts 17 D7
Bradfield Essex 31 E8
Bradfield Norf 39 B8
Bradfield W Berks 18 D3
Bradfield Combust Suff 30 C5
Bradfield Green Ches 43 G9
Bradfield Heath Essex 31 F8
Bradfield St Clare Suff 30 C6
Bradfield St George Suff 30 B6
Bradford Corn 4 D2
Bradford Derbys 44 F6
Bradford Devon 6 F3
Bradford Northumb 71 G10
Bradford W Yorks 51 F7
Bradford Abbas Dorset 8 C4
Bradford Leigh Wilts 16 E5
Bradford-on-Avon Wilts 16 E5
Bradford on Tone Som 7 D10
Bradford Peverell Dorset 8 E5
Brading I o W 10 F5
Bradley Derbys 44 H6
Bradley Hants 18 G3
Bradley NE Lincs 46 B6
Bradley Staffs 34 D4
Bradley W Mid 34 F5
Bradley W Yorks 51 G7
Bradley Green Worcs 26 B6
Bradley in the Moors Staffs 35 A6
Bradlow Hereford 26 E4
Bradmore Notts 36 B1
Bradmore W Mid 34 F4
Bradninch Devon 7 F9
Bradnop Staffs 44 G4
Bradpole Dorset 8 E3
Bradshaw Gtr Man 43 A10
Bradshaw W Yorks 44 A4
Bradstone Devon 4 C4
Bradwall Green Ches 43 F10
Bradway S Yorks 45 D7
Bradwell Derbys 44 D5
Bradwell Essex 30 F5
Bradwell M Keynes 28 E5
Bradwell Norf 39 E11
Bradwell Staffs 44 H2
Bradwell Grove Oxon 27 H9
Bradwell on Sea Essex 31 H7
Bradwell Waterside Essex 30 H6
Bradworthy Devon 6 E2
Bradworthy Cross Devon 6 E2
Brae Dumfries 60 F4
Brae Highld 91 J13
Brae Highld 92 J7
Brae Shetland 96 G5
Brae of Achnahaird Highld 92 H3
Brae Roy Lodge Highld 80 D5
Braeantra Highld 87 D8
Braedownie Angus 82 F4
Braefield Highld 86 H7
Braegrum Perth 76 E3
Braehead Dumfries 55 D7
Braehead Orkney 95 H6
Braehead Orkney 95 D5
Braehead S Lnrk 69 G7
Braehead S Lnrk 69 E8
Braehead of Lunan Angus 77 B9
Braehoulland Shetland 96 F4
Braehungie Highld 94 G3
Braelangwell Lodge Highld 87 B8
Braemar Aberds 82 D3
Braemore Highld 94 G2
Braemore Highld 86 D4
Braes of Enzie Moray 88 C3
Braeside Invclyd 73 F11
Braeswick Orkney 95 E7
Braewick Shetland 96 H5
Brafferton Darl 58 D3
Brafferton N Yorks 51 B10
Brafield-on-the-Green Northants 28 C5
Bragar W Isles 91 C7
Bragbury End Herts 29 F9
Bragleenmore Argyll 74 E2
Braichmelyn Gwyn 41 D8
Braid Edin 69 D11
Braides Lancs 49 D4
Braidley N Yorks 50 A6
Braidwood S Lnrk 69 F7
Braigo Argyll 64 B3
Brailsford Derbys 35 A8
Brainshaugh Northumb 63 C8
Braintree Essex 30 F4
Braiseworth Suff 31 A8
Braishfield Hants 10 B2
Braithwaite Cumb 56 D4
Braithwaite S Yorks 45 A10
Braithwaite W Yorks 50 E6
Braithwell S Yorks 45 C9
Bramber W Sus 11 C10
Bramcote Notts 35 B11
Bramcote Warks 35 G10
Bramdean Hants 10 B5
Bramerton Norf 39 E8
Bramfield Herts 29 G9
Bramfield Suff 31 A10
Bramford Suff 31 D8
Bramhall Gtr Man 44 D2
Bramham W Yorks 51 E10
Bramhope W Yorks 51 E8
Bramley Hants 18 F3
Bramley Sur 19 G7
Bramley S Yorks 45 C8
Bramley W Yorks 51 F8
Bramling Kent 21 F9
Brampford Speke Devon 7 G8
Brampton Cambs 29 A9
Brampton Cumb 57 D8
Brampton Cumb 61 G11
Brampton Derbys 45 E7
Brampton Hereford 25 E11
Brampton Lincs 46 E2
Brampton Norf 39 C8
Brampton Suff 39 G10
Brampton S Yorks 45 B8
Brampton Abbotts Hereford 26 F3
Brampton Ash Northants 36 G3
Brampton Bryan Hereford 25 A10
Brampton en le Morthen S Yorks 45 D8
Bramshall Staffs 35 B6
Bramshaw Hants 10 C1
Bramshill Hants 18 E4
Bramshott Hants 11 A7
Bran End Essex 30 F3
Branault Highld 79 E8
Brancaster Norf 38 A3
Brancaster Staithe Norf 38 A3
Brancepeth Durham 58 C3
Branch End Northumb 62 G6
Branchill Moray 87 F13
Brand Green Glos 26 F4
Branderburgh Moray 88 A2
Brandesburton E Yorks 53 E7
Brandeston Suff 31 B9
Brandhill Shrops 33 H10
Brandis Corner Devon 6 F3
Brandiston Norf 39 C7
Brandon Durham 58 C3
Brandon Lincs 46 H3
Brandon Northumb 62 B6
Brandon Suff 38 G3
Brandon Warks 35 H10
Brandon Bank Norf 38 G2
Brandon Creek Norf 38 F2
Brandon Parva Norf 39 E6
Brandsby N Yorks 52 B1
Brandy Wharf Lincs 46 C4
Brane Corn 2 G3
Branksome Poole 9 E9
Branksome Park Poole 9 E9
Bransby Lincs 46 E2
Branscombe Devon 7 H10
Bransford Worcs 26 C4
Bransgore Hants 9 E10
Branshill Clack 69 A7
Bransholme Hull 53 F7
Branson's Cross Worcs 27 A7
Branston Leics 36 C4
Branston Lincs 46 F4
Branston Staffs 35 C8
Branston Booths Lincs 46 F4
Branstone I o W 10 F4
Bransty Cumb 56 E1
Brant Broughton Lincs 46 G3
Brantham Suff 31 E8
Branthwaite Cumb 56 D2
Branthwaite Cumb 56 C4
Brantingham E Yorks 52 G5
Branton Northumb 62 B6
Branton S Yorks 45 B10
Branxholm Park Borders 61 B10
Branxholme Borders 61 B10
Branxton Northumb 71 G7
Brassey Green Ches 43 F8
Brassington Derbys 44 G6
Brasted Kent 19 F11
Brasted Chart Kent 19 F11
Brathens Aberds 83 D8
Bratoft Lincs 47 F8
Brattleby Lincs 46 D3
Bratton Telford 34 D2
Bratton Wilts 16 F6
Bratton Clovelly Devon 6 G3
Bratton Fleming Devon 6 C5
Bratton Seymour Som 8 B5
Braughing Herts 29 F10
Braunston Northants 28 B2
Braunston-in-Rutland Rutland 36 E4
Braunstone Town Leics 36 E1
Braunton Devon 6 C3
Brawby N Yorks 52 B3
Brawl Highld 93 C11
Brawlbin Highld 94 E2
Bray Windsor 18 D6
Bray Shop Corn 4 D4
Bray Wick Windsor 18 D5
Braybrooke Northants 36 G3
Braye Ald 11
Brayford Devon 6 C5
Braystones Cumb 56 F2
Braythorn N Yorks 51 E8
Brayton N Yorks 52 F2
Brazacott Corn 6 G1
Breach Kent 20 E5
Breachacha Castle Argyll 78 F4
Breachwood Green Herts 29 F8
Breacleit W Isles 90 D6
Breaden Heath Shrops 33 B10
Breadsall Derbys 35 B9
Breadstone Glos 16 A4
Breage Corn 2 G5
Breakachy Highld 86 G7
Bream Glos 26 H3
Breamore Hants 9 C10
Brean Som 15 F8
Breanais W Isles 90 E4
Brearton N Yorks 51 C9
Breascleit W Isles 90 D7
Breaston Derbys 35 B10
Brechfa Carms 23 C10
Brechin Angus 77 A8
Breck of Cruan Orkney 95 G4
Breckan Orkney 95 H3
Breckrey Highld 85 B10
Brecon = Aberhonddu Powys 25 F7
Bredbury Gtr Man 44 C3
Brede E Sus 13 E7
Bredenbury Hereford 26 C3
Bredfield Suff 31 C9
Bredgar Kent 20 E5
Bredhurst Kent 20 E4
Bredicot Worcs 26 C6
Bredon Worcs 26 E6
Bredon's Norton Worcs 26 E6
Bredwardine Hereford 25 D10
Breedon on the Hill Leics 35 C10
Breibhig W Isles 84 J1
Breibhig W Isles 91 D9
Breich W Loth 69 D8
Breightmet Gtr Man 43 B10
Breighton E Yorks 52 F3
Breinton Hereford 25 E11
Breinton Common Hereford 25 D11
Breiwick Shetland 96 J6
Bremhill Wilts 16 D6
Bremirehoull Shetland 96 L6
Brenchley Kent 12 B5
Brendon Devon 7 B6
Brenkley T & W 63 F8
Brent Eleigh Suff 30 D6
Brent Knoll Som 15 F9
Brent Pelham Herts 29 E11
Brentford London 19 D8
Brentingby Leics 36 D3
Brentwood Essex 20 B2
Brenzett Kent 13 D9
Brereton Staffs 35 D6
Brereton Green Ches 43 F10
Brereton Heath Ches 44 F2
Bressingham Norf 39 G6
Bretby Derbys 35 C8
Bretford Warks 35 H10
Bretforton Worcs 27 D7
Bretherdale Head Cumb 57 F7
Bretherton Lancs 49 G4
Brettabister Shetland 96 H6
Brettenham Norf 38 G5
Brettenham Suff 30 C6
Bretton Derbys 44 E6
Bretton Flint 42 F6
Brewer Street Sur 19 F10
Brewlands Bridge Angus 76 A4
Brewood Staffs 34 E4
Briach Moray 87 F13
Briants Puddle Dorset 9 E7
Brick End Essex 30 F2
Brickendon Herts 29 H10
Bricket Wood Herts 19 A8
Bricklehampton Worcs 26 D6
Bride I o M 48 B4
Bridekirk Cumb 56 C3
Bridell Pembs 22 B6
Bridestowe Devon 4 C6
Brideswell Aberds 88 E5
Bridford Devon 5 C9
Bridfordmills Devon 5 C9
Bridge Kent 21 F8
Bridge End Lincs 37 B7
Bridge Green Essex 29 E11
Bridge Hewick N Yorks 51 B9
Bridge of Alford Aberds 83 B7
Bridge of Allan Stirl 75 H10
Bridge of Avon Moray 88 E1
Bridge of Awe Argyll 74 E3
Bridge of Balgie Perth 75 C8
Bridge of Cally Perth 76 B4
Bridge of Canny Aberds 83 D8
Bridge of Craigisla Angus 76 B5
Bridge of Dee Dumfries 55 D10
Bridge of Don Aberdeen 83 B11
Bridge of Dun Angus 77 B9
Bridge of Dye Aberds 83 E8
Bridge of Earn Perth 76 F4
Bridge of Ericht Perth 75 B8
Bridge of Feugh Aberds 83 D9
Bridge of Forss Highld 93 C13
Bridge of Gairn Aberds 82 D5
Bridge of Gaur Perth 75 B8
Bridge of Muchalls Aberds 83 D10
Bridge of Oich Highld 80 C5
Bridge of Orchy Argyll 74 D5
Bridge of Waith Orkney 95 G3
Bridge of Walls Shetland 96 H4
Bridge of Weir Renfs 68 D2
Bridge Sollers Hereford 25 D11
Bridge Street Suff 30 D5
Bridge Trafford Ches 43 E7
Bridge Yate S Glos 16 D3
Bridgefoot Angus 76 D6
Bridgefoot Cumb 56 D2
Bridgehampton Som 8 B4
Bridgehill Durham 58 A1
Bridgemary Hants 10 D4
Bridgemont Derbys 44 D4
Bridgend Aberds 88 E5
Bridgend Aberds 83 B7
Bridgend Angus 83 G7
Bridgend Argyll 73 D7
Bridgend Argyll 64 B4
Bridgend Argyll 65 E8
Bridgend Cumb 56 E5
Bridgend Fife 76 F6
Bridgend Moray 88 E3
Bridgend N Lnrk 68 C5
Bridgend Pembs 22 B6
Bridgend W Loth 69 C9
Bridgend = Pen-y-bont ar Ogwr Bridgend 14 D5
Bridgend of Lintrathen Angus 76 B5
Bridgerule Devon 6 F1
Bridges Shrops 33 F9
Bridgeton Glasgow 68 D5
Bridgetown Corn 4 C4
Bridgetown Som 7 C8
Bridgham Norf 38 G5
Bridgnorth Shrops 34 F3
Bridgtown Staffs 34 E5
Bridgwater Som 15 H9
Bridlington E Yorks 53 C7
Bridport Dorset 8 E3
Bridstow Hereford 26 F2
Brierfield Lancs 50 F4
Brierley Glos 26 G3
Brierley Hereford 25 C11
Brierley S Yorks 45 A8
Brierley Hill W Mid 34 G5
Briery Hill Bl Gwent 25 H8
Brig o'Turk Stirl 75 G8
Brigg N Lincs 46 B4
Briggswath N Yorks 59 F9
Brigham Cumb 56 C2
Brigham E Yorks 53 D6
Brighouse W Yorks 51 G7
Brighstone I o W 10 F3
Brightgate Derbys 44 G6
Brighthampton Oxon 17 A10
Brightling E Sus 12 D5
Brightlingsea Essex 31 G7
Brighton Brighton 12 F2
Brighton Corn 3 D8
Brighton Hill Hants 18 G3
Brightons Falk 69 C8
Brightwalton W Berks 17 D11
Brightwell Suff 31 D9
Brightwell Baldwin Oxon 18 B3
Brightwell cum Sotwell Oxon 18 B2
Brignall Durham 58 E1
Brigsley NE Lincs 46 B6
Brigsteer Cumb 57 H6
Brigstock Northants 36 G5
Brill Bucks 28 G3
Brilley Hereford 25 D9
Brimaston Pembs 22 D4
Brimfield Hereford 26 B2
Brimington Derbys 45 E8
Brimley Devon 5 D8
Brimpsfield Glos 26 G6
Brimpton W Berks 18 E2
Brims Orkney 95 K3
Brimscombe Glos 16 A5
Brimstage Mers 42 D6
Brinacory Highld 79 B10
Brind E Yorks 52 F3
Brindister Shetland 96 H4
Brindister Shetland 96 K6
Brindle Lancs 50 G2
Brindley Ford Staffs 44 G2
Brineton Staffs 34 D4
Bringhurst Leics 36 F4
Brington Cambs 37 H6
Brinian Orkney 95 F5
Briningham Norf 38 B6
Brinkhill Lincs 47 E7
Brinkley Cambs 30 C3
Brinklow Warks 35 H10
Brinkworth Wilts 17 C7

Cas – Com 121

Castle Eden Durham 58 C5
Castle Forbes Aberds 83 B8
Castle Frome Hereford 26 D3
Castle Green Sur 18 E6
Castle Gresley Derbys 35 D8
Castle Heaton Northumb 71 F8
Castle Hedingham Essex 30 E4
Castle Hill Kent 12 B5
Castle Huntly Perth 76 E6
Castle Kennedy Dumfries 54 D4
Castle O'er Dumfries 61 D8
Castle Pulverbatch Shrops 33 E10
Castle Rising Norf 38 C2
Castle Stuart Highld 87 G10
Castlebay = Bagh a Chaisteil W Isles 84 J1
Castlebythe Pembs 22 D5
Castlecary N Lnrk 68 C6
Castlecraig Highld 87 E11
Castlefairn Dumfries 60 E3
Castleford W Yorks 51 G10
Castlehill Borders 69 G11
Castlehill Highld 94 D3
Castlehill W Dunb 68 C2
Castlemaddy Dumfries 67 H8
Castlemartin Pembs 22 G4
Castlemilk Dumfries 61 F7
Castlemilk Glasgow 68 E5
Castlemorris Pembs 22 C4
Castlemorton Worcs 26 E4
Castleside Durham 58 B1
Castlethorpe M Keynes 28 D5
Castleton Angus 76 C6
Castleton Argyll 73 E7
Castleton Derbys 44 D5
Castleton Gtr Man 44 A2
Castleton Newport 15 C8
Castleton N Yorks 59 F7
Castletown Ches 43 G7
Castletown Highld 94 D3
Castletown Highld 87 G10
Castletown I o M 48 F2
Castletown T & W 63 H9
Castleweary Borders 61 C10
Castley N Yorks 51 E8
Caston Norf 38 F5
Castor P'boro 37 F7
Catacol N Ayrs 66 B2
Catbrain S Glos 16 C2
Catbrook Mon 15 A11
Catchall Corn 2 G3
Catchems Corner W Mid 35 H8
Catchgate Durham 58 A2
Catcleugh Northumb 62 C3
Catcliffe S Yorks 45 D8
Catcott Som 15 H9
Caterham Sur 19 F10
Catfield Norf 39 C9
Catfirth Shetland 96 H6
Catford London 19 D10
Catforth Lancs 49 F4
Cathays Cardiff 15 D7
Cathcart Glasgow 68 D4
Cathedine Powys 25 F8
Catherington Hants 10 C5
Catherton Shrops 34 H2
Catlodge Highld 81 D8
Catlowdy Cumb 61 F10
Catmore W Berks 17 C11
Caton Lancs 49 C5
Caton Green Lancs 49 C5
Catrine E Ayrs 67 D8
Cat's Ash Newport 15 B9
Catsfield E Sus 12 E6
Catshill Worcs 26 A6
Cattal N Yorks 51 D10
Cattawade Suff 31 E8
Catterall Lancs 49 E4
Catterick N Yorks 58 G3
Catterick Bridge N Yorks 58 G3
Catterick Garrison N Yorks 58 G2
Catterlen Cumb 57 C6
Catterline Aberds 83 F10
Catterton N Yorks 51 E11
Catthorpe Leics 36 H1
Cattistock Dorset 8 E4
Catton Northumb 62 H4
Catton N Yorks 51 B9
Catwick E Yorks 53 E7
Catworth Cambs 29 A7
Caudlesprings Norf 38 E5
Caulcott Oxon 28 F2
Cauldcots Angus 77 C9
Cauldhame Stirl 68 A5
Cauldmill Borders 61 B11
Cauldon Staffs 44 H4
Caulkerbush Dumfries 60 H5
Caulside Dumfries 61 E10
Caunsall Worcs 34 G4
Caunton Notts 45 G11
Causeway End Dumfries 55 C7
Causeway Foot W Yorks 51 F6
Causeway-head Stirl 75 H10
Causewayend S Lnrk 69 G9
Causewayhead Cumb 56 A3
Causey Park Bridge Northumb 63 D7
Causeyend Aberds 83 B11
Cautley Cumb 57 G8
Cavendish Suff 30 D5
Cavendish Bridge Leics 35 C10
Cavenham Suff 30 B4
Caversfield Oxon 28 F2
Caversham Reading 18 D4
Caverswall Staffs 34 A5
Cavil E Yorks 52 F3
Cawdor Highld 87 F11
Cawkwell Lincs 46 E6
Cawood N Yorks 52 F1
Cawsand Corn 4 F5
Cawston Norf 39 C7
Cawthorne S Yorks 44 B6
Cawthorpe Lincs 37 C6
Cawton N Yorks 52 B2
Caxton Cambs 29 C10
Caynham Shrops 26 A2
Caythorpe Lincs 46 H3
Caythorpe Notts 45 H10
Cayton N Yorks 53 A6
Ceann a Bhaigh W Isles 84 B2
Ceann a Deas Loch Baghasdail W Isles 84 G2
Ceann Shiphoirt W Isles 91 F7
Ceann Tarabhaigh W Isles 90 F7
Ceannacroc Lodge Highld 80 B4
Cearsiadair W Isles 91 E8
Cefn Berain Conwy 42 F2
Cefn-brith Conwy 42 G2
Cefn Canol Powys 33 B8
Cefn-coch Conwy 41 D10
Cefn Coch Powys 33 C7
Cefn-coed-y-cymmer M Tydf 25 H7
Cefn Cribbwr Bridgend 14 C4
Cefn Cross Bridgend 14 C4
Cefn-ddwysarn Gwyn 32 B5
Cefn Einion Shrops 33 G8
Cefn-gorwydd Powys 24 D6
Cefn-mawr Wrex 33 A8
Cefn-y-bedd Flint 42 G6
Cefn-y-pant Carms 22 D6
Cefneithin Carms 23 E10
Cei-bach Ceredig 23 A9
Ceinewydd = New Quay Ceredig 23 A8
Ceint Anglesey 40 C6
Cellan Ceredig 24 D3
Cellarhead Staffs 44 H3
Cemaes Anglesey 40 A5
Cemmaes Powys 32 E4
Cemmaes Road Powys 32 E4
Cenarth Carms 23 B7
Cenin Gwyn 40 F6
Central Invclyd 73 F11
Ceos W Isles 91 E8
Ceres Fife 77 F7
Cerne Abbas Dorset 8 D5
Cerney Wick Glos 17 B7
Cerrigceinwen Anglesey 40 C6
Cerrigydrudion Conwy 42 H2
Cessford Borders 62 A3
Ceunant Gwyn 41 D7
Chaceley Glos 26 E5
Chacewater Corn 3 E6
Chackmore Bucks 28 E3
Chacombe Northants 27 D11
Chad Valley W Mid 34 G6
Chadderton Gtr Man 44 B3
Chadderton Fold Gtr Man 44 B2
Chaddesden Derby 35 B9
Chaddesley Corbett Worcs 26 A5
Chaddleworth W Berks 17 D11
Chadlington Oxon 27 F10
Chadshunt Warks 27 C10
Chadwell Leics 36 C3
Chadwell St Mary Thurrock 20 D3
Chadwick End W Mid 27 A9
Chadwick Green Mers 43 C8
Chaffcombe Som 8 C2
Chagford Devon 5 C8
Chailey E Sus 12 E2
Chain Bridge Lincs 37 A9
Chainbridge Cambs 37 E10
Chainhurst Kent 20 G4
Chalbury Dorset 9 D9
Chalbury Common Dorset 9 D9
Chaldon Sur 19 F10
Chaldon Herring Dorset 9 F6
Chale I o W 10 G3
Chale Green I o W 10 G3
Chalfont Common Bucks 19 B7
Chalfont St Giles Bucks 18 B6
Chalfont St Peter Bucks 19 B7
Chalford Glos 16 A5
Chalgrove Oxon 18 B3
Chalk Kent 20 D3
Challacombe Devon 6 B5
Challoch Dumfries 54 C6
Challock Kent 21 F7
Chalton Beds 29 F7
Chalton Hants 10 C6
Chalvington E Sus 12 F4
Chancery Ceredig 32 H1
Chandler's Ford Hants 10 B3
Channel Tunnel Kent 21 H8
Channerwick Shetland 96 L6
Chantry Som 16 G4
Chantry Suff 31 D8
Chapel Fife 69 A11
Chapel Allerton Som 15 F10
Chapel Allerton W Yorks 51 F9
Chapel Amble Corn 3 B8
Chapel Brampton Northants 28 B4
Chapel Chorlton Staffs 34 B4
Chapel-en-le-Frith Derbys 44 D4
Chapel End Warks 35 F9
Chapel Green Warks 35 G8
Chapel Green Warks 27 B11
Chapel Haddlesey N Yorks 52 G1
Chapel Head Cambs 37 G9
Chapel Hill Aberds 89 E10
Chapel Hill Lincs 46 G6
Chapel Hill Mon 15 B11
Chapel Hill N Yorks 51 E9
Chapel Lawn Shrops 33 H9
Chapel-le-Dale N Yorks 50 B3
Chapel Milton Derbys 44 D4
Chapel of Garioch Aberds 83 A9
Chapel Row W Berks 18 E2
Chapel St Leonards Lincs 47 E9
Chapel Stile Cumb 56 F5
Chapelgate Lincs 37 C10
Chapelhall N Lnrk 68 D6
Chapelhill Dumfries 60 D6
Chapelhill Highld 87 D11
Chapelhill N Ayrs 66 B5
Chapelhill Perth 76 E5
Chapelhill Perth 76 D3
Chapelknowe Dumfries 61 F9
Chapelton Angus 77 C9
Chapelton Devon 6 D4
Chapelton Highld 81 B11
Chapelton S Lnrk 68 F5
Chapeltown Blkburn 50 H3
Chapeltown Moray 82 A4
Chapeltown S Yorks 45 C7
Chapmans Well Devon 6 G2
Chapmanslade Wilts 16 G5
Chapmore End Herts 29 G10
Chappel Essex 30 F5
Chard Som 8 D2
Chardstock Devon 8 D2
Charfield S Glos 16 B4
Charford Worcs 26 B6
Charing Kent 20 G6
Charing Cross Dorset 9 C10
Charing Heath Kent 20 G6
Charingworth Glos 27 E9
Charlbury Oxon 27 G10
Charlcombe Bath 16 E4
Charlecote Warks 27 C9
Charles Devon 6 C5
Charles Tye Suff 31 C7
Charlesfield Dumfries 61 G7
Charleston Angus 76 C6
Charleston Renfs 68 D3
Charlestown Aberdeen 83 C11
Charlestown Corn 3 D9
Charlestown Derbys 44 C4
Charlestown Dorset 8 G5
Charlestown Fife 69 B9
Charlestown Gtr Man 44 B2
Charlestown Highld 87 G9
Charlestown Highld 85 A13
Charlestown W Yorks 50 G5
Charlestown of Aberlour Moray 88 D2
Charlesworth Derbys 44 C4
Charleton Devon 5 G8
Charlton London 19 D11
Charlton Hants 17 G10
Charlton Herts 29 F8
Charlton Northants 28 E2
Charlton Northumb 62 E4
Charlton Som 16 F3
Charlton Telford 34 D1
Charlton Wilts 9 B8
Charlton Wilts 17 F8
Charlton Wilts 16 C6
Charlton Worcs 27 D7
Charlton W Sus 11 C7
Charlton Abbots Glos 27 F7
Charlton Adam Som 8 B4
Charlton-All-Saints Wilts 9 B10
Charlton Down Dorset 8 E5
Charlton Horethorne Som 8 B5
Charlton Kings Glos 26 F6
Charlton Mackerell Som 8 B4
Charlton Marshall Dorset 9 D7
Charlton Musgrove Som 8 B6
Charlton on Otmoor Oxon 28 G2
Charltons Redcar 59 E7
Charlwood Sur 19 G9
Charlynch Som 7 C11
Charminster Dorset 8 E5
Charmouth Dorset 8 E2
Charndon Bucks 28 F3
Charney Bassett Oxon 17 B10
Charnock Richard Lancs 50 H1
Charsfield Suff 31 C9
Chart Corner Kent 20 F4
Chart Sutton Kent 20 G5
Charter Alley Hants 18 F2
Charterhouse Som 15 F10
Charterville Allotments Oxon 27 G10
Chartham Kent 21 F8
Chartham Hatch Kent 21 F8
Chartridge Bucks 18 A6
Charvil Wokingham 18 D4
Charwelton Northants 28 C2
Chasetown Staffs 34 E6
Chastleton Oxon 27 F9
Chasty Devon 6 F2
Chatburn Lancs 50 E3
Chatcull Staffs 34 B3
Chatham Medway 20 E4
Chathill Northumb 71 H10
Chattenden Medway 20 D4
Chatteris Cambs 37 G9
Chattisham Suff 31 D7
Chatto Borders 62 B3
Chatton Northumb 71 H9
Chawleigh Devon 7 E6
Chawley Oxon 17 A11
Chawston Beds 29 C8
Chawton Hants 18 H4
Cheadle Gtr Man 44 D2
Cheadle Staffs 34 A6
Cheadle Heath Gtr Man 44 D2
Cheadle Hulme Gtr Man 44 D2
Cheam London 19 E9
Cheapside Sur 19 F7
Chearsley Bucks 28 G4
Chebsey Staffs 34 C4
Checkendon Oxon 18 C3
Checkley Ches 43 H10
Checkley Hereford 26 E2
Checkley Staffs 34 B6
Chedburgh Suff 30 C4
Cheddar Som 15 F10
Cheddington Bucks 28 G6
Cheddleton Staffs 44 G3
Cheddon Fitzpaine Som 8 B1
Chedglow Wilts 16 B6
Chedgrave Norf 39 F9
Chedington Dorset 8 D3
Chediston Suff 39 H9
Chedworth Glos 27 G7
Chedzoy Som 15 H9
Cheeklaw Borders 70 E6
Cheeseman's Green Kent 13 C9
Cheglinch Devon 6 B4
Cheldon Devon 7 E6
Chelford Ches 44 E2
Chell Heath Stoke 44 G2
Chellaston Derby 35 B9
Chellington Beds 28 C6
Chelmarsh Shrops 34 G3
Chelmer Village Essex 30 H4
Chelmondiston Suff 31 E9
Chelmorton Derbys 44 F5
Chelmsford Essex 30 H4
Chelsea London 19 D9
Chelsfield London 19 E11
Chelsworth Suff 30 D6
Cheltenham Glos 26 F6
Chelveston Northants 28 B6
Chelvey N Som 15 E10
Chelwood Bath 16 E3
Chelwood Common E Sus 12 D3
Chelwood Gate E Sus 12 D3
Chelworth Wilts 16 B6
Chelworth Green Wilts 17 B7
Chemistry Shrops 33 A11
Chenies Bucks 19 B7
Cheny Longville Shrops 33 G10
Chepstow = Cas-gwent Mon 15 B11
Chequerfield W Yorks 51 G10
Cherhill Wilts 17 D7
Cherington Glos 16 B6
Cherington Warks 27 E9
Cheriton Devon 7 B6
Cheriton Hants 10 B4
Cheriton Kent 21 H8
Cheriton Swansea 23 G9
Cheriton Bishop Devon 7 G6
Cheriton Fitzpaine Devon 7 F7
Cheriton or Stackpole Elidor Pembs 22 G4
Cherrington Telford 34 C2
Cherry Burton E Yorks 52 E5
Cherry Hinton Cambs 29 C11
Cherry Orchard Worcs 26 C5
Cherry Willingham Lincs 46 E4
Cherrybank Perth 76 E4
Chertsey Sur 19 E7
Cheselbourne Dorset 9 E6
Chesham Bucks 18 A6
Chesham Bois Bucks 18 B6
Cheshunt Herts 19 A10
Cheslyn Hay Staffs 34 E5
Chessington London 19 E8
Chester Ches 43 F7
Chester-Le-Street Durham 58 A3
Chester Moor Durham 58 B3
Chesterblade Som 16 G3
Chesterfield Derbys 45 E7
Chesters Borders 62 B2
Chesters Borders 62 A2
Chesterton Cambs 37 F7
Chesterton Cambs 29 B11
Chesterton Glos 17 A7
Chesterton Oxon 28 F2
Chesterton Shrops 34 F3
Chesterton Staffs 44 H2
Chesterton Warks 27 C10
Chesterwood Northumb 62 G4
Chestfield Kent 21 E8
Cheston Devon 5 F7
Cheswardine Shrops 34 C3
Cheswick Northumb 71 F9
Chetnole Dorset 8 D5
Chettiscombe Devon 7 E8
Chettisham Cambs 37 G11
Chettle Dorset 9 C8
Chetton Shrops 34 F2
Chetwode Bucks 28 F3
Chetwynd Aston Telford 34 D3
Cheveley Cambs 30 B3
Chevening Kent 19 F11
Chevington Suff 30 C4
Chevithorne Devon 7 E8
Chew Magna Bath 16 E2
Chew Stoke Bath 16 E2
Chewton Keynsham Bath 16 E3
Chewton Mendip Som 16 F2
Chicheley M Keynes 28 D6
Chichester W Sus 11 D7
Chickerell Dorset 8 F5
Chicklade Wilts 9 A8
Chicksgrove Wilts 9 A8
Chidden Hants 10 C5
Chiddingfold Sur 18 H6
Chiddingly E Sus 12 E4
Chiddingstone Kent 19 G11
Chiddingstone Causeway Kent 20 G2
Chiddingstone Hoath Kent 12 B3
Chideock Dorset 8 E3
Chidham W Sus 11 D6
Chidswell W Yorks 51 G8
Chieveley W Berks 17 D11
Chignall St James Essex 30 H3
Chignall Smealy Essex 30 G3
Chigwell Essex 19 B11
Chigwell Row Essex 19 B11
Chilbolton Hants 17 H10
Chilcomb Hants 10 B4
Chilcombe Dorset 8 E4
Chilcompton Som 16 F3
Chilcote Leics 35 D8
Child Okeford Dorset 9 C7
Childer Thornton Ches 42 E6
Childrey Oxon 17 C10
Child's Ercall Shrops 34 C2
Childswickham Worcs 27 E7
Childwall Mers 43 D7
Childwick Green Herts 29 G8
Chilfrome Dorset 8 E4
Chilgrove W Sus 11 C7
Chilham Kent 21 F7
Chilhampton Wilts 9 A9
Chilla Devon 6 F3
Chillaton Devon 4 C5
Chillenden Kent 21 F9
Chillerton I o W 10 F3
Chillesford Suff 31 C10
Chillingham Northumb 71 H9
Chillington Devon 5 G8
Chillington Som 8 C2
Chilmark Wilts 9 A8
Chilson Oxon 27 G10
Chilsworthy Corn 4 D5
Chilsworthy Devon 6 F2
Chilthorne Domer Som 8 C4
Chiltington E Sus 12 E2
Chilton Bucks 28 G3
Chilton Durham 58 D3
Chilton Oxon 17 C11
Chilton Cantelo Som 8 B4
Chilton Foliat Wilts 17 D10
Chilton Lane Durham 58 C4
Chilton Polden Som 15 H9
Chilton Street Suff 30 D4
Chilton Trinity Som 15 H8
Chilvers Coton Warks 35 F9
Chilwell Notts 35 B11
Chilworth Hants 10 C3
Chilworth Sur 19 G7
Chimney Oxon 17 A10
Chineham Hants 18 F3
Chingford London 19 B10
Chinley Derbys 44 D4
Chinley Head Derbys 44 D4
Chinnor Oxon 18 A4
Chipnall Shrops 34 B3
Chippenhall Green Suff 39 H8
Chippenham Cambs 30 B3
Chippenham Wilts 16 D6
Chipperfield Herts 19 A7
Chipping Herts 29 E10
Chipping Lancs 50 E2
Chipping Campden Glos 27 E8
Chipping Hill Essex 30 G5
Chipping Norton Oxon 27 F10
Chipping Ongar Essex 20 A2
Chipping Sodbury S Glos 16 C4
Chipping Warden Northants 27 D11
Chipstable Som 7 D9
Chipstead Kent 19 F11
Chipstead Sur 19 F9
Chirbury Shrops 33 F8
Chirk = Y Waun Wrex 33 B8
Chirk Bank Shrops 33 B8
Chirmorrie S Ayrs 54 B5
Chirnside Borders 71 E7
Chirnsidebridge Borders 71 E7
Chirton Wilts 17 F7
Chisbury Wilts 17 E9
Chiselborough Som 8 C3
Chiseldon Swindon 17 D8
Chiserley W Yorks 50 G6
Chislehampton Oxon 18 B2
Chislehurst London 19 D11
Chislet Kent 21 E9
Chiswell Green Herts 19 A8
Chiswick London 19 D9
Chiswick End Cambs 29 D10
Chisworth Derbys 44 C3
Chithurst W Sus 11 B7
Chittering Cambs 29 A11
Chitterne Wilts 16 G6
Chittlehamholt Devon 6 D5
Chittlehampton Devon 6 D5
Chittoe Wilts 16 E6
Chivenor Devon 6 C4
Chobham Sur 18 E6
Choicelee Borders 70 E6
Cholderton Wilts 17 G9
Cholesbury Bucks 28 H6
Chollerford Northumb 62 F5
Chollerton Northumb 62 F5
Cholmondeston Ches 43 F9
Cholsey Oxon 18 C2
Cholstrey Hereford 25 C11
Chop Gate N Yorks 59 G6
Choppington Northumb 63 E8
Chopwell T & W 63 H7
Chorley Ches 43 G8
Chorley Lancs 50 H1
Chorley Shrops 34 G2
Chorley Staffs 35 D6
Chorleywood Herts 19 B7
Chorlton cum Hardy Gtr Man 44 C2
Chorlton Lane Ches 43 H7
Choulton Shrops 33 G9
Chowdene T & W 63 H8
Chowley Ches 43 G7
Chrishall Essex 29 E11
Christchurch Cambs 37 F10
Christchurch Dorset 9 E10
Christchurch Glos 26 G2
Christchurch Newport 15 C9
Christian Malford Wilts 16 D6
Christleton Ches 43 F7
Christmas Common Oxon 18 B4
Christon N Som 15 F9
Christon Bank Northumb 63 A8
Christow Devon 5 C9
Chryston N Lnrk 68 C5
Chudleigh Devon 5 D9
Chudleigh Knighton Devon 5 D9
Chulmleigh Devon 6 E5
Chunal Derbys 44 C4
Church Lancs 50 G3
Church Aston Telford 34 D3
Church Brampton Northants 28 B4
Church Broughton Derbys 35 B8
Church Crookham Hants 18 F5
Church Eaton Staffs 34 D4
Church End Beds 28 F6
Church End Beds 29 E8
Church End Beds 28 E6
Church End Cambs 37 G8
Church End Cambs 37 E9
Church End E Yorks 53 D6
Church End Essex 30 D2
Church End Essex 30 F4
Church End Hants 18 F3
Church End Lincs 37 B8
Church End Warks 35 F8
Church End Warks 35 F8
Church End Wilts 17 D7
Church Enstone Oxon 27 F10
Church Fenton N Yorks 51 F11
Church Green Devon 7 G10
Church Green Norf 39 F6
Church Gresley Derbys 35 D8
Church Hanborough Oxon 27 G11
Church Hill Ches 43 F9
Church Houses N Yorks 59 G7
Church Knowle Dorset 9 F8
Church Laneham Notts 46 E2
Church Langton Leics 36 F3
Church Lawford Warks 35 H10
Church Lawton Ches 44 G2
Church Leigh Staffs 34 B6
Church Lench Worcs 27 C7
Church Mayfield Staffs 35 A7
Church Minshull Ches 43 F9
Church Norton W Sus 11 E7
Church Preen Shrops 33 F11
Church Pulverbatch Shrops 33 E10
Church Stoke Powys 33 F8
Church Stowe Northants 28 C3
Church Street Kent 20 D4
Church Stretton Shrops 33 F10
Church Town N Lincs 45 B11
Church Town Sur 19 F10
Church Village Rhondda 14 C6
Church Warsop Notts 45 F9
Churcham Glos 26 G4
Churchbank Shrops 33 H8
Churchbridge Staffs 34 E5
Churchdown Glos 26 G5
Churchend Essex 30 F3
Churchend Essex 21 B7
Churchend S Glos 16 B4
Churchfield W Mid 34 F6
Churchgate Street Essex 29 G11
Churchill Devon 6 B4
Churchill Devon 8 D2
Churchill N Som 15 F10
Churchill Oxon 27 F9
Churchill Worcs 34 H4
Churchill Worcs 26 C6
Churchinford Som 7 E11
Churchover Warks 35 G11
Churchstanton Som 7 E10
Churchstow Devon 5 G8
Churchtown Derbys 44 F6
Churchtown I o M 48 C4
Churchtown Lancs 49 E4
Churchtown Mers 49 H3
Churnsike Lodge Northumb 62 F2
Churston Ferrers Torbay 5 F10
Churt Sur 18 H5
Churton Ches 43 G7
Churwell W Yorks 51 G8
Chute Standen Wilts 17 F10
Chwilog Gwyn 40 G6
Chyandour Corn 2 F3
Cilan Uchaf Gwyn 40 H4
Cilcain Flint 42 F4
Cilcennin Ceredig 24 B2
Cilfor Gwyn 41 G8
Cilfrew Neath 14 A3
Cilfynydd Rhondda 14 B6
Cilgerran Pembs 22 B6
Cilgwyn Carms 24 F4
Cilgwyn Gwyn 40 E6
Cilgwyn Pembs 22 C5
Ciliau Aeron Ceredig 23 A9
Cill Donnain W Isles 84 F2
Cille Bhrighde W Isles 84 G2
Cille Pheadair W Isles 84 G2
Cilmery Powys 25 C7
Cilsan Carms 23 D10
Ciltalgarth Gwyn 41 F10
Cilwendeg Pembs 23 C7
Cilybebyll Neath 14 A3
Cilycwm Carms 24 E4
Cimla Neath 14 B3
Cinderford Glos 26 G3
Cippyn Pembs 22 B6
Circebost W Isles 90 D6
Cirencester Glos 17 A7
Ciribhig W Isles 90 C6
City Powys 33 G8
City Dulas Anglesey 40 B6
City of London = London, City of London 19 C10
Clachaig Argyll 73 E10
Clachan Argyll 72 H6
Clachan Argyll 72 B6
Clachan Argyll 79 G11
Clachan Argyll 74 F4
Clachan Highld 85 E10
Clachan W Isles 84 D2
Clachan na Luib W Isles 84 B3
Clachan of Campsie E Dunb 68 C5
Clachan of Glendaruel Argyll 73 E8
Clachan-Seil Argyll 72 B6
Clachan Strachur Argyll 73 C9
Clachaneasy Dumfries 54 B6
Clachanmore Dumfries 54 E3
Clachbreck Argyll 72 F6
Clachnabrain Angus 82 G5
Clachtoll Highld 92 G3
Clackmannan Clack 69 A8
Clacton-on-Sea Essex 31 G8
Cladach Chireboist W Isles 84 B2
Claddach-knockline W Isles 84 B2
Cladich Argyll 74 E3
Claggan Highld 79 G9
Claggan Highld 80 F3
Claigan Highld 84 C7
Claines Worcs 26 C5
Clandown Bath 16 F3
Clanfield Hants 10 C5
Clanfield Oxon 17 A9
Clanville Hants 17 G10
Claonaig Argyll 73 H7
Claonel Highld 93 J8
Clap Hill Kent 13 C9
Clapgate Dorset 9 D9
Clapgate Herts 29 F11
Clapham Beds 29 C7
Clapham London 19 D9
Clapham N Yorks 50 C3
Clapham W Sus 11 D9
Clappers Borders 71 E8
Clappersgate Cumb 56 F5
Clapton Som 8 D3
Clapton-in-Gordano N Som 15 D10
Clapton-on-the-Hill Glos 27 G8
Clapworthy Devon 6 D5
Clara Vale T & W 63 G7
Clarach Ceredig 32 G2
Clarbeston Pembs 22 D5
Clarbeston Road Pembs 22 D5
Clarborough Notts 45 D11
Clardon Highld 94 D3
Clare Suff 30 D4
Clarebrand Dumfries 55 C10
Clarencefield Dumfries 60 G6
Clarilaw Borders 61 B11
Clark's Green Sur 19 H8
Clarkston E Renf 68 E4
Clashandorran Highld 87 G8
Clashcoig Highld 87 B9
Clashindarroch Aberds 88 E4
Clashmore Highld 92 F3
Clashmore Highld 87 C10
Clashnessie Highld 92 F3
Clashnoir Moray 82 A4
Clate Shetland 96 G7
Clathy Perth 76 F2
Clatt Aberds 83 A7
Clatter Powys 32 F5
Clatterford I o W 10 F3
Clatterin Bridge Aberds 83 F8
Clatworthy Som 7 C9
Claughton Lancs 49 E5
Claughton Lancs 50 C1
Claughton Mers 42 D6
Claverdon Warks 27 B8
Claverham N Som 15 E10
Clavering Essex 29 E11
Claverley Shrops 34 F3
Claverton Bath 16 E4
Clawdd-newydd Denb 42 G3
Clawthorpe Cumb 49 B5
Clawton Devon 6 G2
Claxby Lincs 46 C5
Claxby Lincs 47 E8
Claxton Norf 39 E9
Claxton N Yorks 52 C2
Clay Common Suff 39 G10
Clay Coton Northants 36 H1
Clay Cross Derbys 45 F7
Clay Hill W Berks 18 D2
Clay Lake Lincs 37 C8
Claybokie Aberds 82 D2
Claybrooke Magna Leics 35 G10
Claybrooke Parva Leics 35 G10
Claydon Oxon 27 C11
Claydon Suff 31 C8
Claygate Dumfries 61 F9
Claygate Kent 12 B6
Claygate Sur 19 E8
Claygate Cross Kent 20 F3
Clayhanger Devon 7 D9
Clayhanger W Mid 34 E6
Clayhidon Devon 7 E10
Clayhill E Sus 13 D7
Clayhill Hants 10 D2
Clayock Highld 94 E3
Claypole Lincs 46 H2
Clayton Staffs 34 A4
Clayton S Yorks 45 B8
Clayton W Sus 12 E1
Clayton W Yorks 51 F7
Clayton Green Lancs 50 G1
Clayton-le-Moors Lancs 50 F3
Clayton-le-Woods Lancs 50 G1
Clayton West W Yorks 44 A6
Clayworth Notts 45 D11
Cleadale Highld 78 C7
Cleadon T & W 63 G9
Clearbrook Devon 4 E6
Clearwell Glos 26 H2
Cleasby N Yorks 58 E3
Cleat Orkney 95 K5
Cleatlam Durham 58 E2
Cleator Cumb 56 E2
Cleator Moor Cumb 56 E2
Clebrig Highld 93 F8
Cleckheaton W Yorks 51 G7
Clee St Margaret Shrops 34 G1
Cleedownton Shrops 34 G1
Cleehill Shrops 34 H1
Cleethorpes NE Lincs 47 B7
Cleeton St Mary Shrops 34 H2
Cleeve N Som 15 E10
Cleeve Hill Glos 26 F6
Cleeve Prior Worcs 27 D7
Clegyrnant Powys 32 E5
Clehonger Hereford 25 E11
Cleish Perth 76 H3
Cleland N Lnrk 69 E7
Clench Common Wilts 17 E8
Clenchwarton Norf 38 C1
Clent Worcs 34 H5
Cleobury Mortimer Shrops 34 H2
Cleobury North Shrops 34 G2
Cleongart Argyll 65 E7
Clephanton Highld 87 F11
Clerklands Borders 61 A11
Clestrain Orkney 95 H4
Cleuch Head Borders 61 B11
Cleughbrae Dumfries 60 F6
Clevancy Wilts 17 D7
Clevedon N Som 15 D10
Cleveley Oxon 27 F10
Cleveleys Lancs 49 E3
Cleverton Wilts 16 C6
Clevis Bridgend 14 D4
Clewer Som 15 F10
Cley next the Sea Norf 38 A6
Cliaid W Isles 84 H1
Cliasmol W Isles 90 G5
Cliburn Cumb 57 D7
Click Mill Orkney 95 F4
Cliddesden Hants 18 G3
Cliff End E Sus 13 E7
Cliffburn Angus 77 C9
Cliffe Medway 20 D4
Cliffe N Yorks 52 F2
Cliffe Woods Medway 20 D4
Clifford Hereford 25 D9
Clifford W Yorks 51 E10
Clifford Chambers Warks 27 C8
Clifford's Mesne Glos 26 F4
Cliffsend Kent 21 E10
Clifton Beds 29 E8
Clifton Bristol 16 D2
Clifton Cumb 57 D7
Clifton Derbys 35 A7
Clifton Lancs 49 F4
Clifton Nottingham 36 B1
Clifton Northumb 63 E8
Clifton N Yorks 51 E7
Clifton Oxon 27 E11
Clifton Stirl 74 D6
Clifton S Yorks 45 C9
Clifton Worcs 26 D5
Clifton York 52 D1
Clifton Campville Staffs 35 D8
Clifton Green Gtr Man 43 B10
Clifton Hampden Oxon 18 B2
Clifton Reynes M Keynes 28 C6
Clifton upon Dunsmore Warks 35 H11
Clifton upon Teme Worcs 26 B4
Cliftoncote Borders 62 A4
Cliftonville Kent 21 D10
Climaen gwyn Neath 24 H4
Climping W Sus 11 D9
Climpy S Lnrk 69 E8
Clink Som 16 G4
Clint N Yorks 51 D8
Clint Green Norf 38 D6
Clintmains Borders 70 G5
Cliobh W Isles 90 D5
Clippesby Norf 39 D10
Clipsham Rutland 36 D5
Clipston Northants 36 G3
Clipstone Notts 45 F9
Clitheroe Lancs 50 E3
Cliuthar W Isles 90 H6
Clive Shrops 33 C11
Clivocast Shetland 96 C8
Clixby Lincs 46 B5
Clocaenog Denb 42 G3
Clochan Moray 88 B4
Clock Face Mers 43 C8
Clockmill Borders 70 E6
Cloddiau Powys 33 E8
Clodock Hereford 25 F10
Clola Aberds 89 D10
Clophill Beds 29 E7
Clopton Northants 37 G6
Clopton Suff 31 C9
Clopton Corner Suff 31 C9
Clopton Green Suff 30 C4
Close Clark I o M 48 E2
Closeburn Dumfries 60 D4
Closworth Som 8 C4
Clothall Herts 29 E9
Clotton Ches 43 F8
Clough Foot W Yorks 50 G5
Cloughton N Yorks 59 G11
Cloughton Newlands N Yorks 59 G11
Clousta Shetland 96 H5
Clouston Orkney 95 G3
Clova Aberds 82 A6
Clova Angus 82 F5
Clove Lodge Durham 57 E11
Clovelly Devon 6 D2
Clovenfords Borders 70 G3
Clovenstone Aberds 83 B9
Clovullin Highld 74 A3
Clow Bridge Lancs 50 G4
Clowne Derbys 45 E8
Clows Top Worcs 26 A4
Cloy Wrex 33 A9
Cluanie Inn Highld 80 B2
Cluanie Lodge Highld 80 B2
Clun Shrops 33 G9
Clunbury Shrops 33 G9
Clunderwen Carms 22 E6
Clune Highld 81 A9
Clunes Highld 80 E4
Clungunford Shrops 33 H9
Clunie Aberds 89 C6
Clunie Perth 76 C4
Clunton Shrops 33 G9
Cluny Fife 76 H5
Cluny Castle Highld 81 D8
Clutton Bath 16 F3
Clutton Ches 43 G7
Clwt-grugoer Conwy 42 F2
Clwt-y-bont Gwyn 41 D7
Clydach Mon 25 G9
Clydach Swansea 14 A2
Clydach Vale Rhondda 14 B5
Clydebank W Dunb 68 C3
Clydey Pembs 23 C7
Clyffe Pypard Wilts 17 D7
Clynder Argyll 73 E11
Clyne Neath 14 A4
Clynelish Highld 93 J11
Clynnog-fawr Gwyn 40 E6
Clyro Powys 25 D9
Clyst Honiton Devon 7 G8
Clyst Hydon Devon 7 F9
Clyst St George Devon 5 C10
Clyst St Lawrence Devon 7 F9
Clyst St Mary Devon 7 G8
Cnoc Amhlaigh W Isles 91 D10
Cnwch-coch Ceredig 32 H2
Coachford Aberds 88 D4
Coad's Green Corn 4 D3
Coal Aston Derbys 45 E7
Coalbrookdale Telford 34 E2
Coalbrookvale Bl Gwent 25 H8
Coalburn S Lnrk 69 G7
Coalburns T & W 63 G7
Coalcleugh Northumb 57 B10
Coaley Glos 16 A4
Coalhall E Ayrs 67 E7
Coalhill Essex 20 B4
Coalpit Heath S Glos 16 C3
Coalport Telford 34 E2
Coalsnaughton Clack 76 H2
Coaltown of Balgonie Fife 76 H5
Coaltown of Wemyss Fife 76 H6
Coalville Leics 35 D10
Coalway Glos 26 G2
Coat Som 8 B3
Coatbridge N Lnrk 68 D6
Coatdyke N Lnrk 68 D6
Coate Swindon 17 C8
Coate Wilts 17 E7
Coates Cambs 37 F9
Coates Glos 16 A6
Coates Lancs 50 E4
Coates Notts 46 D2
Coates W Sus 11 C8
Coatham Redcar 59 D6
Coatham Mundeville Darl 58 D3
Coatsgate Dumfries 60 C6
Cobbaton Devon 6 D5
Cobbler's Green Norf 39 F8
Coberley Glos 26 G6
Cobham Kent 20 E3
Cobham Sur 19 E8
Cobholm Island Norf 39 E11
Cobleland Stirl 75 H8
Cobnash Hereford 25 B11
Coburty Aberds 89 B9
Cock Bank Wrex 42 H6
Cock Bridge Aberds 82 C4
Cock Clarks Essex 20 A5
Cockayne N Yorks 59 G7
Cockayne Hatley Cambs 29 D9
Cockburnspath Borders 70 C6
Cockenzie and Port Seton E Loth 70 C3
Cockerham Lancs 49 D4
Cockermouth Cumb 56 C3
Cockernhoe Green Herts 29 F8
Cockfield Durham 58 D2
Cockfield Suff 30 C6
Cockfosters London 19 B9
Cocking W Sus 11 C7
Cockington Torbay 5 E9
Cocklake Som 15 G10
Cockley Beck Cumb 56 F4
Cockley Cley Norf 38 E3
Cockshutt Shrops 33 C10
Cockthorpe Norf 38 A5
Cockwood Devon 5 C10
Cockyard Hereford 25 E11
Codda Corn 4 D2
Coddenham Suff 31 C8
Coddington Ches 43 G7
Coddington Hereford 26 D4
Coddington Notts 46 G2
Codford St Mary Wilts 16 H6
Codford St Peter Wilts 16 H6
Codicote Herts 29 G9
Codmore Hill W Sus 11 B9
Codnor Derbys 45 H8
Codrington S Glos 16 D4
Codsall Staffs 34 E4
Codsall Wood Staffs 34 E4
Coed Duon = Blackwood Caerph 15 B7
Coed Mawr Gwyn 41 C7
Coed Morgan Mon 25 G10
Coed-Talon Flint 42 G5
Coed-y-bryn Ceredig 23 B8
Coed-y-paen Mon 15 B9
Coed-yr-ynys Powys 25 F8
Coed Ystumgwern Gwyn 32 C1
Coedely Rhondda 14 C6
Coedkernew Newport 15 C8
Coedpoeth Wrex 42 G5
Coedway Powys 33 D9
Coelbren Powys 24 G5
Coffinswell Devon 5 E9
Cofton Hackett Worcs 34 H6
Cogan V Glam 15 D7
Cogenhoe Northants 28 B5
Cogges Oxon 27 H10
Coggeshall Essex 30 F5
Coggeshall Hamlet Essex 30 F5
Coggins Mill E Sus 12 D4
Coig Peighinnean W Isles 91 A10
Coig Peighinnean Bhuirgh W Isles 91 B9
Coignafearn Lodge Highld 81 B8
Coilacriech Aberds 82 D5
Coilantogle Stirl 75 G8
Coilleag W Isles 84 G2
Coillore Highld 85 E8
Coity Bridgend 14 C5
Col W Isles 91 C9
Col Uarach W Isles 91 D9
Colaboll Highld 93 H8
Colan Corn 3 C7
Colaton Raleigh Devon 7 H9
Colbost Highld 84 D7
Colburn N Yorks 58 G2
Colby Cumb 57 D8
Colby I o M 48 E2
Colby Norf 39 B8
Colchester Essex 31 F7
Colcot V Glam 15 E7
Cold Ash W Berks 18 E2
Cold Ashby Northants 36 H2
Cold Ashton S Glos 16 D4
Cold Aston Glos 27 G8
Cold Blow Pembs 22 E6
Cold Brayfield M Keynes 28 C6
Cold Hanworth Lincs 46 D4
Cold Harbour Lincs 36 B5
Cold Hatton Telford 34 C2
Cold Hesledon Durham 58 B5
Cold Higham Northants 28 C3
Cold Kirby N Yorks 51 A11
Cold Newton Leics 36 E3
Cold Northcott Corn 4 C3
Cold Norton Essex 20 A5
Cold Overton Leics 36 D4
Coldbackie Highld 93 D9
Coldbeck Cumb 57 F9
Coldblow London 20 D2
Coldean Brighton 12 F2
Coldeast Devon 5 D9
Colden W Yorks 50 G5
Colden Common Hants 10 B3
Coldfair Green Suff 31 B11
Coldham Cambs 37 E10
Coldharbour Glos 16 A2
Coldharbour Kent 20 F2
Coldharbour Sur 19 G8
Coldingham Borders 71 D8
Coldrain Perth 76 G3
Coldred Kent 21 G9
Coldridge Devon 6 F5
Coldstream Angus 76 D6
Coldstream Borders 71 G7
Coldwaltham W Sus 11 C9
Coldwells Aberds 89 D11
Coldwells Croft Aberds 83 A7
Coldyeld Shrops 33 F9
Cole Som 8 A5
Cole Green Herts 29 G9
Cole Henley Hants 17 F11
Colebatch Shrops 33 G9
Colebrook Devon 7 F9
Colebrooke Devon 7 G6
Coleby Lincs 46 F3
Coleby N Lincs 52 H4
Coleford Devon 7 F6
Coleford Glos 26 G2
Coleford Som 16 G3
Colehill Dorset 9 D9
Coleman's Hatch E Sus 12 C3
Colemere Shrops 33 B10
Colemore Hants 10 A6
Coleorton Leics 35 D10
Colerne Wilts 16 D5
Cole's Green Suff 31 B9
Coles Green Suff 31 D7
Colesbourne Glos 26 G6
Colesden Beds 29 C8
Coleshill Bucks 18 B6
Coleshill Oxon 17 B9
Coleshill Warks 35 G8
Colestocks Devon 7 F9
Colgate W Sus 11 A11
Colgrain Argyll 68 B2
Colinsburgh Fife 77 G7
Colinton Edin 69 D11
Colintraive Argyll 73 F9
Colkirk Norf 38 C5
Collace Perth 76 D5
Collafirth Shetland 96 G6
Collaton St Mary Torbay 5 F9
College Milton S Lnrk 68 E5
Collessie Fife 76 F5
Collier Row London 20 B2
Collier Street Kent 20 G4
Collier's End Herts 29 F10
Collier's Green Kent 13 C6
Colliery Row T & W 58 B4
Collieston Aberds 89 F10
Collin Dumfries 60 F6
Collingbourne Ducis Wilts 17 F9
Collingbourne Kingston Wilts 17 F9
Collingham Notts 46 F2
Collingham W Yorks 51 E9
Collington Hereford 26 B3
Collingtree Northants 28 C4
Collins Green Warr 43 C8
Colliston Angus 77 C9
Collycroft Warks 35 G9
Collynie Aberds 89 E8
Collyweston Northants 36 E5
Colmonell S Ayrs 66 H4
Colmworth Beds 29 C8
Coln Rogers Glos 27 H7
Coln St Aldwyn's Glos 27 H8
Coln St Dennis Glos 27 G7
Colnabaichin Aberds 82 C4
Colnbrook Slough 19 D7
Colne Cambs 37 H9
Colne Lancs 50 E4
Colne Edge Lancs 50 E4
Colne Engaine Essex 30 E5
Colney Norf 39 E7
Colney Heath Herts 29 H9
Colney Street Herts 19 A8
Colpy Aberds 89 E6
Colquhar Borders 70 F2
Colsterdale N Yorks 51 A7
Colsterworth Lincs 36 C5
Colston Bassett Notts 36 B3
Coltfield Moray 87 E14
Colthouse Cumb 56 G5
Coltishall Norf 39 D8
Coltness N Lnrk 69 E7
Colton Cumb 56 H5
Colton Norf 39 E7
Colton N Yorks 51 E11
Colton Staffs 35 C6
Colton W Yorks 51 F9
Colva Powys 25 C9
Colvend Dumfries 55 D11
Colvister Shetland 96 D7
Colwall Green Hereford 26 D4
Colwall Stone Hereford 26 D4
Colwell Northumb 62 F5
Colwich Staffs 34 C6
Colwick Notts 36 A2
Colwinston V Glam 14 D5
Colworth W Sus 11 D8
Colwyn Bay = Bae Colwyn Conwy 41 C10
Colyford Devon 8 E1
Colyton Devon 8 E1
Combe Hereford 25 B10
Combe Oxon 27 G11
Combe W Berks 17 E10
Combe Common Sur 18 H6
Combe Down Bath 16 E4
Combe Florey Som 7 C10
Combe Hay Bath 16 F4
Combe Martin Devon 6 B4
Combe Moor Hereford 25 B10
Combe Raleigh Devon 7 F10
Combe St Nicholas Som 8 C2
Combeinteignhead Devon 5 D10
Comberbach Ches 43 E9
Comberton Cambs 29 C10
Comberton Hereford 25 B11
Combpyne Devon 8 E1
Combridge Staffs 35 B6
Combrook Warks 27 C10
Combs Derbys 44 E4
Combs Suff 31 C7
Combs Ford Suff 31 C7
Combwich Som 15 G8
Comers Aberds 83 C8
Comins Coch Ceredig 32 G2
Commercial End Cambs 30 B2
Commins Capel Betws Ceredig 24 C3
Commins Coch Powys 32 E4
Common Edge Blkpool 49 F3
Common Side Derbys 45 E7
Commondale N Yorks 59 E7
Commonmoor Corn 4 E3
Commonside Ches 43 E8
Compstall Gtr Man 44 C3
Compton Devon 5 E9
Compton Hants 10 B3
Compton Sur 18 G5
Compton Sur 18 G6
Compton W Berks 18 D2
Compton Wilts 17 F8
Compton W Sus 11 C6
Compton Abbas Dorset 9 C7
Compton Abdale Glos 27 G7
Compton Bassett Wilts 17 D7
Compton Beauchamp Oxon 17 C9
Compton Bishop Som 15 F9
Compton Chamberlayne Wilts 9 B9

Derringstone Kent 21 G9
Derrington Staffs 34 C4
Derriton Devon 6 F2
Derry Hill Wilts 16 D6
Derryguaig Argyll 78 H7
Derrythorpe N Lincs 46 B2
Dersingham Norf 38 B2
Dervaig Argyll 78 F7
Derwen Denb 42 G3
Derwenlas Powys 32 F3
Desborough Northants 36 G4
Desford Leics 35 E10
Detchant Northumb 71 G9
Detling Kent 20 F4
Deuddwr Powys 33 D8
Devauden Mon 15 B10
Devil's Bridge Ceredig 32 H3
Devizes Wilts 17 E7
Devol Invclyd 68 C2
Devonport Plym 4 F5
Devonside Clack 76 H2
Devoran Corn 3 F6
Dewar Borders 70 F2
Dewlish Dorset 9 E6
Dewsbury W Yorks 51 G8
Dewsbury Moor W Yorks 51 G8
Dewshall Court Hereford 25 E11
Dhoon I o M 48 D4
Dhoor I o M 48 C4
Dhowin I o M 48 B4
Dial Post W Sus 11 C10
Dibden Hants 10 D3
Dibden Purlieu Hants 10 D3
Dickleburgh Norf 39 G7
Didbrook Glos 27 E7
Didcot Oxon 18 C2
Diddington Cambs 29 B8
Diddlebury Shrops 33 G11
Didley Hereford 25 E11
Didling W Sus 11 C7
Didmarton Glos 16 C5
Didsbury Gtr Man 44 C2
Didworthy Devon 5 E7
Digby Lincs 46 G4
Digg Highld 85 B9
Diggle Gtr Man 44 B4
Digmoor Lancs 43 B7
Digswell Park Herts 29 G9
Dihewyd Ceredig 23 A9
Dilham Norf 39 C9
Dilhorne Staffs 34 A5
Dillarburn S Lnrk 69 F7
Dillington Cambs 29 B8
Dilston Northumb 62 G5
Dilton Marsh Wilts 16 G5
Dilwyn Hereford 25 C11
Dinas Carms 23 C7
Dinas Gwyn 40 G4
Dinas Cross Pembs 22 C5
Dinas Dinlle Gwyn 40 E6
Dinas-Mawddwy Gwyn 32 D4
Dinas Powys V Glam 15 D7
Dinbych = Denbigh Denb 42 F3
Dinbych-y-Pysgod = Tenby Pembs 22 F6
Dinder Som 16 G2
Dinedor Hereford 26 E2
Dingestow Mon 25 G11
Dingle Mers 42 D6
Dingleden Kent 13 C7
Dingley Northants 36 G3
Dingwall Highld 87 F8
Dinlabyre Borders 61 D11
Dinmael Conwy 32 A6
Dinnet Aberds 82 D6
Dinnington Som 8 C3
Dinnington S Yorks 45 D9
Dinnington T & W 63 F8
Dinorwic Gwyn 41 D7
Dinton Bucks 28 G4
Dinton Wilts 9 A9
Dinwoodie Mains Dumfries 61 D7
Dinworthy Devon 6 E2
Dippen N Ayrs 66 D3
Dippenhall Sur 18 G5
Dipple Moray 88 C3
Dipple S Ayrs 66 F5
Diptford Devon 5 F8
Dipton Durham 58 A2
Dirdhu Highld 82 A2
Dirleton E Loth 70 B4
Dirt Pot Northumb 57 B10
Discoed Powys 25 B9
Diseworth Leics 35 C10
Dishes Orkney 95 F7
Dishforth N Yorks 51 B9
Disley Ches 44 D3
Diss Norf 39 H7
Disserth Powys 25 C7
Distington Cumb 56 D2
Ditchampton Wilts 9 A9
Ditcheat Som 16 H3
Ditchingham Norf 39 F9
Ditchling E Sus 12 E2
Ditherington Shrops 33 D11
Dittisham Devon 5 F9
Ditton Halton 43 D7
Ditton Kent 20 F4
Ditton Green Cambs 30 C3
Ditton Priors Shrops 34 G2
Divach Highld 81 A6
Divlyn Carms 24 E4
Dixton Glos 26 E6
Dixton Mon 26 G2
Dobcross Gtr Man 44 B3
Dobwalls Corn 4 E3
Doc Penfro = Pembroke Dock Pembs 22 F4
Doccombe Devon 5 C8
Dochfour Ho. Highld 87 H9
Dochgarroch Highld 87 G9
Docking Norf 38 B3
Docklow Hereford 26 C2
Dockray Cumb 56 D5
Dockroyd W Yorks 50 F6
Dodburn Borders 61 C10
Doddinghurst Essex 20 B2
Doddington Cambs 37 F9
Doddington Kent 20 F6
Doddington Lincs 46 E3
Doddington Northumb 71 G8
Doddington Shrops 34 H2
Doddiscombsleigh Devon 5 C9
Dodford Northants 28 B3
Dodford Worcs 26 A6
Dodington S Glos 16 C4
Dodleston Ches 42 F6
Dods Leigh Staffs 34 B6
Dodworth S Yorks 45 B7
Doe Green Warr 43 D8
Doe Lea Derbys 45 F8
Dog Village Devon 7 G4
Dogdyke Lincs 46 G6
Dogmersfield Hants 18 F4
Dogridge Wilts 17 C7
Dogsthorpe P'boro 37 E7
Dol-fôr Powys 32 E4
Dôl-y-Bont Ceredig 32 G2
Dol-y-cannau Powys 25 D9
Dolanog Powys 33 D6
Dolau Powys 25 B8
Dolau Rhondda 14 C5
Dolbenmaen Gwyn 41 F7
Dolfach Powys 32 E5
Dolfor Powys 33 G7
Dolgarrog Conwy 41 D9
Dolgellau Gwyn 32 D3
Dolgran Carms 23 C9
Dolhendre Gwyn 41 G10
Doll Highld 93 J11
Dollar Clack 76 H2
Dolley Green Powys 25 B9
Dollwen Ceredig 32 G2
Dolphin Flint 42 E4
Dolphinholme Lancs 49 D5
Dolphinton S Lnrk 69 F10
Dolton Devon 6 E4
Dolwen Conwy 41 C10
Dolwen Powys 32 E5
Dolwyd Conwy 41 C10
Dolwyddelan Conwy 41 E9
Dolyhir Powys 25 C9
Doncaster S Yorks 45 B9
Dones Green Ches 43 E9
Donhead St Andrew Wilts 9 B8
Donhead St Mary Wilts 9 B8
Donibristle Fife 69 B10
Donington Lincs 37 B8
Donington on Bain Lincs 46 D6
Donington South Ing Lincs 37 B8
Donisthorpe Leics 35 D9
Donkey Town Sur 18 E6
Donnington Glos 27 F8
Donnington Hereford 26 E4
Donnington Shrops 34 E1
Donnington Telford 34 D3
Donnington W Berks 17 E11
Donnington W Sus 11 D7
Donnington Wood Telford 34 D3
Donyatt Som 8 C2
Doonfoot S Ayrs 66 E6
Dorback Lodge Highld 82 B2
Dorchester Dorset 8 E5
Dorchester Oxon 18 B2
Dordon Warks 35 E8
Dore S Yorks 45 D7
Dores Highld 87 H8
Dorking Sur 19 G8
Dormansland Sur 12 B3
Dormanstown Redcar 59 D6
Dormington Hereford 26 D2
Dormston Worcs 26 C6
Dornal S Ayrs 54 B5
Dorney Bucks 18 D6
Dornie Highld 85 F13
Dornoch Highld 87 C10
Dornock Dumfries 61 G8
Dorrery Highld 94 E2
Dorridge W Mid 35 H7
Dorrington Lincs 46 G4
Dorrington Shrops 33 E10
Dorsington Warks 27 D8
Dorstone Hereford 25 D10
Dorton Bucks 28 G3
Dorusduain Highld 80 A1
Dosthill Staffs 35 F8
Dottery Dorset 8 E3
Doublebois Corn 4 E2
Dougarie N Ayrs 66 C1
Doughton Glos 16 B5
Douglas I o M 48 E3
Douglas S Lnrk 69 G7
Douglas & Angus Dundee 77 D7
Douglas Water S Lnrk 69 G7
Douglas West S Lnrk 69 G7
Douglastown Angus 77 C7
Doulting Som 16 G3
Dounby Orkney 95 F3
Doune Highld 92 J7
Doune Stirl 75 G10
Doune Park Aberds 89 B7
Douneside Aberds 82 C6
Dounie Highld 87 B8
Dounreay Highld 93 C12
Dousland Devon 4 E6
Dovaston Shrops 33 C9
Dove Holes Derbys 44 E4
Dovenby Cumb 56 C2
Dover Kent 21 G10
Dovercourt Essex 31 E9
Doverdale Worcs 26 B5
Doveridge Derbys 35 B7
Doversgreen Sur 19 G9
Dowally Perth 76 C3
Dowbridge Lancs 49 F4
Dowdeswell Glos 26 G6
Dowlais M Tydf 25 H7
Dowland Devon 6 E4
Dowlish Wake Som 8 C2
Down Ampney Glos 17 B8
Down Hatherley Glos 26 F5
Down St Mary Devon 7 F6
Down Thomas Devon 4 F6
Downcraig Ferry N Ayrs 73 H10
Downderry Corn 4 F4
Downe London 19 E11
Downend I o W 10 F4
Downend S Glos 16 D3
Downend W Berks 17 D11
Downfield Dundee 76 D6
Downgate Corn 4 D4
Downham Essex 20 B4
Downham Lancs 50 E3
Downham Northumb 71 G7
Downham Market Norf 38 E2
Downhead Som 16 G3
Downhill Perth 76 D3
Downhill T & W 63 H9
Downholland Cross Lancs 42 B6
Downholme N Yorks 58 G2
Downies Aberds 83 D11
Downley Bucks 18 B5
Downside Som 16 G3
Downside Sur 19 F8
Downton Hants 10 E1
Downton Wilts 9 B10
Downton on the Rock Hereford 25 A11
Dowsby Lincs 37 C7
Dowsdale Lincs 37 D8
Dowthwaitehead Cumb 56 D5
Doxey Staffs 34 C5
Doxford Northumb 63 A7
Doxford Park T & W 58 A4
Doynton S Glos 16 D4
Draffan S Lnrk 68 F6
Dragonby N Lincs 46 A3
Drakeland Corner Devon 5 F6
Drakemyre N Ayrs 66 A5
Drake's Broughton Worcs 26 D6
Drakes Cross Worcs 35 H6
Drakewalls Corn 4 D5
Draughton Northants 36 H3
Draughton N Yorks 50 D6
Drax N Yorks 52 G2
Draycote Warks 27 A11
Draycott Derbys 35 B10
Draycott Glos 27 E8
Draycott Som 15 F10
Draycott in the Clay Staffs 35 C7
Draycott in the Moors Staffs 34 A5
Drayford Devon 7 E6
Drayton Leics 36 F4
Drayton Lincs 37 B8
Drayton Norf 39 D7
Drayton Oxon 27 D11
Drayton Oxon 17 B11
Drayton Ptsmth 10 D5
Drayton Som 8 B3
Drayton Worcs 34 H5
Drayton Bassett Staffs 35 E7
Drayton Beauchamp Bucks 28 G6
Drayton Parslow Bucks 28 F5
Drayton St Leonard Oxon 18 B2
Dre-fach Ceredig 23 B10
Dre-fach Carms 24 G3
Drebley N Yorks 51 D6
Dreemskerry I o M 48 C4
Dreenhill Pembs 22 E4
Drefach Carms 23 C8
Drefach Carms 23 E10
Drefelin Carms 23 C8
Dreghorn N Ayrs 67 C6
Drellingore Kent 21 G9
Drem E Loth 70 C4
Dresden Stoke 34 A5
Dreumasdal W Isles 84 E2
Drewsteignton Devon 7 G6
Driby Lincs 47 E7
Driffield E Yorks 52 D6
Driffield Glos 17 B7
Drigg Cumb 56 G2
Drighlington W Yorks 51 G8
Drimnin Highld 79 F8
Drimpton Dorset 8 D3
Drimsynie Argyll 74 G4
Drinisiadar W Isles 90 H6
Drinkstone Suff 30 B6
Drinkstone Green Suff 30 B6
Drishaig Argyll 74 F4
Drissaig Argyll 73 B8
Drochil Borders 69 F10
Drointon Staffs 34 C6
Droitwich Spa Worcs 26 B5
Droman Highld 92 D4
Dron Perth 76 F4
Dronfield Derbys 45 E7
Dronfield Woodhouse Derbys 45 E7
Drongan E Ayrs 67 E7
Dronley Angus 76 D6
Droxford Hants 10 C5
Droylsden Gtr Man 44 C3
Druid Denb 32 A6
Druidston Pembs 22 E3
Druimarbin Highld 80 F2
Druimavuic Argyll 74 C3
Druimdrishaig Argyll 72 F6
Druimindarroch Highld 79 C9
Druimyeon More Argyll 65 C7
Drum Argyll 73 F8
Drum Perth 76 G3
Drumbeg Highld 92 F4
Drumblade Aberds 88 D5
Drumblair Aberds 89 D6
Drumbuie Dumfries 55 A8
Drumbuie Highld 85 E12
Drumburgh Cumb 61 H8
Drumburn Dumfries 60 G5
Drumchapel Glasgow 68 C4
Drumchardine Highld 87 G8
Drumchork Highld 91 J13
Drumclog S Lnrk 68 G5
Drumderfit Highld 87 F9
Drumeldrie Fife 77 G7
Drumelzier Borders 69 G10
Drumfearn Highld 85 G11
Drumgask Highld 81 D8
Drumgley Angus 77 B7
Drumguish Highld 81 D9
Drumin Moray 88 E1
Drumlasie Aberds 83 C8
Drumlemble Argyll 65 G7
Drumligair Aberds 83 B11
Drumlithie Aberds 83 E9
Drummoddie Dumfries 54 E6
Drummond Highld 87 E9
Drummore Dumfries 54 F4
Drummuir Moray 88 D3
Drummuir Castle Moray 88 D3
Drumnadrochit Highld 81 A7
Drumnagorrach Moray 88 C5
Drumoak Aberds 83 D9
Drumpark Dumfries 60 E4
Drumphail Dumfries 54 C5
Drumrash Dumfries 55 B9
Drumrunie Highld 92 J4
Drums Aberds 89 F9
Drumsallie Highld 80 F1
Drumstinchall Dumfries 55 D11
Drumsturdy Angus 77 D7
Drumtochty Castle Aberds 83 F8
Drumtroddan Dumfries 54 E6
Drumuie Highld 85 D9
Drumuillie Highld 81 A11
Drumvaich Stirl 75 G9
Drumwhindle Aberds 89 E9
Drunkendub Angus 77 C9
Drury Flint 42 F5
Drury Square Norf 38 D5
Dry Doddington Lincs 46 H2
Dry Drayton Cambs 29 B10
Drybeck Cumb 57 E8
Drybridge Moray 88 B4
Drybridge N Ayrs 67 C6
Drybrook Glos 26 G3
Dryburgh Borders 70 G4
Dryhope Borders 61 A8
Drylaw Edin 69 C11
Drym Corn 2 F5
Drymen Stirl 68 B3
Drymuir Aberds 89 D9
Drynoch Highld 85 E9
Dryslwyn Carms 23 D10
Dryton Shrops 34 E1
Dubford Aberds 89 B8
Dubton Angus 77 B8
Duchally Highld 92 H6
Duchlage Argyll 73 E11
Duck Corner Suff 31 D10
Duckington Ches 43 G7
Ducklington Oxon 27 H10
Duckmanton Derbys 45 E8
Duck's Cross Beds 29 C8
Duddenhoe End Essex 29 E11
Duddingston Edin 69 C11
Duddington Northants 36 E5
Duddleswell E Sus 12 D3
Duddo Northumb 71 F8
Duddon Ches 43 F8
Duddon Bridge Cumb 56 H4
Dudleston Shrops 33 B9
Dudleston Heath Shrops 33 B9
Dudley T & W 63 F8
Dudley W Mid 34 F5
Dudley Port W Mid 34 F5
Duffield Derbys 35 A9
Duffryn Newport 15 C8
Duffryn Neath 14 B4
Dufftown Moray 88 E3
Duffus Moray 88 B1
Dufton Cumb 57 D8
Duggleby N Yorks 52 C4
Duirinish Highld 85 E12
Duisdalemore Highld 85 G12
Duisky Highld 80 F2
Dukestown Bl Gwent 25 G8
Dukinfield Gtr Man 44 C3
Dulas Anglesey 40 B6
Dulcote Som 16 G2
Dulford Devon 7 F9
Dull Perth 75 C11
Dullatur N Lnrk 68 C6
Dullingham Cambs 30 C3
Dulnain Bridge Highld 82 A1
Duloe Beds 29 B8
Duloe Corn 4 F3
Dulsie Highld 87 G12
Dulverton Som 7 D8
Dulwich London 19 D10
Dumbarton W Dunb 68 C2
Dumbleton Glos 27 E7
Dumcrieff Dumfries 61 C7
Dumfries Dumfries 60 F5
Dumgoyne Stirl 68 B4
Dummer Hants 18 G2
Dumpford W Sus 11 B7
Dumpton Kent 21 E10
Dun Angus 77 B9
Dun Charlabhaigh W Isles 90 C6
Dunain Ho. Highld 87 G9
Dunalastair Perth 75 B10
Dunan Highld 85 F10
Dunans Argyll 73 D9
Dunball Som 15 G9
Dunbar E Loth 70 C5
Dunbeath Highld 94 H3
Dunbeg Argyll 79 H11
Dunblane Stirl 75 G10
Dunbog Fife 76 F5
Duncanston Aberds 83 A7
Duncanston Highld 87 F8
Dunchurch Warks 27 A11
Duncote Northants 28 C3
Duncow Dumfries 60 E5
Duncraggan Stirl 75 G8
Duncrievie Perth 76 G4
Duncton W Sus 11 C8
Dundas Ho. Orkney 95 K5
Dundee Dundee 77 D7
Dundee Airport Dundee 76 E6
Dundeugh Dumfries 67 H8
Dundon Som 8 A3
Dundonald S Ayrs 67 C6
Dundonnell Highld 86 C3
Dundonnell Hotel Highld 86 C3
Dundonnell House Highld 86 C4
Dundraw Cumb 56 B4
Dundreggan Highld 80 B5
Dundreggan Lodge Highld 80 B5
Dundrennan Dumfries 55 E10
Dundry N Som 16 E2
Dunecht Aberds 83 C9
Dunfermline Fife 69 B9
Dunfield Glos 17 B8
Dunford Bridge S Yorks 44 B5
Dungworth S Yorks 44 D6
Dunham Notts 46 E2
Dunham-on-the-Hill Ches 43 E7
Dunham Town Gtr Man 43 D10
Dunhampton Worcs 26 B5
Dunholme Lincs 46 E4
Dunino Fife 77 F8
Dunipace Falk 69 B7
Dunira Perth 75 E10
Dunkeld Perth 76 C3
Dunkerton Bath 16 F4
Dunkeswell Devon 7 F10
Dunkeswick N Yorks 51 E9
Dunkirk Kent 21 F7
Dunkirk Norf 39 C8
Dunk's Green Kent 20 F3
Dunlappie Angus 83 G7
Dunley Hants 17 F11
Dunley Worcs 26 B4
Dunlichity Lodge Highld 87 H9
Dunlop E Ayrs 67 B7
Dunmaglass Lodge Highld 81 A7
Dunmore Argyll 72 G6
Dunmore Falk 69 B7
Dunnet Highld 94 C4
Dunnichen Angus 77 C8
Dunninald Angus 77 B10
Dunning Perth 76 F3
Dunnington E Yorks 53 D7
Dunnington Warks 27 C7
Dunnington York 52 D2
Dunnockshaw Lancs 50 G4
Dunollie Argyll 79 H11
Dunoon Argyll 73 F10
Dunragit Dumfries 54 D4
Dunrostan Argyll 72 E6
Duns Borders 70 E6
Duns Tew Oxon 27 F11
Dunsby Lincs 37 C7
Dunscore Dumfries 60 E4
Dunscroft S Yorks 45 B10
Dunsdale Redcar 59 E7
Dunsden Green Oxon 18 D4
Dunsfold Sur 19 H7
Dunsford Devon 5 C9
Dunshalt Fife 76 F5
Dunshillock Aberds 89 D9
Dunskey Ho. Dumfries 54 D3
Dunsley N Yorks 59 E9
Dunsmore Bucks 28 H5
Dunsop Bridge Lancs 50 D2
Dunstable Beds 29 F7
Dunstall Staffs 35 C7
Dunstall Common Worcs 26 D5
Dunstall Green Suff 30 B4
Dunstan Northumb 63 B8
Dunstan Steads Northumb 63 A8
Dunster Som 7 B8
Dunston Lincs 46 F4
Dunston Norf 39 E8
Dunston Staffs 34 D5
Dunston T & W 63 G8
Dunsville S Yorks 45 B10
Dunswell E Yorks 53 F6
Dunsyre S Lnrk 69 F9
Dunterton Devon 4 D4
Duntisbourne Abbots Glos 26 H6
Duntisbourne Leer Glos 26 H6
Duntish Dorset 8 D5
Duntocher W Dunb 68 C3
Dunton Beds 29 D9
Dunton Bucks 28 F5
Dunton Norf 38 B4
Dunton Bassett Leics 35 F11
Dunton Green Kent 20 F2
Dunton Wayletts Essex 20 B3
Duntulm Highld 85 A9
Dunure S Ayrs 66 E5
Dunvant Swansea 23 G10
Dunvegan Highld 84 D7
Dunwich Suff 31 A11
Dunwood Staffs 44 G3
Dupplin Castle Perth 76 F3
Durdar Cumb 56 A6
Durgates E Sus 12 C5
Durham Durham 58 B3
Durham Tees Valley Airport Stockton 58 E4
Durisdeer Dumfries 60 C4
Durisdeermill Dumfries 60 C4
Durkar W Yorks 51 H9
Durleigh Som 15 H8
Durley Hants 10 C4
Durley Wilts 17 E9
Durnamuck Highld 86 B3
Durness Highld 92 C7
Durno Aberds 83 A9
Duror Highld 74 B2
Durran Argyll 73 C8
Durran Highld 94 D3
Durrington Wilts 17 G8
Durrington W Sus 11 D10
Dursley Glos 16 B4
Durston Som 8 B1
Durweston Dorset 9 D7
Dury Shetland 96 G6
Duston Northants 28 B4
Duthil Highld 81 A11
Dutlas Powys 33 H8
Duton Hill Essex 30 F3
Dutson Corn 4 C4
Dutton Ches 43 E8
Duxford Cambs 29 D11
Duxford Oxon 17 B10
Dwygyfylchi Conwy 41 C9
Dwyran Anglesey 40 D6
Dyce Aberdeen 83 B10
Dye House Northumb 62 H5
Dyffryn Bridgend 14 B4
Dyffryn Carms 23 D8
Dyffryn Pembs 22 C4
Dyffryn Ardudwy Gwyn 32 C1
Dyffryn Castell Ceredig 32 G3
Dyffryn Ceidrych Carms 24 F4
Dyffryn Cellwen Neath 24 H5
Dyke Lincs 37 C7
Dyke Moray 87 F12
Dykehead Angus 76 A6
Dykehead N Lnrk 69 E7
Dykehead Stirl 75 H8
Dykelands Aberds 83 G9
Dykends Angus 76 B5
Dykeside Aberds 89 D7
Dykesmains N Ayrs 66 B5
Dylife Powys 32 F4
Dymchurch Kent 13 D9
Dymock Glos 26 E4
Dyrham S Glos 16 D4
Dysart Fife 70 A2
Dyserth Denb 42 E3

E

Eachwick Northumb 63 F7
Eadar Dha Fhadhail W Isles 90 D5
Eagland Hill Lancs 49 E4
Eagle Lincs 46 F2
Eagle Barnsdale Lincs 46 F2
Eagle Moor Lincs 46 F2
Eaglescliffe Stockton 58 E5
Eaglesfield Cumb 56 D2
Eaglesfield Dumfries 61 F8
Eaglesham E Renf 68 E4
Eaglethorpe Northants 37 F6
Eairy I o M 48 E2
Eakley Lanes M Keynes 28 C5
Eakring Notts 45 F10
Ealand N Lincs 45 A11
Ealing London 19 C8
Eals Northumb 62 H2
Eamont Bridge Cumb 57 D7
Earby Lancs 50 E5
Earcroft Blkburn 50 G2
Eardington Shrops 34 F3
Eardisland Hereford 25 C11
Eardisley Hereford 25 D10
Eardiston Shrops 33 C9
Eardiston Worcs 26 B3
Earith Cambs 29 A10
Earl Shilton Leics 35 F10
Earl Soham Suff 31 B9
Earl Sterndale Derbys 44 F4
Earl Stonham Suff 31 C8
Earle Northumb 71 H8
Earley Wokingham 18 D4
Earlham Norf 39 E8
Earlish Highld 85 B8
Earls Barton Northants 28 B5
Earls Colne Essex 30 F5
Earl's Croome Worcs 26 D5
Earl's Green Suff 31 B7
Earlsdon W Mid 35 H9
Earlsferry Fife 77 H7
Earlsfield Lincs 36 B5
Earlsford Aberds 89 E8
Earlsheaton W Yorks 51 G8
Earlsmill Moray 87 F12
Earlston Borders 70 G4
Earlston E Ayrs 67 C7
Earlswood Mon 15 B10
Earlswood Sur 19 G9
Earlswood Warks 27 A8
Earnley W Sus 11 E7
Earsairidh W Isles 84 J2
Earsdon T & W 63 F9
Earsham Norf 39 G9
Earswick York 52 D2
Eartham W Sus 11 D8
Easby N Yorks 59 F6
Easby N Yorks 58 F2
Easdale Argyll 72 B6
Easebourne W Sus 11 B7
Easenhall Warks 35 H10
Eashing Sur 18 G6
Easington Bucks 28 G3
Easington Durham 58 B5
Easington E Yorks 53 H9
Easington Northumb 71 G10
Easington Oxon 27 E11
Easington Oxon 18 B3
Easington Redcar 59 E8
Easington Colliery Durham 58 B5
Easington Lane T & W 58 B4
Easingwold N Yorks 51 C11
Easole Street Kent 21 F9
Eassie Angus 76 C6
East Aberthaw V Glam 14 E6
East Adderbury Oxon 27 E11
East Allington Devon 5 G8
East Anstey Devon 7 D7
East Appleton N Yorks 58 G3
East Ardsley W Yorks 51 G9
East Ashling W Sus 11 D7
East Auchronie Aberds 83 C10
East Ayton N Yorks 59 H10
East Bank Bl Gwent 25 H9
East Barkwith Lincs 46 D5
East Barming Kent 20 F4
East Barnby N Yorks 59 E9
East Barnet London 19 B9
East Barns E Loth 70 C6
East Barsham Norf 38 B5
East Beckham Norf 39 B7
East Bedfont London 19 D7
East Bergholt Suff 31 E7
East Bilney Norf 38 D5
East Blatchington E Sus 12 F3
East Boldre Hants 10 D2
East Brent Som 15 F9
East Bridgford Notts 36 A2
East Buckland Devon 6 C5
East Budleigh Devon 7 H9
East Burrafirth Shetland 96 H5
East Burton Dorset 9 F7
East Butsfield Durham 58 B2
East Butterwick N Lincs 46 B2
East Cairnbeg Aberds 83 F9
East Calder W Loth 69 D9
East Carleton Norf 39 E7
East Carlton Northants 36 G4
East Carlton W Yorks 51 E8
East Chaldon Dorset 9 F6
East Challow Oxon 17 C10
East Chiltington E Sus 12 E2
East Chinnock Som 8 C3
East Chisenbury Wilts 17 F8
East Clandon Sur 19 F7
East Claydon Bucks 28 F4
East Clyne Highld 93 J12
East Coker Som 8 C4
East Combe Som 7 C10
East Common N Yorks 52 F2
East Compton Som 16 G3
East Cottingwith E Yorks 52 E3
East Cowes I o W 10 E4
East Cowick E Yorks 52 G2
East Cowton N Yorks 58 F4
East Cramlington Northumb 63 F8
East Cranmore Som 16 G3
East Creech Dorset 9 F8
East Croachy Highld 81 A8
East Croftmore Highld 81 B11
East Curthwaite Cumb 56 B5
East Dean E Sus 12 G4
East Dean Hants 10 B1
East Dean W Sus 11 C8
East Down Devon 6 B5
East Drayton Notts 45 E11
East Ella Hull 53 G6
East End Dorset 9 E8
East End E Yorks 53 G8
East End Hants 10 E2
East End Hants 10 B5
East End Hants 17 E11
East End Herts 29 F11
East End Kent 13 C7
East End N Som 15 D10
East End Oxon 27 G10
East Farleigh Kent 20 F4
East Farndon Northants 36 G3
East Ferry Lincs 46 C2
East Fortune E Loth 70 C4
East Garston W Berks 17 D10
East Ginge Oxon 17 C11
East Goscote Leics 36 D2
East Grafton Wilts 17 E9
East Grimstead Wilts 9 B11
East Grinstead W Sus 12 C2
East Guldeford E Sus 13 D8
East Haddon Northants 28 B3
East Hagbourne Oxon 18 C2
East Halton N Lincs 53 H7
East Ham London 19 C11
East Hanney Oxon 17 B11
East Hanningfield Essex 20 A4
East Hardwick W Yorks 51 H10
East Harling Norf 38 G5
East Harlsey N Yorks 58 G5
East Harnham Wilts 9 B10
East Harptree Bath 16 F2
East Hartford Northumb 63 F8
East Harting W Sus 11 C6
East Hatley Cambs 29 C9
East Hauxwell N Yorks 58 G2
East Haven Angus 77 D8
East Heckington Lincs 37 A7
East Hedleyhope Durham 58 B2
East Hendred Oxon 17 C11
East Herrington T & W 58 A4
East Heslerton N Yorks 52 B5
East Hoathly E Sus 12 E4
East Horrington Som 16 G2
East Horsley Sur 19 F7
East Horton Northumb 71 G9
East Huntspill Som 15 G9
East Hyde Beds 29 G8
East Ilkerton Devon 6 B6
East Ilsley W Berks 17 C11
East Keal Lincs 47 F7
East Kennett Wilts 17 E8
East Keswick W Yorks 51 E9
East Kilbride S Lnrk 68 E5
East Kirkby Lincs 47 F7
East Knapton N Yorks 52 B4
East Knighton Dorset 9 F7
East Knoyle Wilts 9 A7
East Kyloe Northumb 71 G9
East Lambrook Som 8 C3
East Lamington Highld 87 D10
East Langdon Kent 21 G10
East Langton Leics 36 F3
East Langwell Highld 93 J10
East Lavant W Sus 11 D7
East Lavington W Sus 11 C8
East Layton N Yorks 58 F2
East Leake Notts 36 C1
East Learmouth Northumb 71 G7
East Leigh Devon 6 F5
East Lexham Norf 38 D4
East Lilburn Northumb 62 A6
East Linton E Loth 70 C4
East Liss Hants 11 B6
East Looe Corn 4 F3
East Lound N Lincs 45 C11
East Lulworth Dorset 9 F7
East Lutton N Yorks 52 C5
East Lydford Som 8 A4
East Mains Aberds 83 D8
East Malling Kent 20 F4
East March Angus 77 D7
East Marden W Sus 11 C7
East Markham Notts 45 E11
East Marton N Yorks 50 D5
East Meon Hants 10 B5
East Mere Devon 7 E8
East Mersea Essex 31 G7
East Mey Highld 94 C5
East Molesey Sur 19 E8
East Morden Dorset 9 E8
East Morton W Yorks 51 E6
East Ness N Yorks 52 B2
East Newton E Yorks 53 F8
East Norton Leics 36 E3
East Nynehead Som 7 D10
East Oakley Hants 18 F2
East Ogwell Devon 5 D9
East Orchard Dorset 9 C7
East Ord Northumb 71 E8
East Panson Devon 6 G2
East Peckham Kent 20 G3
East Pennard Som 16 H2
East Perry Cambs 29 B8
East Portlemouth Devon 5 H8
East Prawle Devon 5 H8
East Preston W Sus 11 D9
East Putford Devon 6 E2
East Quantoxhead Som 7 B10
East Rainton T & W 58 B4
East Ravendale NE Lincs 46 C6
East Raynham Norf 38 C4
East Rhidorroch Lodge Highld 86 B5
East Rigton W Yorks 51 E9
East Rounton N Yorks 58 F5
East Row N Yorks 59 E9
East Rudham Norf 38 C4
East Runton Norf 39 A7
East Ruston Norf 39 C9
East Saltoun E Loth 70 D3
East Sleekburn Northumb 63 E8
East Somerton Norf 39 D10
East Stockwith Lincs 45 C11
East Stoke Dorset 9 F7
East Stoke Notts 45 H11
East Stour Dorset 9 B7
East Stourmouth Kent 21 E9
East Stowford Devon 6 D5
East Stratton Hants 18 H2
East Studdal Kent 21 G10
East Suisnish Highld 85 E10
East Taphouse Corn 4 E2
East-the-Water Devon 6 D3
East Thirston Northumb 63 D7
East Tilbury Thurrock 20 D3
East Tisted Hants 10 A6
East Torrington Lincs 46 D5
East Tuddenham Norf 39 D6
East Tytherley Hants 10 B1
East Tytherton Wilts 16 D6
East Village Devon 7 F7
East Wall Shrops 33 F11
East Walton Norf 38 D3
East Wellow Hants 10 B2
East Wemyss Fife 76 H6
East Whitburn W Loth 69 D8
East Williamston Pembs 22 F5
East Winch Norf 38 D2
East Winterslow Wilts 9 A11
East Wittering W Sus 11 E6
East Witton N Yorks 58 H2
East Woodburn Northumb 62 E5
East Woodhay Hants 17 E11
East Worldham Hants 18 H4
East Worlington Devon 7 E6
East Worthing W Sus 11 D10
Eastbourne E Sus 12 G5
Eastbridge Suff 31 B11
Eastburn W Yorks 50 E6
Eastbury Herts 19 B7
Eastbury W Berks 17 D10
Eastby N Yorks 50 D6
Eastchurch Kent 20 D6
Eastcombe Glos 16 A5
Eastcote London 19 C8
Eastcote Northants 28 C3
Eastcote W Mid 35 H7
Eastcott Corn 6 E1
Eastcott Wilts 17 F7
Eastcourt Wilts 16 B6
Eastcourt Wilts 17 E9
Easter Ardross Highld 87 D9
Easter Balmoral Aberds 82 D4
Easter Boleskine Highld 81 A7
Easter Compton S Glos 16 C2
Easter Cringate Stirl 68 B6
Easter Davoch Aberds 82 C6
Easter Earshaig Dumfries 60 C6
Easter Fearn Highld 87 C9
Easter Galcantray Highld 87 G11
Easter Howgate Midloth 69 D11
Easter Howlaws Borders 70 F6
Easter Kinkell Highld 87 F8
Easter Lednathie Angus 76 A6
Easter Milton Highld 87 F12
Easter Moniack Highld 87 G8
Easter Ord Aberds 83 C10
Easter Quarff Shetland 96 K6
Easter Rhynd Perth 76 F4
Easter Row Stirl 75 H10
Easter Silverford Aberds 89 B7
Easter Skeld Shetland 96 J5
Easter Whyntie Aberds 88 B6
Eastergate W Sus 11 D8
Easterhouse Glasgow 68 D5
Eastern Green W Mid 35 G8
Easterton Wilts 17 F7
Eastertown Som 15 F9
Eastertown of Auchleuchries Aberds 89 E10
Eastfield N Lnrk 69 D7
Eastfield N Yorks 52 A6
Eastfield Hall Northumb 63 C8
Eastgate Durham 57 C11
Eastgate Norf 39 C7
Eastham Mers 42 D6
Eastham Ferry Mers 42 D6
Easthampstead Brack 18 E5
Eastheath Wokingham 18 E5
Easthope Shrops 34 F1
Easthorpe Essex 30 F6
Easthorpe Leics 36 B4
Easthorpe Notts 45 G11
Easthouses Midloth 70 D2
Eastington Devon 7 F6
Eastington Glos 26 H4
Eastington Glos 27 G8
Eastleach Martin Glos 27 H9
Eastleach Turville Glos 27 H8
Eastleigh Devon 6 D3
Eastleigh Hants 10 C3
Eastling Kent 20 F6
Eastmoor Derbys 45 E7
Eastmoor Norf 38 E3
Eastney Ptsmth 10 E5
Eastnor Hereford 26 E4
Eastoft N Lincs 52 H4
Eastoke Hants 10 E6
Easton Cambs 29 A8
Easton Cumb 61 H8
Easton Cumb 61 F10
Easton Devon 5 C8
Easton Dorset 8 G5
Easton Hants 10 A4
Easton Lincs 36 C5
Easton Norf 39 D7
Easton Som 15 G11
Easton Suff 31 C9
Easton Wilts 16 D5
Easton Grey Wilts 16 C5
Easton-in-Gordano N Som 15 D11
Easton Maudit Northants 28 C5
Easton on the Hill Northants 36 E6
Easton Royal Wilts 17 E9
Eastpark Dumfries 60 G6
Eastrea Cambs 37 F8
Eastriggs Dumfries 61 G8
Eastrington E Yorks 52 G3
Eastry Kent 21 F10
Eastville Bristol 16 D3
Eastville Lincs 47 G8
Eastwell Leics 36 C3
Eastwick Herts 29 G11
Eastwick Shetland 96 F5
Eastwood Notts 45 H8
Eastwood Sthend 20 C5
Eastwood W Yorks 50 G5
Eathorpe Warks 27 B10
Eaton Ches 43 F8
Eaton Ches 44 F2
Eaton Leics 36 C3
Eaton Norf 39 E8
Eaton Notts 45 E11
Eaton Oxon 17 A11
Eaton Shrops 33 G9
Eaton Shrops 33 G11
Eaton Bishop Hereford 25 E11
Eaton Bray Beds 28 F6
Eaton Constantine Shrops 34 E1
Eaton Green Beds 28 F6
Eaton Hastings Oxon 17 B9
Eaton on Tern Shrops 34 C2
Eaton Socon Cambs 29 C8
Eavestone N Yorks 51 C8
Ebberston N Yorks 52 A4
Ebbesbourne Wake Wilts 9 B8
Ebbw Vale = Glyn Ebwy Bl Gwent 25 H8
Ebchester Durham 63 H7
Ebford Devon 5 C10
Ebley Glos 26 H5
Ebnal Ches 43 H7
Ebrington Glos 27 D8
Ecchinswell Hants 17 F11
Ecclaw Borders 70 D6
Ecclefechan Dumfries 61 F7
Eccles Borders 70 F6
Eccles Gtr Man 43 C10
Eccles Kent 20 E4
Eccles on Sea Norf 39 C10
Eccles Road Norf 38 F6
Ecclesall S Yorks 45 D7
Ecclesfield S Yorks 45 C7
Ecclesgreig Aberds 83 G9
Eccleshall Staffs 34 C4
Eccleshill W Yorks 51 F7
Ecclesmachan W Loth 69 C9
Eccleston Ches 43 F7
Eccleston Lancs 49 H5
Eccleston Mers 43 C7
Eccleston Park Mers 43 C7
Eccup W Yorks 51 E8
Echt Aberds 83 C9
Eckford Borders 70 H6
Eckington Derbys 45 E8
Eckington Worcs 26 D6
Ecton Northants 28 B5
Edale Derbys 44 D5
Edburton W Sus 11 C11
Edderside Cumb 56 B2
Edderton Highld 87 C10
Eddistone Devon 6 D1
Eddleston Borders 69 F11
Eden Park London 19 E10
Edenbridge Kent 19 G11
Edenfield Lancs 50 H3
Edenhall Cumb 57 C7
Edenham Lincs 37 C6
Edensor Derbys 44 F6
Edentaggart Argyll 68 A2
Edenthorpe S Yorks 45 B10
Edentown Cumb 61 H9
Ederline Argyll 73 C7
Edern Gwyn 40 G4
Edgarley Som 15 H11
Edgbaston W Mid 35 G6
Edgcott Bucks 28 F3
Edgcott Som 7 C7
Edge Shrops 33 E9
Edge End Glos 26 G2
Edge Green Ches 43 G7
Edge Hill Mers 42 D6
Edgebolton Shrops 34 C1
Edgefield Norf 39 B6
Edgefield Street Norf 39 B6
Edgeside Lancs 50 G4
Edgeworth Glos 26 H6
Edgmond Telford 34 D3
Edgmond Marsh Telford 34 C3
Edgton Shrops 33 G9
Edgware London 19 B8
Edgworth Blkburn 50 H3
Edinample Stirl 75 E8
Edinbane Highld 85 C8
Edinburgh Edin 69 C11
Edinburgh Airport Edin 69 C10
Edingale Staffs 35 D8
Edingight Ho. Moray 88 C5
Edingley Notts 45 G10
Edingthorpe Norf 39 B9
Edingthorpe Green Norf 39 B9
Edington Som 15 H9
Edington Wilts 16 F6
Edintore Moray 88 D4
Edith Weston Rutland 36 E5
Edithmead Som 15 G9
Edlesborough Bucks 28 G6
Edlingham Northumb 63 C7
Edlington Lincs 46 E6
Edmondsham Dorset 9 C9
Edmondsley Durham 58 B3
Edmondthorpe Leics 36 D4
Edmonstone Orkney 95 F6
Edmonton London 19 B10
Edmundbyers Durham 58 A1
Ednam Borders 70 G6
Ednaston Derbys 35 A8
Edradynate Perth 75 B11
Edrom Borders 71 E7
Edstaston Shrops 33 B11
Edstone Warks 27 B8
Edvin Loach Hereford 26 C3
Edwalton Notts 36 B1
Edwardstone Suff 30 D6
Edwinsford Carms 24 E3
Edwinstowe Notts 45 F10
Edworth Beds 29 D9
Edwyn Ralph Hereford 26 C3
Edzell Angus 83 G7
Efail Isaf Rhondda 14 C6
Efailnewydd Gwyn 40 G5
Efailwen Carms 22 D6
Efenechtyd Denb 42 G4
Effingham Sur 19 F8
Effirth Shetland 96 H5
Efford Devon 7 F7
Egdon Worcs 26 C6
Egerton Gtr Man 43 A10
Egerton Kent 20 G6
Egerton Forstal Kent 20 G5
Eggborough N Yorks 52 G1
Eggbuckland Plym 4 F6
Eggington Beds 28 F6
Egginton Derbys 35 C8
Egglescliffe Stockton 58 E5
Eggleston Durham 57 D11
Egham Sur 19 D7
Egleton Rutland 36 E4
Eglingham Northumb 63 B7
Egloshayle Corn 3 B8
Egloskerry Corn 4 C3
Eglwys-Brewis V Glam 14 E6
Eglwys Cross Wrex 33 A10
Eglwys Fach Ceredig 32 F2
Eglwysbach Conwy 41 C10
Eglwyswen Pembs 22 C6
Eglwyswrw Pembs 22 C6
Egmanton Notts 45 F11
Egremont Cumb 56 E2
Egremont Mers 42 C6
Egton N Yorks 59 F9
Egton Bridge N Yorks 59 F9
Eight Ash Green Essex 30 F6
Eignaig Highld 79 G10
Eil Highld 81 B10
Eilanreach Highld 85 G13
Eilean Darach Highld 86 C4
Eileanach Lodge Highld 87 E8
Einacleite W Isles 90 E6
Eisgean W Isles 91 F8
Eisingrug Gwyn 41 G8
Elan Village Powys 24 B6
Elberton S Glos 16 C3
Elburton Plym 4 F6
Elcho Perth 76 E4
Elcombe Swindon 17 C8
Eldernell Cambs 37 F9
Eldersfield Worcs 26 E5
Elderslie Renfs 68 D3
Eldon Durham 58 D3
Eldrick S Ayrs 54 A5
Eldroth N Yorks 50 C3
Eldwick W Yorks 51 E7
Elfhowe Cumb 56 G6
Elford Northumb 71 G10
Elford Staffs 35 D7
Elgin Moray 88 B2
Elgol Highld 85 G10
Elham Kent 21 G8
Elie Fife 77 G7
Elim Anglesey 40 B5
Eling Hants 10 C2
Elishader Highld 85 B10
Elishaw Northumb 62 D4
Elkesley Notts 45 E10
Elkstone Glos 26 G6
Ellan Highld 81 A10
Elland W Yorks 51 G7
Ellary Argyll 72 F6
Ellastone Staffs 35 A7
Ellemford Borders 70 D6
Ellenbrook I o M 48 E3
Ellenhall Staffs 34 C4
Ellen's Green Sur 19 H7
Ellerbeck N Yorks 58 G5
Ellerburn N Yorks 52 A4
Ellerby N Yorks 59 E8
Ellerdine Heath Telford 34 C2
Ellerhayes Devon 7 F8
Elleric Argyll 74 C3
Ellerker E Yorks 52 G5
Ellerton E Yorks 52 F3
Ellerton Shrops 34 C3
Ellesborough Bucks 28 H5
Ellesmere Shrops 33 B10
Ellesmere Port Ches 43 E7
Ellingham Norf 39 F9
Ellingham Northumb 71 H10
Ellingstring N Yorks 51 A7
Ellington Cambs 29 A8
Ellington Northumb 63 D8
Elliot Angus 77 D9
Ellisfield Hants 18 G3
Ellistown Leics 35 D10
Ellon Aberds 89 E9
Ellonby Cumb 56 C6
Ellough Suff 39 G10
Elloughton E Yorks 52 G5
Ellwood Glos 26 H2
Elm Cambs 37 E10
Elm Hill Dorset 9 B7
Elm Park London 20 C2
Elmbridge Worcs 26 B6
Elmdon Essex 29 E11
Elmdon W Mid 35 G7
Elmdon Heath W Mid 35 G7
Elmers End London 19 E10
Elmesthorpe Leics 35 F10
Elmfield I o W 10 E5
Elmhurst Staffs 35 D7
Elmley Castle Worcs 26 D6
Elmley Lovett Worcs 26 B5
Elmore Glos 26 G4
Elmore Back Glos 26 G4
Elmscott Devon 6 D1
Elmsett Suff 31 D7
Elmstead Market Essex 31 F7
Elmsted Kent 13 B10
Elmstone Kent 21 E9
Elmstone Hardwicke Glos 26 F6
Elmswell E Yorks 52 D5
Elmswell Suff 30 B6
Elmton Derbys 45 E9
Elphin Highld 92 H5
Elphinstone E Loth 70 C2
Elrick Aberds 83 C10
Elrig Dumfries 54 E6
Elsdon Northumb 62 D5
Elsecar S Yorks 45 C7
Elsenham Essex 30 F2
Elsfield Oxon 28 G2
Elsham N Lincs 46 A4
Elsing Norf 39 D6
Elslack N Yorks 50 E5
Elson Shrops 33 B9
Elsrickle S Lnrk 69 F9
Elstead Sur 18 G6
Elsted W Sus 11 C7
Elsthorpe Lincs 37 C6
Elstob Durham 58 D4
Elston Notts 45 H11
Elston Wilts 17 G7
Elstone Devon 6 E5
Elstow Beds 29 D7
Elstree Herts 19 B8
Elstronwick E Yorks 53 F8
Elswick Lancs 49 F4
Elsworth Cambs 29 B10
Elterwater Cumb 56 F5
Eltham London 19 D11
Eltisley Cambs 29 C9
Elton Cambs 37 F6

Elton Ches 43 E7
Elton Derbys 44 F6
Elton Glos 26 G4
Elton Hereford 25 A11
Elton Notts 36 B3
Elton Stockton 58 E5
Elton Green Ches 43 E7
Elvanfoot S Lnrk 60 B5
Elvaston Derbys 35 B10
Elveden Suff 38 H4
Elvingston E Loth 70 C3
Elvington Kent 21 F9
Elvington York 52 E2
Elwick Hrtlpl 58 C5
Elwick Northumb 71 G10
Elworth Ches 43 F10
Elworthy Som 7 C9
Ely Cambs 37 G11
Ely Cardiff 15 D7
Emberton M Keynes 28 D5
Embleton Cumb 56 C3
Embleton Northumb 63 A8
Embo Highld 87 B11
Embo Street Highld 87 B11
Emborough Som 16 F3
Embsay N Yorks 50 D6
Emery Down Hants 10 D1
Emley W Yorks 44 A6
Emmbrook Wokingham 18 E4
Emmer Green Reading 18 D4
Emmington Oxon 18 A4
Emneth Norf 37 E10
Emneth Hungate Norf 37 E11
Empingham Rutland 36 E5
Empshott Hants 11 A6
Emstrey Shrops 33 D11
Emsworth Hants 10 D6
Enborne W Berks 17 E11
Enchmarsh Shrops 33 F11
Enderby Leics 35 F11
Endmoor Cumb 49 A5
Endon Staffs 44 G3
Endon Bank Staffs 44 G3
Enfield London 19 B10
Enfield Wash London 19 B10
Enford Wilts 17 F8
Engamoor Shetland 96 H4
Engine Common S Glos 16 C3
Englefield W Berks 18 D3
Englefield Green Sur 18 D6
Englesea-brook Ches 43 G10
English Bicknor Glos 26 G2
English Frankton Shrops 33 C10
Englishcombe Bath 16 E4
Enham Alamein Hants 17 G10
Enmore Som 8 A1
Ennerdale Bridge Cumb 56 E2
Enoch Dumfries 60 C4
Enochdhu Perth 76 A3
Ensay Argyll 78 G6
Ensbury Bmouth 9 E9
Ensdon Shrops 33 D10
Ensis Devon 6 D4
Enstone Oxon 27 F10
Enterkinfoot Dumfries 60 C4
Enterpen N Yorks 58 F5
Enville Staffs 34 G4
Eolaigearraidh W Isles 84 H2
Eorabus Argyll 78 J6
Eòropaidh W Isles 91 A10
Epperstone Notts 45 H10
Epping Essex 19 A11
Epping Green Essex 29 H11
Epping Green Herts 29 H9
Epping Upland Essex 19 A11
Eppleby N Yorks 58 E2
Eppleworth E Yorks 52 F6
Epsom Sur 19 E9
Epwell Oxon 27 D10
Epworth N Lincs 45 B11
Epworth Turbary N Lincs 45 B11
Erbistock Wrex 33 A9
Erbusaig Highld 85 F12
Erchless Castle Highld 86 G7
Erdington W Mid 35 F7
Eredine Argyll 73 C8
Eriboll Highld 92 D7
Ericstane Dumfries 60 B6
Eridge Green E Sus 12 C4
Erines Argyll 73 F7
Eriswell Suff 38 H3
Erith London 20 D2
Erlestoke Wilts 16 F6
Ermine Lincs 46 E3
Ermington Devon 5 F7
Erpingham Norf 39 B7
Errogie Highld 81 A7
Errol Perth 76 E5
Erskine Renfs 68 C3
Erskine Bridge Renfs 68 C3
Ervie Dumfries 54 C3
Erwarton Suff 31 E9
Erwood Powys 25 D7
Eryholme N Yorks 58 F4
Eryrys Denb 42 G5
Escomb Durham 58 D2
Escrick N Yorks 52 E2
Esgairdawe Carms 24 D3
Esgairgeiliog Powys 32 E3
Esh Durham 58 B2
Esh Winning Durham 58 B2
Esher Sur 19 E8
Esholt W Yorks 51 E7
Eshott Northumb 63 D8
Eshton N Yorks 50 D5
Esk Valley N Yorks 59 F9
Eskadale Highld 86 H7
Eskbank Midloth 70 D2
Eskdale Green Cumb 56 F3
Eskdalemuir Dumfries 61 D8
Eske E Yorks 53 E6
Eskham Lincs 47 C7
Esprick Lancs 49 F4
Essendine Rutland 36 D6
Essendon Herts 29 H9
Essich Highld 87 H9
Essington Staffs 34 E5
Esslemont Aberds 89 F9
Eston Redcar 59 E6
Eswick Shetland 96 H6
Etal Northumb 71 G8
Etchilhampton Wilts 17 E7
Etchingham E Sus 12 D6
Etchinghill Kent 21 H8
Etchinghill Staffs 34 D6
Ethie Castle Angus 77 C9
Ethie Mains Angus 77 C9
Etling Green Norf 38 D6
Eton Windsor 18 D6
Eton Wick Windsor 18 D6
Etteridge Highld 81 D8
Ettersgill Durham 57 D10
Ettingshall W Mid 34 F5
Ettington Warks 27 D9
Etton E Yorks 52 E5
Etton P'boro 37 E7
Ettrick Borders 61 B8
Ettrickbridge Borders 61 A9
Ettrickhill Borders 61 B8
Etwall Derbys 35 B8
Euston Suff 38 H4
Euximoor Drove Cambs 37 F10
Euxton Lancs 50 H1
Evanstown Bridgend 14 C5
Evanton Highld 87 E9
Evedon Lincs 46 H4
Evelix Highld 87 B10
Evenjobb Powys 25 B9
Evenley Northants 28 E2
Evenlode Glos 27 F9
Evenwood Durham 58 D2
Evenwood Gate Durham 58 D2
Everbay Orkney 95 F7
Evercreech Som 16 H3
Everdon Northants 28 C2
Everingham E Yorks 52 E4
Everleigh Wilts 17 F9
Everley N Yorks 59 H10
Eversholt Beds 28 E6
Evershot Dorset 8 D4
Eversley Hants 18 E4
Eversley Cross Hants 18 E4
Everthorpe E Yorks 52 F5
Everton Beds 29 C9
Everton Hants 10 E1
Everton Mers 42 C6
Everton Notts 45 C10
Evertown Dumfries 61 F9
Evesbatch Hereford 26 D3
Evesham Worcs 27 D7
Evington Leicester 36 E2
Ewden Village S Yorks 44 C6
Ewell Sur 19 E9
Ewell Minnis Kent 21 G9
Ewelme Oxon 18 B3
Ewen Glos 17 B7
Ewenny V Glam 14 D5
Ewerby Lincs 46 H5
Ewerby Thorpe Lincs 46 H5
Ewes Dumfries 61 D9
Ewesley Northumb 62 D6
Ewhurst Sur 19 G7
Ewhurst Green E Sus 13 D6
Ewhurst Green Sur 19 H7
Ewloe Flint 42 F6
Ewloe Green Flint 42 F5
Ewood Blkburn 50 G2
Eworthy Devon 6 G3
Ewshot Hants 18 G5
Ewyas Harold Hereford 25 F10
Exbourne Devon 6 F5
Exbury Hants 10 E3
Exebridge Som 7 D8
Exelby N Yorks 58 H3
Exeter Devon 7 G8
Exeter International Airport Devon 7 G8
Exford Som 7 C7
Exhall Warks 27 C8
Exley Head W Yorks 50 F6
Exminster Devon 5 C10
Exmouth Devon 5 C11
Exnaboe Shetland 96 M5
Exning Suff 30 B3
Exton Devon 5 C10
Exton Hants 10 B5
Exton Rutland 36 D5
Exton Som 7 C8
Exwick Devon 7 G8
Eyam Derbys 44 E6
Eydon Northants 28 C2
Eye Hereford 25 B11
Eye P'boro 37 E8
Eye Suff 31 A8
Eye Green P'boro 37 E8
Eyemouth Borders 71 D8
Eyeworth Beds 29 D9
Eyhorne Street Kent 20 F5
Eyke Suff 31 C10
Eynesbury Cambs 29 C8
Eynort Highld 85 F8
Eynsford Kent 20 E2
Eynsham Oxon 27 H11
Eype Dorset 8 E3
Eyre Highld 85 C9
Eyre Highld 85 E10
Eythorne Kent 21 G9
Eyton Hereford 25 B11
Eyton Shrops 33 G9
Eyton Wrex 33 A9
Eyton upon the Weald Moors Telford 34 D2

F

Faccombe Hants 17 F10
Faceby N Yorks 58 F5
Facit Lancs 50 H4
Faddiley Ches 43 G8
Fadmoor N Yorks 59 H7
Faerdre Swansea 14 A2
Failand N Som 15 D4
Failford S Ayrs 67 D7
Failsworth Gtr Man 44 B2
Fain Highld 86 D4
Fair Green Norf 38 D2
Fair Hill Cumb 57 C7
Fair Oak Hants 10 C3
Fair Oak Green Hants 18 E3
Fairbourne Gwyn 32 D2
Fairburn N Yorks 51 G10
Fairfield Derbys 44 E4
Fairfield Stockton 58 E5
Fairfield Worcs 27 D7
Fairfield Worcs 34 H5
Fairford Glos 17 A8
Fairhaven Lancs 49 G3
Fairlie N Ayrs 73 H11
Fairlight E Sus 13 E7
Fairlight Cove E Sus 13 E7
Fairmile Devon 7 G9
Fairmilehead Edin 69 D11
Fairoak Staffs 34 B3
Fairseat Kent 20 E3
Fairstead Essex 30 G4
Fairstead Norf 39 C8
Fairwarp E Sus 12 D3
Fairy Cottage I o M 48 D4
Fairy Cross Devon 6 D3
Fakenham Norf 38 C5
Fakenham Magna Suff 38 H5
Fala Midloth 70 D3
Fala Dam Midloth 70 D3
Falahill Borders 70 E2
Falcon Hereford 26 E3
Faldingworth Lincs 46 D4
Falfield S Glos 16 B3
Falkenham Suff 31 E9
Falkirk Falk 69 C7
Falkland Fife 76 G5
Falla Borders 62 B3
Fallgate Derbys 45 F7
Fallin Stirl 69 A7
Fallowfield Gtr Man 44 C2
Fallsidehill Borders 70 F5
Falmer E Sus 12 F2
Falmouth Corn 3 F7
Falsgrave N Yorks 59 H11
Falstone Northumb 62 E3
Fanagmore Highld 92 E4
Fangdale Beck N Yorks 59 G6
Fangfoss E Yorks 52 D3
Fankerton Falk 68 B6
Fanmore Argyll 78 G7
Fannich Lodge Highld 86 E5
Fans Borders 70 F5
Far Bank S Yorks 45 A10
Far Bletchley M Keynes 28 E5
Far Cotton Northants 28 C4
Far Forest Worcs 26 A4
Far Laund Derbys 45 H7
Far Sawrey Cumb 56 G5
Farcet Cambs 37 F8
Farden Shrops 34 H1
Fareham Hants 10 D4
Farewell Staffs 35 D6
Farforth Lincs 47 E7
Faringdon Oxon 17 B9
Farington Lancs 49 G5
Farlam Cumb 61 H11
Farlary Highld 93 J10
Farleigh N Som 15 E10
Farleigh Sur 19 E10
Farleigh Hungerford Som 16 F5
Farleigh Wallop Hants 18 G3
Farlesthorpe Lincs 47 E8
Farleton Cumb 49 A5
Farleton Lancs 50 C1
Farley Shrops 33 E9
Farley Staffs 35 A6
Farley Wilts 9 B11
Farley Green Sur 19 G7
Farley Hill Luton 29 F7
Farley Hill Wokingham 18 E4
Farleys End Glos 26 G4
Farlington N Yorks 52 C2
Farlow Shrops 34 G2
Farmborough Bath 16 E3
Farmcote Glos 27 F7
Farmcote Shrops 34 F3
Farmington Glos 27 G8
Farmoor Oxon 27 H11
Farmtown Moray 88 C5
Farnborough London 19 E11
Farnborough Hants 18 F5
Farnborough Warks 27 D11
Farnborough W Berks 17 C11
Farnborough Green Hants 18 F5
Farncombe Sur 18 G6
Farndish Beds 28 B6
Farndon Ches 43 G7
Farndon Notts 45 G11
Farnell Angus 77 B9
Farnham Dorset 9 C8
Farnham Essex 29 F11
Farnham N Yorks 51 C9
Farnham Suff 31 B10
Farnham Sur 18 G5
Farnham Common Bucks 18 C6
Farnham Green Essex 29 F11
Farnham Royal Bucks 18 C6
Farnhill N Yorks 50 E6
Farningham Kent 20 E2
Farnley N Yorks 51 E8
Farnley W Yorks 51 F8
Farnley Tyas W Yorks 44 A5
Farnsfield Notts 45 G10
Farnworth Gtr Man 43 B10
Farnworth Halton 43 D8
Farr Highld 87 H9
Farr Highld 81 C10
Farr Highld 93 C10
Farr House Highld 87 H9
Farringdon Devon 7 G9
Farrington Gurney Bath 16 F3
Farsley W Yorks 51 F8
Farthinghoe Northants 28 E2
Farthingloe Kent 21 G9
Farthingstone Northants 28 C3
Fartown W Yorks 51 H7
Farway Devon 7 G10
Fasag Highld 85 C13
Fascadale Highld 79 D8
Faslane Port Argyll 73 E11
Fasnacloich Argyll 74 C3
Fasnakyle Ho. Highld 80 A5
Fassfern Highld 80 F2
Fatfield T & W 58 A4
Fattahead Aberds 89 C6
Faugh Cumb 57 A7
Fauldhouse W Loth 69 D8
Faulkbourne Essex 30 G4
Faulkland Som 16 F4
Fauls Shrops 34 B1
Faversham Kent 21 E7
Favillar Moray 88 E2
Fawdington N Yorks 51 B10
Fawfieldhead Staffs 44 F4
Fawkham Green Kent 20 E2
Fawler Oxon 27 G10
Fawley Bucks 18 C4
Fawley Hants 10 D3
Fawley W Berks 17 C10
Fawley Chapel Hereford 26 F2
Faxfleet E Yorks 52 G4
Faygate W Sus 11 A11
Fazakerley Mers 43 C6
Fazeley Staffs 35 E8
Fearby N Yorks 51 A7
Fearn Highld 87 D11
Fearn Lodge Highld 87 C9
Fearn Station Highld 87 D11
Fearnan Perth 75 C10
Fearnbeg Highld 85 C12
Fearnhead Warr 43 C9
Fearnmore Highld 85 B12
Featherstone Staffs 34 E5
Featherstone W Yorks 51 G10
Featherwood Northumb 62 C4
Feckenham Worcs 27 B7
Feering Essex 30 F5
Feetham N Yorks 57 G11
Feizor N Yorks 50 C3
Felbridge Sur 12 C2
Felbrigg Norf 39 B8
Felcourt Sur 12 B2
Felden Herts 19 A7
Felin-Crai Powys 24 F5
Felindre Ceredig 23 A10
Felindre Carms 23 D10
Felindre Carms 24 E3
Felindre Carms 24 F4
Felindre Carms 23 C8
Felindre Powys 33 G7
Felindre Swansea 14 A2
Felindre Farchog Pembs 22 C6
Felinfach Ceredig 23 A10
Felinfach Powys 25 E7
Felinfoel Carms 23 F10
Felingwm isaf Carms 23 D10
Felingwm uchaf Carms 23 D10
Felinwynt Ceredig 23 A7
Felixkirk N Yorks 51 A10
Felixstowe Suff 31 E9
Felixstowe Ferry Suff 31 E10
Felkington Northumb 71 F8
Felkirk W Yorks 45 A7
Fell Side Cumb 56 C5
Felling T & W 63 G8
Felmersham Beds 28 C6
Felmingham Norf 39 C8
Felpham W Sus 11 E8
Felsham Suff 30 C6
Felsted Essex 30 F3
Feltham London 19 D8
Felthorpe Norf 39 D7
Felton Hereford 26 D2
Felton Northumb 63 C7
Felton N Som 15 E11
Felton Butler Shrops 33 D9
Feltwell Norf 38 F3
Fen Ditton Cambs 29 B11
Fen Drayton Cambs 29 B10
Fen End W Mid 35 H8
Fen Side Lincs 47 G7
Fenay Bridge W Yorks 51 H7
Fence Lancs 50 F4
Fence Houses T & W 58 A4
Fengate Norf 39 C7
Fengate P'boro 37 F8
Fenham Northumb 71 F9
Fenhouses Lincs 37 A8
Feniscliffe Blkburn 50 G2
Feniscowles Blkburn 50 G2
Feniton Devon 7 G10
Fenlake Beds 29 D7
Fenny Bentley Derbys 44 G5
Fenny Bridges Devon 7 G10
Fenny Compton Warks 27 C11
Fenny Drayton Leics 35 F9
Fenny Stratford M Keynes 28 E5
Fenrother Northumb 63 D7
Fenstanton Cambs 29 B10
Fenton Cambs 37 H9
Fenton Lincs 46 G2
Fenton Lincs 46 E2
Fenton Stoke 34 A4
Fenton Barns E Loth 70 B4
Fenton Town Northumb 71 G8
Fenwick E Ayrs 67 B7
Fenwick Northumb 62 F6
Fenwick Northumb 71 F9
Fenwick S Yorks 52 H1
Feochaig Argyll 65 G8
Feock Corn 3 F7
Feolin Ferry Argyll 72 G3
Ferindonald Highld 85 H11
Feriniquarrie Highld 84 C6
Ferlochan Argyll 74 C2
Fern Angus 77 A7
Ferndale Rhondda 14 B6
Ferndown Dorset 9 D9
Ferness Highld 87 G12
Ferney Green Cumb 56 G6
Fernham Oxon 17 B9
Fernhill Heath Worcs 26 C5
Fernhurst W Sus 11 B7
Fernie Fife 76 F6
Ferniegair S Lnrk 68 E6
Fernilea Highld 85 E8
Fernilee Derbys 44 E4
Ferrensby N Yorks 51 C9
Ferring W Sus 11 D9
Ferry Hill Cambs 37 G9
Ferry Point Highld 87 C10
Ferrybridge W Yorks 51 G10
Ferryden Angus 77 B10
Ferryhill Aberdeen 83 C11
Ferryhill Durham 58 C3
Ferryhill Station Durham 58 C4
Ferryside Carms 23 E8
Fersfield Norf 39 G6
Fersit Highld 80 F5
Ferwig Ceredig 22 B6
Feshiebridge Highld 81 C10
Fetcham Sur 19 F8
Fetlar Airport Shetland 96 D8
Fetterangus Aberds 89 C9
Fettercairn Aberds 83 F8
Fettes Highld 87 F8
Fewcott Oxon 28 F2
Fewston N Yorks 51 D7
Ffair-Rhos Ceredig 24 B4
Ffairfach Carms 24 F3
Ffaldybrenin Carms 24 D3
Ffarmers Carms 24 D3
Ffawyddog Powys 25 G9
Fforest Carms 23 F10
Fforest-fach Swansea 14 B2
Ffos-y-ffin Ceredig 24 B1
Ffostrasol Ceredig 23 B8
Ffridd-Uchaf Gwyn 41 E7
Ffrith Flint 42 G5
Ffrwd Gwyn 40 E6
Ffynnon ddrain Carms 23 D9
Ffynnon-oer Ceredig 23 A10
Ffynnongroyw Flint 42 D4
Fidden Argyll 78 J6
Fiddes Aberds 83 E10
Fiddington Glos 26 E6
Fiddington Som 7 B11
Fiddleford Dorset 9 C7
Fiddlers Hamlet Essex 19 A11
Field Staffs 34 B6
Field Broughton Cumb 49 A3
Field Dalling Norf 38 B6
Field Head Leics 35 E10
Fifehead Magdalen Dorset 9 B6
Fifehead Neville Dorset 9 C6
Fifield Oxon 27 G9
Fifield Wilts 17 F8
Fifield Windsor 18 D6
Fifield Bavant Wilts 9 B9
Figheldean Wilts 17 G8
Filands Wilts 16 C6
Filby Norf 39 D10
Filey N Yorks 53 A7
Filgrave M Keynes 28 D5
Filkins Oxon 17 A9
Filleigh Devon 6 D5
Filleigh Devon 7 E6
Fillingham Lincs 46 D3
Fillongley Warks 35 G8
Filton S Glos 16 D3
Fimber E Yorks 52 C4
Finavon Angus 77 B7
Finchairn Argyll 73 C8
Fincham Norf 38 E2
Finchampstead Wokingham 18 E4
Finchdean Hants 10 C6
Finchingfield Essex 30 E3
Finchley London 19 B9
Findern Derbys 35 B9
Findhorn Moray 87 E13
Findhorn Bridge Highld 81 A10
Findo Gask Perth 76 E3
Findochty Moray 88 B4
Findon Aberds 83 D11
Findon W Sus 11 D10
Findon Mains Highld 87 E9
Findrack Ho. Aberds 83 C8
Finedon Northants 28 A6
Fingal Street Suff 31 B9
Fingask Aberds 83 A9
Fingerpost Worcs 26 A4
Fingest Bucks 18 B4
Finghall N Yorks 58 H2
Fingland Cumb 61 H8
Fingland Dumfries 60 B3
Finglesham Kent 21 F10
Fingringhoe Essex 31 F7
Finlarig Stirl 75 D8
Finmere Oxon 28 E3
Finnart Perth 75 B8
Finningham Suff 31 B7
Finningley S Yorks 45 C10
Finnygaud Aberds 88 C5
Finsbury London 19 C10
Finstall Worcs 26 B6
Finsthwaite Cumb 56 H5
Finstock Oxon 27 G10
Finstown Orkney 95 G4
Fintry Aberds 89 C7
Fintry Dundee 77 D7
Fintry Stirl 68 B5
Finzean Aberds 83 D8
Fionnphort Argyll 78 J6
Fionnsbhagh W Isles 90 J5
Fir Tree Durham 58 C2
Firbeck S Yorks 45 D9
Firby N Yorks 58 H3
Firby N Yorks 52 C3
Firgrove Gtr Man 44 A3
Firsby Lincs 47 F8
Firsdown Wilts 9 A11
First Coast Highld 86 B2
Fishbourne I o W 10 E4
Fishbourne W Sus 11 D7
Fishburn Durham 58 C4
Fishcross Clack 75 H11
Fisher Place Cumb 56 E5
Fisherford Aberds 89 E6
Fisher's Pond Hants 10 B3
Fisherstreet W Sus 11 A8
Fisherton Highld 87 F10
Fisherton S Ayrs 66 E5
Fishguard = Abergwaun Pembs 22 C4
Fishlake S Yorks 45 A10
Fishleigh Barton Devon 6 D4
Fishponds Bristol 16 D3
Fishpool Glos 26 F3
Fishtoft Lincs 37 A9
Fishtoft Drove Lincs 47 H7
Fishtown of Usan Angus 77 B10
Fishwick Borders 71 E8
Fiskavaig Highld 85 E8
Fiskerton Lincs 46 E4
Fiskerton Notts 45 G11
Fitling E Yorks 53 F8
Fittleton Wilts 17 G8
Fittleworth W Sus 11 C9
Fitton End Cambs 37 D10
Fitz Shrops 33 D10
Fitzhead Som 7 D10
Fitzwilliam W Yorks 51 H10
Fiunary Highld 79 G9
Five Acres Glos 26 G2
Five Ashes E Sus 12 D4
Five Oak Green Kent 20 G3
Five Oaks Jersey 11
Five Oaks W Sus 11 B9
Five Roads Carms 23 F9
Fivecrosses Ches 43 E8
Fivehead Som 8 B2
Flack's Green Essex 30 G4
Flackwell Heath Bucks 18 C5
Fladbury Worcs 26 D6
Fladdabister Shetland 96 K6
Flagg Derbys 44 F5
Flamborough E Yorks 53 B8
Flamstead Herts 29 G7
Flamstead End Herts 19 A10
Flansham W Sus 11 D8
Flanshaw W Yorks 51 G9
Flasby N Yorks 50 D5
Flash Staffs 44 F4
Flashader Highld 85 C8
Flask Inn N Yorks 59 F10
Flaunden Herts 19 A7
Flawborough Notts 36 A3
Flawith N Yorks 51 C10
Flax Bourton N Som 15 E11
Flaxby N Yorks 51 D9
Flaxholme Derbys 35 A9
Flaxley Glos 26 G3
Flaxpool Som 7 C10
Flaxton N Yorks 52 C2
Fleckney Leics 36 F2
Flecknoe Warks 28 B2
Fledborough Notts 46 E2
Fleet Hants 18 F5
Fleet Hants 10 D6
Fleet Lincs 37 C9
Fleet Hargate Lincs 37 C9
Fleetham Northumb 71 H10
Fleetlands Hants 10 D4
Fleetville Herts 29 H8
Fleetwood Lancs 49 E3
Flemingston V Glam 14 D6
Flemington S Lnrk 68 E5
Flempton Suff 30 B5
Fleoideabhagh W Isles 90 J5
Fletchertown Cumb 56 B4
Fletching E Sus 12 D3
Flexbury Corn 4 A3
Flexford Sur 18 G6
Flimby Cumb 56 C2
Flimwell E Sus 12 C6
Flint = Y Fflint Flint 42 E5
Flint Mountain Flint 42 E5
Flintham Notts 45 H11
Flinton E Yorks 53 F8
Flintsham Hereford 25 C10
Flitcham Norf 38 C3
Flitton Beds 29 E7
Flitwick Beds 29 E7
Flixborough N Lincs 46 A2
Flixborough Stather N Lincs 46 A2
Flixton Gtr Man 43 C10
Flixton N Yorks 52 B6
Flixton Suff 39 G9
Flockton W Yorks 44 A6
Flodaigh W Isles 84 C3
Flodden Northumb 71 G8
Flodigarry Highld 85 A9
Flood's Ferry Cambs 37 F9
Flookburgh Cumb 49 B3
Florden Norf 39 F7
Flore Northants 28 B3
Flotterton Northumb 62 C5
Flowton Suff 31 D7
Flush House W Yorks 44 B5
Flushing Aberds 89 D11
Flushing Corn 3 F7
Flyford Flavell Worcs 26 C6
Foals Green Suff 31 A9
Fobbing Thurrock 20 C4
Fochabers Moray 88 C3
Fochriw Caerph 25 H8
Fockerby N Lincs 52 H4
Fodderletter Moray 82 A3
Fodderty Highld 87 F8
Foel Powys 32 D5
Foel-gastell Carms 23 E10
Foffarty Angus 77 C7
Foggathorpe E Yorks 52 F3
Fogo Borders 70 F6
Fogorig Borders 70 F6
Foindle Highld 92 E4
Folda Angus 76 A4
Fole Staffs 34 B6
Foleshill W Mid 35 G9
Folke Dorset 8 C5
Folkestone Kent 21 H9
Folkingham Lincs 37 B6
Folkington E Sus 12 F4
Folksworth Cambs 37 G7
Folkton N Yorks 53 B6
Folla Rule Aberds 89 E7
Follifoot N Yorks 51 D9
Folly Gate Devon 6 G4
Fonthill Bishop Wilts 9 A8
Fonthill Gifford Wilts 9 A8
Fontmell Magna Dorset 9 C7
Fontwell W Sus 11 D8
Foolow Derbys 44 E5
Foots Cray London 19 D11
Forbestown Aberds 82 B5
Force Mills Cumb 56 G5
Forcett N Yorks 58 E2
Ford Argyll 73 C7
Ford Bucks 28 H4
Ford Devon 6 D3
Ford Glos 27 F7
Ford Northumb 71 G8
Ford Shrops 33 D10
Ford Staffs 44 G4
Ford Wilts 16 D5
Ford W Sus 11 D8
Ford End Essex 30 G3
Ford Street Som 7 E10
Fordcombe Kent 12 B4
Fordell Fife 69 B10
Forden Powys 33 E8
Forder Green Devon 5 E8
Fordham Cambs 30 A3
Fordham Essex 30 F6
Fordham Norf 38 F2
Fordhouses W Mid 34 E5
Fordingbridge Hants 9 C10
Fordon E Yorks 52 B6
Fordoun Aberds 83 F9
Ford's Green Suff 31 B7
Fordstreet Essex 30 F6
Fordwells Oxon 27 G10
Fordwich Kent 21 F8
Fordyce Aberds 88 B5
Forebridge Staffs 34 C5
Forest Durham 57 C10
Forest Becks Lancs 50 D3
Forest Gate London 19 C11
Forest Green Sur 19 G8
Forest Hall Cumb 57 F7
Forest Head Cumb 61 H11
Forest Hill Oxon 28 H2
Forest Lane Head N Yorks 51 D9
Forest Lodge Argyll 74 C5
Forest Lodge Highld 82 B2
Forest Lodge Perth 81 F11
Forest Mill Clack 69 A8
Forest Row E Sus 12 C3
Forest Town Notts 45 F9
Forestburn Gate Northumb 62 D6
Foresterseat Moray 88 C1
Forestside W Sus 11 C6
Forfar Angus 77 B7
Forgandenny Perth 76 F3
Forge Powys 32 F3
Forge Side Torf 25 H9
Forgewood N Lnrk 68 E6
Forgie Moray 88 C3
Forglen Ho. Aberds 89 C6
Formby Mers 42 B6
Forncett End Norf 39 F7
Forncett St Mary Norf 39 F7
Forncett St Peter Norf 39 F7
Forneth Perth 76 C3
Fornham All Saints Suff 30 B5
Fornham St Martin Suff 30 B5
Forres Moray 87 F13
Forrest Lodge Dumfries 67 H8
Forrestfield N Lnrk 69 D7
Forsbrook Staffs 34 A5
Forse Highld 94 G4
Forse Ho. Highld 94 G4
Forsinain Highld 93 E12
Forsinard Highld 93 E11
Forsinard Station Highld 93 E11
Forston Dorset 8 E5
Fort Augustus Highld 80 C5
Fort George Guern 11
Fort George Highld 87 F10
Fort William Highld 80 F3
Forteviot Perth 76 F3
Forth S Lnrk 69 E8
Forth Road Bridge Fife 69 C10
Forthampton Glos 26 E5
Fortingall Perth 75 C10
Forton Hants 17 G11
Forton Lancs 49 D4
Forton Shrops 33 D10
Forton Som 8 D2
Forton Staffs 34 C3
Forton Heath Shrops 33 D10
Fortrie Aberds 89 D6
Fortrose Highld 87 F10
Fortuneswell Dorset 8 G5
Forty Green Bucks 18 B6
Forty Hill London 19 B10
Forward Green Suff 31 C7
Fosbury Wilts 17 F10
Fosdyke Lincs 37 B9
Foss Perth 75 B10
Foss Cross Glos 27 H7
Fossebridge Glos 27 G7
Foster Street Essex 29 H11
Fosterhouses S Yorks 45 A10
Foston Derbys 35 B7
Foston Lincs 36 A4
Foston N Yorks 52 C2
Foston on the Wolds E Yorks 53 D7
Fotherby Lincs 47 C7
Fotheringhay Northants 37 F6
Foubister Orkney 95 H6
Foul Mile E Sus 12 E5
Foulby W Yorks 51 H9
Foulden Borders 71 E8
Foulden Norf 38 F3
Foulis Castle Highld 87 E8
Foulridge Lancs 50 E4
Foulsham Norf 38 C6
Fountainhall Borders 70 F3
Four Ashes Staffs 34 G4
Four Ashes Suff 31 A7
Four Crosses Powys 33 E6
Four Crosses Powys 33 D8
Four Crosses Wrex 42 G5
Four Elms Kent 19 G11
Four Forks Som 7 C11
Four Gotes Cambs 37 D10
Four Lane Ends Ches 43 F8
Four Lanes Corn 2 F5
Four Marks Hants 10 A5
Four Mile Bridge Anglesey 40 C4
Four Oaks E Sus 13 D7
Four Oaks W Mid 35 F7
Four Oaks W Mid 35 H8
Four Roads Carms 23 F9
Four Roads I o M 48 F2
Four Throws Kent 13 D6
Fourlane Ends Derbys 45 G7
Fourlanes End Ches 44 G2
Fourpenny Highld 87 B11
Fourstones Northumb 62 G4
Fovant Wilts 9 B9
Foveran Aberds 89 F9
Fowey Corn 4 F2
Fowley Common Warr 43 C9
Fowlis Angus 76 D6
Fowlis Wester Perth 76 E2
Fowlmere Cambs 29 D11
Fownhope Hereford 26 E2
Fox Corner Sur 18 F6
Fox Lane Hants 18 F5
Fox Street Essex 31 F7
Foxbar Renfs 68 D3
Foxcombe Hill Oxon 17 A11
Foxdale I o M 48 E2
Foxearth Essex 30 D5
Foxfield Cumb 56 H4
Foxham Wilts 16 D6
Foxhole Corn 3 D8
Foxhole Swansea 14 B2
Foxholes N Yorks 52 B6
Foxhunt Green E Sus 12 E4
Foxley Norf 38 C6
Foxley Wilts 16 C5
Foxt Staffs 44 H4
Foxton Cambs 29 D11
Foxton Durham 58 D4
Foxton Leics 36 F3
Foxup N Yorks 50 B4
Foxwist Green Ches 43 F9
Foxwood Shrops 34 H2
Foy Hereford 26 F2
Foyers Highld 81 A6
Fraddam Corn 2 F4
Fraddon Corn 3 D8
Fradley Staffs 35 D7
Fradswell Staffs 34 B5
Fraisthorpe E Yorks 53 C7
Framfield E Sus 12 D3
Framingham Earl Norf 39 E8
Framingham Pigot Norf 39 E8
Framlingham Suff 31 B9
Frampton Dorset 8 E5
Frampton Lincs 37 B9
Frampton Cotterell S Glos 16 C3
Frampton Mansell Glos 16 A6
Frampton on Severn Glos 26 H4
Frampton West End Lincs 37 A8
Framsden Suff 31 C8
Framwellgate Moor Durham 58 B3
Franche Worcs 34 H4
Frankby Mers 42 D5
Frankley Worcs 34 G5
Frank's Bridge Powys 25 C8
Frankton Warks 27 A11
Frant E Sus 12 C4
Fraserburgh Aberds 89 B9
Frating Green Essex 31 F7
Fratton Ptsmth 10 E5
Freathy Corn 4 F4
Freckenham Suff 30 A3
Freckleton Lancs 49 G4
Freeby Leics 36 C4
Freehay Staffs 34 A6
Freeland Oxon 27 G11
Freester Shetland 96 H6
Freethorpe Norf 39 E10
Freiston Lincs 37 A9
Fremington Devon 6 C4
Fremington N Yorks 58 G1
Frenchay S Glos 16 D3
Frenchbeer Devon 5 C7
Frenich Stirl 75 G7
Frensham Sur 18 G5
Fresgoe Highld 93 C12
Freshfield Mers 42 B5
Freshford Bath 16 E4
Freshwater I o W 10 F2
Freshwater Bay I o W 10 F2
Freshwater East Pembs 22 G5
Fressingfield Suff 39 H8
Freston Suff 31 E8
Freswick Highld 94 D5
Fretherne Glos 26 H4
Frettenham Norf 39 D8
Freuchie Fife 76 G5
Freuchies Angus 76 A5
Freystrop Pembs 22 E4
Friar's Gate E Sus 12 C3
Friarton Perth 76 E4
Friday Bridge Cambs 37 E10
Friday Street E Sus 12 F5
Fridaythorpe E Yorks 52 D4
Friern Barnet London 19 B9
Friesland Argyll 78 F4
Friesthorpe Lincs 46 D4
Frieston Lincs 46 H3
Frieth Bucks 18 B4
Frilford Oxon 17 B11
Frilsham W Berks 18 D2
Frimley Sur 18 F5
Frimley Green Sur 18 F5
Frindsbury Medway 20 D4
Fring Norf 38 B3
Fringford Oxon 28 F3
Frinsted Kent 20 F5
Frinton-on-Sea Essex 31 F9
Friockheim Angus 77 C8
Friog Gwyn 32 D2
Frisby on the Wreake Leics 36 D2
Friskney Lincs 47 G8
Friskney Eaudike Lincs 47 G8
Friskney Tofts Lincs 47 G8
Friston E Sus 12 G4
Friston Suff 31 B11
Fritchley Derbys 45 G7
Frith Bank Lincs 47 H7
Frith Common Worcs 26 B3
Fritham Hants 9 C11
Frithelstock Devon 6 E3
Frithelstock Stone Devon 6 E3
Frithville Lincs 47 G7
Frittenden Kent 13 B7
Frittiscombe Devon 5 G9
Fritton Norf 39 F8
Fritton Norf 39 E10
Fritwell Oxon 28 F2
Frizinghall W Yorks 51 F7
Frizington Cumb 56 E2
Frocester Glos 16 A4
Frodesley Shrops 33 E11
Frodingham N Lincs 46 A2
Frodsham Ches 43 E8
Frogden Borders 70 H6
Froggatt Derbys 44 E6
Froghall Staffs 44 H4
Frogmore Devon 5 G8
Frogmore Hants 18 F5
Frognall Lincs 37 D7
Frogshail Norf 39 B8
Frolesworth Leics 35 F11
Frome Som 16 G4
Frome St Quintin Dorset 8 D4
Fromes Hill Hereford 26 D3
Fron Denb 42 F3
Fron Gwyn 41 E7
Fron Gwyn 40 G5
Fron Powys 25 B7
Fron Powys 33 E8
Fron Powys 33 F7
Froncysyllte Wrex 33 A8
Frongoch Gwyn 32 B5
Frostenden Suff 39 G10
Frosterley Durham 58 C1
Frotoft Orkney 95 F5
Froxfield Wilts 17 E9
Froxfield Green Hants 10 B6
Froyle Hants 18 G4
Fryerning Essex 20 A3
Fryton N Yorks 52 B2
Fulbeck Lincs 46 G3
Fulbourn Cambs 30 C2
Fulbrook Oxon 27 G9
Fulford Som 7 D11
Fulford Staffs 34 B5
Fulford York 52 E2
Fulham London 19 D9
Fulking W Sus 11 C11
Full Sutton E Yorks 52 D3
Fullarton Glasgow 68 D5
Fullarton N Ayrs 66 C6
Fuller Street Essex 30 G4
Fuller's Moor Ches 43 G7
Fullerton Hants 17 H10
Fulletby Lincs 46 E6
Fullwood E Ayrs 67 A7
Fulmer Bucks 18 C6
Fulmodestone Norf 38 B5
Fulnetby Lincs 46 E4
Fulstow Lincs 47 C7
Fulwell T & W 63 H9
Fulwood Lancs 49 F5
Fulwood S Yorks 45 D7
Fundenhall Norf 39 F7
Fundenhall Street Norf 39 F7
Funtington W Sus 11 D6
Funtley Hants 10 D4
Funtullich Perth 75 E10
Funzie Shetland 96 D8
Furley Devon 8 D1
Furnace Argyll 73 C9
Furnace Carms 23 F10
Furnace End Warks 35 F8
Furneaux Pelham Herts 29 F11
Furness Vale Derbys 44 D4
Furze Platt Windsor 18 C5
Furzehill Devon 7 B6
Fyfett Som 7 E11
Fyfield Essex 30 H2
Fyfield Glos 17 A9
Fyfield Hants 17 G9
Fyfield Oxon 17 B11
Fyfield Wilts 17 E8
Fylingthorpe N Yorks 59 F10
Fyvie Aberds 89 E7

G

Gabhsann bho Dheas W Isles 91 B9
Gabhsann bho Thuath W Isles 91 B9
Gablon Highld 87 B10
Gabroc Hill E Ayrs 67 A7
Gaddesby Leics 36 D2
Gadebridge Herts 29 H7
Gaer Powys 25 F8
Gaerllwyd Mon 15 B10
Gaerwen Anglesey 40 C6
Gagingwell Oxon 27 F11
Gaick Lodge Highld 81 E9
Gailey Staffs 34 D5
Gainford Durham 58 E2
Gainsborough Lincs 46 C2
Gainsborough Suff 31 D8
Gainsford End Essex 30 E4
Gairloch Highld 85 A13
Gairlochy Highld 80 E3
Gairney Bank Perth 76 H4
Gairnshiel Lodge Aberds 82 C4
Gaisgill Cumb 57 F8
Gaitsgill Cumb 56 B5
Galashiels Borders 70 G3
Galgate Lancs 49 D4
Galhampton Som 8 B5
Gallaberry Dumfries 60 E5
Gallachoille Argyll 72 E6
Gallanach Argyll 79 J11
Gallanach Argyll 78 E5
Gallantry Bank Ches 43 G8
Gallatown Fife 69 A11
Galley Common Warks 35 F9
Galley Hill Cambs 29 B10
Galleyend Essex 20 A4
Galleywood Essex 20 A4
Gallin Perth 75 C8
Gallowfauld Angus 77 C7
Gallows Green Staffs 35 A6
Galltair Highld 85 F13
Galmisdale Highld 78 C7
Galmpton Devon 5 G7
Galmpton Torbay 5 F9
Galphay N Yorks 51 B8
Galston E Ayrs 67 C8
Galtrigill Highld 84 C6
Gamblesby Cumb 57 C8
Gamesley Derbys 44 C4
Gamlingay Cambs 29 C9
Gammersgill N Yorks 51 A6
Gamston Notts 45 E11
Ganarew Hereford 26 G2
Ganavan Argyll 79 H11
Gang Corn 4 E4
Ganllwyd Gwyn 32 C3
Gannochy Angus 83 F7
Gannochy Perth 76 E4
Gansclet Highld 94 F5
Ganstead E Yorks 53 F7
Ganthorpe N Yorks 52 B2
Ganton N Yorks 52 B5
Garbat Highld 86 E7
Garbhallt Argyll 73 D9
Garboldisham Norf 38 G6
Garden City Flint 42 F6
Garden Village Wrex 42 G6
Garden Village W Yorks 51 F10
Gardenstown Aberds 89 B7
Garderhouse Shetland 96 J5
Gardham E Yorks 52 E5
Gardin Shetland 96 G6
Gare Hill Som 16 G4
Garelochhead Argyll 73 D11
Garford Oxon 17 B11
Garforth W Yorks 51 F10
Gargrave N Yorks 50 D5
Gargunnock Stirl 68 A6
Garlic Street Norf 39 G8
Garlieston Dumfries 55 E7
Garlinge Green Kent 21 F8
Garlogie Aberds 83 C9
Garmond Aberds 89 C8
Garmony Argyll 79 G9
Garmouth Moray 88 B3
Garn-yr-erw Torf 25 G9
Garnant Carms 24 G3
Garndiffaith Torf 15 A8
Garndolbenmaen Gwyn 40 F6
Garnedd Conwy 41 E9
Garnett Bridge Cumb 57 G7
Garnfadryn Gwyn 40 G4
Garnkirk N Lnrk 68 D5
Garnlydan Bl Gwent 25 G8
Garnswllt Swansea 24 H3
Garrabost W Isles 91 D10
Garraron Argyll 73 C7
Garras Corn 2 G6
Garreg Gwyn 41 F8
Garrick Perth 75 F11
Garrigill Cumb 57 B9
Garriston N Yorks 58 G2
Garroch Dumfries 55 A8
Garrogie Lodge Highld 81 B7
Garros Highld 85 B9
Garrow Perth 75 C11
Garryhorn Dumfries 67 G8
Garsdale Cumb 57 H9
Garsdale Head Cumb 57 G9
Garsdon Wilts 16 C6
Garshall Green Staffs 34 B5
Garsington Oxon 18 A2
Garstang Lancs 49 E4
Garston Mers 43 D7
Garswood Mers 43 C8
Gartcosh N Lnrk 68 D5
Garth Bridgend 14 B4
Garth Gwyn 41 C7
Garth Powys 24 D6
Garth Shetland 96 H4
Garth Wrex 33 A8
Garth Row Cumb 57 G7
Garthamlock Glasgow 68 D5
Garthbrengy Powys 25 E7
Garthdee Aberdeen 83 C11
Gartheli Ceredig 23 A10
Garthmyl Powys 33 F7
Garthorpe Leics 36 C4
Garthorpe N Lincs 52 H4
Gartly Aberds 88 E5
Gartmore Stirl 75 H8
Gartnagrenach Argyll 72 H6
Gartness N Lnrk 68 D6
Gartness Stirl 68 B4
Gartocharn W Dunb 68 B3
Garton E Yorks 53 F8
Garton-on-the-Wolds E Yorks 52 D5
Gartsherrie N Lnrk 68 D6
Gartymore Highld 93 H13
Garvald E Loth 70 C4
Garvamore Highld 81 D7
Garvard Argyll 72 D2
Garvault Hotel Highld 93 F10
Garve Highld 86 E6
Garvestone Norf 38 E6
Garvock Aberds 83 F9
Garvock Invclyd 73 F11
Garway Hereford 25 F11
Garway Hill Hereford 25 F11
Gaskan Highld 79 D10
Gastard Wilts 16 E5
Gasthorpe Norf 38 G5
Gatcombe I o W 10 F3
Gate Burton Lincs 46 D2
Gate Helmsley N Yorks 52 D2
Gateacre Mers 43 D7
Gatebeck Cumb 57 H7
Gateford Notts 45 D9
Gateforth N Yorks 52 G1
Gatehead E Ayrs 67 C6
Gatehouse Northumb 62 E3
Gatehouse of Fleet Dumfries 55 D9
Gatelawbridge Dumfries 60 D5
Gateley Norf 38 C5
Gatenby N Yorks 58 H4
Gateshead T & W 63 G8
Gatesheath Ches 43 F7
Gateside Aberds 83 B8
Gateside Angus 77 C7
Gateside E Renf 68 E3
Gateside Fife 76 G4
Gateside N Ayrs 67 A6
Gathurst Gtr Man 43 B8
Gatley Gtr Man 44 D2
Gattonside Borders 70 G4
Gaufron Powys 24 B6
Gaulby Leics 36 E2
Gauldry Fife 76 E6
Gaunt's Common Dorset 9 D9
Gautby Lincs 46 E5
Gavinton Borders 70 E6
Gawber S Yorks 45 B7
Gawcott Bucks 28 E3
Gawsworth Ches 44 F2
Gawthorpe W Yorks 51 G8
Gawthrop Cumb 57 H8
Gawthwaite Cumb 49 A2
Gay Street W Sus 11 B9
Gaydon Warks 27 C10
Gayfield Orkney 95 C5
Gayhurst M Keynes 28 D5
Gayle N Yorks 57 H10
Gayles N Yorks 58 F2
Gayton Mers 42 D5
Gayton Norf 38 D3
Gayton Northants 28 C4
Gayton Staffs 34 C5
Gayton le Marsh Lincs 47 D8
Gayton le Wold Lincs 46 D6
Gayton Thorpe Norf 38 D3
Gaywood Norf 38 C2
Gazeley Suff 30 B4
Geanies House Highld 87 D11
Gearraidh Bhailteas W Isles 84 F2
Gearraidh Bhaird W Isles 91 E8
Gearraidh na h-Aibhne W Isles 90 D7
Gearraidh na Monadh W Isles 84 G2
Geary Highld 84 B7
Geddes House Highld 87 F11
Gedding Suff 30 C6
Geddington Northants 36 G4
Gedintailor Highld 85 E10
Gedling Notts 36 A2
Gedney Lincs 37 C10
Gedney Broadgate Lincs 37 C10
Gedney Drove End Lincs 37 C10
Gedney Dyke Lincs 37 C10
Gedney Hill Lincs 37 D9
Gee Cross Gtr Man 44 C3
Geilston Argyll 68 C2
Geirinis W Isles 84 D2
Geise Highld 94 D3
Geisiadar W Isles 90 D6
Geldeston Norf 39 F9
Gell Conwy 41 D10
Gelli Pembs 22 E5
Gelli Rhondda 14 B5
Gellideg M Tydf 25 H7
Gellifor Denb 42 F4
Gelligaer Caerph 15 B7
Gellilydan Gwyn 41 G8
Gellinudd Neath 14 A3
Gellyburn Perth 76 D3
Gellywen Carms 23 D7

Gelston Dumfries 55 D10
Gelston Lincs 36 A5
Gembling E Yorks 53 D7
Gentleshaw Staffs 35 D6
Geocrab W Isles 90 H6
George Green Bucks 19 C7
George Nympton Devon 6 D6
Georgefield Dumfries 61 D8
Georgeham Devon 6 C3
Georgetown Bl Gwent 25 H8
Gerlan Gwyn 41 D8
Germansweek Devon 6 G3
Germoe Corn 2 G4
Gerrans Corn 3 F7
Gerrards Cross Bucks 19 C7
Gestingthorpe Essex 30 E5
Geuffordd Powys 33 D8
Gib Hill Ches 43 E9
Gibbet Hill Warks 35 G11
Gibbshill Dumfries 60 F3
Gidea Park London 20 C2
Gidleigh Devon 5 C7
Giffnock E Renf 68 E4
Gifford E Loth 70 D4
Giffordland N Ayrs 66 B5
Giffordtown Fife 76 F5
Giggleswick N Yorks 50 C4
Gilberdyke E Yorks 52 G4
Gilchriston E Loth 70 D3
Gilcrux Cumb 56 C3
Gildersome W Yorks 51 G8
Gildingwells S Yorks 45 D9
Gileston V Glam 14 E6
Gilfach Caerph 15 B7
Gilfach Goch Rhondda 14 C5
Gilfachrheda Ceredig 23 A9
Gillamoor N Yorks 59 H7
Gillar's Green Mers 43 C7
Gillen Highld 84 C7
Gilling East N Yorks 52 B2
Gilling West N Yorks 58 F2
Gillingham Dorset 9 B7
Gillingham Medway 20 E4
Gillingham Norf 39 F10
Gillock Highld 94 E4
Gillow Heath Staffs 44 G2
Gills Highld 94 C5
Gill's Green Kent 13 C6
Gilmanscleuch Borders 61 A9
Gilmerton Edin 69 D11
Gilmerton Perth 75 E11
Gilmonby Durham 57 E11
Gilmorton Leics 36 G1
Gilmourton S Lnrk 68 F5
Gilsland Cumb 62 G2
Gilsland Spa Cumb 62 G2
Gilston Borders 70 E3
Gilston Herts 29 G11
Gilwern Mon 25 G9
Gimingham Norf 39 B8
Giosla W Isles 90 E6
Gipping Suff 31 B7
Gipsey Bridge Lincs 46 H6
Girdle Toll N Ayrs 66 B6
Girlsta Shetland 96 H6
Girsby N Yorks 58 F4
Girtford Beds 29 C8
Girthon Dumfries 55 D9
Girton Cambs 29 B11
Girton Notts 46 F2
Girvan S Ayrs 66 G4
Gisburn Lancs 50 E4
Gisleham Suff 39 G11
Gislingham Suff 31 A7
Gissing Norf 39 G7
Gittisham Devon 7 G10
Gladestry Powys 25 C9
Gladsmuir E Loth 70 C3
Glais Swansea 14 A3
Glaisdale N Yorks 59 F8
Glame Highld 85 D10
Glamis Angus 76 C6
Glan Adda Gwyn 41 C7
Glan-Conwy Conwy 41 E10
Glan Conwy Conwy 41 C10
Glan-Duar Carms 23 B10
Glan-Dwyfach Gwyn 40 F6
Glan Gors Anglesey 40 C6
Glan-rhyd Gwyn 40 E6
Glan-traeth Anglesey 40 C4
Glan-y-don Flint 42 E4
Glan-y-nant Powys 32 G5
Glan-y-wern Gwyn 41 G8
Glan-yr-afon Anglesey 41 B8
Glan-yr-afon Gwyn 32 A5
Glan-yr-afon Gwyn 32 A6
Glanaman Carms 24 G3
Glandford Norf 38 A6
Glandwr Pembs 22 D6
Glandy Cross Carms 22 D6
Glandyfi Ceredig 32 F2
Glangrwyney Powys 25 G9
Glanmule Powys 33 F7
Glanrafon Ceredig 32 G2
Glanrhyd Gwyn 40 G4
Glanrhyd Pembs 22 B6
Glanton Northumb 62 B6
Glanton Pike Northumb 62 B6
Glanvilles Wootton Dorset 8 D5
Glapthorn Northants 36 F6
Glapwell Derbys 45 F8
Glas-allt Shiel Aberds 82 E4
Glasbury Powys 25 E8
Glaschoil Highld 87 H13
Glascoed Denb 42 E2
Glascoed Mon 15 A9
Glascoed Powys 33 D7
Glascorrie Aberds 82 D5
Glascote Staffs 35 E8
Glascwm Powys 25 C8
Glasdrum Argyll 74 C3
Glasfryn Conwy 42 G2
Glasgow Glasgow 68 D4
Glasgow Airport Renfs 68 D3
Glasgow Prestwick International Airport S Ayrs 67 D6
Glashvin Highld 85 B9
Glasinfryn Gwyn 41 D7
Glasnacardoch Highld 79 B9
Glasnakille Highld 85 G10
Glasphein Highld 84 D6
Glaspwll Powys 32 F3
Glassburn Highld 86 H6
Glasserton Dumfries 55 F7
Glassford S Lnrk 68 F6
Glasshouse Hill Glos 26 F4
Glasshouses N Yorks 51 C7
Glasslie Fife 76 G5
Glasson Cumb 61 G8
Glasson Lancs 49 D4
Glassonby Cumb 57 C7
Glasterlaw Angus 77 B8
Glaston Rutland 36 E4
Glastonbury Som 15 H11
Glatton Cambs 37 G7
Glazebrook Warr 43 C9
Glazebury Warr 43 C9
Glazeley Shrops 34 G3
Gleadless S Yorks 45 D7
Gleadsmoss Ches 44 F2
Gleann Tholàstaidh W Isles 91 C10
Gleaston Cumb 49 B2
Gleiniant Powys 32 F5
Glemsford Suff 30 D5
Glen Dumfries 55 D8
Glen Dumfries 60 F4
Glen Auldyn I o M 48 C4
Glen Bernisdale Highld 85 D9
Glen Ho. Borders 69 G11
Glen Mona I o M 48 D4
Glen Nevis House Highld 80 F3
Glen Parva Leics 36 F1
Glen Sluain Argyll 73 D9
Glen Tanar House Aberds 82 D6
Glen Trool Lodge Dumfries 55 A7
Glen Village Falk 69 C7
Glen Vine I o M 48 E3
Glenamachrie Argyll 74 E2
Glenbarr Argyll 65 E7
Glenbeg Highld 79 E8
Glenbeg Highld 82 A2
Glenbervie Aberds 83 E9
Glenboig N Lnrk 68 D6
Glenborrodale Highld 79 E9
Glenbranter Argyll 73 D10
Glenbreck Borders 60 A6
Glenbrein Lodge Highld 81 B6
Glenbrittle House Highld 85 F9
Glenbuchat Lodge Aberds 82 B5
Glenbuck E Ayrs 68 H6
Glenburn Renfs 68 D3
Glencalvie Lodge Highld 86 C7
Glencanisp Lodge Highld 92 G4
Glencaple Dumfries 60 G5
Glencarron Lodge Highld 86 F3
Glencarse Perth 76 E4
Glencassley Castle Highld 92 J7
Glenceitlein Highld 74 C4
Glencoe Highld 74 B3
Glencraig Fife 76 H4
Glencripesdale Highld 79 F9
Glencrosh Dumfries 60 E3
Glendavan Ho. Aberds 82 C6
Glendevon Perth 76 G2
Glendoe Lodge Highld 80 C6
Glendoebeg Highld 80 C6
Glendoick Perth 76 E5
Glendoll Lodge Angus 82 F4
Glendoune S Ayrs 66 G4
Glenduckie Fife 76 F5
Glendye Lodge Aberds 83 E8
Gleneagles Hotel Perth 76 F2
Gleneagles House Perth 76 G2
Glenegedale Argyll 64 C4
Glenelg Highld 85 G13
Glenernie Moray 87 G13
Glenfarg Perth 76 F4
Glenfarquhar Lodge Aberds 83 E9
Glenferness House Highld 87 G12
Glenfeshie Lodge Highld 81 D10
Glenfield Leics 35 E11
Glenfinnan Highld 79 C11
Glenfoot Perth 76 F4
Glenfyne Lodge Argyll 74 F5
Glengap Dumfries 55 D9
Glengarnock N Ayrs 66 A6
Glengorm Castle Argyll 78 F7
Glengrasco Highld 85 D9
Glenhead Farm Angus 76 A5
Glenhoul Dumfries 67 H9
Glenhurich Highld 79 E11
Glenkerry Borders 61 B8
Glenkiln Dumfries 60 F4
Glenkindie Aberds 82 B6
Glenlatterach Moray 88 C1
Glenlee Dumfries 55 A9
Glenlichorn Perth 75 F10
Glenlivet Moray 82 A3
Glenlochsie Perth 82 F2
Glenloig N Ayrs 66 C2
Glenluce Dumfries 54 D5
Glenmallan Argyll 74 H5
Glenmarksie Highld 86 F6
Glenmassan Argyll 73 E10
Glenmavis N Lnrk 68 D6
Glenmaye I o M 48 E2
Glenmidge Dumfries 60 E4
Glenmore Argyll 73 B7
Glenmore Highld 85 D9
Glenmore Lodge Highld 82 C1
Glenmoy Angus 77 A7
Glenogil Angus 77 A7
Glenprosen Lodge Angus 82 G4
Glenprosen Village Angus 82 G5
Glenquiech Angus 77 A7
Glenreasdell Mains Argyll 73 H7
Glenree N Ayrs 66 D2
Glenridding Cumb 56 E5
Glenrossal Highld 92 J7
Glenrothes Fife 76 G5
Glensanda Highld 79 G11
Glensaugh Aberds 83 F8
Glenshero Lodge Highld 81 D7
Glenstockadale Dumfries 54 C3
Glenstriven Argyll 73 F9
Glentaggart S Lnrk 69 H7
Glentham Lincs 46 C4
Glentirranmuir Stirl 68 A5
Glenton Aberds 83 A8
Glentress Borders 69 G11
Glentromie Lodge Highld 81 D9
Glentrool Village Dumfries 54 B6
Glentruan I o M 48 B4
Glentruim House Highld 81 D8
Glentworth Lincs 46 D3
Glenuig Highld 79 D9
Glenurquhart Highld 87 E10
Glespin S Lnrk 69 H7
Gletness Shetland 96 H6
Glewstone Hereford 26 F2
Glinton P'boro 37 E7
Glooston Leics 36 F3
Glororum Northumb 71 G10
Glossop Derbys 44 C4
Gloster Hill Northumb 63 C8
Gloucester Glos 26 G5
Gloucestershire Airport Glos 26 F5
Gloup Shetland 96 C7
Glusburn N Yorks 50 E6
Glutt Lodge Highld 93 F12
Glutton Bridge Derbys 44 F4
Glympton Oxon 27 F11
Glyn-Ceiriog Wrex 33 B8
Glyn-cywarch Gwyn 41 G8
Glyn Ebwy = Ebbw Vale Bl Gwent 25 H8
Glyn-neath = Glynedd Neath 24 H5
Glynarthen Ceredig 23 B8
Glynbrochan Powys 32 G5
Glyncoch Rhondda 14 B6
Glyncorrwg Neath 14 B4
Glynde E Sus 12 F3
Glyndebourne E Sus 12 E3
Glyndyfrdwy Denb 33 A7
Glynedd = Glyn-neath Neath 24 H5
Glynogwr Bridgend 14 C5
Glyntaff Rhondda 14 C6
Glyntawe Powys 24 G5
Gnosall Staffs 34 C4
Gnosall Heath Staffs 34 C4
Goadby Leics 36 F3
Goadby Marwood Leics 36 C3
Goat Lees Kent 21 G7
Goatacre Wilts 17 D7
Goathill Dorset 8 C5
Goathland N Yorks 59 F9
Goathurst Som 8 A1
Gobernuisgach Lodge Highld 92 E7
Gobhaig W Isles 90 G5
Gobowen Shrops 33 B9
Godalming Sur 18 G6
Godley Gtr Man 44 C3
Godmanchester Cambs 29 A9
Godmanstone Dorset 8 E4
Godmersham Kent 21 F7
Godney Som 15 G10
Godolphin Cross Corn 2 F5
Godre'r-graig Neath 24 H4
Godshill Hants 9 C10
Godshill I o W 10 F4
Godstone Sur 19 F10
Godwinscroft Hants 9 E10
Goetre Mon 25 H10
Goferydd Anglesey 40 B4
Goff's Oak Herts 19 A10
Gogar Edin 69 C10
Goginan Ceredig 32 G2
Golan Gwyn 41 F7
Golant Corn 4 F2
Golberdon Corn 4 D4
Golborne Gtr Man 43 C9
Golcar W Yorks 51 H7
Gold Hill Norf 37 F11
Goldcliff Newport 15 C9
Golden Cross E Sus 12 E4
Golden Green Kent 20 G3
Golden Grove Carms 23 E10
Golden Hill Hants 10 E1
Golden Pot Hants 18 G4
Golden Valley Glos 26 F6
Goldenhill Stoke 44 G2
Golders Green London 19 C9
Goldhanger Essex 30 H6
Golding Shrops 33 E11
Goldington Beds 29 C7
Goldsborough N Yorks 51 D9
Goldsborough N Yorks 59 E9
Goldsithney Corn 2 F4
Goldsworthy Devon 6 D2
Goldthorpe S Yorks 45 B8
Gollanfield Highld 87 F11
Golspie Highld 93 J11
Golval Highld 93 C11
Gomeldon Wilts 17 H8
Gomersal W Yorks 51 G8
Gomshall Sur 19 G7
Gonalston Notts 45 H10
Gonfirth Shetland 96 G5
Good Easter Essex 30 G3
Gooderstone Norf 38 E3
Goodleigh Devon 6 C5
Goodmanham E Yorks 52 E4
Goodnestone Kent 21 E7
Goodnestone Kent 21 F9
Goodrich Hereford 26 G2
Goodrington Torbay 5 F9
Goodshaw Lancs 50 G4
Goodwick = Wdig Pembs 22 C4
Goodworth Clatford Hants 17 G10
Goole E Yorks 52 G3
Goonbell Corn 2 E6
Goonhavern Corn 3 D6
Goose Eye W Yorks 50 E6
Goose Green Gtr Man 43 B8
Goose Green Norf 39 G7
Goose Green W Sus 11 C10
Gooseham Corn 6 E1
Goosey Oxon 17 B10
Goosnargh Lancs 50 F1
Goostrey Ches 43 E10
Gorcott Hill Warks 27 B7
Gord Shetland 96 L6
Gordon Borders 70 F5
Gordonbush Highld 93 J11
Gordonsburgh Moray 88 B4
Gordonstoun Moray 88 B1
Gordonstown Aberds 88 C5
Gordonstown Aberds 89 E7
Gore Kent 21 F10
Gore Cross Wilts 17 F7
Gore Pit Essex 30 G5
Gorebridge Midloth 70 D2
Gorefield Cambs 37 D10
Gorey Jersey 11
Gorgie Edin 69 C11
Goring Oxon 18 C3
Goring-by-Sea W Sus 11 D10
Goring Heath Oxon 18 D3
Gorleston-on-Sea Norf 39 E11
Gornalwood W Mid 34 F5
Gorrachie Aberds 89 C7
Gorran Churchtown Corn 3 E8
Gorran Haven Corn 3 E9
Gorrenberry Borders 61 D10
Gors Ceredig 32 H2
Gorse Hill Swindon 17 C8
Gorsedd Flint 42 E4
Gorseinon Swansea 23 G10
Gorseness Orkney 95 G5
Gorsgoch Ceredig 23 A9
Gorslas Carms 23 E10
Gorsley Glos 26 F3
Gorstan Highld 86 E6
Gorstanvorran Highld 79 D11
Gorsteyhill Staffs 43 G10
Gorsty Hill Staffs 35 C7
Gortantaoid Argyll 64 A4
Gorton Gtr Man 44 C2
Gosbeck Suff 31 C8
Gosberton Lincs 37 B8
Gosberton Clough Lincs 37 C7
Gosfield Essex 30 F4
Gosford Hereford 26 B2
Gosforth Cumb 56 F2
Gosforth T & W 63 G8
Gosmore Herts 29 F8
Gosport Hants 10 E5
Gossabrough Shetland 96 E7
Gossington Glos 16 A4
Goswick Northumb 71 F9
Gotham Notts 35 B11
Gotherington Glos 26 F6
Gott Shetland 96 J6
Goudhurst Kent 12 C6
Goulceby Lincs 46 E6
Gourdas Aberds 89 D7
Gourdon Aberds 83 F10
Gourock Invclyd 73 F11
Govan Glasgow 68 D4
Govanhill Glasgow 68 D4
Goveton Devon 5 G8
Govilon Mon 25 G9
Gowanhill Aberds 89 B10
Gowdall E Yorks 52 G2
Gowerton Swansea 23 G10
Gowkhall Fife 69 B9
Gowthorpe E Yorks 52 D3
Goxhill E Yorks 53 E7
Goxhill N Lincs 53 G7
Goxhill Haven N Lincs 53 G7
Goybre Neath 14 C3
Grabhair W Isles 91 F8
Graby Lincs 37 C6
Grade Corn 2 H6
Graffham W Sus 11 C8
Grafham Cambs 29 B8
Grafham Sur 19 G7
Grafton Hereford 25 E11
Grafton N Yorks 51 C10
Grafton Oxon 17 A9
Grafton Shrops 33 D10
Grafton Worcs 26 B2
Grafton Flyford Worcs 26 C6
Grafton Regis Northants 28 D4
Grafton Underwood Northants 36 G5
Grafty Green Kent 20 G5
Graianrhyd Denb 42 G5
Graig Conwy 41 C10
Graig Denb 42 E3
Graig-fechan Denb 42 G4
Grain Medway 20 D5
Grainsby Lincs 46 C6
Grainthorpe Lincs 47 C7
Grampound Corn 3 E8
Grampound Road Corn 3 D8
Gramsdal W Isles 84 C3
Granborough Bucks 28 F4
Granby Notts 36 B3
Grandborough Warks 27 B11
Grandtully Perth 76 B2
Grange Cumb 56 E4
Grange E Ayrs 67 C7
Grange Medway 20 E4
Grange Mers 42 D5
Grange Perth 76 E5
Grange Crossroads Moray 88 C4
Grange Hall Moray 87 E13
Grange Hill Essex 19 B11
Grange Moor W Yorks 51 H8
Grange of Lindores Fife 76 F5
Grange-over-Sands Cumb 49 B4
Grange Villa Durham 58 A3
Grangemill Derbys 44 G6
Grangemouth Falk 69 B8
Grangepans Falk 69 B9
Grangetown Cardiff 15 D7
Grangetown Redcar 59 D6
Granish Highld 81 B11
Gransmoor E Yorks 53 D7
Granston Pembs 22 C3
Grantchester Cambs 29 C11
Grantham Lincs 36 B5
Grantley N Yorks 51 C8
Grantlodge Aberds 83 B9
Granton Dumfries 60 C6
Granton Edin 69 C11
Grantown-on-Spey Highld 82 A2
Grantshouse Borders 71 D7
Grappenhall Warr 43 D9
Grasby Lincs 46 B4
Grasmere Cumb 56 F5
Grasscroft Gtr Man 44 B3
Grassendale Mers 43 D6
Grassholme Durham 57 D11
Grassington N Yorks 50 C6
Grassmoor Derbys 45 F8
Grassthorpe Notts 45 F11
Grateley Hants 17 G9
Gratwich Staffs 34 B6
Graveley Cambs 29 B9
Graveley Herts 29 F9
Gravelly Hill W Mid 35 F7
Gravels Shrops 33 E9
Graven Shetland 96 F6
Graveney Kent 21 E7
Gravesend Herts 29 F11
Gravesend Kent 20 D3
Grayingham Lincs 46 C3
Grayrigg Cumb 57 G7
Grays Thurrock 20 D3
Grayshott Hants 18 H5
Grayswood Sur 11 A8
Graythorp Hrtlpl 58 D6
Grazeley Wokingham 18 E3
Greasbrough S Yorks 45 C8
Greasby Mers 42 D5
Great Abington Cambs 30 D2
Great Addington Northants 28 A6
Great Alne Warks 27 C8
Great Altcar Lancs 42 B6
Great Amwell Herts 29 G10
Great Asby Cumb 57 E8
Great Ashfield Suff 30 B6
Great Ayton N Yorks 59 E6
Great Baddow Essex 20 A4
Great Bardfield Essex 30 E3
Great Barford Beds 29 C8
Great Barr W Mid 34 F6
Great Barrington Glos 27 G9
Great Barrow Ches 43 F7
Great Barton Suff 30 B5
Great Barugh N Yorks 52 B3
Great Bavington Northumb 62 E5
Great Bealings Suff 31 D9
Great Bedwyn Wilts 17 E9
Great Bentley Essex 31 F8
Great Billing Northants 28 B5
Great Bircham Norf 38 B3
Great Blakenham Suff 31 C8
Great Blencow Cumb 56 C6
Great Bolas Telford 34 C2
Great Bookham Sur 19 F8
Great Bourton Oxon 27 D11
Great Bowden Leics 36 G3
Great Bradley Suff 30 C3
Great Braxted Essex 30 G5
Great Bricett Suff 31 C7
Great Brickhill Bucks 28 E6
Great Bridge W Mid 34 F5
Great Bridgeford Staffs 34 C4
Great Brington Northants 28 B3
Great Bromley Essex 31 F7
Great Broughton Cumb 56 C2
Great Broughton N Yorks 59 F6
Great Budworth Ches 43 E9
Great Burdon Darl 58 E4
Great Burgh Sur 19 F9
Great Burstead Essex 20 B3
Great Busby N Yorks 58 F6
Great Canfield Essex 30 G2
Great Carlton Lincs 47 D8
Great Casterton Rutland 36 E6
Great Chart Kent 13 B8
Great Chatwell Staffs 34 D3
Great Chesterford Essex 30 D2
Great Cheverell Wilts 16 F6
Great Chishill Cambs 29 E11
Great Clacton Essex 31 G8
Great Cliff W Yorks 51 H9
Great Clifton Cumb 56 D2
Great Coates NE Lincs 46 B6
Great Comberton Worcs 26 D6
Great Corby Cumb 56 A6
Great Cornard Suff 30 D5
Great Cowden E Yorks 53 E8
Great Coxwell Oxon 17 B9
Great Crakehall N Yorks 58 G3
Great Cransley Northants 36 H4
Great Cressingham Norf 38 E4
Great Crosby Mers 42 C6
Great Cubley Derbys 35 B7
Great Dalby Leics 36 D3
Great Denham Beds 29 D7
Great Doddington Northants 28 B5
Great Dunham Norf 38 D4
Great Dunmow Essex 30 F3
Great Durnford Wilts 17 H8
Great Easton Essex 30 F3
Great Easton Leics 36 F4
Great Eccleston Lancs 49 E4
Great Edstone N Yorks 52 A3
Great Ellingham Norf 38 F6
Great Elm Som 16 G4
Great Eversden Cambs 29 C10
Great Fencote N Yorks 58 G3
Great Finborough Suff 31 C7
Great Fransham Norf 38 D4
Great Gaddesden Herts 29 G7
Great Gidding Cambs 37 G7
Great Givendale E Yorks 52 D4
Great Glemham Suff 31 B10
Great Glen Leics 36 F2
Great Gonerby Lincs 36 B4
Great Gransden Cambs 29 C9
Great Green Norf 39 G8
Great Green Suff 30 C6
Great Habton N Yorks 52 B3
Great Hale Lincs 37 A7
Great Hallingbury Essex 30 G2
Great Hampden Bucks 18 A5
Great Harrowden Northants 28 A5
Great Harwood Lancs 50 F3
Great Haseley Oxon 18 A3
Great Hatfield E Yorks 53 E7
Great Haywood Staffs 34 C6
Great Heath W Mid 35 G9
Great Heck N Yorks 52 G1
Great Henny Essex 30 E5
Great Hinton Wilts 16 F6
Great Hockham Norf 38 F5
Great Holland Essex 31 G9
Great Horkesley Essex 30 E6
Great Hormead Herts 29 F10
Great Horton W Yorks 51 F7
Great Horwood Bucks 28 E4
Great Houghton Northants 28 C4
Great Houghton S Yorks 45 B8
Great Hucklow Derbys 44 E5
Great Kelk E Yorks 53 D7
Great Kimble Bucks 28 H5
Great Kingshill Bucks 18 B5
Great Langton N Yorks 58 G3
Great Leighs Essex 30 G4
Great Lever Gtr Man 43 B10
Great Limber Lincs 46 B5
Great Linford M Keynes 28 D5
Great Livermere Suff 30 A5
Great Longstone Derbys 44 E6
Great Lumley Durham 58 B3
Great Lyth Shrops 33 E10
Great Malvern Worcs 26 D4
Great Maplestead Essex 30 E5
Great Marton Blkpool 49 F3
Great Massingham Norf 38 C3
Great Melton Norf 39 E7
Great Milton Oxon 18 A3
Great Missenden Bucks 18 A5
Great Mitton Lancs 50 F3
Great Mongeham Kent 21 F10
Great Moulton Norf 39 F7
Great Munden Herts 29 F10
Great Musgrave Cumb 57 E9
Great Ness Shrops 33 D9
Great Notley Essex 30 F4
Great Oakley Essex 31 F8
Great Oakley Northants 36 G4
Great Offley Herts 29 F8
Great Ormside Cumb 57 E9
Great Orton Cumb 56 A5
Great Ouseburn N Yorks 51 C10
Great Oxendon Northants 36 G3
Great Oxney Green Essex 30 H3
Great Palgrave Norf 38 D4
Great Parndon Essex 29 H11
Great Paxton Cambs 29 B9
Great Plumpton Lancs 49 F3
Great Plumstead Norf 39 D9
Great Ponton Lincs 36 B5
Great Preston W Yorks 51 G10
Great Raveley Cambs 37 G8
Great Rissington Glos 27 G8
Great Rollright Oxon 27 E10
Great Ryburgh Norf 38 C5
Great Ryle Northumb 62 B6
Great Ryton Shrops 33 E10
Great Saling Essex 30 F4
Great Salkeld Cumb 57 C7
Great Sampford Essex 30 E3
Great Sankey Warr 43 D8
Great Saxham Suff 30 B4
Great Shefford W Berks 17 D10
Great Shelford Cambs 29 C11
Great Smeaton N Yorks 58 F4
Great Snoring Norf 38 B5
Great Somerford Wilts 16 C6
Great Stainton Darl 58 D4
Great Stambridge Essex 20 B5
Great Staughton Cambs 29 B8
Great Steeping Lincs 47 F8
Great Stonar Kent 21 F10
Great Strickland Cumb 57 D7
Great Stukeley Cambs 29 A9
Great Sturton Lincs 46 E6
Great Sutton Ches 43 E6
Great Sutton Shrops 33 G11
Great Swinburne Northumb 62 F5
Great Tew Oxon 27 F10
Great Tey Essex 30 F5
Great Thurkleby N Yorks 51 B10
Great Thurlow Suff 30 C3
Great Torrington Devon 6 E3
Great Tosson Northumb 62 C6
Great Totham Essex 30 G5
Great Totham Essex 30 G5
Great Tows Lincs 46 C6
Great Urswick Cumb 49 B2
Great Wakering Essex 20 C6
Great Waldingfield Suff 30 D6
Great Walsingham Norf 38 B5
Great Waltham Essex 30 G3
Great Warley Essex 20 B2
Great Washbourne Glos 26 E6
Great Weldon Northants 36 G5
Great Welnetham Suff 30 C5
Great Wenham Suff 31 E7
Great Whittington Northumb 62 F6
Great Wigborough Essex 30 G6
Great Wilbraham Cambs 30 C2
Great Wishford Wilts 17 H7
Great Witcombe Glos 26 G6
Great Witley Worcs 26 B4
Great Wolford Warks 27 E9
Great Wratting Suff 30 D3
Great Wymondley Herts 29 F9
Great Wyrley Staffs 34 E5
Great Wytheford Shrops 34 D1
Great Yarmouth Norf 39 E11
Great Yeldham Essex 30 E4
Greater Doward Hereford 26 G2
Greatford Lincs 37 D6
Greatgate Staffs 35 A6
Greatham Hants 11 A6
Greatham Hrtlpl 58 D5
Greatham W Sus 11 C9
Greatstone on Sea Kent 13 D9
Greatworth Northants 28 D2
Greave Lancs 50 G4
Greeba I o M 48 D3
Green Denb 42 F3
Green End Beds 29 C8
Green Hammerton N Yorks 51 D10
Green Lane Powys 33 F7
Green Ore Som 16 F2
Green St Green London 19 E11
Green Street Herts 19 B8
Greenbank Shetland 96 C7
Greenburn W Loth 69 D8
Greendikes Northumb 71 H9
Greenfield Beds 29 E7
Greenfield Flint 42 E4
Greenfield Gtr Man 44 B3
Greenfield Highld 80 C4
Greenfield Oxon 18 B4
Greenford London 19 C8
Greengairs N Lnrk 68 C6
Greenham W Berks 17 E11
Greenhaugh Northumb 62 E3
Greenhead Northumb 62 G2
Greenhill Falk 69 C7
Greenhill London 19 C8
Greenhill Kent 21 E8
Greenhill Leics 35 D10
Greenhills N Ayrs 67 A6
Greenhithe Kent 20 D2
Greenholm E Ayrs 67 C8
Greenholme Cumb 57 F7
Greenhouse Borders 61 A11
Greenhow Hill N Yorks 51 C7
Greenigoe Orkney 95 H5
Greenland Highld 94 D4
Greenlands Bucks 18 C4
Greenlaw Aberds 89 C6
Greenlaw Borders 70 F6
Greenlea Dumfries 60 F6
Greenloaning Perth 75 G11
Greenmount Gtr Man 43 A10
Greenmow Shetland 96 L6
Greenock Invclyd 73 F11
Greenock West Invclyd 73 F11
Greenodd Cumb 49 A3
Greenrow Cumb 56 A3
Greens Norton Northants 28 D3
Greenside T & W 63 G7
Greensidehill Northumb 62 B5
Greenstead Green Essex 30 F5
Greensted Essex 20 A2
Greenwich London 19 D10
Greet Glos 27 E7
Greete Shrops 26 A2
Greetham Lincs 47 E7
Greetham Rutland 36 D5
Greetland W Yorks 51 G6
Gregg Hall Cumb 56 G6
Gregson Lane Lancs 50 G1
Greinetobht W Isles 84 A3
Greinton Som 15 H10
Gremista Shetland 96 J6
Grenaby I o M 48 E2
Grendon Northants 28 B5
Grendon Warks 35 E8
Grendon Common Warks 35 F8
Grendon Green Hereford 26 C2
Grendon Underwood Bucks 28 F3
Grenofen Devon 4 D5
Grenoside S Yorks 45 C7
Greosabhagh W Isles 90 H6
Gresford Wrex 42 G6
Gresham Norf 39 B7
Greshornish Highld 85 C8
Gressenhall Norf 38 D5
Gressingham Lancs 50 C1
Gresty Green Ches 43 G10
Greta Bridge Durham 58 E1
Gretna Dumfries 61 G9
Gretna Green Dumfries 61 G9
Gretton Glos 27 E7
Gretton Northants 36 F4
Gretton Shrops 33 F11
Grewelthorpe N Yorks 51 B8
Grey Green N Lincs 45 B11
Greygarth N Yorks 51 B7
Greynor Carms 23 F10
Greysouthen Cumb 56 D2
Greystoke Cumb 56 C6
Greystone Angus 77 C8
Greystone Dumfries 60 F5
Greywell Hants 18 F4
Griais W Isles 91 C9
Grianan W Isles 91 D9
Gribthorpe E Yorks 52 F3
Gridley Corner Devon 6 G2
Griff Warks 35 G9
Griffithstown Torf 15 B8
Grimbister Orkney 95 G4
Grimblethorpe Lincs 46 D6
Grimeford Village Lancs 43 A9
Grimethorpe S Yorks 45 B8
Griminis W Isles 84 C2
Grimister Shetland 96 D6
Grimley Worcs 26 B5
Grimness Orkney 95 J5
Grimoldby Lincs 47 D7
Grimpo Shrops 33 C9
Grimsargh Lancs 50 F1
Grimsbury Oxon 27 D11
Grimsby NE Lincs 46 A6
Grimscote Northants 28 C3
Grimscott Corn 6 F1
Grimsthorpe Lincs 36 C6
Grimston E Yorks 53 F8
Grimston Leics 36 C2
Grimston Norf 38 C3
Grimston York 52 D2
Grimstone Dorset 8 E5
Grinacombe Moor Devon 6 G3
Grindale E Yorks 53 B7
Grindigar Orkney 95 H6
Grindiscol Shetland 96 K6
Grindle Shrops 34 E3
Grindleford Derbys 44 E6
Grindleton Lancs 50 E3
Grindley Staffs 34 C6
Grindley Brook Shrops 33 A11
Grindlow Derbys 44 E5
Grindon Northumb 71 F8
Grindon Staffs 44 G4
Grindonmoor Gate Staffs 44 G4
Gringley on the Hill Notts 45 C11
Grinsdale Cumb 61 H9
Grinshill Shrops 33 C11
Grinton N Yorks 58 G1
Griomsidar W Isles 91 E8
Grishipoll Argyll 78 F4
Grisling Common E Sus 12 D3
Gristhorpe N Yorks 53 A6
Griston Norf 38 F5
Gritley Orkney 95 H6
Grittenham Wilts 17 C7
Grittleton Wilts 16 C5
Grizebeck Cumb 49 A2
Grizedale Cumb 56 G5
Grobister Orkney 95 F7
Groby Leics 35 E11
Groes Conwy 42 F3
Groes Neath 14 C3
Groes-faen Rhondda 14 C6
Groes-lwyd Powys 33 D8
Groesffordd Marli Denb 42 E3
Groeslon Gwyn 41 D7
Groeslon Gwyn 40 E6
Grogport Argyll 65 D9
Gromford Suff 31 C10
Gronant Flint 42 D3
Groombridge E Sus 12 C4
Grosmont Mon 25 F11
Grosmont N Yorks 59 F9
Groton Suff 30 D6
Groudle Glen I o M 48 E4
Grougfoot Falk 69 C9
Grouville Jersey 11
Grove Dorset 8 G6
Grove Kent 21 E9
Grove Notts 45 E11
Grove Oxon 17 B11
Grove Park London 19 D11
Grove Vale W Mid 34 F6
Grovesend Swansea 23 F10
Grudie Highld 86 E6
Gruids Highld 93 J8
Gruinard House Highld 86 B2
Grula Highld 85 F8
Gruline Argyll 79 G8
Grunasound Shetland 96 K5
Grundisburgh Suff 31 C9
Grunsagill Lancs 50 D3
Gruting Shetland 96 J4
Grutness Shetland 96 N6
Gualachulain Highld 74 C4
Gualin Ho. Highld 92 D6
Guardbridge Fife 77 F7
Guarlford Worcs 26 D5
Guay Perth 76 C3
Guernsey Airport Guern 11
Guestling Green E Sus 13 E7
Guestling Thorn E Sus 13 E7
Guestwick Norf 39 C6
Guestwick Green Norf 39 C6
Guide Blkburn 50 G3
Guide Post Northumb 63 E8
Guilden Morden Cambs 29 D9
Guilden Sutton Ches 43 F7
Guildford Sur 18 G6
Guildtown Perth 76 D4
Guilsborough Northants 28 A3
Guilsfield Powys 33 D8
Guilton Kent 21 F9
Guineaford Devon 6 C4
Guisborough Redcar 59 E7
Guiseley W Yorks 51 E7
Guist Norf 38 C5
Guith Orkney 95 E6
Guiting Power Glos 27 F7
Gulberwick Shetland 96 K6
Gullane E Loth 70 B3
Gulval Corn 2 F3
Gulworthy Devon 4 D5
Gumfreston Pembs 22 F6
Gumley Leics 36 F2
Gummow's Shop Corn 3 D7
Gun Hill E Sus 12 E4
Gunby E Yorks 52 F3
Gunby Lincs 36 C5
Gundleton Hants 10 A5
Gunn Devon 6 C5
Gunnerside N Yorks 57 G11
Gunnerton Northumb 62 F5
Gunness N Lincs 46 A2
Gunnislake Corn 4 D5
Gunnista Shetland 96 J7
Gunthorpe Norf 38 B6
Gunthorpe Notts 36 A2
Gunthorpe P'boro 37 E7
Gunville I o W 10 F3
Gunwalloe Corn 2 G5
Gurnard I o W 10 E3
Gurnett Ches 44 E3
Gurney Slade Som 16 G3
Gurnos Powys 24 H4
Gussage All Saints Dorset 9 C9
Gussage St Michael Dorset 9 C8
Guston Kent 21 G10
Gutcher Shetland 96 D7
Guthrie Angus 77 B8
Guyhirn Cambs 37 E9
Guyhirn Gull Cambs 37 E9
Guy's Head Lincs 37 C10
Guy's Marsh Dorset 9 B7
Guyzance Northumb 63 C8
Gwaenysgor Flint 42 D3
Gwalchmai Anglesey 40 C5
Gwaun-Cae-Gurwen Neath 24 G4
Gwaun-Leision Neath 24 G4
Gwbert Ceredig 22 B6
Gweek Corn 2 G6
Gwehelog Mon 15 A9
Gwenddwr Powys 25 D7
Gwennap Corn 2 F6
Gwenter Corn 2 H6
Gwernaffield Flint 42 F5
Gwernesney Mon 15 A10
Gwernogle Carms 23 C10
Gwernymynydd Flint 42 F5
Gwersyllt Wrex 42 G6
Gwespyr Flint 42 D4
Gwithian Corn 2 E4
Gwredog Anglesey 40 B6
Gwyddelwern Denb 42 H3
Gwyddgrug Carms 23 C9
Gwydyr Uchaf Conwy 41 D9
Gwynfryn Wrex 42 G5
Gwystre Powys 25 B7
Gwytherin Conwy 41 D10
Gyfelia Wrex 42 H6
Gyffin Conwy 41 C9
Gyre Orkney 95 H4
Gyrn-goch Gwyn 40 F6

H

Habberley Shrops 33 E9
Habergham Lancs 50 F4
Habrough NE Lincs 46 A5
Haceby Lincs 36 B6
Hacheston Suff 31 C10
Hackbridge London 19 E9
Hackenthorpe S Yorks 45 D8
Hackford Norf 39 E6
Hackforth N Yorks 58 G3
Hackland Orkney 95 F4
Hackleton Northants 28 C5
Hackness N Yorks 59 G10
Hackness Orkney 95 J4
Hackney London 19 C10
Hackthorn Lincs 46 D3
Hackthorpe Cumb 57 D7
Haconby Lincs 37 C7
Hacton London 20 C2
Hadden Borders 70 G6
Haddenham Bucks 28 H4
Haddenham Cambs 37 H10
Haddington E Loth 70 C4
Haddington Lincs 46 F3
Haddiscoe Norf 39 F10
Haddon Cambs 37 F7
Haddon Ches 44 F3
Hade Edge W Yorks 44 B5
Hademore Staffs 35 E7
Hadfield Derbys 44 C4
Hadham Cross Herts 29 G11
Hadham Ford Herts 29 F11
Hadleigh Essex 20 C5
Hadleigh Suff 31 D7
Hadley Telford 34 D2
Hadley End Staffs 35 C7
Hadlow Kent 20 G3
Hadlow Down E Sus 12 D4
Hadnall Shrops 33 D11
Hadstock Essex 30 D2
Hady Derbys 45 E7
Hadzor Worcs 26 B6
Haffenden Quarter Kent 13 B7
Hafod-Dinbych Conwy 41 E10
Hafod-lom Conwy 41 C10
Haggate Lancs 50 F4
Haggbeck Cumb 61 F10
Haggerston Northumb 71 F9
Haggrister Shetland 96 F5
Hagley Hereford 26 D2
Hagley Worcs 34 G5
Hagworthingham Lincs 47 F7
Haigh Gtr Man 43 B9
Haigh S Yorks 44 A6
Haigh Moor W Yorks 51 G8
Haighton Green Lancs 50 F1
Hail Weston Cambs 29 B8
Haile Cumb 56 F2
Hailes Glos 27 E7
Hailey Herts 29 G10
Hailey Oxon 27 G10
Hailsham E Sus 12 F4
Haimer Highld 94 D3
Hainault London 19 B11
Hainford Norf 39 D8
Hainton Lincs 46 D5
Hairmyres S Lnrk 68 E5
Haisthorpe E Yorks 53 C7
Hakin Pembs 22 F3
Halam Notts 45 G10
Halbeath Fife 69 B10
Halberton Devon 7 E9
Halcro Highld 94 D4
Hale Gtr Man 43 D10
Hale Halton 43 D7
Hale Hants 9 C10
Hale Bank Halton 43 D7
Hale Street Kent 20 G3
Halebarns Gtr Man 43 D10
Hales Norf 39 F9
Hales Staffs 34 B3
Hales Place Kent 21 F8
Halesfield Telford 34 E3
Halesgate Lincs 37 C9
Halesowen W Mid 34 G5
Halesworth Suff 39 H9
Halewood Mers 43 D7
Halford Shrops 33 G10
Halford Warks 27 D9
Halfpenny Furze Carms 23 E7
Halfpenny Green Staffs 34 F4
Halfway Carms 24 E3
Halfway Carms 24 E5
Halfway W Berks 17 E11
Halfway Bridge W Sus 11 B8
Halfway House Shrops 33 D9
Halfway Houses Kent 20 D6
Halifax W Yorks 51 G6
Halket E Ayrs 67 A7
Halkirk Highld 94 E3
Halkyn Flint 42 E5
Hall Dunnerdale Cumb 56 G4
Hall Green W Mid 35 G7
Hall Green W Yorks 51 H9
Hall Grove Herts 29 G9
Hall of Tankerness Orkney 95 H6
Hall of the Forest Shrops 33 G8
Halland E Sus 12 E3
Hallaton Leics 36 F3
Hallatrow Bath 16 F3
Hallbankgate Cumb 61 H11
Hallen S Glos 15 C11
Halliburton Borders 70 F5
Hallin Highld 84 C7
Halling Medway 20 E4
Hallington Lincs 47 D7
Hallington Northumb 62 F5
Halliwell Gtr Man 43 A10
Halloughton Notts 45 G10
Hallow Worcs 26 C5
Hallrule Borders 61 B11
Halls E Loth 70 C5
Hall's Green Herts 29 F9
Hallsands Devon 5 H9
Hallthwaites Cumb 56 H3
Hallworthy Corn 4 C2
Hallyburton House Perth 76 D5
Hallyne Borders 69 F10
Halmer End Staffs 43 H10
Halmore Glos 16 A3
Halmyre Mains Borders 69 F10
Halnaker W Sus 11 D8
Halsall Lancs 42 A6
Halse Northants 28 D2
Halse Som 7 D10
Halsetown Corn 2 F4
Halsham E Yorks 53 G8
Halsinger Devon 6 C4
Halstead Essex 30 E5
Halstead Kent 19 E11
Halstead Leics 36 E3
Halstock Dorset 8 D4
Haltham Lincs 46 F6
Haltoft End Lincs 47 H7
Halton Bucks 28 G5
Halton Halton 43 D8
Halton Lancs 49 C5
Halton Northumb 62 G5
Halton Wrex 33 B9
Halton W Yorks 51 F9
Halton East N Yorks 50 D6
Halton Gill N Yorks 50 B4
Halton Holegate Lincs 47 F8
Halton Lea Gate Northumb 62 H2
Halton West N Yorks 50 D4
Haltwhistle Northumb 62 G3
Halvergate Norf 39 E10
Halwell Devon 5 F8
Halwill Devon 6 G3
Halwill Junction Devon 6 F3
Ham Devon 7 F11
Ham Glos 16 B3
Ham London 19 D8
Ham Highld 94 C4
Ham Kent 21 F10
Ham Shetland 96 K1
Ham Wilts 17 E10
Ham Common Dorset 9 B7
Ham Green Hereford 26 D4
Ham Green Kent 13 D7
Ham Green Kent 20 E5
Ham Green N Som 15 D11
Ham Green Worcs 27 B7
Ham Street Som 8 A4
Hamble-le-Rice Hants 10 D3
Hambleden Bucks 18 C4
Hambledon Hants 10 C5
Hambledon Sur 18 H6
Hambleton Lancs 49 E3
Hambleton N Yorks 52 F1
Hambridge Som 8 B2
Hambrook S Glos 16 D3
Hambrook W Sus 11 D6
Hameringham Lincs 47 F7
Hamerton Cambs 37 H7
Hametoun Shetland 96 K1
Hamilton S Lnrk 68 E6
Hammer W Sus 11 A7
Hammerpot W Sus 11 D9
Hammersmith London 19 D9
Hammerwich Staffs 35 E6
Hammerwood E Sus 12 C3
Hammond Street Herts 19 A10
Hammoon Dorset 9 C7
Hamnavoe Shetland 96 E4
Hamnavoe Shetland 96 K5
Hamnavoe Shetland 96 E6
Hamnavoe Shetland 96 F6
Hampden National Stadium Glasgow 68 D4
Hampden Park E Sus 12 F5
Hampden End Essex 30 E2
Hampnett Glos 27 G7
Hampole S Yorks 45 A9
Hampreston Dorset 9 E9
Hampstead London 19 C9
Hampstead Norreys W Berks 18 D2
Hampsthwaite N Yorks 51 D8
Hampton London 19 E8
Hampton Shrops 34 G3
Hampton Worcs 27 D7
Hampton Bishop Hereford 26 E2
Hampton Heath Ches 43 H7
Hampton in Arden W Mid 35 G8
Hampton Loade Shrops 34 G3
Hampton Lovett Worcs 26 B5
Hampton Lucy Warks 27 C9
Hampton on the Hill Warks 27 B9
Hampton Poyle Oxon 28 G2
Hamrow Norf 38 C5
Hamsey E Sus 12 E3
Hamsey Green Sur 19 F10
Hamstall Ridware Staffs 35 D7
Hamstead I o W 10 E3
Hamstead W Mid 34 F6
Hamstead Marshall W Berks 17 E11
Hamsterley Durham 58 C2
Hamsterley Durham 63 H7
Hamstreet Kent 13 C9
Hamworthy Poole 9 E8
Hanbury Staffs 35 C7
Hanbury Worcs 26 B6
Hanbury Woodend Staffs 35 C7
Hanby Lincs 36 B6
Hanchurch Staffs 34 A4
Handbridge Ches 43 F7
Handcross W Sus 12 D1
Handforth Ches 44 D2
Handley Ches 43 G7
Handsacre Staffs 35 D6
Handsworth S Yorks 45 D8
Handsworth W Mid 34 F6
Handy Cross Devon 6 D3
Hanford Stoke 34 A4
Hanging Langford Wilts 17 H7
Hangleton W Sus 11 D9
Hanham S Glos 16 D3
Hankelow Ches 43 H9
Hankerton Wilts 16 B6
Hankham E Sus 12 F5
Hanley Stoke 44 H2
Hanley Castle Worcs 26 D5
Hanley Child Worcs 26 B3
Hanley Swan Worcs 26 D5
Hanley William Worcs 26 B3
Hanlith N Yorks 50 C5
Hanmer Wrex 33 B10

Hornsea Bridge E Yorks 53 E8
Hornsey London 19 C10
Hornton Oxon 27 D10
Horrabridge Devon 4 E6
Horringer Suff 30 B5
Horringford I o W 10 F4
Horse Bridge Staffs 44 G3
Horsebridge Devon 4 D5
Horsebridge Hants 10 A2
Horsebrook Staffs 34 D4
Horsehay Telford 34 E2
Horseheath Cambs 30 D3
Horsehouse N Yorks 50 A6
Horsell Sur 18 F6
Horseman's Green Wrex 33 A10
Horseway Cambs 37 G10
Horsey Norf 39 C10
Horsford Norf 39 D7
Horsforth W Yorks 51 F8
Horsham Worcs 26 C4
Horsham W Sus 11 A10
Horsham St Faith Norf 39 D8
Horsington Lincs 46 F5
Horsington Som 8 B6
Horsley Derbys 35 A9
Horsley Glos 16 B5
Horsley Northumb 62 G6
Horsley Northumb 62 D4
Horsley Cross Essex 31 F8
Horsley Woodhouse Derbys 35 A9
Horsleycross Street Essex 31 F8
Horsleyhill Borders 61 B11
Horsleyhope Durham 58 B1
Horsmonden Kent 12 B5
Horspath Oxon 18 A2
Horstead Norf 39 D8
Horsted Keynes W Sus 12 D2
Horton Bucks 28 G6
Horton Dorset 9 D9
Horton Lancs 50 D4
Horton Northants 28 C5
Horton Shrops 33 C10
Horton S Glos 16 C4
Horton Som 8 C2
Horton Staffs 44 G3
Horton Swansea 23 H9
Horton Wilts 17 E7
Horton Windsor 19 D7
Horton-cum-Studley Oxon 28 G2
Horton Green Ches 43 H7
Horton Heath Hants 10 C3
Horton in Ribblesdale N Yorks 50 B4
Horton Kirby Kent 20 E2
Hortonlane Shrops 33 D10
Horwich Gtr Man 43 A9
Horwich End Derbys 44 D4
Horwood Devon 6 D4
Hose Leics 36 C3
Hoselaw Borders 71 G7
Hoses Cumb 56 G4
Hosh Perth 75 E11
Hosta W Isles 84 A2
Hoswick Shetland 96 L6
Hotham E Yorks 52 F4
Hothfield Kent 20 G6
Hoton Leics 36 C1
Houbie Shetland 96 D8
Houdston S Ayrs 66 G4
Hough Ches 43 G10
Hough Ches 44 E2
Hough Green Halton 43 D7
Hough-on-the-Hill Lincs 46 H3
Hougham Lincs 36 A4
Houghton Cambs 29 A9
Houghton Cumb 61 H10
Houghton Hants 10 A2
Houghton Pembs 22 F4
Houghton W Sus 11 C9
Houghton Conquest Beds 29 D7
Houghton Green E Sus 13 D8
Houghton Green Warr 43 C9
Houghton-le-Side Darl 58 D3
Houghton-Le-Spring T & W 58 B4
Houghton on the Hill Leics 36 E2
Houghton Regis Beds 29 F7
Houghton St Giles Norf 38 B5
Houlland Shetland 96 H5
Houlland Shetland 96 F7
Houlsyke N Yorks 59 F8
Hound Hants 10 D3
Hound Green Hants 18 F4
Houndslow Borders 70 F5
Houndwood Borders 71 D7
Hounslow London 19 D8
Hounslow Green Essex 30 G3
Housay Shetland 96 F8
House of Daviot Highld 87 G10
House of Glenmuick Aberds 82 D5
Housetter Shetland 96 E5
Houss Shetland 96 K5
Houston Renfs 68 D3
Houstry Highld 94 G3
Houton Orkney 95 H4
Hove Brighton 12 F1
Hoveringham Notts 45 H10
Hoveton Norf 39 D9
Hovingham N Yorks 52 B2
How Cumb 61 H11
How Caple Hereford 26 E3
How End Beds 29 D7
How Green Kent 19 G11
Howbrook S Yorks 45 C7
Howden Borders 62 A2
Howden E Yorks 52 G3
Howden-le-Wear Durham 58 C2
Howe Highld 94 D5
Howe Norf 39 E8
Howe N Yorks 51 A9
Howe Bridge Gtr Man 43 B9
Howe Green Essex 20 A4
Howe of Teuchar Aberds 89 D7
Howe Street Essex 30 G3
Howe Street Essex 30 E3
Howell Lincs 46 H5
Howey Powys 25 C7
Howgate Midloth 69 E11
Howick Northumb 63 B8
Howle Durham 58 D1
Howle Telford 34 C2
Howlett End Essex 30 E2
Howley Som 8 D1
Hownam Borders 62 B3
Hownam Mains Borders 62 A3
Howpasley Borders 61 C9
Howsham N Lincs 46 B4
Howsham N Yorks 52 C3
Howslack Dumfries 60 C6
Howtel Northumb 71 G7
Howton Hereford 25 F11
Howtown Cumb 56 E6
Howwood Renfs 68 D2
Hoxne Suff 39 H7
Hoy Orkney 95 H3
Hoylake Mers 42 D5
Hoyland S Yorks 45 B7
Hoylandswaine S Yorks 44 B6
Hubberholme N Yorks 50 B5
Hubbert's Bridge Lincs 37 A8
Huby N Yorks 51 E8
Huby N Yorks 52 C1
Hucclecote Glos 26 G5
Hucking Kent 20 F5
Hucknall Notts 45 H9
Huddersfield W Yorks 51 H7
Huddington Worcs 26 C6
Hudswell N Yorks 58 F2
Huggate E Yorks 52 D4
Hugglescote Leics 35 D10
Hugh Town Scilly 2 C3
Hughenden Valley Bucks 18 B5
Hughley Shrops 34 F1
Huish Devon 6 E4
Huish Wilts 17 E8
Huish Champflower Som 7 D9
Huish Episcopi Som 8 B3
Huisinis W Isles 90 F4
Hulcott Bucks 28 G5
Hulland Derbys 44 H6
Hulland Ward Derbys 44 H6
Hullavington Wilts 16 C5
Hullbridge Essex 20 B5
Hulme Gtr Man 44 C2
Hulme End Staffs 44 G5
Hulme Walfield Ches 44 F2
Hulver Street Suff 39 G10
Hulverstone I o W 10 F2
Humber Hereford 26 C2
Humber Bridge E Yorks 52 G6
Humberside International Airport N Lincs 46 A4
Humberston NE Lincs 47 B7
Humbie E Loth 70 D3
Humbleton E Yorks 53 F8
Humbleton Northumb 71 H8
Humby Lincs 36 B6
Hume Borders 70 F6
Humshaugh Northumb 62 F5
Huna Highld 94 C5
Huncoat Lancs 50 F3
Huncote Leics 35 F11
Hundalee Borders 62 B2
Hunderthwaite Durham 57 D11
Hundle Houses Lincs 46 G6
Hundleby Lincs 47 F7
Hundleton Pembs 22 F4
Hundon Suff 30 D4
Hundred Acres Hants 10 C4
Hundred End Lancs 49 G4
Hundred House Powys 25 C8
Hungarton Leics 36 E2
Hungerford Hants 9 C10
Hungerford W Berks 17 E10
Hungerford Newtown W Berks 17 D10
Hungerton Lincs 36 C4
Hungladder Highld 85 A8
Hunmanby N Yorks 53 B6
Hunmanby Moor N Yorks 53 B7
Hunningham Warks 27 B10
Hunny Hill I o W 10 F3
Hunsdon Herts 29 G11
Hunsingore N Yorks 51 D10
Hunslet W Yorks 51 F9
Hunsonby Cumb 57 C7
Hunspow Highld 94 C4
Hunstanton Norf 38 A2
Hunstanworth Durham 57 B11
Hunsterson Ches 43 H9
Hunston Suff 30 B6
Hunston W Sus 11 D7
Hunstrete Bath 16 E3
Hunt End Worcs 27 B7
Hunter's Quay Argyll 73 F10
Hunthill Lodge Angus 82 F6
Hunting-tower Perth 76 E3
Huntingdon Cambs 29 A9
Huntingfield Suff 31 A10
Huntingford Dorset 9 A7
Huntington E Loth 70 C3
Huntington Hereford 25 C9
Huntington Staffs 34 D5
Huntington York 52 D2
Huntley Glos 26 G4
Huntly Aberds 88 E5
Huntlywood Borders 70 F5
Hunton Kent 20 G4
Hunton N Yorks 58 G2
Hunt's Corner Norf 39 G6
Hunt's Cross Mers 43 D7
Huntsham Devon 7 D9
Huntspill Som 15 G9
Huntworth Som 8 A2
Hunwick Durham 58 C2
Hunworth Norf 39 B6
Hurdsfield Ches 44 E3
Hurley Warks 35 F8
Hurley Windsor 18 C5
Hurlford E Ayrs 67 C7
Hurliness Orkney 95 K3
Hurn Dorset 9 E10
Hurn's End Lincs 47 H8
Hursley Hants 10 B3
Hurst N Yorks 58 F1
Hurst Som 8 C3
Hurst Wokingham 18 D4
Hurst Green E Sus 12 D6
Hurst Green Lancs 50 F2
Hurst Wickham W Sus 12 E1
Hurstbourne Priors Hants 17 G11
Hurstbourne Tarrant Hants 17 F10
Hurstpierpoint W Sus 12 E1
Hurstwood Lancs 50 F4
Hurtmore Sur 18 G6
Hurworth Place Darl 58 F3
Hury Durham 57 E11
Husabost Highld 84 C7
Husbands Bosworth Leics 36 G2
Husborne Crawley Beds 28 E6
Husthwaite N Yorks 51 B11
Hutchwns Bridgend 14 D4
Huthwaite Notts 45 G8
Huttoft Lincs 47 E9
Hutton Borders 71 E8
Hutton Cumb 56 D6
Hutton E Yorks 52 D6
Hutton Essex 20 B3
Hutton Lancs 49 G4
Hutton N Som 15 F9
Hutton Buscel N Yorks 52 A5
Hutton Conyers N Yorks 51 B9
Hutton Cranswick E Yorks 52 D6
Hutton End Cumb 56 C6
Hutton Gate Redcar 59 E6
Hutton Henry Durham 58 C5
Hutton-le-Hole N Yorks 59 G8
Hutton Magna Durham 58 E2
Hutton Roof Cumb 56 C5
Hutton Roof Cumb 50 B1
Hutton Rudby N Yorks 58 F5
Hutton Sessay N Yorks 51 B10
Hutton Village Redcar 59 E6
Hutton Wandesley N Yorks 51 D11
Huxley Ches 43 F8
Huxter Shetland 96 H5
Huxter Shetland 96 G7
Huxton Borders 71 D7
Huyton Mers 43 C7
Hwlffordd = Haverfordwest Pembs 22 E4
Hycemoor Cumb 56 H2
Hyde Glos 16 A5
Hyde Gtr Man 44 C3
Hyde Hants 9 C10
Hyde Heath Bucks 18 A6
Hyde Park S Yorks 45 B9
Hydestile Sur 18 G6
Hylton Castle T & W 63 H9
Hyndford Bridge S Lnrk 69 F8
Hynish Argyll 78 H2
Hyssington Powys 33 F9
Hythe Hants 10 D3
Hythe Kent 21 H8
Hythe End Windsor 19 D7
Hythie Aberds 89 C10

I

Ibberton Dorset 9 D6
Ible Derbys 44 G6
Ibsley Hants 9 D10
Ibstock Leics 35 D10
Ibstone Bucks 18 B4
Ibthorpe Hants 17 F10
Ibworth Hants 18 F2
Ichrachan Argyll 74 D3
Ickburgh Norf 38 F4
Ickenham London 19 C7
Ickford Bucks 28 H3
Ickham Kent 21 F9
Ickleford Herts 29 E8
Icklesham E Sus 13 E7
Ickleton Cambs 29 D11
Icklingham Suff 30 A4
Ickwell Green Beds 29 D8
Icomb Glos 27 F9
Idbury Oxon 27 G9
Iddesleigh Devon 6 F4
Ide Devon 7 G7
Ide Hill Kent 19 F11
Ideford Devon 5 D9
Iden E Sus 13 D8
Iden Green Kent 13 C7
Iden Green Kent 12 C6
Idle W Yorks 51 F7
Idlicote Warks 27 D9
Idmiston Wilts 17 H8
Idole Carms 23 E9
Idridgehay Derbys 44 H6
Idrigill Highld 85 B8
Idstone Oxon 17 C9
Idvies Angus 77 C8
Iffley Oxon 18 A2
Ifield W Sus 19 H9
Ifold W Sus 11 A9
Iford E Sus 12 F3
Ifton Heath Shrops 33 B9
Ightfield Shrops 34 B1
Ightham Kent 20 F2
Iken Suff 31 C11
Ilam Staffs 44 G5
Ilchester Som 8 B4
Ilderton Northumb 62 A6
Ilford London 19 C11
Ilfracombe Devon 6 B4
Ilkeston Derbys 35 A10
Ilketshall St Andrew Suff 39 G9
Ilketshall St Lawrence Suff 39 G9
Ilketshall St Margaret Suff 39 G9
Ilkley W Yorks 51 E7
Illey W Mid 34 G5
Illingworth W Yorks 51 G6
Illogan Corn 2 E5
Illston on the Hill Leics 36 F3
Ilmer Bucks 28 H4
Ilmington Warks 27 D9
Ilminster Som 8 C2
Ilsington Devon 5 D8
Ilston Swansea 23 G10
Ilton N Yorks 51 B7
Ilton Som 8 C2
Imachar N Ayrs 66 B1
Imeraval Argyll 64 D4
Immingham NE Lincs 46 A5
Impington Cambs 29 B11
Ince Ches 43 E7
Ince Blundell Mers 42 B6
Ince in Makerfield Gtr Man 43 B8
Inch of Arnhall Aberds 83 F8
Inchbare Angus 83 G8
Inchberry Moray 88 C3
Inchbraoch Angus 77 B10
Incheril Highld 86 E3
Inchgrundle Angus 82 F6
Inchina Highld 86 B2
Inchinnan Renfs 68 D3
Inchkinloch Highld 93 E8
Inchlaggan Highld 80 C3
Inchlumpie Highld 87 D8
Inchmore Highld 86 G6
Inchnacardoch Hotel Highld 80 B5
Inchnadamph Highld 92 G5
Inchree Highld 74 A3
Inchture Perth 76 E5
Inchyra Perth 76 E4
Indian Queens Corn 3 D8
Inerval Argyll 64 D4
Ingatestone Essex 20 B3
Ingbirchworth S Yorks 44 B6
Ingestre Staffs 34 C5
Ingham Lincs 46 D3
Ingham Norf 39 C9
Ingham Suff 30 A5
Ingham Corner Norf 39 C9
Ingleborough Norf 37 D10
Ingleby Derbys 35 C9
Ingleby Lincs 46 E2
Ingleby Arncliffe N Yorks 58 F5
Ingleby Barwick Stockton 58 E5
Ingleby Greenhow N Yorks 59 F6
Inglemire Hull 53 F6
Inglesbatch Bath 16 E4
Inglesham Swindon 17 B9
Ingleton Durham 58 D2
Ingleton N Yorks 50 B2
Inglewhite Lancs 49 E5
Ingliston Edin 69 C10
Ingoe Northumb 62 F6
Ingol Lancs 49 F5
Ingoldisthorpe Norf 38 B2
Ingoldmells Lincs 47 F9
Ingoldsby Lincs 36 B6
Ingon Warks 27 C9
Ingram Northumb 62 B6
Ingrave Essex 20 B3
Ingrow W Yorks 51 F6
Ings Cumb 56 G6
Ingst S Glos 16 C2
Ingworth Norf 39 C7
Inham's End Cambs 37 F8
Inkberrow Worcs 27 C7
Inkpen W Berks 17 E10
Inkstack Highld 94 C4
Inn Cumb 56 F6
Innellan Argyll 73 F10
Innerleithen Borders 70 G2
Innerleven Fife 76 G6
Innermessan Dumfries 54 C3
Innerwick E Loth 70 C6
Innerwick Perth 75 C8
Innis Chonain Argyll 74 E4
Insch Aberds 83 A8
Insh Highld 81 C10
Inshore Highld 92 C6
Inskip Lancs 49 F4
Instoneville S Yorks 45 A9
Instow Devon 6 C3
Intake S Yorks 45 B9
Inver Aberds 82 D4
Inver Highld 87 C11
Inver Perth 76 C3
Inver Mallie Highld 80 E3
Inverailort Highld 79 C10
Inveraldie Angus 77 D7
Inveralligin Highld 85 C13
Inverallochy Aberds 89 B10
Inveran Highld 87 B8
Inveraray Argyll 73 C9
Inverarish Highld 85 E10
Inverarity Angus 77 C7
Inverarnan Stirl 74 F6
Inverasdale Highld 91 J13
Inverbeg Argyll 74 H6
Inverbervie Aberds 83 F10
Inverboyndie Aberds 89 B6
Inverbroom Highld 86 C4
Invercassley Highld 92 J7
Invercauld House Aberds 82 D3
Inverchaolain Argyll 73 F9
Invercharnan Highld 74 C4
Inverchoran Highld 86 F5
Invercreran Argyll 74 C3
Inverdruie Highld 81 B11
Inverebrie Aberds 89 E9
Invereck Argyll 73 E10
Inverernan Ho. Aberds 82 B5
Invereshie House Highld 81 C10
Inveresk E Loth 70 C2
Inverey Aberds 82 E2
Inverfarigaig Highld 81 A7
Invergarry Highld 80 C5
Invergelder Aberds 82 D4
Invergeldie Perth 75 E10
Invergordon Highld 87 E10
Invergowrie Perth 76 D6
Inverguseran Highld 85 H12
Inverhadden Perth 75 B9
Inverharroch Moray 88 E3
Inverherive Stirl 74 E6
Inverie Highld 79 B10
Inverinan Argyll 73 B8
Inverinate Highld 85 F14
Inverkeilor Angus 77 C9
Inverkeithing Fife 69 B10
Inverkeithny Aberds 89 D6
Inverkip Invclyd 73 F11
Inverkirkaig Highld 92 H3
Inverlael Highld 86 C4
Inverlochlarig Stirl 75 F7
Inverlochy Argyll 74 E4
Inverlochy Highld 80 F3
Inverlussa Argyll 72 E5
Invermark Lodge Angus 82 E6
Invermoidart Highld 79 D9
Invermoriston Highld 80 B6
Invernaver Highld 93 C10
Inverneill Argyll 73 E7
Inverness Highld 87 G9
Inverness Airport Highld 87 F10
Invernettie Aberds 89 D11
Invernoaden Argyll 73 D10
Inveroran Hotel Argyll 74 C5
Inverpolly Lodge Highld 92 H3
Inverquharity Angus 77 B7
Inverquhomery Aberds 89 D10
Inverroy Highld 80 E4
Inversanda Highld 74 B2
Invershiel Highld 80 B1
Invershin Highld 87 B8
Inversnaid Hotel Stirl 74 G6
Inverugie Aberds 89 D11
Inveruglas Argyll 74 G6
Inveruglass Highld 81 C10
Inverurie Aberds 83 A9
Invervar Perth 75 C9
Inverythan Aberds 89 D7
Inwardleigh Devon 6 G4
Inworth Essex 30 G5
Iochdar W Isles 84 D2
Iping W Sus 11 B7
Ipplepen Devon 5 E9
Ipsden Oxon 18 C3
Ipsley Worcs 27 B7
Ipstones Staffs 44 G4
Ipswich Suff 31 D8
Irby Mers 42 D5
Irby in the Marsh Lincs 47 F8
Irby upon Humber NE Lincs 46 B5
Irchester Northants 28 B6
Ireby Cumb 56 C4
Ireby Lancs 50 B2
Ireland Orkney 95 H4
Ireland Shetland 96 L5
Ireland's Cross Shrops 34 A3
Ireleth Cumb 49 B2
Ireshopeburn Durham 57 C10
Irlam Gtr Man 43 C10
Irnham Lincs 36 C6
Iron Acton S Glos 16 C3
Iron Cross Warks 27 C7
Ironbridge Telford 34 E2
Irongray Dumfries 60 F5
Ironmacannie Dumfries 55 B9
Ironside Aberds 89 C8
Ironville Derbys 45 G8
Irstead Norf 39 C9
Irthington Cumb 61 G10
Irthlingborough Northants 28 A6
Irton N Yorks 52 A6
Irvine N Ayrs 66 C6
Isauld Highld 93 C12
Isbister Orkney 95 F3
Isbister Orkney 95 G4
Isbister Shetland 96 D5
Isbister Shetland 96 G7
Isfield E Sus 12 E3
Isham Northants 28 A5
Islay Airport Argyll 64 C4
Isle Abbotts Som 8 B2
Isle Brewers Som 8 B2
Isle of Man Airport I o M 48 F2
Isle of Whithorn Dumfries 55 F7
Isleham Cambs 30 A3
Isleornsay Highld 85 G12
Islesburgh Shetland 96 G5
Islesteps Dumfries 60 F5
Isleworth London 19 D8
Isley Walton Leics 35 C10
Islibhig W Isles 90 E4
Islington London 19 C10
Islip Northants 36 H5
Islip Oxon 28 G2
Istead Rise Kent 20 E3
Isycoed Wrex 43 G7
Itchen Soton 10 C3
Itchen Abbas Hants 10 A4
Itchen Stoke Hants 10 A4
Itchingfield W Sus 11 B10
Itchington S Glos 16 C3
Itteringham Norf 39 B7
Itton Devon 6 G5
Itton Common Mon 15 B10
Ivegill Cumb 56 B6
Iver Bucks 19 C7
Iver Heath Bucks 19 C7
Iveston Durham 58 A2
Ivinghoe Bucks 28 G6
Ivinghoe Aston Bucks 28 G6
Ivington Hereford 25 C11
Ivington Green Hereford 25 C11
Ivy Chimneys Essex 19 A11
Ivy Cross Dorset 9 B7
Ivy Hatch Kent 20 F2
Ivybridge Devon 5 F7
Ivychurch Kent 13 D9
Iwade Kent 20 E6
Iwerne Courtney or Shroton Dorset 9 C7
Iwerne Minster Dorset 9 C7
Ixworth Suff 30 A6
Ixworth Thorpe Suff 30 A6

J

Jack Hill N Yorks 51 D8
Jack in the Green Devon 7 G9
Jacksdale Notts 45 G8
Jackstown Aberds 89 E7
Jacobstow Corn 4 B2
Jacobstowe Devon 6 F4
Jameston Pembs 22 G5
Jamestown Dumfries 61 D9
Jamestown Highld 86 F7
Jamestown W Dunb 68 B2
Jarrow T & W 63 G9
Jarvis Brook E Sus 12 D4
Jasper's Green Essex 30 F4
Java Argyll 79 H10
Jawcraig Falk 69 C7
Jaywick Essex 31 G8
Jealott's Hill Brack 18 D5
Jedburgh Borders 62 A2
Jeffreyston Pembs 22 F5
Jellyhill E Dunb 68 C5
Jemimaville Highld 87 E10
Jersey Airport Jersey 11
Jersey Farm Herts 29 H8
Jesmond T & W 63 G8
Jevington E Sus 12 F4
Jockey End Herts 29 G7
John o'Groats Highld 94 C5
Johnby Cumb 56 C6
John's Cross E Sus 12 D6
Johnshaven Aberds 83 G9
Johnston Pembs 22 E4
Johnstone Renfs 68 D3
Johnstonebridge Dumfries 60 D6
Johnstown Carms 23 E9
Johnstown Wrex 42 H6
Joppa Edin 70 C2
Joppa S Ayrs 67 E7
Jordans Bucks 18 B6
Jordanthorpe S Yorks 45 D7
Jump S Yorks 45 B7
Jumpers Green Dorset 9 E10
Juniper Green Edin 69 D10
Jurby East I o M 48 C3
Jurby West I o M 48 C3

K

Kaber Cumb 57 E9
Kaimend S Lnrk 69 F8
Kaimes Edin 69 D11
Kalemouth Borders 70 H6
Kames Argyll 73 F8
Kames Argyll 73 B7
Kames E Ayrs 68 H5
Kea Corn 3 E7
Keadby N Lincs 46 A2
Keal Cotes Lincs 47 F7
Kearsley Gtr Man 43 B10
Kearstwick Cumb 50 A2
Kearton N Yorks 57 G11
Kearvaig Highld 92 B5
Keasden N Yorks 50 C3
Keckwick Halton 43 D8
Keddington Lincs 47 D7
Kedington Suff 30 D4
Kedleston Derbys 35 A9
Keelby Lincs 46 A5
Keele Staffs 44 H2
Keeley Green Beds 29 D7
Keeston Pembs 22 E4
Keevil Wilts 16 F6
Kegworth Leics 35 C10
Kehelland Corn 2 E5
Keig Aberds 83 B8
Keighley W Yorks 51 E6
Keil Highld 74 B2
Keilarsbrae Clack 69 A7
Keilhill Aberds 89 C7
Keillmore Argyll 72 E5
Keillor Perth 76 C5
Keillour Perth 76 E2
Keills Argyll 64 B5
Keils Argyll 72 G4
Keinton Mandeville Som 8 A4
Keir Mill Dumfries 60 D4
Keisby Lincs 36 C6
Keiss Highld 94 D5
Keith Moray 88 C4
Keith Inch Aberds 89 D11
Keithock Angus 77 A9
Kelbrook Lancs 50 E5
Kelby Lincs 36 A6
Keld Cumb 57 E7
Keld N Yorks 57 F10
Keldholme N Yorks 59 H8
Kelfield N Lincs 46 B2
Kelfield N Yorks 52 F1
Kelham Notts 45 G11
Kellan Argyll 79 G8
Kellas Angus 77 D7
Kellas Moray 88 C1
Kellaton Devon 5 H9
Kelleth Cumb 57 F8
Kelleythorpe E Yorks 52 D5
Kelling Norf 39 A6
Kellingley N Yorks 51 G11
Kellington N Yorks 52 G1
Kelloe Durham 58 C4
Kelloholm Dumfries 60 B3
Kelly Devon 4 C4
Kelly Bray Corn 4 D4
Kelmarsh Northants 36 H3
Kelmscot Oxon 17 B9
Kelsale Suff 31 B10
Kelsall Ches 43 F8
Kelsall Hill Ches 43 F8
Kelshall Herts 29 E10
Kelsick Cumb 56 A3
Kelso Borders 70 G6
Kelstedge Derbys 45 F7
Kelstern Lincs 46 C6
Kelston Bath 16 E4
Keltneyburn Perth 75 C10
Kelton Dumfries 60 F5
Kelty Fife 69 A10
Kelvedon Essex 30 G5
Kelvedon Hatch Essex 20 B2
Kelvin S Lnrk 68 E5
Kelvinside Glasgow 68 D4
Kelynack Corn 2 F2
Kemback Fife 77 F7
Kemberton Shrops 34 E3
Kemble Glos 16 B6
Kemerton Worcs 26 E6
Kemeys Commander Mon 15 A9
Kemnay Aberds 83 B9
Kemp Town Brighton 12 F2
Kempley Glos 26 F3
Kemps Green Warks 27 A8
Kempsey Worcs 26 D5
Kempsford Glos 17 B8
Kempshott Hants 18 F3
Kempston Beds 29 D7
Kempston Hardwick Beds 29 D7
Kempton Shrops 33 G9
Kemsing Kent 20 F2
Kemsley Kent 20 E6
Kenardington Kent 13 C8
Kenchester Hereford 25 D11
Kencot Oxon 17 A9
Kendal Cumb 57 G7
Kendoon Dumfries 67 H9
Kendray S Yorks 45 B7
Kenfig Bridgend 14 C4
Kenfig Hill Bridgend 14 C4
Kenilworth Warks 27 A9
Kenknock Stirl 75 D7
Kenley London 19 F10
Kenley Shrops 34 E1
Kenmore Highld 85 C12
Kenmore Perth 75 C10
Kenn Devon 5 C10
Kenn N Som 15 E10
Kennacley W Isles 90 H6
Kennacraig Argyll 73 G7
Kennerleigh Devon 7 F7
Kennet Clack 69 A8
Kennethmont Aberds 83 A7
Kennett Cambs 30 B3
Kennford Devon 5 C10
Kenninghall Norf 38 G6
Kenninghall Heath Norf 38 G6
Kennington Kent 13 B9
Kennington Oxon 18 A2
Kennoway Fife 76 G6
Kenny Hill Suff 38 H2
Kennythorpe N Yorks 52 C3
Kenovay Argyll 78 G2
Kensaleyre Highld 85 C9
Kensington London 19 D9
Kensworth Beds 29 G7
Kensworth Common Beds 29 G7
Kent International Airport Kent 21 E10
Kent Street E Sus 13 E6
Kent Street Kent 20 F3
Kent Street W Sus 11 B11
Kentallen Highld 74 B3
Kentchurch Hereford 25 F11
Kentford Suff 30 B4
Kentisbeare Devon 7 F9
Kentisbury Devon 6 B5
Kentisbury Ford Devon 6 B5
Kentmere Cumb 56 F6
Kenton Devon 5 C10
Kenton Suff 31 B8
Kenton T & W 63 G8
Kenton Bankfoot T & W 63 G8
Kentra Highld 79 E9
Kents Bank Cumb 49 B3
Kent's Green Glos 26 F4
Kent's Oak Hants 10 B2
Kenwick Shrops 33 B10
Kenwyn Corn 3 E7
Keoldale Highld 92 C6
Keppanach Highld 74 A3
Keppoch Highld 85 F14
Keprigan Argyll 65 G7
Kepwick N Yorks 58 G5
Kerchesters Borders 70 G6
Keresley W Mid 35 G9
Kernborough Devon 5 G8
Kerne Bridge Hereford 26 G2
Kerris Corn 2 G3
Kerry Powys 33 G7
Kerrycroy Argyll 73 G10
Kerry's Gate Hereford 25 E10
Kerrysdale Highld 85 A13
Kersall Notts 45 F11
Kersey Suff 31 D7
Kershopefoot Cumb 61 E10
Kersoe Worcs 26 E6
Kerswell Devon 7 F9
Kerswell Green Worcs 26 D5
Kesgrave Suff 31 D9
Kessingland Suff 39 G11
Kessingland Beach Suff 39 G11
Kessington E Dunb 68 C4
Kestle Corn 3 E8
Kestle Mill Corn 3 D7
Keston London 19 E11
Keswick Cumb 56 D4
Keswick Norf 39 E8
Keswick Norf 39 B9
Ketley Telford 34 D2
Ketley Bank Telford 34 D2
Ketsby Lincs 47 E7
Kettering Northants 36 H4
Ketteringham Norf 39 E7
Kettins Perth 76 D5
Kettlebaston Suff 30 C6
Kettlebridge Fife 76 G6
Kettleburgh Suff 31 B9
Kettlehill Fife 76 G6
Kettleholm Dumfries 61 F7
Kettleness N Yorks 59 E9
Kettleshume Ches 44 E3
Kettlesing Bottom N Yorks 51 D8
Kettlesing Head N Yorks 51 D8
Kettlestone Norf 38 B5
Kettlethorpe Lincs 46 E2
Kettletoft Orkney 95 E7
Kettlewell N Yorks 50 B5
Ketton Rutland 36 E5
Kew London 19 D8
Kew Br. London 19 D8
Kewstoke N Som 15 E9
Kexbrough S Yorks 45 B7
Kexby Lincs 46 D2
Kexby York 52 D3
Key Green Ches 44 F2
Keyham Leics 36 E2
Keyhaven Hants 10 E2
Keyingham E Yorks 53 G8
Keymer W Sus 12 E2
Keynsham Bath 16 E3
Keysoe Beds 29 B7
Keysoe Row Beds 29 B7
Keyston Cambs 36 H6
Keyworth Notts 36 B2
Kibblesworth T & W 63 H8
Kibworth Beauchamp Leics 36 F2
Kibworth Harcourt Leics 36 F2
Kidbrooke London 19 D11
Kiddemore Green Staffs 34 E4
Kidderminster Worcs 34 H4
Kiddington Oxon 27 F11
Kidlington Oxon 27 G11
Kidmore End Oxon 18 D3
Kidsgrove Staffs 44 G2
Kidstones N Yorks 50 A5
Kidwelly = Cydweli Carms 23 F9
Kiel Crofts Argyll 74 D2
Kielder Northumb 62 D2
Kierfiold Ho. Orkney 95 G3
Kilbagie Clack 69 B8
Kilbarchan Renfs 68 D3
Kilbeg Highld 85 H11
Kilberry Argyll 72 G6
Kilbirnie N Ayrs 66 A6
Kilbride Argyll 79 J11
Kilbride Argyll 74 E2
Kilbride Highld 85 F10
Kilburn Angus 82 G5
Kilburn Derbys 45 H7
Kilburn London 19 C9
Kilburn N Yorks 51 B11
Kilby Leics 36 F2
Kilchamaig Argyll 73 G7
Kilchattan Argyll 72 D2
Kilchattan Bay Argyll 66 A4
Kilchenzie Argyll 65 F7
Kilcheran Argyll 79 H11
Kilchiaran Argyll 64 B3
Kilchoan Argyll 72 B6
Kilchoan Highld 78 E7
Kilchoman Argyll 64 B3
Kilchrenan Argyll 74 E3
Kilconquhar Fife 77 G7
Kilcot Glos 26 F3
Kilcoy Highld 87 F8
Kilcreggan Argyll 73 E11
Kildale N Yorks 59 F7
Kildalloig Argyll 65 G8
Kildary Highld 87 D10
Kildermorie Lodge Highld 87 D8
Kildonan N Ayrs 66 D3
Kildonan Lodge Highld 93 G12
Kildonnan Highld 78 C7
Kildrummy Aberds 82 B6
Kildwick N Yorks 50 E6
Kilfinan Argyll 73 F8
Kilfinnan Highld 80 D4
Kilgetty Pembs 22 F6
Kilgwrrwg Common Mon 15 B10
Kilham E Yorks 53 C6
Kilham Northumb 71 G7
Kilkenneth Argyll 78 G2
Kilkerran Argyll 65 G8
Kilkhampton Corn 6 E1
Killamarsh Derbys 45 D8
Killay Swansea 14 B2
Killbeg Argyll 79 G9
Killean Argyll 65 D7
Killearn Stirl 68 B4
Killen Highld 87 F9
Killerby Darl 58 E2
Killichonan Perth 75 B8
Killiechonate Highld 80 E4
Killiechronan Argyll 79 G8
Killiecrankie Perth 76 A2
Killiemor Argyll 78 H7
Killiemore House Argyll 78 J7
Killilan Highld 86 H2
Killimster Highld 94 E5
Killin Stirl 75 D8
Killin Lodge Highld 81 C7
Killinallan Argyll 64 A4
Killinghall N Yorks 51 D8
Killington Cumb 57 H8
Killingworth T & W 63 F8
Killmahumaig Argyll 72 D6
Killochyett Borders 70 F3
Killocraw Argyll 65 E7
Killundine Highld 79 G8
Kilmacolm Invclyd 68 D2
Kilmaha Argyll 73 C8
Kilmahog Stirl 75 G9
Kilmalieu Highld 79 F11
Kilmaluag Highld 85 A9
Kilmany Fife 76 E6
Kilmarie Highld 85 G10
Kilmarnock E Ayrs 67 C7
Kilmaron Castle Fife 76 F6
Kilmartin Argyll 73 D7
Kilmaurs E Ayrs 67 B7
Kilmelford Argyll 73 B7
Kilmeny Argyll 64 B4
Kilmersdon Som 16 F3
Kilmeston Hants 10 B4
Kilmichael Argyll 65 F7
Kilmichael Glassary Argyll 73 D7
Kilmichael of Inverlussa Argyll 72 E6
Kilmington Devon 8 E1
Kilmington Wilts 16 H4
Kilmonivaig Highld 80 E3
Kilmorack Highld 86 G7
Kilmore Argyll 79 J11
Kilmore Highld 85 H11
Kilmory Argyll 72 F6
Kilmory Highld 79 D8
Kilmory Highld 85 H8
Kilmory N Ayrs 66 D2
Kilmuir Highld 84 D7
Kilmuir Highld 87 G9
Kilmuir Highld 87 D10
Kilmuir Highld 85 A8
Kilmun Argyll 73 E10
Kilmun Argyll 73 B8
Kiln Pit Hill Northumb 58 A1
Kilncadzow S Lnrk 69 F7
Kilndown Kent 12 C6
Kilnhurst S Yorks 45 C8
Kilninian Argyll 78 G6
Kilninver Argyll 79 J11
Kilnsea E Yorks 53 H10
Kilnsey N Yorks 50 C5
Kilnwick E Yorks 52 E5
Kilnwick Percy E Yorks 52 D4
Kiloran Argyll 72 D2
Kilpatrick N Ayrs 66 D2
Kilpeck Hereford 25 E11
Kilphedir Highld 93 H12
Kilpin E Yorks 52 G3
Kilpin Pike E Yorks 52 G3
Kilrenny Fife 77 G8
Kilsby Northants 28 A2
Kilspindie Perth 76 E5
Kilsyth N Lnrk 68 C6
Kiltarlity Highld 87 G8
Kilton Notts 45 E9
Kilton Som 7 B10
Kilton Thorpe Redcar 59 E7
Kilvaxter Highld 85 B8
Kilve Som 7 B10
Kilvington Notts 36 A3
Kilwinning N Ayrs 66 B6
Kimber worth S Yorks 45 C8
Kimberley Norf 39 E6
Kimberley Notts 35 A11
Kimble Wick Bucks 28 H5
Kimblesworth Durham 58 B3
Kimbolton Cambs 29 B7
Kimbolton Hereford 26 B2
Kimcote Leics 36 G1
Kimmeridge Dorset 9 G8
Kimmerston Northumb 71 G8
Kimpton Hants 17 G9
Kimpton Herts 29 G8
Kinbrace Highld 93 F11
Kinbuck Stirl 75 G10
Kincaple Fife 77 F7
Kincardine Fife 69 B8
Kincardine Highld 87 C9
Kincardine Bridge Fife 69 B8
Kincardine O'Neil Aberds 83 D7
Kinclaven Perth 76 D4
Kincorth Aberdeen 83 C11
Kincorth Ho. Moray 87 E13
Kincraig Highld 81 C10
Kincraigie Perth 76 C2
Kindallachan Perth 76 C2
Kineton Glos 27 F7
Kineton Warks 27 C10
Kinfauns Perth 76 E4
King Edward Aberds 89 C7
King Sterndale Derbys 44 E4
Kingairloch Highld 79 F11
Kingarth Argyll 73 H9
Kingcoed Mon 25 H11
Kingerby Lincs 46 C4
Kingham Oxon 27 F9
Kingholm Quay Dumfries 60 F5
Kinghorn Fife 69 B11
Kingie Highld 80 C3
Kinglassie Fife 76 H5
Kingoodie Perth 76 E6
King's Acre Hereford 25 D11
King's Bromley Staffs 35 D7
King's Caple Hereford 26 F2
King's Cliffe Northants 36 F6
King's Coughton Warks 27 C7
King's Heath W Mid 35 G6
Kings Hedges Cambs 29 B11
Kings Langley Herts 19 A7
King's Lynn Norf 38 C2
King's Meaburn Cumb 57 D8
King's Mills Wrex 42 H6
Kings Muir Borders 69 G11
King's Newnham Warks 35 H10
King's Newton Derbys 35 C9
King's Norton Leics 36 E2
King's Norton W Mid 35 H6
King's Nympton Devon 6 E5
King's Pyon Hereford 25 C11
King's Ripton Cambs 37 H8
King's Somborne Hants 10 A2
King's Stag Dorset 8 C6
King's Stanley Glos 16 A5
King's Sutton Northants 27 E11
King's Thorn Hereford 26 E2
King's Walden Herts 29 F8
Kings Worthy Hants 10 A3
Kingsand Corn 4 F5
Kingsbarns Fife 77 F8
Kingsbridge Devon 5 G8
Kingsbridge Som 7 C8
Kingsburgh Highld 85 C8
Kingsbury London 19 C9
Kingsbury Warks 35 F8
Kingsbury Episcopi Som 8 B3
Kingsclere Hants 18 F2
Kingscote Glos 16 B5
Kingscott Devon 6 E4
Kingscross N Ayrs 66 D3
Kingsdon Som 8 B4
Kingsdown Kent 21 G10
Kingseat Fife 69 A10
Kingsey Bucks 28 H4
Kingsfold W Sus 19 H8
Kingsford E Ayrs 67 B7
Kingsford Worcs 34 G4
Kingsforth N Lincs 52 H6
Kingsgate Kent 21 D10
Kingsheanton Devon 6 C4
Kingshouse Hotel Highld 74 B5
Kingside Hill Cumb 56 A3
Kingskerswell Devon 5 E9
Kingskettle Fife 76 G6
Kingsland Anglesey 40 B4
Kingsland Hereford 25 B11
Kingsley Ches 43 E8
Kingsley Hants 18 H4
Kingsley Staffs 44 H4
Kingsley Green W Sus 11 A7
Kingsley Holt Staffs 44 H4
Kingsley Park Northants 28 B4
Kingsmuir Angus 77 C7
Kingsmuir Fife 77 G8
Kingsnorth Kent 13 C9
Kingstanding W Mid 35 F6
Kingsteignton Devon 5 D9
Kingsthorpe Northants 28 B4
Kingston Cambs 29 C10
Kingston Devon 5 G7
Kingston Dorset 9 D6
Kingston Dorset 9 G8
Kingston E Loth 70 B4
Kingston Hants 9 D10
Kingston I o W 10 F3
Kingston Kent 21 F8
Kingston Moray 88 B3
Kingston Bagpuize Oxon 17 B11
Kingston Blount Oxon 18 B4
Kingston by Sea W Sus 11 D11
Kingston Deverill Wilts 16 H5
Kingston Gorse W Sus 11 D9
Kingston Lisle Oxon 17 C10
Kingston Maurward Dorset 8 E6
Kingston near Lewes E Sus 12 F2
Kingston on Soar Notts 35 C11
Kingston Russell Dorset 8 E4
Kingston St Mary Som 7 D11
Kingston Seymour N Som 15 E10
Kingston Upon Hull Hull 53 G6
Kingston upon Thames London 19 E8
Kingston Vale London 19 D9
Kingstone Hereford 25 E11
Kingstone Som 8 C2
Kingstone Staffs 35 C6
Kingstown Cumb 61 H9
Kingswear Devon 5 F9
Kingswells Aberdeen 83 C10
Kingswinford W Mid 34 G4
Kingswood Bucks 28 G3
Kingswood Glos 16 B4
Kingswood Hereford 25 C9
Kingswood Kent 20 F5
Kingswood Powys 33 E8
Kingswood S Glos 16 D3
Kingswood Sur 19 F9
Kingswood Warks 27 A8
Kingthorpe Lincs 46 E5
Kington Hereford 25 C9
Kington Worcs 26 C6
Kington Langley Wilts 16 D6
Kington Magna Dorset 9 B6
Kington St Michael Wilts 16 D6
Kingussie Highld 81 C9
Kingweston Som 8 A4
Kininvie Ho. Moray 88 D3
Kinkell Bridge Perth 76 F2
Kinknockie Aberds 89 D10
Kinlet Shrops 34 G3
Kinloch Fife 76 F5
Kinloch Highld 78 B6
Kinloch Highld 92 F6
Kinloch Highld 85 G11
Kinloch Perth 76 C4
Kinloch Perth 76 C5
Kinloch Hourn Highld 80 C1
Kinloch Laggan Highld 81 E7
Kinloch Lodge Highld 93 D8
Kinloch Rannoch Perth 75 B9
Kinlochan Highld 79 E11
Kinlochard Stirl 75 G7
Kinlochbeoraid Highld 79 C11
Kinlochbervie Highld 92 D5
Kinlocheil Highld 80 F1
Kinlochewe Highld 86 E3
Kinlochleven Highld 74 A4
Kinlochmoidart Highld 79 D10
Kinlochmorar Highld 79 B11
Kinlochmore Highld 74 A4
Kinlochspelve Argyll 79 J9
Kinloid Highld 79 C9
Kinloss Moray 87 E13
Kinmel Bay Conwy 42 D2
Kinmuck Aberds 83 B10
Kinmundy Aberds 83 B10
Kinnadie Aberds 89 D9
Kinnaird Perth 76 E5
Kinnaird Castle Angus 77 B9
Kinneff Aberds 83 F10
Kinnelhead Dumfries 60 C6
Kinnell Angus 77 B9
Kinnerley Shrops 33 C9
Kinnersley Hereford 25 D10
Kinnersley Worcs 26 D5
Kinnerton Powys 25 B9
Kinnesswood Perth 76 G4
Kinninvie Durham 58 D1
Kinnordy Angus 76 B6
Kinoulton Notts 36 B2
Kinross Perth 76 G4
Kinrossie Perth 76 D4
Kinsbourne Green Herts 29 G8
Kinsey Heath Ches 34 A2
Kinsham Hereford 25 B10
Kinsham Worcs 26 E6
Kinsley W Yorks 45 A8
Kinson Bmouth 9 E9
Kintbury W Berks 17 E10
Kintessack Moray 87 E12
Kintillo Perth 76 F4
Kintocher Aberds 83 C7
Kinton Hereford 25 A11
Kinton Shrops 33 D9
Kintore Aberds 83 B9
Kintour Argyll 64 C5
Kintra Argyll 78 J6
Kintra Argyll 64 D4
Kintraw Argyll 73 C7
Kinuachdrachd Argyll 72 D6
Kinveachy Highld 81 B11
Kinver Staffs 34 G4
Kippax W Yorks 51 F10
Kippen Stirl 68 A5
Kippford or Scaur Dumfries 55 D11
Kirbister Orkney 95 H4
Kirbister Orkney 95 F7
Kirbuster Orkney 95 F3
Kirby Bedon Norf 39 E8
Kirby Bellars Leics 36 D3
Kirby Cane Norf 39 F9
Kirby Cross Essex 31 F9
Kirby Grindalythe N Yorks 52 C5
Kirby Hill N Yorks 51 C9
Kirby Hill N Yorks 58 F2
Kirby Knowle N Yorks 58 H5
Kirby-le-Soken Essex 31 F9
Kirby Misperton N Yorks 52 B3
Kirby Muxloe Leics 35 E11
Kirby Row Norf 39 F9
Kirby Sigston N Yorks 58 G5
Kirby Underdale E Yorks 52 D4
Kirby Wiske N Yorks 51 A9
Kirdford W Sus 11 B9
Kirk Highld 94 E4
Kirk Bramwith S Yorks 45 A10
Kirk Deighton N Yorks 51 D9
Kirk Ella E Yorks 52 G6
Kirk Hallam Derbys 35 A10
Kirk Hammerton N Yorks 51 D10
Kirk Ireton Derbys 44 G6
Kirk Langley Derbys 35 B8
Kirk Merrington Durham 58 C3
Kirk Michael I o M 48 C3
Kirk of Shotts N Lnrk 69 D7
Kirk Sandall S Yorks 45 B10
Kirk Smeaton N Yorks 51 H11
Kirk Yetholm Borders 71 H7
Kirkabister Shetland 96 K6
Kirkandrews Dumfries 55 E9
Kirkandrews upon Eden Cumb 61 H9
Kirkbampton Cumb 61 H9
Kirkbean Dumfries 60 H5
Kirkbride Cumb 61 H7
Kirkbuddo Angus 77 C8
Kirkburn Borders 69 G11
Kirkburn E Yorks 52 D5
Kirkburton W Yorks 44 A5
Kirkby Lincs 46 C4
Kirkby Mers 43 C7

Kirkby N Yorks 59 F6
Kirkby Fleetham N Yorks 58 G3
Kirkby Green Lincs 46 G4
Kirkby In Ashfield Notts 45 G9
Kirkby-in-Furness Cumb 49 A2
Kirkby la Thorpe Lincs 46 H5
Kirkby Lonsdale Cumb 50 B2
Kirkby Malham N Yorks 50 C4
Kirkby Mallory Leics 35 E10
Kirkby Malzeard N Yorks 51 B8
Kirkby Mills N Yorks 59 H8
Kirkby on Bain Lincs 46 F6
Kirkby Overblow N Yorks 51 E9
Kirkby Stephen Cumb 57 F9
Kirkby Thore Cumb 57 D8
Kirkby Underwood Lincs 37 C6
Kirkby Wharfe N Yorks 51 E11
Kirkbymoorside N Yorks 59 H7
Kirkcaldy Fife 69 A11
Kirkcambeck Cumb 61 G11
Kirkcarswell Dumfries 55 E10
Kirkcolm Dumfries 54 C3
Kirkconnel Dumfries 60 G5
Kirkconnell Dumfries 60 G5
Kirkcowan Dumfries 54 C6
Kirkcudbright Dumfries 55 D9
Kirkdale Mers 42 C6
Kirkfieldbank S Lnrk 69 F7
Kirkgunzeon Dumfries 55 C11
Kirkham Lancs 49 F4
Kirkham N Yorks 52 C3
Kirkhamgate W Yorks 51 G8
Kirkharle Northumb 62 E6
Kirkheaton Northumb 62 F6
Kirkheaton W Yorks 51 H7
Kirkhill Angus 77 A9
Kirkhill Highld 87 G8
Kirkhill Midloth 69 D11
Kirkhill Moray 88 E2
Kirkhope Borders 61 A9
Kirkhouse Borders 70 G2
Kirkiboll Highld 93 D8
Kirkibost Highld 85 G10
Kirkinch Angus 76 C6
Kirkinner Dumfries 55 D7
Kirkintilloch E Dunb 68 C5
Kirkland Cumb 56 E2
Kirkland Cumb 57 C8
Kirkland Dumfries 60 D4
Kirkland Dumfries 60 B3
Kirkleatham Redcar 59 D6
Kirklevington Stockton 58 F5
Kirkley Suff 39 F11
Kirklington Notts 45 G10
Kirklington N Yorks 51 A9
Kirklinton Cumb 61 G10
Kirkliston Edin 69 C10
Kirkmaiden Dumfries 54 F4
Kirkmichael Perth 76 B3
Kirkmichael S Ayrs 66 F6
Kirkmuirhill S Lnrk 68 F6
Kirknewton Northumb 71 G8
Kirknewton W Loth 69 D10
Kirkney Aberds 88 E5
Kirkoswald Cumb 57 B7
Kirkoswald S Ayrs 66 F5
Kirkpatrick Durham Dumfries 60 F3
Kirkpatrick-Fleming Dumfries 61 F8
Kirksanton Cumb 49 A1
Kirkstall W Yorks 51 F8
Kirkstead Lincs 46 F5
Kirkstile Aberds 88 E5
Kirkstyle Highld 94 C5
Kirkton Aberds 83 A8
Kirkton Aberds 89 D6
Kirkton Angus 77 C7
Kirkton Angus 77 D7
Kirkton Borders 61 B11
Kirkton Dumfries 60 E5
Kirkton Fife 76 E6
Kirkton Highld 85 F13
Kirkton Highld 86 G2
Kirkton Highld 87 B10
Kirkton Highld 87 F10
Kirkton Perth 76 F2
Kirkton S Lnrk 60 A5
Kirkton Stirl 75 G8
Kirkton Manor Borders 69 G11
Kirkton of Airlie Angus 76 B6
Kirkton of Auchterhouse Angus 76 D6
Kirkton of Auchterless Aberds 89 D7
Kirkton of Barevan Highld 87 G11
Kirkton of Bourtie Aberds 89 F8
Kirkton of Collace Perth 76 D4
Kirkton of Craig Angus 77 B10
Kirkton of Culsalmond Aberds 89 E6
Kirkton of Durris Aberds 83 D9
Kirkton of Glenbuchat Aberds 82 B5
Kirkton of Glenisla Angus 76 A5
Kirkton of Kingoldrum Angus 76 B6
Kirkton of Largo Fife 77 G7
Kirkton of Lethendy Perth 76 C4
Kirkton of Logie Buchan Aberds 89 F9
Kirkton of Maryculter Aberds 83 D10
Kirkton of Menmuir Angus 77 A8
Kirkton of Monikie Angus 77 D8
Kirkton of Oyne Aberds 83 A8
Kirkton of Rayne Aberds 83 A8
Kirkton of Skene Aberds 83 C10
Kirkton of Tough Aberds 83 B8
Kirktonhill Borders 70 E3
Kirktown Aberds 89 C10
Kirktown of Alvah Aberds 89 B6
Kirktown of Deskford Moray 88 B5
Kirktown of Fetteresso Aberds 83 E10
Kirktown of Mortlach Moray 88 E3
Kirktown of Slains Aberds 89 F10
Kirkurd Borders 69 F10
Kirkwall Orkney 95 G5
Kirkwall Airport Orkney 95 H5
Kirkwhelpington Northumb 62 E5
Kirmington N Lincs 46 A5
Kirmond le Mire Lincs 46 C5
Kirn Argyll 73 F10
Kirriemuir Angus 76 B6
Kirstead Green Norf 39 F8
Kirtlebridge Dumfries 61 F8
Kirtleton Dumfries 61 E8
Kirtling Cambs 30 C3
Kirtling Green Cambs 30 C3
Kirtlington Oxon 27 G11
Kirtomy Highld 93 C10
Kirton Lincs 37 B9
Kirton Notts 45 F10
Kirton Suff 31 E9
Kirton End Lincs 37 A8
Kirton Holme Lincs 37 A8
Kirton in Lindsey N Lincs 46 C3
Kislingbury Northants 28 C3
Kites Hardwick Warks 27 B11
Kittisford Som 7 D9
Kittle Swansea 23 H10
Kitt's Green W Mid 35 G7
Kitt's Moss Gtr Man 44 D2
Kittybrewster Aberdeen 83 C11
Kitwood Hants 10 A5
Kivernoll Hereford 25 E11
Kiveton Park S Yorks 45 D8
Knaith Lincs 46 D2
Knaith Park Lincs 46 D2
Knap Corner Dorset 9 B7
Knaphill Sur 18 F6
Knapp Perth 76 D5
Knapp Som 8 B2
Knapthorpe Notts 45 G11
Knapton Norf 39 B9
Knapton York 52 D1
Knapton Green Hereford 25 C11
Knapwell Cambs 29 B10
Knaresborough N Yorks 51 D9
Knarsdale Northumb 57 A8
Knauchland Moray 88 C5
Knaven Aberds 89 D8
Knayton N Yorks 58 H5
Knebworth Herts 29 F9
Knedlington E Yorks 52 G3
Kneesall Notts 45 F11
Kneesworth Cambs 29 D10
Kneeton Notts 45 H11
Knelston Swansea 23 H9
Knenhall Staffs 34 B5
Knettishall Suff 38 G5
Knightacott Devon 6 C5
Knightcote Warks 27 C10
Knightley Dale Staffs 34 C4
Knighton Devon 4 G6
Knighton Leicester 36 E1
Knighton Staffs 34 C3
Knighton Staffs 34 A3
Knighton = Tref-y-Clawdd Powys 25 A9
Knightswood Glasgow 68 D4
Knightwick Worcs 26 C4
Knill Hereford 25 B9
Knipton Leics 36 B4
Knitsley Durham 58 B2
Kniveton Derbys 44 G6
Knock Argyll 79 H8
Knock Cumb 57 D8
Knock Moray 88 C5
Knockally Highld 94 H3
Knockan Highld 92 H5
Knockandhu Moray 82 A4
Knockando Moray 88 D1
Knockando Ho. Moray 88 D2
Knockbain Highld 87 F9
Knockbreck Highld 84 B7
Knockbrex Dumfries 55 E8
Knockdee Highld 94 D3
Knockdolian S Ayrs 66 H4
Knockenkelly N Ayrs 66 D3
Knockentiber E Ayrs 67 C6
Knockespock Ho. Aberds 83 A7
Knockfarrel Highld 87 F8
Knockglass Dumfries 54 D3
Knockholt Kent 19 F11
Knockholt Pound Kent 19 F11
Knockie Lodge Highld 80 B6
Knockin Shrops 33 C9
Knockinlaw E Ayrs 67 C7
Knocklearn Dumfries 60 F3
Knocknaha Argyll 65 G7
Knocknain Dumfries 54 C2
Knockrome Argyll 72 F4
Knocksharry I o M 48 D2
Knodishall Suff 31 B11
Knolls Green Ches 44 E2
Knolton Wrex 33 B9
Knolton Bryn Wrex 33 B9
Knook Wilts 16 G6
Knossington Leics 36 E4
Knott End-on-Sea Lancs 49 E3
Knotting Beds 29 B7
Knotting Green Beds 29 B7
Knottingley W Yorks 51 G11
Knotts Cumb 56 D6
Knotts Lancs 50 D3
Knotty Ash Mers 43 C7
Knotty Green Bucks 18 B6
Knowbury Shrops 26 A2
Knowe Dumfries 54 B6
Knowehead Dumfries 67 G9
Knowes of Elrick Aberds 88 C6
Knowesgate Northumb 62 E5
Knoweton N Lnrk 68 E6
Knowhead Aberds 89 C9
Knowl Hill Windsor 18 D5
Knowle Bristol 16 D3
Knowle Devon 7 C4
Knowle Devon 7 H9
Knowle Devon 6 C3
Knowle Shrops 26 A2
Knowle W Mid 35 H7
Knowle Green Lancs 50 F2
Knowle Park W Yorks 51 E6
Knowlton Dorset 9 C9
Knowlton Kent 21 F9
Knowsley Mers 43 C7
Knowstone Devon 7 D7
Knox Bridge Kent 13 B6
Knucklas Powys 25 A9
Knuston Northants 28 B6
Knutsford Ches 43 E10
Knutton Staffs 44 H2
Knypersley Staffs 44 G2
Kuggar Corn 2 H6
Kyle of Lochalsh Highld 85 F12
Kyleakin Highld 85 F12
Kylerhea Highld 85 F12
Kylesknoydart Highld 79 B11
Kylesku Highld 92 F5
Kylesmorar Highld 79 B11
Kylestrome Highld 92 F5
Kyllachy House Highld 81 A9
Kynaston Shrops 33 C9
Kynnersley Telford 34 D2
Kyre Magna Worcs 26 B3

L

La Fontenelle Guern 11
La Planque Guern 11
Labost W Isles 91 C7
Lacasaidh W Isles 91 E8
Lacasdal W Isles 91 D9
Laceby NE Lincs 46 B6
Lacey Green Bucks 18 B5
Lach Dennis Ches 43 E10
Lackford Suff 30 A4
Lacock Wilts 16 E6
Ladbroke Warks 27 C11
Laddingford Kent 20 G3
Lade Bank Lincs 47 G7
Ladock Corn 3 D7
Lady Orkney 95 D7
Ladybank Fife 76 F6
Ladykirk Borders 71 F7
Ladysford Aberds 89 B9
Laga Highld 79 E9
Lagalochan Argyll 73 B7
Lagavulin Argyll 64 D5
Lagg Argyll 72 F4
Lagg N Ayrs 66 D2
Laggan Argyll 64 C3
Laggan Highld 80 D4
Laggan Highld 81 D8
Laggan Highld 79 D10
Laggan S Ayrs 54 A5
Lagganulva Argyll 78 G7
Laide Highld 91 H13
Laigh Fenwick E Ayrs 67 B7
Laigh Glengall S Ayrs 66 E6
Laighmuir E Ayrs 67 B7
Laindon Essex 20 C3
Lair Highld 86 G3
Lairg Highld 93 J8
Lairg Lodge Highld 93 J8
Lairg Muir Highld 93 J8
Lairgmore Highld 87 H8
Laisterdyke W Yorks 51 F7
Laithes Cumb 56 C6
Lake I o W 10 F4
Lake Wilts 17 H8
Lakenham Norf 39 E8
Lakenheath Suff 38 G3
Lakesend Norf 37 F11
Lakeside Cumb 56 H5
Laleham Sur 19 E7
Laleston Bridgend 14 D4
Lamarsh Essex 30 E5
Lamas Norf 39 C8
Lambden Borders 70 F6
Lamberhurst Kent 12 C5
Lamberhurst Quarter Kent 12 C5
Lamberton Borders 71 E8
Lambeth London 19 D10
Lambhill Glasgow 68 D4
Lambley Notts 45 H10
Lambley Northumb 62 H2
Lamborough Hill Oxon 17 A11
Lambourn W Berks 17 D10
Lambourne End Essex 19 B11
Lambs Green W Sus 19 H9
Lambston Pembs 22 E4
Lambton T & W 58 A3
Lamerton Devon 4 D5
Lamesley T & W 63 H8
Laminess Orkney 95 E7
Lamington Highld 87 D10
Lamington S Lnrk 69 G8
Lamlash N Ayrs 66 C3
Lamloch Dumfries 67 G8
Lamonby Cumb 56 C6
Lamorna Corn 2 G3
Lamorran Corn 3 E7
Lampardbrook Suff 31 B9
Lampeter = Llanbedr Pont Steffan Ceredig 23 B10
Lampeter Velfrey Pembs 22 E6
Lamphey Pembs 22 F5
Lamplugh Cumb 56 D2
Lamport Northants 28 A4
Lamyatt Som 16 H3
Lana Devon 6 G2
Lanark S Lnrk 69 F7
Lancaster Lancs 49 C4
Lanchester Durham 58 B2
Lancing W Sus 11 D10
Landbeach Cambs 29 B11
Landcross Devon 6 D3
Landerberry Aberds 83 C9
Landford Wilts 10 C1
Landford Manor Wilts 10 B1
Landimore Swansea 23 G9
Landkey Devon 6 C4
Landore Swansea 14 B2
Landrake Corn 4 E4
Land's End Airport Corn 2 G2
Landscove Devon 5 E8
Landshipping Pembs 22 E5
Landshipping Quay Pembs 22 E5
Landulph Corn 4 E5
Landwade Suff 30 B3
Lane Corn 3 C7
Lane End Bucks 18 B5
Lane End Cumb 56 G3
Lane End Dorset 9 E7
Lane End Hants 10 B4
Lane End I o W 10 F5
Lane End Lancs 50 E4
Lane Ends Lancs 50 F3
Lane Ends Lancs 50 D3
Lane Ends N Yorks 50 E5
Lane Head Derbys 44 E5
Lane Head Durham 58 E2
Lane Head Gtr Man 43 C9
Lane Head W Yorks 44 B5
Lane Side Lancs 50 G3
Laneast Corn 4 C3
Laneham Notts 46 E2
Lanehead Durham 57 B10
Lanehead Northumb 62 E3
Lanercost Cumb 61 G11
Laneshaw Bridge Lancs 50 E5
Lanfach Caerph 15 B8
Langar Notts 36 B3
Langbank Renfs 68 C2
Langbar N Yorks 51 D6
Langburnshiels Borders 61 C11
Langcliffe N Yorks 50 C4
Langdale Highld 93 E9
Langdale End N Yorks 59 G10
Langdon Corn 4 C4
Langdon Beck Durham 57 C10
Langdon Hills Essex 20 C3
Langdyke Fife 76 G6
Langenhoe Essex 31 G7
Langford Beds 29 D8
Langford Devon 7 F9
Langford Essex 30 H5
Langford Notts 46 G2
Langford Oxon 17 A9
Langford Budville Som 7 D10
Langham Essex 31 E7
Langham Norf 38 A6
Langham Rutland 36 D4
Langham Suff 30 B6
Langhaugh Borders 69 G11
Langho Lancs 50 F3
Langholm Dumfries 61 E9
Langleeford Northumb 62 A5
Langley Ches 44 E3
Langley Hants 10 D3
Langley Herts 29 F9
Langley Kent 20 F5
Langley Northumb 62 G4
Langley Slough 19 D7
Langley Warks 27 B8
Langley W Sus 11 B7
Langley Burrell Wilts 16 D6
Langley Common Derbys 35 B8
Langley Heath Kent 20 F5
Langley Lower Green Essex 29 E11
Langley Marsh Som 7 D9
Langley Park Durham 58 B3
Langley Street Norf 39 E9
Langley Upper Green Essex 29 E11
Langney E Sus 12 F5
Langold Notts 45 D9
Langore Corn 4 C4
Langport Som 8 B3
Langrick Lincs 46 H6
Langridge Bath 16 E4
Langridge Ford Devon 6 D4
Langrigg Cumb 56 B3
Langrish Hants 10 B6
Langsett S Yorks 44 B6
Langshaw Borders 70 G4
Langside Perth 75 F10
Langskaill Orkney 95 D5
Langstone Hants 10 D6
Langstone Newport 15 B9
Langthorne N Yorks 58 G3
Langthorpe N Yorks 51 C9
Langthwaite N Yorks 58 F1
Langtoft E Yorks 52 C6
Langtoft Lincs 37 D7
Langton Durham 58 E2
Langton Lincs 46 F6
Langton Lincs 47 E7
Langton N Yorks 52 C3
Langton by Wragby Lincs 46 E5
Langton Green Kent 12 C4
Langton Green Suff 31 A8
Langton Herring Dorset 8 F5
Langton Matravers Dorset 9 G9
Langtree Devon 6 E3
Langwathby Cumb 57 C7
Langwell Ho. Highld 94 H3
Langwell Lodge Highld 92 J4
Langwith Derbys 45 F9
Langwith Junction Derbys 45 F9
Langworth Lincs 46 E4
Lanivet Corn 3 C9
Lanlivery Corn 4 F1
Lanner Corn 2 F6
Lanreath Corn 4 F2
Lansallos Corn 4 F2
Lansdown Glos 26 F6
Lanteglos Highway Corn 4 F2
Lanton Borders 62 A2
Lanton Northumb 71 G8
Lapford Devon 7 F6
Laphroaig Argyll 64 D4
Lapley Staffs 34 D4
Lapworth Warks 27 A8
Larachbeg Highld 79 G9
Larbert Falk 69 B7
Larden Green Ches 43 G8
Largie Aberds 88 E6
Largiemore Argyll 73 E8
Largoward Fife 77 G7
Largs N Ayrs 73 H11
Largybeg N Ayrs 66 D3
Largymore N Ayrs 66 D3
Larkfield Invclyd 73 F11
Larkhall S Lnrk 68 E6
Larkhill Wilts 17 G8
Larling Norf 38 G5
Larriston Borders 61 D11
Lartington Durham 58 E1
Lary Aberds 82 C5
Lasham Hants 18 G3
Lashenden Kent 13 B7
Lassington Glos 26 F4
Lassodie Fife 69 A10
Lastingham N Yorks 59 G8
Latcham Som 15 G10
Latchford Herts 29 F10
Latchford Warr 43 D9
Latchingdon Essex 20 A5
Latchley Corn 4 D5
Lately Common Warr 43 C9
Lathbury M Keynes 28 D5
Latheron Highld 94 G3
Latheronwheel Highld 94 G3
Latheronwheel Ho. Highld 94 G3
Lathones Fife 77 G7
Latimer Bucks 19 B7
Latteridge S Glos 16 C3
Lattiford Som 8 B5
Latton Wilts 17 B7
Latton Bush Essex 29 H11
Lauchintilly Aberds 83 B9
Lauder Borders 70 F4
Laugharne Carms 23 E8
Laughterton Lincs 46 E2
Laughton E Sus 12 E4
Laughton Leics 36 G2
Laughton Lincs 37 B6
Laughton Lincs 46 C2
Laughton Common S Yorks 45 D9
Laughton en le Morthen S Yorks 45 D9
Launcells Corn 6 F1
Launceston Corn 4 C4
Launton Oxon 28 F3
Laurencekirk Aberds 83 F9
Laurieston Dumfries 55 C9
Laurieston Falk 69 C8
Lavendon M Keynes 28 C6
Lavenham Suff 30 D6
Laverhay Dumfries 61 D7
Laversdale Cumb 61 G10
Laverstock Wilts 9 A10
Laverstoke Hants 17 G11
Laverton Glos 27 E7
Laverton N Yorks 51 B8
Laverton Som 16 F4
Lavister Wrex 42 G6
Law S Lnrk 69 E7
Lawers Perth 75 D9
Lawers Perth 75 E10
Lawford Essex 31 E7
Lawhitton Corn 4 C4
Lawkland N Yorks 50 C3
Lawley Telford 34 E2
Lawnhead Staffs 34 C4
Lawrenny Pembs 22 F5
Lawshall Suff 30 C5
Lawton Hereford 25 C11
Laxey I o M 48 D4
Laxfield Suff 31 A9
Laxfirth Shetland 96 J6
Laxfirth Shetland 96 H6
Laxford Bridge Highld 92 E5
Laxo Shetland 96 G6
Laxobigging Shetland 96 F6
Laxton E Yorks 52 G3
Laxton Notts 45 F11
Laxton Northants 36 F5
Laycock W Yorks 50 E6
Layer Breton Essex 30 G6
Layer de la Haye Essex 30 F6
Layer Marney Essex 30 G6
Layham Suff 31 D7
Laylands Green W Berks 17 E10
Laytham E Yorks 52 F3
Layton Blkpool 49 F3
Lazenby Redcar 59 D6
Lazonby Cumb 57 C7
Le Planel Guern 11
Le Villocq Guern 11
Lea Derbys 45 G7
Lea Hereford 26 F3
Lea Lincs 46 D2
Lea Shrops 33 G9
Lea Shrops 33 E10
Lea Wilts 16 C6
Lea Marston Warks 35 F8
Lea Town Lancs 49 F4
Leabrooks Derbys 45 G8
Leac a Li W Isles 90 H6
Leachkin Highld 87 G9
Leadburn Midloth 69 E11
Leaden Roding Essex 30 G2
Leadenham Lincs 46 G3
Leadgate Cumb 57 B9
Leadgate Durham 58 A2
Leadgate Northumb 63 H7
Leadhills S Lnrk 60 B4
Leafield Oxon 27 G10
Leagrave Luton 29 F7
Leake N Yorks 58 G5
Leake Commonside Lincs 47 G7
Lealholm N Yorks 59 F8
Lealt Argyll 72 D5
Lealt Highld 85 B10
Leamington Hastings Warks 27 B11
Leamonsley Staffs 35 E7
Leamside Durham 58 B4
Leanaig Highld 87 F8
Leargybreck Argyll 72 F4
Leasgill Cumb 49 A4
Leasingham Lincs 46 H4
Leasingthorne Durham 58 D3
Leasowe Mers 42 C5
Leatherhead Sur 19 F8
Leatherhead Common Sur 19 F8
Leathley N Yorks 51 E8
Leaton Shrops 33 D10
Leaveland Kent 21 F7
Leavening N Yorks 52 C3
Leaves Green London 19 E11
Leazes Durham 63 H7
Lebberston N Yorks 53 A6
Lechlade-on-Thames Glos 17 B9
Leck Lancs 50 B2
Leckford Hants 17 H10
Leckfurin Highld 93 D10
Leckgruinart Argyll 64 B3
Leckhampstead Bucks 28 E4
Leckhampstead W Berks 17 D11
Leckhampstead Thicket W Berks 17 D11
Leckhampton Glos 26 G6
Leckie Highld 86 E3
Leckmelm Highld 86 B4
Leckwith V Glam 15 D7
Leconfield E Yorks 52 E6
Ledaig Argyll 74 D2
Ledburn Bucks 28 F6
Ledbury Hereford 26 E4
Ledcharrie Stirl 75 E8
Ledgemoor Hereford 25 C11
Ledicot Hereford 25 B11
Ledmore Highld 92 H5
Lednagullin Highld 93 C10
Ledsham Ches 42 E6
Ledsham W Yorks 51 G10
Ledston W Yorks 51 G10
Ledston Luck W Yorks 51 F10
Ledwell Oxon 27 F11
Lee Argyll 78 J7
Lee Devon 6 B3
Lee Hants 10 C2
Lee Lancs 50 D1
Lee Shrops 33 B10
Lee Brockhurst Shrops 33 C11
Lee Clump Bucks 18 A6
Lee Mill Devon 5 F7
Lee Moor Devon 5 E6
Lee-on-the-Solent Hants 10 D4
Leeans Shetland 96 J5
Leebotten Shetland 96 L6
Leebotwood Shrops 33 F10
Leece Cumb 49 C2
Leechpool Pembs 22 E4
Leeds Kent 20 F5
Leeds W Yorks 51 F8
Leeds Bradford International Airport W Yorks 51 E8
Leedstown Corn 2 F5
Leek Staffs 44 G3
Leek Wootton Warks 27 B9
Leekbrook Staffs 44 G3
Leeming N Yorks 58 H3
Leeming Bar N Yorks 58 G3
Lees Derbys 35 B8
Lees Gtr Man 44 B3
Lees W Yorks 50 F6
Leeswood Flint 42 F5
Legbourne Lincs 47 D7
Legerwood Borders 70 F4
Legsby Lincs 46 D5
Leicester Leicester 36 E1
Leicester Forest East Leics 35 E11
Leigh Dorset 8 D5
Leigh Glos 26 F5
Leigh Gtr Man 43 B9
Leigh Kent 20 G2
Leigh Shrops 33 E9
Leigh Sur 19 G9
Leigh Wilts 17 B7
Leigh Worcs 26 C4
Leigh Beck Essex 20 C5
Leigh Common Som 8 B6
Leigh Delamere Wilts 16 D5
Leigh Green Kent 13 C8
Leigh on Sea Sthend 20 C5
Leigh Park Hants 10 D6
Leigh Sinton Worcs 26 C4
Leigh upon Mendip Som 16 G3
Leigh Woods N Som 16 D2
Leighswood W Mid 35 E6
Leighterton Glos 16 B5
Leighton N Yorks 51 B7
Leighton Powys 33 E8
Leighton Shrops 34 E2
Leighton Som 16 G4
Leighton Bromswold Cambs 37 H7
Leighton Buzzard Beds 28 F6
Leinthall Earls Hereford 25 B11
Leinthall Starkes Hereford 25 B11
Leintwardine Hereford 25 A11
Leire Leics 35 F11
Leirinmore Highld 92 C7
Leiston Suff 31 B11
Leitfie Perth 76 C5
Leith Edin 69 C11
Leitholm Borders 70 F6
Lelant Corn 2 F4
Lelley E Yorks 53 F8
Lem Hill Worcs 26 A4
Lemmington Hall Northumb 63 B7
Lempitlaw Borders 70 G6
Lenchwick Worcs 27 D7
Lendalfoot S Ayrs 66 H4
Lendrick Lodge Stirl 75 G8
Lenham Kent 20 F5
Lenham Heath Kent 20 G6
Lennel Borders 71 F7
Lennoxtown E Dunb 68 C5
Lenton Lincs 36 B6
Lenton Nottingham 36 B1
Lentran Highld 87 G8
Lenwade Norf 39 D6
Leny Ho. Stirl 75 G9
Lenzie E Dunb 68 C5
Leoch Angus 76 D6
Leochel-Cushnie Aberds 83 B7
Leominster Hereford 25 C11
Leonard Stanley Glos 16 A5
Leorin Argyll 64 D4
Lepe Hants 10 E3
Lephin Highld 84 D6
Lephinchapel Argyll 73 D8
Lephinmore Argyll 73 D8
Leppington N Yorks 52 C3
Lepton W Yorks 51 H8
Lerryn Corn 4 F2
Lerwick Shetland 96 J6
Lerwick (Tingwall) Airport Shetland 96 J6
Lesbury Northumb 63 B8
Leslie Aberds 83 A7
Leslie Fife 76 G5
Lesmahagow S Lnrk 69 G7
Lesnewth Corn 4 B2
Lessendrum Aberds 88 D5
Lessingham Norf 39 C9
Lessonhall Cumb 56 A4
Leswalt Dumfries 54 C3
Letchmore Heath Herts 19 B8
Letchworth Herts 29 E9
Letcombe Bassett Oxon 17 C10
Letcombe Regis Oxon 17 C10
Letham Angus 77 C8
Letham Falk 69 B7
Letham Fife 76 F6
Letham Perth 76 E3
Letham Grange Angus 77 C9
Lethenty Aberds 89 D8
Letheringham Suff 31 C9
Letheringsett Norf 39 B6
Lettaford Devon 5 C8
Lettan Orkney 95 D8
Letterewe Highld 86 D2
Letterfearn Highld 85 F13
Letterfinlay Highld 80 D4
Lettermorar Highld 79 C10
Lettermore Argyll 78 G7
Letters Highld 86 C4
Letterston Pembs 22 D4
Lettoch Highld 82 B2
Lettoch Highld 87 H13
Letton Hereford 25 D10
Letton Hereford 25 A10
Letton Green Norf 38 E5
Letty Green Herts 29 G9
Letwell S Yorks 45 D9
Leuchars Fife 77 E7
Leuchars Ho. Moray 88 B2
Leumrabhagh W Isles 91 F8
Levan Invclyd 73 F11
Levaneap Shetland 96 G6
Levedale Staffs 34 D4
Leven E Yorks 53 E7
Leven Fife 76 G6
Levencorroch N Ayrs 66 D3
Levens Cumb 57 H6
Levens Green Herts 29 F10
Levenshulme Gtr Man 44 C2
Levenwick Shetland 96 L6
Leverburgh = An t-Ob W Isles 90 J5
Leverington Cambs 37 D10
Leverton Lincs 47 H8
Leverton Highgate Lincs 47 H8
Leverton Lucasgate Lincs 47 H8
Leverton Outgate Lincs 47 H8
Levington Suff 31 E9
Levisham N Yorks 59 G9
Levishie Highld 80 B6
Lew Oxon 27 H10
Lewannick Corn 4 C3
Lewdown Devon 4 C5
Lewes E Sus 12 E3
Leweston Pembs 22 D4
Lewisham London 19 D10
Lewiston Highld 81 A7
Lewistown Bridgend 14 C5
Lewknor Oxon 18 B4
Leworthy Devon 6 F2
Leworthy Devon 6 C5
Lewtrenchard Devon 4 C5
Lexden Essex 30 F6
Ley Aberds 83 B7
Ley Corn 4 E2
Leybourne Kent 20 F3
Leyburn N Yorks 58 G2
Leyfields Staffs 35 E8
Leyhill Bucks 18 A6
Leyland Lancs 49 G5
Leylodge Aberds 83 B9
Leymoor W Yorks 51 H7
Leys Aberds 89 C10
Leys Perth 76 D5
Leys Castle Highld 87 G9
Leys of Cossans Angus 76 C6
Leysdown-on-Sea Kent 21 D7
Leysmill Angus 77 C9
Leysters Pole Hereford 26 B2
Leyton London 19 C10
Leytonstone London 19 C10
Lezant Corn 4 D4
Leziate Norf 38 D2
Lhanbryde Moray 88 B2
Liatrie Highld 86 H5
Libanus Powys 24 F6
Libberton S Lnrk 69 F8
Liberton Edin 69 D11
Liceasto W Isles 90 H6
Lichfield Staffs 35 E7
Lickey Worcs 34 H5
Lickey End Worcs 26 A6
Lickfold W Sus 11 B8
Liddel Orkney 95 K5
Liddesdale Highld 79 F10
Liddington Swindon 17 C9
Lidgate Suff 30 C4
Lidget S Yorks 45 B10
Lidget Green W Yorks 51 F7
Lidgett Notts 45 F10
Lidlington Beds 28 E6
Lidstone Oxon 27 F10
Lieurary Highld 94 D2
Liff Angus 76 D6
Lifton Devon 4 C4
Liftondown Devon 4 C4
Lighthorne Warks 27 C10
Lightwater Sur 18 E6
Lightwood Stoke 34 A5
Lightwood Green Ches 34 A2
Lightwood Green Wrex 33 A9
Lilbourne Northants 36 H1
Lilburn Tower Northumb 62 A6
Lilleshall Telford 34 D3
Lilley Herts 29 F8
Lilley W Berks 17 D11
Lilliesleaf Borders 61 A11
Lillingstone Dayrell Bucks 28 E4
Lillingstone Lovell Bucks 28 D4
Lillington Dorset 8 C5
Lillington Warks 27 B10
Lilliput Poole 9 E9
Lilstock Som 7 B10
Lilyhurst Shrops 34 D3
Limbury Luton 29 F7
Limebrook Hereford 25 B10
Limefield Gtr Man 44 A2
Limekilnburn S Lnrk 68 E6
Limekilns Fife 69 B9
Limerigg Falk 69 C7
Limerstone I o W 10 F3
Limington Som 8 B4
Limpenhoe Norf 39 E9
Limpley Stoke Wilts 16 E4
Limpsfield Sur 19 F11
Limpsfield Chart Sur 19 F11
Linby Notts 45 G9
Linchmere W Sus 11 A7
Lincluden Dumfries 60 F5
Lincoln Lincs 46 E3
Lincomb Worcs 26 B5
Lincombe Devon 5 F8
Lindal in Furness Cumb 49 B2
Lindale Cumb 49 A4
Lindean Borders 70 G3
Lindfield W Sus 12 D2
Lindford Hants 18 H5
Lindifferon Fife 76 F6
Lindley W Yorks 51 H7
Lindley Green N Yorks 51 E8
Lindores Fife 76 F5
Lindridge Worcs 26 B3
Lindsell Essex 30 F3
Lindsey Suff 30 D6
Linford Hants 9 D10
Linford Thurrock 20 D3
Lingague I o M 48 E2
Lingards Wood W Yorks 44 A4
Lingbob W Yorks 51 F6
Lingdale Redcar 59 E7
Lingen Hereford 25 B10
Lingfield Sur 12 B2
Lingreabhagh W Isles 90 J5
Lingwood Norf 39 E9
Linicro Highld 85 B8
Linkenholt Hants 17 F10
Linkhill Kent 13 D7
Linkinhorne Corn 4 D4
Linklater Orkney 95 K5
Linksness Orkney 95 H3
Linktown Fife 69 A11
Linley Shrops 33 F9
Linley Green Hereford 26 C3
Linlithgow W Loth 69 C9
Linlithgow Bridge W Loth 69 C8
Linshiels Northumb 62 C4
Linsiadar W Isles 90 D7
Linsidemore Highld 87 B8
Linslade Beds 28 F6
Linstead Parva Suff 39 H9
Linstock Cumb 61 H10
Linthwaite W Yorks 44 A5
Lintlaw Borders 71 E7
Lintmill Moray 88 B5
Linton Borders 70 H6
Linton Cambs 30 D2
Linton Derbys 35 D8
Linton Hereford 26 F3
Linton Kent 20 G4
Linton Northumb 63 D8
Linton N Yorks 50 C5
Linton W Yorks 51 E9
Linton-on-Ouse N Yorks 51 C10
Linwood Hants 9 D10
Linwood Lincs 46 D5
Linwood Renfs 68 D3
Lionacleit W Isles 84 D2
Lional W Isles 91 A10
Liphook Hants 11 A7
Liscard Mers 42 C6
Liscombe Som 7 C7
Liskeard Corn 4 E3
L'Islet Guern 11
Liss Hants 11 B6
Liss Forest Hants 11 B6
Lissett E Yorks 53 D7
Lissington Lincs 46 D5
Lisvane Cardiff 15 C7
Liswerry Newport 15 C9
Litcham Norf 38 D4
Litchborough Northants 28 C3
Litchfield Hants 17 F11
Litherland Mers 42 C6
Litlington Cambs 29 D10
Litlington E Sus 12 F4
Little Abington Cambs 30 D2
Little Addington Northants 28 A6
Little Alne Warks 27 B8
Little Altcar Mers 42 B6
Little Asby Cumb 57 F8
Little Assynt Highld 92 G4
Little Aston Staffs 35 E6
Little Atherfield I o W 10 F3
Little Ayre Orkney 95 J4
Little-ayre Shetland 96 G5
Little Ayton N Yorks 59 E6
Little Baddow Essex 30 H4
Little Badminton S Glos 16 C5
Little Ballinluig Perth 76 B2
Little Bampton Cumb 61 H8
Little Bardfield Essex 30 E3
Little Barford Beds 29 C8
Little Barningham Norf 39 B7
Little Barrington Glos 27 G9
Little Barrow Ches 43 F7
Little Barugh N Yorks 52 B3
Little Bavington Northumb 62 F5
Little Bealings Suff 31 D9
Little Bedwyn Wilts 17 E9
Little Bentley Essex 31 F8
Little Berkhamsted Herts 29 H9
Little Billing Northants 28 B5
Little Birch Hereford 26 E2
Little Blakenham Suff 31 D8
Little Blencow Cumb 56 C6
Little Bollington Ches 43 D10
Little Bookham Sur 19 F8
Little Bowden Leics 36 G3
Little Bradley Suff 30 C3
Little Brampton Shrops 33 G9
Little Brechin Angus 77 A8
Little Brickhill M Keynes 28 E6
Little Brington Northants 28 B3
Little Bromley Essex 31 F7
Little Broughton Cumb 56 C2
Little Budworth Ches 43 F8
Little Burstead Essex 20 B3
Little Bytham Lincs 36 D6
Little Carlton Lincs 47 D7
Little Carlton Notts 45 G11
Little Casterton Rutland 36 E6
Little Cawthorpe Lincs 47 D7
Little Chalfont Bucks 18 B6
Little Chart Kent 20 G6
Little Chesterford Essex 30 D2
Little Cheverell Wilts 16 F6
Little Chishill Cambs 29 E11
Little Clacton Essex 31 G8
Little Clifton Cumb 56 D2
Little Colp Aberds 89 D7
Little Comberton Worcs 26 D6
Little Common E Sus 12 F6
Little Compton Warks 27 E9
Little Cornard Suff 30 E5
Little Cowarne Hereford 26 C3
Little Coxwell Oxon 17 B9
Little Crakehall N Yorks 58 G3
Little Cressingham Norf 38 E4
Little Crosby Mers 42 B6
Little Dalby Leics 36 D3
Little Dawley Telford 34 E2
Little Dens Aberds 89 D10
Little Dewchurch Hereford 26 E2
Little Downham Cambs 37 G11
Little Driffield E Yorks 52 D6
Little Dunham Norf 38 D4
Little Dunkeld Perth 76 C3
Little Dunmow Essex 30 F3
Little Easton Essex 30 F3
Little Eaton Derbys 35 A9
Little Eccleston Lancs 49 E4
Little Ellingham Norf 38 F6
Little End Essex 20 A2
Little Eversden Cambs 29 C10
Little Faringdon Oxon 17 A9
Little Fencote N Yorks 58 G3
Little Fenton N Yorks 51 F11
Little Finborough Suff 31 C7
Little Fransham Norf 38 D5
Little Gaddesden Herts 28 G6
Little Gidding Cambs 37 G7
Little Glemham Suff 31 C10
Little Glenshee Perth 76 D2
Little Gransden Cambs 29 C9
Little Green Som 16 G4
Little Grimsby Lincs 47 C7
Little Gruinard Highld 86 C2
Little Habton N Yorks 52 B3
Little Hadham Herts 29 F11
Little Hale Lincs 37 A7
Little Hallingbury Essex 29 G11
Little Hampden Bucks 18 A5
Little Harrowden Northants 28 A5
Little Haseley Oxon 18 A3
Little Hatfield E Yorks 53 E7
Little Hautbois Norf 39 C8
Little Haven Pembs 22 E3
Little Hay Staffs 35 E7
Little Hayfield Derbys 44 D4
Little Haywood Staffs 34 C6
Little Heath W Mid 35 G9
Little Hereford Hereford 26 B2
Little Horkesley Essex 30 E6
Little Horsted E Sus 12 E3
Little Horton W Yorks 51 F7
Little Horwood Bucks 28 E4
Little Houghton Northants 28 C5
Little Houghton S Yorks 45 B8
Little Hucklow Derbys 44 E5
Little Hulton Gtr Man 43 B10
Little Humber E Yorks 53 G7
Little Hungerford W Berks 18 D2
Little Irchester Northants 28 B6
Little Kimble Bucks 28 H5
Little Kineton Warks 27 C10
Little Kingshill Bucks 18 B5
Little Langdale Cumb 56 F5
Little Langford Wilts 17 H7
Little Laver Essex 30 H2
Little Leigh Ches 43 E9
Little Leighs Essex 30 G4
Little Lever Gtr Man 43 B10
Little London Bucks 28 G3
Little London E Sus 12 E4
Little London Hants 17 G10
Little London Hants 18 F3
Little London Lincs 37 C8
Little London Lincs 37 C10
Little London Norf 39 C7
Little London Powys 32 G6
Little Longstone Derbys 44 E5
Little Lynturk Aberds 83 B7
Little Malvern Worcs 26 D4
Little Maplestead Essex 30 E5
Little Marcle Hereford 26 E3
Little Marlow Bucks 18 C5
Little Marsden Lancs 50 F4
Little Massingham Norf 38 C3
Little Melton Norf 39 E7
Little Mill Mon 15 A9
Little Milton Oxon 18 A3
Little Missenden Bucks 18 B6
Little Musgrave Cumb 57 E9
Little Ness Shrops 33 D10
Little Neston Ches 42 E5
Little Newcastle Pembs 22 D4
Little Newsham Durham 58 E2
Little Oakley Essex 31 F9
Little Oakley Northants 36 G4
Little Orton Cumb 61 H9
Little Ouseburn N Yorks 51 C10
Little Paxton Cambs 29 B8
Little Petherick Corn 3 B8
Little Pitlurg Moray 88 D4
Little Plumpton Lancs 49 F3
Little Plumstead Norf 39 D9
Little Ponton Lincs 36 B5
Little Raveley Cambs 37 H8
Little Reedness E Yorks 52 G4
Little Ribston N Yorks 51 D9
Little Rissington Glos 27 G8
Little Ryburgh Norf 38 C5
Little Ryle Northumb 62 B6
Little Salkeld Cumb 57 C7
Little Sampford Essex 30 E3
Little Sandhurst Brack 18 E5
Little Saxham Suff 30 B4
Little Scatwell Highld 86 F6
Little Sessay N Yorks 51 B10
Little Shelford Cambs 29 C11
Little Singleton Lancs 49 F3
Little Skillymarno Aberds 89 C9
Little Smeaton N Yorks 51 H11
Little Snoring Norf 38 B5
Little Sodbury S Glos 16 C4
Little Somborne Hants 10 A2
Little Somerford Wilts 16 C6
Little Stainforth N Yorks 50 C4
Little Stainton Darl 58 D4
Little Stanney Ches 43 E7
Little Staughton Beds 29 B8
Little Steeping Lincs 47 F8
Little Stoke Staffs 34 B5
Little Stonham Suff 31 B8
Little Stretton Leics 36 E2
Little Stretton Shrops 33 F10
Little Strickland Cumb 57 E7
Little Stukeley Cambs 37 H8
Little Sutton Ches 42 E6
Little Tew Oxon 27 F10
Little Thetford Cambs 37 H11
Little Thirkleby N Yorks 51 B10
Little Thurlow Suff 30 C3
Little Thurrock Thurrock 20 D3
Little Torboll Highld 87 B10
Little Torrington Devon 6 E3
Little Totham Essex 30 G5
Little Toux Aberds 88 C5
Little Town Cumb 56 E4
Little Town Lancs 50 F2
Little Urswick Cumb 49 B2
Little Wakering Essex 20 C6
Little Walden Essex 30 D2
Little Waldingfield Suff 30 D6
Little Walsingham Norf 38 B5
Little Waltham Essex 30 G4
Little Warley Essex 20 B3
Little Weighton E Yorks 52 F5
Little Weldon Northants 36 G5
Little Welnetham Suff 30 B5
Little Wenlock Telford 34 E2
Little Whittingham Green Suff 39 H8
Little Wilbraham Cambs 30 C2
Little Wishford Wilts 17 H7
Little Witley Worcs 26 B4
Little Wittenham Oxon 18 B2
Little Wolford Warks 27 E9
Little Wratting Suff 30 D3
Little Wymington Beds 28 B6
Little Wymondley Herts 29 F9
Little Wyrley Staffs 34 E6
Little Yeldham Essex 30 E4
Littlebeck N Yorks 59 F9
Littleborough Gtr Man 50 H5
Littleborough Notts 45 D11
Littlebourne Kent 21 F9
Littlebredy Dorset 8 F4
Littlebury Essex 30 E2
Littlebury Green Essex 29 E11
Littledean Glos 26 G3
Littleferry Highld 87 B11
Littleham Devon 5 C11
Littleham Devon 6 D3
Littlehampton W Sus 11 D9
Littlehempston Devon 5 E9
Littlehoughton Northumb 63 B8
Littlemill Aberds 82 D5
Littlemill E Ayrs 67 E7
Littlemill Highld 87 F12
Littlemill Northumb 63 B8
Littlemoor Dorset 8 F5
Littlemore Oxon 18 A2
Littleover Derby 35 B9
Littleport Cambs 38 G1
Littlestone on Sea Kent 13 D9
Littlethorpe Leics 35 F11
Littlethorpe N Yorks 51 C9
Littleton Ches 43 F7
Littleton Hants 10 A3
Littleton Perth 76 D5
Littleton Som 8 A3
Littleton Sur 19 E7
Littleton Sur 18 G6
Littleton Drew Wilts 16 C5
Littleton-on-Severn S Glos 16 C2
Littleton Pannell Wilts 17 F7
Littletown Durham 58 B4
Littlewick Green Windsor 18 D5
Littleworth Beds 29 D7
Littleworth Glos 16 A5
Littleworth Oxon 17 B10
Littleworth Staffs 34 D6
Littleworth Worcs 26 C5
Litton Derbys 44 E5
Litton N Yorks 50 B5
Litton Som 16 F2
Litton Cheney Dorset 8 E4
Liurbost W Isles 91 E8
Liverpool Mers 42 C6
Liverpool John Lennon Airport Mers 43 D7
Liversedge W Yorks 51 G8
Liverton Devon 5 D9
Liverton Redcar 59 E8
Livingston W Loth 69 D9
Livingston Village W Loth 69 D9
Lixwm Flint 42 E4
Lizard Corn 2 H6
Llaingoch Anglesey 40 B4
Llaithddu Powys 33 G6
Llan Powys 32 E4
Llan Ffestiniog Gwyn 41 F9
Llan-y-pwll Wrex 42 G6
Llanaber Gwyn 32 D2
Llanaelhaearn Gwyn 40 F5
Llanafan Ceredig 24 A3
Llanafan-fawr Powys 24 C6
Llanallgo Anglesey 40 B6
Llanandras = Presteigne Powys 25 B10
Llanarmon Gwyn 40 G6
Llanarmon Dyffryn Ceiriog Wrex 33 B7
Llanarmon-yn-Ial Denb 42 G4
Llanarth Ceredig 23 A9
Llanarth Mon 25 G10
Llanarthne Carms 23 D10
Llanasa Flint 42 D4

Llanbabo Anglesey 40 B5
Llanbadarn Fawr Ceredig 32 G2
Llanbadarn Fynydd Powys 33 H7
Llanbadarn-y-Garreg Powys 25 D8
Llanbadoc Mon 15 B9
Llanbadrig Anglesey 40 A5
Llanbeder Newport 15 B9
Llanbedr Gwyn 32 C1
Llanbedr Powys 25 D8
Llanbedr Powys 25 F9
Llanbedr-Dyffryn-Clwyd Denb 42 G4
Llanbedr Pont Steffan = Lampeter Ceredig 23 B10
Llanbedr-y-cennin Conwy 41 D9
Llanbedrgoch Anglesey 41 B7
Llanbedrog Gwyn 40 G5
Llanberis Gwyn 41 D7
Llanbethêry V Glam 14 E6
Llanbister Powys 25 A8
Llanblethian V Glam 14 D5
Llanboidy Carms 23 D7
Llanbradach Caerph 15 B7
Llanbrynmair Powys 32 E4
Llancarfan V Glam 14 D6
Llancayo Mon 15 A9
Llancloudy Hereford 25 F11
Llancynfelyn Ceredig 32 F2
Llandaff Cardiff 15 D7
Llandanwg Gwyn 32 C1
Llandarcy Neath 14 B3
Llandawke Carms 23 E7
Llanddaniel Fab Anglesey 40 C6
Llanddarog Carms 23 E10
Llanddeiniol Ceredig 24 A2
Llanddeiniolen Gwyn 41 D7
Llandderfel Gwyn 32 B5
Llanddeusant Anglesey 40 B5
Llanddeusant Carms 24 F4
Llanddew Powys 25 E7
Llanddewi Swansea 23 H9
Llanddewi-Brefi Ceredig 24 C3
Llanddewi Rhydderch Mon 25 G10
Llanddewi Velfrey Pembs 22 E6
Llanddewi'r Cwm Powys 25 D7
Llanddoged Conwy 41 D10
Llanddona Anglesey 41 C7
Llanddowror Carms 23 E7
Llanddulas Conwy 42 E2
Llanddwywe Gwyn 32 C1
Llanddyfnan Anglesey 41 C7
Llandefaelog Fach Powys 25 E7
Llandefaelog-tre'r-graig Powys 25 F8
Llandefalle Powys 25 E8
Llandegai Gwyn 41 C7
Llandegfan Anglesey 41 C7
Llandegla Denb 42 G4
Llandegley Powys 25 B8
Llandegveth Mon 15 B9
Llandegwning Gwyn 40 G4
Llandeilo Carms 24 F3
Llandeilo Graban Powys 25 D7
Llandeilo'r Fan Powys 24 E5
Llandeloy Pembs 22 D3
Llandenny Mon 15 A10
Llandevenny Mon 15 C10
Llandewednock Corn 2 H6
Llandewi Ystradenny Powys 25 B8
Llandinabo Hereford 26 F2
Llandinam Powys 32 G6
Llandissilio Pembs 22 D6
Llandogo Mon 15 A11
Llandough V Glam 14 D5
Llandough V Glam 15 D7
Llandovery = Llanymddyfri Carms 24 E4
Llandow V Glam 14 D5
Llandre Ceredig 32 G2
Llandre Carms 24 D3
Llandrillo Denb 32 B6
Llandrillo-yn-Rhos Conwy 41 B10
Llandrindod = Llandrindod Wells Powys 25 B7
Llandrindod Wells = Llandrindod Powys 25 B7
Llandrinio Powys 33 D8
Llandudno Conwy 41 B9
Llandudno Junction = Cyffordd Llandudno Conwy 41 C9
Llandwrog Gwyn 40 E6
Llandybie Carms 24 G3
Llandyfaelog Carms 23 E9
Llandyfan Carms 24 G3
Llandyfriog Ceredig 23 B8
Llandyfrydog Anglesey 40 B6
Llandygwydd Ceredig 23 B7
Llandynan Denb 42 H4
Llandyrnog Denb 42 F4
Llandysilio Powys 33 D8
Llandyssil Powys 33 F7
Llandysul Ceredig 23 B9
Llanedeyrn Cardiff 15 C8
Llanedi Carms 23 F10
Llaneglwys Powys 25 E7
Llanegryn Gwyn 32 E1
Llanegwad Carms 23 D10
Llaneilian Anglesey 40 A6
Llanelian-yn-Rhos Conwy 41 C10
Llanelidan Denb 42 G4
Llanelieu Powys 25 E8
Llanellen Mon 25 G10
Llanelli Carms 23 G10
Llanelltyd Gwyn 32 D3
Llanelly Mon 25 G9
Llanelly Hill Mon 25 G9
Llanelwedd Powys 25 C7
Llanelwy = St Asaph Denb 42 E3
Llanenddwyn Gwyn 32 C1
Llanengan Gwyn 40 H4
Llanerchymedd Anglesey 40 B6
Llanerfyl Powys 32 E6
Llanfachraeth Anglesey 40 B5
Llanfachreth Gwyn 32 C3
Llanfaelog Anglesey 40 C5
Llanfaelrhys Gwyn 40 H4
Llanfaenor Mon 25 G11
Llanfaes Anglesey 41 C8
Llanfaes Powys 25 F7
Llanfaethlu Anglesey 40 B5
Llanfaglan Gwyn 40 D6
Llanfair Gwyn 32 C1
Llanfair-ar-y-bryn Carms 24 E5
Llanfair Caereinion Powys 33 E7
Llanfair Clydogau Ceredig 24 C3
Llanfair-Dyffryn-Clwyd Denb 42 G4
Llanfair Kilgheddin Mon 25 H10
Llanfair-Nant-Gwyn Pembs 22 C6
Llanfair Talhaiarn Conwy 42 E2
Llanfair Waterdine Shrops 33 H8
Llanfair-ym-Muallt = Builth Wells Powys 25 C7
Llanfairfechan Conwy 41 C8
Llanfairpwll-gwyngyll Anglesey 41 C7
Llanfairyneubwll Anglesey 40 C5
Llanfairynghornwy Anglesey 40 A5
Llanfallteg Carms 22 E6
Llanfaredd Powys 25 C7
Llanfarian Ceredig 32 H1
Llanfechain Powys 33 C7
Llanfechan Powys 24 C6
Llanfechell Anglesey 40 A5
Llanfendigaid Gwyn 32 E1
Llanferres Denb 42 F4
Llanfflewyn Anglesey 40 B5
Llanfihangel-ar-arth Carms 23 C9
Llanfihangel-Crucorney Mon 25 F10
Llanfihangel Glyn Myfyr Conwy 42 H2
Llanfihangel Nant Bran Powys 24 E6
Llanfihangel-nant-Melan Powys 25 C8
Llanfihangel Rhydithon Powys 25 B8
Llanfihangel Rogiet Mon 15 C10
Llanfihangel Tal-y-llyn Powys 25 F8
Llanfihangel-uwch-Gwili Carms 23 D9
Llanfihangel-y-Creuddyn Ceredig 32 H2
Llanfihangel-y-pennant Gwyn 41 F7
Llanfihangel-y-pennant Gwyn 32 E2
Llanfihangel-y-traethau Gwyn 41 G7
Llanfihangel-yn-Ngwynfa Powys 33 D6
Llanfihangel yn Nhowyn Anglesey 40 C5
Llanfilo Powys 25 E8
Llanfoist Mon 25 G9
Llanfor Gwyn 32 B5
Llanfrechfa Torf 15 B9
Llanfrothen Gwyn 41 F8
Llanfrynach Powys 25 F7
Llanfwrog Anglesey 40 B5
Llanfwrog Denb 42 G4
Llanfyllin Powys 33 D7
Llanfynydd Carms 23 D10
Llanfynydd Flint 42 G5
Llanfyrnach Pembs 23 C7
Llangadfan Powys 32 D6
Llangadog Carms 24 F4
Llangadwaladr Anglesey 40 D5
Llangadwaladr Powys 33 B7
Llangaffo Anglesey 40 D6
Llangain Carms 23 E8
Llangammarch Wells Powys 24 D6
Llangan V Glam 14 D5
Llangarron Hereford 26 F2
Llangasty Talyllyn Powys 25 F8
Llangathen Carms 23 D10
Llangattock Powys 25 G9
Llangattock Lingoed Mon 25 F10
Llangattock nigh Usk Mon 25 H10
Llangattock-Vibon-Avel Mon 25 G11
Llangedwyn Powys 33 C7
Llangefni Anglesey 40 C6
Llangeinor Bridgend 14 C5
Llangeitho Ceredig 24 C3
Llangeler Carms 23 C8
Llangelynin Gwyn 32 E1
Llangendeirne Carms 23 E9
Llangennech Carms 23 F10
Llangennith Swansea 23 G9
Llangenny Powys 25 G9
Llangernyw Conwy 41 D10
Llangian Gwyn 40 H4
Llanglydwen Carms 22 D6
Llangoed Anglesey 41 C8
Llangoedmor Ceredig 22 B6
Llangollen Denb 33 A8
Llangolman Pembs 22 D6
Llangors Powys 25 F8
Llangovan Mon 25 H11
Llangower Gwyn 32 B5
Llangrannog Ceredig 23 A8
Llangristiolus Anglesey 40 C6
Llangrove Hereford 26 G2
Llangua Mon 25 F10
Llangunllo Powys 25 A9
Llangunnor Carms 23 E9
Llangurig Powys 32 H5
Llangwm Conwy 32 A5
Llangwm Mon 15 A10
Llangwm Pembs 22 F4
Llangwnnadl Gwyn 40 G4
Llangwyfan Denb 42 F4
Llangwyfan-isaf Anglesey 40 D5
Llangwyllog Anglesey 40 C6
Llangwyryfon Ceredig 24 A2
Llangybi Ceredig 24 C3
Llangybi Gwyn 40 F6
Llangybi Mon 15 B9
Llangyfelach Swansea 14 B2
Llangynhafal Denb 42 F4
Llangynidr Powys 25 G8
Llangynin Carms 23 E7
Llangynog Carms 23 E8
Llangynog Powys 33 C6
Llangynwyd Bridgend 14 C4
Llanhamlach Powys 25 F7
Llanharan Rhondda 14 C6
Llanharry Rhondda 14 C6
Llanhennock Mon 15 B9
Llanhiledd = Llanhilleth Bl Gwent 15 A8
Llanhilleth = Llanhiledd Bl Gwent 15 A8
Llanidloes Powys 32 G5
Llaniestyn Gwyn 40 G4
Llanifyny Powys 32 G4
Llanigon Powys 25 E9
Llanilar Ceredig 24 A3
Llanilid Rhondda 14 C5
Llanilltud Fawr = Llantwit Major V Glam 14 E5
Llanishen Cardiff 15 C7
Llanishen Mon 15 A10
Llanllawddog Carms 23 D9
Llanllechid Gwyn 41 D8
Llanllowell Mon 15 B9
Llanllugan Powys 33 E6
Llanllwch Carms 23 E8
Llanllwchaiarn Powys 33 F7
Llanllwni Carms 23 C9
Llanllyfni Gwyn 40 E6
Llanmadoc Swansea 23 G9
Llanmaes V Glam 14 E5
Llanmartin Newport 15 C9
Llanmihangel V Glam 14 D5
Llanmorlais Swansea 23 G10
Llannefydd Conwy 42 E2
Llannon Carms 23 F10
Llannor Gwyn 40 G5
Llanon Ceredig 24 B2
Llanover Mon 25 H10
Llanpumsaint Carms 23 D9
Llanreithan Pembs 22 D3
Llanrhaeadr Denb 42 F3
Llanrhaeadr-ym-Mochnant Powys 33 C7
Llanrhian Pembs 22 C3
Llanrhidian Swansea 23 G9
Llanrhos Conwy 41 B9
Llanrhyddlad Anglesey 40 B5
Llanrhystud Ceredig 24 B2
Llanrosser Hereford 25 E9
Llanrothal Hereford 25 G11
Llanrug Gwyn 41 D7
Llanrumney Cardiff 15 C8
Llanrwst Conwy 41 D10
Llansadurnen Carms 23 E7
Llansadwrn Anglesey 41 C7
Llansadwrn Carms 24 E3
Llansaint Carms 23 F8
Llansamlet Swansea 14 B2
Llansannan Conwy 42 F2
Llansannor V Glam 14 D5
Llansantffraed Ceredig 24 B2
Llansantffraed Powys 25 F8
Llansantffraed Cwmdeuddwr Powys 24 B6
Llansantffraed-in-Elvel Powys 25 C7
Llansantffraid-ym-Mechain Powys 33 C8
Llansawel Carms 24 E3
Llansilin Powys 33 C8
Llansoy Mon 15 A10
Llanspyddid Powys 25 F7
Llanstadwell Pembs 22 F4
Llansteffan Carms 23 E8
Llanstephan Powys 25 D8
Llantarnam Torf 15 B9
Llanteg Pembs 22 E6
Llanthony Mon 25 F9
Llantilio Crossenny Mon 25 G10
Llantilio Pertholey Mon 25 G10
Llantood Pembs 22 B6
Llantrisant Anglesey 40 B5
Llantrisant Mon 15 B9
Llantrisant Rhondda 14 C6
Llantrithyd V Glam 14 D6
Llantwit Fardre Rhondda 14 C6
Llantwit Major = Llanilltud Fawr V Glam 14 E5
Llanuwchllyn Gwyn 41 G10
Llanvaches Newport 15 B10
Llanvair Discoed Mon 15 B10
Llanvapley Mon 25 G10
Llanvetherine Mon 25 G10
Llanveynoe Hereford 25 E10
Llanvihangel Gobion Mon 25 H10
Llanvihangel-Ystern-Llewern Mon 25 G11
Llanwarne Hereford 26 F2
Llanwddyn Powys 32 D6
Llanwenog Ceredig 23 B9
Llanwern Newport 15 C9
Llanwinio Carms 23 D7
Llanwnda Gwyn 40 E6
Llanwnda Pembs 22 C4
Llanwnnen Ceredig 23 B10
Llanwnog Powys 32 F6
Llanwrda Carms 24 E4
Llanwrin Powys 32 E3
Llanwrthwl Powys 24 B6
Llanwrtud = Llanwrtyd Wells Powys 24 D5
Llanwrtyd Powys 24 D5
Llanwrtyd Wells = Llanwrtud Powys 24 D5
Llanwyddelan Powys 33 E6
Llanyblodwel Shrops 33 C8
Llanybri Carms 23 E8
Llanybydder Carms 23 B10
Llanycefn Pembs 22 D5
Llanychaer Pembs 22 C4
Llanycil Gwyn 32 B5
Llanycrwys Carms 24 D3
Llanymawddwy Gwyn 32 D5
Llanymddyfri = Llandovery Carms 24 E4
Llanymynech Powys 33 C8
Llanynghenedl Anglesey 40 B5
Llanynys Denb 42 F4
Llanyre Powys 25 B7
Llanystumdwy Gwyn 40 G6
Llanywern Powys 25 F8
Llawhaden Pembs 22 E5
Llawnt Shrops 33 B8
Llawr Dref Gwyn 40 H4
Llawryglyn Powys 32 F5
Llay Wrex 42 G6
Llechcynfarwy Anglesey 40 B5
Llecheiddior Gwyn 40 F6
Llechfaen Powys 25 F7
Llechryd Caerph 25 H8
Llechryd Ceredig 23 B7
Llechrydau Powys 33 B8
Lledrod Ceredig 24 A3
Llenmerewig Powys 33 F7
Llethrid Swansea 23 G10
Llidiad Nenog Carms 23 C10
Llidiardau Gwyn 41 G10
Llidiart-y-parc Denb 33 A7
Llithfaen Gwyn 40 F5
Llong Flint 42 F5
Llowes Powys 25 D8
Llundain-fach Ceredig 23 A10
Llwydcoed Rhondda 14 A5
Llwyn Shrops 33 G8
Llwyn-du Mon 25 G9
Llwyn-hendy Carms 23 G10
Llwyn-têg Carms 23 F10
Llwyn-y-brain Carms 22 E6
Llwyn-y-groes Ceredig 23 A10
Llwyncelyn Ceredig 23 A9
Llwyndafydd Ceredig 23 A8
Llwynderw Powys 33 E8
Llwyndyrys Gwyn 40 F5
Llwyngwril Gwyn 32 E1
Llwynmawr Wrex 33 B8
Llwynypia Rhondda 14 B5
Llynclys Shrops 33 C8
Llynfaes Anglesey 40 C6
Llys-y-frân Pembs 22 D5
Llysfaen Conwy 41 C10
Llyswen Powys 25 E8
Llysworney V Glam 14 D5
Llywel Powys 24 E5
Loan Falk 69 C8
Loanend Northumb 71 E8
Loanhead Midloth 69 D11
Loans S Ayrs 66 C6
Loans of Tullich Highld 87 D11
Lobb Devon 6 C3
Loch a Charnain W Isles 84 D3
Loch a'Ghainmhich W Isles 91 E7
Loch Baghasdail = Lochboisdale W Isles 84 G2
Loch Choire Lodge Highld 93 F9
Loch Euphoirt W Isles 84 B3
Loch Head Dumfries 54 E6
Loch Loyal Lodge Highld 93 E9
Loch nam Madadh = Lochmaddy W Isles 84 B4
Loch Sgioport W Isles 84 E3
Lochailort Highld 79 C10
Lochaline Highld 79 G9
Lochanhully Highld 81 A11
Lochans Dumfries 54 D3
Locharbriggs Dumfries 60 E5
Lochassynt Lodge Highld 92 G4
Lochavich Ho. Argyll 73 B8
Lochawe Argyll 74 E4
Lochboisdale = Loch Baghasdail W Isles 84 G2
Lochbuie Argyll 79 J9
Lochcarron Highld 85 E13
Lochdhu Highld 93 E13
Lochdochart House Stirl 75 E7
Lochdon Argyll 79 H10
Lochdrum Highld 86 D5
Lochead Argyll 72 F6
Lochearnhead Stirl 75 E8
Lochee Dundee 76 D6
Lochend Highld 87 H8
Lochend Highld 94 D4
Locherben Dumfries 60 D5
Lochfoot Dumfries 60 F4
Lochgair Argyll 73 D8
Lochgarthside Highld 81 B7
Lochgelly Fife 69 A10
Lochgilphead Argyll 73 E7
Lochgoilhead Argyll 74 G5
Lochhill Moray 88 B2
Lochindorb Lodge Highld 87 H12
Lochinver Highld 92 G3
Lochlane Perth 75 E11
Lochluichart Highld 86 E6
Lochmaben Dumfries 60 E6
Lochmaddy = Loch nam Madadh W Isles 84 B4
Lochmore Cottage Highld 94 F2
Lochmore Lodge Highld 92 F5
Lochore Fife 76 H4
Lochportain W Isles 84 A4
Lochranza N Ayrs 66 A2
Lochs Crofts Moray 88 B3
Lochside Aberds 77 A10
Lochside Highld 92 D7
Lochside Highld 93 F11
Lochside Highld 87 F11
Lochslin Highld 87 C11
Lochstack Lodge Highld 92 E5
Lochton Aberds 83 D9
Lochty Angus 77 A8
Lochty Fife 77 G8
Lochty Perth 76 E3
Lochuisge Highld 79 F10
Lochurr Dumfries 60 E3
Lochwinnoch Renfs 68 E2
Lochwood Dumfries 60 D6
Lochyside Highld 80 F3
Lockengate Corn 3 C9
Lockerbie Dumfries 61 E7
Lockeridge Wilts 17 E8
Lockerley Hants 10 B1
Locking N Som 15 F9
Lockinge Oxon 17 C11
Lockington E Yorks 52 E5
Lockington Leics 35 C10
Lockleywood Shrops 34 C2
Locks Heath Hants 10 D4
Lockton N Yorks 59 G9
Lockwood W Yorks 51 H7
Loddington Leics 36 E3
Loddington Northants 36 H4
Loddiswell Devon 5 G8
Loddon Norf 39 F9
Lode Cambs 30 B2
Loders Dorset 8 E3
Lodsworth W Sus 11 B8
Lofthouse N Yorks 51 B7
Lofthouse W Yorks 51 G9
Loftus Redcar 59 E8
Logan E Ayrs 67 D8
Logan Mains Dumfries 54 E3
Loganlea W Loth 69 D8
Loggerheads Staffs 34 B3
Logie Angus 77 A9
Logie Fife 77 E7
Logie Moray 87 F13
Logie Coldstone Aberds 82 C6
Logie Hill Highld 87 D10
Logie Newton Aberds 89 E6
Logie Pert Angus 77 A9
Logiealmond Lodge Perth 76 D2
Logierait Perth 76 B2
Login Carms 22 D6
Lolworth Cambs 29 B10
Lonbain Highld 85 C11
Londesborough E Yorks 52 E4
London, City of = City of London London 19 C10
London City Airport London 19 C11
London Colney Herts 19 A8
London Gatwick Airport W Sus 12 B1
London Heathrow Airport London 19 D7
London Luton Airport Luton 29 F8
London Stansted Airport Essex 30 F2
Londonderry N Yorks 58 H4
Londonthorpe Lincs 36 B5
Londubh Highld 91 J13
Lonemore Highld 87 C10
Long Ashton N Som 15 D11
Long Bennington Lincs 36 A4
Long Bredy Dorset 8 E4
Long Buckby Northants 28 B3
Long Clawson Leics 36 C3
Long Common Hants 10 C4
Long Compton Staffs 34 C4
Long Compton Warks 27 E9
Long Crendon Bucks 28 H3
Long Crichel Dorset 9 C8
Long Ditton Sur 19 E8
Long Drax N Yorks 52 G2
Long Duckmanton Derbys 45 E8
Long Eaton Derbys 35 B10
Long Green Worcs 26 E5
Long Hanborough Oxon 27 G11
Long Itchington Warks 27 B11
Long Lawford Warks 35 H10
Long Load Som 8 B3
Long Marston Herts 28 G5
Long Marston N Yorks 51 D11
Long Marston Warks 27 D8
Long Marton Cumb 57 D8
Long Melford Suff 30 D5
Long Newnton Glos 16 B6
Long Newton E Loth 70 D4
Long Preston N Yorks 50 D4
Long Riston E Yorks 53 E7
Long Sight Gtr Man 44 B3
Long Stratton Norf 39 F7
Long Street M Keynes 28 D4
Long Sutton Hants 18 G4
Long Sutton Lincs 37 C10
Long Sutton Som 8 B3
Long Thurlow Suff 31 B7
Long Whatton Leics 35 C10
Long Wittenham Oxon 18 B2
Longbar N Ayrs 66 A6
Longbenton T & W 63 G8
Longborough Glos 27 F8
Longbridge Warks 27 B9
Longbridge W Mid 34 H6
Longbridge Deverill Wilts 16 G5
Longburton Dorset 8 C5
Longcliffe Derbys 44 G6
Longcot Oxon 17 B9
Longcroft Falk 68 C6
Longden Shrops 33 E10
Longdon Staffs 35 D6
Longdon Worcs 26 E5
Longdon Green Staffs 35 D6
Longdon on Tern Telford 34 D2
Longdown Devon 7 G7
Longdowns Corn 2 F6
Longfield Kent 20 E3
Longfield Shetland 96 M5
Longford Derbys 35 B8
Longford Glos 26 F5
Longford London 19 D7
Longford Shrops 34 B2
Longford Telford 34 D3
Longford W Mid 35 G9
Longfordlane Derbys 35 B8
Longforgan Perth 76 E6
Longformacus Borders 70 E5
Longframlington Northumb 63 C7
Longham Dorset 9 E9
Longham Norf 38 D5
Longhaven Aberds 89 E11
Longhill Aberds 89 C9
Longhirst Northumb 63 E8
Longhope Glos 26 G3
Longhope Orkney 95 J4
Longhorsley Northumb 63 D7
Longhoughton Northumb 63 B8
Longlane Derbys 35 B8
Longlane W Berks 17 D11
Longlevens Glos 26 F5
Longley W Yorks 44 B5
Longley Green Worcs 26 C4
Longmanhill Aberds 89 B7
Longmoor Camp Hants 11 A6
Longmorn Moray 88 C2
Longnewton Borders 70 H4
Longnewton Stockton 58 E4
Longney Glos 26 G4
Longniddry E Loth 70 C3
Longnor Shrops 33 E10
Longnor Staffs 44 F4
Longparish Hants 17 G11
Longport Stoke 44 H2
Longridge Lancs 50 F2
Longridge Staffs 34 D5
Longridge W Loth 69 D8
Longriggend N Lnrk 69 C7
Longsdon Staffs 44 G3
Longshaw Gtr Man 43 B8
Longside Aberds 89 D10
Longstanton Cambs 29 B10
Longstock Hants 17 H10
Longstone Pembs 22 F6
Longstowe Cambs 29 C10
Longthorpe P'boro 37 F7
Longthwaite Cumb 56 D6
Longton Lancs 49 G4
Longton Stoke 34 A5
Longtown Cumb 61 G9
Longtown Hereford 25 F10
Longview Mers 43 C7
Longville in the Dale Shrops 33 F11
Longwick Bucks 28 H4
Longwitton Northumb 62 E6
Longwood Shrops 34 E2
Longworth Oxon 17 B10
Longyester E Loth 70 D4
Lonmay Aberds 89 C10
Lonmore Highld 84 D7
Looe Corn 4 F3
Loose Kent 20 F4
Loosley Row Bucks 18 A5
Lopcombe Corner Wilts 17 H9
Lopen Som 8 C3
Loppington Shrops 33 C10
Lopwell Devon 4 E5
Lorbottle Northumb 62 C6
Lorbottle Hall Northumb 62 C6
Lornty Perth 76 C4
Loscoe Derbys 45 H8
Losgaintir W Isles 90 H5
Lossiemouth Moray 88 A2
Lossit Argyll 64 C2
Lostford Shrops 34 B2
Lostock Gralam Ches 43 E9
Lostock Green Ches 43 E9
Lostock Hall Lancs 49 G5
Lostock Junction Gtr Man 43 B9
Lostwithiel Corn 4 F2
Loth Orkney 95 E7
Lothbeg Highld 93 H12
Lothersdale N Yorks 50 E5
Lothmore Highld 93 H12
Loudwater Bucks 18 B6
Loughborough Leics 35 D11
Loughor Swansea 23 G10
Loughton Essex 19 B11
Loughton M Keynes 28 E5
Loughton Shrops 34 G2
Lound Lincs 37 D6
Lound Notts 45 D10
Lound Suff 39 F11
Lount Leics 35 D9
Louth Lincs 47 D7
Love Clough Lancs 50 G4
Lovedean Hants 10 C5
Lover Wilts 9 B11
Loversall S Yorks 45 C9
Loves Green Essex 20 A3
Lovesome Hill N Yorks 58 G4
Loveston Pembs 22 F5
Lovington Som 8 A4
Low Ackworth W Yorks 51 H10
Low Barlings Lincs 46 E4
Low Bentham N Yorks 50 C2
Low Bradfield S Yorks 44 C6
Low Bradley N Yorks 50 E6
Low Braithwaite Cumb 56 B6
Low Brunton Northumb 62 F5
Low Burnham N Lincs 45 B11
Low Burton N Yorks 51 A8
Low Buston Northumb 63 C8
Low Catton E Yorks 52 D3
Low Clanyard Dumfries 54 F4
Low Coniscliffe Darl 58 E3
Low Crosby Cumb 61 H10
Low Dalby N Yorks 59 H9
Low Dinsdale Darl 58 E4
Low Ellington N Yorks 51 A8
Low Etherley Durham 58 D2
Low Fell T & W 63 H8
Low Fulney Lincs 37 C8
Low Garth N Yorks 59 F8
Low Gate Northumb 62 G5
Low Grantley N Yorks 51 B8
Low Habberley Worcs 34 H4
Low Ham Som 8 B3
Low Hesket Cumb 56 B6
Low Hesleyhurst Northumb 62 D6
Low Hutton N Yorks 52 C3
Low Laithe N Yorks 51 C7
Low Leighton Derbys 44 D4
Low Lorton Cumb 56 D3
Low Marishes N Yorks 52 B4
Low Marnham Notts 46 F2
Low Mill N Yorks 59 G7
Low Moor Lancs 50 E3
Low Moor W Yorks 51 G7
Low Moorsley T & W 58 B4
Low Newton Cumb 49 A4
Low Newton-by-the-Sea Northumb 63 A8
Low Row Cumb 56 C5
Low Row Cumb 61 G11
Low Row N Yorks 57 G11
Low Salchrie Dumfries 54 C3
Low Smerby Argyll 65 F8
Low Torry Fife 69 B9
Low Worsall N Yorks 58 F4
Low Wray Cumb 56 F5
Lowbridge House Cumb 57 F7
Lowca Cumb 56 D1
Lowdham Notts 45 H10
Lowe Shrops 33 B11
Lowe Hill Staffs 44 G3
Lower Aisholt Som 7 C11
Lower Arncott Oxon 28 G3
Lower Ashton Devon 5 C9
Lower Assendon Oxon 18 C4
Lower Badcall Highld 92 E4
Lower Bartle Lancs 49 F4
Lower Basildon W Berks 18 D3
Lower Beeding W Sus 11 B11
Lower Benefield Northants 36 G5
Lower Boddington Northants 27 C11
Lower Brailes Warks 27 E10
Lower Breakish Highld 85 F11
Lower Broadheath Worcs 26 C5
Lower Bullingham Hereford 26 E2
Lower Cam Glos 16 A4
Lower Chapel Powys 25 E7
Lower Chute Wilts 17 F10
Lower Cragabus Argyll 64 D4
Lower Crossings Derbys 44 D4
Lower Cumberworth W Yorks 44 B6
Lower Cwm-twrch Powys 24 G4
Lower Darwen Blkburn 50 G2
Lower Dean Beds 29 B7
Lower Diabaig Highld 85 B12
Lower Dicker E Sus 12 E4
Lower Dinchope Shrops 33 G10
Lower Down Shrops 33 G9
Lower Drift Corn 2 G3
Lower Dunsforth N Yorks 51 C10
Lower Egleton Hereford 26 D3
Lower Elkstone Staffs 44 G4
Lower End Beds 28 F6
Lower Everleigh Wilts 17 F8
Lower Farringdon Hants 18 H4
Lower Foxdale I o M 48 E2
Lower Frankton Shrops 33 B9
Lower Froyle Hants 18 G4
Lower Gledfield Highld 87 B8
Lower Green Norf 38 B5
Lower Hacheston Suff 31 C10
Lower Halistra Highld 84 C7
Lower Halstow Kent 20 E5
Lower Hardres Kent 21 F8
Lower Hawthwaite Cumb 56 H4
Lower Heath Ches 44 F2
Lower Hempriggs Moray 87 E14
Lower Hergest Hereford 25 C9
Lower Heyford Oxon 27 F11
Lower Higham Kent 20 D4
Lower Holbrook Suff 31 E8
Lower Hordley Shrops 33 C9
Lower Horsebridge E Sus 12 E4
Lower Killeyan Argyll 64 D3
Lower Kingswood Sur 19 F9
Lower Kinnerton Ches 42 F6
Lower Langford N Som 15 E10
Lower Largo Fife 77 G7
Lower Leigh Staffs 34 B6
Lower Lemington Glos 27 E9
Lower Lenie Highld 81 A7
Lower Lydbrook Glos 26 G2
Lower Lye Hereford 25 B11
Lower Machen Newport 15 C8
Lower Maes-coed Hereford 25 E10
Lower Mayland Essex 20 A6
Lower Midway Derbys 35 C9
Lower Milovaig Highld 84 C6
Lower Moor Worcs 26 D6
Lower Nazeing Essex 29 H10
Lower Netchwood Shrops 34 F2
Lower Ollach Highld 85 E10
Lower Penarth V Glam 15 D7
Lower Penn Staffs 34 F4
Lower Pennington Hants 10 E2
Lower Peover Ches 43 E10
Lower Pexhill Ches 44 E2
Lower Place Gtr Man 44 A3
Lower Quinton Warks 27 D8
Lower Rochford Worcs 26 B3
Lower Seagry Wilts 16 C6
Lower Shelton Beds 28 D6
Lower Shiplake Oxon 18 D4
Lower Shuckburgh Warks 27 B11
Lower Slaughter Glos 27 F8
Lower Stanton St Quintin Wilts 16 C6
Lower Stoke Medway 20 D5
Lower Stondon Beds 29 E8
Lower Stow Bedon Norf 38 F5
Lower Street Norf 39 B8
Lower Street Norf 39 D9
Lower Strensham Worcs 26 D6
Lower Stretton Warr 43 D9
Lower Sundon Beds 29 F7
Lower Swanwick Hants 10 D3
Lower Swell Glos 27 F8
Lower Tean Staffs 34 B6
Lower Thurlton Norf 39 F10
Lower Tote Highld 85 B10
Lower Town Pembs 22 C4
Lower Tysoe Warks 27 D10
Lower Upham Hants 10 C4
Lower Vexford Som 7 C10
Lower Weare Som 15 F10
Lower Welson Hereford 25 C9
Lower Whitley Ches 43 E9
Lower Wield Hants 18 G3
Lower Winchendon Bucks 28 G4
Lower Withington Ches 44 F2
Lower Woodend Bucks 18 C5
Lower Woodford Wilts 9 A10
Lower Wyche Worcs 26 D4
Lowesby Leics 36 E3
Lowestoft Suff 39 F11
Loweswater Cumb 56 D3
Lowford Hants 10 C3
Lowgill Cumb 57 G8
Lowgill Lancs 50 C2
Lowick Northants 36 G5
Lowick Northumb 71 G9
Lowick Bridge Cumb 56 H4
Lowick Green Cumb 56 H4
Lowlands Torf 15 B8
Lowmoor Row Cumb 57 D8
Lownie Moor Angus 77 C7
Lowsonford Warks 27 B8
Lowther Cumb 57 D7
Lowthorpe E Yorks 53 C6
Lowton Gtr Man 43 C9
Lowton Common Gtr Man 43 C9
Loxbeare Devon 7 E8
Loxhill Sur 19 H7
Loxhore Devon 6 C5
Loxley Warks 27 C9
Loxton N Som 15 F9
Loxwood W Sus 11 A9
Lubcroy Highld 92 J6
Lubenham Leics 36 G3
Luccombe Som 7 B8
Luccombe Village I o W 10 G4
Lucker Northumb 71 G10
Luckett Corn 4 D4
Luckington Wilts 16 C5
Lucklawhill Fife 77 E7
Luckwell Bridge Som 7 C8
Lucton Hereford 25 B11
Ludag W Isles 84 G2
Ludborough Lincs 46 C6
Ludchurch Pembs 22 E6
Luddenden W Yorks 50 G6
Luddenden Foot W Yorks 50 G6
Luddesdown Kent 20 E3
Luddington N Lincs 52 H4
Luddington Warks 27 C8
Luddington in the Brook Northants 37 G7
Lude House Perth 81 G10
Ludford Lincs 46 D6
Ludford Shrops 26 A2
Ludgershall Bucks 28 G3
Ludgershall Wilts 17 F9
Ludgvan Corn 2 F4
Ludham Norf 39 D9
Ludlow Shrops 26 A2
Ludwell Wilts 9 B8
Ludworth Durham 58 B4
Luffincott Devon 6 G2
Lugar E Ayrs 67 D8
Lugg Green Hereford 25 B11
Luggate Burn E Loth 70 C5
Luggiebank N Lnrk 68 C6
Lugton E Ayrs 67 A7
Lugwardine Hereford 26 D2
Luib Highld 85 F10
Lulham Hereford 25 D11
Lullenden Sur 12 B3
Lullington Derbys 35 D8
Lullington Som 16 F4
Lulsgate Bottom N Som 15 E11
Lulsley Worcs 26 C4
Lumb W Yorks 50 G6
Lumby N Yorks 51 F10
Lumloch E Dunb 68 D5
Lumphanan Aberds 83 C7
Lumphinnans Fife 69 A10
Lumsdaine Borders 71 D7
Lumsden Aberds 82 A6
Lunan Angus 77 B9
Lunanhead Angus 77 B7
Luncarty Perth 76 E3
Lund E Yorks 52 E5
Lund N Yorks 52 F2
Lund Shetland 96 C7
Lunderton Aberds 89 D11
Lundie Angus 76 D5
Lundie Highld 80 B3
Lundin Links Fife 77 G7
Lunga Argyll 72 C6
Lunna Shetland 96 G6
Lunning Shetland 96 G7
Lunnon Swansea 23 H10
Lunsford's Cross E Sus 12 E6
Lunt Mers 42 B6
Luntley Hereford 25 C10
Luppitt Devon 7 F10
Lupset W Yorks 51 H9
Lupton Cumb 50 A1
Lurgashall W Sus 11 B8
Lusby Lincs 47 F7
Luson Devon 5 G7
Luss Argyll 68 A2
Lussagiven Argyll 72 E5
Lusta Highld 85 C7
Lustleigh Devon 5 C8
Luston Hereford 25 B11
Luthermuir Aberds 83 G8
Luthrie Fife 76 F6
Luton Devon 5 D10
Luton Luton 29 F7
Luton Medway 20 E4
Lutterworth Leics 35 G11
Lutton Devon 5 F6
Lutton Lincs 37 C10
Lutton Northants 37 G7
Lutworthy Devon 7 E6
Luxborough Som 7 C8
Luxulyan Corn 4 F1
Lybster Highld 94 G4
Lydbury North Shrops 33 G9
Lydcott Devon 6 C5
Lydd Kent 13 D9
Lydd on Sea Kent 13 D9
Lydden Kent 21 G9
Lyddington Rutland 36 F4
Lyde Green Hants 18 F4
Lydeard St Lawrence Som 7 C10
Lydford Devon 4 C6
Lydford-on-Fosse Som 8 A4
Lydgate W Yorks 50 G5
Lydham Shrops 33 F9
Lydiard Green Wilts 17 C7
Lydiard Millicent Wilts 17 C7
Lydiate Mers 42 B6
Lydlinch Dorset 8 C6
Lydney Glos 16 A3
Lydstep Pembs 22 G5
Lye W Mid 34 G5
Lye Green Bucks 18 A6
Lye Green E Sus 12 C4
Lyford Oxon 17 B10
Lymbridge Green Kent 13 B10
Lyme Regis Dorset 8 E2
Lyminge Kent 21 G8
Lymington Hants 10 E2
Lyminster W Sus 11 D9
Lymm Warr 43 D9
Lymore Hants 10 E1
Lympne Kent 13 C10
Lympsham Som 15 F9
Lympstone Devon 5 C10
Lynchat Highld 81 C9
Lyndale Ho. Highld 85 C8
Lyndhurst Hants 10 D2
Lyndon Rutland 36 E5
Lyne Sur 19 E7
Lyne Down Hereford 26 E3
Lyne of Gorthleck Highld 81 A7
Lyne of Skene Aberds 83 B9
Lyneal Shrops 33 B10
Lyneham Oxon 27 F9
Lyneham Wilts 17 D7
Lynemore Highld 82 A2
Lynemouth Northumb 63 D8
Lyness Orkney 95 J4
Lyng Norf 39 D6
Lyng Som 8 B2
Lynmouth Devon 7 B6
Lynsted Kent 20 E6
Lynton Devon 6 B6
Lyon's Gate Dorset 8 D5
Lyonshall Hereford 25 C10
Lytchett Matravers Dorset 9 E8
Lytchett Minster Dorset 9 E8
Lyth Highld 94 D4
Lytham Lancs 49 G3
Lytham St Anne's Lancs 49 G3
Lythe N Yorks 59 E9
Lythes Orkney 95 K5

M

Mabe Burnthouse Corn 3 F6
Mabie Dumfries 60 F5
Mablethorpe Lincs 47 D9
Macclesfield Ches 44 E3
Macclesfield Forest Ches 44 E3
Macduff Aberds 89 B7
Mace Green Suff 31 D8
Macharioch Argyll 65 H8
Machen Caerph 15 C8
Machrihanish Argyll 65 F7
Machynlleth Powys 32 E3
Machynys Carms 23 G10
Mackerel's Common W Sus 11 B9
Mackworth Derbys 35 B9
Macmerry E Loth 70 C3
Madderty Perth 76 E2
Maddiston Falk 69 C8
Madehurst W Sus 11 C8
Madeley Staffs 34 A3
Madeley Telford 34 E2
Madeley Heath Staffs 43 H10
Madeley Park Staffs 34 A3
Madingley Cambs 29 B10
Madley Hereford 25 E11
Madresfield Worcs 26 D5
Madron Corn 2 F3
Maen-y-groes Ceredig 23 A8
Maenaddwyn Anglesey 40 B6
Maenclochog Pembs 22 D5
Maendy V Glam 14 D6
Maentwrog Gwyn 41 F8
Maer Staffs 34 B3
Maerdy Conwy 32 A6
Maerdy Rhondda 14 B5
Maes-Treylow Powys 25 B9
Maesbrook Shrops 33 C8
Maesbury Shrops 33 C9
Maesbury Marsh Shrops 33 C9
Maesgwyn-Isaf Powys 33 D7
Maesgwynne Carms 23 D7
Maeshafn Denb 42 F5
Maesllyn Ceredig 23 B8
Maesmynis Powys 25 D7
Maesteg Bridgend 14 B4
Maestir Ceredig 23 B10
Maesy cwmmer Caerph 15 B7
Maesybont Carms 23 E10
Maesycrugiau Carms 23 B9
Maesymeillion Ceredig 23 B9
Magdalen Laver Essex 20 A2
Maggieknockater Moray 88 D3
Magham Down E Sus 12 E5
Maghull Mers 43 B6
Magor Mon 15 C10
Magpie Green Suff 39 H6
Maiden Bradley Wilts 16 H5
Maiden Law Durham 58 B2
Maiden Newton Dorset 8 E4
Maiden Wells Pembs 22 G4
Maidencombe Torbay 5 E10
Maidenhall Suff 31 D8
Maidenhead Windsor 18 C5
Maidens S Ayrs 66 F5
Maiden's Green Brack 18 D5
Maidensgrave Suff 31 D9
Maidenwell Corn 4 D2
Maidenwell Lincs 47 E7
Maidford Northants 28 C3
Maids Moreton Bucks 28 E4
Maidstone Kent 20 F4
Maidwell Northants 36 H3
Mail Shetland 96 L6
Main Powys 33 D7
Maindee Newport 15 C9
Mains of Airies Dumfries 54 C2
Mains of Allardice Aberds 83 F10
Mains of Annochie Aberds 89 D9
Mains of Ardestie Angus 77 D8
Mains of Balhall Angus 77 A8
Mains of Ballindarg Angus 77 B7
Mains of Balnakettle Aberds 83 F8
Mains of Birness Aberds 89 E9
Mains of Burgie Moray 87 F13
Mains of Clunas Highld 87 G11
Mains of Crichie Aberds 89 D9
Mains of Dalvey Highld 87 H14
Mains of Dellavaird Aberds 83 E9
Mains of Drum Aberds 83 D10
Mains of Edingight Moray 88 C5
Mains of Fedderate Aberds 89 D8
Mains of Inkhorn Aberds 89 E9
Mains of Mayen Moray 88 D5
Mains of Melgund Angus 77 B8
Mains of Thornton Aberds 83 F8
Mains of Watten Highld 94 E4
Mainsforth Durham 58 C4
Mainsriddle Dumfries 60 H5
Mainstone Shrops 33 G8
Maisemore Glos 26 F5
Malacleit W Isles 84 A2
Malborough Devon 5 H8
Malcoff Derbys 44 D4
Maldon Essex 30 H5
Malham N Yorks 50 C5
Maligar Highld 85 B9
Mallaig Highld 79 B9
Malleny Mills Edin 69 D10
Malling Stirl 75 G8
Malltraeth Anglesey 40 D6
Mallwyd Gwyn 32 D4
Malmesbury Wilts 16 C6
Malmsmead Devon 7 B6
Malpas Ches 43 H7
Malpas Corn 3 E7
Malpas Newport 15 B9
Malswick Glos 26 F4
Maltby Stockton 58 E5
Maltby S Yorks 45 C9
Maltby le Marsh Lincs 47 D8
Malting Green Essex 30 F6
Maltman's Hill Kent 13 B8
Malton N Yorks 52 B3
Malvern Link Worcs 26 D4
Malvern Wells Worcs 26 D4
Mamble Worcs 26 A3
Man-moel Caerph 15 A7
Manaccan Corn 3 G6
Manafon Powys 33 E7
Manais W Isles 90 J6
Manar Ho. Aberds 83 A9
Manaton Devon 5 C8
Manby Lincs 47 D7
Mancetter Warks 35 F9
Manchester Gtr Man 44 C2
Manchester Airport Gtr Man 44 D2
Mancot Flint 42 F6
Mandally Highld 80 C4
Manea Cambs 37 G10
Manfield N Yorks 58 E3
Mangaster Shetland 96 F5
Mangotsfield S Glos 16 D3
Mangurstadh W Isles 90 D5
Mankinholes W Yorks 50 G5
Manley Ches 43 E8
Mannal Argyll 78 G2
Mannerston W Loth 69 C9
Manningford Bohune Wilts 17 F8
Manningford Bruce Wilts 17 F8
Manningham W Yorks 51 F7
Mannings Heath W Sus 11 B11
Mannington Dorset 9 D9
Manningtree Essex 31 E7
Mannofield Aberdeen 83 C11
Manor Estate S Yorks 45 D7
Manor Park London 19 C11
Manorbier Pembs 22 G5
Manordeilo Carms 24 F3
Manorhill Borders 70 G5
Manorowen Pembs 22 C4
Mansel Lacy Hereford 25 D11
Manselfield Swansea 23 H10
Mansell Gamage Hereford 25 D10
Mansergh Cumb 50 A2
Mansfield E Ayrs 67 E9
Mansfield Notts 45 F9
Mansfield Woodhouse Notts 45 F9
Mansriggs Cumb 49 A2
Manston Dorset 9 C7
Manston Kent 21 E10
Manston W Yorks 51 F9
Manswood Dorset 9 D8
Manthorpe Lincs 37 D6
Manthorpe Lincs 36 B5
Manton N Lincs 46 B3
Manton Notts 45 E9
Manton Rutland 36 E4
Manton Wilts 17 E8
Manuden Essex 29 F11
Maperton Som 8 B5
Maple Cross Herts 19 B7
Maplebeck Notts 45 F11
Mapledurham Oxon 18 D3
Mapledurwell Hants 18 F3
Maplehurst W Sus 11 B10
Maplescombe Kent 20 E2
Mapleton Derbys 44 H5
Mapperley Derbys 35 A10
Mapperley Park Nottingham 36 A1
Mapperton Dorset 8 E4
Mappleborough Green Warks 27 B7
Mappleton E Yorks 53 E8
Mappowder Dorset 8 D6
Mar Lodge Aberds 82 D2
Maraig W Isles 90 G6
Marazanvose Corn 3 D7
Marazion Corn 2 F4
Marbhig W Isles 91 F9
Marbury Ches 43 H8
March Cambs 37 F10
March S Lnrk 60 B5
Marcham Oxon 17 B11

Marchamley Shrops 34 C1
Marchington Staffs 35 B7
Marchington Woodlands Staffs 35 C7
Marchroes Gwyn 40 H5
Marchwiel Wrex 42 H6
Marchwood Hants 10 C2
Marcross V Glam 14 E5
Marden Hereford 26 D2
Marden Kent 12 B6
Marden T & W 63 F9
Marden Wilts 17 F7
Marden Beech Kent 12 B6
Marden Thorn Kent 12 B6
Mardy Mon 25 G10
Marefield Leics 36 E3
Mareham le Fen Lincs 46 F6
Mareham on the Hill Lincs 46 F6
Marehay Derbys 45 H7
Marehill W Sus 11 C9
Maresfield E Sus 12 D3
Marfleet Hull 53 G7
Marford Wrex 42 G6
Margam Neath 14 C3
Margaret Marsh Dorset 9 C7
Margaret Roding Essex 30 G2
Margaretting Essex 20 A3
Margate Kent 21 D10
Margnaheglish N Ayrs 66 C3
Margrove Park Redcar 59 E7
Marham Norf 38 D3
Marhamchurch Corn 4 A3
Marholm P'boro 37 E7
Mariandyrys Anglesey 41 B8
Marianglas Anglesey 41 B7
Mariansleigh Devon 7 D6
Marionburgh Aberds 83 C9
Marishader Highld 85 B9
Marjoriebanks Dumfries 60 E6
Mark Dumfries 54 D4
Mark S Ayrs 54 B3
Mark Som 15 G9
Mark Causeway Som 15 G9
Mark Cross E Sus 12 E3
Mark Cross E Sus 12 C4
Markbeech Kent 12 B3
Markby Lincs 47 E8
Market Bosworth Leics 35 E10
Market Deeping Lincs 37 E7
Market Drayton Shrops 34 B2
Market Harborough Leics 36 G3
Market Lavington Wilts 17 F7
Market Overton Rutland 36 D4
Market Rasen Lincs 46 D5
Market Stainton Lincs 46 E6
Market Warsop Notts 45 F9
Market Weighton E Yorks 52 E4
Market Weston Suff 38 H5
Markethill Perth 76 D5
Markfield Leics 35 D10
Markham Caerph 15 A7
Markham Moor Notts 45 E11
Markinch Fife 76 G5
Markington N Yorks 51 C8
Marks Tey Essex 30 F6
Marksbury Bath 16 E3
Markyate Herts 29 G7
Marland Gtr Man 44 A2
Marlborough Wilts 17 E8
Marlbrook Hereford 26 C2
Marlbrook Worcs 26 A6
Marlcliff Warks 27 C7
Marldon Devon 5 E9
Marlesford Suff 31 C10
Marley Green Ches 43 H8
Marley Hill T & W 63 H8
Marley Mount Hants 10 E1
Marlingford Norf 39 E7
Marloes Pembs 22 F2
Marlow Bucks 18 C5
Marlow Hereford 33 H10
Marlow Bottom Bucks 18 C5
Marlpit Hill Kent 19 G11
Marlpool Derbys 45 H8
Marnhull Dorset 9 C6
Marnoch Aberds 88 C5
Marnock N Lnrk 68 D6
Marple Gtr Man 44 D3
Marple Bridge Gtr Man 44 D3
Marr S Yorks 45 B9
Marrel Highld 93 H13
Marrick N Yorks 58 G1
Marrister Shetland 96 G7
Marros Carms 23 F7
Marsden T & W 63 G9
Marsden W Yorks 44 A4
Marsett N Yorks 57 H11
Marsh Devon 8 C1
Marsh W Yorks 50 F6
Marsh Baldon Oxon 18 B2
Marsh Gibbon Bucks 28 F3
Marsh Green Devon 7 G9
Marsh Green Kent 12 B3
Marsh Green Staffs 44 G2
Marsh Lane Derbys 45 E8
Marsh Street Som 7 B8
Marshall's Heath Herts 29 G8
Marshalsea Dorset 8 D2
Marshalswick Herts 29 H8
Marsham Norf 39 C7
Marshaw Lancs 50 D1
Marshborough Kent 21 F10
Marshbrook Shrops 33 G10
Marshchapel Lincs 47 C7
Marshfield Newport 15 C8
Marshfield S Glos 16 D4
Marshgate Corn 4 B2
Marshland St James Norf 37 E11
Marshside Mers 49 H3
Marshwood Dorset 8 E2
Marske N Yorks 58 F2
Marske-by-the-Sea Redcar 59 D7
Marston Ches 43 E9
Marston Hereford 25 C10
Marston Lincs 36 A4
Marston Oxon 28 H2
Marston Staffs 34 D4
Marston Staffs 34 C5
Marston Warks 35 F8
Marston Wilts 16 F6
Marston Doles Warks 27 C11
Marston Green W Mid 35 G7
Marston Magna Som 8 B4
Marston Meysey Wilts 17 B8
Marston Montgomery Derbys 35 B7
Marston Moretaine Beds 28 D6
Marston on Dove Derbys 35 C8
Marston St Lawrence Northants 28 D2
Marston Stannett Hereford 26 C2
Marston Trussell Northants 36 G2
Marstow Hereford 26 G2
Marsworth Bucks 28 G6
Marten Wilts 17 F9
Marthall Ches 44 E2
Martham Norf 39 D10
Martin Hants 9 C9
Martin Kent 21 G10
Martin Lincs 46 G5
Martin Lincs 46 F6
Martin Dales Lincs 46 F5
Martin Drove End Hants 9 B9
Martin Hussingtree Worcs 26 B5
Martin Mill Kent 21 G10
Martinhoe Devon 6 B5
Martinhoe Cross Devon 6 B5
Martinscroft Warr 43 D9
Martinstown Dorset 8 F5
Martlesham Suff 31 D9
Martlesham Heath Suff 31 D9
Martletwy Pembs 22 E5
Martley Worcs 26 C4
Martock Som 8 C3
Marton Ches 44 F2
Marton E Yorks 53 F7
Marton Lincs 46 D2
Marton M'bro 58 E6
Marton N Yorks 51 C10
Marton N Yorks 52 A3
Marton Shrops 33 E8
Marton Shrops 33 C10
Marton Warks 27 B11
Marton-le-Moor N Yorks 51 B9
Martyr Worthy Hants 10 A4
Martyr's Green Sur 19 F7
Marwick Orkney 95 F3
Marwood Devon 6 C4
Mary Tavy Devon 4 D6
Marybank Highld 86 F7
Maryburgh Highld 87 F8
Maryhill Glasgow 68 D4
Marykirk Aberds 83 G8
Marylebone Gtr Man 43 B8
Marypark Moray 88 E1
Maryport Cumb 56 C2
Maryport Dumfries 54 F4
Maryton Angus 77 B9
Marywell Aberds 83 D7
Marywell Aberds 83 D11
Marywell Angus 77 C9
Masham N Yorks 51 A8
Mashbury Essex 30 G3
Masongill N Yorks 50 B2
Masonhill S Ayrs 67 D6
Mastin Moor Derbys 45 E8
Mastrick Aberdeen 83 C10
Matching Essex 30 G2
Matching Green Essex 30 G2
Matching Tye Essex 30 G2
Matfen Northumb 62 F6
Matfield Kent 12 B5
Mathern Mon 15 B11
Mathon Hereford 26 D4
Mathry Pembs 22 C3
Matlaske Norf 39 B7
Matlock Derbys 44 F6
Matlock Bath Derbys 44 G6
Matson Glos 26 G5
Matterdale End Cumb 56 D5
Mattersey Notts 45 D10
Mattersey Thorpe Notts 45 D10
Mattingley Hants 18 F4
Mattishall Norf 39 D6
Mattishall Burgh Norf 39 D6
Mauchline E Ayrs 67 D7
Maud Aberds 89 D9
Maugersbury Glos 27 F9
Maughold I o M 48 C4
Mauld Highld 86 H7
Maulden Beds 29 E7
Maulds Meaburn Cumb 57 E8
Maunby N Yorks 58 H4
Maund Bryan Hereford 26 C2
Maundown Som 7 D9
Mautby Norf 39 D10
Mavis Enderby Lincs 47 F7
Maw Green Ches 43 G10
Mawbray Cumb 56 B2
Mawdesley Lancs 43 A7
Mawdlam Bridgend 14 C4
Mawgan Corn 2 G6
Mawla Corn 2 E6
Mawnan Corn 3 G6
Mawnan Smith Corn 3 G6
Mawsley Northants 36 H4
Maxey P'boro 37 E7
Maxstoke Warks 35 G8
Maxton Borders 70 G5
Maxton Kent 21 G10
Maxwellheugh Borders 70 G6
Maxwelltown Dumfries 60 F5
Maxworthy Corn 6 G1
May Bank Staffs 44 H2
Mayals Swansea 14 B2
Maybole S Ayrs 66 F6
Mayfield E Sus 12 D4
Mayfield Midloth 70 D2
Mayfield Staffs 44 H5
Mayfield W Loth 69 D8
Mayford Sur 18 F6
Mayland Essex 20 A6
Maynard's Green E Sus 12 E4
Maypole Mon 25 G11
Maypole Scilly 2 C3
Maypole Green Essex 30 F6
Maypole Green Norf 39 F10
Maypole Green Suff 31 B9
Maywick Shetland 96 L5
Meadle Bucks 28 H5
Meadowtown Shrops 33 E9
Meaford Staffs 34 B4
Meal Bank Cumb 57 G7
Mealabost W Isles 91 D9
Mealabost Bhuirgh W Isles 91 B9
Mealsgate Cumb 56 B4
Meanwood W Yorks 51 F8
Mearbeck N Yorks 50 C4
Meare Som 15 G10
Meare Green Som 8 B2
Mears Ashby Northants 28 B5
Measham Leics 35 D9
Meath Green Sur 12 B2
Meathop Cumb 49 A4
Meaux E Yorks 53 F6
Meavy Devon 4 E6
Medbourne Leics 36 F3
Medburn Northumb 63 F7
Meddon Devon 6 E1
Meden Vale Notts 45 F9
Medlam Lincs 47 G7
Medmenham Bucks 18 C5
Medomsley Durham 58 A2
Medstead Hants 18 H3
Meer End W Mid 27 A9
Meerbrook Staffs 44 F3
Meers Bridge Lincs 47 D8
Meesden Herts 29 E11
Meeth Devon 6 F4
Meggethead Borders 61 A7
Meidrim Carms 23 D7
Meifod Denb 42 G3
Meifod Powys 33 D7
Meigle N Ayrs 73 G10
Meigle Perth 76 C5
Meikle Earnock S Lnrk 68 E6
Meikle Ferry Highld 87 C10
Meikle Forter Angus 76 A4
Meikle Gluich Highld 87 C9
Meikle Pinkerton E Loth 70 C6
Meikle Strath Aberds 83 F8
Meikle Tarty Aberds 89 F9
Meikle Wartle Aberds 89 E7
Meikleour Perth 76 D4
Meinciau Carms 23 E9
Meir Stoke 34 A5
Meir Heath Staffs 34 A5
Melbourn Cambs 29 D10
Melbourne Derbys 35 C9
Melbourne E Yorks 52 E3
Melbourne S Lnrk 69 F9
Melbury Abbas Dorset 9 B7
Melbury Bubb Dorset 8 D4
Melbury Osmond Dorset 8 D4
Melbury Sampford Dorset 8 D4
Melby Shetland 96 H3
Melchbourne Beds 29 B7
Melcombe Bingham Dorset 9 D6
Melcombe Regis Dorset 8 F5
Meldon Devon 6 G4
Meldon Northumb 63 E7
Meldreth Cambs 29 D10
Meldrum Ho. Aberds 89 F8
Melfort Argyll 73 B7
Melgarve Highld 81 D6
Meliden Denb 42 D3
Melin-y-coed Conwy 41 D10
Melin-y-ddôl Powys 33 E6
Melin-y-grug Powys 33 E6
Melin-y-Wig Denb 42 H3
Melinbyrhedyn Powys 32 F4
Melincourt Neath 14 A4
Melkinthorpe Cumb 57 D7
Melkridge Northumb 62 G3
Melksham Wilts 16 E6
Melldalloch Argyll 73 F8
Melling Lancs 50 B1
Melling Mers 43 B6
Melling Mount Mers 43 B7
Mellis Suff 31 A8
Mellon Charles Highld 91 H13
Mellon Udrigle Highld 91 H13
Mellor Gtr Man 44 D3
Mellor Lancs 50 F2
Mellor Brook Lancs 50 F2
Mells Som 16 G4
Melmerby Cumb 57 C8
Melmerby N Yorks 51 B9
Melmerby N Yorks 58 H1
Melplash Dorset 8 E3
Melrose Borders 70 G4
Melsetter Orkney 95 K3
Melsonby N Yorks 58 F2
Meltham W Yorks 44 A5
Melton Suff 31 C9
Melton Constable Norf 38 B6
Melton Mowbray Leics 36 D3
Melton Ross N Lincs 46 A4
Meltonby E Yorks 52 D3
Melvaig Highld 91 J12
Melverley Shrops 33 D9
Melverley Green Shrops 33 D9
Melvich Highld 93 C11
Membury Devon 8 D1
Memsie Aberds 89 B9
Memus Angus 77 B7
Menabilly Corn 4 F1
Menai Bridge = Porthaethwy Anglesey 41 C7
Mendham Suff 39 G8
Mendlesham Suff 31 B8
Mendlesham Green Suff 31 B7
Menheniot Corn 4 E3
Mennock Dumfries 60 C4
Menston W Yorks 51 E7
Menstrie Clack 75 H11
Menthorpe N Yorks 52 F2
Mentmore Bucks 28 G6
Meoble Highld 79 C10
Meole Brace Shrops 33 D10
Meols Mers 42 C5
Meonstoke Hants 10 C5
Meopham Kent 20 E3
Meopham Station Kent 20 E3
Mepal Cambs 37 G10
Meppershall Beds 29 E8
Merbach Hereford 25 D10
Mere Ches 43 D10
Mere Wilts 9 A7
Mere Brow Lancs 49 H4
Mere Green W Mid 35 F7
Mereclough Lancs 50 F4
Mereside Blkpool 49 F3
Mereworth Kent 20 F3
Mergie Aberds 83 E9
Meriden W Mid 35 G8
Merkadale Highld 85 E8
Merkland Dumfries 60 F3
Merkland S Ayrs 66 G5
Merkland Lodge Highld 92 G7
Merley Poole 9 E9
Merlin's Bridge Pembs 22 E4
Merrington Shrops 33 C10
Merrion Pembs 22 G4
Merriott Som 8 C3
Merrivale Devon 4 D6
Merrow Sur 19 F7
Merrymeet Corn 4 E3
Mersham Kent 13 C9
Merstham Sur 19 F9
Merston W Sus 11 D7
Merstone I o W 10 F4
Merther Corn 3 E7
Merthyr Carms 23 D8
Merthyr Cynog Powys 24 E6
Merthyr-Dyfan V Glam 15 E7
Merthyr Mawr Bridgend 14 D4
Merthyr Tudful = Merthyr Tydfil M Tydf 25 H7
Merthyr Tydfil = Merthyr Tudful M Tydf 25 H7
Merthyr Vale M Tydf 14 B6
Merton Devon 6 E4
Merton London 19 D9
Merton Norf 38 F5
Merton Oxon 28 G2
Mervinslaw Borders 62 B2
Meshaw Devon 7 E6
Messing Essex 30 G5
Messingham N Lincs 46 B2
Metfield Suff 39 G8
Metheringham Lincs 46 F4
Methil Fife 76 H6
Methlem Gwyn 40 G3
Methley W Yorks 51 G9
Methlick Aberds 89 E8
Methven Perth 76 E3
Methwold Norf 38 F3
Methwold Hythe Norf 38 F3
Mettingham Suff 39 G9
Mevagissey Corn 3 E9
Mewith Head N Yorks 50 C3
Mexborough S Yorks 45 B8
Mey Highld 94 C4
Meysey Hampton Glos 17 B8
Miabhag W Isles 90 H6
Miabhag W Isles 90 G5
Miabhig W Isles 90 D5
Michaelchurch Hereford 26 F2
Michaelchurch Escley Hereford 25 E10
Michaelchurch on Arrow Powys 25 C9
Michaelston-le-Pit V Glam 15 D7
Michaelston-y-Fedw Newport 15 C8
Michaelstow Corn 4 D1
Michealston-super-Ely Cardiff 15 D7
Micheldever Hants 18 H2
Michelmersh Hants 10 B2
Mickfield Suff 31 B8
Mickle Trafford Ches 43 F7
Micklebring S Yorks 45 C9
Mickleby N Yorks 59 E9
Mickleham Sur 19 F8
Mickleover Derby 35 B9
Micklethwaite W Yorks 51 E7
Mickleton Durham 57 D11
Mickleton Glos 27 D8
Mickletown W Yorks 51 G9
Mickley N Yorks 51 B8
Mickley Square Northumb 62 G6
Mid Ardlaw Aberds 89 B9
Mid Auchinlech Invclyd 68 C2
Mid Beltie Aberds 83 C8
Mid Calder W Loth 69 D9
Mid Cloch Forbie Aberds 89 C7
Mid Clyth Highld 94 G4
Mid Lavant W Sus 11 D7
Mid Main Highld 86 H7
Mid Urchany Highld 87 G11
Mid Walls Shetland 96 H4
Mid Yell Shetland 96 D7
Midbea Orkney 95 D5
Middle Assendon Oxon 18 C4
Middle Aston Oxon 27 F11
Middle Barton Oxon 27 F11
Middle Cairncake Aberds 89 D8
Middle Claydon Bucks 28 F4
Middle Drums Angus 77 B8
Middle Handley Derbys 45 E8
Middle Littleton Worcs 27 D7
Middle Maes-coed Hereford 25 E10
Middle Mill Pembs 22 D3
Middle Rasen Lincs 46 D4
Middle Rigg Perth 76 G3
Middle Tysoe Warks 27 D10
Middle Wallop Hants 17 H9
Middle Winterslow Wilts 9 A11
Middle Woodford Wilts 17 H8
Middlebie Dumfries 61 F8
Middleforth Green Lancs 49 G5
Middleham N Yorks 58 H2
Middlehope Shrops 33 G10
Middlemarsh Dorset 8 D5
Middlemuir Aberds 89 F9
Middlesbrough M'bro 58 D5
Middleshaw Cumb 57 H7
Middleshaw Dumfries 61 F7
Middlesmoor N Yorks 51 B6
Middlestone Durham 58 C3
Middlestone Moor Durham 58 C3
Middlestown W Yorks 51 H8
Middlethird Borders 70 F5
Middleton Aberds 83 B10
Middleton Argyll 78 G2
Middleton Cumb 57 H8
Middleton Derbys 44 G6
Middleton Derbys 44 F5
Middleton Essex 30 E5
Middleton Gtr Man 44 B2
Middleton Hants 17 G11
Middleton Hereford 26 B2
Middleton Lancs 49 D4
Middleton Midloth 70 E2
Middleton Norf 38 D2
Middleton Northants 36 G4
Middleton Northumb 62 E6
Middleton Northumb 71 G10
Middleton N Yorks 59 H8
Middleton Perth 76 G4
Middleton Perth 76 C4
Middleton Shrops 33 H11
Middleton Shrops 33 F8
Middleton Shrops 33 C9
Middleton Suff 31 B11
Middleton Swansea 23 H9
Middleton Warks 35 F7
Middleton W Yorks 51 G8
Middleton W Yorks 51 E7
Middleton Cheney Northants 27 D11
Middleton Green Staffs 34 B5
Middleton Hall Northumb 71 H8
Middleton-in-Teesdale Durham 57 D11
Middleton Moor Suff 31 B11
Middleton-on-Leven N Yorks 58 F5
Middleton-on-Sea W Sus 11 D8
Middleton on the Hill Hereford 26 B2
Middleton-on-the-Wolds E Yorks 52 E5
Middleton One Row Darl 58 E4
Middleton Priors Shrops 34 F2
Middleton Quernham N Yorks 51 B9
Middleton St George Darl 58 E4
Middleton Scriven Shrops 34 G2
Middleton Stoney Oxon 28 F2
Middleton Tyas N Yorks 58 F3
Middletown Cumb 56 F1
Middletown Powys 33 D9
Middlewich Ches 43 F9
Middlewood Green Suff 31 B7
Middlezoy Som 8 A2
Middridge Durham 58 D3
Midfield Highld 93 C8
Midge Hall Lancs 49 G5
Midgeholme Cumb 62 H2
Midgham W Berks 18 E2
Midgley W Yorks 50 G6
Midgley W Yorks 44 A6
Midhopestones S Yorks 44 C6
Midhurst W Sus 11 B7
Midlem Borders 70 H4
Midmar Aberds 83 C8
Midsomer Norton Bath 16 F3
Midton Invclyd 73 F11
Midtown Highld 93 C8
Midtown Highld 91 J13
Midtown of Buchromb Moray 88 D3
Midville Lincs 47 G7
Midway Ches 44 D3
Migdale Highld 87 B9
Migvie Aberds 82 C6
Milarrochy Stirl 68 A3
Milborne Port Som 8 C5
Milborne St Andrew Dorset 9 E7
Milborne Wick Som 8 B5
Milbourne Northumb 63 F7
Milburn Cumb 57 D8
Milbury Heath S Glos 16 B3
Milcombe Oxon 27 E11
Milden Suff 30 D6
Mildenhall Suff 30 A4
Mildenhall Wilts 17 E9
Mile Cross Norf 39 D8
Mile Elm Wilts 16 E6
Mile End Essex 30 F6
Mile End Glos 26 G2
Mile Oak Brighton 11 D11
Milebrook Powys 25 A10
Milebush Kent 20 G4
Mileham Norf 38 D5
Milesmark Fife 69 B9
Milfield Northumb 71 G8
Milford Derbys 45 H7
Milford Devon 6 D1
Milford Powys 33 F6
Milford Staffs 34 C5
Milford Sur 18 G6
Milford Wilts 9 B10
Milford Haven = Aberdaugleddau Pembs 22 F4
Milford on Sea Hants 10 E1
Milkwall Glos 26 H2
Milkwell Wilts 9 B8
Mill Bank W Yorks 50 G6
Mill Common Suff 39 G10
Mill End Bucks 18 C4
Mill End Herts 29 E10
Mill Green Essex 20 A3
Mill Green Norf 39 G7
Mill Green Suff 30 D6
Mill Hill London 19 B9
Mill Lane Hants 18 F4
Mill of Kingoodie Aberds 89 F8
Mill of Muiresk Aberds 89 D6
Mill of Sterin Aberds 82 D5
Mill of Uras Aberds 83 E10
Mill Place N Lincs 46 B3
Mill Side Cumb 49 A4
Mill Street Norf 39 D6
Milland W Sus 11 B7
Millarston Renfs 68 D3
Millbank Aberds 89 D11
Millbank Highld 94 D3
Millbeck Cumb 56 D4
Millbounds Orkney 95 E6
Millbreck Aberds 89 D10
Millbridge Sur 18 G5
Millbrook Beds 29 E7
Millbrook Corn 4 F5
Millbrook Soton 10 C2
Millburn S Ayrs 67 D7
Millcombe Devon 5 G9
Millcorner E Sus 13 D7
Milldale Staffs 44 G5
Millden Lodge Angus 83 F7
Milldens Angus 77 B8
Millerhill Midloth 70 D2
Miller's Dale Derbys 44 E5
Miller's Green Derbys 44 G6
Millgreen Shrops 34 C2
Millhalf Hereford 25 D9
Millhayes Devon 7 F11
Millhead Lancs 49 B4
Millheugh S Lnrk 68 E6
Millholme Cumb 57 G7
Millhouse Argyll 73 F8
Millhouse Cumb 56 C5
Millhouse Green S Yorks 44 B6
Millhousebridge Dumfries 61 E7
Millhouses S Yorks 45 D7
Millikenpark Renfs 68 D3
Millin Cross Pembs 22 E4
Millington E Yorks 52 D4
Millmeece Staffs 34 B4
Millom Cumb 49 A1
Millook Corn 4 B2
Millpool Corn 4 D2
Millport N Ayrs 66 A4
Millquarter Dumfries 55 A9
Millthorpe Lincs 37 B7
Millthrop Cumb 57 G8
Milltimber Aberdeen 83 C10
Milltown Corn 4 F2
Milltown Derbys 45 F7
Milltown Devon 6 C4
Milltown Dumfries 61 F9
Milltown of Aberdalgie Perth 76 E3
Milltown of Auchindoun Moray 88 D3
Milltown of Craigston Aberds 89 C7
Milltown of Edinvillie Moray 88 D2
Milltown of Kildrummy Aberds 82 B6
Milltown of Rothiemay Moray 88 D5
Milltown of Towie Aberds 82 B6
Milnathort Perth 76 G4
Milner's Heath Ches 43 F7
Milngavie E Dunb 68 C4
Milnrow Gtr Man 44 A3
Milnshaw Lancs 50 G3
Milnthorpe Cumb 49 A4
Milo Carms 23 E10
Milson Shrops 26 A3
Milstead Kent 20 F6
Milston Wilts 17 G8
Milton Angus 76 C6
Milton Cambs 29 B11
Milton Cumb 61 G11
Milton Derbys 35 C9
Milton Dumfries 54 D5
Milton Dumfries 60 F4
Milton Dumfries 60 E4
Milton Highld 86 F6
Milton Highld 86 H7
Milton Highld 87 G8
Milton Highld 94 E5
Milton Highld 87 D10
Milton Moray 88 B5
Milton Notts 45 E11
Milton N Som 15 E9
Milton Oxon 27 E11
Milton Oxon 17 B11
Milton Pembs 22 F5
Milton Perth 76 F2
Milton Ptsmth 10 E5
Milton Stirl 75 G8
Milton Stoke 44 G3
Milton W Dunb 68 C3
Milton Abbas Dorset 9 D7
Milton Abbot Devon 4 D5
Milton Bridge Midloth 69 D11
Milton Bryan Beds 28 E6
Milton Clevedon Som 16 H3
Milton Coldwells Aberds 89 E9
Milton Combe Devon 4 E5
Milton Damerel Devon 6 E2
Milton End Glos 17 A8
Milton Ernest Beds 29 C7
Milton Green Ches 43 G7
Milton Hill Oxon 17 B11
Milton Keynes M Keynes 28 E5
Milton Keynes Village M Keynes 28 E5
Milton Lilbourne Wilts 17 E8
Milton Malsor Northants 28 C4
Milton Morenish Perth 75 D9
Milton of Auchinhove Aberds 83 C7
Milton of Balgonie Fife 76 G6
Milton of Buchanan Stirl 68 A3
Milton of Campfield Aberds 83 C8
Milton of Campsie E Dunb 68 C5
Milton of Corsindae Aberds 83 C8
Milton of Cushnie Aberds 83 B7
Milton of Dalcapon Perth 76 B2
Milton of Edradour Perth 76 B2
Milton of Gollanfield Highld 87 F10
Milton of Lesmore Aberds 82 A6
Milton of Logie Aberds 82 C6
Milton of Murtle Aberdeen 83 C10
Milton of Noth Aberds 83 A7
Milton of Tullich Aberds 82 D5
Milton on Stour Dorset 9 B6
Milton Regis Kent 20 E6
Milton under Wychwood Oxon 27 G9
Miltonduff Moray 88 B1
Miltonhill Moray 87 E13
Miltonise Dumfries 54 B4
Milverton Som 7 D10
Milverton Warks 27 B10
Milwich Staffs 34 B5
Minard Argyll 73 D8
Minchinhampton Glos 16 A5
Mindrum Northumb 71 G7
Minehead Som 7 B8
Minera Wrex 42 G5
Minety Wilts 17 B7
Minffordd Gwyn 41 G7
Minffordd Gwyn 32 D3
Minffordd Gwyn 41 C7
Miningsby Lincs 47 F7
Minions Corn 4 D3
Minishant S Ayrs 66 E6
Minllyn Gwyn 32 D4
Minnes Aberds 89 F9
Minngearraidh W Isles 84 F2
Minnigaff Dumfries 55 C7
Minnonie Aberds 89 B7
Minskip N Yorks 51 C9
Minstead Hants 10 C1
Minsted W Sus 11 B7
Minster Kent 20 D6
Minster Kent 21 E10
Minster Lovell Oxon 27 G10
Minsterley Shrops 33 E9
Minsterworth Glos 26 G4
Minterne Magna Dorset 8 D5
Minting Lincs 46 E5
Mintlaw Aberds 89 D10
Minto Borders 61 A11
Minton Shrops 33 F10
Minwear Pembs 22 E5
Minworth W Mid 35 F7
Mirbister Orkney 95 F4
Mirehouse Cumb 56 E1
Mireland Highld 94 D5
Mirfield W Yorks 51 H8
Miserden Glos 26 H6
Miskin Rhondda 14 C6
Misson Notts 45 C10
Misterton Leics 36 G1
Misterton Notts 45 C11
Misterton Som 8 D3
Mistley Essex 31 E8
Mitcham London 19 E9
Mitchel Troy Mon 25 G11
Mitcheldean Glos 26 G3
Mitchell Corn 3 D7
Mitcheltroy Common Mon 25 H11
Mitford Northumb 63 E7
Mithian Corn 2 D6
Mitton Staffs 34 D4
Mixbury Oxon 28 E3
Moat Cumb 61 F10
Moats Tye Suff 31 C7
Mobberley Ches 44 E2
Mobberley Staffs 34 A6
Moccas Hereford 25 D10
Mochdre Conwy 41 C10
Mochdre Powys 33 G6
Mochrum Dumfries 54 E6
Mockbeggar Hants 9 D10
Mockerkin Cumb 56 D2
Modbury Devon 5 F7
Moddershall Staffs 34 B5
Moelfre Anglesey 41 B7
Moelfre Powys 33 C7
Moffat Dumfries 60 C6
Moggerhanger Beds 29 D8
Moira Leics 35 D9
Mol-chlach Highld 85 G9
Molash Kent 21 F7
Mold = Yr Wyddgrug Flint 42 F5
Moldgreen W Yorks 51 H7
Molehill Green Essex 30 F2
Molescroft E Yorks 52 E6
Molesden Northumb 63 E7
Molesworth Cambs 37 H6
Moll Highld 85 E10
Molland Devon 7 D7
Mollington Ches 43 E6
Mollington Oxon 27 D11
Mollinsburn N Lnrk 68 C6
Monachty Ceredig 24 B2
Monachylemore Stirl 75 F7
Monar Lodge Highld 86 G5
Monaughty Powys 25 B9
Monboddo House Aberds 83 F9
Mondynes Aberds 83 F9
Monevechadan Argyll 74 G4
Monewden Suff 31 C9
Moneydie Perth 76 E3
Moniaive Dumfries 60 D3
Monifieth Angus 77 D7
Monikie Angus 77 D7
Monimail Fife 76 F5
Monington Pembs 22 B6
Monk Bretton S Yorks 45 B7
Monk Fryston N Yorks 51 G11
Monk Sherborne Hants 18 F3
Monk Soham Suff 31 B9
Monk Street Essex 30 F3
Monken Hadley London 19 B9
Monkhopton Shrops 34 F2
Monkland Hereford 25 C11
Monkleigh Devon 6 D3
Monknash V Glam 14 D5
Monkokehampton Devon 6 F4
Monks Eleigh Suff 30 D6
Monk's Gate W Sus 11 B11
Monks Heath Ches 44 E2
Monks Kirby Warks 35 G10
Monks Risborough Bucks 18 A5
Monkseaton T & W 63 F9
Monkshill Aberds 89 D7
Monksilver Som 7 C9
Monkspath W Mid 35 H7
Monkswood Mon 15 A9
Monkton Devon 7 F10
Monkton Kent 21 E9
Monkton Pembs 22 F4
Monkton S Ayrs 67 D6
Monkton Combe Bath 16 E4
Monkton Deverill Wilts 16 H5
Monkton Farleigh Wilts 16 E5
Monkton Heathfield Som 8 B1
Monkton Up Wimborne Dorset 9 C9
Monkwearmouth T & W 63 H9
Monkwood Hants 10 A5
Monmouth = Trefynwy Mon 26 G2
Monmouth Cap Mon 25 F10
Monnington on Wye Hereford 25 D10
Monreith Dumfries 54 E6
Monreith Mains Dumfries 54 E6
Mont Saint Guern 11
Montacute Som 8 C3
Montcoffer Ho. Aberds 89 B6
Montford Argyll 73 G10
Montford Shrops 33 D10
Montford Bridge Shrops 33 D10
Montgarrie Aberds 83 B7
Montgomery = Trefaldwyn Powys 33 F8
Montrave Fife 76 G6
Montrose Angus 77 B10
Montsale Essex 21 B7
Monxton Hants 17 G10
Monyash Derbys 44 F5
Monymusk Aberds 83 B8
Monzie Perth 75 E11
Monzie Castle Perth 75 E11
Moodiesburn N Lnrk 68 C5
Moonzie Fife 76 F6
Moor Allerton W Yorks 51 F8
Moor Crichel Dorset 9 D8
Moor End E Yorks 52 F4
Moor End York 52 D2
Moor Monkton N Yorks 51 D11
Moor of Granary Moray 87 F13
Moor of Ravenstone Dumfries 54 E6
Moor Row Cumb 56 E2
Moor Street Kent 20 E5
Moorby Lincs 46 F6
Moordown Bmouth 9 E9
Moore Halton 43 D8
Moorend Glos 16 A4
Moorends S Yorks 52 H2
Moorgate S Yorks 45 C8
Moorgreen Notts 45 H8
Moorhall Derbys 45 E7
Moorhampton Hereford 25 D10
Moorhead W Yorks 51 F7
Moorhouse Cumb 61 H9
Moorhouse Notts 45 F11
Moorlinch Som 15 H9
Moorsholm Redcar 59 E7
Moorside Gtr Man 44 B3
Moorthorpe W Yorks 45 A8
Moortown Hants 9 D10
Moortown I o W 10 F3
Moortown Lincs 46 C4
Morangie Highld 87 C10
Morar Highld 79 B9
Morborne Cambs 37 F7
Morchard Bishop Devon 7 F6
Morcombelake Dorset 8 E3
Morcott Rutland 36 E5
Morda Shrops 33 C8
Morden Dorset 9 E8
Morden London 19 E9
Mordiford Hereford 26 E2
Mordon Durham 58 D4
More Shrops 33 F9
Morebath Devon 7 D8
Morebattle Borders 62 A3
Morecambe Lancs 49 C4
Morefield Highld 86 B4
Moreleigh Devon 5 F8
Morenish Perth 75 D8
Moresby Cumb 56 D1
Moresby Parks Cumb 56 E1
Morestead Hants 10 B4
Moreton Dorset 9 F7
Moreton Essex 30 H2
Moreton Mers 42 C5
Moreton Oxon 18 A3
Moreton Staffs 34 D3
Moreton Corbet Shrops 34 C1
Moreton-in-Marsh Glos 27 E9
Moreton Jeffries Hereford 26 D3
Moreton Morrell Warks 27 C10
Moreton on Lugg Hereford 26 D2
Moreton Pinkney Northants 28 D2
Moreton Say Shrops 34 B2
Moreton Valence Glos 26 H4
Moretonhampstead Devon 5 C8
Morfa Carms 23 E10
Morfa Carms 23 G10
Morfa Bach Carms 23 E8
Morfa Bychan Gwyn 41 G7
Morfa Dinlle Gwyn 40 E6
Morfa Glas Neath 24 H5
Morfa Nefyn Gwyn 40 F4
Morfydd Denb 42 H4
Morgan's Vale Wilts 9 B10
Moriah Ceredig 32 H2
Morland Cumb 57 D7
Morley Derbys 35 A9
Morley Durham 58 D2
Morley W Yorks 51 G8
Morley Green Ches 44 D2
Morley St Botolph Norf 39 F6
Morningside Edin 69 C11
Morningside N Lnrk 69 E7
Morningthorpe Norf 39 F8
Morpeth Northumb 63 E8
Morphie Aberds 77 A10
Morrey Staffs 35 D7
Morris Green Essex 30 E4
Morriston Swansea 14 B2
Morston Norf 38 A6
Mortehoe Devon 6 B3
Mortimer W Berks 18 E3
Mortimer West End Hants 18 E3
Mortimer's Cross Hereford 25 B11
Mortlake London 19 D9
Morton Cumb 56 A5
Morton Derbys 45 F8
Morton Lincs 37 C6
Morton Lincs 46 C2
Morton Lincs 46 F2
Morton Norf 39 D7
Morton Notts 45 G11
Morton Shrops 33 C8
Morton S Glos 16 B3
Morton Bagot Warks 27 B8
Morton-on-Swale N Yorks 58 G4
Morvah Corn 2 F3
Morval Corn 4 F3
Morvich Highld 80 A1
Morvich Highld 93 J10
Morville Shrops 34 F2
Morville Heath Shrops 34 F2
Morwenstow Corn 6 E1
Mosborough S Yorks 45 D8
Moscow E Ayrs 67 B7
Mosedale Cumb 56 C5
Moseley W Mid 35 G6
Moseley W Mid 34 F5
Moseley Worcs 26 C5
Moss Argyll 78 G2
Moss Highld 79 E9
Moss S Yorks 45 A9
Moss Wrex 42 G6
Moss Bank Mers 43 C8
Moss Edge Lancs 49 E4
Moss End Brack 18 D5
Moss of Barmuckity Moray 88 B2
Moss Pit Staffs 34 C5
Moss-side Highld 87 F11
Moss Side Lancs 49 F3
Mossat Aberds 82 B6
Mossbank Shetland 96 F6
Mossbay Cumb 56 D1
Mossblown S Ayrs 67 D7
Mossbrow Gtr Man 43 D10
Mossburnford Borders 62 B2
Mossdale Dumfries 55 B9
Mossend N Lnrk 68 D6
Mosser Cumb 56 D3
Mossfield Highld 87 D9
Mossgiel E Ayrs 67 D7
Mossiende Angus 77 B7
Mossley Ches 44 F2
Mossley Gtr Man 44 B3
Mossley Hill Mers 43 D6
Mosstodloch Moray 88 C3
Mosston Angus 77 C8
Mossy Lea Lancs 43 A8
Mosterton Dorset 8 D3
Moston Gtr Man 44 B2
Moston Shrops 34 C1
Moston Green Ches 43 F10
Mostyn Flint 42 D4
Mostyn Quay Flint 42 D4
Motcombe Dorset 9 B7
Mothecombe Devon 5 G7
Motherby Cumb 56 D6
Motherwell N Lnrk 68 E6
Mottingham London 19 D11
Mottisfont Hants 10 B2
Mottistone I o W 10 F3
Mottram in Longdendale Gtr Man 44 C3
Mottram St Andrew Ches 44 E2
Mouilpied Guern 11
Mouldsworth Ches 43 E8
Moulin Perth 76 B2
Moulsecoomb Brighton 12 F2
Moulsford Oxon 18 C2
Moulsoe M Keynes 28 D6
Moulton Ches 43 F9
Moulton Lincs 37 C9
Moulton Northants 28 B4
Moulton N Yorks 58 F3
Moulton Suff 30 B3
Moulton V Glam 14 D6
Moulton Chapel Lincs 37 D8
Moulton Eaugate Lincs 37 D9
Moulton St Mary Norf 39 E9
Moulton Seas End Lincs 37 C9
Mounie Castle Aberds 83 A9
Mount Corn 3 D6
Mount Corn 4 E2
Mount Highld 87 G12
Mount Bures Essex 30 E6
Mount Canisp Highld 87 D10
Mount Hawke Corn 2 E6
Mount Pleasant Ches 44 G2
Mount Pleasant Derbys 45 H7
Mount Pleasant Derbys 35 D8
Mount Pleasant Flint 42 E5
Mount Pleasant Hants 10 E1
Mount Pleasant W Yorks 51 G8
Mount Sorrel Wilts 9 B9
Mount Tabor W Yorks 51 G6
Mountain W Yorks 51 F6
Mountain Ash = Aberpennar Rhondda 14 B6
Mountain Cross Borders 69 F10
Mountain Water Pembs 22 D4
Mountbenger Borders 70 H2
Mountfield E Sus 12 D6
Mountgerald Highld 87 E8
Mountjoy Corn 3 C7
Mountnessing Essex 20 B3
Mounton Mon 15 B11
Mountsorrel Leics 36 D1
Mousehole Corn 2 G3
Mousen Northumb 71 G10
Mouswald Dumfries 60 F6
Mow Cop Ches 44 G2
Mowhaugh Borders 62 A4
Mowsley Leics 36 G2
Moxley W Mid 34 F5
Moy Highld 80 E6
Moy Highld 87 H10
Moy Hall Highld 87 H10
Moy Ho. Moray 87 E13
Moy Lodge Highld 80 E6
Moyles Court Hants 9 D10
Moylgrove Pembs 22 B6
Muasdale Argyll 65 D7
Much Birch Hereford 26 E2
Much Cowarne Hereford 26 D3
Much Dewchurch Hereford 25 E11
Much Hadham Herts 29 G11
Much Hoole Lancs 49 G4
Much Marcle Hereford 26 E3
Much Wenlock Shrops 34 E2
Muchalls Aberds 83 D11
Muchelney Som 8 B3
Muchlarnick Corn 4 F3
Muchrachd Highld 86 H5
Muckernich Highld 87 F8
Mucking Thurrock 20 C3
Muckleford Dorset 8 E5
Mucklestone Staffs 34 B3
Muckleton Shrops 34 C1
Muckletown Aberds 83 A7
Muckley Corner Staffs 35 E6
Muckton Lincs 47 D7
Mudale Highld 93 F8
Muddiford Devon 6 C4
Mudeford Dorset 9 E10
Mudford Som 8 C4
Mudgley Som 15 G10
Mugdock Stirl 68 C4
Mugeary Highld 85 E9
Mugginton Derbys 35 A8
Muggleswick Durham 58 B1
Muie Highld 93 J9
Muir Aberds 82 E2
Muir of Fairburn Highld 86 F7
Muir of Fowlis Aberds 83 B7
Muir of Ord Highld 87 F8
Muir of Pert Angus 77 D7
Muirden Aberds 89 C7
Muirdrum Angus 77 D8
Muirhead Angus 76 D6
Muirhead Fife 76 G5
Muirhead N Lnrk 68 D5
Muirhead S Ayrs 66 C6
Muirhouselaw Borders 70 H5
Muirhouses Falk 69 B9
Muirkirk E Ayrs 68 H5
Muirmill Stirl 68 B6
Muirshearlich Highld 80 E3
Muirskie Aberds 83 D10
Muirtack Aberds 89 E9
Muirton Highld 87 E10
Muirton Perth 76 E4
Muirton Perth 76 F2
Muirton Mains Highld 86 F7
Muirton of Ardblair Perth 76 C4
Muirton of Ballochy Angus 77 A9
Muiryfold Aberds 89 C7
Muker N Yorks 57 G11
Mulbarton Norf 39 E7
Mulben Moray 88 C3
Mulindry Argyll 64 C4
Mullardoch House Highld 86 H5
Mullion Corn 2 H5
Mullion Cove Corn 2 H5
Mumby Lincs 47 E9
Munderfield Row Hereford 26 C3
Munderfield Stocks Hereford 26 C3
Mundesley Norf 39 B9
Mundford Norf 38 F4
Mundham Norf 39 F9
Mundon Essex 20 A5
Mundurno Aberdeen 83 B11
Munerigie Highld 80 C4
Muness Shetland 96 C8
Mungasdale Highld 86 B2
Mungrisdale Cumb 56 C5
Munlochy Highld 87 F9
Munsley Hereford 26 D3
Munslow Shrops 33 G11
Murchington Devon 5 C7
Murcott Oxon 28 G2
Murkle Highld 94 D3
Murlaggan Highld 80 D2
Murlaggan Highld 80 E5
Murra Orkney 95 H3
Murrayfield Edin 69 C11
Murrow Cambs 37 E9
Mursley Bucks 28 F5
Murthill Angus 77 B7
Murthly Perth 76 D3
Murton Cumb 57 D9
Murton Durham 58 B4
Murton Northumb 71 F8
Murton York 52 D2
Musbury Devon 8 E1
Muscoates N Yorks 52 A2
Musdale Argyll 74 E2
Musselburgh E Loth 70 C2
Muston Leics 36 B4
Muston N Yorks 53 B6
Mustow Green Worcs 26 A5
Mutehill Dumfries 55 E9
Mutford Suff 39 G10
Muthill Perth 75 F11
Mutterton Devon 7 F9
Muxton Telford 34 D3
Mybster Highld 94 E3
Myddfai Carms 24 F4
Myddle Shrops 33 C10
Mydroilyn Ceredig 23 A9
Myerscough Lancs 49 F4
Mylor Bridge Corn 3 F7
Mynachlog-ddu Pembs 22 C6
Myndtown Shrops 33 G9
Mynydd Bach Ceredig 32 H3
Mynydd-bach Mon 15 B10
Mynydd Bodafon Anglesey 40 B6
Mynydd-isa Flint 42 F5
Mynyddygarreg Carms 23 F9
Mynytho Gwyn 40 G5
Myrebird Aberds 83 D9
Myrelandhorn Highld 94 E4
Myreside Perth 76 E5
Myrtle Hill Carms 24 E4
Mytchett Sur 18 F5
Mytholm W Yorks 50 G5
Mytholmroyd W Yorks 50 G6
Myton-on-Swale N Yorks 51 C10
Mytton Shrops 33 D10

N

Na Gearrannan W Isles 90 C6
Naast Highld 91 J13
Naburn York 52 E1
Nackington Kent 21 F8
Nacton Suff 31 D9
Nafferton E Yorks 53 D6
Nailbridge Glos 26 G3
Nailsbourne Som 7 D11
Nailsea N Som 15 D10
Nailstone Leics 35 E10
Nailsworth Glos 16 B5
Nairn Highld 87 F11
Nalderswood Sur 19 G9
Nancegollan Corn 2 F5
Nancledra Corn 2 F3
Nanhoron Gwyn 40 G4
Nannau Gwyn 32 C3
Nannerch Flint 42 F4
Nanpantan Leics 35 D11
Nanpean Corn 3 D8
Nanstallon Corn 3 C9
Nant-ddu Powys 25 G7

Nant-glas Powys 24 B6
Nant Peris Gwyn 41 E8
Nant Uchaf Denb 42 G3
Nant-y-Bai Carms 24 D4
Nant-y-cafn Neath 24 H5
Nant-y-derry Mon 25 H10
Nant-y-ffin Carms 23 C10
Nant-y-moel Bridgend 14 B5
Nant-y-pandy Conwy 41 C8
Nanternis Ceredig 23 A8
Nantgaredig Carms 23 D9
Nantgarw Rhondda 15 C7
Nantglyn Denb 42 F3
Nantgwyn Powys 32 H5
Nantlle Gwyn 41 E7
Nantmawr Shrops 33 C8
Nantmel Powys 25 B7
Nantmor Gwyn 41 F8
Nantwich Ches 43 G9
Nantycaws Carms 23 E9
Nantyffyllon Bridgend 14 B4
Nantyglo Bl Gwent 25 G8
Naphill Bucks 18 B5
Nappa N Yorks 50 D4
Napton on the Hill Warks 27 B11
Narberth = Arberth Pembs 22 E6
Narborough Leics 35 F11
Narborough Norf 38 D3
Nasareth Gwyn 40 E6
Naseby Northants 36 H2
Nash Bucks 28 E4
Nash Hereford 25 B10
Nash Newport 15 C9
Nash Shrops 26 A3
Nash Lee Bucks 28 H5
Nassington Northants 37 F6
Nasty Herts 29 F10
Nateby Cumb 57 F9
Nateby Lancs 49 E4
Natland Cumb 57 H7
Naughton Suff 31 D7
Naunton Glos 27 F8
Naunton Worcs 26 E5
Naunton Beauchamp Worcs 26 C6
Navenby Lincs 46 G3
Navestock Heath Essex 20 B2
Navestock Side Essex 20 B2
Navidale Highld 93 H13
Nawton N Yorks 52 A2
Nayland Suff 30 E6
Nazeing Essex 29 H11
Neacroft Hants 9 E10
Neal's Green Warks 35 G9
Neap Shetland 96 H7
Near Sawrey Cumb 56 G5
Neasham Darl 58 E4
Neath = Castell-Nedd Neath 14 B3
Neath Abbey Neath 14 B3
Neatishead Norf 39 C9
Nebo Anglesey 40 A6
Nebo Ceredig 24 B2
Nebo Conwy 41 E10
Nebo Gwyn 40 E6
Necton Norf 38 E4
Nedd Highld 92 F4
Nedderton Northumb 63 E8
Nedging Tye Suff 31 D7
Needham Norf 39 G8
Needham Market Suff 31 C7
Needingworth Cambs 29 A10
Needwood Staffs 35 C7
Neen Savage Shrops 34 H2
Neen Sollars Shrops 26 A3
Neenton Shrops 34 G2
Nefyn Gwyn 40 F5
Neilston E Renf 68 E3
Neinthirion Powys 32 E5
Neithrop Oxon 27 D11
Nelly Andrews Green Powys 33 E8
Nelson Caerph 15 B7
Nelson Lancs 50 F4
Nelson Village Northumb 63 F8
Nemphlar S Lnrk 69 F7
Nempnett Thrubwell Bath 15 E11
Nene Terrace Lincs 37 E8
Nenthall Cumb 57 B9
Nenthead Cumb 57 B9
Nenthorn Borders 70 G5
Nerabus Argyll 64 C3
Nercwys Flint 42 F5
Nerston S Lnrk 68 E5
Nesbit Northumb 71 G8
Ness Ches 42 E6
Nesscliffe Shrops 33 D9
Neston Ches 42 E5
Neston Wilts 16 E5
Nether Alderley Ches 44 E2
Nether Blainslie Borders 70 F4
Nether Booth Derbys 44 D5
Nether Broughton Leics 36 C2
Nether Burrow Lancs 50 B2
Nether Cerne Dorset 8 E5
Nether Compton Dorset 8 C4
Nether Crimond Aberds 89 F8
Nether Dalgliesh Borders 61 C8
Nether Dallachy Moray 88 B3
Nether Exe Devon 7 F8
Nether Glasslaw Aberds 89 C8
Nether Handwick Angus 76 C6
Nether Haugh S Yorks 45 C8
Nether Heage Derbys 45 G7
Nether Heyford Northants 28 C3
Nether Hindhope Borders 62 B3
Nether Howecleuch S Lnrk 60 B6
Nether Kellet Lancs 49 C5
Nether Kinmundy Aberds 89 D10
Nether Langwith Notts 45 E9
Nether Leask Aberds 89 E10
Nether Lenshie Aberds 89 D6
Nether Monynut Borders 70 D6
Nether Padley Derbys 44 E6
Nether Park Aberds 89 C10
Nether Poppleton York 52 D1
Nether Silton N Yorks 58 G5
Nether Stowey Som 7 C10
Nether Urquhart Fife 76 G4
Nether Wallop Hants 17 H10
Nether Wasdale Cumb 56 F3
Nether Whitacre Warks 35 F8
Nether Worton Oxon 27 E11
Netheravon Wilts 17 G8
Netherbrae Aberds 89 C7
Netherbrough Orkney 95 G4
Netherburn S Lnrk 69 F7
Netherbury Dorset 8 E3
Netherby Cumb 61 F9
Netherby N Yorks 51 E9
Nethercote Warks 28 B2
Nethercott Devon 6 C3
Netherend Glos 16 A2
Netherfield E Sus 12 E6
Netherhampton Wilts 9 B10
Netherlaw Dumfries 55 E10
Netherley Aberds 83 D10
Netherley Mers 43 D7
Nethermill Dumfries 60 E6
Nethermuir Aberds 89 D9
Netherplace E Renf 68 E4
Netherseal Derbys 35 D8
Netherthird E Ayrs 67 E8
Netherthong W Yorks 44 B5
Netherthorpe S Yorks 45 D9
Netherton Angus 77 B8
Netherton Devon 5 D9
Netherton Hants 17 F10
Netherton Mers 42 B6
Netherton Northumb 62 C5
Netherton Oxon 17 B11
Netherton Perth 76 B4
Netherton Stirl 68 C4
Netherton W Mid 34 G5
Netherton Worcs 26 D6
Netherton W Yorks 44 A5
Netherton W Yorks 51 H8
Nethertown Cumb 56 F1
Nethertown Highld 94 C5
Netherwitton Northumb 63 D7
Netherwood E Ayrs 68 H5
Nethy Bridge Highld 82 A2
Netley Hants 10 D3
Netley Marsh Hants 10 C2
Netteswell Essex 29 G11
Nettlebed Oxon 18 C4
Nettlebridge Som 16 G3
Nettlecombe Dorset 8 E4
Nettleden Herts 29 G7
Nettleham Lincs 46 E4
Nettlestead Kent 20 F3
Nettlestead Green Kent 20 F3
Nettlestone I o W 10 E5
Nettlesworth Durham 58 B3
Nettleton Lincs 46 B5
Nettleton Wilts 16 D5
Neuadd Carms 24 F3
Nevendon Essex 20 B4
Nevern Pembs 22 B5
New Abbey Dumfries 60 G5
New Aberdour Aberds 89 B8
New Addington London 19 E10
New Alresford Hants 10 A4
New Alyth Perth 76 C5
New Arley Warks 35 G8
New Ash Green Kent 20 E3
New Barn Kent 20 E3
New Barnetby N Lincs 46 A4
New Barton Northants 28 B5
New Bewick Northumb 62 A6
New-bigging Angus 77 D8
New Bilton Warks 35 H10
New Bolingbroke Lincs 47 G7
New Boultham Lincs 46 E3
New Bradwell M Keynes 28 D5
New Brancepeth Durham 58 B3
New Bridge Wrex 33 A8
New Brighton Flint 42 F5
New Brighton Mers 42 C6
New Brinsley Notts 45 G8
New Broughton Wrex 42 G6
New Buckenham Norf 39 F6
New Byth Aberds 89 C8
New Catton Norf 39 D8
New Cheriton Hants 10 B4
New Costessey Norf 39 D7
New Cowper Cumb 56 B3
New Cross Ceredig 32 H2
New Cross London 19 D10
New Cumnock E Ayrs 67 E9
New Deer Aberds 89 D8
New Delaval Northumb 63 F8
New Duston Northants 28 B4
New Earswick York 52 D2
New Edlington S Yorks 45 C9
New Elgin Moray 88 B2
New Ellerby E Yorks 53 F7
New Eltham London 19 D11
New End Worcs 27 C7
New Farnley W Yorks 51 F8
New Ferry Mers 42 D6
New Fryston W Yorks 51 G10
New Galloway Dumfries 55 B9
New Gilston Fife 77 G7
New Grimsby Scilly 2 C2
New Hainford Norf 39 D8
New Hartley Northumb 63 F9
New Haw Sur 19 E7
New Hedges Pembs 22 F6
New Herrington T & W 58 A4
New Hinksey Oxon 18 A2
New Holkham Norf 38 B4
New Holland N Lincs 53 G6
New Houghton Derbys 45 F8
New Houghton Norf 38 C3
New Houses N Yorks 50 B4
New Humberstone Leicester 36 E2
New Hutton Cumb 57 G7
New Hythe Kent 20 F4
New Inn Carms 23 C9
New Inn Mon 15 A10
New Inn Pembs 22 C5
New Inn Torf 15 B9
New Invention Shrops 33 H8
New Invention W Mid 34 E5
New Kelso Highld 86 G2
New Kingston Notts 35 C11
New Lanark S Lnrk 69 F7
New Lane Lancs 43 A7
New Lane End Warr 43 C9
New Leake Lincs 47 G8
New Leeds Aberds 89 C9
New Longton Lancs 49 G5
New Luce Dumfries 54 C4
New Malden London 19 E9
New Marske Redcar 59 D7
New Marton Shrops 33 B9
New Micklefield W Yorks 51 F10
New Mill Aberds 83 E9
New Mill Herts 28 G6
New Mill Wilts 17 E8
New Mill W Yorks 44 B5
New Mills Ches 43 D10
New Mills Corn 3 D7
New Mills Derbys 44 D3
New Mills Powys 33 E6
New Milton Hants 9 E11
New Moat Pembs 22 D5
New Ollerton Notts 45 F10
New Oscott W Mid 35 F6
New Park N Yorks 51 D8
New Pitsligo Aberds 89 C8
New Polzeath Corn 3 B8
New Quay = Ceinewydd Ceredig 23 A8
New Rackheath Norf 39 D8
New Radnor Powys 25 B9
New Rent Cumb 56 C6
New Ridley Northumb 62 H6
New Road Side N Yorks 50 E5
New Romney Kent 13 D9
New Rossington S Yorks 45 C10
New Row Ceredig 24 A4
New Row Lancs 50 F2
New Row N Yorks 59 E7
New Sarum Wilts 9 A10
New Silksworth T & W 58 A4
New Stevenston N Lnrk 68 E6
New Street Staffs 44 G4
New Street Lane Shrops 34 B2
New Swanage Dorset 9 F9
New Totley S Yorks 45 E7
New Town E Loth 70 C3
New Tredegar = Tredegar Newydd Caerph 15 A7
New Trows S Lnrk 69 G7
New Ulva Argyll 72 E6
New Walsoken Cambs 37 E10
New Waltham NE Lincs 46 B6
New Whittington Derbys 45 E7
New Wimpole Cambs 29 D10
New Winton E Loth 70 C3
New Yatt Oxon 27 G10
New York Lincs 46 G6
New York N Yorks 51 C7
Newall W Yorks 51 E7
Newark Orkney 95 D8
Newark P'boro 37 E8
Newark-on-Trent Notts 45 G11
Newarthill N Lnrk 68 E6
Newbarns Cumb 49 B2
Newbattle Midloth 70 D2
Newbiggin Cumb 56 G2
Newbiggin Cumb 49 C2
Newbiggin Cumb 56 D6
Newbiggin Cumb 57 B7
Newbiggin Cumb 57 D8
Newbiggin Durham 57 D11
Newbiggin N Yorks 57 G11
Newbiggin N Yorks 57 H11
Newbiggin-by-the-Sea Northumb 63 E9
Newbiggin-on-Lune Cumb 57 F9
Newbigging Angus 77 D7
Newbigging Angus 77 D7
Newbigging S Lnrk 69 F9
Newbold Derbys 45 E7
Newbold Leics 35 D10
Newbold on Avon Warks 35 H10
Newbold on Stour Warks 27 D9
Newbold Pacey Warks 27 C9
Newbold Verdon Leics 35 E10
Newborough Anglesey 40 D6
Newborough P'boro 37 E8
Newborough Staffs 35 C7
Newbottle Northants 28 E2
Newbottle T & W 58 A4
Newbourne Suff 31 D9
Newbridge Caerph 15 B8
Newbridge Ceredig 23 A10
Newbridge Corn 2 F3
Newbridge Corn 4 E4
Newbridge Dumfries 60 F5
Newbridge Edin 69 C10
Newbridge Hants 10 C1
Newbridge I o W 10 F3
Newbridge Pembs 22 C4
Newbridge Green Worcs 26 E5
Newbridge-on-Usk Mon 15 B9
Newbridge on Wye Powys 25 C7
Newbrough Northumb 62 G4
Newbuildings Devon 7 F6
Newburgh Aberds 89 F9
Newburgh Aberds 89 C9
Newburgh Borders 61 B9
Newburgh Fife 76 F5
Newburgh Lancs 43 A7
Newburn T & W 63 G7
Newbury W Berks 17 E11
Newbury Park London 19 C11
Newby Cumb 57 D7
Newby Lancs 50 E4
Newby N Yorks 50 B3
Newby N Yorks 58 E6
Newby N Yorks 59 G11
Newby Bridge Cumb 56 H5
Newby East Cumb 61 H10
Newby West Cumb 56 A5
Newby Wiske N Yorks 58 H4
Newcastle Mon 25 G11
Newcastle Shrops 33 G8
Newcastle Emlyn = Castell Newydd Emlyn Carms 23 B8
Newcastle International Airport T & W 63 F7
Newcastle-under-Lyme Staffs 44 H2
Newcastle Upon Tyne T & W 63 G8
Newcastleton = Copshaw Holm Borders 61 E10
Newchapel Pembs 23 C7
Newchapel Powys 32 G5
Newchapel Staffs 44 G2
Newchapel Sur 12 B2
Newchurch Carms 23 D8
Newchurch I o W 10 F4
Newchurch Kent 13 C9
Newchurch Lancs 50 F4
Newchurch Mon 15 B10
Newchurch Powys 25 C9
Newchurch Staffs 35 C7
Newcott Devon 8 D1
Newcraighall Edin 70 C2
Newdigate Sur 19 G8
Newell Green Brack 18 D5
Newenden Kent 13 D7
Newent Glos 26 F4
Newerne Glos 16 A3
Newfield Durham 58 C3
Newfield Highld 87 D10
Newford Scilly 2 C3
Newfound Hants 18 F2
Newgale Pembs 22 D3
Newgate Norf 39 A6
Newgate Street Herts 19 A10
Newhall Ches 43 H9
Newhall Derbys 35 C8
Newhall House Highld 87 E9
Newhall Point Highld 87 E10
Newham Northumb 71 H10
Newham Hall Northumb 71 H10
Newhaven Derbys 44 G5
Newhaven Edin 69 C11
Newhaven E Sus 12 F3
Newhey Gtr Man 44 A3
Newholm N Yorks 59 E9
Newhouse N Lnrk 68 D6
Newick E Sus 12 D3
Newingreen Kent 13 C10
Newington Kent 20 E5
Newington Kent 21 H8
Newington Kent 21 E10
Newington Notts 45 C10
Newington Oxon 18 B3
Newington Shrops 33 G10
Newland Glos 26 H2
Newland Hull 53 F6
Newland N Yorks 52 G2
Newland Worcs 26 D4
Newlandrig Midloth 70 D2
Newlands Borders 61 D11
Newlands Highld 87 G10
Newlands Moray 88 C3
Newlands Northumb 62 H6
Newland's Corner Sur 19 G7
Newlands of Geise Highld 94 D2
Newlands of Tynet Moray 88 B3
Newlands Park Anglesey 40 B4
Newlandsmuir S Lnrk 68 E5
Newlot Orkney 95 G6
Newlyn Corn 2 G3
Newmachar Aberds 83 B10
Newmains N Lnrk 69 E7
Newmarket Suff 30 B3
Newmarket W Isles 91 D9
Newmill Borders 61 B10
Newmill Corn 2 F3
Newmill Moray 88 C4
Newmill of Inshewan Angus 77 A7
Newmills of Boyne Aberds 88 C5
Newmiln Perth 76 D4
Newmilns E Ayrs 67 C8
Newnham Cambs 29 C11
Newnham Glos 26 G3
Newnham Hants 18 F4
Newnham Herts 29 E9
Newnham Kent 20 F6
Newnham Northants 28 C2
Newnham Bridge Worcs 26 B3
Newpark Fife 77 F7
Newport Devon 6 C4
Newport E Yorks 52 F4
Newport Essex 30 E2
Newport Highld 94 H3
Newport I o W 10 F4
Newport Norf 39 D11
Newport Telford 34 D3
Newport = Casnewydd Newport 15 C9
Newport = Trefdraeth Pembs 22 C5
Newport-on-Tay Fife 77 E7
Newport Pagnell M Keynes 28 D5
Newpound Common W Sus 11 B9
Newquay Corn 3 C7
Newquay Airport Corn 3 C7
Newsbank Ches 44 F2
Newseat Aberds 89 E7
Newseat Aberds 89 D10
Newsham Northumb 63 F9
Newsham N Yorks 58 E2
Newsham N Yorks 51 A9
Newsholme E Yorks 52 G3
Newsholme Lancs 50 D4
Newsome W Yorks 44 A5
Newstead Borders 70 G4
Newstead Notts 45 G9
Newstead Northumb 71 H10
Newthorpe N Yorks 51 F10
Newton Argyll 73 D9
Newton Borders 62 A2
Newton Bridgend 14 D4
Newton Cambs 29 D11
Newton Cambs 37 D10
Newton Cardiff 15 D8
Newton Ches 43 G8
Newton Ches 43 F7
Newton Ches 43 E8
Newton Cumb 49 B2
Newton Derbys 45 G8
Newton Dorset 9 C6
Newton Dumfries 61 D7
Newton Dumfries 61 F8
Newton Gtr Man 44 C3
Newton Hereford 25 E10
Newton Hereford 26 C2
Newton Highld 87 E10
Newton Highld 92 F5
Newton Highld 94 F5
Newton Highld 87 G10
Newton Lancs 49 F4
Newton Lancs 50 B2
Newton Lancs 50 D2
Newton Lincs 50 B1
Newton Lincs 36 B6
Newton Moray 88 B1
Newton Norf 38 D4
Newton Notts 36 A2
Newton Northants 36 G4
Newton Northumb 62 G6
Newton Perth 75 D11
Newton S Lnrk 68 D5
Newton S Lnrk 69 G8
Newton Staffs 34 C6
Newton Suff 30 D6
Newton Swansea 14 C2
Newton S Yorks 45 B9
Newton Warks 35 H11
Newton Wilts 9 B11
Newton W Loth 69 C9
Newton Abbot Devon 5 D9
Newton Arlosh Cumb 61 H7
Newton Aycliffe Durham 58 D3
Newton Bewley Hrtlpl 58 D5
Newton Blossomville M Keynes 28 C6
Newton Bromswold Northants 28 B6
Newton Burgoland Leics 35 E9
Newton by Toft Lincs 46 D4
Newton Ferrers Devon 4 G6
Newton Flotman Norf 39 F8
Newton Hall Northumb 62 G6
Newton Harcourt Leics 36 F2
Newton Heath Gtr Man 44 B2
Newton Ho. Aberds 83 A8
Newton Kyme N Yorks 51 E10
Newton-le-Willows Mers 43 C8
Newton-le-Willows N Yorks 58 H3
Newton Longville Bucks 28 E5
Newton Mearns E Renf 68 E4
Newton Morrell N Yorks 58 F3
Newton Mulgrave N Yorks 59 E8
Newton of Ardtoe Highld 79 D9
Newton of Balcanquhal Perth 76 F4
Newton of Falkland Fife 76 G5
Newton on Ayr S Ayrs 66 D6
Newton on Ouse N Yorks 51 D11
Newton-on-Rawcliffe N Yorks 59 G9
Newton-on-the-Moor Northumb 63 C7
Newton on Trent Lincs 46 E2
Newton Park Argyll 73 G10
Newton Poppleford Devon 7 H9
Newton Purcell Oxon 28 E3
Newton Regis Warks 35 E8
Newton Reigny Cumb 57 C6
Newton St Cyres Devon 7 G7
Newton St Faith Norf 39 D8
Newton St Loe Bath 16 E4
Newton St Petrock Devon 6 E3
Newton Solney Derbys 35 C8
Newton Stacey Hants 17 G11
Newton Stewart Dumfries 55 C7
Newton Tony Wilts 17 G9
Newton Tracey Devon 6 D4
Newton under Roseberry Redcar 59 E6
Newton upon Derwent E Yorks 52 E3
Newton Valence Hants 10 A6
Newtonairds Dumfries 60 E4
Newtongrange Midloth 70 D2
Newtonhill Aberds 83 D11
Newtonhill Highld 87 G8
Newtonmill Angus 77 A9
Newtonmore Highld 81 D9
Newtown Argyll 73 C9
Newtown Ches 43 E8
Newtown Corn 2 G6
Newtown Cumb 56 B2
Newtown Cumb 61 G11
Newtown Derbys 44 D3
Newtown Devon 7 D6
Newtown Glos 16 A3
Newtown Glos 26 E6
Newtown Hants 10 C1
Newtown Hants 10 B2
Newtown Hants 10 C5
Newtown Hants 17 E11
Newtown Hants 10 C4
Newtown Hants 10 D3
Newtown Hereford 26 D3
Newtown Highld 80 C5
Newtown I o M 48 E3
Newtown I o W 10 E3
Newtown Northumb 62 C6
Newtown Northumb 71 H9
Newtown Northumb 71 G8
Newtown Poole 9 E9
Newtown Shrops 33 B10
Newtown Staffs 44 F3
Newtown Staffs 44 F4
Newtown Wilts 9 B8
Newtown = Y Drenewydd Powys 33 F7
Newtown Linford Leics 35 E11
Newtown St Boswells Borders 70 G4
Newtown Unthank Leics 35 E10
Newtyle Angus 76 C5
Neyland Pembs 22 F4
Niarbyl I o M 48 E2
Nibley S Glos 16 C3
Nibley Green Glos 16 B4
Nibon Shetland 96 F5
Nicholashayne Devon 7 E10
Nicholaston Swansea 23 H10
Nidd N Yorks 51 C9
Nigg Aberdeen 83 C11
Nigg Highld 87 D11
Nigg Ferry Highld 87 E10
Nightcott Som 7 D7
Nilig Denb 42 G3
Nine Ashes Essex 20 A2
Nine Mile Burn Midloth 69 E10
Nine Wells Pembs 22 D2
Ninebanks Northumb 57 A9
Ninfield E Sus 12 E6
Ningwood I o W 10 F2
Nisbet Borders 70 H5
Nisthouse Orkney 95 G4
Nisthouse Shetland 96 G7
Niton I o W 10 G4
Nitshill Glasgow 68 D4
No Man's Heath Ches 43 H8
No Man's Heath Warks 35 E8
Noak Hill London 20 B2
Noblethorpe S Yorks 44 B6
Nobottle Northants 28 B3
Nocton Lincs 46 F4
Noke Oxon 28 G2
Nolton Pembs 22 E3
Nolton Haven Pembs 22 E3
Nomansland Devon 7 E7
Nomansland Wilts 10 C1
Noneley Shrops 33 C10
Nonikiln Highld 87 D9
Nonington Kent 21 F9
Noonsbrough Shetland 96 H4
Norbreck Blkpool 49 E3
Norbridge Hereford 26 D4
Norbury Ches 43 H8
Norbury Derbys 35 A7
Norbury Shrops 33 F9
Norbury Staffs 34 C3
Nordelph Norf 38 E1
Norden Gtr Man 44 A2
Norden Heath Dorset 9 F8
Nordley Shrops 34 F2
Norham Northumb 71 F8
Norley Ches 43 E8
Norleywood Hants 10 E2
Norman Cross Cambs 37 F7
Normanby N Lincs 52 H4
Normanby N Yorks 52 A3
Normanby Redcar 59 E6
Normanby-by-Spital Lincs 46 D4
Normanby by Stow Lincs 46 D2
Normanby le Wold Lincs 46 C5
Normandy Sur 18 F6
Norman's Bay E Sus 12 F5
Norman's Green Devon 7 F9
Normanstone Suff 39 F11
Normanton Derby 35 B9
Normanton Leics 36 A4
Normanton Lincs 46 H3
Normanton Notts 45 G11
Normanton Rutland 36 E5
Normanton W Yorks 51 G9
Normanton le Heath Leics 35 D9
Normanton on Soar Notts 35 C11
Normanton-on-the-Wolds Notts 36 B2
Normanton on Trent Notts 45 F11
Normoss Lancs 49 F3
Norney Sur 18 G6
Norrington Common Wilts 16 E5
Norris Green Mers 43 C6
Norris Hill Leics 35 D9
North Anston S Yorks 45 D9
North Aston Oxon 27 F11
North Baddesley Hants 10 C2
North Ballachulish Highld 74 A3
North Barrow Som 8 B5
North Barsham Norf 38 B5
North Benfleet Essex 20 C4
North Bersted W Sus 11 D8
North Berwick E Loth 70 B4
North Boarhunt Hants 10 C5
North Bovey Devon 5 C8
North Bradley Wilts 16 F5
North Brentor Devon 4 C5
North Brewham Som 16 H4
North Buckland Devon 6 B3
North Burlingham Norf 39 D9
North Cadbury Som 8 B5
North Cairn Dumfries 54 B2
North Carlton Lincs 46 E3
North Carrine Argyll 65 H7
North Cave E Yorks 52 F4
North Cerney Glos 27 H7
North Charford Wilts 9 C10
North Charlton Northumb 63 A7
North Cheriton Som 8 B5
North Cliff E Yorks 53 E8
North Cliffe E Yorks 52 F4
North Clifton Notts 46 E2
North Cockerington Lincs 47 C7
North Coker Som 8 C4
North Collafirth Shetland 96 E5
North Common E Sus 12 D2
North Connel Argyll 74 D2
North Cornelly Bridgend 14 C4
North Cotes Lincs 47 B7
North Cove Suff 39 G10
North Cowton N Yorks 58 F3
North Crawley M Keynes 28 D6
North Cray London 19 D11
North Creake Norf 38 B4
North Curry Som 8 B2
North Dalton E Yorks 52 D5
North Dawn Orkney 95 H5
North Deighton N Yorks 51 D9
North Duffield N Yorks 52 F2
North Elkington Lincs 46 C6
North Elmham Norf 38 C5
North Elmshall W Yorks 45 A8
North End Bucks 28 F5
North End E Yorks 53 F8
North End Essex 30 G3
North End Hants 17 E11
North End Lincs 37 A8
North End N Som 15 E10
North End Ptsmth 10 D5
North End Som 8 B1
North End W Sus 11 D10
North Erradale Highld 91 J12
North Fambridge Essex 20 B5
North Fearns Highld 85 E10
North Featherstone W Yorks 51 G10
North Ferriby E Yorks 52 G5
North Frodingham E Yorks 53 D7
North Gluss Shetland 96 F5
North Gorley Hants 9 C10
North Green Norf 39 G8
North Green Suff 31 B10
North Greetwell Lincs 46 E4
North Grimston N Yorks 52 C4
North Halley Orkney 95 H6
North Halling Medway 20 E4
North Hayling Hants 10 D6
North Hazelrigg Northumb 71 G9
North Heasley Devon 7 C6
North Heath W Sus 11 B9
North Hill Cambs 37 H10
North Hill Corn 4 D3
North Hinksey Oxon 27 H11
North Holmwood Sur 19 G8
North Howden E Yorks 52 F3
North Huish Devon 5 F8
North Hykeham Lincs 46 F3
North Johnston Pembs 22 E4
North Kelsey Lincs 46 B4
North Kelsey Moor Lincs 46 B4
North Kessock Highld 87 G9
North Killingholme N Lincs 53 H7
North Kilvington N Yorks 58 H5
North Kilworth Leics 36 G2
North Kirkton Aberds 89 C11
North Kiscadale N Ayrs 66 D3
North Kyme Lincs 46 G5
North Lancing W Sus 11 D10
North Lee Bucks 28 H5
North Leigh Oxon 27 G10
North Leverton with Habblesthorpe Notts 45 D11
North Littleton Worcs 27 D7
North Lopham Norf 38 G6
North Luffenham Rutland 36 E5
North Marden W Sus 11 C7
North Marston Bucks 28 F4
North Middleton Midloth 70 E2
North Middleton Northumb 62 A6
North Molton Devon 7 D6
North Moreton Oxon 18 C2
North Mundham W Sus 11 D7
North Muskham Notts 45 G11
North Newbald E Yorks 52 F5
North Newington Oxon 27 E11
North Newnton Wilts 17 F8
North Newton Som 8 A1
North Nibley Glos 16 B4
North Oakley Hants 18 F2
North Ockendon London 20 C2
North Ormesby M'bro 58 D6
North Ormsby Lincs 46 C6
North Otterington N Yorks 58 H4
North Owersby Lincs 46 C4
North Perrott Som 8 D3
North Petherton Som 8 A1
North Petherwin Corn 4 C3
North Pickenham Norf 38 E4
North Piddle Worcs 26 C6
North Poorton Dorset 8 E4
North Port Argyll 74 E3
North Queensferry Fife 69 B10
North Radworthy Devon 7 C6
North Rauceby Lincs 46 H4
North Reston Lincs 47 D7
North Rigton N Yorks 51 E8
North Rode Ches 44 F2
North Roe Shetland 96 E5
North Ronaldsay Airport Orkney 95 C8
North Runcton Norf 38 D2
North Sandwick Shetland 96 D7
North Scale Cumb 49 C1
North Scarle Lincs 46 F2
North Seaton Northumb 63 E8
North Shian Argyll 74 C2
North Shields T & W 63 G9
North Shoebury Sthend 20 C6
North Shore Blkpool 49 F3
North Side Cumb 56 D2
North Side P'boro 37 F8
North Skelton Redcar 59 E7
North Somercotes Lincs 47 C8
North Stainley N Yorks 51 B8
North Stainmore Cumb 57 E10
North Stifford Thurrock 20 C3
North Stoke Bath 16 E4
North Stoke Oxon 18 C3
North Stoke W Sus 11 C9
North Street Hants 10 A5
North Street Kent 21 F7
North Street Medway 20 D5
North Street W Berks 18 D3
North Sunderland Northumb 71 G11
North Tamerton Corn 6 G2
North Tawton Devon 6 F5
North Thoresby Lincs 46 C6
North Tidworth Wilts 17 G9
North Togston Northumb 63 C8
North Tuddenham Norf 38 D6
North Walbottle T & W 63 G7
North Walsham Norf 39 B8
North Waltham Hants 18 G2
North Warnborough Hants 18 F4
North Water Bridge Angus 83 G8
North Watten Highld 94 E4
North Weald Bassett Essex 19 A11
North Wheatley Notts 45 D11
North Whilborough Devon 5 E9
North Wick Bath 16 E2
North Willingham Lincs 46 D5
North Wingfield Derbys 45 F8
North Witham Lincs 36 C5
North Woolwich London 19 D11
North Wootton Dorset 8 C5
North Wootton Norf 38 C2
North Wootton Som 16 G2
North Wraxall Wilts 16 D5
North Wroughton Swindon 17 C8
Northacre Norf 38 F5
Northallerton N Yorks 58 G4
Northam Devon 6 D3
Northam Soton 10 C3
Northampton Northants 28 B4
Northaw Herts 19 A9
Northbeck Lincs 37 A6
Northborough P'boro 37 E7
Northbourne Kent 21 F10
Northbridge Street E Sus 12 D6
Northchapel W Sus 11 B8
Northchurch Herts 28 H6
Northcott Devon 6 G2
Northdown Kent 21 D10
Northdyke Orkney 95 F3
Northend Bath 16 E4
Northend Bucks 18 B4
Northend Warks 27 C10
Northenden Gtr Man 44 C2
Northfield Aberdeen 83 C11
Northfield Borders 71 D8
Northfield E Yorks 52 G6
Northfield W Mid 34 H6
Northfields Lincs 36 E6
Northfleet Kent 20 D3
Northgate Lincs 37 C7
Northhouse Borders 61 C10
Northiam E Sus 13 D7
Northill Beds 29 D8
Northington Hants 18 H2
Northlands Lincs 47 G7
Northlea Durham 58 A5
Northleach Glos 27 G8
Northleigh Devon 7 G10
Northlew Devon 6 G4
Northmoor Oxon 17 A11
Northmoor Green or Moorland Som 8 A2
Northmuir Angus 76 B6
Northney Hants 10 D6
Northolt London 19 C8
Northop Flint 42 F5
Northop Hall Flint 42 F5
Northorpe Lincs 37 D6
Northorpe Lincs 37 B8
Northorpe Lincs 46 C2
Northover Som 15 H10
Northover Som 8 B4
Northowram W Yorks 51 G7
Northport Dorset 9 F8
Northpunds Shetland 96 L6
Northrepps Norf 39 B8
Northtown Orkney 95 J5
Northway Glos 26 E6
Northwich Ches 43 E9
Northwick S Glos 16 C2
Northwold Norf 38 F3
Northwood Derbys 44 F6
Northwood London 19 B7
Northwood I o W 10 E3
Northwood Kent 21 E10
Northwood Shrops 33 B10
Northwood Green Glos 26 G4
Norton E Sus 12 F3
Norton Glos 26 F5
Norton Halton 43 D8
Norton Herts 29 E9
Norton I o W 10 F2
Norton Mon 25 G11
Norton Notts 45 E9
Norton Northants 28 B3
Norton Powys 25 B10
Norton Shrops 33 G10
Norton Shrops 34 E1
Norton Shrops 34 E3
Norton Shrops 34 F3
Norton Stockton 58 D5
Norton Suff 30 B6
Norton S Yorks 51 H11
Norton Wilts 16 C5
Norton Worcs 26 C5
Norton Worcs 27 D7
Norton W Sus 11 E7
Norton W Sus 11 D8
Norton Bavant Wilts 16 G6
Norton Bridge Staffs 34 B4
Norton Canes Staffs 34 E6
Norton Canon Hereford 25 D10
Norton Corner Norf 39 C6
Norton Disney Lincs 46 G2
Norton East Staffs 34 E6
Norton Ferris Wilts 16 H4
Norton Fitzwarren Som 7 D10
Norton Green I o W 10 F2
Norton Hawkfield Bath 16 E2
Norton Heath Essex 20 A3
Norton in Hales Shrops 34 B3
Norton-in-the-Moors Stoke 44 G2
Norton-Juxta-Twycross Leics 35 E9
Norton-le-Clay N Yorks 51 B10
Norton Lindsey Warks 27 B9
Norton Malreward Bath 16 E3
Norton Mandeville Essex 20 A2
Norton-on-Derwent N Yorks 52 B3
Norton St Philip Som 16 F4
Norton sub Hamdon Som 8 C3
Norton Woodseats S Yorks 45 D7
Norwell Notts 45 F11
Norwell Woodhouse Notts 45 F11
Norwich Norf 39 E8
Norwich International Airport Norf 39 D8
Norwick Shetland 96 B8
Norwood Derbys 45 D8
Norwood Hill Sur 19 G9
Norwoodside Cambs 37 F10
Noseley Leics 36 F3
Noss Shetland 96 M5
Noss Mayo Devon 4 G6
Nosterfield N Yorks 51 A8
Nostie Highld 85 F13
Notgrove Glos 27 F8
Nottage Bridgend 14 D4
Nottingham Nottingham 36 B1
Nottingham East Midlands Airport Leics 35 C10
Nottington Dorset 8 F5
Notton Wilts 16 E6
Notton W Yorks 45 A7
Nounsley Essex 30 G4
Noutard's Green Worcs 26 B4
Novar House Highld 87 E9
Nox Shrops 33 D10
Nuffield Oxon 18 C3
Nun Hills Lancs 50 G4
Nun Monkton N Yorks 51 D11
Nunburnholme E Yorks 52 E4
Nuncargate Notts 45 G9
Nuneaton Warks 35 F9
Nuneham Courtenay Oxon 18 B2
Nunney Som 16 G4
Nunnington N Yorks 52 B2
Nunnykirk Northumb 62 D6
Nunsthorpe NE Lincs 46 B6
Nunthorpe M'bro 59 E6
Nunthorpe York 52 D2
Nunton Wilts 9 B10
Nunwick N Yorks 51 B9
Nupend Glos 26 H4
Nursling Hants 10 C2
Nursted Hants 11 B6
Nutbourne W Sus 11 C9
Nutbourne W Sus 11 D6
Nutfield Sur 19 F10
Nuthall Notts 35 A11
Nuthampstead Herts 29 E11
Nuthurst W Sus 11 B10
Nutley E Sus 12 D3
Nutley Hants 18 G3
Nutwell S Yorks 45 B10
Nybster Highld 94 D5
Nyetimber W Sus 11 E7
Nyewood W Sus 11 B7
Nymet Rowland Devon 6 F6
Nymet Tracey Devon 7 F6
Nympsfield Glos 16 A5
Nynehead Som 7 D10
Nyton W Sus 11 D8

O

Oad Street Kent 20 E5
Oadby Leics 36 E2
Oak Cross Devon 6 G4
Oakamoor Staffs 35 A6
Oakbank W Loth 69 D9
Oakdale Caerph 15 B7
Oake Som 7 D10
Oaken Staffs 34 E4
Oakenclough Lancs 49 E5
Oakengates Telford 34 D3
Oakenholt Flint 42 E5
Oakenshaw Durham 58 C3
Oakenshaw W Yorks 51 G7
Oakerthorpe Derbys 45 G7
Oakes W Yorks 51 H7
Oakfield Torf 15 B9
Oakford Ceredig 23 A9
Oakford Devon 7 D8
Oakfordbridge Devon 7 D8
Oakgrove Ches 44 F3
Oakham Rutland 36 E4
Oakhanger Hants 18 H4
Oakhill Som 16 G3
Oakhurst Kent 20 F2
Oakington Cambs 29 B11
Oaklands Herts 29 G9
Oaklands Powys 25 C7
Oakle Street Glos 26 G4
Oakley Beds 29 C7
Oakley Bucks 28 G3
Oakley Fife 69 B9
Oakley Hants 18 F2
Oakley Oxon 18 A4
Oakley Poole 9 E9
Oakley Suff 39 H7
Oakley Green Windsor 18 D6
Oakley Park Powys 32 G5
Oakmere Ches 43 F8
Oakridge Glos 16 A6
Oakridge Hants 18 F3
Oaks Shrops 33 E10
Oaks Green Derbys 35 B7
Oaksey Wilts 16 B6
Oakthorpe Leics 35 D9
Oakwoodhill Sur 19 H8
Oakworth W Yorks 50 F6
Oape Highld 92 J7
Oare Kent 21 E7
Oare Som 7 B7
Oare W Berks 18 D2
Oare Wilts 17 E8
Oasby Lincs 36 B6
Oathlaw Angus 77 B7
Oatlands N Yorks 51 D9
Oban Argyll 79 J11
Oban Highld 79 C11
Oborne Dorset 8 C5
Obthorpe Lincs 37 D6
Occlestone Green Ches 43 F9
Occold Suff 31 A8
Ochiltree E Ayrs 67 D8
Ochtermuthill Perth 75 F11
Ochtertyre Perth 75 E11
Ockbrook Derbys 35 B10
Ockham Sur 19 F7
Ockle Highld 79 D8
Ockley Sur 19 H8
Ocle Pychard Hereford 26 D2
Octon E Yorks 52 C6
Octon Cross Roads E Yorks 52 C6
Odcombe Som 8 C4
Odd Down Bath 16 E4
Oddendale Cumb 57 E7
Odder Lincs 46 E3
Oddingley Worcs 26 C6
Oddington Glos 27 F9
Oddington Oxon 28 G2
Odell Beds 28 C6
Odie Orkney 95 F7
Odiham Hants 18 F4
Odstock Wilts 9 B10
Odstone Leics 35 E9
Offchurch Warks 27 B10
Offenham Worcs 27 D7
Offham E Sus 12 E2
Offham Kent 20 F3
Offham W Sus 11 D9
Offord Cluny Cambs 29 B9
Offord Darcy Cambs 29 B9
Offton Suff 31 D7
Offwell Devon 7 G10
Ogbourne Maizey Wilts 17 D8
Ogbourne St Andrew Wilts 17 D8
Ogbourne St George Wilts 17 D9
Ogil Angus 77 A7
Ogle Northumb 63 F7
Ogmore V Glam 14 D4
Ogmore-by-Sea V Glam 14 D4
Ogmore Vale Bridgend 14 B5
Okeford Fitzpaine Dorset 9 C7
Okehampton Devon 6 G4
Okehampton Camp Devon 6 G4
Okraquoy Shetland 96 K6
Old Northants 28 A4
Old Aberdeen Aberdeen 83 C11
Old Alresford Hants 10 A4
Old Arley Warks 35 F8
Old Basford Nottingham 35 A11
Old Basing Hants 18 F3
Old Bewick Northumb 62 A6
Old Bolingbroke Lincs 47 F7
Old Bramhope W Yorks 51 E8
Old Brampton Derbys 45 E7
Old Bridge of Tilt Perth 81 G10
Old Bridge of Urr Dumfries 55 C10
Old Buckenham Norf 39 F6
Old Burghclere Hants 17 F11
Old Byland N Yorks 59 H6
Old Cassop Durham 58 C4
Old Castleton Borders 61 D11
Old Catton Norf 39 D8
Old Clee NE Lincs 46 B6
Old Cleeve Som 7 B9
Old Clipstone Notts 45 F10
Old Colwyn Conwy 41 C10
Old Coulsdon London 19 F10
Old Crombie Aberds 88 C5
Old Dailly S Ayrs 66 G5
Old Dalby Leics 36 C2
Old Deer Aberds 89 D9
Old Denaby S Yorks 45 C8
Old Edlington S Yorks 45 C9
Old Eldon Durham 58 D3
Old Ellerby E Yorks 53 F7
Old Felixstowe Suff 31 E10
Old Fletton P'boro 37 F7
Old Glossop Derbys 44 C4
Old Goole E Yorks 52 G3
Old Hall Powys 32 G5
Old Heath Essex 31 F7
Old Heathfield E Sus 12 D4
Old Hill W Mid 34 G5
Old Hunstanton Norf 38 A2
Old Hurst Cambs 37 H8
Old Hutton Cumb 57 H7
Old Kea Corn 3 E7
Old Kilpatrick W Dunb 68 C3
Old Kinnernie Aberds 83 C9
Old Knebworth Herts 29 F9
Old Langho Lancs 50 F3
Old Laxey I o M 48 D4
Old Leake Lincs 47 G8
Old Malton N Yorks 52 B3
Old Micklefield W Yorks 51 F10
Old Milton Hants 9 E11
Old Milverton Warks 27 B9
Old Monkland N Lnrk 68 D6
Old Netley Hants 10 D3
Old Philpstoun W Loth 69 C9
Old Quarrington Durham 58 C4
Old Radnor Powys 25 C9
Old Rattray Aberds 89 C10
Old Rayne Aberds 83 A8
Old Romney Kent 13 D9
Old Sodbury S Glos 16 C4
Old Somerby Lincs 36 B5
Old Stratford Northants 28 D4
Old Thirsk N Yorks 51 A10
Old Town Cumb 57 B6
Old Town Cumb 50 A1
Old Town Northumb 62 D4
Old Town Scilly 2 C3
Old Trafford Gtr Man 44 C2
Old Tupton Derbys 45 F7
Old Warden Beds 29 D8
Old Weston Cambs 37 H6
Old Whittington Derbys 45 E7
Old Wick Highld 94 E5
Old Windsor Windsor 18 D6
Old Wives Lees Kent 21 F7
Old Woking Sur 19 F7
Old Woodhall Lincs 46 F6
Oldany Highld 92 F4
Oldberrow Warks 27 B8
Oldborough Devon 7 F6
Oldbury Shrops 34 F3
Oldbury Warks 35 F9
Oldbury W Mid 34 G5
Oldbury-on-Severn S Glos 16 B3
Oldbury on the Hill Glos 16 C5
Oldcastle Bridgend 14 D5
Oldcastle Mon 25 F10
Oldcotes Notts 45 D9
Oldfallow Staffs 34 D5
Oldfield Worcs 26 B5
Oldford Som 16 F4
Oldham Gtr Man 44 B3
Oldhamstocks E Loth 70 C6
Oldland S Glos 16 D3
Oldmeldrum Aberds 89 F8
Oldshore Beg Highld 92 D4
Oldshoremore Highld 92 D5
Oldstead N Yorks 51 A11
Oldtown Aberds 83 A7

South Luffenham Rutland 36 E5
South Malling E Sus 12 E3
South Marston Swindon 17 C8
South Middleton Northumb 62 A5
South Milford N Yorks 51 F10
South Millbrex Aberds 89 D8
South Milton Devon 5 G8
South Mimms Herts 19 A9
South Molton Devon 6 D6
South Moreton Oxon 18 C2
South Mundham W Sus 11 D7
South Muskham Notts 45 G11
South Newbald E Yorks 52 F5
South Newington Oxon 27 E11
South Newton Wilts 9 A9
South Normanton Derbys 45 G8
South Norwood London 19 E10
South Nutfield Sur 19 G10
South Ockendon Thurrock 20 C2
South Ormsby Lincs 47 E7
South Otterington N Yorks 58 H4
South Owersby Lincs 46 C4
South Oxhey Herts 19 B8
South Perrott Dorset 8 D3
South Petherton Som 8 C3
South Petherwin Corn 4 C4
South Pickenham Norf 38 E4
South Pool Devon 5 G8
South Port Argyll 74 E3
South Radworthy Devon 7 C6
South Rauceby Lincs 46 H4
South Raynham Norf 38 C4
South Reston Lincs 47 D8
South Runcton Norf 38 E2
South Scarle Notts 46 F2
South Shian Argyll 74 C2
South Shields T & W 63 G9
South Shore Blkpool 49 F3
South Somercotes Lincs 47 C8
South Stainley N Yorks 51 C9
South Stainmore Cumb 57 E10
South Stifford Thurrock 20 D3
South Stoke Oxon 18 C2
South Stoke W Sus 11 D9
South Street E Sus 12 E2
South Street London 19 F11
South Street Kent 21 E8
South Street Kent 21 F7
South Tawton Devon 6 G5
South Thoresby Lincs 47 E8
South Tidworth Wilts 17 G9
South Town Hants 18 H3
South View Hants 18 F3
South Walsham Norf 39 D9
South Warnborough Hants 18 G4
South Weald Essex 20 B2
South Weston Oxon 18 B4
South Wheatley Corn 4 B3
South Wheatley Notts 45 D11
South Whiteness Shetland 96 J5
South Widcombe Bath 16 F2
South Wigston Leics 36 F1
South Willingham Lincs 46 D5
South Wingfield Derbys 45 G7
South Witham Lincs 36 D5
South Wonston Hants 17 H11
South Woodham Ferrers Essex 20 B5
South Wootton Norf 38 C2
South Wraxall Wilts 16 E5
South Zeal Devon 6 G5
Southall London 19 C8
Southam Glos 26 F6
Southam Warks 27 B11
Southampton Soton 10 C3
Southampton International Airport Hants 10 C3
Southborough Kent 12 B4
Southbourne Bmouth 9 E10
Southbourne W Sus 11 D6
Southburgh Norf 38 E5
Southburn E Yorks 52 D5
Southchurch Sthend 20 C6
Southcott Wilts 17 F8
Southcourt Bucks 28 G5
Southdean Borders 62 C2
Southdene Mers 43 C7
Southease E Sus 12 F3
Southend Argyll 65 H7
Southend W Berks 18 D2
Southend Wilts 17 D8
Southend Airport Essex 20 C5
Southend-on-Sea Sthend 20 C5
Southernden Kent 20 G5
Southerndown V Glam 14 D4
Southerness Dumfries 60 H5
Southery Norf 38 F2
Southfield Northumb 63 F8
Southfleet Kent 20 D3
Southgate Ceredig 32 H1
Southgate London 19 B9
Southgate Norf 39 C7
Southgate Swansea 23 H10
Southill Beds 29 D8
Southleigh Devon 7 G11
Southminster Essex 20 B6
Southmoor Oxon 17 B10
Southoe Cambs 29 B8
Southolt Suff 31 B8
Southorpe P'boro 37 E6
Southowram W Yorks 51 G7
Southport Mers 49 H3
Southpunds Shetland 96 L6
Southrepps Norf 39 B8
Southrey Lincs 46 F5
Southrop Glos 17 A8
Southrope Hants 18 G3
Southsea Ptsmth 10 E5
Southstoke Bath 16 E4
Southtown Norf 39 E11
Southtown Orkney 95 J5
Southwaite Cumb 56 B6
Southwark London 19 D10
Southwater W Sus 11 B10
Southwater Street W Sus 11 B10
Southway Som 15 G11
Southwell Dorset 8 G5
Southwell Notts 45 G10
Southwick Hants 10 D5
Southwick Northants 36 F6
Southwick T & W 63 H9
Southwick Wilts 16 F5
Southwick W Sus 11 D11
Southwold Suff 39 H11
Southwood Norf 39 E9
Southwood Som 8 A4
Soval Lodge W Isles 91 E8
Sowber Gate N Yorks 58 H4
Sowerby N Yorks 51 A10
Sowerby W Yorks 50 G6
Sowerby Bridge W Yorks 51 G6
Sowerby Row Cumb 56 C5
Sowood W Yorks 51 H6
Sowton Devon 7 G8
Soyal Highld 87 B8
Spa Common Norf 39 B8
Spacey Houses N Yorks 51 D9
Spadeadam Farm Cumb 61 F11
Spalding Lincs 37 C8
Spaldington E Yorks 52 F3
Spaldwick Cambs 29 A8
Spalford Notts 46 F2
Spanby Lincs 37 B6
Sparham Norf 39 D6
Spark Bridge Cumb 49 A3
Sparkford Som 8 B5
Sparkhill W Mid 35 G6
Sparkwell Devon 5 F6
Sparrow Green Norf 38 D5
Sparrowpit Derbys 44 D4
Sparsholt Hants 10 A3
Sparsholt Oxon 17 C10
Spartylea Northumb 57 B10
Spaunton N Yorks 59 H8
Spaxton Som 7 C11
Spean Bridge Highld 80 E4
Spear Hill W Sus 11 C10
Speen Bucks 18 B5
Speen W Berks 17 E11
Speeton N Yorks 53 B7
Speke Mers 43 D7
Speldhurst Kent 12 B4
Spellbrook Herts 29 G11
Spelsbury Oxon 27 F10
Spelter Bridgend 14 B4
Spencers Wood Wokingham 18 E4
Spennithorne N Yorks 58 H2
Spennymoor Durham 58 C3
Spetchley Worcs 26 C5
Spetisbury Dorset 9 D8
Spexhall Suff 39 G9
Spey Bay Moray 88 B3
Speybridge Highld 82 A2
Speyview Moray 88 D2
Spilsby Lincs 47 F8
Spindlestone Northumb 71 G10
Spinkhill Derbys 45 E8
Spinningdale Highld 87 C9
Spirthill Wilts 16 D6
Spital Hill S Yorks 45 C10
Spital in the Street Lincs 46 D3
Spithurst E Sus 12 E3
Spittal Dumfries 54 D6
Spittal E Loth 70 C3
Spittal Highld 94 E3
Spittal Northumb 71 E9
Spittal Pembs 22 D4
Spittal Stirl 68 B4
Spittal of Glenmuick Aberds 82 E5
Spittal of Glenshee Perth 82 F3
Spittalfield Perth 76 C4
Spixworth Norf 39 D8
Splayne's Green E Sus 12 D3
Spofforth N Yorks 51 D9
Spon End W Mid 35 H9
Spon Green Flint 42 F5
Spondon Derby 35 B10
Spooner Row Norf 39 F6
Sporle Norf 38 D4
Spott E Loth 70 C5
Spratton Northants 28 A4
Spreakley Sur 18 G5
Spreyton Devon 6 G5
Spridlington Lincs 46 D4
Spring Vale S Yorks 44 B6
Spring Valley I o M 48 E3
Springburn Glasgow 68 D5
Springfield Dumfries 61 G9
Springfield Essex 30 H4
Springfield Fife 76 F6
Springfield Moray 87 F13
Springfield W Mid 35 G6
Springhill Staffs 34 E5
Springholm Dumfries 55 C11
Springkell Dumfries 61 F8
Springside N Ayrs 67 C6
Springthorpe Lincs 46 D2
Springwell T & W 63 H8
Sproatley E Yorks 53 F7
Sproston Green Ches 43 F10
Sprotbrough S Yorks 45 B9
Sproughton Suff 31 D8
Sprouston Borders 70 G6
Sprowston Norf 39 D8
Sproxton Leics 36 C4
Sproxton N Yorks 52 A2
Spurstow Ches 43 G8
Spynie Moray 88 B2
Squires Gate Blkpool 49 F3
Srannda W Isles 90 J5
Sronphadruig Lodge Perth 81 F9
Stableford Shrops 34 F3
Stableford Staffs 34 B4
Stacey Bank S Yorks 44 C6
Stackhouse N Yorks 50 C4
Stackpole Pembs 22 G4
Staddiscombe Devon 4 F6
Staddlethorpe E Yorks 52 G4
Stadhampton Oxon 18 B3
Stadhlaigearraidh W Isles 84 E2
Staffield Cumb 57 B7
Staffin Highld 85 B9
Stafford Staffs 34 C5
Stagsden Beds 28 D6
Stainburn Cumb 56 D2
Stainburn N Yorks 51 E8
Stainby Lincs 36 C5
Staincross S Yorks 45 A7
Staindrop Durham 58 D2
Staines Sur 19 D7
Stainfield Lincs 37 C6
Stainfield Lincs 46 E5
Stainforth N Yorks 50 C4
Stainforth S Yorks 45 A10
Staining Lancs 49 F3
Stainland W Yorks 51 H6
Stainsacre N Yorks 59 F10
Stainsby Derbys 45 F8
Stainton Cumb 57 D7
Stainton Cumb 57 D6
Stainton Durham 58 E1
Stainton M'bro 58 E5
Stainton N Yorks 58 G2
Stainton S Yorks 45 C9
Stainton by Langworth Lincs 46 E4
Stainton le Vale Lincs 46 C5
Stainton with Adgarley Cumb 49 B2
Staintondale N Yorks 59 G10
Stair Cumb 56 D4
Stair E Ayrs 67 D7
Stairhaven Dumfries 54 D5
Staithes N Yorks 59 E8
Stake Pool Lancs 49 E4
Stakeford Northumb 63 E8
Stalbridge Dorset 8 C6
Stalbridge Weston Dorset 8 C6
Stalham Norf 39 C9
Stalham Green Norf 39 C9
Stalisfield Green Kent 20 F6
Stalling Busk N Yorks 57 H11
Stallingborough NE Lincs 46 A5
Stalmine Lancs 49 E3
Stalybridge Gtr Man 44 C3
Stambourne Essex 30 E4
Stambourne Green Essex 30 E4
Stamford Lincs 36 E6
Stamford Bridge Ches 43 F7
Stamford Bridge E Yorks 52 D3
Stamfordham Northumb 62 F6
Stanah Cumb 56 E5
Stanborough Herts 29 G9
Stanbridge Beds 28 F6
Stanbridge Dorset 9 D9
Stanbrook Worcs 26 D5
Stanbury W Yorks 50 F6
Stand Gtr Man 43 B10
Stand N Lnrk 68 D6
Standburn Falk 69 C8
Standeford Staffs 34 E5
Standen Kent 13 B7
Standford Hants 11 A7
Standingstone Cumb 56 C2
Standish Gtr Man 43 A8
Standlake Oxon 17 A10
Standon Hants 10 B3
Standon Herts 29 F10
Standon Staffs 34 B4
Stane N Lnrk 69 E7
Stanfield Norf 38 C5
Stanford Beds 29 D8
Stanford Kent 13 C10
Stanford Bishop Hereford 26 C3
Stanford Bridge Worcs 26 B4
Stanford Dingley W Berks 18 D2
Stanford in the Vale Oxon 17 B10
Stanford-le-Hope Thurrock 20 C3
Stanford on Avon Northants 36 H1
Stanford on Soar Notts 35 C11
Stanford on Teme Worcs 26 B4
Stanford Rivers Essex 20 A2
Stanfree Derbys 45 E8
Stanghow Redcar 59 E7
Stanground P'boro 37 F7
Stanhoe Norf 38 B4
Stanhope Borders 69 H10
Stanhope Durham 57 C11
Stanion Northants 36 G5
Stanley Derbys 35 A10
Stanley Durham 58 A2
Stanley Lancs 43 B7
Stanley Perth 76 D4
Stanley Staffs 44 G3
Stanley W Yorks 51 G9
Stanley Common Derbys 35 A10
Stanley Gate Lancs 43 B7
Stanley Hill Hereford 26 D3
Stanlow Ches 43 E7
Stanmer Brighton 12 F2
Stanmore London 19 B8
Stanmore Hants 10 B3
Stanmore W Berks 17 D11
Stannergate Dundee 77 D7
Stanningley W Yorks 51 F8
Stannington Northumb 63 F8
Stannington S Yorks 45 D7
Stansbatch Hereford 25 B10
Stansfield Suff 30 C4
Stanstead Suff 30 D5
Stanstead Abbotts Herts 29 G10
Stansted Kent 20 E3
Stansted Mountfitchet Essex 30 F2
Stanton Glos 27 E7
Stanton Mon 25 F10
Stanton Northumb 63 E7
Stanton Staffs 44 H5
Stanton Suff 30 A6
Stanton by Bridge Derbys 35 C9
Stanton-by-Dale Derbys 35 B10
Stanton Drew Bath 16 E2
Stanton Fitzwarren Swindon 17 B8
Stanton Harcourt Oxon 27 H11
Stanton Hill Notts 45 F8
Stanton in Peak Derbys 44 F6
Stanton Lacy Shrops 33 H10
Stanton Long Shrops 34 F1
Stanton-on-the-Wolds Notts 36 B2
Stanton Prior Bath 16 E3
Stanton St Bernard Wilts 17 E7
Stanton St John Oxon 28 H2
Stanton St Quintin Wilts 16 D6
Stanton Street Suff 30 B6
Stanton under Bardon Leics 35 D10
Stanton upon Hine Heath Shrops 34 C1
Stanton Wick Bath 16 E3
Stanwardine in the Fields Shrops 33 C10
Stanwardine in the Wood Shrops 33 C10
Stanway Essex 30 F6
Stanway Glos 27 E7
Stanway Green Suff 31 A9
Stanwell Sur 19 D7
Stanwell Moor Sur 19 D7
Stanwick Northants 28 A6
Stanwick-St-John N Yorks 58 E2
Stanwix Cumb 61 H10
Stanydale Shetland 96 H4
Staoinebrig W Isles 84 E2
Stape N Yorks 59 G8
Stapehill Dorset 9 D9
Stapeley Ches 43 H9
Stapenhill Staffs 35 C8
Staple Kent 21 F9
Staple Som 7 B10
Staple Cross E Sus 13 D6
Staple Fitzpaine Som 8 C1
Staplefield W Sus 12 D1
Stapleford Cambs 29 C11
Stapleford Herts 29 G10
Stapleford Leics 36 D4
Stapleford Lincs 46 G2
Stapleford Notts 35 B10
Stapleford Wilts 17 H7
Stapleford Abbotts Essex 20 B2
Stapleford Tawney Essex 20 B2
Staplegrove Som 7 D11
Staplehay Som 7 D11
Staplehurst Kent 13 B6
Staplers I o W 10 F4
Stapleton Bristol 16 D3
Stapleton Cumb 61 F11
Stapleton Hereford 25 B10
Stapleton Leics 35 F10
Stapleton N Yorks 58 E3
Stapleton Shrops 33 E10
Stapleton Som 8 B3
Stapley Som 7 E10
Staploe Beds 29 B8
Staplow Hereford 26 D3
Star Fife 76 G6
Star Pembs 23 C7
Star Som 15 F10
Stara Orkney 95 F3
Starbeck N Yorks 51 D9
Starbotton N Yorks 50 B5
Starcross Devon 5 C10
Stareton Warks 27 A10
Starkholmes Derbys 45 G7
Starlings Green Essex 29 E11
Starston Norf 39 G8
Startforth Durham 58 E1
Startley Wilts 16 C6
Stathe Som 8 B2
Stathern Leics 36 B3
Station Town Durham 58 C5
Staughton Green Cambs 29 B8
Staughton Highway Cambs 29 B8
Staunton Glos 26 G2
Staunton Glos 26 F4
Staunton in the Vale Notts 36 A4
Staunton on Arrow Hereford 25 B10
Staunton on Wye Hereford 25 D10
Staveley Cumb 56 H5
Staveley Cumb 56 G6
Staveley Derbys 45 E8
Staveley N Yorks 51 C9
Staverton Devon 5 E8
Staverton Glos 26 F5
Staverton Northants 28 B2
Staverton Wilts 16 E5
Staverton Bridge Glos 26 F5
Stawell Som 15 H9
Staxigoe Highld 94 E5
Staxton N Yorks 52 B6
Staylittle Powys 32 F4
Staynall Lancs 49 E3
Staythorpe Notts 45 G11
Stean N Yorks 51 B6
Stearsby N Yorks 52 B2
Steart Som 15 G8
Stebbing Essex 30 F3
Stebbing Green Essex 30 F3
Stedham W Sus 11 B7
Steele Road Borders 61 D11
Steen's Bridge Hereford 26 C2
Steep Hants 10 B6
Steep Marsh Hants 11 B6
Steeple Dorset 9 F8
Steeple Essex 20 A6
Steeple Ashton Wilts 16 F6
Steeple Aston Oxon 27 F11
Steeple Barton Oxon 27 F11
Steeple Bumpstead Essex 30 D3
Steeple Claydon Bucks 28 F3
Steeple Gidding Cambs 37 G7
Steeple Langford Wilts 17 H7
Steeple Morden Cambs 29 D9
Steeton W Yorks 50 E6
Stein Highld 84 C7
Steinmanhill Aberds 89 D7
Stelling Minnis Kent 21 G8
Stemster Highld 94 D3
Stemster Ho. Highld 94 D3
Stenalees Corn 3 D9
Stenhousemuir Falk 69 B7
Stenigot Lincs 46 D6
Stenness Shetland 96 F4
Stenscholl Highld 85 B9
Stenso Orkney 95 F4
Stenson Derbys 35 C9
Stenton E Loth 70 C5
Stenton Fife 76 H5
Stenwith Lincs 36 B4
Stepaside Pembs 22 F6
Stepping Hill Gtr Man 44 D3
Steppingley Beds 29 E7
Stepps N Lnrk 68 D5
Sterndale Moor Derbys 44 F5
Sternfield Suff 31 B10
Sterridge Devon 6 B4
Stert Wilts 17 F7
Stetchworth Cambs 30 C3
Stevenage Herts 29 F9
Stevenston N Ayrs 66 B5
Steventon Hants 18 G2
Steventon Oxon 17 B11
Stevington Beds 28 C6
Stewartby Beds 29 D7
Stewarton Argyll 65 G7
Stewarton E Ayrs 67 B7
Stewkley Bucks 28 F5
Stewton Lincs 47 D7
Steyne Cross I o W 10 F5
Steyning W Sus 11 C10
Steynton Pembs 22 F4
Stibb Corn 6 E1
Stibb Cross Devon 6 E3
Stibb Green Wilts 17 E9
Stibbard Norf 38 C5
Stibbington Cambs 37 F6
Stichill Borders 70 G6
Sticker Corn 3 D8
Stickford Lincs 47 G7
Sticklepath Devon 6 G5
Stickney Lincs 47 G7
Stiffkey Norf 38 A5
Stifford's Bridge Hereford 26 D4
Stillingfleet N Yorks 52 E1
Stillington N Yorks 52 C1
Stillington Stockton 58 D4
Stilton Cambs 37 G7
Stinchcombe Glos 16 B4
Stinsford Dorset 8 E6
Stirchley Telford 34 E3
Stirkoke Ho. Highld 94 E5
Stirling Aberds 89 D11
Stirling Stirl 68 A6
Stisted Essex 30 F4
Stithians Corn 2 F6
Stittenham Highld 87 D9
Stivichall W Mid 35 H9
Stixwould Lincs 46 F5
Stoak Ches 43 E7
Stobieside S Lnrk 68 G5
Stobo Borders 69 G10
Stoborough Dorset 9 F8
Stoborough Green Dorset 9 F8
Stobshiel E Loth 70 D3
Stobswood Northumb 63 D8
Stock Essex 20 B3
Stock Green Worcs 26 C6
Stock Wood Worcs 27 C7
Stockbridge Hants 10 A2
Stockbury Kent 20 E5
Stockcross W Berks 17 E11
Stockdalewath Cumb 56 B5
Stockerston Leics 36 F4
Stockheath Hants 10 D6
Stockiemuir Stirl 68 B4
Stocking Pelham Herts 29 F11
Stockingford Warks 35 F9
Stockland Devon 8 D1
Stockland Bristol Som 15 G8
Stockleigh English Devon 7 F7
Stockleigh Pomeroy Devon 7 F7
Stockley Wilts 17 E7
Stocklinch Som 8 C2
Stockport Gtr Man 44 C2
Stocksbridge S Yorks 44 C6
Stocksfield Northumb 62 G6
Stockton Hereford 26 B2
Stockton Norf 39 F9
Stockton Shrops 33 E8
Stockton Shrops 34 F3
Stockton Warks 27 B11
Stockton Wilts 16 H6
Stockton Heath Warr 43 D9
Stockton-on-Tees Stockton 58 E5
Stockton on Teme Worcs 26 B4
Stockton on the Forest York 52 D2
Stodmarsh Kent 21 E9
Stody Norf 39 B6
Stoer Highld 92 G3
Stoford Som 8 C4
Stoford Wilts 17 H7
Stogumber Som 7 C9
Stogursey Som 7 B11
Stoke Devon 6 D1
Stoke Hants 17 F11
Stoke Hants 10 D6
Stoke Medway 20 D5
Stoke Suff 31 D8
Stoke Abbott Dorset 8 D3
Stoke Albany Northants 36 G4
Stoke Ash Suff 31 A8
Stoke Bardolph Notts 36 A2
Stoke Bliss Worcs 26 B3
Stoke Bruerne Northants 28 D4
Stoke by Clare Suff 30 D4
Stoke-by-Nayland Suff 30 E6
Stoke Canon Devon 7 G8
Stoke Charity Hants 17 H11
Stoke Climsland Corn 4 D4
Stoke D'Abernon Sur 19 F8
Stoke Doyle Northants 36 G6
Stoke Dry Rutland 36 F4
Stoke Farthing Wilts 9 B9
Stoke Ferry Norf 38 F3
Stoke Fleming Devon 5 G9
Stoke Gabriel Devon 5 F9
Stoke Gifford S Glos 16 D3
Stoke Golding Leics 35 F9
Stoke Goldington M Keynes 28 D5
Stoke Green Bucks 18 C6
Stoke Hammond Bucks 28 F5
Stoke Heath Shrops 34 C2
Stoke Holy Cross Norf 39 E8
Stoke Lacy Hereford 26 D3
Stoke Lyne Oxon 28 F2
Stoke Mandeville Bucks 28 G5
Stoke Newington London 19 C10
Stoke on Tern Shrops 34 C2
Stoke-on-Trent Stoke 44 H2
Stoke Orchard Glos 26 F6
Stoke Poges Bucks 18 C6
Stoke Prior Hereford 26 C2
Stoke Prior Worcs 26 B6
Stoke Rivers Devon 6 C5
Stoke Rochford Lincs 36 C5
Stoke Row Oxon 18 C3
Stoke St Gregory Som 8 B2
Stoke St Mary Som 8 B1
Stoke St Michael Som 16 G3
Stoke St Milborough Shrops 34 G1
Stoke sub Hamdon Som 8 C3
Stoke Talmage Oxon 18 B3
Stoke Trister Som 8 B6
Stoke Wake Dorset 9 D6
Stokeford Dorset 9 F7
Stokeham Notts 45 E11
Stokeinteignhead Devon 5 D10
Stokenchurch Bucks 18 B4
Stokenham Devon 5 G9
Stokesay Shrops 33 G10
Stokesby Norf 39 D10
Stokesley N Yorks 59 F6
Stolford Som 7 B11
Ston Easton Som 16 F3
Stondon Massey Essex 20 A2
Stone Bucks 28 G4
Stone Glos 16 B3
Stone Kent 13 D8
Stone Kent 20 D2
Stone Staffs 34 B5
Stone S Yorks 45 D9
Stone Worcs 34 H4
Stone Allerton Som 15 F10
Stone Bridge Corner P'boro 37 E8
Stone Chair W Yorks 51 G7
Stone Cross E Sus 12 F5
Stone Cross Kent 21 F10
Stone-edge Batch N Som 15 D10
Stone House Cumb 57 H9
Stone Street Kent 20 F2
Stone Street Suff 30 E6
Stone Street Suff 39 G9
Stonebroom Derbys 45 G8
Stoneferry Hull 53 F7
Stonefield S Lnrk 68 E5
Stonegate E Sus 12 D5
Stonegate N Yorks 59 F8
Stonegrave N Yorks 52 B2
Stonehaugh Northumb 62 F3
Stonehaven Aberds 83 E10
Stonehouse Glos 26 H5
Stonehouse Northumb 62 H2
Stonehouse S Lnrk 68 F6
Stoneleigh Warks 27 A10
Stonely Cambs 29 B8
Stoner Hill Hants 10 B6
Stone's Green Essex 31 F8
Stonesby Leics 36 C4
Stonesfield Oxon 27 G10
Stonethwaite Cumb 56 E4
Stoney Cross Hants 10 C1
Stoney Middleton Derbys 44 E6
Stoney Stanton Leics 35 F10
Stoney Stoke Som 8 A6
Stoney Stratton Som 16 H3
Stoney Stretton Shrops 33 E9
Stoneybreck Shetland 96 N8
Stoneyburn W Loth 69 D8
Stoneygate Aberds 89 E10
Stoneygate Leicester 36 E2
Stoneyhills Essex 20 B6
Stoneykirk Dumfries 54 D3
Stoneywood Aberdeen 83 B10
Stoneywood Falk 68 B6
Stonganess Shetland 96 C7
Stonham Aspal Suff 31 C8
Stonnall Staffs 35 E6
Stonor Oxon 18 C4
Stonton Wyville Leics 36 F3
Stony Cross Hereford 26 D4
Stony Stratford M Keynes 28 D4
Stonyfield Highld 87 D9
Stoodleigh Devon 7 E8
Stopes S Yorks 44 D6
Stopham W Sus 11 C9
Stopsley Luton 29 F8
Stores Corner Suff 31 D10
Storeton Mers 42 D6
Stornoway W Isles 91 D9
Stornoway Airport W Isles 91 D9
Storridge Hereford 26 D4
Storrington W Sus 11 C9
Storrs Cumb 56 G5
Storth Cumb 49 A4
Storwood E Yorks 52 E3
Stotfield Moray 88 A2
Stotfold Beds 29 E9
Stottesdon Shrops 34 G2
Stoughton Leics 36 E2
Stoughton Sur 18 F6
Stoughton W Sus 11 C7
Stoul Highld 79 B10
Stoulton Worcs 26 D6
Stour Provost Dorset 9 B6
Stour Row Dorset 9 B7
Stourbridge W Mid 34 G5
Stourpaine Dorset 9 D7
Stourport on Severn Worcs 26 A5
Stourton Staffs 34 G4
Stourton Warks 27 E9
Stourton Wilts 9 A6
Stourton Caundle Dorset 8 C6
Stove Orkney 95 E7
Stove Shetland 96 L6
Stoven Suff 39 G10
Stow Borders 70 F3
Stow Lincs 46 D2
Stow Lincs 37 B6
Stow Bardolph Norf 38 E2
Stow Bedon Norf 38 F5
Stow cum Quy Cambs 30 B2
Stow Longa Cambs 29 A8
Stow Maries Essex 20 B5
Stow-on-the-Wold Glos 27 F8
Stowbridge Norf 38 E2
Stowe Shrops 25 A10
Stowe-by-Chartley Staffs 34 C6
Stowe Green Glos 26 H2
Stowell Som 8 B5
Stowford Devon 4 C5
Stowlangtoft Suff 30 B6
Stowmarket Suff 31 C7
Stowting Kent 13 B10
Stowupland Suff 31 C7
Straad Argyll 73 G9
Strachan Aberds 83 D8
Stradbroke Suff 31 A9
Stradishall Suff 30 C4
Stradsett Norf 38 E2
Stragglethorpe Lincs 46 G3
Straid S Ayrs 66 G4
Straith Dumfries 60 E4
Straiton Edin 69 D11
Straiton S Ayrs 67 F6
Straloch Aberds 89 F8
Straloch Perth 76 A3
Stramshall Staffs 35 B6
Strang I o M 48 E3
Stranraer Dumfries 54 C3
Stratfield Mortimer W Berks 18 E3
Stratfield Saye Hants 18 E3
Stratfield Turgis Hants 18 F3
Stratford London 19 C10
Stratford St Andrew Suff 31 B10
Stratford St Mary Suff 31 E7
Stratford Sub Castle Wilts 9 A10
Stratford Tony Wilts 9 B9
Stratford-upon-Avon Warks 27 C8
Strath Highld 94 E4
Strath Highld 85 A12
Strathan Highld 80 D1
Strathan Highld 93 C8
Strathan Highld 92 G3
Strathaven S Lnrk 68 F6
Strathblane Stirl 68 C4
Strathcanaird Highld 92 J4
Strathcarron Highld 86 G2
Strathcoil Argyll 79 H9
Strathdon Aberds 82 B5
Strathellie Aberds 89 B10
Strathkinness Fife 77 F7
Strathmashie House Highld 81 D7
Strathmiglo Fife 76 F5
Strathmore Lodge Highld 94 F3
Strathpeffer Highld 86 F7
Strathrannoch Highld 86 D6
Strathtay Perth 76 B2
Strathvaich Lodge Highld 86 D6
Strathwhillan N Ayrs 66 C3
Strathy Highld 93 C11
Strathyre Stirl 75 F8
Stratton Corn 4 A3
Stratton Dorset 8 E5
Stratton Glos 17 A7
Stratton Audley Oxon 28 F3
Stratton on the Fosse Som 16 F3
Stratton St Margaret Swindon 17 C8
Stratton St Michael Norf 39 F8
Stratton Strawless Norf 39 C8
Stravithie Fife 77 F8
Streat E Sus 12 E2
Streatham London 19 D10
Streatley Beds 29 F7
Streatley W Berks 18 C2
Street Lancs 49 D5
Street N Yorks 59 F8
Street Som 15 H10
Street Dinas Shrops 33 B9
Street End Kent 21 F8
Street End W Sus 11 E7
Street Gate T & W 63 H8
Street Lydan Wrex 33 B10
Streethay Staffs 35 D7
Streetlam N Yorks 58 G4
Streetly W Mid 35 F6
Streetly End Cambs 30 D3
Strefford Shrops 33 G10
Strelley Notts 35 A11
Strensall York 52 C2
Stretcholt Som 15 G8
Strete Devon 5 G9
Stretford Gtr Man 44 C2
Strethall Essex 29 E11
Stretham Cambs 30 A2
Strettington W Sus 11 D7
Stretton Ches 43 G7
Stretton Derbys 45 F7
Stretton Rutland 36 D5
Stretton Staffs 34 D4
Stretton Staffs 35 C8
Stretton Warr 43 D9
Stretton Grandison Hereford 26 D3
Stretton-on-Dunsmore Warks 27 A11
Stretton-on-Fosse Warks 27 E9
Stretton Sugwas Hereford 25 D11
Stretton under Fosse Warks 35 G10
Stretton Westwood Shrops 34 F1
Strichen Aberds 89 C9
Strines Gtr Man 44 D3
Stringston Som 7 B10
Strixton Northants 28 B6
Stroat Glos 16 B2
Stromeferry Highld 85 E13
Stromemore Highld 85 E13
Stromness Orkney 95 H3
Stronaba Highld 80 E4
Stronachlachar Stirl 75 F7
Stronchreggan Highld 80 F2
Stronchrubie Highld 92 H5
Strone Argyll 73 E10
Strone Highld 81 A7
Strone Highld 80 E3
Strone Invclyd 73 F11
Stronmilchan Argyll 74 E4
Stronsay Airport Orkney 95 F7
Strontian Highld 79 E11
Strood Medway 20 E4
Strood Green Sur 19 G9
Strood Green W Sus 11 B9
Strood Green W Sus 11 A10
Stroud Glos 26 H5
Stroud Hants 10 B6
Stroud Green Essex 20 B5
Stroxton Lincs 36 B5
Struan Highld 85 E8
Struan Perth 81 G10
Strubby Lincs 47 D8
Strumpshaw Norf 39 E9
Strutherhill S Lnrk 68 F6
Struy Highld 86 H6
Stryt-issa Wrex 42 H5
Stuartfield Aberds 89 D9
Stub Place Cumb 56 G2
Stubbington Hants 10 D4
Stubbins Lancs 50 H3
Stubbs Cross Kent 13 C8
Stubb's Green Norf 39 F8
Stubbs Green Norf 39 F9
Stubhampton Dorset 9 C8
Stubton Lincs 46 H2
Stuckgowan Argyll 74 G6
Stuckton Hants 9 C10
Stud Green Windsor 18 D5
Studham Beds 29 G7
Studland Dorset 9 F9
Studley Warks 27 B7
Studley Wilts 16 D6
Studley Roger N Yorks 51 B8
Stump Cross Essex 30 D2
Stuntney Cambs 38 H1
Sturbridge Staffs 34 B4
Sturmer Essex 30 D3
Sturminster Marshall Dorset 9 D8
Sturminster Newton Dorset 9 C6
Sturry Kent 21 E8
Sturton N Lincs 46 B3
Sturton by Stow Lincs 46 D2
Sturton le Steeple Notts 45 D11
Stuston Suff 39 H7
Stutton N Yorks 51 E10
Stutton Suff 31 E8
Styal Ches 44 D2
Styrrup Notts 45 C10
Suainebost W Isles 91 A10
Suardail W Isles 91 D9
Succoth Aberds 88 E4
Succoth Argyll 74 G5
Suckley Worcs 26 C4
Suckquoy Orkney 95 K5
Sudborough Northants 36 G5
Sudbourne Suff 31 C11
Sudbrook Lincs 36 A5
Sudbrook Mon 15 C11
Sudbrooke Lincs 46 E4
Sudbury Derbys 35 B7
Sudbury London 19 C8
Sudbury Suff 30 D5
Suddie Highld 87 F9
Sudgrove Glos 26 H6
Suffield Norf 39 B8
Suffield N Yorks 59 G10
Sugnall Staffs 34 B3
Suladale Highld 85 C8
Sulaisiadar W Isles 91 D10
Sulby I o M 48 C3
Sulgrave Northants 28 D2
Sulham W Berks 18 D3
Sulhamstead W Berks 18 E3
Sulland Orkney 95 D6
Sullington W Sus 11 C9
Sullom Shetland 96 F5
Sullom Voe Oil Terminal Shetland 96 F5
Sully V Glam 15 E7
Sumburgh Shetland 96 N6
Sumburgh Airport Shetland 96 M5
Summer Bridge N Yorks 51 C8
Summer-house Darl 58 E3
Summercourt Corn 3 D7
Summerfield Norf 38 B3
Summergangs Hull 53 F7
Summerleaze Mon 15 C10
Summersdale W Sus 11 D7
Summerseat Gtr Man 43 A10
Summertown Oxon 28 H2
Summit Gtr Man 44 B3
Sunbury-on-Thames Sur 19 E8
Sundaywell Dumfries 60 E4
Sunderland Argyll 64 B3
Sunderland Cumb 56 C3
Sunderland T & W 63 H9
Sunderland Bridge Durham 58 C3
Sundhope Borders 70 H2
Sundon Park Luton 29 F7
Sundridge Kent 19 F11
Sunipol Argyll 78 F6
Sunk Island E Yorks 53 H8
Sunningdale Windsor 18 E6
Sunninghill Windsor 18 E6
Sunningwell Oxon 17 A11
Sunniside Durham 58 C2
Sunniside T & W 63 H8
Sunnyhurst Blkburn 50 G2
Sunnylaw Stirl 75 H10
Sunnyside W Sus 12 C2
Sunton Wilts 17 F9
Surbiton London 19 E8
Surby I o M 48 E2
Surfleet Lincs 37 C8
Surfleet Seas End Lincs 37 C8
Surlingham Norf 39 E9
Sustead Norf 39 B7
Susworth Lincs 46 B2
Sutcombe Devon 6 E2
Suton Norf 39 F6
Sutors of Cromarty Highld 87 E11
Sutterby Lincs 47 E7
Sutterton Lincs 37 B8
Sutton Beds 29 D9
Sutton Cambs 37 H10
Sutton London 19 E9
Sutton Kent 21 G10
Sutton Mers 43 C8
Sutton Norf 39 C9
Sutton Notts 36 B3
Sutton Notts 45 D10
Sutton N Yorks 51 G10
Sutton Oxon 27 H11
Sutton P'boro 37 F6
Sutton Shrops 34 G3
Sutton Shrops 34 B2
Sutton Som 8 A5
Sutton Staffs 34 C3
Sutton Suff 31 D10
Sutton Sur 19 G7
Sutton S Yorks 45 A9
Sutton W Sus 11 C8
Sutton at Hone Kent 20 D2
Sutton Bassett Northants 36 F3
Sutton Benger Wilts 16 D6
Sutton Bonington Notts 35 C11
Sutton Bridge Lincs 37 C10
Sutton Cheney Leics 35 E10
Sutton Coldfield W Mid 35 F7
Sutton Courtenay Oxon 18 B2
Sutton Crosses Lincs 37 C10
Sutton Grange N Yorks 51 B8
Sutton Green Sur 19 F7
Sutton Howgrave N Yorks 51 B9
Sutton In Ashfield Notts 45 G8
Sutton-in-Craven N Yorks 50 E6
Sutton in the Elms Leics 35 F11
Sutton Ings Hull 53 F7
Sutton Lane Ends Ches 44 E3
Sutton Leach Mers 43 C8
Sutton Maddock Shrops 34 E3
Sutton Mallet Som 15 H9
Sutton Mandeville Wilts 9 B8
Sutton Manor Mers 43 C8
Sutton Montis Som 8 B5
Sutton on Hull Hull 53 F7
Sutton on Sea Lincs 47 D9
Sutton-on-the-Forest N Yorks 52 C1
Sutton on the Hill Derbys 35 B8
Sutton on Trent Notts 45 F11
Sutton St Edmund Lincs 37 D9
Sutton St James Lincs 37 D9
Sutton St Nicholas Hereford 26 D2
Sutton Scarsdale Derbys 45 F8
Sutton Scotney Hants 17 H11
Sutton under Brailes Warks 27 E10
Sutton-under-Whitestonecliffe N Yorks 51 A10
Sutton upon Derwent E Yorks 52 E3
Sutton Valence Kent 20 G5
Sutton Veny Wilts 16 G5
Sutton Waldron Dorset 9 C7
Sutton Weaver Ches 43 E8
Sutton Wick Bath 16 F2
Swaby Lincs 47 E7
Swadlincote Derbys 35 D9
Swaffham Norf 38 E4
Swaffham Bulbeck Cambs 30 B2
Swaffham Prior Cambs 30 B2
Swafield Norf 39 B8
Swainby N Yorks 58 F5
Swainshill Hereford 25 D11
Swainsthorpe Norf 39 E8
Swainswick Bath 16 E4
Swalcliffe Oxon 27 E10
Swalecliffe Kent 21 E8
Swallow Lincs 46 B5
Swallowcliffe Wilts 9 B8
Swallowfield Wokingham 18 E4
Swallownest S Yorks 45 D8
Swallows Cross Essex 20 B3
Swan Green Ches 43 E10
Swan Green Suff 31 A9
Swanage Dorset 9 G9
Swanbister Orkney 95 H4
Swanbourne Bucks 28 F5
Swanland E Yorks 52 G5
Swanley Kent 20 E2
Swanley Village Kent 20 E2
Swanmore Hants 10 C4
Swannington Leics 35 D10
Swannington Norf 39 D7
Swanscombe Kent 20 D3
Swansea = Abertawe Swansea 14 B2
Swanton Abbott Norf 39 C8
Swanton Morley Norf 38 D6
Swanton Novers Norf 38 B6
Swanton Street Kent 20 F5
Swanwick Derbys 45 G8
Swanwick Hants 10 D4
Swarby Lincs 36 A6
Swardeston Norf 39 E8
Swarister Shetland 96 E7
Swarkestone Derbys 35 C9
Swarland Northumb 63 C7
Swarland Estate Northumb 63 C7
Swarthmoor Cumb 49 B2
Swathwick Derbys 45 F7
Swaton Lincs 37 B7
Swavesey Cambs 29 B10
Sway Hants 10 E1
Swayfield Lincs 36 C5
Swaythling Soton 10 C3
Sweet Green Worcs 26 B3
Sweetham Devon 7 G7
Sweethouse Corn 4 E1
Sweffling Suff 31 B10
Swepstone Leics 35 D9
Swerford Oxon 27 E10
Swettenham Ches 44 F2
Swetton N Yorks 51 B7
Swffryd Bl Gwent 15 B8
Swiftsden E Sus 12 D6
Swilland Suff 31 C8
Swillington W Yorks 51 F9
Swimbridge Devon 6 D5
Swimbridge Newland Devon 6 C5
Swinbrook Oxon 27 G9
Swinderby Lincs 46 F2
Swindon Glos 26 F6
Swindon Staffs 34 F4
Swindon Swindon 17 C8
Swine E Yorks 53 F7
Swinefleet E Yorks 52 G3
Swineshead Beds 29 B7
Swineshead Lincs 37 A8
Swineshead Bridge Lincs 37 A8
Swiney Highld 94 G4
Swinford Leics 36 H1
Swinford Oxon 27 H11
Swingate Notts 35 A11
Swingfield Minnis Kent 21 G9
Swingfield St Kent 21 G9
Swinhoe Northumb 71 H11
Swinhope Lincs 46 C6
Swining Shetland 96 G6
Swinithwaite N Yorks 58 H1
Swinnow Moor W Yorks 51 F8
Swinscoe Staffs 44 H5
Swinside Hall Borders 62 B3
Swinstead Lincs 36 C6
Swinton Borders 71 F7
Swinton Gtr Man 43 B10
Swinton N Yorks 51 B8
Swinton N Yorks 52 B3
Swinton S Yorks 45 C8
Swintonmill Borders 71 F7
Swithland Leics 35 D11
Swordale Highld 87 E8
Swordland Highld 79 B10
Swordly Highld 93 C10
Sworton Heath Ches 43 D9
Swydd-ffynnon Ceredig 24 B3
Swynnerton Staffs 34 B4
Swyre Dorset 8 F4
Sychtyn Powys 32 E5
Syde Glos 26 G6
Sydenham London 19 D10
Sydenham Oxon 18 A4
Sydenham Damerel Devon 4 D5
Syderstone Norf 38 B4
Sydling St Nicholas Dorset 8 E5
Sydmonton Hants 17 F11
Syerston Notts 45 H11
Syke Gtr Man 50 H4
Sykehouse S Yorks 52 H2
Sykes Lancs 50 D2
Syleham Suff 39 H8
Sylen Carms 23 F10
Symbister Shetland 96 G7
Symington S Ayrs 67 C6
Symington S Lnrk 69 G8
Symonds Yat Hereford 26 G2
Symondsbury Dorset 8 E3
Synod Inn Ceredig 23 A9
Syre Highld 93 E9
Syreford Glos 27 F7
Syresham Northants 28 D3
Syston Leics 36 D2
Syston Lincs 36 A5
Sytchampton Worcs 26 B5
Sywell Northants 28 B5

T

Taagan Highld 86 E3
Tàbost W Isles 91 A10
Tabost W Isles 91 F8
Tackley Oxon 27 F11
Tacleit W Isles 90 D6
Tacolneston Norf 39 F7
Tadcaster N Yorks 51 E10
Taddington Derbys 44 E5
Taddiport Devon 6 E3
Tadley Hants 18 E3
Tadlow Beds 29 D9
Tadmarton Oxon 27 E10
Tadworth Sur 19 F9
Tafarn-y-gelyn Denb 42 F4
Tafarnau-bach Bl Gwent 25 G8
Taff's Well Rhondda 15 C7
Tafolwern Powys 32 E4
Tai Conwy 41 D9
Tai-bach Powys 33 C7
Tai-mawr Conwy 32 A5
Tai-Ucha Denb 42 G3
Taibach Neath 14 C3
Taigh a Ghearraidh W Isles 84 A2
Tain Highld 87 C10
Tain Highld 94 D4
Tainant Wrex 42 H5
Tainlon Gwyn 40 E6
Tai'r-Bull Powys 24 F6
Tairbeart = Tarbert W Isles 90 G6
Tairgwaith Neath 24 G4
Takeley Essex 30 F2
Takeley Street Essex 30 F2
Tal-sarn Ceredig 23 A10
Tal-y-bont Ceredig 32 G2
Tal-y-Bont Conwy 41 D9
Tal-y-bont Gwyn 41 C8
Tal-y-bont Gwyn 32 C1
Tal-y-cafn Conwy 41 C9
Tal-y-llyn Gwyn 32 E3
Tal-y-wern Powys 32 E4
Talachddu Powys 25 E7
Talacre Flint 42 D4
Talardd Gwyn 32 C4
Talaton Devon 7 G9
Talbenny Pembs 22 E3
Talbot Green Rhondda 14 C6
Talbot Village Poole 9 E9
Tale Devon 7 F9
Talerddig Powys 32 E5
Talgarreg Ceredig 23 A9
Talgarth Powys 25 E8
Talisker Highld 85 E8
Talke Staffs 44 G2
Talkin Cumb 61 H11
Talla Linnfoots Borders 61 A7
Talladale Highld 86 D2
Tallarn Green Wrex 33 A10
Tallentire Cumb 56 C3
Talley Carms 24 E3
Tallington Lincs 37 E6
Talmine Highld 93 C8
Talog Carms 23 D8
Talsarn Carms 24 F4
Talsarnau Gwyn 41 G8
Talskiddy Corn 3 C8
Talwrn Anglesey 40 C6
Talwrn Wrex 42 H5
Talybont-on-Usk Powys 25 F8
Talygarn Rhondda 14 C6
Talyllyn Powys 25 F8

Talysarn Gwyn 40 E6
Talywain Torf 15 A8
Tame Bridge N Yorks 58 F6
Tamerton Foliot Plym 4 E5
Tamworth Staffs 35 E8
Tan Hinon Powys 32 G4
Tan-lan Conwy 41 D9
Tan-lan Gwyn 41 F8
Tan-y-bwlch Gwyn 41 F8
Tan-y-fron Conwy 42 F2
Tan-y-graig Anglesey 41 C7
Tan-y-graig Gwyn 40 G5
Tan-y-groes Ceredig 23 B7
Tan-y-pistyll Powys 33 C6
Tan-yr-allt Gwyn 40 E6
Tandem W Yorks 51 H7
Tanden Kent 13 C8
Tandridge Sur 19 F10
Tanerdy Carms 23 D9
Tanfield Durham 63 H7
Tanfield Lea Durham 58 A2
Tangasdal W Isles 84 J1
Tangiers Pembs 22 E4
Tangley Hants 17 F10
Tanglwst Carms 23 C8
Tangmere W Sus 11 D8
Tangwick Shetland 96 F4
Tankersley S Yorks 45 B7
Tankerton Kent 21 E8
Tannach Highld 94 F5
Tannachie Aberds 83 E9
Tannadice Angus 77 B7
Tannington Suff 31 B9
Tansley Derbys 45 G7
Tansley Knoll Derbys 45 F7
Tansor Northants 37 F6
Tantobie Durham 58 A2
Tanton N Yorks 58 E6
Tanworth-in-Arden Warks 27 A8
Tanygrisiau Gwyn 41 F8
Tanyrhydiau Ceredig 24 B4
Taobh a Chaolais W Isles 84 G2
Taobh a Thuath Loch Aineort W Isles 84 F2
Taobh a Tuath Loch Baghasdail W Isles 84 F2
Taobh a'Ghlinne W Isles 91 F8
Taobh Tuath W Isles 90 J4
Taplow Bucks 18 C6
Tapton Derbys 45 E7
Tarbat Ho. Highld 87 D10
Tarbert Argyll 72 E5
Tarbert Argyll 73 G7
Tarbert Argyll 65 C7
Tarbert = Tairbeart W Isles 90 G6
Tarbet Argyll 74 G6
Tarbet Highld 92 E4
Tarbet Highld 79 B10
Tarbock Green Mers 43 D7
Tarbolton S Ayrs 67 D7
Tarbrax S Lnrk 69 E9
Tardebigge Worcs 27 B7
Tarfside Angus 82 F6
Tarland Aberds 82 C6
Tarleton Lancs 49 G4
Tarlogie Highld 87 C10
Tarlscough Lancs 43 A7
Tarlton Glos 16 B6
Tarnbrook Lancs 50 D1
Tarporley Ches 43 F8
Tarr Som 7 C10
Tarrant Crawford Dorset 9 D8
Tarrant Gunville Dorset 9 C8
Tarrant Hinton Dorset 9 C8
Tarrant Keyneston Dorset 9 D8
Tarrant Launceston Dorset 9 D8
Tarrant Monkton Dorset 9 D8
Tarrant Rawston Dorset 9 D8
Tarrant Rushton Dorset 9 D8
Tarrel Highld 87 C11
Tarring Neville E Sus 12 F3
Tarrington Hereford 26 D3
Tarsappie Perth 76 E4
Tarskavaig Highld 85 H10
Tarves Aberds 89 E8
Tarvie Highld 86 F7
Tarvie Perth 76 A3
Tarvin Ches 43 F7
Tasburgh Norf 39 F8
Tasley Shrops 34 F2
Taston Oxon 27 F10
Tatenhill Staffs 35 C8
Tathall End M Keynes 28 D5
Tatham Lancs 50 C2
Tathwell Lincs 47 D7
Tatling End Bucks 19 C7
Tatsfield Sur 19 F11
Tattenhall Ches 43 G7
Tattenhoe M Keynes 28 E5
Tatterford Norf 38 C4
Tattersett Norf 38 B4
Tattershall Lincs 46 G6
Tattershall Bridge Lincs 46 G5
Tattershall Thorpe Lincs 46 G6
Tattingstone Suff 31 E8
Tatworth Som 8 D2
Taunton Som 7 D11
Taverham Norf 39 D7
Tavernspite Pembs 22 E6
Tavistock Devon 4 D5
Taw Green Devon 6 G5
Tawstock Devon 6 D4
Taxal Derbys 44 E4
Tay Bridge Dundee 77 E7
Tayinloan Argyll 65 D7
Taymouth Castle Perth 75 C10
Taynish Argyll 72 E6
Taynton Glos 26 F4
Taynton Oxon 27 G9
Taynuilt Argyll 74 D3
Tayport Fife 77 E7
Tayvallich Argyll 72 E6
Tealby Lincs 46 C5
Tealing Angus 77 D7
Teangue Highld 85 H11
Teanna Mhachair W Isles 84 B2
Tebay Cumb 57 F8
Tebworth Beds 28 F6
Tedburn St Mary Devon 7 G7
Teddington Glos 26 E6
Teddington London 19 D8
Tedstone Delamere Hereford 26 C3
Tedstone Wafre Hereford 26 C3
Teeton Northants 28 A3
Teffont Evias Wilts 9 A8
Teffont Magna Wilts 9 A8
Tegryn Pembs 23 C7
Teigh Rutland 36 D4
Teigncombe Devon 5 C7
Teigngrace Devon 5 D9
Teignmouth Devon 5 D10
Telford Telford 34 E2
Telham E Sus 13 E6
Tellisford Som 16 F5
Telscombe E Sus 12 F2
Telscombe Cliffs E Sus 12 F2
Templand Dumfries 60 E6
Temple Corn 4 D2
Temple Glasgow 68 D4
Temple Midloth 70 E2
Temple Balsall W Mid 35 H8
Temple Bar Ceredig 23 A10
Temple Bar Carms 23 E10
Temple Cloud Bath 16 F3
Temple Combe Som 8 B6
Temple Ewell Kent 21 G9
Temple Grafton Warks 27 C8
Temple Guiting Glos 27 F7
Temple Herdewyke Warks 27 C10
Temple Hirst N Yorks 52 G2
Temple Normanton Derbys 45 F8
Temple Sowerby Cumb 57 D8
Templehall Fife 69 A11
Templeton Devon 7 E7
Templeton Pembs 22 E6
Templeton Bridge Devon 7 E7
Templetown Durham 58 A2
Tempsford Beds 29 C8
Ten Mile Bank Norf 38 F2
Tenbury Wells Worcs 26 B2
Tenby = Dinbych-y-Pysgod Pembs 22 F6
Tendring Essex 31 F8
Tendring Green Essex 31 F8
Tenston Orkney 95 G3
Tenterden Kent 13 C7
Terling Essex 30 G4
Ternhill Shrops 34 B2
Terregles Banks Dumfries 60 F5
Terrick Bucks 28 H5
Terrington N Yorks 52 B2
Terrington St Clement Norf 37 D11
Terrington St John Norf 37 D11
Teston Kent 20 F4
Testwood Hants 10 C2
Tetbury Glos 16 B5
Tetbury Upton Glos 16 B5
Tetchill Shrops 33 B9
Tetcott Devon 6 G2
Tetford Lincs 47 E7
Tetney Lincs 47 B7
Tetney Lock Lincs 47 B7
Tetsworth Oxon 18 A3
Tettenhall W Mid 34 F4
Teuchan Aberds 89 E10
Teversal Notts 45 F8
Teversham Cambs 29 C11
Teviothead Borders 61 C10
Tewel Aberds 83 E10
Tewin Herts 29 G9
Tewkesbury Glos 26 E5
Teynham Kent 20 E6
Thackthwaite Cumb 56 D3
Thainston Aberds 83 F8
Thakeham W Sus 11 C10
Thame Oxon 28 H4
Thames Ditton Sur 19 E8
Thames Haven Thurrock 20 C4
Thamesmead London 19 C11
Thanington Kent 21 F8
Thankerton S Lnrk 69 G8
Tharston Norf 39 F7
Thatcham W Berks 18 E2
Thatto Heath Mers 43 C8
Thaxted Essex 30 E3
The Aird Highld 85 C9
The Arms Norf 38 F4
The Bage Hereford 25 D9
The Balloch Perth 75 F11
The Barony Orkney 95 F3
The Bog Shrops 33 F9
The Bourne Sur 18 G5
The Braes Highld 85 E10
The Broad Hereford 25 B11
The Butts Som 16 G4
The Camp Glos 26 H6
The Camp Herts 29 H8
The Chequer Wrex 33 A10
The City Bucks 18 B4
The Common Wilts 9 A11
The Craigs Highld 86 B7
The Cronk I o M 48 C3
The Dell Suff 39 F10
The Den N Ayrs 66 A6
The Eals Northumb 62 E3
The Eaves Glos 26 H3
The Flatt Cumb 61 F11
The Four Alls Shrops 34 B2
The Garths Shetland 96 B8
The Green Cumb 49 A1
The Green Wilts 9 A7
The Grove Dumfries 60 F5
The Hall Shetland 96 D8
The Haven W Sus 11 A9
The Heath Norf 39 C7
The Heath Suff 31 E8
The Hill Cumb 49 A1
The Howe Cumb 56 H6
The Howe I o M 48 F1
The Hundred Hereford 26 B2
The Lee Bucks 18 A6
The Lhen I o M 48 B3
The Marsh Powys 33 F9
The Marsh Wilts 17 C7
The Middles Durham 58 A3
The Moor Kent 13 D6
The Mumbles = Y Mwmbwls Swansea 14 C2
The Murray S Lnrk 68 E5
The Neuk Aberds 83 D9
The Oval Bath 16 E4
The Pole of Itlaw Aberds 89 C6
The Quarry Glos 16 B4
The Rhos Pembs 22 E5
The Rock Telford 34 E2
The Ryde Herts 29 H9
The Sands Sur 18 G5
The Stocks Kent 13 D8
The Throat Wokingham 18 E5
The Vauld Hereford 26 D2
The Wyke Shrops 34 E3
Theakston N Yorks 58 H4
Thealby N Lincs 46 A2
Theale Som 15 G10
Theale W Berks 18 D3
Thearne E Yorks 53 F6
Theberton Suff 31 B11
Theddingworth Leics 36 G2
Theddlethorpe All Saints Lincs 47 D8
Theddlethorpe St Helen Lincs 47 D8
Thelbridge Barton Devon 7 E6
Thelnetham Suff 38 H6
Thelveton Norf 39 G7
Thelwall Warr 43 D9
Themelthorpe Norf 39 C6
Thenford Northants 28 D2
Therfield Herts 29 E10
Thetford Lincs 37 D7
Thetford Norf 38 G4
Theydon Bois Essex 19 B11
Thickwood Wilts 16 D5
Thimbleby Lincs 46 F6
Thimbleby N Yorks 58 G5
Thingwall Mers 42 D5
Thirdpart N Ayrs 66 B4
Thirlby N Yorks 51 A10
Thirlestane Borders 70 F4
Thirn N Yorks 58 H3
Thirsk N Yorks 51 A10
Thirtleby E Yorks 53 F7
Thistleton Lancs 49 F4
Thistleton Rutland 36 D5
Thistley Green Suff 38 H2
Thixendale N Yorks 52 C4
Thockrington Northumb 62 F5
Tholomas Drove Cambs 37 E9
Tholthorpe N Yorks 51 C10
Thomas Chapel Pembs 22 F6
Thomas Close Cumb 56 B6
Thomastown Aberds 88 E5
Thompson Norf 38 F5
Thomshill Moray 88 C2
Thong Kent 20 D3
Thongsbridge W Yorks 44 B5
Thoralby N Yorks 58 H1
Thoresway Lincs 46 C5
Thorganby Lincs 46 C6
Thorganby N Yorks 52 E2
Thorgill N Yorks 59 G8
Thorington Suff 31 A11
Thorington Street Suff 31 E7
Thorlby N Yorks 50 D5
Thorley Herts 29 G11
Thorley Street Herts 29 G11
Thorley Street I o W 10 F2
Thormanby N Yorks 51 B10
Thornaby on Tees Stockton 58 E5
Thornage Norf 38 B6
Thornborough Bucks 28 E4
Thornborough N Yorks 51 B8
Thornbury Devon 6 F3
Thornbury Hereford 26 C3
Thornbury S Glos 16 B3
Thornbury W Yorks 51 F7
Thornby Northants 36 H2
Thorncliffe Staffs 44 G4
Thorncombe Dorset 8 D2
Thorncombe Dorset 9 D7
Thorncombe Street Sur 19 G7
Thorncote Green Beds 29 D8
Thorncross I o W 10 F3
Thorndon Suff 31 B8
Thorndon Cross Devon 6 G4
Thorne S Yorks 45 A10
Thorne St Margaret Som 7 D9
Thorner W Yorks 51 E9
Thorney Notts 46 E2
Thorney P'boro 37 E8
Thorney Crofts E Yorks 53 G8
Thorney Green Suff 31 B7
Thorney Hill Hants 9 E10
Thorney Toll Cambs 37 E9
Thornfalcon Som 8 B1
Thornford Dorset 8 C5
Thorngumbald E Yorks 53 G8
Thornham Norf 38 A3
Thornham Magna Suff 31 A8
Thornham Parva Suff 31 A8
Thornhaugh P'boro 37 E6
Thornhill Caerph 15 C7
Thornhill Cumb 56 F2
Thornhill Derbys 44 D5
Thornhill Dumfries 60 D4
Thornhill Soton 10 C3
Thornhill Stirl 75 H9
Thornhill W Yorks 51 H8
Thornhill Edge W Yorks 51 H8
Thornhill Lees W Yorks 51 H8
Thornholme E Yorks 53 C7
Thornley Durham 58 C2
Thornley Durham 58 C4
Thornliebank E Renf 68 E4
Thorns Suff 30 C4
Thorns Green Ches 43 D10
Thornsett Derbys 44 D4
Thornthwaite Cumb 56 D4
Thornthwaite N Yorks 51 D7
Thornton Angus 76 C6
Thornton Bucks 28 E4
Thornton E Yorks 52 E3
Thornton Fife 76 H5
Thornton Lancs 49 E3
Thornton Leics 35 E10
Thornton Lincs 46 F6
Thornton Mers 42 B6
Thornton M'bro 58 E5
Thornton Northumb 71 F8
Thornton Pembs 22 F4
Thornton W Yorks 51 F7
Thornton Curtis N Lincs 53 H6
Thornton Heath London 19 E10
Thornton Hough Mers 42 D6
Thornton in Craven N Yorks 50 E5
Thornton-le-Beans N Yorks 58 G4
Thornton-le-Clay N Yorks 52 C2
Thornton-le-Dale N Yorks 52 A4
Thornton le Moor Lincs 46 C4
Thornton-le-Moor N Yorks 58 H4
Thornton-le-Moors Ches 43 E7
Thornton-le-Street N Yorks 58 H5
Thornton Rust N Yorks 57 H11
Thornton Steward N Yorks 58 H2
Thornton Watlass N Yorks 58 H3
Thorntonhall S Lnrk 68 E4
Thorntonloch E Loth 70 C6
Thorntonpark Northumb 71 F8
Thornwood Common Essex 19 A11
Thornydykes Borders 70 F5
Thoroton Notts 36 A3
Thorp Arch W Yorks 51 E10
Thorpe Derbys 44 G5
Thorpe E Yorks 52 E5
Thorpe Lincs 47 D8
Thorpe Norf 39 F10
Thorpe Notts 45 H11
Thorpe N Yorks 50 C6
Thorpe Sur 19 E7
Thorpe Abbotts Norf 39 H7
Thorpe Acre Leics 35 C11
Thorpe Arnold Leics 36 C3
Thorpe Audlin W Yorks 51 H10
Thorpe Bassett N Yorks 52 B4
Thorpe Bay Sthend 20 C6
Thorpe by Water Rutland 36 F4
Thorpe Common Suff 31 E9
Thorpe Constantine Staffs 35 E8
Thorpe Culvert Lincs 47 F8
Thorpe End Norf 39 D8
Thorpe Fendykes Lincs 47 F8
Thorpe Green Essex 31 F8
Thorpe Green Suff 30 C6
Thorpe Hesley S Yorks 45 C7
Thorpe in Balne S Yorks 45 A9
Thorpe in the Fallows Lincs 46 D3
Thorpe Langton Leics 36 F3
Thorpe Larches Durham 58 D4
Thorpe-le-Soken Essex 31 F8
Thorpe le Street E Yorks 52 E4
Thorpe Malsor Northants 36 H4
Thorpe Mandeville Northants 28 D2
Thorpe Market Norf 39 B8
Thorpe Marriot Norf 39 D7
Thorpe Morieux Suff 30 C6
Thorpe on the Hill Lincs 46 F3
Thorpe St Andrew Norf 39 E8
Thorpe St Peter Lincs 47 F8
Thorpe Salvin S Yorks 45 D9
Thorpe Satchville Leics 36 D3
Thorpe Thewles Stockton 58 D5
Thorpe Tilney Lincs 46 G5
Thorpe Underwood N Yorks 51 D10
Thorpe Waterville Northants 36 G6
Thorpe Willoughby N Yorks 52 F1
Thorpeness Suff 31 C11
Thorrington Essex 31 G7
Thorverton Devon 7 F8
Thrandeston Suff 39 H7
Thrapston Northants 36 H5
Thrashbush N Lnrk 68 D6
Threapland Cumb 56 C3
Threapland N Yorks 50 C5
Threapwood Ches 43 H7
Threapwood Staffs 34 A6
Three Ashes Hereford 26 F2
Three Bridges W Sus 12 C1
Three Burrows Corn 2 E6
Three Chimneys Kent 13 C7
Three Cocks Powys 25 E8
Three Crosses Swansea 23 G10
Three Cups Corner E Sus 12 D5
Three Holes Norf 37 E11
Three Leg Cross E Sus 12 C5
Three Legged Cross Dorset 9 D9
Three Oaks E Sus 13 E7
Threehammer Common Norf 39 D9
Threekingham Lincs 37 B6
Threemile Cross Wokingham 18 E4
Threemilestone Corn 3 E6
Threemiletown W Loth 69 C9
Threlkeld Cumb 56 D5
Threshfield N Yorks 50 C5
Thrigby Norf 39 D10
Thringarth Durham 57 D11
Thringstone Leics 35 D10
Thrintoft N Yorks 58 G4
Thriplow Cambs 29 D11
Throckenholt Lincs 37 E9
Throcking Herts 29 E10
Throckley T & W 63 G7
Throckmorton Worcs 26 D6
Throphill Northumb 63 E7
Thropton Northumb 62 C6
Throsk Stirl 69 A7
Throwleigh Devon 6 G5
Throwley Kent 20 F6
Thrumpton Notts 35 B11
Thrumster Highld 94 F5
Thrunton Northumb 62 B6
Thrupp Glos 16 A5
Thrupp Oxon 27 G11
Thrushelton Devon 4 C5
Thrussington Leics 36 D2
Thruxton Hants 17 G9
Thruxton Hereford 25 E11
Thrybergh S Yorks 45 C8
Thulston Derbys 35 B10
Thundergay N Ayrs 66 B1
Thundersley Essex 20 C4
Thundridge Herts 29 G10
Thurcaston Leics 36 D1
Thurcroft S Yorks 45 D8
Thurgarton Norf 39 B7
Thurgarton Notts 45 H10
Thurgoland S Yorks 44 B6
Thurlaston Leics 35 F11
Thurlaston Warks 27 A11
Thurlbear Som 8 B1
Thurlby Lincs 37 D7
Thurlby Lincs 46 F3
Thurleigh Beds 29 C7
Thurlestone Devon 5 G7
Thurloxton Som 8 A1
Thurlstone S Yorks 44 B6
Thurlton Norf 39 F10
Thurlwood Ches 44 G2
Thurmaston Leics 36 E2
Thurnby Leics 36 E2
Thurne Norf 39 D10
Thurnham Kent 20 F5
Thurnham Lancs 49 D4
Thurning Norf 39 C6
Thurning Northants 37 G6
Thurnscoe S Yorks 45 B8
Thurnscoe East S Yorks 45 B8
Thursby Cumb 56 A5
Thursford Norf 38 B5
Thursley Sur 18 H6
Thurso Highld 94 D3
Thurso East Highld 94 D3
Thurstaston Mers 42 D5
Thurston Suff 30 B6
Thurstonfield Cumb 61 H9
Thurstonland W Yorks 44 A5
Thurton Norf 39 E9
Thurvaston Derbys 35 B8
Thuxton Norf 38 E6
Thwaite N Yorks 57 G10
Thwaite Suff 31 B8
Thwaite St Mary Norf 39 F9
Thwaites W Yorks 51 E6
Thwaites Brow W Yorks 51 E6
Thwing E Yorks 53 B6
Tibbermore Perth 76 E3
Tibberton Glos 26 F4
Tibberton Telford 34 C2
Tibberton Worcs 26 C6
Tibenham Norf 39 G7
Tibshelf Derbys 45 F8
Tibthorpe E Yorks 52 D5
Ticehurst E Sus 12 C5
Tichborne Hants 10 A4
Tickencote Rutland 36 E5
Tickenham N Som 15 D10
Tickhill S Yorks 45 C9
Ticklerton Shrops 33 F10
Ticknall Derbys 35 C9
Tickton E Yorks 53 E6
Tidcombe Wilts 17 F9
Tiddington Oxon 18 A3
Tiddington Warks 27 C9
Tidebrook E Sus 12 D5
Tideford Corn 4 F4
Tideford Cross Corn 4 E4
Tidenham Glos 16 B2
Tideswell Derbys 44 E5
Tidmarsh W Berks 18 D3
Tidmington Warks 27 E9
Tidpit Hants 9 C9
Tidworth Wilts 17 G9
Tiers Cross Pembs 22 E4
Tiffield Northants 28 C3
Tifty Aberds 89 D7
Tigerton Angus 77 A8
Tigh-na-Blair Perth 75 F10
Tighnabruaich Argyll 73 F8
Tighnafiline Highld 91 J13
Tigley Devon 5 E8
Tilbrook Cambs 29 B7
Tilbury Thurrock 20 D3
Tilbury Juxta Clare Essex 30 D4
Tile Cross W Mid 35 G7
Tile Hill W Mid 35 H8
Tilehurst Reading 18 D3
Tilford Sur 18 G5
Tilgate W Sus 12 C1
Tilgate Forest Row W Sus 12 C1
Tillathrowie Aberds 88 E4
Tilley Shrops 33 C11
Tillicoultry Clack 76 H2
Tillingham Essex 20 A6
Tillington Hereford 25 D11
Tillington W Sus 11 B8
Tillington Common Hereford 25 D11
Tillyarblet Angus 83 G7
Tillybirloch Aberds 83 C8
Tillycorthie Aberds 89 F9
Tillydrine Aberds 83 D8
Tillyfour Aberds 83 B7
Tillyfourie Aberds 83 B8
Tillygarmond Aberds 83 D8
Tillygreig Aberds 89 F8
Tillykerrie Aberds 89 F8
Tilmanstone Kent 21 F10
Tilney All Saints Norf 38 D1
Tilney High End Norf 38 D1
Tilney St Lawrence Norf 37 D11
Tilshead Wilts 17 G7
Tilstock Shrops 33 B11
Tilston Ches 43 G7
Tilstone Fearnall Ches 43 F8
Tilsworth Beds 28 F6
Tilton on the Hill Leics 36 E3
Timberland Lincs 46 G5
Timbersbrook Ches 44 F2
Timberscombe Som 7 B8
Timble N Yorks 51 D7
Timperley Gtr Man 43 D10
Timsbury Bath 16 F3
Timsbury Hants 10 B2
Timsgearraidh W Isles 90 D5
Timworth Green Suff 30 B5
Tincleton Dorset 9 E6
Tindale Cumb 62 H2
Tingewick Bucks 28 E3
Tingley W Yorks 51 G8
Tingrith Beds 29 E7
Tingwall Orkney 95 F4
Tinhay Devon 4 C4
Tinshill W Yorks 51 F8
Tinsley S Yorks 45 C8
Tintagel Corn 4 C1
Tintern Parva Mon 15 A11
Tintinhull Som 8 C4
Tintwistle Derbys 44 C4
Tinwald Dumfries 60 E6
Tinwell Rutland 36 E6
Tipperty Aberds 89 F9
Tipsend Norf 37 F11
Tipton W Mid 34 F5
Tipton St John Devon 7 G9
Tiptree Essex 30 G5
Tir-y-dail Carms 24 G3
Tirabad Powys 24 D5
Tiraghoil Argyll 78 J6
Tiree Airport Argyll 78 G2
Tirley Glos 26 F5
Tirphil Caerph 15 A7
Tirril Cumb 57 D7
Tisbury Wilts 9 B8
Tisman's Common W Sus 11 A9
Tissington Derbys 44 G5
Titchberry Devon 6 D1
Titchfield Hants 10 D4
Titchmarsh Northants 36 H6
Titchwell Norf 38 A3
Tithby Notts 36 B2
Titley Hereford 25 B10
Titlington Northumb 63 B7
Titsey Sur 19 F11
Tittensor Staffs 34 B4
Tittleshall Norf 38 C4
Tiverton Ches 43 F8
Tiverton Devon 7 E8
Tivetshall St Margaret Norf 39 G7
Tivetshall St Mary Norf 39 G7
Tividale W Mid 34 F5
Tivy Dale S Yorks 44 B6
Tixall Staffs 34 C5
Tixover Rutland 36 E5
Toab Orkney 95 H6
Toab Shetland 96 M5
Toadmoor Derbys 45 G7
Tobermory Argyll 79 F8
Toberonochy Argyll 72 C6
Tobha Mor W Isles 84 E2
Tobhtarol W Isles 90 D6
Tobson W Isles 90 D6
Tocher Aberds 89 E6
Tockenham Wilts 17 D7
Tockenham Wick Wilts 17 C7
Tockholes Blkburn 50 G2
Tockington S Glos 16 C3
Tockwith N Yorks 51 D10
Todber Dorset 9 B7
Todding Hereford 33 H10
Toddington Beds 29 F7
Toddington Glos 27 E7
Todenham Glos 27 E9
Todhills Cumb 61 G9
Todlachie Aberds 83 B8
Todmorden W Yorks 50 G5
Todrig Borders 61 B10
Todwick S Yorks 45 D8
Toft Cambs 29 C10
Toft Lincs 37 D6
Toft Hill Durham 58 D2
Toft Hill Lincs 46 F6
Toft Monks Norf 39 F10
Toft next Newton Lincs 46 D4
Toftrees Norf 38 C4
Tofts Highld 94 D5
Toftwood Norf 38 D5
Togston Northumb 63 C8
Tokavaig Highld 85 G11
Tokers Green Oxon 18 D4
Tolastadh a Chaolais W Isles 90 D6
Tolastadh bho Thuath W Isles 91 C10
Toll Bar S Yorks 45 B9
Toll End W Mid 34 F5
Toll of Birness Aberds 89 E10
Tolland Som 7 C10
Tollard Royal Wilts 9 C8
Tollbar End W Mid 35 H9
Toller Fratrum Dorset 8 E4
Toller Porcorum Dorset 8 E4
Tollerton Notts 36 B2
Tollerton N Yorks 51 C11
Tollesbury Essex 30 G6
Tolleshunt D'Arcy Essex 30 G6
Tolleshunt Major Essex 30 G6
Tolm W Isles 91 D9
Tolpuddle Dorset 9 E6
Tolvah Highld 81 D10
Tolworth London 19 E8
Tomatin Highld 81 A10
Tombreck Highld 87 H9
Tomchrasky Highld 80 B4
Tomdoun Highld 80 C3
Tomich Highld 80 A5
Tomich Highld 87 D9
Tomich House Highld 87 G8
Tomintoul Aberds 82 D3
Tomintoul Moray 82 B3
Tomnaven Moray 88 E4
Tomnavoulin Moray 82 A4
Ton-Pentre Rhondda 14 B5
Tonbridge Kent 20 G2
Tondu Bridgend 14 C4
Tonfanau Gwyn 32 E1
Tong Shrops 34 E3
Tong W Yorks 51 F8
Tong Norton Shrops 34 E3
Tonge Leics 35 C10
Tongham Sur 18 G5
Tongland Dumfries 55 D9
Tongue Highld 93 D8
Tongue End Lincs 37 D7
Tongwynlais Cardiff 15 C7
Tonna Neath 14 B3
Tonwell Herts 29 G10
Tonypandy Rhondda 14 B5
Tonyrefail Rhondda 14 C6
Toot Baldon Oxon 18 A2
Toot Hill Essex 20 A2
Toothill Hants 10 C2
Top of Hebers Gtr Man 44 B2
Topcliffe N Yorks 51 B10
Topcroft Norf 39 F8
Topcroft Street Norf 39 F8
Toppesfield Essex 30 E4
Toppings Gtr Man 43 A10
Topsham Devon 5 C10
Torbay Torbay 5 F10
Torbeg N Ayrs 66 D2
Torboll Farm Highld 87 B10
Torbrex Stirl 68 A6
Torbryan Devon 5 E9
Torcross Devon 5 G9
Tore Highld 87 F9
Torinturk Argyll 73 G7
Torksey Lincs 46 E2
Torlum W Isles 84 C2
Torlundy Highld 80 F3
Tormarton S Glos 16 D4
Tormisdale Argyll 64 C2
Tormitchell S Ayrs 66 G5
Tormore N Ayrs 66 C1
Tornagrain Highld 87 G10
Tornahaish Aberds 82 C4
Tornaveen Aberds 83 C8
Torness Highld 81 A7
Toronto Durham 58 C2
Torpenhow Cumb 56 C4
Torphichen W Loth 69 C8
Torphins Aberds 83 C8
Torpoint Corn 4 F5
Torquay Torbay 5 E10
Torquhan Borders 70 F3
Torran Argyll 73 C7
Torran Highld 85 D10
Torran Highld 87 D10
Torrance E Dunb 68 C5
Torrans Argyll 78 J7
Torranyard N Ayrs 67 B6
Torre Torbay 5 E10
Torridon Highld 86 F2
Torridon Ho. Highld 85 C13
Torrin Highld 85 F10
Torrisdale Highld 93 C9
Torrisdale-Square Argyll 65 E8
Torrish Highld 93 H12
Torrisholme Lancs 49 C4
Torroble Highld 93 J8
Torry Aberdeen 83 C11
Torry Aberds 88 E4
Torryburn Fife 69 B9
Torterston Aberds 89 D10
Torthorwald Dumfries 60 F6
Tortington W Sus 11 D9
Tortworth S Glos 16 B4
Torvaig Highld 85 D9
Torver Cumb 56 G4
Torwood Falk 69 B7
Torworth Notts 45 D10
Tosberry Devon 6 D1
Toscaig Highld 85 E12
Toseland Cambs 29 B9
Tosside N Yorks 50 D3
Tostock Suff 30 B6
Totaig Highld 84 C7
Totaig Highld 85 F13
Tote Highld 85 D9
Totegan Highld 93 C11
Tothill Lincs 47 D8
Totland I o W 10 F2
Totnes Devon 5 E9
Toton Notts 35 B11
Totronald Argyll 78 F4
Totscore Highld 85 B8
Tottenham London 19 B10
Tottenhill Norf 38 D2
Tottenhill Row Norf 38 D2
Totteridge London 19 B9
Totternhoe Beds 28 F6
Tottington Gtr Man 43 A10
Totton Hants 10 C2
Touchen End Windsor 18 D5
Tournaig Highld 91 J13
Toux Aberds 89 C9
Tovil Kent 20 F4
Tow Law Durham 58 C2
Toward Argyll 73 G10
Towcester Northants 28 D3
Towednack Corn 2 F3
Tower End Norf 38 D2
Towersey Oxon 28 H4
Towie Aberds 82 B6
Towie Aberds 89 B8
Towiemore Moray 88 D3
Town End Cambs 37 F10
Town End Cumb 49 A4
Town Row E Sus 12 C4
Town Yetholm Borders 71 H7
Townend W Dunb 68 C3
Towngate Lincs 37 D7
Townhead Cumb 57 C7
Townhead Dumfries 55 E9
Townhead S Ayrs 66 F5
Townhead S Yorks 44 B5
Townhead of Greenlaw Dumfries 55 C10
Townhill Fife 69 B10
Townsend Bucks 28 H4
Townsend Herts 29 H8
Townshend Corn 2 F4
Towthorpe York 52 D2
Towton N Yorks 51 F10
Towyn Conwy 42 E2
Toxteth Mers 42 D6
Toynton All Saints Lincs 47 F7
Toynton Fen Side Lincs 47 F7
Toynton St Peter Lincs 47 F8
Toy's Hill Kent 19 F11
Trabboch E Ayrs 67 D7
Traboe Corn 2 G6
Tradespark Highld 87 F11
Tradespark Orkney 95 H5
Trafford Park Gtr Man 43 C10
Trallong Powys 24 F6
Tranent E Loth 70 C3
Tranmere Mers 42 D6
Trantlebeg Highld 93 D11
Trantlemore Highld 93 D11
Tranwell Northumb 63 E7
Trapp Carms 24 G3
Traprain E Loth 70 C4
Traquair Borders 70 G2
Trawden Lancs 50 F5
Trawsfynydd Gwyn 41 G9
Tre-Gibbon Rhondda 24 H6
Tre-Taliesin Ceredig 32 F2
Tre-vaughan Carms 23 D8
Tre-wyn Mon 25 F10
Trealaw Rhondda 14 B6
Treales Lancs 49 F4
Trearddur Anglesey 40 C4
Treaslane Highld 85 C8
Trebanog Rhondda 14 B6
Trebanos Neath 14 A3
Trebartha Corn 4 D3
Trebarwith Corn 4 C1
Trebetherick Corn 3 B8
Treborough Som 7 C9
Trebudannon Corn 3 C7
Trebullett Corn 4 D4
Treburley Corn 4 D4
Trebyan Corn 4 E1
Trecastle Powys 24 F5
Trecenydd Caerph 15 C7
Trecwn Pembs 22 C4
Trecynon Rhondda 14 A5
Tredavoe Corn 2 G3
Treddiog Pembs 22 D3
Tredegar Bl Gwent 25 H8
Tredegar Newydd = New Tredegar Caerph 15 A7
Tredington Glos 26 F6
Tredington Warks 27 D9
Tredinnick Corn 3 B8
Tredomen Powys 25 E8
Tredunnock Mon 15 B9
Tredustan Powys 25 E8
Treen Corn 2 G2
Treeton S Yorks 45 D8
Tref-y-Clawdd = Knighton Powys 25 A9
Trefaldwyn = Montgomery Powys 33 F8
Trefasser Pembs 22 C3
Trefdraeth Anglesey 40 C6
Trefdraeth = Newport Pembs 22 C5
Trefecca Powys 25 E8
Trefechan Ceredig 32 G1
Trefeglwys Powys 32 F5
Trefenter Ceredig 24 B3
Treffgarne Pembs 22 D4
Treffynnon Pembs 22 D3
Treffynnon = Holywell Flint 42 E4
Trefgarn Owen Pembs 22 D3
Trefil Bl Gwent 25 G8
Trefilan Ceredig 23 A10
Trefin Pembs 22 C3
Treflach Shrops 33 C8
Trefnanney Powys 33 D8
Trefnant Denb 42 E3
Trefonen Shrops 33 C8
Trefor Anglesey 40 B5
Trefor Gwyn 40 F5
Treforest Rhondda 14 C6
Trefriw Conwy 41 D9
Trefynwy = Monmouth Mon 26 G2
Tregadillett Corn 4 C3
Tregaian Anglesey 40 C6
Tregare Mon 25 G11
Tregaron Ceredig 24 C3
Tregarth Gwyn 41 D8
Tregeare Corn 4 C3
Tregeiriog Wrex 33 B7
Tregele Anglesey 40 A5
Tregidden Corn 3 G6
Treglemais Pembs 22 D3
Tregole Corn 4 B2
Tregonetha Corn 3 C8
Tregony Corn 3 E8
Tregoss Corn 3 C8
Tregoyd Powys 25 E9
Tregroes Ceredig 23 B9
Tregurrian Corn 3 C7
Tregynon Powys 33 F6
Trehafod Rhondda 14 B6
Treharris M Tydf 14 B6
Treherbert Rhondda 14 B5
Trekenner Corn 4 D4
Treknow Corn 4 C1
Trelan Corn 2 H6
Trelash Corn 4 B2
Trelassick Corn 3 D7
Trelawnyd Flint 42 E3
Trelech Carms 23 C7
Treleddyd-fawr Pembs 22 D2
Trelewis M Tydf 15 B7
Treligga Corn 4 C1
Trelights Corn 3 B8
Trelill Corn 3 B9
Trelissick Corn 3 F7
Trellech Mon 26 H2
Trelleck Grange Mon 15 A10
Trelogan Flint 42 D4
Trelystan Powys 33 E8
Tremadog Gwyn 41 F7
Tremail Corn 4 C2
Tremain Ceredig 23 B7
Tremaine Corn 4 C3
Tremar Corn 4 E3
Trematon Corn 4 F4
Tremeirchion Denb 42 E3
Trenance Corn 3 C7
Trenarren Corn 3 E9
Trench Telford 34 D2
Treneglos Corn 4 C3
Trenewan Corn 4 F2
Trent Dorset 8 C4
Trent Vale Stoke 34 A4
Trentham Stoke 34 A4
Trentishoe Devon 6 B5
Treoes V Glam 14 D5
Treorchy = Treorci Rhondda 14 B5
Treorci = Treorchy Rhondda 14 B5
Tre'r-ddôl Ceredig 32 F2
Trerule Foot Corn 4 F4
Tresaith Ceredig 23 A7
Tresawle Corn 3 E7
Trescott Staffs 34 F4
Trescowe Corn 2 F4
Tresham Glos 16 B4
Tresillian Corn 3 E7
Tresinwen Pembs 22 B4
Treskinnick Cross Corn 4 B3
Tresmeer Corn 4 C3
Tresparrett Corn 4 B2
Tresparrett Posts Corn 4 B2
Tressait Perth 75 A11
Tresta Shetland 96 H5
Tresta Shetland 96 D8
Treswell Notts 45 E11
Trethosa Corn 3 D8
Trethurgy Corn 3 D9
Tretio Pembs 22 D2
Tretire Hereford 26 F2
Tretower Powys 25 F8
Treuddyn Flint 42 G5
Trevalga Corn 4 C1
Trevalyn Wrex 43 G6
Trevanson Corn 3 B8
Trevarren Corn 3 C8
Trevarrian Corn 3 C7
Trevarrick Corn 3 E8
Trevaughan Carms 22 E6
Treveighan Corn 4 D1
Trevellas Corn 2 D6
Treverva Corn 3 F6
Trevethin Torf 15 A8
Trevigro Corn 4 E4
Treviscoe Corn 3 D8
Trevone Corn 3 B7
Trewarmett Corn 4 C1
Trewassa Corn 4 C2
Trewellard Corn 2 F2
Trewen Corn 4 C3
Trewennack Corn 2 G5
Trewern Powys 33 D8
Trewethern Corn 3 B9
Trewidland Corn 4 F3
Trewint Corn 4 C3
Trewint Corn 4 B2
Trewithian Corn 3 F7
Trewoofe Corn 2 G3
Trewoon Corn 3 D8
Treworga Corn 3 E7
Treworlas Corn 3 F7
Treyarnon Corn 3 B7
Treyford W Sus 11 C7
Trezaise Corn 3 D8
Triangle W Yorks 50 G6
Trickett's Cross Dorset 9 D9
Triffleton Pembs 22 D4
Trimdon Durham 58 C4
Trimdon Colliery Durham 58 C4
Trimdon Grange Durham 58 C4
Trimingham Norf 39 B8
Trimley Lower Street Suff 31 E9
Trimley St Martin Suff 31 E9
Trimley St Mary Suff 31 E9
Trimpley Worcs 34 H3
Trimsaran Carms 23 F9
Trimstone Devon 6 B3
Trinafour Perth 75 A10
Trinant Caerph 15 A8
Tring Herts 28 G6
Tring Wharf Herts 28 G6
Trinity Angus 77 A9
Trinity Jersey 11
Trisant Ceredig 32 H3
Trislaig Highld 80 F2
Trispen Corn 3 D7
Tritlington Northumb 63 D8
Trochry Perth 76 C2
Trodigal Argyll 65 F7
Troed-rhiwdalar Powys 24 C6
Troedyraur Ceredig 23 B8
Troedyrhiw M Tydf 14 A6
Tromode I o M 48 E3
Trondavoe Shetland 96 F5
Troon Corn 2 F5
Troon S Ayrs 66 C6
Trosaraidh W Isles 84 G2
Trossachs Hotel Stirl 75 G8
Troston Suff 30 A5
Trottiscliffe Kent 20 E3
Trotton W Sus 11 B7
Troutbeck Cumb 56 F6
Troutbeck Cumb 56 D5
Troutbeck Bridge Cumb 56 F6
Trow Green Glos 26 H2
Trowbridge Wilts 16 F5
Trowell Notts 35 B10
Trowle Common Wilts 16 F5
Trowley Bottom Herts 29 G7
Trows Borders 70 G5
Trowse Newton Norf 39 E8
Trudoxhill Som 16 G4
Trull Som 7 D11
Trumaisgearraidh W Isles 84 A3
Trumpan Highld 84 B7
Trumpet Hereford 26 E3
Trumpington Cambs 29 C11
Trunch Norf 39 B8
Trunnah Lancs 49 E3
Truro Corn 3 E7
Trusham Devon 5 C9
Trusley Derbys 35 B8
Trusthorpe Lincs 47 D9
Trysull Staffs 34 F4
Tubney Oxon 17 B11
Tuckenhay Devon 5 F9
Tuckhill Shrops 34 G3
Tuckingmill Corn 2 E5
Tuddenham Suff 30 A4
Tuddenham St Martin Suff 31 D8
Tudeley Kent 20 G3
Tudhoe Durham 58 C3
Tudorville Hereford 26 F2
Tudweiliog Gwyn 40 G4
Tuesley Sur 18 G6
Tuffley Glos 26 G5
Tufton Hants 17 G11
Tufton Pembs 22 D5
Tugby Leics 36 E3
Tugford Shrops 34 G1
Tullibardine Perth 76 F2
Tullibody Clack 75 H11
Tullich Argyll 73 B9
Tullich Highld 81 A8
Tullich Muir Highld 87 D10
Tulliemet Perth 76 B2
Tulloch Aberds 83 F9
Tulloch Aberds 89 E8
Tulloch Perth 76 E3
Tulloch Castle Highld 87 E8
Tullochgorm Argyll 73 D8
Tulloes Angus 77 C8
Tullybannocher Perth 75 E10
Tullybelton Perth 76 D3
Tullyfergus Perth 76 C5
Tullymurdoch Perth 76 B4
Tullynessle Aberds 83 B7
Tumble Carms 23 E10
Tumby Woodside Lincs 46 G6
Tummel Bridge Perth 75 B10
Tunga W Isles 91 D9
Tunstall E Yorks 53 F9
Tunstall Kent 20 E5
Tunstall Lancs 50 B2
Tunstall Norf 39 E10
Tunstall N Yorks 58 G3
Tunstall Stoke 44 G2
Tunstall Suff 31 C10
Tunstall T & W 58 A4
Tunstead Derbys 44 E5
Tunstead Gtr Man 44 B4
Tunstead Norf 39 C8
Tunworth Hants 18 G3
Tupsley Hereford 26 D2
Tupton Derbys 45 F7
Tur Langton Leics 36 F3
Turgis Green Hants 18 F3
Turin Angus 77 B8
Turkdean Glos 27 G8
Turleigh Wilts 16 E5
Turn Lancs 50 H4
Turnastone Hereford 25 E10
Turnberry S Ayrs 66 F5
Turnditch Derbys 44 H6
Turners Hill W Sus 12 C2
Turners Puddle Dorset 9 E7
Turnford Herts 19 A10
Turnhouse Edin 69 C10
Turnworth Dorset 9 D7
Turriff Aberds 89 C7
Turton Bottoms Blkburn 50 H3
Turves Cambs 37 F9
Turvey Beds 28 C6
Turville Bucks 18 B4
Turville Heath Bucks 18 B4
Turweston Bucks 28 E3
Tushielaw Borders 61 B9
Tutbury Staffs 35 C8
Tutnall Worcs 26 A6
Tutshill Glos 15 B11
Tuttington Norf 39 C8
Tutts Clump W Berks 18 D2
Tuxford Notts 45 E11
Twatt Orkney 95 F3
Twatt Shetland 96 H5
Twechar E Dunb 68 C6
Tweedmouth Northumb 71 E8
Tweedsmuir Borders 60 A6
Twelve Heads Corn 3 E6
Twemlow Green Ches 43 F10
Twenty Lincs 37 C7
Twerton Bath 16 E4
Twickenham London 19 D8
Twigworth Glos 26 F5
Twineham W Sus 12 E1
Twinhoe Bath 16 F4
Twinstead Essex 30 E5
Twinstead Green Essex 30 E5
Twiss Green Warr 43 C9
Twiston Lancs 50 E4
Twitchen Devon 7 C6
Twitchen Shrops 33 H9
Two Bridges Devon 5 D7
Two Dales Derbys 44 F6
Two Mills Ches 42 E6
Twycross Leics 35 E9
Twyford Bucks 28 F3
Twyford Derbys 35 C9
Twyford Hants 10 B3
Twyford Leics 36 D3
Twyford Lincs 36 C5
Twyford Norf 38 C6
Twyford Wokingham 18 D4
Twyford Common Hereford 26 E2
Twyn-y-Sheriff Mon 25 H11
Twynholm Dumfries 55 D9
Twyning Glos 26 E5
Twyning Green Glos 26 E6
Twynllanan Carms 24 F4
Twynmynydd Carms 24 G3
Twywell Northants 36 H5
Ty-draw Conwy 41 E10
Ty-hen Carms 23 D8
Ty-hen Gwyn 40 G3
Ty-mawr Anglesey 40 B6
Ty Mawr Carms 23 B10
Ty Mawr Cwm Conwy 42 H2
Ty-nant Conwy 32 A5
Ty-nant Gwyn 32 C5
Ty-uchaf Powys 32 C6
Tyberton Hereford 25 E10
Tyburn W Mid 35 F7
Tycroes Carms 24 G3
Tycrwyn Powys 33 D7
Tydd Gote Lincs 37 D10
Tydd St Giles Cambs 37 D10
Tydd St Mary Lincs 37 D10
Tyddewi = St David's Pembs 22 D2
Tyddyn-mawr Gwyn 41 F7
Tye Green Essex 30 E2
Tye Green Essex 30 F4
Tye Green Essex 29 H11
Tyldesley Gtr Man 43 B9
Tyler Hill Kent 21 E8
Tylers Green Bucks 18 B6
Tylorstown Rhondda 14 B6
Tylwch Powys 32 G5
Tyn-y-celyn Wrex 33 B7
Tyn-y-coed Shrops 33 C8
Tyn-y-fedwen Powys 33 B7
Tyn-y-ffridd Powys 33 B7
Tyn-y-graig Powys 25 C7
Ty'n-y-groes Conwy 41 C9
Ty'n-y-maes Gwyn 41 D8
Tyn-y-pwll Anglesey 40 B6
Ty'n-yr-eithin Ceredig 24 B3
Tyncelyn Ceredig 24 B3
Tyndrum Stirl 74 D6
Tyne Tunnel T & W 63 G9
Tyneham Dorset 9 F7
Tynehead Midloth 70 E2
Tynemouth T & W 63 G9
Tynewydd Rhondda 14 B5
Tyninghame E Loth 70 C5
Tynron Dumfries 60 D4
Tynygongl Anglesey 41 B7
Tynygraig Ceredig 24 B3
Tŷ'r-felin-isaf Conwy 41 D10
Tyrie Aberds 89 B9
Tyringham M Keynes 28 D5
Tythecott Devon 6 E3
Tythegston Bridgend 14 D4
Tytherington Ches 44 E3
Tytherington Som 16 G4
Tytherington S Glos 16 C3
Tytherington Wilts 16 G6
Tytherleigh Devon 8 D2
Tywardreath Corn 4 F1
Tywyn Conwy 41 C9
Tywyn Gwyn 32 E1

U

Uachdar W Isles 84 C2
Uags Highld 85 E12
Ubbeston Green Suff 31 A10
Ubley Bath 15 F11
Uckerby N Yorks 58 F3
Uckfield E Sus 12 D3

Uckington Glos 26 F6
Uddingston S Lnrk 68 D5
Uddington S Lnrk 69 G7
Udimore E Sus 13 E7
Udny Green Aberds 89 F8
Udny Station Aberds 89 F9
Udston S Lnrk 68 E5
Udstonhead S Lnrk 68 F6
Uffcott Wilts 17 D8
Uffculme Devon 7 E9
Uffington Lincs 37 E6
Uffington Oxon 17 C10
Uffington Shrops 33 D11
Ufford P'boro 37 E6
Ufford Suff 31 C9
Ufton Warks 27 B10
Ufton Nervet W Berks 18 E3
Ugadale Argyll 65 F8
Ugborough Devon 5 F7
Uggeshall Suff 39 G10
Ugglebarnby N Yorks 59 F9
Ughill S Yorks 44 C6
Ugley Essex 30 F2
Ugley Green Essex 30 F2
Ugthorpe N Yorks 59 E8
Uidh W Isles 84 J1
Uig Argyll 73 E10
Uig Highld 85 B8
Uig Highld 84 C6
Uigen W Isles 90 D5
Uigshader Highld 85 D9
Uisken Argyll 78 K6
Ulbster Highld 94 F5
Ulceby Lincs 47 E8
Ulceby N Lincs 46 A5
Ulceby Skitter N Lincs 46 A5
Ulcombe Kent 20 G5
Uldale Cumb 56 C4
Uley Glos 16 B4
Ulgham Northumb 63 D8
Ullapool Highld 86 B4
Ullenhall Warks 27 B8
Ullenwood Glos 26 G6
Ulleskelf N Yorks 51 E11
Ullesthorpe Leics 35 G11
Ulley S Yorks 45 D8
Ullingswick Hereford 26 D2
Ullinish Highld 85 E8
Ullock Cumb 56 D2
Ulnes Walton Lancs 49 H5
Ulpha Cumb 56 G3
Ulrome E Yorks 53 D7
Ulsta Shetland 96 E6
Ulva House Argyll 78 H7
Ulverston Cumb 49 B2
Ulwell Dorset 9 F9
Umberleigh Devon 6 D5
Unapool Highld 92 F5
Unasary W Isles 84 F2
Underbarrow Cumb 56 G6
Undercliffe W Yorks 51 F7
Underhoull Shetland 96 C7
Underriver Kent 20 F2
Underwood Notts 45 G8
Undy Mon 15 C10
Unifirth Shetland 96 H4
Union Cottage Aberds 83 D10
Union Mills I o M 48 E3
Union Street E Sus 12 C6
Unst Airport Shetland 96 C8
Unstone Derbys 45 E7
Unstone Green Derbys 45 E7
Unthank Cumb 56 C6
Unthank Cumb 57 B8
Unthank End Cumb 56 C6
Up Cerne Dorset 8 D5
Up Exe Devon 7 F8
Up Hatherley Glos 26 F6
Up Holland Lancs 43 B8
Up Marden W Sus 11 C6
Up Nately Hants 18 F3
Up Somborne Hants 10 A2
Up Sydling Dorset 8 D5
Upavon Wilts 17 F8
Upchurch Kent 20 E5
Upcott Hereford 25 C10
Upend Cambs 30 C3
Upgate Norf 39 D7
Uphall W Loth 69 C9
Uphall Station W Loth 69 C9
Upham Devon 7 F7
Upham Hants 10 B4
Uphampton Worcs 26 B5
Uphill N Som 15 F9
Uplawmoor E Renf 68 E3
Upleadon Glos 26 F4
Upleatham Redcar 59 E7
Uplees Kent 20 E6
Uploders Dorset 8 E4
Uplowman Devon 7 E9
Uplyme Devon 8 E2
Upminster London 20 C2
Upnor Medway 20 D4
Upottery Devon 7 F11
Upper Affcot Shrops 33 G10
Upper Ardchronie Highld 87 C9
Upper Arley Worcs 34 G3
Upper Arncott Oxon 28 G3
Upper Astrop Northants 28 E2
Upper Badcall Highld 92 E4
Upper Basildon W Berks 18 D2
Upper Beeding W Sus 11 C10
Upper Benefield Northants 36 G5
Upper Bighouse Highld 93 D11
Upper Boddington Northants 27 C11
Upper Borth Ceredig 32 G2
Upper Boyndlie Aberds 89 B9
Upper Brailes Warks 27 E10
Upper Breakish Highld 85 F11
Upper Breinton Hereford 25 D11
Upper Broadheath Worcs 26 C5
Upper Broughton Notts 36 C2
Upper Bucklebury W Berks 18 E2
Upper Burnhaugh Aberds 83 D10
Upper Caldecote Beds 29 D8
Upper Catesby Northants 28 C2
Upper Chapel Powys 25 D7
Upper Church Village Rhondda 14 C6
Upper Chute Wilts 17 F9
Upper Clatford Hants 17 G10
Upper Clynnog Gwyn 40 F6
Upper Cumberworth W Yorks 44 B6
Upper Cwm-twrch Powys 24 G4
Upper Cwmbran Torf 15 B8
Upper Dallachy Moray 88 B3
Upper Dean Beds 29 B7
Upper Denby W Yorks 44 B6
Upper Denton Cumb 62 G3
Upper Derraid Highld 87 H13
Upper Dicker E Sus 12 F4
Upper Dovercourt Essex 31 E9
Upper Druimfin Argyll 79 F8
Upper Dunsforth N Yorks 51 C10
Upper Eathie Highld 87 E10
Upper Elkstone Staffs 44 G4
Upper End Derbys 44 E4
Upper Farringdon Hants 18 H4
Upper Framilode Glos 26 G4
Upper Glenfintaig Highld 80 E4
Upper Gornal W Mid 34 F5
Upper Gravenhurst Beds 29 E8
Upper Green Mon 25 G10
Upper Green W Berks 17 E10
Upper Grove Common Hereford 26 F2
Upper Hackney Derbys 44 F6
Upper Hale Sur 18 G5
Upper Halistra Highld 84 C7
Upper Halling Medway 20 E3
Upper Hambleton Rutland 36 E5
Upper Hardres Court Kent 21 F8
Upper Hartfield E Sus 12 C3
Upper Haugh S Yorks 45 C8
Upper Heath Shrops 34 G1
Upper Hellesdon Norf 39 D8
Upper Helmsley N Yorks 52 D2
Upper Hergest Hereford 25 C9
Upper Heyford Northants 28 C3
Upper Heyford Oxon 27 F11
Upper Hill Hereford 25 C11
Upper Hopton W Yorks 51 H7
Upper Horsebridge E Sus 12 E4
Upper Hulme Staffs 44 F4
Upper Inglesham Swindon 17 B9
Upper Inverbrough Highld 87 H11
Upper Killay Swansea 23 G10
Upper Knockando Moray 88 D1
Upper Lambourn W Berks 17 C10
Upper Leigh Staffs 34 B6
Upper Lenie Highld 81 A7
Upper Lochton Aberds 83 D8
Upper Longdon Staffs 35 D6
Upper Lybster Highld 94 G4
Upper Lydbrook Glos 26 G3
Upper Maes-coed Hereford 25 E10
Upper Midway Derbys 35 C8
Upper Milovaig Highld 84 D6
Upper Minety Wilts 17 B7
Upper Mitton Worcs 26 A5
Upper North Dean Bucks 18 B5
Upper Obney Perth 76 D3
Upper Ollach Highld 85 E10
Upper Padley Derbys 44 E6
Upper Pollicott Bucks 28 G4
Upper Poppleton York 52 D1
Upper Quinton Warks 27 D8
Upper Ratley Hants 10 B2
Upper Rissington Glos 27 G9
Upper Rochford Worcs 26 B3
Upper Sandaig Highld 85 G12
Upper Sanday Orkney 95 H6
Upper Sapey Hereford 26 B3
Upper Seagry Wilts 16 C6
Upper Shelton Beds 28 D6
Upper Sheringham Norf 39 A7
Upper Skelmorlie N Ayrs 73 G11
Upper Slaughter Glos 27 F8
Upper Soudley Glos 26 G3
Upper Stondon Beds 29 E8
Upper Stowe Northants 28 C3
Upper Stratton Swindon 17 C8
Upper Street Hants 9 C10
Upper Street Norf 39 D9
Upper Street Norf 39 D9
Upper Street Suff 31 E8
Upper Strensham Worcs 26 E6
Upper Sundon Beds 29 F7
Upper Swell Glos 27 F8
Upper Tean Staffs 34 B6
Upper Tillyrie Perth 76 G4
Upper Tooting London 19 D9
Upper Tote Highld 85 C10
Upper Town N Som 15 E11
Upper Treverward Shrops 33 H8
Upper Tysoe Warks 27 D10
Upper Upham Wilts 17 D9
Upper Wardington Oxon 27 D11
Upper Weald M Keynes 28 E4
Upper Weedon Northants 28 C3
Upper Wield Hants 18 H3
Upper Winchendon Bucks 28 G4
Upper Witton W Mid 35 F6
Upper Woodend Aberds 83 B8
Upper Woodford Wilts 17 H8
Upper Wootton Hants 18 F2
Upper Wyche Worcs 26 D4
Uppercourt Cumb 56 A6
Uppermill Gtr Man 44 B3
Uppersound Shetland 96 J6
Upperthong W Yorks 44 B5
Upperthorpe N Lincs 45 B11
Upperton W Sus 11 B8
Uppertown Derbys 45 F7
Uppertown Highld 94 C5
Uppertown Orkney 95 J5
Uppingham Rutland 36 F4
Uppington Shrops 34 E2
Upsall N Yorks 58 H5
Upshire Essex 19 A11
Upstreet Kent 21 E9
Upthorpe Suff 30 A6
Upton Cambs 37 H7
Upton Ches 43 F7
Upton Corn 6 F1
Upton Dorset 8 F6
Upton Dorset 9 E8
Upton Hants 10 C2
Upton Hants 17 F10
Upton Leics 35 F9
Upton Lincs 46 D2
Upton Mers 42 D5
Upton Norf 39 D9
Upton Notts 45 G11
Upton Notts 45 E11
Upton Northants 28 B4
Upton Oxon 18 C2
Upton P'boro 37 E7
Upton Slough 18 D6
Upton Som 7 D8
Upton W Yorks 45 A8
Upton Bishop Hereford 26 F3
Upton Cheyney S Glos 16 E3
Upton Cressett Shrops 34 F2
Upton Cross Corn 4 D3
Upton Grey Hants 18 G3
Upton Hellions Devon 7 F7
Upton Lovell Wilts 16 G6
Upton Magna Shrops 34 D1
Upton Noble Som 16 H4
Upton Pyne Devon 7 G8
Upton St Leonard's Glos 26 G5
Upton Scudamore Wilts 16 G5
Upton Snodsbury Worcs 26 C6
Upton upon Severn Worcs 26 D5
Upton Warren Worcs 26 B6
Upwaltham W Sus 11 C8
Upware Cambs 30 A2
Upwell Norf 37 E10
Upwey Dorset 8 F5
Upwood Cambs 37 G8
Uradale Shetland 96 K6
Urafirth Shetland 96 F5
Urchfont Wilts 17 F7
Urdimarsh Hereford 26 D2
Ure Shetland 96 F4
Ure Bank N Yorks 51 B9
Urgha W Isles 90 H6
Urishay Common Hereford 25 E10
Urlay Nook Stockton 58 E4
Urmston Gtr Man 43 C10
Urpeth Durham 58 A3
Urquhart Highld 87 F8
Urquhart Moray 88 B2
Urra N Yorks 59 F6
Urray Highld 87 F8
Ushaw Moor Durham 58 B3
Usk = Brynbuga Mon 15 A9
Usselby Lincs 46 C4
Usworth T & W 63 H9
Utkinton Ches 43 F8
Utley W Yorks 50 E6
Uton Devon 7 G7
Utterby Lincs 47 C7
Uttoxeter Staffs 35 B6
Uwchmynydd Gwyn 40 H3
Uxbridge London 19 C7
Uyeasound Shetland 96 C7
Uzmaston Pembs 22 E4

V

Valley Anglesey 40 C4
Valley Truckle Corn 4 C1
Valleyfield Dumfries 55 D9
Valsgarth Shetland 96 B8
Valtos Highld 85 B10
Van Powys 32 G5
Vange Essex 20 C4
Varteg Torf 25 H9
Vatten Highld 85 D7
Vaul Argyll 78 G3
Vaynor M Tydf 25 G7
Veensgarth Shetland 96 J6
Velindre Powys 25 E8
Vellow Som 7 C9
Veness Orkney 95 F6
Venn Green Devon 6 E2
Venn Ottery Devon 7 G9
Vennington Shrops 33 E9
Venny Tedburn Devon 7 G7
Ventnor I o W 10 G4
Vernham Dean Hants 17 F10
Vernham Street Hants 17 F10
Vernolds Common Shrops 33 G10
Verwood Dorset 9 D9
Veryan Corn 3 F8
Vicarage Devon 7 H11
Vickerstown Cumb 49 C1
Victoria Corn 3 C8
Victoria S Yorks 44 B5
Vidlin Shetland 96 G6
Viewpark N Lnrk 68 D6
Vigo Village Kent 20 E3
Vinehall Street E Sus 13 D6
Vine's Cross E Sus 12 E4
Viney Hill Glos 26 H3
Virginia Water Sur 18 E6
Virginstow Devon 6 G2
Vobster Som 16 G4
Voe Shetland 96 G6
Voe Shetland 96 E5
Vowchurch Hereford 25 E10
Voxter Shetland 96 F5
Voy Orkney 95 G3

W

Wackerfield Durham 58 D2
Wacton Norf 39 F7
Wadbister Shetland 96 J6
Wadborough Worcs 26 D6
Waddesdon Bucks 28 G4
Waddingham Lincs 46 C3
Waddington Lancs 50 E3
Waddington Lincs 46 F3
Wadebridge Corn 3 B8
Wadeford Som 8 C2
Wadenhoe Northants 36 G6
Wadesmill Herts 29 G10
Wadhurst E Sus 12 C5
Wadshelf Derbys 45 E7
Wadsley S Yorks 45 C7
Wadsley Bridge S Yorks 45 C7
Wadworth S Yorks 45 C9
Waen Denb 42 F4
Waen Denb 42 F2
Waen Fach Powys 33 D8
Waen Goleugoed Denb 42 E3
Wag Highld 93 G13
Wainfleet All Saints Lincs 47 G8
Wainfleet Bank Lincs 47 G8
Wainfleet St Mary Lincs 47 G9
Wainfleet Tofts Lincs 47 G8
Wainhouse Corner Corn 4 B2
Wainscott Medway 20 D4
Wainstalls W Yorks 50 G6
Waitby Cumb 57 F9
Waithe Lincs 46 B6
Wake Lady Green N Yorks 59 G7
Wakefield W Yorks 51 G9
Wakerley Northants 36 F5
Wakes Colne Essex 30 F5
Walberswick Suff 31 A11
Walberton W Sus 11 D8
Walbottle T & W 63 G7
Walcot Lincs 37 B6
Walcot N Lincs 52 G4
Walcot Shrops 33 G9
Walcot Telford 34 D1
Walcot Swindon 17 C8
Walcot Green Norf 39 G7
Walcote Leics 36 G1
Walcote Warks 27 C8
Walcott Lincs 46 G5
Walcott Norf 39 B9
Walden N Yorks 50 A6
Walden Head N Yorks 50 A5
Walden Stubbs N Yorks 52 H1
Waldersey Cambs 37 E10
Walderslade Medway 20 E4
Walderton W Sus 11 C6
Walditch Dorset 8 E3
Waldley Derbys 35 B7
Waldridge Durham 58 A3
Waldringfield Suff 31 D9
Waldringfield Heath Suff 31 D9
Waldron E Sus 12 E4
Wales S Yorks 45 D8
Walesby Lincs 46 C5
Walesby Notts 45 E10
Walford Hereford 25 A10
Walford Hereford 26 F2
Walford Shrops 33 C10
Walford Heath Shrops 33 D10
Walgherton Ches 43 H9
Walgrave Northants 28 A5
Walhampton Hants 10 E2
Walk Mill Lancs 50 F4
Walkden Gtr Man 43 B10
Walker T & W 63 G8
Walker Barn Ches 44 E3
Walker Fold Lancs 50 E2
Walkerburn Borders 70 G2
Walkeringham Notts 45 C11
Walkerith Lincs 45 C11
Walkern Herts 29 F9
Walker's Green Hereford 26 D2
Walkerville N Yorks 58 G3
Walkford Dorset 9 E11
Walkhampton Devon 4 E6
Walkington E Yorks 52 F5
Walkley S Yorks 45 D7
Wall Northumb 62 G5
Wall Staffs 35 E7
Wall Bank Shrops 33 F11
Wall Heath W Mid 34 G4
Wall under Heywood Shrops 33 F11
Wallaceton Dumfries 60 E4
Wallacetown S Ayrs 66 F5
Wallacetown S Ayrs 66 D6
Wallands Park E Sus 12 E3
Wallasey Mers 42 C6
Wallcrouch E Sus 12 C5
Wallingford Oxon 18 C3
Wallington London 19 E9
Wallington Hants 10 D4
Wallington Herts 29 E9
Wallis Pembs 22 D5
Walliswood Sur 19 H8
Walls Shetland 96 J4
Wallsend T & W 63 G8
Wallston V Glam 15 D7
Wallyford E Loth 70 C2
Walmer Kent 21 F10
Walmer Bridge Lancs 49 G4
Walmersley Gtr Man 44 A2
Walmley W Mid 35 F7
Walney Island Airport Cumb 49 B1
Walpole Suff 31 A10
Walpole Cross Keys Norf 37 D11
Walpole Highway Norf 37 D11
Walpole Marsh Norf 37 D10
Walpole St Andrew Norf 37 D11
Walpole St Peter Norf 37 D11
Walsall W Mid 34 F6
Walsall Wood W Mid 34 E6
Walsden W Yorks 50 G5
Walsgrave on Sowe W Mid 35 G9
Walsham le Willows Suff 30 A6
Walshaw Gtr Man 43 A10
Walshford N Yorks 51 D10
Walsoken Cambs 37 D10
Walston S Lnrk 69 F9
Walsworth Herts 29 E9
Walters Ash Bucks 18 B5
Walterston V Glam 14 D6
Walterstone Hereford 25 F10
Waltham Kent 21 G8
Waltham NE Lincs 46 B6
Waltham Abbey Essex 19 A10
Waltham Chase Hants 10 C4
Waltham Cross Herts 19 A10
Waltham on the Wolds Leics 36 C4
Waltham St Lawrence Windsor 18 D5
Walthamstow London 19 C10
Walton Cumb 61 G11
Walton Derbys 45 F7
Walton Leics 36 G1
Walton Mers 42 C6
Walton M Keynes 28 E5
Walton P'boro 37 E7
Walton Powys 25 C9
Walton Som 15 H10
Walton Staffs 34 B4
Walton Suff 31 E9
Walton Telford 34 D1
Walton Warks 27 C9
Walton W Yorks 51 H9
Walton W Yorks 51 E10
Walton Cardiff Glos 26 E6
Walton East Pembs 22 D5
Walton-in-Gordano N Som 15 D10
Walton-le-Dale Lancs 50 G1
Walton-on-Thames Sur 19 E8
Walton on the Hill Staffs 34 C5
Walton on the Hill Sur 19 F9
Walton-on-the-Naze Essex 31 F9
Walton on the Wolds Leics 36 D1
Walton-on-Trent Derbys 35 D8
Walton West Pembs 22 E3
Walwen Flint 42 E5
Walwick Northumb 62 F5
Walworth Darl 58 E3
Walworth Gate Darl 58 D3
Walwyn's Castle Pembs 22 E3
Wambrook Som 8 D1
Wanborough Sur 18 G6
Wanborough Swindon 17 C9
Wandsworth London 19 D9
Wangford Suff 39 H10
Wanlockhead Dumfries 60 B4
Wansford E Yorks 53 D6
Wansford P'boro 37 F6
Wanstead London 19 C11
Wanstrow Som 16 G4
Wanswell Glos 16 A3
Wantage Oxon 17 C10
Wapley S Glos 16 D4
Wappenbury Warks 27 B10
Wappenham Northants 28 D3
Warbleton E Sus 12 E5
Warblington Hants 10 D6
Warborough Oxon 18 B2
Warboys Cambs 37 G9
Warbreck Blkpool 49 F3
Warbstow Corn 4 B3
Warburton Gtr Man 43 D10
Warcop Cumb 57 E9
Ward End W Mid 35 G7
Ward Green Suff 31 B7
Warden Kent 21 D7
Warden Northumb 62 G5
Wardhill Orkney 95 F7
Wardington Oxon 27 D11
Wardlaw Borders 61 B8
Wardle Ches 43 G9
Wardle Gtr Man 50 H5
Wardley Rutland 36 E4
Wardlow Derbys 44 E5
Wardy Hill Cambs 37 G10
Ware Herts 29 G10
Ware Kent 21 E9
Wareham Dorset 9 F8
Warehorne Kent 13 C8
Waren Mill Northumb 71 G10
Warenford Northumb 71 H10
Warenton Northumb 71 G10
Wareside Herts 29 G10
Waresley Cambs 29 C9
Waresley Worcs 26 A5
Warfield Brack 18 D5
Warfleet Devon 5 F9
Wargrave Wokingham 18 D4
Warham Norf 38 A5
Warhill Gtr Man 44 C3
Wark Northumb 62 F4
Wark Northumb 71 G7
Warkleigh Devon 6 D5
Warkton Northants 36 H4
Warkworth Northants 27 D11
Warkworth Northumb 63 C8
Warlaby N Yorks 58 G4
Warland W Yorks 50 G5
Warleggan Corn 4 E2
Warlingham Sur 19 F10
Warmfield W Yorks 51 G9
Warmingham Ches 43 F10
Warmington Northants 37 F6
Warmington Warks 27 D11
Warminster Wilts 16 G5
Warmlake Kent 20 F5
Warmley S Glos 16 D3
Warmley Tower S Glos 16 D3
Warmonds Hill Northants 28 B6
Warmsworth S Yorks 45 B9
Warmwell Dorset 9 F6
Warndon Worcs 26 C5
Warnford Hants 10 B5
Warnham W Sus 11 A10
Warninglid W Sus 11 B11
Warren Ches 44 E2
Warren Pembs 22 G4
Warren Heath Suff 31 D9
Warren Row Windsor 18 C5
Warren Street Kent 20 F6
Warrington M Keynes 28 C5
Warrington Warr 43 D9
Warsash Hants 10 D3
Warslow Staffs 44 G4
Warter E Yorks 52 D4
Warthermarske N Yorks 51 B8
Warthill N Yorks 52 D2
Wartling E Sus 12 F5
Wartnaby Leics 36 C3
Warton Lancs 49 G4
Warton Lancs 49 B4
Warton Northumb 62 C6
Warton Warks 35 E8
Warwick Warks 27 B9
Warwick Bridge Cumb 61 H10
Warwick on Eden Cumb 61 H10
Wasbister Orkney 95 E4
Wasdale Head Cumb 56 F3
Wash Common W Berks 17 E11
Washaway Corn 3 C9
Washbourne Devon 5 F8
Washfield Devon 7 E8
Washfold N Yorks 58 F1
Washford Som 7 B9
Washford Pyne Devon 7 E7
Washingborough Lincs 46 E4
Washington T & W 63 H9
Washington W Sus 11 C10
Wasing W Berks 18 E2
Waskerley Durham 58 B1
Wasperton Warks 27 C9
Wasps Nest Lincs 46 F4
Wass N Yorks 52 B1
Watchet Som 7 B9
Watchfield Oxon 17 B9
Watchfield Som 15 G9
Watchgate Cumb 57 G7
Watchhill Cumb 56 B3
Watcombe Torbay 5 E10
Watendlath Cumb 56 E4
Water Devon 5 C8
Water Lancs 50 G4
Water End E Yorks 52 F3
Water End Herts 29 G7
Water End Herts 19 A9
Water Newton Cambs 37 F7
Water Orton Warks 35 F7
Water Stratford Bucks 28 E3
Water Yeat Cumb 56 H4
Waterbeach Cambs 29 B11
Waterbeck Dumfries 61 F8
Waterden Norf 38 B4
Waterfall Staffs 44 G4
Waterfoot E Renf 68 E4
Waterfoot Lancs 50 G4
Waterford Hants 10 E2
Waterford Herts 29 G10
Waterhead Cumb 56 F5
Waterhead Dumfries 61 D7
Waterheads Borders 69 E11
Waterhouses Durham 58 B2
Waterhouses Staffs 44 G4
Wateringbury Kent 20 F3
Waterloo Gtr Man 44 B3
Waterloo Highld 85 F11
Waterloo Mers 42 C6
Waterloo N Lnrk 69 E7
Waterloo Norf 39 D8
Waterloo Perth 76 D3
Waterloo Poole 9 E9
Waterloo Shrops 33 B11
Waterloo Port Gwyn 40 D6
Waterlooville Hants 10 D5
Watermeetings S Lnrk 60 B5
Watermillock Cumb 56 D6
Waterperry Oxon 28 H3
Waterrow Som 7 D9
Water's Nook Gtr Man 43 B9
Waters Upton Telford 34 D2
Watersfield W Sus 11 C9
Waterside Aberds 89 F10
Waterside Blkburn 50 G3
Waterside Cumb 56 B4
Waterside E Ayrs 67 F7
Waterside E Ayrs 67 B7
Waterside E Dunb 68 C5
Waterside E Renf 68 E4
Waterstock Oxon 28 H3
Waterston Pembs 22 F4
Watford Herts 19 B8
Watford Northants 28 B3
Watford Gap W Mid 35 E7
Wath N Yorks 51 C7
Wath N Yorks 51 B9
Wath N Yorks 52 B2
Wath Brow Cumb 56 E2
Wath upon Dearne S Yorks 45 B8
Watley's End S Glos 16 C3
Watlington Norf 38 D2
Watlington Oxon 18 B3
Watnall Notts 45 H9
Watten Highld 94 E4
Wattisfield Suff 31 A7
Wattisham Suff 31 C7
Wattlesborough Heath Shrops 33 D9
Watton E Yorks 52 D6
Watton Norf 38 E5
Watton at Stone Herts 29 G10
Wattston N Lnrk 68 C6
Wattstown Rhondda 14 B6
Wauchan Highld 80 E1
Waulkmill Lodge Orkney 95 H4
Waun Powys 32 E4
Waun-y-clyn Carms 23 F9
Waunarlwydd Swansea 14 B2
Waunclunda Carms 24 E3
Waunfawr Gwyn 41 E7
Waungron Swansea 23 F10
Waunlwyd Bl Gwent 25 H8
Wavendon M Keynes 28 E6
Waverbridge Cumb 56 B4
Waverton Ches 43 F7
Waverton Cumb 56 B4
Wavertree Mers 43 D6
Wawne E Yorks 53 F6
Waxham Norf 39 C10
Waxholme E Yorks 53 G9
Way Kent 21 E10
Way Village Devon 7 E7
Wayfield Medway 20 E4
Wayford Som 8 D3
Waymills Shrops 34 A1
Wayne Green Mon 25 G11
Wdig = Goodwick Pembs 22 C4
Weachyburn Aberds 89 C6
Weald Oxon 17 A10
Wealdstone London 19 C8
Weardley W Yorks 51 E8
Weare Som 15 F10
Weare Giffard Devon 6 D3
Wearhead Durham 57 C10
Weasdale Cumb 57 F8
Weasenham All Saints Norf 38 C4
Weasenham St Peter Norf 38 C4
Weatherhill Sur 12 B2
Weaverham Ches 43 E9
Weaverthorpe N Yorks 52 B5
Webheath Worcs 27 B7
Wedderlairs Aberds 89 E8
Wedderlie Borders 70 E5
Weddington Warks 35 F9
Wedhampton Wilts 17 F7
Wedmore Som 15 G10
Wednesbury W Mid 34 F5
Wednesfield W Mid 34 E5
Weedon Bucks 28 G5
Weedon Bec Northants 28 C3
Weedon Lois Northants 28 D3
Weeford Staffs 35 E7
Week Devon 7 E6
Week St Mary Corn 4 B3
Weeke Hants 10 A3
Weekley Northants 36 G4
Weel E Yorks 53 F6
Weeley Essex 31 F8
Weeley Heath Essex 31 F8
Weem Perth 75 C11
Weeping Cross Staffs 34 C5
Weethley Gate Warks 27 C7
Weeting Norf 38 G3
Weeton E Yorks 53 G9
Weeton Lancs 49 F3
Weeton N Yorks 51 E8
Weetwood Hall Northumb 71 H9
Weir Lancs 50 G4
Weir Quay Devon 4 E5
Welborne Norf 39 E6
Welbourn Lincs 46 G3
Welburn N Yorks 52 C3
Welburn N Yorks 52 A2
Welbury N Yorks 58 F4
Welby Lincs 36 B5
Welches Dam Cambs 37 G10
Welcombe Devon 6 E1
Weld Bank Lancs 50 H1
Weldon Northumb 63 D7
Welford Northants 36 G2
Welford W Berks 17 D11
Welford-on-Avon Warks 27 C8
Welham Leics 36 F3
Welham Notts 45 D11
Welham Green Herts 29 H9
Well Hants 18 G4
Well Lincs 47 E8
Well N Yorks 51 A8
Well End Bucks 18 C5
Well Heads W Yorks 51 F6
Well Hill Kent 19 E11
Well Town Devon 7 F8
Welland Worcs 26 D4
Wellbank Angus 77 D7
Welldale Dumfries 61 G7
Wellesbourne Warks 27 C9
Welling London 19 D11
Wellingborough Northants 28 B5
Wellingham Norf 38 C4
Wellingore Lincs 46 G3
Wellington Cumb 56 F2
Wellington Hereford 25 D11
Wellington Som 7 D10
Wellington Telford 34 D2
Wellington Heath Hereford 26 D4
Wellington Hill W Yorks 51 F9
Wellow Bath 16 F4
Wellow I o W 10 F2
Wellow Notts 45 F10
Wellpond Green Herts 29 F11
Wells Som 15 G11
Wells Green Ches 43 G9
Wells-Next-The-Sea Norf 38 A5
Wellsborough Leics 35 E9
Wellswood Torbay 5 E10
Wellwood Fife 69 B9
Welney Norf 37 F11
Welsh Bicknor Hereford 26 G2
Welsh End Shrops 33 B11
Welsh Frankton Shrops 33 B9
Welsh Hook Pembs 22 D4
Welsh Newton Hereford 25 G11
Welsh St Donats V Glam 14 D6
Welshampton Shrops 33 B10
Welshpool = Y Trallwng Powys 33 E8
Welton Cumb 56 B5
Welton E Yorks 52 G5
Welton Lincs 46 E4
Welton Northants 28 B2
Welton Hill Lincs 46 D4
Welton le Marsh Lincs 47 F8
Welton le Wold Lincs 46 D6
Welwick E Yorks 53 G9
Welwyn Herts 29 G9
Welwyn Garden City Herts 29 G9
Wem Shrops 33 C11
Wembdon Som 15 H8
Wembley London 19 C8
Wembury Devon 4 G6
Wembworthy Devon 6 F5
Wemyss Bay Invclyd 73 G10
Wenallt Ceredig 24 A3
Wenallt Gwyn 32 A5
Wendens Ambo Essex 30 E2
Wendlebury Oxon 28 G2
Wendling Norf 38 D5
Wendover Bucks 28 H5
Wendron Corn 2 F5
Wendy Cambs 29 D10
Wenfordbridge Corn 4 D1
Wenhaston Suff 39 H10
Wennington Cambs 37 H8
Wennington London 20 C2
Wennington Lancs 50 B2
Wensley Derbys 44 F6
Wensley N Yorks 58 H1
Wentbridge W Yorks 51 H10
Wentnor Shrops 33 F9
Wentworth Cambs 37 H10
Wentworth S Yorks 45 C7
Wenvoe V Glam 15 D7
Weobley Hereford 25 C11
Weobley Marsh Hereford 25 C11
Wereham Norf 38 E2
Wergs W Mid 34 E4
Wern Powys 32 D5
Wern Powys 33 D8
Wernffrwd Swansea 23 G10
Wernyrheolydd Mon 25 G10
Werrington Corn 4 C4
Werrington P'boro 37 E7
Werrington Staffs 44 H3
Wervin Ches 43 E7
Wesham Lancs 49 F4
Wessington Derbys 45 G7
West Acre Norf 38 D3
West Adderbury Oxon 27 E11
West Allerdean Northumb 71 F8
West Alvington Devon 5 G8
West Amesbury Wilts 17 G8
West Anstey Devon 7 D7
West Ashby Lincs 46 E6
West Ashling W Sus 11 D7
West Ashton Wilts 16 F5
West Auckland Durham 58 D2
West Ayton N Yorks 52 A5
West Bagborough Som 7 C10
West Barkwith Lincs 46 D5
West Barnby N Yorks 59 E9
West Barns E Loth 70 C5
West Barsham Norf 38 B5
West Bay Dorset 8 E3
West Beckham Norf 39 B7
West Bedfont Sur 19 D7
West Benhar N Lnrk 69 D7
West Bergholt Essex 30 F6
West Bexington Dorset 8 F4
West Bilney Norf 38 D3
West Blatchington Brighton 12 F1
West Bowling W Yorks 51 F7
West Bradford Lancs 50 E3
West Bradley Som 16 H2
West Bretton W Yorks 44 A6
West Bridgford Notts 36 B1
West Bromwich W Mid 34 F6
West Buckland Devon 6 C5
West Buckland Som 7 D10
West Burrafirth Shetland 96 H4
West Burton N Yorks 58 H1
West Burton W Sus 11 C8
West Butterwick N Lincs 46 B2
West Byfleet Sur 19 E7
West Caister Norf 39 D11
West Calder W Loth 69 D9
West Camel Som 8 B4
West Challow Oxon 17 C10
West Chelborough Dorset 8 D4
West Chevington Northumb 63 D8
West Chiltington W Sus 11 C9
West Chiltington Common W Sus 11 C9
West Chinnock Som 8 C3
West Chisenbury Wilts 17 F8
West Clandon Sur 19 F7
West Cliffe Kent 21 G10
West Clyne Highld 93 J11
West Clyth Highld 94 G4
West Coker Som 8 C4
West Compton Dorset 8 E4
West Compton Som 16 G2
West Cowick E Yorks 52 G2
West Cranmore Som 16 G3
West Cross Swansea 14 C2
West Cullery Aberds 83 C9
West Curry Corn 6 G1
West Curthwaite Cumb 56 B5
West Darlochan Argyll 65 F7
West Dean Wilts 10 B1
West Dean W Sus 11 C7
West Deeping Lincs 37 E7
West Derby Mers 43 C6
West Dereham Norf 38 E2
West Didsbury Gtr Man 44 C2
West Ditchburn Northumb 63 A7
West Down Devon 6 B4
West Drayton London 19 D7
West Drayton Notts 45 E11
West Ella E Yorks 52 G6
West End Beds 28 C6
West End E Yorks 52 F5
West End E Yorks 53 F7
West End Hants 10 C3
West End Lancs 50 G3
West End Norf 38 E5
West End Norf 39 D11
West End N Som 15 E10
West End N Yorks 51 D7
West End Oxon 17 A11
West End S Lnrk 69 F8
West End Suff 39 G10
West End Sur 18 E6
West End S Yorks 45 B10
West End Wilts 9 B8
West End Wilts 16 D6
West End W Sus 11 C11
West End Green Hants 18 E3
West Farleigh Kent 20 F4
West Felton Shrops 33 C9
West Fenton E Loth 70 B3
West Ferry Dundee 77 D7
West Firle E Sus 12 F3
West Ginge Oxon 17 C11
West Grafton Wilts 17 E9
West Green Hants 18 F4
West Greenskares Aberds 89 B7
West Grimstead Wilts 9 B11
West Grinstead W Sus 11 B10
West Haddlesey N Yorks 52 G1
West Haddon Northants 28 A3
West Hagbourne Oxon 18 C2
West Hagley Worcs 34 G5
West Hall Cumb 61 G11
West Hallam Derbys 35 A10
West Halton N Lincs 52 G5
West Ham London 19 C11
West Handley Derbys 45 E7
West Hanney Oxon 17 B11
West Hanningfield Essex 20 B4
West Hardwick W Yorks 51 H10
West Harnham Wilts 9 B10
West Harptree Bath 16 F2
West Hatch Som 8 B1
West Head Norf 38 E1
West Heath Ches 44 F2
West Heath Hants 18 F5
West Heath Hants 18 F2
West Helmsdale Highld 93 H13
West Hendred Oxon 17 C11
West Heslerton N Yorks 52 B5
West Hill Devon 7 G9
West Hill E Yorks 53 C7
West Hill N Som 15 D10
West Hoathly W Sus 12 C2
West Holme Dorset 9 F7
West Horndon Essex 20 C3
West Horrington Som 16 G2
West Horsley Sur 19 F7
West Horton Northumb 71 G9
West Hougham Kent 21 G9
West Houlland Shetland 96 H4
West-houses Derbys 45 G8
West Huntington York 52 D2
West Hythe Kent 13 C10
West Ilsley W Berks 17 C11
West Itchenor W Sus 11 D6
West Keal Lincs 47 F7
West Kennett Wilts 17 E8
West Kilbride N Ayrs 66 B5
West Kingsdown Kent 20 E2
West Kington Wilts 16 D5
West Kinharrachie Aberds 89 E9
West Kirby Mers 42 D5
West Knapton N Yorks 52 B4
West Knighton Dorset 8 F6
West Knoyle Wilts 9 A7
West Kyloe Northumb 71 F9
West Lambrook Som 8 C3
West Langdon Kent 21 G10
West Langwell Highld 93 J9
West Lavington Wilts 17 F7
West Lavington W Sus 11 B7
West Layton N Yorks 58 F2
West Lea Durham 58 B5
West Leake Notts 35 C11
West Learmouth Northumb 71 G7
West Leigh Devon 6 F5
West Lexham Norf 38 D4
West Lilling N Yorks 52 C2
West Linton Borders 69 E10
West Liss Hants 11 B6
West Littleton S Glos 16 D4
West Looe Corn 4 F3
West Luccombe Som 7 B7
West Lulworth Dorset 9 F7
West Lutton N Yorks 52 C5
West Lydford Som 8 A4
West Lyng Som 8 B2
West Lynn Norf 38 C2
West Malling Kent 20 F3
West Malvern Worcs 26 D4
West Marden W Sus 11 C6
West Marina E Sus 13 F6
West Markham Notts 45 E11
West Marsh NE Lincs 46 A6
West Marton N Yorks 50 D4
West Meon Hants 10 B5
West Mersea Essex 31 G7
West Milton Dorset 8 E4
West Minster Kent 20 D6
West Molesey Sur 19 E8
West Monkton Som 8 B1
West Moors Dorset 9 D9
West Morriston Borders 70 F5
West Muir Angus 77 A8
West Ness N Yorks 52 B2
West Newham Northumb 62 F6
West Newton E Yorks 53 F7
West Newton Norf 38 C2
West Norwood London 19 D10
West Ogwell Devon 5 D9
West Orchard Dorset 9 C7
West Overton Wilts 17 E8
West Park Hrtlpl 58 C5
West Parley Dorset 9 E9
West Peckham Kent 20 F3
West Pelton Durham 58 A3
West Pennard Som 15 H11
West Pentire Corn 3 C6
West Perry Cambs 29 B8
West Putford Devon 6 E2
West Quantoxhead Som 7 B10
West Rainton Durham 58 B4
West Rasen Lincs 46 D4
West Raynham Norf 38 C4
West Retford Notts 45 D10
West Rounton N Yorks 58 F5
West Row Suff 38 H2
West Rudham Norf 38 C4
West Runton Norf 39 A7
West Saltoun E Loth 70 D3
West Sandwick Shetland 96 E6
West Scrafton N Yorks 51 A6
West Sleekburn Northumb 63 E8
West Somerton Norf 39 D10
West Stafford Dorset 8 F6
West Stockwith Notts 45 C11
West Stoke W Sus 11 D7
West Stonesdale N Yorks 57 F10
West Stoughton Som 15 G10
West Stour Dorset 9 B6
West Stourmouth Kent 21 E9
West Stow Suff 30 A5
West Stowell Wilts 17 E8
West Strathan Highld 93 C8
West Stratton Hants 18 G2
West Street Kent 20 F6
West Tanfield N Yorks 51 B8
West Taphouse Corn 4 E2
West Tarbert Argyll 73 G7
West Thirston Northumb 63 D7
West Thorney W Sus 11 D6
West Thurrock Thurrock 20 D2
West Tilbury Thurrock 20 D3
West Tisted Hants 10 B5
West Tofts Norf 38 F4
West Tofts Perth 76 D4
West Torrington Lincs 46 D5
West Town Hants 10 E6
West Town N Som 15 E10
West Tytherley Hants 10 B1
West Tytherton Wilts 16 D6
West Walton Norf 37 D10
West Walton Highway Norf 37 D10
West Wellow Hants 10 C1
West Wemyss Fife 70 A2
West Wick N Som 15 E9
West Wickham Cambs 30 D3
West Wickham London 19 E10
West Williamston Pembs 22 F5
West Willoughby Lincs 36 A5
West Winch Norf 38 D2
West Winterslow Wilts 9 A11
West Wittering W Sus 11 E6
West Witton N Yorks 58 H1
West Woodburn Northumb 62 E4
West Woodhay W Berks 17 E10
West Woodlands Som 16 G4
West Worldham Hants 18 H4
West Worlington Devon 7 E6
West Worthing W Sus 11 D10
West Wratting Cambs 30 C3
West Wycombe Bucks 18 B5
West Wylam Northumb 63 G7
West Yell Shetland 96 E6
Westacott Devon 6 C4
Westbere Kent 21 E8
Westborough Lincs 36 A4
Westbourne Bmouth 9 E9
Westbourne Suff 31 D8
Westbourne W Sus 11 D6
Westbrook W Berks 17 D11
Westbury Bucks 28 E3
Westbury Shrops 33 E9
Westbury Wilts 16 F5
Westbury Leigh Wilts 16 F5
Westbury-on-Severn Glos 26 G4
Westbury on Trym Bristol 16 D2
Westbury-sub-Mendip Som 15 G11
Westby Lancs 49 F3
Westcliff-on-Sea Sthend 20 C5
Westcombe Som 16 H3
Westcote Glos 27 F9
Westcott Bucks 28 G4
Westcott Devon 7 F9
Westcott Sur 19 G8
Westcott Barton Oxon 27 F11
Westdean E Sus 12 G4
Westdene Brighton 12 F1
Wester Aberchalder Highld 81 A7
Wester Balgedie Perth 76 G4
Wester Culbeuchly Aberds 89 B6
Wester Dechmont W Loth 69 C9
Wester Denoon Angus 76 C6
Wester Fintray Aberds 83 B10
Wester Gruinards Highld 87 B8
Wester Lealty Highld 87 D9
Wester Milton Highld 87 F12
Wester Newburn Fife 77 G7
Wester Quarff Shetland 96 K6
Wester Skeld Shetland 96 J4
Westerdale Highld 94 E3
Westerdale N Yorks 59 F7
Westerfield Shetland 96 H5
Westerfield Suff 31 D8
Westergate W Sus 11 D8
Westerham Kent 19 F11
Westerhope T & W 63 G7
Westerleigh S Glos 16 D4
Westerton Angus 77 B9
Westerton Durham 58 C3
Westerton W Sus 11 D7
Westerwick Shetland 96 J4
Westfield Cumb 56 D1
Westfield E Sus 13 E7
Westfield Hereford 26 D4
Westfield Highld 94 D2
Westfield N Lnrk 68 C6
Westfield Norf 38 E5
Westfield W Loth 69 C8
Westfields Dorset 8 D6
Westfields of Rattray Perth 76 C4
Westgate Durham 57 C11
Westgate N Lincs 45 B11
Westgate Norf 38 A4
Westgate Norf 38 A5
Westgate on Sea Kent 21 D10
Westhall Aberds 83 A8
Westhall Suff 39 G10
Westham Dorset 8 G5
Westham E Sus 12 F5
Westham Som 15 G10
Westhampnett W Sus 11 D7
Westhay Som 15 G10
Westhead Lancs 43 B7
Westhide Hereford 26 D2
Westhill Aberds 83 C10
Westhill Highld 87 G10
Westhope Hereford 25 C11
Westhope Shrops 33 G10
Westhorpe Lincs 37 B8
Westhorpe Suff 31 B7
Westhoughton Gtr Man 43 B9
Westhouse N Yorks 50 B2
Westhumble Sur 19 F8
Westing Shetland 96 C7
Westlake Devon 5 F7
Westleigh Devon 6 D3
Westleigh Devon 7 E9
Westleigh Gtr Man 43 B9
Westleton Suff 31 B11
Westley Shrops 33 E9
Westley Suff 30 B5
Westley Waterless Cambs 30 C3
Westlington Bucks 28 G4
Westlinton Cumb 61 G9
Westmarsh Kent 21 E9
Westmeston E Sus 12 E2
Westmill Herts 29 F10
Westminster London 19 D10
Westmuir Angus 76 B6
Westness Orkney 95 F4
Westnewton Cumb 56 B3
Westnewton Northumb 71 G8
Westoe T & W 63 G9
Weston Bath 16 E4
Weston Ches 43 G10
Weston Devon 7 H10
Weston Dorset 8 G5
Weston Halton 43 D8
Weston Hants 10 B6
Weston Herts 29 E9
Weston Lincs 37 C8
Weston Notts 45 F11
Weston Northants 28 D2
Weston N Yorks 51 E7
Weston Shrops 34 F1
Weston Shrops 34 C1
Weston Shrops 33 C9
Weston Staffs 34 C5

Weston W Berks 17 D10
Weston Beggard Hereford 26 D2
Weston by Welland Northants 36 F3
Weston Colville Cambs 30 C3
Weston Coyney Stoke 34 A5
Weston Favell Northants 28 B4
Weston Green Cambs 30 C3
Weston Green Norf 39 D7
Weston Heath Shrops 34 D3
Weston Hills Lincs 37 C8
Weston-in-Gordano N Som 15 D10
Weston Jones Staffs 34 C3
Weston Longville Norf 39 D7
Weston Lullingfields Shrops 33 C10
Weston-on-the-Green Oxon 28 G2
Weston-on-Trent Derbys 35 C10
Weston Patrick Hants 18 G3
Weston Rhyn Shrops 33 B8
Weston-Sub-Edge Glos 27 D8
Weston-super-Mare N Som 15 E9
Weston Turville Bucks 28 G5
Weston under Lizard Staffs 34 D4
Weston under Penyard Hereford 26 F3
Weston under Wetherley Warks 27 B10
Weston Underwood Derbys 35 A8
Weston Underwood M Keynes 28 C5
Westonbirt Glos 16 C5
Westoncommon Shrops 33 C10
Westoning Beds 29 E7
Westonzoyland Som 8 A2
Westow N Yorks 52 C3
Westport Argyll 65 F7
Westport Som 8 C2
Westray Airport Orkney 95 C5
Westrigg W Loth 69 D8
Westruther Borders 70 F5
Westry Cambs 37 F9
Westville Notts 45 H9
Westward Cumb 56 B4
Westward Ho! Devon 6 D3
Westwell Kent 20 G6
Westwell Oxon 27 H9
Westwell Leacon Kent 20 G6
Westwick Cambs 29 B11
Westwick Durham 58 E1
Westwick Norf 39 C8
Westwood Devon 7 G9
Westwood Wilts 16 E5
Westwoodside N Lincs 45 C11
Wetheral Cumb 56 A6
Wetherby W Yorks 51 E10
Wetherden Suff 31 B7
Wetheringsett Suff 31 B8
Wethersfield Essex 30 E4
Wethersta Shetland 96 G5
Wetherup Street Suff 31 B8
Wetley Rocks Staffs 44 H3
Wetton Staffs 44 G5
Wetwang E Yorks 52 D5
Wetwood Staffs 34 B3
Wexcombe Wilts 17 F9
Wexham Street Bucks 18 C6
Weybourne Norf 39 A7
Weybread Suff 39 G8
Weybridge Sur 19 E7
Weycroft Devon 8 E2
Weydale Highld 94 D3
Weyhill Hants 17 G10
Weymouth Dorset 8 G5
Whaddon Bucks 28 E5
Whaddon Cambs 29 D10
Whaddon Glos 26 G5
Whaddon Wilts 9 B10
Whale Cumb 57 D7
Whaley Derbys 45 E9
Whaley Bridge Derbys 44 D4
Whaley Thorns Derbys 45 E9
Whaligoe Highld 94 F5
Whalley Lancs 50 F3
Whalsay Airport Shetland 96 G7
Whalton Northumb 63 E7
Wham N Yorks 50 C3
Whaplode Lincs 37 C9
Whaplode Drove Lincs 37 D9
Whaplode St Catherine Lincs 37 C9
Wharfe N Yorks 50 C3
Wharles Lancs 49 F4
Wharncliffe Side S Yorks 44 C6
Wharram le Street N Yorks 52 C4
Wharton Ches 43 F9
Wharton Green Ches 43 F9
Whashton N Yorks 58 F2
Whatcombe Dorset 9 D7
Whatcote Warks 27 D10
Whatfield Suff 31 D7
Whatley Som 8 D2
Whatley Som 16 G4
Whatlington E Sus 13 E6
Whatstandwell Derbys 45 G7
Whatton Notts 36 B3
Whauphill Dumfries 55 E7
Whaw N Yorks 57 F11
Wheatacre Norf 39 F10
Wheatcroft Derbys 45 G7
Wheathampstead Herts 29 G8
Wheathill Shrops 34 G2
Wheatley Devon 7 G8
Wheatley Hants 18 G4
Wheatley Oxon 28 H2
Wheatley S Yorks 45 B9
Wheatley Hill Durham 58 C4
Wheaton Aston Staffs 34 D4
Wheddon Cross Som 7 C8
Wheedlemont Aberds 82 A6
Wheelerstreet Sur 18 G6
Wheelock Ches 43 G10
Wheelock Heath Ches 43 G10
Wheelton Lancs 50 G2
Wheen Angus 82 F5
Wheldrake York 52 E2
Whelford Glos 17 B8
Whelpley Hill Bucks 18 A6
Whempstead Herts 29 F10
Whenby N Yorks 52 C2
Whepstead Suff 30 C5
Wherstead Suff 31 D8
Wherwell Hants 17 G10
Wheston Derbys 44 E5
Whetsted Kent 20 G3
Whetstone Leics 36 F1
Whicham Cumb 49 A1

Whichford Warks 27 E10
Whickham T & W 63 G8
Whiddon Down Devon 6 G5
Whigstreet Angus 77 C7
Whilton Northants 28 B3
Whim Farm Borders 69 E11
Whimble Devon 6 F2
Whimple Devon 7 G9
Whimpwell Green Norf 39 C9
Whinburgh Norf 38 E6
Whinnieliggate Dumfries 55 D10
Whinnyfold Aberds 89 E10
Whippingham I o W 10 E4
Whipsnade Beds 29 G7
Whipton Devon 7 G8
Whirlow S Yorks 45 D7
Whisby Lincs 46 F3
Whissendine Rutland 36 D4
Whissonsett Norf 38 C5
Whistlefield Argyll 73 D10
Whistlefield Argyll 73 D11
Whistley Green Wokingham 18 D4
Whiston Mers 43 C7
Whiston Northants 28 B5
Whiston Staffs 34 D4
Whiston Staffs 44 H4
Whiston S Yorks 45 D8
Whitbeck Cumb 49 A1
Whitbourne Hereford 26 C4
Whitburn T & W 63 G10
Whitburn W Loth 69 D8
Whitburn Colliery T & W 63 G10
Whitby Ches 43 E6
Whitby N Yorks 59 E9
Whitbyheath Ches 43 E6
Whitchurch Bath 16 E3
Whitchurch Bucks 28 F4
Whitchurch Cardiff 15 C7
Whitchurch Devon 4 D5
Whitchurch Hants 17 G11
Whitchurch Hereford 26 G2
Whitchurch Oxon 18 D3
Whitchurch Pembs 22 D2
Whitchurch Shrops 33 A11
Whitchurch Canonicorum Dorset 8 E2
Whitchurch Hill Oxon 18 D3
Whitcombe Dorset 8 F6
Whitcott Keysett Shrops 33 G8
White Coppice Lancs 50 H2
White Lackington Dorset 8 E6
White Ladies Aston Worcs 26 C6
White Lund Lancs 49 C4
White Mill Carms 23 D9
White Ness Shetland 96 J5
White Notley Essex 30 G4
White Pit Lincs 47 E7
White Post Notts 45 G10
White Rocks Hereford 25 F11
White Roding Essex 30 G2
White Waltham Windsor 18 D5
Whiteacen Moray 88 D2
Whiteacre Heath Warks 35 F8
Whitebridge Highld 81 B6
Whitebrook Mon 26 H2
Whiteburn Borders 70 F4
Whitecairn Dumfries 54 D5
Whitecairns Aberds 83 B11
Whitecastle S Lnrk 69 F9
Whitechapel Lancs 50 E1
Whitecleat Orkney 95 H6
Whitecraig E Loth 70 C2
Whitecroft Glos 26 H3
Whitecross Corn 3 B8
Whitecross Falk 69 C8
Whitecross Som 8 B4
Whiteface Highld 87 C10
Whitefarland N Ayrs 66 B1
Whitefaulds S Ayrs 66 F5
Whitefield Gtr Man 44 B2
Whitefield Perth 76 D4
Whiteford Aberds 83 A9
Whitegate Ches 43 F9
Whitehall Blkburn 50 G3
Whitehall W Sus 11 B10
Whitehall Village Orkney 95 F7
Whitehaven Cumb 56 E1
Whitehill Hants 11 A6
Whitehills Aberds 89 B6
Whitehills S Lnrk 68 E5
Whitehough Derbys 44 D4
Whitehouse Aberds 83 B8
Whitehouse Argyll 73 G7
Whiteinch Glasgow 68 D4
Whitekirk E Loth 70 B4
Whitelaw S Ayrs 68 E5
Whiteleas T & W 63 G9
Whiteley Bank I o W 10 F4
Whiteley Green Ches 44 E3
Whiteley Village Sur 19 E7
Whitemans Green W Sus 12 D2
Whitemire Moray 87 F12
Whitemoor Corn 3 D8
Whitemore Staffs 44 F2
Whitenap Hants 10 B2
Whiteoak Green Oxon 27 G10
Whiteparish Wilts 9 B11
Whiterashes Aberds 89 F8
Whiterow Highld 94 F5
Whiteshill Glos 26 H5
Whiteside Northumb 62 G3
Whiteside W Loth 69 D8
Whitesmith E Sus 12 E4
Whitestaunton Som 8 C1
Whitestone Devon 7 G7
Whitestone Devon 6 B4
Whitestone Aberds 83 D9
Whitestones Aberds 89 C8
Whitestreet Green Suff 30 E6
Whitewall Corner N Yorks 52 B3
Whiteway Bath 16 E3
Whiteway Glos 26 G6
Whitewell Aberds 89 B9
Whitewell Lancs 50 E2
Whitewell Bottom Lancs 50 G4
Whiteworks Devon 5 D7
Whitfield Kent 21 G10
Whitfield Northants 28 E3
Whitfield Northumb 62 H3
Whitfield S Glos 16 B3
Whitford Devon 8 E1
Whitford Flint 42 E4
Whitgift E Yorks 52 G4
Whitgreave Staffs 34 C4
Whithorn Dumfries 55 E7
Whiting Bay N Ayrs 66 D3
Whitkirk W Yorks 51 F9
Whitland Carms 23 E7
Whitletts S Ayrs 67 D6
Whitley N Yorks 52 G1
Whitley Reading 18 D4
Whitley Wilts 16 E5
Whitley Bay T & W 63 F9
Whitley Chapel Northumb 62 H5

Whitley Lower W Yorks 51 H8
Whitley Row Kent 19 F11
Whitlock's End W Mid 35 H7
Whitminster Glos 26 H4
Whitmore Staffs 34 A4
Whitnage Devon 7 E9
Whitnash Warks 27 B10
Whitney-on-Wye Hereford 25 D9
Whitrigg Cumb 56 A3
Whitrigg Cumb 61 H8
Whitsbury Hants 9 C10
Whitsome Borders 71 E7
Whitson Newport 15 C9
Whitstable Kent 21 E8
Whitstone Corn 6 G1
Whittingham Northumb 62 B6
Whittingslow Shrops 33 G10
Whittington Glos 27 F7
Whittington Lancs 50 B2
Whittington Norf 38 F3
Whittington Shrops 33 B9
Whittington Staffs 34 G4
Whittington Staffs 35 E7
Whittington Worcs 26 C5
Whittle-le-Woods Lancs 50 G1
Whittlebury Northants 28 D3
Whittlesey Cambs 37 F8
Whittlesford Cambs 29 D11
Whittlestone Head Blkburn 50 H3
Whitton Borders 62 A3
Whitton N Lincs 52 G5
Whitton Northumb 62 C6
Whitton Powys 25 B9
Whitton Shrops 26 A2
Whitton Stockton 58 D4
Whitton Suff 31 D8
Whittonditch Wilts 17 D9
Whittonstall Northumb 62 H6
Whitway Hants 17 F11
Whitwell Derbys 45 E9
Whitwell Herts 29 F8
Whitwell I o W 10 G4
Whitwell N Yorks 58 G3
Whitwell Rutland 36 E5
Whitwell-on-the-Hill N Yorks 52 C3
Whitwell Street Norf 39 C7
Whitwick Leics 35 D10
Whitwood W Yorks 51 G10
Whitworth Lancs 50 H4
Whixall Shrops 33 B11
Whixley N Yorks 51 D10
Whoberley W Mid 35 H9
Whorlton Durham 58 E2
Whorlton N Yorks 58 F5
Whygate Northumb 62 F3
Whyle Hereford 26 B2
Whyteleafe Sur 19 F10
Wibdon Glos 16 B2
Wibsey W Yorks 51 F7
Wibtoft Leics 35 G10
Wichenford Worcs 26 B4
Wichling Kent 20 F6
Wick Bmouth 9 E10
Wick Devon 7 F10
Wick Highld 94 E5
Wick Shetland 96 K6
Wick V Glam 14 D5
Wick Wilts 9 B10
Wick Worcs 26 D6
Wick W Sus 11 D9
Wick Airport Highld 94 E5
Wick Hill Wokingham 18 E4
Wick St Lawrence N Som 15 E9
Wicken Cambs 30 A2
Wicken Northants 28 E4
Wicken Bonhunt Essex 29 E11
Wicken Green Village Norf 38 B4
Wickenby Lincs 46 D4
Wickersley S Yorks 45 C8
Wickford Essex 20 B4
Wickham Hants 10 C4
Wickham W Berks 17 D10
Wickham Bishops Essex 30 G5
Wickham Market Suff 31 C10
Wickham St Paul Essex 30 E5
Wickham Skeith Suff 31 B7
Wickham Street Suff 30 C4
Wickham Street Suff 31 B7
Wickhambreaux Kent 21 F9
Wickhambrook Suff 30 C4
Wickhamford Worcs 27 D7
Wickhampton Norf 39 E10
Wicklewood Norf 39 E6
Wickmere Norf 39 B7
Wickwar S Glos 16 C4
Widdington Essex 30 E2
Widdrington Northumb 63 D8
Widdrington Station Northumb 63 D8
Wide Open T & W 63 F8
Widecombe in the Moor Devon 5 D8
Widegates Corn 4 F3
Widemouth Bay Corn 4 A3
Widewall Orkney 95 J5
Widford Essex 30 H3
Widford Herts 29 G11
Widham Wilts 17 C7
Widmer End Bucks 18 B5
Widmerpool Notts 36 C2
Widnes Halton 43 D8
Wigan Gtr Man 43 B8
Wiggaton Devon 7 G10
Wiggenhall St Germans Norf 38 D1
Wiggenhall St Mary Magdalen Norf 38 D1
Wiggenhall St Mary the Virgin Norf 38 D1
Wigginton Herts 28 G6
Wigginton Oxon 27 E10
Wigginton Staffs 35 E8
Wigginton York 52 D1
Wigglesworth N Yorks 50 D4
Wiggonby Cumb 56 A4
Wiggonholt W Sus 11 C9
Wighill N Yorks 51 E10
Wighton Norf 38 B5
Wigley Hants 10 C2
Wigmore Hereford 25 B11
Wigmore Medway 20 E5
Wigsley Notts 46 E2
Wigsthorpe Northants 36 G6
Wigston Leics 36 F2
Wigthorpe Notts 45 D9
Wigtoft Lincs 37 B8
Wigton Cumb 56 B4
Wigtown Dumfries 55 C7
Wigtwizzle S Yorks 44 C6
Wike W Yorks 51 E9
Wike Well End S Yorks 45 A10
Wilbarston Northants 36 G4
Wilberfoss E Yorks 52 D3
Wilberlee W Yorks 44 A4
Wilburton Cambs 29 A11
Wilby Norf 38 G6

Wilby Northants 28 B5
Wilby Suff 31 A9
Wilcot Wilts 17 E8
Wilcott Shrops 33 D9
Wilcrick Newport 15 C10
Wilday Green Derbys 45 E7
Wildboarclough Ches 44 F3
Wilden Beds 29 C7
Wilden Worcs 26 A5
Wildhern Hants 17 F10
Wildhill Herts 29 H9
Wildmoor Worcs 34 H5
Wildsworth Lincs 46 C2
Wilford Notts 36 B1
Wilkesley Ches 34 A2
Wilkhaven Highld 87 C12
Wilkieston W Loth 69 D10
Willand Devon 7 E9
Willaston Ches 42 E6
Willaston Ches 43 G9
Willen M Keynes 28 D5
Willenhall W Mid 35 H9
Willenhall W Mid 34 F5
Willerby E Yorks 52 F6
Willerby N Yorks 52 B6
Willersey Glos 27 E8
Willersley Hereford 25 D10
Willesborough Kent 13 B9
Willesborough Lees Kent 13 B9
Willesden London 19 C9
Willett Som 7 C10
Willey Shrops 34 F2
Willey Warks 35 G10
Willey Green Sur 18 F6
Williamscott Oxon 27 D11
Willian Herts 29 E9
Willingale Essex 30 H2
Willingdon E Sus 12 F4
Willingham Cambs 29 A11
Willingham by Stow Lincs 46 D2
Willington Beds 29 D8
Willington Derbys 35 C8
Willington Durham 58 C2
Willington T & W 63 G9
Willington Warks 27 E9
Willington Corner Ches 43 F8
Willisham Tye Suff 31 C7
Willitoft E Yorks 52 F3
Williton Som 7 B9
Willoughbridge Staffs 34 A3
Willoughby Lincs 47 E8
Willoughby Warks 28 B2
Willoughby-on-the-Wolds Notts 36 C2
Willoughby Waterleys Leics 36 F1
Willoughton Lincs 46 C3
Willows Green Essex 30 G4
Willsbridge S Glos 16 D3
Willsworthy Devon 4 C6
Wilmcote Warks 27 C8
Wilmington Devon 7 G11
Wilmington E Sus 12 F4
Wilmington Kent 20 D2
Wilminstone Devon 4 D5
Wilmslow Ches 44 D2
Wilnecote Staffs 35 E8
Wilpshire Lancs 50 F2
Wilsden W Yorks 51 F6
Wilsford Lincs 36 A6
Wilsford Wilts 17 F8
Wilsford Wilts 17 H8
Wilsill N Yorks 51 C7
Wilsley Pound Kent 13 C6
Wilsom Hants 18 H4
Wilson Leics 35 C10
Wilsontown S Lnrk 69 E8
Wilstead Beds 29 D7
Wilsthorpe Lincs 37 D6
Wilstone Herts 28 G6
Wilton Borders 61 B10
Wilton Cumb 56 E2
Wilton N Yorks 52 A4
Wilton Redcar 59 E6
Wilton Wilts 17 E9
Wilton Wilts 17 H7
Wimbish Essex 30 E2
Wimbish Green Essex 30 E3
Wimblebury Staffs 34 D6
Wimbledon London 19 D9
Wimblington Cambs 37 F10
Wimborne Minster Dorset 9 E9
Wimborne St Giles Dorset 9 C9
Wimbotsham Norf 38 E2
Wimpson Soton 10 C2
Wimpstone Warks 27 D9
Wincanton Som 8 B6
Wincham Ches 43 E9
Winchburgh W Loth 69 C9
Winchcombe Glos 27 F7
Winchelsea E Sus 13 E8
Winchelsea Beach E Sus 13 E8
Winchester Hants 10 B3
Winchet Hill Kent 13 B6
Winchfield Hants 18 F4
Winchmore Hill Bucks 18 B6
Winchmore Hill London 19 B10
Wincle Ches 44 F3
Wincobank S Yorks 45 C7
Windermere Cumb 56 G6
Winderton Warks 27 D10
Windhill Highld 87 G8
Windhouse Shetland 96 D6
Windlehurst Gtr Man 44 D3
Windlesham Sur 18 E6
Windley Derbys 45 H7
Windmill Hill E Sus 12 E5
Windmill Hill Som 8 C2
Windrush Glos 27 G8
Windsor N Lincs 45 A11
Windsor Windsor 18 D6
Windsoredge Glos 16 A5
Windygates Fife 76 G6
Windyknowe W Loth 69 D8
Windywalls Borders 70 G6
Wineham W Sus 11 B11
Winestead E Yorks 53 G8
Winewall Lancs 50 E5
Winfarthing Norf 39 G7
Winford I o W 10 F4
Winford N Som 15 E11
Winforton Hereford 25 D9
Winfrith Newburgh Dorset 9 F7
Wing Bucks 28 F5
Wing Rutland 36 E4
Wingate Durham 58 C4
Wingates Gtr Man 43 B9
Wingates Northumb 63 D7
Wingerworth Derbys 45 F7
Wingfield Beds 29 F7
Wingfield Suff 39 H8
Wingfield Wilts 16 F5
Wingham Kent 21 F9
Wingmore Kent 21 G8
Wingrave Bucks 28 G5
Winkburn Notts 45 G11
Winkfield Brack 18 D5
Winkfield Row Brack 18 D5
Winkhill Staffs 44 G4
Winkleigh Devon 6 F5
Winksley N Yorks 51 B8
Winmarleigh Lancs 49 E4
Winnal Hereford 25 E11
Winnall Hants 10 B3
Winnersh Wokingham 18 D4
Winscales Cumb 56 D2
Winscombe N Som 15 F10
Winsford Ches 43 F9
Winsford Som 7 C8
Winsham Som 8 D2
Winshill Staffs 35 C8
Winskill Cumb 57 C7
Winslade Hants 18 G3
Winsley Wilts 16 E5
Winslow Bucks 28 F4
Winson Glos 27 H7
Winson Green W Mid 34 G6
Winsor Hants 10 C2
Winster Cumb 56 G6
Winster Derbys 44 F6
Winston Durham 58 E2
Winston Suff 31 B8
Winstone Glos 26 H6
Winswell Devon 6 E3
Winter Gardens Essex 20 C4
Winterborne Bassett Wilts 17 D8
Winterborne Clenston Dorset 9 D7
Winterborne Herringston Dorset 8 F5
Winterborne Houghton Dorset 9 D7
Winterborne Kingston Dorset 9 E7
Winterborne Monkton Dorset 8 F5
Winterborne Monkton Wilts 17 D8
Winterborne Stickland Dorset 9 D7
Winterborne Whitechurch Dorset 9 D7
Winterborne Zelston Dorset 9 E7
Winterbourne W Berks 17 D11
Winterbourne S Glos 16 C3
Winterbourne Abbas Dorset 8 E5
Winterbourne Dauntsey Wilts 9 A10
Winterbourne Down S Glos 16 D3
Winterbourne Earls Wilts 9 A10
Winterbourne Gunner Wilts 17 H8
Winterbourne Steepleton Dorset 8 F5
Winterbourne Stoke Wilts 17 G7
Winterburn N Yorks 50 D5
Winteringham N Lincs 52 G5
Winterley Ches 43 G10
Wintersett W Yorks 51 H9
Wintershill Hants 10 C4
Winterton N Lincs 52 H5
Winterton-on-Sea Norf 39 D10
Winthorpe Lincs 47 F9
Winthorpe Notts 46 G2
Winton Bmouth 9 E9
Winton Cumb 57 E9
Winton N Yorks 58 G5
Wintringham N Yorks 52 B4
Winwick Cambs 37 G7
Winwick Northants 28 A3
Winwick Warr 43 C9
Wirksworth Derbys 44 G6
Wirksworth Moor Derbys 45 G7
Wirswall Ches 33 A11
Wisbech Cambs 37 E10
Wisbech St Mary Cambs 37 E10
Wisborough Green W Sus 11 B9
Wiseton Notts 45 D11
Wishaw N Lnrk 68 E6
Wishaw Warks 35 F7
Wisley Sur 19 F7
Wispington Lincs 46 E6
Wissenden Kent 13 B8
Wissett Suff 39 H9
Wistanstow Shrops 33 G10
Wistanswick Shrops 34 C2
Wistaston Ches 43 G9
Wistaston Green Ches 43 G9
Wiston Pembs 22 E5
Wiston S Lnrk 69 G8
Wiston W Sus 11 C10
Wistow Cambs 37 G8
Wistow N Yorks 52 F1
Wiswell Lancs 50 F3
Witcham Cambs 37 G10
Witchampton Dorset 9 D8
Witchford Cambs 37 H11
Witham Essex 30 G5
Witham Friary Som 16 G4
Witham on the Hill Lincs 37 D6
Withcall Lincs 46 D6
Withdean Brighton 12 F2
Witherenden Hill E Sus 12 D5
Witheridge Devon 7 E7
Witherley Leics 35 F9
Withern Lincs 47 D8
Withernsea E Yorks 53 G9
Withernwick E Yorks 53 E7
Withersdale Street Suff 39 G8
Withersfield Suff 30 D3
Witherslack Cumb 49 A4
Withiel Corn 3 C8
Withiel Florey Som 7 C8
Withington Glos 27 G7
Withington Gtr Man 44 C2
Withington Hereford 26 D2
Withington Shrops 34 D1
Withington Staffs 34 B6
Withington Green Ches 44 E2
Withleigh Devon 7 E8
Withnell Lancs 50 G2
Withybrook Warks 35 G10
Withycombe Som 7 B9
Withycombe Raleigh Devon 5 C11
Withyham E Sus 12 C3
Withypool Som 7 C7
Witley Sur 18 H6
Witnesham Suff 31 C8
Witney Oxon 27 G10
Wittersham Kent 13 D7
Witton Worcs 26 B5
Witton Bridge Norf 39 B9
Witton Gilbert Durham 58 B3

Witton-le-Wear Durham 58 C2
Witton Park Durham 58 C2
Wiveliscombe Som 7 D9
Wivelrod Hants 18 H3
Wivelsfield E Sus 12 D2
Wivelsfield Green E Sus 12 E2
Wivenhoe Essex 31 F7
Wivenhoe Cross Essex 31 F7
Wiveton Norf 38 A6
Wix Essex 31 F8
Wixford Warks 27 C7
Wixhill Shrops 34 C1
Wixoe Suff 30 D4
Woburn Beds 28 E6
Woburn Sands M Keynes 28 E6
Wokefield Park W Berks 18 E3
Woking Sur 19 F7
Wokingham Wokingham 18 E5
Wolborough Devon 5 D9
Wold Newton E Yorks 52 B6
Wold Newton NE Lincs 46 C6
Woldingham Sur 19 F10
Wolfclyde S Lnrk 69 G9
Wolferton Norf 38 C2
Wolfhill Perth 76 D4
Wolf's Castle Pembs 22 D4
Wolfsdale Pembs 22 D4
Woll Borders 61 A10
Wollaston Northants 28 B6
Wollaston Shrops 33 D9
Wollaton Nottingham 35 B11
Wollerton Shrops 34 B2
Wollescote W Mid 34 G5
Wolsingham Durham 58 C1
Wolstanton Staffs 44 H2
Wolston Warks 35 H10
Wolvercote Oxon 27 H11
Wolverhampton W Mid 34 F5
Wolverley Shrops 33 B10
Wolverley Worcs 34 H4
Wolverton Hants 18 F2
Wolverton M Keynes 28 D5
Wolverton Warks 27 B9
Wolverton Common Hants 18 F2
Wolvesnewton Mon 15 B10
Wolvey Warks 35 G10
Wolviston Stockton 58 D5
Wombleton N Yorks 52 A2
Wombourne Staffs 34 F4
Wombwell S Yorks 45 B7
Womenswold Kent 21 F9
Womersley N Yorks 51 H11
Wonastow Mon 25 G11
Wonersh Sur 19 G7
Wonson Devon 5 C7
Wonston Hants 17 H11
Wooburn Bucks 18 C6
Wooburn Green Bucks 18 C6
Wood Dalling Norf 39 C6
Wood End Herts 29 F10
Wood End Warks 27 A8
Wood End Warks 35 H8
Wood Enderby Lincs 46 F6
Wood Field Sur 19 E8
Wood Green London 19 B10
Wood Hayes W Mid 34 E5
Wood Lanes Ches 44 D3
Wood Norton Norf 38 C6
Wood Street Norf 39 C9
Wood Street Sur 18 F6
Wood Walton Cambs 37 G8
Woodacott Devon 6 F2
Woodale N Yorks 50 B6
Woodbank Argyll 65 G7
Woodbastwick Norf 39 D9
Woodbeck Notts 45 E11
Woodborough Notts 45 H10
Woodborough Wilts 17 F8
Woodbridge Dorset 8 C6
Woodbridge Suff 31 D9
Woodbury Devon 5 C11
Woodbury Salterton Devon 5 C11
Woodchester Glos 16 A5
Woodchurch Kent 13 C8
Woodchurch Mers 42 D5
Woodcombe Som 7 B8
Woodcote Oxon 18 C3
Woodcott Hants 17 F11
Woodcutts Dorset 9 C8
Woodditton Cambs 30 C3
Woodeaton Oxon 28 G2
Woodend Cumb 56 G3
Woodend Northants 28 D3
Woodend W Sus 11 D7
Woodend Green Northants 28 D3
Woodfalls Wilts 9 B10
Woodfield Oxon 28 F2
Woodfield S Ayrs 66 D6
Woodford Corn 6 E1
Woodford Devon 5 F8
Woodford Glos 16 B3
Woodford Gtr Man 44 D2
Woodford Northants 36 H5
Woodford London 19 B11
Woodford Bridge London 19 B11
Woodford Halse Northants 28 C2
Woodgate Norf 38 D6
Woodgate W Mid 34 G5
Woodgate W Mid 34 G5
Woodgate Worcs 26 B6
Woodgate W Sus 11 D8
Woodgreen Hants 9 C10
Woodhall Herts 29 G9
Woodhall Involyd 68 C2
Woodhall N Yorks 57 G11
Woodhall Spa Lincs 46 F5
Woodham Sur 19 E7
Woodham Ferrers Essex 20 B4
Woodham Mortimer Essex 20 A5
Woodham Walter Essex 30 H5
Woodhaven Fife 77 E7
Woodhey Gtr Man 50 H3
Woodhill Shrops 34 G3
Woodhouse Leics 35 D11
Woodhouse S Yorks 45 D8
Woodhouse W Yorks 51 F8
Woodhouse W Yorks 51 G10
Woodhouse Eaves Leics 35 D11
Woodhouse Park Gtr Man 44 D2
Woodhouselee Midloth 69 D11
Woodhouselees Dumfries 61 F9
Woodhouses Staffs 35 D7
Woodhurst Cambs 37 H9
Woodingdean Brighton 12 F2
Woodkirk W Yorks 51 G8
Woodland Devon 5 E8

Woodlands Aberds 83 D9
Woodlands Aberds 9 D9
Woodlands Hants 10 C2
Woodlands Highld 87 E8
Woodlands N Yorks 51 D9
Woodlands S Yorks 45 B9
Woodlands Park Windsor 18 D5
Woodlands St Mary W Berks 17 D10
Woodlane Staffs 35 C7
Woodleigh Devon 5 G8
Woodlesford W Yorks 51 G9
Woodley Gtr Man 44 C3
Woodley Wokingham 18 D4
Woodmancote Glos 16 B4
Woodmancote Glos 27 H7
Woodmancote Glos 26 F6
Woodmancote W Sus 11 C11
Woodmancote W Sus 12 E1
Woodmancott Hants 18 G2
Woodmansey E Yorks 53 F6
Woodmansterne Sur 19 F9
Woodminton Wilts 9 B9
Woodnesborough Kent 21 F10
Woodnewton Northants 36 F6
Woodplumpton Lancs 49 F5
Woodrising Norf 38 E5
Wood's Green E Sus 12 C5
Woodseaves Shrops 34 B2
Woodseaves Staffs 34 C3
Woodsend Wilts 17 D9
Woodsetts S Yorks 45 D9
Woodsford Dorset 9 E6
Woodside Aberdeen 83 C11
Woodside Aberds 89 D10
Woodside Brack 18 D6
Woodside Fife 77 G7
Woodside Hands 10 E2
Woodside Herts 29 H9
Woodside Perth 76 D5
Woodside of Arbeadie Aberds 83 D9
Woodstock Oxon 27 G11
Woodstock Pembs 22 D5
Woodthorpe Derbys 45 E8
Woodthorpe Leics 35 D11
Woodthorpe Lincs 47 D8
Woodthorpe York 52 E1
Woodton Norf 39 F8
Woodtown Devon 6 D3
Woodtown Devon 6 D3
Woodvale Mers 42 A6
Woodville Derbys 35 D9
Woodyates Dorset 9 C9
Woofferton Shrops 26 B2
Wookey Som 15 G11
Wookey Hole Som 15 G11
Wool Dorset 9 F7
Woolacombe Devon 6 B3
Woolage Green Kent 21 G9
Woolaston Glos 16 B2
Woolavington Som 15 G9
Woolbeding W Sus 11 B7
Wooldale W Yorks 44 B5
Wooler Northumb 71 H8
Woolfardisworthy Devon 6 D2
Woolfardisworthy Devon 7 F7
Woolfords Cottages S Lnrk 69 E9
Woolhampton W Berks 18 E2
Woolhope Hereford 26 E3
Woolhope Cockshoot Hereford 26 E3
Woolland Dorset 9 D6
Woollaton Devon 6 E3
Woolley Bath 16 E4
Woolley Cambs 29 A8
Woolley Corn 6 E1
Woolley Derbys 45 F7
Woolley W Yorks 45 A7
Woolmer Green Herts 29 G9
Woolmere Green Worcs 26 B6
Woolpit Suff 30 B6
Woolscott Warks 27 B11
Woolsington T & W 63 G7
Woolstanton Ches 43 G9
Woolstaston Shrops 33 F10
Woolsthorpe Lincs 36 B4
Woolsthorpe Lincs 36 C5
Woolston Devon 5 G8
Woolston Shrops 33 C9
Woolston Shrops 33 G10
Woolston Soton 10 C3
Woolston Warr 43 D9
Woolstone M Keynes 28 E5
Woolstone Oxon 17 C9
Woolton Mers 43 D7
Woolton Hill Hants 17 E11
Woolverstone Suff 31 E8
Woolverton Som 16 F4
Woolwich London 19 D11
Woolwich Ferry London 19 D11
Woonton Hereford 25 C10
Wooperton Northumb 62 A6
Woore Shrops 34 A3
Wootten Green Suff 31 A9
Wootton Beds 29 D7
Wootton Hants 9 E11
Wootton Hereford 25 C10
Wootton Kent 21 G9
Wootton N Lincs 52 H6
Wootton Northants 28 C4
Wootton Oxon 27 H11
Wootton Oxon 27 G11
Wootton Shrops 33 C9
Wootton Shrops 33 C10
Wootton Staffs 34 C4
Wootton Staffs 44 H5
Wootton Bassett Wilts 17 C7
Wootton Bridge I o W 10 E4
Wootton Common I o W 10 E4
Wootton Courtenay Som 7 B8
Wootton Fitzpaine Dorset 8 E2
Wootton Rivers Wilts 17 E8
Wootton St Lawrence Hants 18 F2
Wootton Wawen Warks 27 B8
Worcester Worcs 26 C5
Worcester Park London 19 E9
Wordsley W Mid 34 G4
Wordwell Suff 30 A5
Work Orkney 95 G5
Workington Cumb 56 D2
Worksop Notts 45 E9
Worlaby N Lincs 46 A4
World's End W Berks 17 D11
Worle N Som 15 E9
Worleston Ches 43 G9
Worlingham Suff 39 G10
Worlington Suff 30 A3
Worlingworth Suff 31 B9
Wormald Green N Yorks 51 C9
Wormbridge Hereford 25 E11
Wormegay Norf 38 D2
Wormelow Tump Hereford 25 E11
Wormhill Derbys 44 E5
Wormingford Essex 30 E6
Worminghall Bucks 28 H3

Wormington Glos 27 E7
Worminster Som 16 G2
Wormit Fife 76 E6
Wormleighton Warks 27 C11
Wormley Herts 29 H10
Wormley Sur 18 H6
Wormley West End Herts 29 H10
Wormshill Kent 20 F5
Wormsley Hereford 25 D11
Worplesdon Sur 18 F6
Worrall S Yorks 45 C7
Worsbrough S Yorks 45 B7
Worsbrough Common S Yorks 45 B7
Worsley Gtr Man 43 B10
Worstead Norf 39 C9
Worsthorne Lancs 50 F4
Worston Lancs 50 E3
Worswell Devon 4 G6
Worth Kent 21 F10
Worth W Sus 12 C2
Worth Matravers Dorset 9 G8
Wortham Suff 39 H6
Worthen Shrops 33 E9
Worthenbury Wrex 43 H7
Worthing Norf 38 D5
Worthing W Sus 11 D10
Worthington Leics 35 C10
Worting Hants 18 F3
Wortley S Yorks 45 C7
Wortley W Yorks 51 F8
Worton N Yorks 57 G11
Worton Wilts 16 F6
Wortwell Norf 39 G8
Wotherton Shrops 33 E8
Wotter Devon 5 E6
Wotton Sur 19 G8
Wotton-under-Edge Glos 16 B4
Wotton Underwood Bucks 28 G3
Woughton on the Green M Keynes 28 E5
Wouldham Kent 20 E4
Wrabness Essex 31 E8
Wrafton Devon 6 C3
Wragby Lincs 46 E5
Wragby W Yorks 51 H10
Wragholme Lincs 47 C7
Wramplingham Norf 39 E7
Wrangbrook W Yorks 45 A8
Wrangham Aberds 89 E6
Wrangle Lincs 47 G8
Wrangle Bank Lincs 47 G8
Wrangle Lowgate Lincs 47 G8
Wrangway Som 7 E10
Wrantage Som 8 B2
Wrawby N Lincs 46 B4
Wraxall Dorset 8 E4
Wraxall N Som 15 D10
Wraxall Som 16 H3
Wray Lancs 50 C2
Wraysbury Windsor 19 D7
Wrayton Lancs 50 B2
Wrea Green Lancs 49 F3
Wreay Cumb 56 B6
Wreay Cumb 56 D6
Wrecclesham Sur 18 G5
Wrecsam = Wrexham Wrex 42 G6
Wrekenton T & W 63 H8
Wrelton N Yorks 59 H8
Wrenbury Ches 43 H8
Wrench Green N Yorks 59 H10
Wreningham Norf 39 F7
Wrentham Suff 39 G10
Wrenthorpe W Yorks 51 G9
Wrentnall Shrops 33 E10
Wressle E Yorks 52 F3
Wressle N Lincs 46 B3
Wrestlingworth Beds 29 D9
Wretham Norf 38 F5
Wretton Norf 38 E2
Wrexham = Wrecsam Wrex 42 G6
Wrexham Industrial Estate Wrex 42 H6
Wribbenhall Worcs 34 H3
Wrightington Bar Lancs 43 A8
Wrinehill Staffs 43 H10
Wrington N Som 15 E10
Writhlington Bath 16 F4
Writtle Essex 30 H3
Wrockwardine Telford 34 D2
Wroot N Lincs 45 B11
Wrotham Kent 20 F3
Wrotham Heath Kent 20 F3
Wroughton Swindon 17 C8
Wroxall I o W 10 G4
Wroxall Warks 27 A9
Wroxeter Shrops 34 E1
Wroxham Norf 39 D9
Wroxton Oxon 27 D11
Wyaston Derbys 35 A7
Wyberton Lincs 37 A9
Wyboston Beds 29 C8
Wybunbury Ches 43 H10
Wych Cross E Sus 12 C3
Wychbold Worcs 26 B6
Wyck Hants 18 H4
Wyck Rissington Glos 27 F8
Wycoller Lancs 50 F5
Wycomb Leics 36 C3
Wycombe Marsh Bucks 18 B5
Wyddial Herts 29 E10
Wye Kent 21 G7
Wyesham Mon 26 G2
Wyfordby Leics 36 D3
Wyke Dorset 9 B6
Wyke Shrops 34 E2
Wyke Sur 18 F6
Wyke W Yorks 51 G7
Wyke Regis Dorset 8 G5
Wykeham N Yorks 52 A5
Wykeham N Yorks 52 B5
Wyken W Mid 35 G9
Wykey Shrops 33 C9
Wylam Northumb 63 G7
Wylde Green W Mid 35 F7
Wyllie Caerph 15 B7
Wylye Wilts 17 H7
Wymering Ptsmth 10 D5
Wymeswold Leics 36 C2
Wymington Beds 28 B6
Wymondham Leics 36 D4
Wymondham Norf 39 E7
Wyndham Bridgend 14 B5
Wynford Eagle Dorset 8 E4
Wyng Orkney 95 J4
Wynyard Village Stockton 58 D5
Wyre Piddle Worcs 26 D6
Wysall Notts 36 C2
Wythall Worcs 27 A7
Wytham Oxon 27 H11
Wythburn Cumb 56 E5
Wythenshawe Gtr Man 44 D2
Wythop Mill Cumb 56 D3
Wyton Cambs 29 A9
Wyverstone Suff 31 B7
Wyverstone Street Suff 31 B7
Wyville Lincs 36 C4
Wyvis Lodge Highld 86 D7

Y

Y Bala = Bala Gwyn 32 B5
Y Barri = Barry V Glam 15 E7
Y Bont-Faen = Cowbridge V Glam 14 D5
Y Drenewydd = Newtown Powys 33 F7
Y Felinheli Gwyn 41 D7
Y Fenni = Abergavenny Mon 25 G9
Y Fflint = Flint Flint 42 E5
Y Ffôr Gwyn 40 G5
Y-Ffrith Denb 42 D3
Y Gelli Gandryll = Hay-on-Wye Powys 25 D9
Y Mwmbwls = The Mumbles Swansea 14 C2
Y Pîl = Pyle Bridgend 14 C4
Y Rhws = Rhoose V Glam 14 E6
Y Rhyl = Rhyl Denb 42 D3
Y Trallwng = Welshpool Powys 33 E8
Y Waun = Chirk Wrex 33 B8
Yaddlethorpe N Lincs 46 B2
Yafford I o W 10 F3
Yafforth N Yorks 58 G4
Yalding Kent 20 F3
Yanworth Glos 27 G7
Yapham E Yorks 52 D3
Yapton W Sus 11 D8
Yarburgh Lincs 47 C7
Yarcombe Devon 8 D1
Yard Som 7 C9
Yardley W Mid 35 G7
Yardley Gobion Northants 28 D4
Yardley Hastings Northants 28 C5
Yardro Powys 25 C9
Yarkhill Hereford 26 D3
Yarlet Staffs 34 C5
Yarlington Som 8 B5
Yarlside Cumb 49 C2
Yarm Stockton 58 E5
Yarmouth I o W 10 F2
Yarnbrook Wilts 16 F5
Yarnfield Staffs 34 B4
Yarnscombe Devon 6 D4
Yarnton Oxon 27 G11
Yarpole Hereford 25 B11
Yarrow Borders 70 H2
Yarrow Feus Borders 70 H2
Yarsop Hereford 25 D11
Yarwell Northants 37 F6
Yate S Glos 16 C4
Yateley Hants 18 E5
Yatesbury Wilts 17 D7
Yattendon W Berks 18 D2
Yatton Hereford 25 B11
Yatton N Som 15 E10
Yatton Keynell Wilts 16 D5
Yaverland I o W 10 F5
Yaxham Norf 38 D6
Yaxley Cambs 37 F7
Yaxley Suff 31 A8
Yazor Hereford 25 D11
Yeading London 19 C8
Yeadon W Yorks 51 E8
Yealand Conyers Lancs 49 B5
Yealand Redmayne Lancs 49 B5
Yealmpton Devon 5 F6
Yearby Redcar 59 D7
Yearsley N Yorks 52 B1
Yeaton Shrops 33 D10
Yeaveley Derbys 35 A7
Yedingham N Yorks 52 B4
Yeldon Beds 29 B7
Yelford Oxon 17 A10
Yelland Devon 6 C3
Yelling Cambs 29 B9
Yelvertoft Northants 36 H1
Yelverton Devon 4 E6
Yelverton Norf 39 E8
Yeo Mill Devon 7 D7
Yeoford Devon 7 G6
Yeolmbridge Corn 4 C4
Yeovil Som 8 C4
Yeovil Marsh Som 8 C4
Yeovilton Som 8 B4
Yerbeston Pembs 22 F5
Yesnaby Orkney 95 G3
Yetlington Northumb 62 C6
Yetminster Dorset 8 C4
Yettington Devon 7 H9
Yetts o'Muckhart Clack 76 G3
Yieldshields S Lnrk 69 E7
Yiewsley London 19 C7
Ynys-meudwy Neath 24 H4
Ynysboeth Rhondda 14 B6
Ynysddu Caerph 15 B7
Ynysgyffylog Gwyn 32 D2
Ynyshir Rhondda 14 B6
Ynyslas Ceredig 32 F2
Ynystawe Swansea 14 A2
Ynysybwl Rhondda 14 B6
Yockenthwaite N Yorks 50 B5
Yockleton Shrops 33 D9
Yokefleet E Yorks 52 G4
Yoker Glasgow 68 D4
Yonder Bognie Aberds 88 D5
York York 52 D1
York Town Sur 18 E5
Yorkletts Kent 21 E7
Yorkley Glos 26 H3
Yorton Shrops 33 C11
Youlgreave Derbys 44 F6
Youlstone Devon 6 E1
Youlthorpe E Yorks 52 D3
Youlton N Yorks 51 C10
Young Wood Lincs 46 E5
Young's End Essex 30 G4
Yoxall Staffs 35 D7
Yoxford Suff 31 B10
Yr Hôb = Hope Flint 42 G6
Yr Wyddgrug = Mold Flint 42 F5
Ysbyty-Cynfyn Ceredig 32 H3
Ysbyty Ifan Conwy 41 E10
Ysbyty Ystwyth Ceredig 24 A4
Ysceifiog Flint 42 E4
Yspitty Carms 23 G10
Ystalyfera Neath 24 H4
Ystrad Rhondda 14 B5
Ystrad Aeron Ceredig 23 A10
Ystrad-mynach Caerph 15 B7
Ystradfellte Powys 24 G6
Ystradffin Carms 24 D4
Ystradgynlais Powys 24 G4
Ystradmeurig Ceredig 24 B4
Ystradowen Carms 24 G4
Ystradowen V Glam 14 D6
Ystumtuen Ceredig 32 H3
Ythanbank Aberds 89 E9
Ythanwells Aberds 89 E6
Ythsie Aberds 89 E8

Z

Zeal Monachorum Devon 6 F6
Zeals Wilts 9 A6
Zelah Corn 3 D7
Zennor Corn 2 F3